DOES HUMAN RIGHTS NEED GOD?

THE EERDMANS RELIGION, ETHICS, AND PUBLIC LIFE SERIES

Jean Bethke Elshtain and John D. Carlson, Series Editors

This series aims to explore dilemmas and debates at the intersection of religion, ethics, and public life. Its high-caliber books will include both single- and multi-authored volumes by scholars, public officials, and policy experts discussing the religious and moral meanings of pressing social issues. At a time when people puzzle over the connections between religious belief and civic practice, this series will offer valuable perspectives to a wide range of readers.

PUBLISHED VOLUMES

Does Human Rights Need God?
   Elizabeth M. Bucar and Barbra Barnett, Editors

Religion and the Death Penalty
   Erik C. Owens, John D. Carlson, and Eric P. Elshtain, Editors

DOES HUMAN RIGHTS NEED GOD?

Edited by

Elizabeth M. Bucar and Barbra Barnett

WILLIAM B. EERDMANS PUBLISHING COMPANY

GRAND RAPIDS, MICHIGAN / CAMBRIDGE, U.K.

Wm. B. Eerdmans Publishing Co.
255 Jefferson Ave. S.E., Grand Rapids, Michigan 49503 /
P.O. Box 163, Cambridge CB3 9PU U.K.

Printed in the United States of America

10 09 08 07 06 05   7 6 5 4 3 2 1

Library of Congress Cataloging-in-Publication Data

Does human rights need God? / edited by Elizabeth M. Bucar and Barbra Barnett.
    p.   cm.   — (The Eerdmans religion, ethics, and public life series)
    Includes bibliographical references and index.
    ISBN 0-8028-2905-8 (pbk.: alk. paper)
    1. Human rights — Religious aspects. 2. Human rights.
    I. Bucar, Elizabeth M.   II. Barnett, Barbra.   III. Series.

BL65.H78.D64   2005
201'.723 — dc22

                  2005050061

www.eerdmans.com

Contents

Series Foreword

This series explores dilemmas and debates at the intersections of religion, ethics, and public life. At a time when religion pervades the public square, concerned citizens puzzle over the connections between their religious beliefs and the moral practices of civic life. The Eerdmans Religion, Ethics, and Public Life Series delivers high caliber books that reflect on the religious and moral dimensions of politics, culture, and society. The series foregrounds the relationship among theological and philosophical scholarship, practical ethics, and policy studies — all contextualized in light of contemporary themes and issues. It does so by integrating a broad array of perspectives from diverse religious faiths, moral traditions, academic disciplines, political persuasions, and professional vocations. Some of the books in the series bring scholars, public leaders and officials, and policy experts together within one volume to discuss the religious and moral meanings of timely issues and to provide a venue in which their work can be mutually informative. In addition to multiauthored volumes, the series also features monographs which make compelling arguments that enrich ongoing conversations or initiate new ones. Books in the series are intended for a wide readership, including academics, clergy, government officials, journalists, students, policy experts, leaders of public institutions, and interested citizens generally.

As the second installment in the series, this book expands our conceptual and practical inquiry into universal human rights — an enduring legacy of twentieth-century political life, yet a still imperiled aspiration for many people in the twenty-first. In recent years, the language of human rights has made tremendous institutional inroads, jostling its way into the lexicon of international politics. As news of intolerable atrocities splashes too frequently across our front pages and television screens, as prominent international rights organizations fill greater space and apply increasing pressure in world affairs, human rights concerns now vie regularly for a place alongside traditional "realist" talk of national security and economic interests. For individuals, nations, governments, and groups of all kinds, human rights has become a new *lingua franca* of global civic life. Whether to advance a cause or claim, to justify the use of force, or to challenge an economic or foreign policy — all require increased fluency in "rights talk," whatever the national accent or local dialect may be.

Yet, despite the shared language of human rights (in the West, at least), there is considerable disagreement over the origins of such rights. There are those for whom religious and moral principles behind the idea of human rights are incidental — even antithetical — to the protections that rights afford. Rights exist. They are universal, absolute, and inviolable. What more need be said? Others, though, argue that haziness about the source of human rights claims invariably entails troubling ambiguity and unsteady commitment to the rights themselves. The editors of this book energetically open up this debate by drawing together a diverse and distinguished cadre of contributors whose insights on these themes are informed by their own experiences, professions, scholarship, and religious and moral traditions. The book's authors hail from many lands, near and far, and speak many native tongues. Some showcase intellectual fluency as leaders in their academic fields. Others have been participants in epic reform movements that have shaped the course of political history. No matter the regional dialect, the language of the discipline, or the particular approach to human rights deployed, these sage voices proffer readers lively, often contrasting, perspectives on questions that cannot be ignored in our complex and religiously pluralistic global age.

JEAN BETHKE ELSHTAIN *and*
JOHN D. CARLSON
Series Editors

Preface

This book began, under the auspices of the Pew Forum on Religion and Public Life, as a lecture series at the University of Chicago during 2002 to 2003, entitled "Does Human Rights Need God?" Several contributors traveled to the University of Chicago, from as far away as South Africa, to deliver public addresses, in addition to providing essays for the book. We are particularly grateful for their willingness to engage with our university community. We also thank Mieke Holkeboer for her early work in conceptualizing and organizing the lecture series.

Given the importance of each of our contributors' respective activities in striving toward a world community in which humans are protected from fundamental violations, we greatly appreciate their willingness to reflect on our organizing question, and to provide us with the thoughtful, well-crafted, provocative essays that follow.

Hannah Timmermans' keen editing skills on behalf of Eerdmans have been much appreciated. John Carlson, who went above and beyond the call of duty of a series editor, provided invaluable advice, encouragement, and substantive feedback. We particularly thank Jean Bethke Elshtain, who made this project possible and guided us to its fruition. She is extraordinarily generous in facilitating opportunities for the professional development of young scholars and continues to be a valued mentor.

Finally, we would like to thank our families and friends for their encouragement and guidance, especially Alexis Zubrow and Emilie Barnett — our most dedicated, and patient, supporters.

Contributors

Khaled Abou El Fadl is a Full Professor of Law at the UCLA School of Law, where he teaches Islamic law, immigration, human rights, international, and national security law. Raised in Egypt and Kuwait, he trained in Islamic legal sciences in Egypt, Kuwait, and the United States. He is a member of the Board of Human Rights Watch, a recent presidential appointee to the United States Commission on International Religious Freedom, and a 2005 Carnegie Foundation Scholar. Dr. Abou El Fadl's most recent books include *Islam and the Challenge of Democracy, And God Knows the Soldiers: The Authoritative and Authoritarian in Islamic Discourses,* and *The Great Theft: Wrestling Islam from the Extremists.*

Barbra Barnett is pursuing her doctoral degree in ethics at the University of Chicago Divinity School and is a former research associate with the Pew Forum on Religion and Public Life. She received her J.D., with honors, from the George Washington University Law School in 1996. Her research interests and writing focus on political virtue and responsibility in religiously pluralistic communities and the role of legal and political institutions in mediating and resolving conflicting claims.

Elizabeth M. Bucar is a doctoral candidate in ethics at the University of Chicago Divinity School. Her research and writing focuses on gender, rhetoric, and comparative religion (Roman Catholicism and Shi'ite Islam). She has served as a research associate with the Pew Forum on Religion and Public Life and as policy analyst for Catholics for a Free Choice.

Jean Bethke Elshtain is Laura Spelman Rockefeller Professor of Social and Political Ethics at the University of Chicago Divinity School. Through her work as a political philosopher she has tried to show the connections between our political and ethical convictions. Her books include *Public Man, Private Woman: Women in Social and Political Thought* and *Just War against Terror: The Burden of American Power in a Violent World*. Professor Elshtain is also a contributing editor for *The New Republic*, a Fellow of the American Academy of Arts and Sciences, Co-Chair of the Pew Forum on Religion and Public Life, Chair of the Council on Civil Society, and a member of the Boards of Trustees of the National Humanities Center and National Endowment for Democracy.

Robert P. George is McCormick Professor of Jurisprudence and Director of the James Madison Program in American Ideals and Institutions at Princeton University. His books include *Making Men Moral: Civil Liberties and Public Morality; In Defense of Natural Law;* and, most recently, *The Clash of Orthodoxies*. He is a former Judicial Fellow at the Supreme Court of the United States, a former presidential appointee to the U.S. Committee on Civil Rights, and currently serves on the President's Council on Bioethics. He is a member of the Council on Foreign Relations.

Vigen Guroian is Professor of Theology and Ethics at Loyola College in Baltimore and a member of the faculty of the Ecumenical Institute of Theology at St. Mary's Seminary and University, where he was named the Distinguished Lecturer in Moral and Religious Education at the Institute (1995-1996). Dr. Guroian has published some one hundred and fifty articles on a range of subjects including liturgy and ethics, marriage and family, children's literature, ecology, genocide, and medical ethics. He is the author of several books including *Incarnate Love: Essays in Orthodox Ethics* and *Inheriting Paradise: Meditations on Gardening*.

Louis Henkin is University Professor Emeritus and Special Service Professor at Columbia University. He is Chairman of the Board of Directors of the Columbia University Center for the Study of Human Rights, and founding Chair and Director of the Columbia Law School's Institute of Human Rights. He has made specialties of the law of American foreign relations and of international and comparative human rights. His publications include *How Nations Behave: Law and Foreign Policy* and *Constitutionalism and Rights: The Influence of the U.S. Constitution Abroad*. Professor Henkin is on the Advisory Panel on International Law for the U.S. Department of State, is a member of the American Philosophical Society, and is a Fellow of the American Academy of Arts and Sciences.

Courtney W. Howland last served as Visiting Scholar in Residence at the International Women's Human Rights Center, Georgetown University Law

Center, where she remained until her retirement. Ms. Howland formerly taught international and comparative law on the rights of women, and her interests have focused on powerful social institutions — predominantly constructed and controlled by men — that marginalize women and shape law and gender roles in society. Her article on religious fundamentalism (reprinted in this volume) prompted an international conference on that topic and a book, *Religious Fundamentalisms and the Human Rights of Women,* which she contributed to and edited.

David Novak holds the J. Richard and Dorothy Shiff Chair of Jewish Studies at the University of Toronto. Professor Novak is primarily engaged in the study of the philosophical aspects of the Jewish legal tradition. He is the author of ten books including *Jewish Social Ethics* and *The Election of Israel: The Idea of the Chosen People.* He serves as secretary-treasurer of the Institute of Religion and Public Life in New York, is on the editorial board of its monthly journal *First Things,* is a founder and vice president of the Panel of Inquiry on Jewish Law of the Union for Traditional Judaism, and is a fellow of the American Academy for Jewish Research and the Academy for Jewish Philosophy. He has served as a pulpit rabbi in several congregations.

Sari Nusseibeh is Minister of Jerusalem Affairs for the Palestinian Authority and President and Professor of Islamic Philosophy at Al-Quds University in East Jerusalem. He is the founder and head of the Palestinian Consultancy Group, undertaking research projects on the management of Palestinian infrastructure. He has written dozens of articles on Jerusalem and the prospects for agreement with Israel and has co-authored *No Trumpets, No Drums* and co-edited *Jerusalem: Points of Friction — And Beyond.* In 2003, Professor Nusseibeh and former Israeli security Shin Bet chief Ami Ayalon devised a statement of basic principles for ending the Palestinian-Israeli conflict. The Ayalon-Nusseibeh Plan is intended to be complementary to the political process and has received significant support and approval.

Martin Palouš is Ambassador of the Czech Republic to the United States, appointed by Czech President Václav Havel in the summer of 2001. Ambassador Palouš was one of the first signatories of Charter 77 and served as spokesman for this dissident human rights group in 1986. He has held a number of teaching positions at Charles University since 1990 and has served as the faculty's Vice Dean. In 1993, Ambassador Palouš joined the Centre for Theoretical Studies, a research center run jointly by Charles University and the Czech Academy of Sciences. Ambassador Palouš is the author of numerous publications, including the chapter on the Czech Republic in the European Commission publication *Democratization in Central and Eastern Europe,* and is a well-known translator of the works of Hannah Arendt.

Robert A. Seiple is founder and chairman of the board of the Institute for Global Engagement, a faith-based think tank that combines strategic analysis with an operational component that seeks solutions to complex political and religious problems in difficult parts of the world. He served as the first ever U.S. Ambassador-at-Large for International Religious Freedom in the U.S. State Department and spent eleven years as President of World Vision, Inc., the largest privately funded relief and development agency in the world.

Max L. Stackhouse is the Rimmer and Ruth deVries Professor of Reformed Theology and Public Life and director of the Kuyper Center for Public Theology at Princeton Theological Seminary. He studies and writes extensively on the relationship of theological ethics to society. Professor Stackhouse serves on the editorial board of a number of journals, including the *Journal of Religious Ethics* and *Religion in Eastern Europe.* He is the author and editor of numerous books including *On Moral Business: Classical and Contemporary Resources for Ethics in Economic Life,* and most recently was primary editor and contributor to a four-volume series entitled *God and Globalization* (volume 4 forthcoming). He is an ordained minister in the United Church of Christ and President of the Berkshire Institute for Theology and the Arts.

Charles Villa-Vicencio is Executive Director of the Institute for Justice and Reconciliation, which is committed to the promotion of democratic co-existence and transitional justice in South Africa and across the African continent. Professor Villa-Vicencio is a widely recognized social ethicist and anti-apartheid activist whose writings provide an inside account of the South African human rights experience. He has published nearly 100 professional articles and a dozen books, including *Spirit of Freedom: South African Leaders on Religion and Politics* and *A Theology of Reconstruction.*

Anthony C. Yu is the Carl Darling Buck Distinguished Service Professor in the Humanities and Professor of Religion and Literature at the University of Chicago Divinity School. Professor Yu's research centers on the comparative study of both literary and religious traditions. He is best known for his four-volume translation of *The Journey to the West,* and his published works include *Rereading the Stone: Desire and the Making of Fiction in "Dream of the Red Chamber"* and *State and Religion in China: Historical and Textual Perspectives.*

INTRODUCTION:
The "Why" of Human Rights

ELIZABETH M. BUCAR AND BARBRA BARNETT

In the wake of the horrors of World War II, the United Nations adopted the Universal Declaration of Human Rights (UDHR) in 1945. The UDHR declared to the world community that there are universal standards of human treatment. It also explicitly guaranteed for all citizens of its signatories protection of a bundle of specific rights. Many consider this event the beginning of a new era marking human rights as the philosophy, language, and politics of our time.

Given the pervasiveness of human rights talk in our contemporary society, one might be tempted to conclude that the world has finally reached undisputed consensus on human rights. Despite widespread agreement that there is a set of rights owed to us as human beings, however, there is still wide disagreement about which rights are contained in this set, as well as who should enforce them and how they should be enforced. These disagreements are particularly fierce across national and regional boundaries. The stark reality is that human rights abuses continue to occur, all around the world. Accounts of abuse of Iraqi prisoners, murder and torture of street children in Brazil, kidnapping and forced prostitution of women in Thailand, and genocide in the Democratic Republic of Congo are just a few recent examples of the atrocities that mark our modern failures to enforce human rights.

How can we make sense of the fact that, in the last twenty years, even as international recognition of human rights has permeated our discourse, in practice human rights abuses are far too often a reality? Perhaps one way to gain purchase on this apparent paradox is to consider not what the UDHR sought to accomplish, but what it failed to address. UDHR had a limited goal, to articulate the specific human rights that member states could agree upon. The limited nature of this project is reflected in French Catholic philosopher Jacques Maritain's comment on the debates preceding its drafting: "We agree

1

on these rights, providing we are not asked why. With the 'why,' the dispute begins."[1] The text of the UDHR follows Maritain's advice, intentionally remaining vague and general on the "why" of human rights. The UDHR affirms that "the inherent dignity [of and] the equal and inalienable rights of all members of the human family is the foundation of freedom, justice and peace in the world," but bases these rights on an unnamed, unspecified, ungrounded "common understanding."[2] Following this early attempt to bracket any rationale for human rights, the world community has simply continued to agree to disagree, fearing perhaps that any discussion of the differences among the various rationales for human rights might undermine the consensus manifested in the UDHR.

As time passed, this practice of ignoring the why has given rise to a number of questions. Is a global commitment to human rights so tenuous that open debate on their foundations will dissolve it? Or, as the editors believe, is it possible that the current failures of human rights protection stem from this concerted effort to avoid addressing the rationale for human rights? Have we reached a point in which human rights are strong enough conceptually to withstand debate of the whys, yet still imperfectly enough enforced in practice that such a debate is demanded?

Taken as a whole, this volume argues that considering the why of human rights does not necessarily devolve into irreconcilable conflict. Even if individuals provide different answers to the question of justification, we must continue to discuss our whys in order to identify points of contact, shared assumptions, areas of future debate, and avenues for future improvement.

There is no single solution to the myriad human rights problems plaguing today's world. No nongovernmental organization, sovereign power, or international organization can single-handedly protect military detainees, the dispossessed, targets of genocide, and victims of the sex industry. Each of these problems has emerged in a particular context. The abuse of Iraqi detainees is not the product of an explicit denial of the existence and importance of human rights. Rather, it betrays an insufficient framework for addressing how a government at war can obtain the intelligence necessary to succeed militarily while maintaining its commitment to respect for human life. The torture and murder of street children by Brazilian police demonstrates the inability of a community to address poverty and crime, not just the inadequacy of legal prohibitions against torture and murder. Young girls who are kidnapped and forced into prostitution are not only victims of the perpetrators of these crimes, but are also victims of an international society that pays lip service to equality between the sexes but ignores the huge economic incentives for selling girls and women as sexual objects. The campaigns of genocide and civil war in central Africa are products of both local histories of hostility and global failures to intervene on behalf of the lives of citizens facing violence and oppression in impoverished regions of the world.

As the abuses outlined above demonstrate, human rights are far too easily neglected. We believe that unless we are able to explain to one another why we think human rights are important — express to each other our "whys" for human rights — the world community will be unable to elicit the widespread and consistent support necessary to prevent human rights abuses. The fact that the underlying foundations of human rights will vary within different discursive and geographic contexts does not mean that discussion of the whys is impossible or unfruitful. On the contrary, it makes such a conversation all the more necessary.

Religion and Human Rights

In seeking to provoke an interesting discussion of the conceptual foundations of human rights, we, the editors, posed the following question to contributors to this volume: "Does human rights need God?" This question may appear puzzling at first glance. Human rights are a bundle of claims each person has simply because of his or her humanness. These claims have been enumerated in international declarations and agreements. How does God enter into it? This volume explores the hypothesis that the rationale for human rights cannot be adequately analyzed without addressing religious perspectives. We consider the following questions regarding the relationship of religion and human rights: Do human rights "require" some sort of theological or religious grounding in order to be coherent, valid, or otherwise sustainable — both in theory and in practice? Does religion strengthen or undermine the case for — or protection of — human rights? Do human rights flourish when based upon principles and practices that are secular, religious, or both?

On what basis can one argue that religion is key to the "why" of human rights? First, this volume defines religion broadly, as a comprehensive, albeit perhaps fragmented, tradition of beliefs and practices about the meaning and appropriate living of human life. Given this account, religion plays a central role in the lives of countless individuals throughout the world. For many, religion has a role in answering all the whys of our lives. It is therefore not surprising that for some religion contributes to the why of human rights. Moreover, the fact that so many countries and people of diverse religious and cultural backgrounds acknowledge the significance of human rights may itself have important and interesting implications for our understanding of religion.

In addition, in certain historically specific contexts, religious ideas have been used to justify both the violation and the defense of human rights. As a result, we see at least four different types of arguments for the proper relationship of religion and human rights. First, religion has no place in human rights theory or practice. Second, religion is a prerequisite of human rights ideas and practices. Third, religion is essential to formulating the theoretical foundations of human rights but detrimental to its practical implementation. Fourth, religion is not essential to theoretically grounded human rights, but implementation of human rights is not possible without the cooperation of religious institutions, communities, and individuals. Despite the very real differences between these arguments, all begin with the assumption that religion has a special relationship to the why of human rights.

Approaches to Religion and Human Rights

There are many other volumes that focus on religion and human rights, and much of this literature relies on a single paradigm for resolving this complex relationship. The "theological approach," used by a number of books, focuses on the voices of religious scholars and theologians who argue that the concept of human rights is religiously grounded.[3] In their volume of collected essays, John Witte and Johan van der Vyver label their subject matter "religious human rights,"[4] examining diverse religious foundational texts and religious legal systems to support a complementarity between religious traditions and human rights. Often these theologians and religion scholars conclude that human rights is fundamentally flawed if not grounded in a religiously sanctified notion of human life.

The theological approach is an important perspective because it identifies a role for religious resources in shoring up human rights, and it is articulated by a number of this volume's contributors. But alone, such a characterization of religion and human rights may overlook important facets and nuances of human rights discourse. For example, one may charge that harmony between religion and human rights is merely the result of the efforts of mainstream religious communities to avoid the perception that they stand against the tide of international sentiment. In addition, a seamless narrative in which protection for human rights is embedded in a religion's texts and traditions may neglect the ambiguities of religious institutions' human rights records. Finally, this approach often includes only religious voices, overlooking secular thinkers' contributions to a conversation about the proper relation between human rights and religion.

Another tack taken in religion and human rights research offers a "historical approach" focusing on religious intolerance and the role of intolerance in violations of other human rights norms, as evidenced by ethnic cleansing and campaigns of genocide.[5] These writings have the advantage of focusing our attention on religious freedom as a specific human right. What is unique about religious practice that makes it worthy of international covenantal guarantee? How should the right to religious freedom be protected?

When presented alone, however, this approach can present religious freedom as *the* issue of human rights and God. It can also slip into the assertion that religious traditions, while relevant to a global discussion on religious pluralism, have no other meaningful contribution to offer human rights. This view is contested by a number of our contributors, who would question the appropriateness of limiting the voices of religious traditions or conceptions of God to issues of "proper religious exercise," arguing that religion touches all aspects of a believer's life. Pursued in isolation, this approach may distract us from recognizing how religious traditions might contribute to a more robust international human rights regime and to a safer world.

A third common approach to the issue of human rights and religion — "the cultural approach" — focuses on the relationship between the universality of a human rights ideal and the diverse articulations of particular religious norms for human life.[6] This approach often focuses on the charge that human rights are an invention of the Christian West and have no role in the non-West, a concept most famously modeled in Samuel Huntington's thesis of the "clash of civilizations."[7] A similar approach grounds volumes exploring the arguments for "Asian values" made by some Asian officials and their supporters who reject the imposition of Western values.[8] Focus on diverse articulations of human rights has the advantage of raising the question of whether human rights has the same meaning within an array of cultural contexts. This is not simply a question of empty rhetoric or semantics: real cultural diversity may be at the root of much debate over human rights and consequent challenges to their implementation.

This cultural approach also explores the rejection by some of any need for a transcendent, or even universal, grounding of human rights. As such, it focuses inquiry on the practical ways in which we fall short of implementing human rights ideals in particular contexts, reminding us that, more often than we would hope, communities either reject sets of rights endorsed by others or disagree about the shape and content of specific rights.

Taken alone the cultural approach has two major drawbacks. First, by focusing on the unique character of a particular cultural or political context, the dynamic and interdependent nature of the modern world is too easily ignored. This also slights the different ways religion and human rights have each contributed to the flourishing of the other in varying degrees, in different historical contexts. Second, by drawing too firm a line between local particularities and universal ideas about human rights, one may actually miss an important insight, namely, that even if human rights are understood, articulated, or implemented in divergent ways, there still may be norms that are shared cross-culturally.

These approaches are essential to any conversation regarding God and human rights, but it is our belief as editors that exclusive focus on one approach at the expense of others oversimplifies this complex and dynamic issue. Accordingly, this volume seeks to guide us through a deep and even-handed investigation that brings all three of these approaches into conversation together and, in so doing, raises the discourse to a new level.

Methodology

In an attempt to move beyond a single approach to the issue of religion and human rights and draw a number of different perspectives into conversation, this volume is organized around a question, "Does human rights need God?" The question is meant to be provocative, particularly in its use of "God." Conceptions of the nature and significance of God differ in various contexts, places, and times. Theism and monotheism, in particular, are not universally accepted. Furthermore, even among monotheistic faiths there is no agreement regarding the role of God in human affairs. In this volume "God" is used both to highlight the fact that human rights are often conceived within a Western Judeo-Christian framework and to challenge the sufficiency of that paradigm. This volume thus seeks to explode the assumption that "Religion = God" by including essays that focus on religious traditions that are not God-centered, and essays that call upon an understanding of God that is not defined in terms of a particular religious tradition. Accordingly, the editors of this volume have not given the term "God" a definition, but rather intend to make its proper meaning one of the topics contested in the conversation.

Leading scholars, human rights advocates, and public officials address our organizing question from within various specific contexts. They offer diverse perspectives — Jewish, Protestant, Eastern Orthodox, Muslim, Confucian, feminist, legal, political, and secular humanist. Their arguments span the philosophical and theological spectrum, and they write from diverse geographical regions — the United States and Canada, New Europe, Asia, the

6

Middle East, and Africa. The contributions comprising this volume also span a wide range of rhetorical strategies and writing styles. Readers will note that some chapters are in the form of legal or philosophical arguments supported by many detailed references, while other contributions are informed by personal reflections. One is even presented in interview format. The breadth of styles of essays is part of the strategy of producing a dialogue among various responses to "Does human rights need God?" in order to demonstrate that this question may not be resolvable with an easy, single, or universal answer.

In addition, this volume is arranged in three categories of response to our organizing question: (1) religious appraisals, (2) secular responses, and (3) regional experiences. Parts I and II contain responses that address the organizing question by examining the role of religious and nonreligious traditions in theoretically grounding human rights. At this level "Does human rights need God?" is taken quite literally: Do human rights ideals require a religious backing in order to be properly grounded? If not, from where do human rights originate?

The chapters in Part III exemplify another approach, asking in what ways religion has been or should be a factor in regional discussions of specific human rights issues. The issue here is practical: What contribution might religious traditions make to the future of an international human rights regime?

The three-part classification of essays is thus meant to signal to readers the importance of both theoretical and practical perspectives. Since Part I contributors can be understood to be addressing this issue from their religious expertise and Part II contributors from their expertise of law, feminism, and philosophy, the reader is reminded that there are both religious and nonreligious approaches to the theoretical dimension of this question. The breadth of theoretical approaches includes addressing the question by taking either God or human rights as the pivotal object of discussion. The division between Parts I and II, which deal with more conceptual issues, and Part III, which addresses specific situated cases of implementation, highlights the importance of both the theoretical and practical dimensions. By including specific regional experiences, we seek to remind readers that the theoretical can never be entirely severed from the practical, and vice versa.

The Range of Responses

In Part I, our exploration into the rationales for human rights begins with religious perspectives. Here the contributors explore whether the concept of human rights needs some sort of theological or religious undergirding and the possible conflicts between human rights and religious understandings of rights and duties.

In Chapter 1, Protestant theologian Max Stackhouse argues for grounding human rights in a Christian understanding of God as the ultimate source of all claims for human dignity. Stackhouse argues that the "standard secularist account" of human rights is deficient for defining and protecting human dignity. He explores instances of how individual religious convictions were necessary to the emergence of popular support for the United Nations and contributed the intellectual and ethical substance for the human rights documents which the UN promulgated. For Stackhouse, if human rights is to have any meaning, the conviction that inalienable rights exist, rights which stand above and beyond rights that are granted by a particular form of political authority, is essential. Accordingly, he explores the strands of biblical thought out of which he claims Western notions of human dignity and human rights emerged in order to demonstrate the profundity of their foundations.

By contrast, Eastern Orthodox theologian Vigen Guroian argues in Chapter 2 that human rights thinking is alien to his tradition. Guroian is critical of the Enlightenment doctrine of the "rights of man" and believes that the only real rights an individual human person has are those articulated and guaranteed by the norms, customs, and laws of his or her political community. In the place of human rights, Guroian holds up Orthodox christology and its vision of redemption for identifying what is normatively human and necessary for the freedom and flourishing of human beings. Moreover, for Guroian, his tradition provides a platform to critique the weaknesses and dangers of contemporary human rights ideas.

David Novak, a prominent scholar of Jewish thought, finds in Chapter 3 that in order to be sustainable, the concept of human rights for him depends upon a theistic scriptural account of human life and value. In exploring the relationship among God, human rights, and democracy, Novak recognizes that in religiously plural democratic communities, such as the United States and Canada, affirmation of human rights may depend upon diverse pre-political convictions and commitments. He describes the sources of his own affirmation of human rights through an exegesis of Judaic Scripture and tradition in order to clarify moral principles that can be argued for rationally.

In Chapter 4 Khaled Abou El Fadl, professor of Islamic law and recent presidential appointee to the U.S. Commission on International Religious Freedom, addresses the compatibility of Islam with democracy and individual rights. Abou El Fadl acknowledges that God is the only sovereign and source of legitimate law in Islam. God's will is not always unequivocal, however. Further, Abou El Fadl argues that Islam requires certain values, not a certain political form. He explains that central to Islam is the responsibility of each human being to combat injustice, as God's vice-regent on earth. He also identifies sources of Islamic recognition of individual rights through an exploration of the necessary elements of a dignified existence. Through this Islamic conception of individual responsibility and human dignity, Abou El Fadl finds constitutional democracy as the best guarantee for combating injustice and protecting basic human rights. At the same time, constitutional democracies contain safeguards against the errors of judgment and temptations associated with human fallibility. In this context, human rights do not negate ultimate divine sovereignty by allowing human beings to create law. Rather, constitutional democracies acknowledge the human ability and responsibility to pursue a just political society that aspires to attain the ideal of divine law, while denying the state the pretense of divinity.

In Chapter 5, distinguished religion and literature scholar Anthony Yu directs our attention to an intriguing problem in defining human rights in terms of God. Chinese civilization is not founded upon a Judeo Christian God. Accordingly, a different paradigm of human rights must be employed to address the concept of human rights in a Chinese religious context. Yu offers a critique and reinterpretation of traditional Confucianism, and demonstrates that religious support for human rights need not depend upon an appeal to theistic transcendence. Yu also challenges the assumption that the conflict between human rights and the Confucian tradition is a simple conflict between communitarian values and concern for individual autonomy. He describes strands of Confucian thought that recognize the reality of self-affirmation, self-love, self-interest, and self-preservation, all grounded in the concept of human desire. For Yu, desire is the defining feature of our common humanity, and the basis of both virtue and vice. Thus, he sees a possibility for growth of human rights ideas from within Chinese tradition and offers reflections on the dynamism of Chinese civilization and culture through an examination of the modern transformation of the Chinese language.

In Part II, contributors provide secular responses to the question "Does human rights need God?" by addressing, from nonreligious standpoints, the impact of religious movements, beliefs, practices, and institutions on human rights. As human rights is a phenomenon that speaks to political life and community, a conversation regarding the relationship between religion and human rights should not be limited to the voices of theologians and religion scholars. Rather, a truly enriching conversation should also include secular voices. This section invites the reader to ask, first, whether the secular project for securing protection for human rights can adequately accommodate religious traditions and, second, how particular religious institutions and traditions may be obstacles to human rights.

In Chapter 6, moral and political philosopher Robert George engages the editors of this volume in a conversation about human rights from a natural law perspective. For George, there are certain basic human goods that contribute to the fulfillment of human individuals and communities. The pursuit of such things as friendship, knowledge, virtue, and aesthetic appreciation are basic constituents of well-being and form the foundation of our moral judgments. These basic goods in turn implicate certain rights that people have by virtue of their humanity. Moreover, by reflecting on the nature of the human person and human life, anyone and everyone can recognize these moral truths — and their related rights — and conform his or her conduct to their terms. Although George is himself a theist, understanding human dignity as ultimately derived from our relationship to a divine creator, the natural law theory George expounds justifies human rights protection on the basis of our humanity, without explicit theological reference.

Legal scholar Louis Henkin contends in Chapter 7 that religion and human rights differ radically in terms of their sources, bases of authority, forms of expression, and substantive norms. Henkin argues that human rights is not, and should not be taken to be, a total ideology. Rather, it has the limited purpose of promoting the good life within national societies in an international political system and thus has as its sources human contemporary life and society. As such, human rights are limited, legal, and formal. But Henkin remains hopeful that a *rapprochement* is possible between human rights and religious communities that share a commitment to promoting human dignity, thus developing and enlarging the overlapping portions of their agendas.

Feminist legal scholar Courtney Howland shows in Chapter 8 how religious fundamentalist movements have capitalized on a perceived tension between religious freedom and gender equality in order to limit women's human rights. Howland offers a detailed examination of contemporary fundamentalist movements in the context of Buddhism, Christianity, Hinduism, Islam, and Judaism. She highlights the common adherence to male superiority and female subservience within these movements and traces their attempts to enact female obedience into domestic law. For Howland, this reality suggests the necessity of grounding protection for human rights in an extra-religious source. She finds that international law provides an adequate paradigm for adjudicating this conflict between international recognition of equality between the sexes and domestic laws based in fundamentalist beliefs.

Part III is comprised of regional responses, exemplifying the complex relationship between God and human rights in particular contexts around the globe. This section considers how, in lived experience, religious, philosophical, and political convictions have joined together to create movements capable of overturning intransigent regimes that systematically deny human rights. It also demonstrates obstacles religious convictions may erect to the cooperative endeavors necessary to protect human rights. This is a section in which remarkable individuals, who have dedicated their daily lives to the cause of human rights, describe their experiences. Their insights regarding the relationship between God and human rights enriches and enlivens our debate. They bridge the theoretical approaches featured in Parts I and II to the needs of practical implementation through their concrete experiences in South Africa, pre-1989 Czechoslovakia, Israel and Palestine, and the United States State Department.

Leading Palestinian intellectual Sari Nusseibeh considers in Chapter 9 whether God is the obstacle to the protection of human rights in the Israeli-Palestinian conflict. In this chapter, Nusseibeh traces the conflicting rights claims, sources of authority for those claims, and their tragic consequences for this tiny parcel of land and its inhabitants. Nusseibeh is critical of a literalist approach, by which religious adherents refuse to subject divine edicts to human reason or to measure them against human consequences. He cites rationalist strands of Islamic thought, which provide authority for subjecting putative divine edicts to the test of human reason. Nusseibeh offers no simple solution, however, to the religious tribalism by which both Muslims and Jews claim to be the exclusive inheritors of the Abrahamic message and homeland, and by which they kill in order to justify and defend that claim.

In Chapter 10 South African scholar and political reformer Charles Villa-Vicencio examines the role of religion and rights in twentieth-century South Africa and offers religious reflection based on his role in the Truth and Reconciliation process. Villa-Vicencio shows how South Africa shifted from an overtly Christian state, which justified apartheid rule on the claim that white colonizers were the carriers of the gospel and civilization, to a constitutional and secular state, characterized by a spirit of renewal, openness, and generalized human fulfillment. For Villa-Vicencio, this spirit of renewal is found in diverse voices, spiritual and secular, religious and material, and is aimed at ensuring that those norms and values that protect the rights of all South Africans are entrenched in what he describes as a "nonreligious theological openness," in contrast to the explicitly religious, exclusionary apartheid system. Whether this openness, which drives the quest to reach beyond what is to what ought to be, is the "God" that human rights requires, depends upon one's understanding of God, Villa-Vicencio concludes.

Martin Palouš, political philosopher and Czech Ambassador to the United States, wonders in Chapter 11 if respect for human rights is evidence of the realm of the divine manifest in human life. He traces up to the modern era the history of Western political philosophy and the development of political communities in which rights-talk emerged. Palouš draws on Aristotle's distinction between the active and contemplative life and the tension between human finitude and human openness to transcendence. For Palouš, Cicero represents an exemplary moderate politician, who was able to apply insights culled from philosophical contemplation to cultivate and humanize the public life, providing a spiritual balance within the political culture. This enlightened politics is necessary if the voice of conscience and freedom is to have a role in political decision-making. For Palouš, the God who safeguards and fosters these ideals in Western politics is the God that human rights requires, and the existence of such a God may be evidenced in the fall of inhumane systems of rule such as totalitarianism.

Finally, in Chapter 12 the first U.S. Ambassador-at-Large for Religious Freedom, Robert Seiple, discusses the legacy of religious freedom in American history. He demonstrates the pivotal role of religious tolerance and freedom of conscience for the American forefathers. Seiple then turns to modern history and discusses the emergence of the International Religious Freedom Act as the logical outgrowth of this legacy, even if its passage and implementation have been fraught with political wrangling. The challenge Seiple presents is how to implement this ideal of respect for difference into our foreign policy decisions. Only by truly exemplifying and realizing the values upon which the United States was built can America live up to its potential and be a source of inspiration — rather than resentment — in the world. This, Seiple argues, is also the key to our national security.

Thematic Currents

This volume represents an attempt to pick up where the drafters of the UDHR left off, by encouraging a conversation among diverse perspectives on the "why" of human rights. In an attempt to demonstrate that such dialogue is both possible and profitable, we offer five broad themes that arise throughout this volume.

Sources of Authority and Moral Anthropology

By and large, this volume's contributors reject the skeptical conclusion that human beings lack any common basis upon which universal human rights can be built, that human beings share only particular, geographic, familial, social, or tribal affinities and loyalties. To the contrary, resonating within each section of this volume is the premise that a source of rights may be found in human nature, whether religiously or nonreligiously conceived. Toward this end, many of these essays explore "a normative human nature . . . concretely manifested in every individual who comes into existence."[9] Each contributor, however, approaches the organizing question from a distinct perspective, and thus relies on different sources of authority for presenting her or his account of human nature.

The organization of the book broadly distinguishes among different sources of authority relevant to the grounding and elaboration of human rights: sources from religious traditions, those from nonreligious disciplines, and geopolitical-specific sources. The sources of authority presented are, however, diverse even within each section. In addition, this volume offers a plurality of ideas about which aspects of the human experience best flesh out an anthropology and provide evidence of a shared human nature. For example, Anthony Yu looks to ancient Chinese philosophers for guidance for the dignity of humanity and finds desire common to all persons "from the highest ruler to the lowliest peasant."[10] Charles Villa-Vicencio draws upon the history of social thought for his exploration into the human condition in which he discovers "a deep anthropological refusal to submit to subjugation . . . an impulse to be free, to reach beyond the confines of control — whether political, intellectual, or spiritual."[11] Louis Henkin argues that the concept of human rights reflects "a universal, contemporary moral intuition."[12] For Henkin, contemporary human social life offers the primary source for locating the form and character of this normative intuition about human dignity.

Other contributors, such as Vigen Guroian, reject the turn to human sources for excavation of the human condition. For Guroian, God is the source of human nature and provides the deepest roots of human flourishing. Note how radically this position differs from the sources for human dignity proffered by Yu, Villa-Vicencio, and Henkin — particularly Villa-Vicencio's, given his emphasis on freedom. Guroian challenges accounts that locate human dignity in human autonomy by offering an Eastern Orthodox understanding that human life properly understood is theonomous, not autonomous, in which human dignity is dependent upon a relation to the divine. For Robert George, the universal human character is found neither exclusively in human sources nor exclusively in our dependence upon the divine. Rather, reason and freedom are the fundamental elements of human dignity, which provides each human being with the duty to, and claim of, respect. Sari Nusseibeh further complicates the issue of sources of authority by highlighting the catastrophic conflicts that may arise when one fails to examine one's sources of authority or dogmatically asserts them over and against competing rights claims.

What is the value of a conversation in which each participant argues from different theoretical or religious starting points, supporting his or her claim with different warrants? This theme suggests that further reflection is necessary on whether engaging a diversity of sources could strengthen human rights discourse by revealing points of profound resonance and recognition. Notwithstanding the diversity of theoretical and religious starting points, there appears to be, as we have said, wide agreement that a source of rights may be found in human nature, whether religiously or nonreligiously conceived. Since human nature is something all humans share, there is reason to hope that conversation among the differing perspectives finally has some common ground to which it may appeal. This theme also suggests the need to consider whether such foundational diversity demands an equally complex paradigm for practical implementation of human rights norms.

Roles of Institutions

A stumbling block to the implementation of human rights is the continuing failure to implement human rights norms into a stable and responsive human rights regime. This question of how to implement human rights theory into effective praxis is of immense importance to several contributors. For example, Vigen Guroian's principal concern about a human rights regime grounded exclusively in human sources stems from his understanding of the human propensity for sin. He worries, "can sinful human beings resist turning their claims to human rights into swords of vengeance or into injurious pretexts for self-aggrandizement?"[13] Guroian, of course, calls for a transcendent referent to counter human sin: God. Other contributors look to human institutions as best suited to resolving conflicts and bringing to fruition a world in which human rights are universally respected.

Several contributors seek institutional checks and balances against human corruption and oppressive regimes. For example, Courtney Howland believes that the United Nations is the appropriate arbiter for resolving rights claims and protecting fundamental human dignity. In particular, she is concerned with the equal rights of women and the potential conflict between those claims and the right to religious freedom. From Howland's perspective, certain fundamentalist religious groups, which ground their authority in transcendent sources, have in fact converted claims for religious freedom into pretexts for subordinating women. Thus, she argues for the importance of international organizations, such as the United Nations, to check the self-aggrandizing moves of these local groups. Howland also references the work of several nongovernmental organizations in collecting and disseminating data on the state of human rights in various parts of the world.

Another institution that may be employed to further the implementation of the human rights ideal is the nation-state. Robert Seiple sees a responsibility incumbent upon national governments to work toward greater protection for human rights globally. The International Religious Freedom Act, a domestic U.S. statute, provides the authority for consideration of violations of religious freedom in other parts of the world as a component of American foreign policy. In effect, the statute institutionalizes an American concern with the right to religious freedom and extends that concern to all religious adherents wherever they may live.

In considering the nation-state as an institution capable of contributing to the implementation of human rights, several authors argue that constitutional democracies are uniquely capable of providing the necessary balance between freedom and order, thus allowing human rights to flourish. For example, Khaled Abou El Fadl argues that an Islamic constitutional democracy "offers the greatest potential for promoting justice and protecting human dignity, without making God responsible for human injustice or the degradation of human beings by one another."[14] David Novak also finds that democratic societies are unique in their affirmation of human rights. Novak further argues that the respect for freedom of conscience, essential to constitutional democracies, allows for the possibility of a "reciprocal tolerance" through which religious and nonreligious members of a democratic political community bring their diverse pre-political commitments to the public sphere. In this respect, the institutional framework of a constitutional democracy fosters positive changes in the relations among diverse communities. Seiple's firsthand report of the challenging process of introducing, passing, and implementing legislation in the U.S. Congress, however, reminds us that constitutional democracies are human institutions subject to the vagaries of the political process, and provide no panacea for human rights.

As for the role of religious institutions in this process, Max Stackhouse explores the positive contribution of the Christian church to human rights. He argues that the church not only supports human rights but is also the embodiment of human rights ideals. Stackhouse further argues that the church "has opened the door to the development of dynamic pluralistic democratic polities that are both protected *by* human rights ideals and laws and provide the organizational infrastructure for the protection *of* human rights of both persons and groups."[15]

The role of institutions raises a number of other issues. If many institutions have a role in human rights, how do they work together? What happens when these institutions disagree about the nature and content of rights, as well as the appropriate means of implementing human rights norms? This theme suggests that the human rights community needs to work with a greater variety of institutions in implementing human rights norms and that it needs to engage in further conversation about these institutions' respective strengths, limitations, and interdependence.

Historical Dynamism

Historical dynamism is a theme that appears frequently throughout this volume. The continually unfolding character of history itself is dynamic. Not merely the accumulated past of settled facts and conditions into which we are born, history is also the ongoing record of human reaction to and interpretation of those facts and conditions. In other words, history reveals the effects of the past on human society in the present, and how our actions in the present affect the course of the future. This theme resonates throughout Sari Nusseibeh's essay, as he carefully traces the two distinct histories that have erupted into the present Israeli-Palestinian conflict. The history of each people, Muslim and Jewish, has conditioned their understanding of the present situation and limits the array of possible decisions for the future.

Historical dynamism also emerges in these pages through the fluidity of the central concepts of analysis: religion and human rights. The historical dynamism of religion first emerges in Part I. As Stackhouse explains, "religions do not exist as self-contained complete monads. They are dynamic and seldom static . . . they constantly interact with and respond to one another as well as to various philosophies and cultures."[16] Anthony Yu's essay on Confucianism and human rights describes the fate of classical Chinese philosophy in the wake of history, including the dismantling of the imperial system of governance and the 1911 revolution. Yu employs a historical methodology to address the perceived conflict between the Western emphasis on the individual and the importance of community emphasized in "Asian Values." This methodology enables Yu to reclaim strands of Confucian philosophy that support individual dignity and worth. Yu's essay is not only a specific historical examination of Confucian discourse on the individual, however; it is also an exploration of the more general ways in which traditions sustain themselves. Yu argues that many aspects of tradition "need to embody modified content or restructured substance if they are to address realistically and effectively the altered social contexts."[17] In fact, these important cultural features often owe their longevity to their ability to change, an apparent paradox that Yu aptly calls "the change-ability of the culturally permanent."[18] In other words, dynamism is what allows traditional practices and beliefs to continue to be relevant in changing contemporary circumstances.

The dynamism of human rights in relation to contemporary geo-political conditions is particularly vivid in Part III of this volume. For example, Martin Palouš reminds us of the emergence of the idea of human rights in the Greek *polis* and then describes the historical situation that permitted the startling emergence of human rights discourse in Czechoslovakia. Similarly, Seiple examines how religious pluralism in the early American colonial period contributed to the emergence of a radically broad conception of religious freedom, which has contemporary applications and repercussions beyond the borders of the United States.

Historical dynamism is also visible throughout this volume in the reflexive relationship among religion, history, and human rights. As religion and human rights are each affected by history, so is history affected by the contemporary shapes taken by religion and human rights. These phenomena, human rights and religion, are particularly potent in transforming the course of history, because each is manifest in the character of the actions of individuals who cherish it. One vivid example of the evolving quest for human rights is described through Charles Villa-Vicencio's account of the Truth and Reconciliation Commission. He describes the pursuit of human rights as "the incentive to be more than we are, or our nations have achieved, at any given time."[19] This shows how the limited and particular incarnations of rights that have been achieved at any particular point in history are only the beginning of the story of human rights. The ideal of human rights provides the inspiration to transform the current situation into a more promising future. In this respect human rights is "a prophecy which procures its own fulfillment."[20] Even Sari Nusseibeh, who details the theological, historical, and tribal obstacles to resolving conflicting rights claims in Palestine/Israel, proclaims the overriding need to "continue seeking an ideal world in the here and now, and not only in the hereafter."[21]

The theme of historical dynamism reminds us that any response to the question "Does human rights need God?" is incomplete unless it can be specified in appropriate ways to differing historical contexts. If we recognize the dynamic aspects of history, religion, and human rights, we may be better situated to understand their interrelations in particular contexts and better able to make informed decisions about the steps that must be taken for the future.

Warming Up Cold Rights

Another important theme throughout the book is an exploration of how the ideal of human rights can be transformed through a discussion of religion. Many of the contributors note that, at times, the dispassionate rights-talk of the international legal community is severed from the actual terrain on which rights battles are fought and won. Rights-talk can be cold, empty rhetoric, ill-equipped for galvanizing the emotions and commitments needed to preserve human dignity. This challenge is raised explicitly by Louis Henkin: "Human rights — cold rights — do not provide warmth, belonging, fitting, significance, do not exclude need for love, friendship, family, charity, sympathy, devotion, sanctity, or for expiation, atonement, forgiveness."[22]

Accordingly, many chapters seek to move beyond "rights-talk" to what Henkin describes as the "larger, deeper areas beyond the common denominator of human rights."[23] In this respect the book's contributors call for that which transcends the legalistic and political negotiation of rights and interests among competing factions, in order to recover that which can open up a possibility of mercy, compassion, reconciliation, redemption, or renewal. This category of reflection, which is beyond the merely human — variously described as God, religion, grace — is fundamental to many contributors. For example, for Abou El Fadl a key element to creating a just society is mercy, which "is a state in which the individual is able to be just with himself or herself, and with others. . . . [M]ercy is tied to a state of true and genuine perception of others . . . is coupled with the need for human beings to be patient and tolerant with each other." It "enables persons to understand and appreciate, and become enriched by the diversity of humanity," and it is, therefore, a constituent element of founding a just society.[24] For his part, Guroian answers his own question, "How can sinful human beings resist turning their claims to human rights into swords of vengeance or into injurious pretexts for self-aggrandizement?" He does so with a call for repentance and forgiveness.[25]

How do these deeper aspects of the human condition relate to the problem of human rights? How can appeal to these sentiments transform the human rights discourse and transform understandings of human nature? For many these dimensions of human life can be explained only through religious symbolism and language. Others disagree. In either case, however, we highlight this theme because the claim by some of our authors that human rights depends on a deeper understanding of human flourishing is another way to state that the why question, to which this book is directed, is important.

Power of Persuasion

The final theme involves the various methods of persuasion employed to argue for a particular relation of human rights and religion. One contributor may argue from a foundational text of his religious tradition; another may emphasize the role of a particular legal institution in implementation; still another contributor may argue historically, or may contend that the question of human rights cannot be properly understood without God. Each of these approaches represents a distinctive pedagogy of persuasion. Even when two authors initially appear similar in their understanding of the relationship between religion and human rights, they employ different grounds and warrants to support their claims.

At first blush this appeal to diverse pedagogies of persuasion might seem to slip into cultural relativism. Recognition that different arguments are more or less persuasive depending upon the particular worldview of a contributor or reader, however, reflects the fact that human rights inhere in each unique, particular, individual human being. This conspicuous diversity of rhetorical strategies resonates with Max Stackhouse's claim that specific human rights are grounded in a special relationship between both first principles and concrete circumstances. Human rights "are, in principle, demanding of a universalistic reference point, but are simultaneously pluralistic in their internal structure."[26] Charles Villa-Vicencio makes a similar point when he urges those of us committed to human rights to promote them "in relation to the needs and challenges of a particular context. [This enables] the universal to become particular — the word to become flesh."[27] This theme calls us to consider whether a single rhetorical account of human rights can be sufficient or necessary.

Perhaps the different pedagogies of persuasion, each with its own specific way of concretizing universal claims, also point to the human capacity to resolve conflicting claims through nonviolent means. Through his or her commitment to a particular rhetorical strategy, in a volume designed to reach a broad and diverse readership, each contributor evidences a hope in the efficacy of persuasion and argumentation. In other words, by agreeing to present her or his argument alongside the arguments of individuals with different backgrounds and perspectives, each contributor seeks to persuade through discourse, engagement, and respectful argumentation.

This commitment to argumentation may in some ways be the product of many contributors' experiences living in constitutional democracies. As Abou El Fadl notes, valuing intellectual and cultural diversity is an ethical virtue crucial to constitutional democracies and requires persuasion and engagement in public discourse. Tolerance and mutual respect may grow out of freedom of expression and the need to find reasons to pursue common goals. In a similar fashion, this volume seeks to highlight ways in which full and free discourse about God and human rights may engender greater mutual respect and cooperation, thus contributing to the creation and maintenance of a stable and responsive human rights regime. The result may reveal that norms of human rights are not necessarily culturally relative, even if the sorts of arguments made about human rights seem to be. In other words, although there are differing pedagogies of persuasion, the discovery that they lead to common conclusions about human rights, so that these rights are not themselves culturally relative, holds open the possibility that common grounds may be discovered regarding answers to the why question. The differing sorts of arguments may, if engagement between them occurs, emerge as appropriate contextual differences specifying agreement on wider dimensions of the human condition in which human rights are grounded, thereby strengthening common commitment to those rights. Only through the conversation can we know whether this latter agreement is possible.

The theme of rhetorical diversity points to a need to continually expand and deepen conversations about human rights. Charting an honest and realistic course to a world in which each human person is in fact guaranteed protection of a universally recognized bundle of rights begins with recognizing and respecting the validity of distinct and sometimes divergent voices. But this theme also highlights a challenge: If forms of persuasion vary, how are we to achieve a universal understanding of human rights? In other words, can mutual respect lead to cooperative action on grounds that all can accept?

Conclusion

This collection of essays seeks to reflect a rich conversation on the why of human rights and thereby provide policymakers and human rights advocates with some tools for understanding the various ways religion can answer or complicate human rights. It also hopes to provide individuals with various ways in which to answer the why, giving human rights concerns a voice in a personal calculus of what needs to be done. Perhaps part of the failure of the human rights regime in practice has been due to a reliance on governments for doing the real work of protecting human rights. In the future, individuals may need to play a more prominent role in combating those forces that tend toward tabling human rights concerns in the interest of limited and short-sighted goals. Finally, this volume is not an attempt to provide a consensus on the why of human rights, but rather to argue that a conversation about the whys is possible, and that agreement on the fact that rights exist might not be enough if we do not ask the why.

Although no single work could be comprehensive, this collection of essays signals the breadth of possible approaches to the conceptual grounding and practical protection of human rights. Theologians, legal scholars, philosophers, statesmen, and policy-makers each address the relationship between religion and human rights from the perspective of her or his particular field of inquiry. The result is a unique compilation of diverse worldviews, each contributing a piece to the complex puzzle that members of diverse societies must solve if the idea of human rights is to become a reality in practice. The chapters in this volume thus represent not only particular perspectives or fields but also essential components of any truly universal human rights regime. Last century, Jacques Maritain lamented that with the "why" the dispute begins. This book signals what we hope will be a new era in human rights, one in which with the "why" the conversation begins.

PART I

RELIGIOUS APPRAISALS

1 Why Human Rights Needs God: A Christian Perspective

MAX L. STACKHOUSE

More than a quarter century ago, I was invited by my church to participate in ecumenical discussions and to serve as a visiting lecturer in the theological academies of sister churches in the German Democratic Republic and in South India. I became fascinated with the way in which different ideational and social traditions treated human rights, including the interpretations of the United Nations Universal Declaration of Human Rights of 1948 (the "Universal Declaration") and its subsequent covenants. Resistance to "Western" definitions of human rights was intense in the Marxist parties of Eastern Europe and, it turned out, both in the leadership of the Congress Party under Indira Gandhi in India, when she declared her "emergency" in 1976, and in the then emerging Hindu Nationalist parties. On the basis of these extended exposures to non-Western interpretations of human rights, I engaged in a comparative study of the roots and conceptual framework that made modern human rights discourse possible.[1] The invitation to contribute to this volume is a welcome opportunity to rethink the issues in view of new conditions.

There are many things that I might say in response to the organizing question of this volume, "Does human rights need God?" But because space is brief, I am going to focus on two matters, perhaps best understood as providing a response to what I perceive as two challenges to the grounding of hu-

This essay expands on motifs offered at a panel on religion and human rights at the Society of Christian Ethics, later published as "The Intellectual Crisis of a Good Idea," *Journal of Religious Ethics* 26, no. 2 (1998): 263-68; and at a talk on Tolerance and Human Rights, given at Andover Newton Theological School, later published as "A Christian Perspective on Human Rights," *Society* 41, no. 2 (2004): 23-29.

man rights norms: secularist ideology and religious pluralism. First, I will address the claim, often advanced from within the human rights community, that human rights do not have and do not require any religious grounding. Diverse versions of "the standard secularist account" find adequate grounding in secular conceptions of human dignity. In contrast to this view I will argue that the foundations of human rights claims are essentially theological. Second, the reality of ethical pluralism caused by the variety of religions has raised the question as to whether human rights are in any sense universal. I will offer a Christian perspective on the sources of human rights in order to show how human rights ideas formulated historically by the Christian biblically based tradition can recognize, learn from, and selectively embrace philosophical and legal insights from other cultures.[2]

Secularist Views: The Intellectual Crisis of a Good Idea

"The standard secularist account" is found among lawyers, political scientists, economists, philosophers, and others whom we meet often in academia and public policy positions. Some turn to it because religion is marginal to their lives. They cannot imagine how it really means much to anyone else or to society at large; others segregate their historical and social thought from their faith, even if they are personally religious. Whatever its roots, it is, I believe, a deficient view, finally incapable of either defining the full scope or limiting the misuses of human rights arguments.

The uses of the terms "religion" and "theology" that appear in this secular account are prejudiced and confused. The word "religion" is not always clearly distinguished from particular religions, and the operative parts of the conflated definition are often self-contradictory. Secular thinkers tend to presume either that religion is a private sentiment which everyone should be allowed to have in his or her own way (in which case it can hardly serve to ground any public and political moral program) or that it is the ideological expression of group identity — a view that did not originate with Ludwig Feuerbach's notion of projection, or contemporary social location theory, but which is today indebted to them. Understood in this second way, religion is, to be sure, a social and political force, but a constructed one — used to legitimate egoism, war, misogyny, colonial exploitation, and violence.

I have no doubt that religion involves personal sentiments and provides the inner structure of personal moral character or that it also has a communal component that makes it a potent social force intimately tied to other social forces. But it follows from neither of these facts that religion is either irrelevant to the pursuit of justice or that religion is the source of the many social evils of the world.

What evidence can we give that religion has done more damage to human well-being than the legal advisors to kings who threw religious saints and martyrs into dungeons, the judges who tried witches against the advice of the clergy, the lawyers who wrote the slave laws, the jurists who drafted the justifications for the division of the world among the colonial powers, or the legal bureaucracies that enforced Hitler's or Papa Doc's or Stalin's or Mao's edicts?

I do not wish to portray religion as pure and innocent nor the powers of the world — such as law, economics, politics, or culture — as evil or sinful. I view them as equally sinful and as equally redeemable. Heaven knows that various religions have shown complicity in evil and that some are inclined to foment or legitimate particular evils because of the way they are internally constituted. But gross evil is present in many areas of life when this or that religion is not present, and it takes a more subtle analysis than we usually get from the accusers of religion under the standard secularist account to discern the degree to which religion mitigates or augments particular evils. George H. Williams was surely right when he said (often in lectures at Havard), "Religion is high voltage; it can energize much or electrocute many." For this reason, religion is the human acknowledgment that we live under a power and morality that we did not construct and may not ignore, and particular religions are sets of ultimate convictions and hypotheses about the nature, character, demands, and implications of that reality. They may be judged by reference to that reality, but otherwise must be treated with greater care and nuance than the accusers show.

"Religion in general" probably had no more to do with the origin and development of human rights ideas than "law in general" generated pluralistic constitutional democracy. That, however, is not at all the same as saying that specific religious convictions about how humans are constituted in the image of God — "endowed" with dignity (as the Universal Declaration says, although it does not say who did the endowing) — and about how God wants us to live, convictions argued in public theological debates about the relation of faith to truth and justice, have had nothing to do with human rights or democracy.

People, of course, use the term "theology" differently. Some use it as a confessional shell to wrap around a religion to make it unassailable to criticism, an intellectual trump to play when precious convictions are challenged. This license to be dogmatic in the less savory sense of the term is the meaning of "theology" most often accepted by the standard secularist account. It assumes that no theological claim or argument of ethic could be universally true without imperialism, for it holds that all theology is irrational and group particular; it denies the fact that every religion can be, and often is, assessed by norms of justice as well as truth and faith in theological terms. These assumptions are not completely unwarranted; some theologians do use theology this way to resist human rights.

Another, deeper view of theology, however, sees it as precisely the proper discipline to evaluate various religious, ethical, and quasi-religious claims to determine whether they are in accord with what humans can reasonably know about God, God's justice, and God's relationship to the world. On these grounds, some religions or aspects of religions, some ethical principles or purposes borne by them, and some morally laden quasi-religious claims (such as some human rights ideologies) can be judged as false or trivial while others can be judged as having greater validity or importance. It is at this point that reason converges with some religious orientations to form theology in such a way that it can judge bad faith from within and provide the moral architecture of civilization without. Theology, thus understood, issues in jurisprudence and the upbuilding of those key institutions of civil society, especially communities of faith, that in turn generated the complex societies that the secularist sees as the sociological source and grounding of human rights. That the jurisprudence and the society at large do not acknowledge these sources (and, indeed, may actually deny them) does not alter what is actually the case.

No known civilization has ever endured that was not rooted in some such beliefs about ultimate reality and what it requires of us, although some cultures are stronger and some are weaker in their capacity to join faith with reason, become self-critical, and shape changing civilizations. They then feed, and feed on, other religions, and prompt revision and reform in them, even if they do not convert everyone. After all, religions do not exist as self-contained complete monads. They are dynamic and seldom static, even if they share certain basic characteristics that allow us to use the word "religion" to point to quite different phenomena. Besides, they constantly interact with and respond to one another as well as to various philosophies and cultures. That is why human rights are discovered as latently or potentially present in other religions also.

A specific investigation into how the Christian tradition has contributed to human rights will be addressed in section two. But as for religion in general, the evidence for its linkage to human rights has been clear for some time, at least since the work of Georg Jellinek, the great Jewish legal historian and friend of the "quasi-Unitarian" Max Weber, the Lutheran Ernst Troeltsch, and the Calvinist Abram Kuyper — all of whom approved the embrace of rights theory by Pope Leo XIII from the 1890s on.[3] Jellinek showed that a theologically refined religious faith, not the repudiation of it, best accounted for the rights established in modern constitutions. Such a faith, publicly articulated, is what had allowed the founders of the United States to declare, quoting a line from one of Locke's most Puritan writings, "We hold these truths to be self-evident, that all men are created equal, that they are endowed by their Creator with certain unalienable rights." It is not hard to show that these theological traditions are the ones to which the authors of the Universal Declaration turned after the terrors of Nazi paganism and in the face of Communist secularism. I do not deny that it has taken more than two centuries for the "all" to revise the operative definition of "men" as including only white, propertied males, but I deny that it was Kant's immaculate conception of human dignity that served as the root of human rights ideas, as a number of secularist advocates of human rights have claimed. He was not in that way Immanuel.

In fresh research, the British scholar-pastor Canon John Nurser has documented in extended detail the ways in which, from 1939 until 1947, leading ecumenical Protestant figures worked with key figures not only in developing the Bretton Woods agreements, anticipating a postwar need for economic stability and development, but also in forming the Commission for a Just and Durable Peace, the Churches' Commission on International Affairs, and later the Joint Committee on Religious Liberty, all under the auspices of the Federal Council of Churches, with close connections to the emerging World Council of Churches and the International Missionary Conference. These organizations, notably led by Lutheran O. Frederick Nolde, Congregationalist Richard Fagley, Baptist M. Searle Bates, and Presbyterian John A. Mackay, among others, were dedicated to shaping what they then called a "new world order" that would honor human rights. They worked closely with Jacob Blaustein and Joseph Proskauer of the American Jewish Committee and with twelve bishops of the Roman Catholic Church to encourage the formation of the United Nations Charter Committee and the committee that drafted the Universal Declaration. Further, they worked through their church and synagogue contacts at the local level to build popular support for the activities of the United Nations. In fact, the more this history is dug out, the clearer it becomes that they supplied much of the intellectual and ethical substance that formed these so-called "secular" documents.[4] Such data is of particular importance, for it helps correct the secularists' slanderous treatment of religion as the cause of human rights violations.

The results of such efforts are what leaders from most of the world's great cultures have now endorsed, what oppressed peoples appeal to for justice, and what are functionally recognizable principles of universal justice.[5] Moreover, there are, at present, more people living under democratically ordered constitutions that seek to protect human rights, and a broader public constituency interested in defending them, than at any point in human history, and little evidence of their fading from normative use soon.[6] Indeed, even those who violate human rights plead special conditions, temporary delays, or hermeneutical differences regarding the relative weight of some as compared to others; they seldom deny their validity as ideals or goals.

In any case, the standard secularist account of autonomous human rights is mistaken. Some hold, indeed, that if human rights discourse has no other grounds than those the secularist account approves, the movement for human rights will and should fade until another time. The reason is that human rights need to be embedded in a wider view of ethics, a deeper view of social history, and a higher view of meaning if they are to be actualized in a more embracing web of duties, virtues, commitments to justice, and concerns for the common good. Without this, rights claims spin out of control and become the Rorschach of every ideological agenda. On this ground, it can be said that the theological view is more universal, reasonable, and inclusive and that the secularist account is more particular, irrational, and narrow.

Clearly, all modern and postmodern thought, including theological thought, insofar as it is critical, is indebted to Kant's several "critiques," even if it engages him critically. Yet it is not at all clear that even this Plato of modernity fully understood the foundations on which he depended, nor can they be explained by reference to "bourgeois societies." The chief — some think the only — contribution of the recent sharp critique of foundationalism is precisely this: It discloses the degree to which the Enlightenment failed to acknowledge how deeply theological its assumptions were and failed to recognize that such theological assumptions were indispensable to the further development of the reason, progress, and respect for dignity that the Enlightenment rationalists advocated.

If we perpetuate these errors, we may make it impossible for human rights to be actualized in the new global society forming in our time. Non-Western cultures will gain evidence for the view that human rights *are* merely the artifacts of a phase of modern Western sentiment or merely philosophical speculations formed out of peculiar sociological conditions. Fortified by such evidence, they may become more entrenched in their resistance to what then appears to them to be a new colonialism. They will not have to face the question as to whether documents such as the Universal Declaration represent an ultimately valid insight about and for humanity, an insight about which they will have to marshal careful evidence and make critical decisions. The sentiment will pass, the speculations will fade, other interests will set the agendas, the international instruments of rights will be revised or ignored, and we will have no basis on which to defend the oppressed, the prisoner, the weak, the dispossessed; to justify civil and political liberties; or to fight for social and economic justice. This, it seems to me, would be a genuinely tragic possibility. We face, I believe, a good idea in a crisis of intellectual thinness.

The Context of Pluralism

Beyond the judgment against the inhumane barbarism of Nazism that triggered the United Nations' Universal Declaration, the great struggles facing human rights and the pluralism of the last third of the previous century had to do with racial justice, the rising parallel movements of equal rights for women, and the worldwide movements for decolonialization. All these took place in the context of a life-and-death confrontation of the "free world" with "world communism," and the development of the idea of "the Third World." The question was whether human rights were in any sense universal, especially in view of the fact of pluralism. It is not, of course, the case that the world became pluralistic all of a sudden — it had been so for as long as we have recorded history — but the direct awareness of other cultures, traditions, customs, moralities, social orders, and religions, brought to us by modern communication, transportation, urbanization, and immigration, made the pluralistic world more present to us.

In some ways the consensus has grown that human rights are universal, at least with regard to race and sex.[7] Racism and sexism are widely condemned although they have not been abolished, and a number of regions are experiencing new diversities that evoke new forms of ethnic consciousness and conflict. Still, the suspicion remains that human rights in other areas of civil and political rights are an invention of the bourgeois West, in spite of the fact that the Soviet world has collapsed, and with it the chief advocates of this view. In some ways, the Soviet threat has been replaced by the rise of Islamist militance, and with it a theocratic rather than a humanistic hope for a revolutionary change that will overthrow the influence of Christianity and of the remaining superpower. This has happened in the context of massive globalization of technology, science, and democratic ideals, and the increased power and range of professionalism, ecological consciousness, media influence, and economic interaction, all of which also bring new challenges to the world religions.

To be sure, many people think about globalization only in economic terms. But a narrowly economic understanding of our present situation denies that the economic challenges are themselves largely a function of educational, technological, legal, communication, and, indeed, moral and spiritual developments and blinds us to one of the most difficult problems of universalistic principles in the face of pluralism, the conflict of values, and the differing definitions of what is human and what is right held by the world religions. On the whole, globalization is the forming of a new and wider human interdependence, extremely complex and highly variegated, to the disadvantage of some, that nevertheless raises the prospect of a new world civilization, and the now unavoidable encounter of the world's cultures and societies and the religious values on which they are based. It requires us to think again about universalistic ethical principles, and whether they are possible and real, what difference they make, and whether they inhibit or enhance the prospects of a genuine and principled pluralism. After all, to speak of "human" rights is to speak categorically, irrespective of social and cultural differences.

On this point, those who defend human rights as global principles have reason to be cautiously optimistic. We can be optimistic because the wider vision of human rights ideas has, at the least, become a part of the *ius gentium,* the operating consensus as to what constitutes proper behavior by states and other formal institutions, and what counts as compelling moral argument in contemporary international discourse. It seemed in the middle years of the twentieth century that a neo-pagan nationalism and the militant anti-liberalism of socialist secularism, both backed by radically historicist philosophies that denied any "essentialist" normative order, could not be contained by theological, ethical, or social wisdom and would bring only holocausts, gulags, and violence to the future. In reality, however, it was often-obscured Judeo-Christian ethical principles, frequently in their religiously neutered Enlightenment formulations, that the nations have increasingly adopted.[8]

Yet if these facts give us reason to be optimistic, it must be a cautious optimism, not only because the rights of many people continue to be savagely violated in many places, but also because the exigencies of earlier battles against domination by colonialized peoples and now against threats of terrorism in many countries seem to justify the use of means that threaten the rights of groups and persons in ways that are more than "collateral damage." For those who seek to defend civil rights and liberties and see them as a way to love their neighbors near and far, the potential erosion of the legal protections of civil rights and liberties is a matter of immediate and pressing practical concern. This is so because it denies that there are inalienable human rights that stand beyond and above civil rights, which are granted by a state and thus can be withdrawn by civil authority. It makes human rights a function of state policy, not a matter of universal principle.

This points to a deeper threat, for it takes human rights outside the realm of universal, meta-legal norms that cannot be repealed by political authority, no matter how powerful. It is a refusal to see human rights in the same class as the prohibition against murder. The world, after all, has known that murder is wrong for many centuries, and every nation has laws against it. People know that murders occur, with very few "justifiable homicides." But they also know that the empirical fact that things happen does not negate the normative principles by which we judge them. Today, the threat to human rights is deeper than an occasional violation; it is a profound intellectual and spiritual problem, for many today doubt that we can have or defend any trans-empirical principles to judge empirical life, and therefore it is helpful to consider the sources of human rights particularly as they allow or disallow pluralism.

A Christian Perspective on the Sources of Human Rights

Certainly we cannot say that all of Judaism or of Christianity has supported human rights. It has been key minorities within these traditions, arguing their case over long periods of time, that have established the normative view. Nor can we say that even these groups have been faithful to the implications of their own heritage at all times, and the horror stories of our pasts also have to be told to mitigate any temptation to triumphalism. Still, intellectual honesty demands recognition of the fact that what passes as "secular," "Western" principles of basic human rights developed nowhere else but out of key strands of the biblically rooted religions. And while many scholars and leaders from other traditions have endorsed them, and found resources in their own traditions that point to quite similar principles, today these views are under suspicion both by some Asian leaders who appeal to "Asian Values" and by some communitarian and postmodern philosophers in the West who have challenged the very idea of human rights. An exploration of the sources of human rights, however, yields three central areas of contribution: (1) relating first principles and concrete circumstances, (2) accenting the regard for the individual, and (3) recognizing the need for the social embodiment of human rights, particularly in the institution of the church.

Universal Reference Point and Pluralistic Structure

Those who doubt the validity of human rights do so on the ground that there neither is nor can be universalistic moral theology, master narrative, or *jus naturale* to support the idea.⁹ That, of course, is a universalistic claim in itself, one that ironically presses toward a universal moral relativism. Thus, they see the West's pressure to affirm human rights as rooted in a positive *jus civile* of a particular civilization or (in some versions) in the philosophical or religious "values" of distinct traditions or historical periods of thought, and doubt that either human-wide "first principles" or universalistic ends can be found if one turns to particular traditions, especially in the face of religious variety and cultural multiplicity. The existence of a diversity of religions and cultures is taken as an argument for a relativism of normative morality. Thus, human rights are seen as a matter of sociohistorical context. While some lament that universal principles cannot be found, many celebrate the fact, making diversity, multiculturalism, and religious distinctives themselves universally positive moral values, although on their own grounds it is difficult to see how they could defend the view, except as a cultural preference. In this situation, to insist that all people be judged according to principles of human rights is seen as an act of cultural imperialism.¹⁰ In addition, some argue that such "values" are altogether too individualistic, and that since abstract individuals do not exist, only concrete persons-in-relationship, we need an ethic based essentially in the particularities of specific community-embedded practices and duties.¹¹

Politically, such arguments can be seen to feed the interests of those states that are the least democratic and the most likely to violate the rights of their own citizens, as recognized by the interfaith Project on Religion and Human Rights. Nearly a decade ago they recognized that

> To date, governmental claims that culture justifies deviating from human rights standards have been made exclusively by states that have demonstrably bad human rights records. State invocations of "culture" and "cultural relativism" seem to be little more than cynical pretexts for rationalizing human rights abuses that particular states would in any case commit. [Some] . . . emulate China in appealing to . . . national sovereignty. . . . [Others] . . . such as Saudi Arabia, . . . maintain that they are following Islamic human rights norms, while failing to adhere to the norms that they officially deem Islamic.¹²

Yet these critics have one valid point that fuels their argument. They are partially correct insofar as they know that abstract principles and abstracted autonomous conceptions of human nature do not and cannot supply a full ethic for humanity or provide the general theory to guide a just and peaceful civil society in a global era. They also know that particular kinds of ethical obligations, rooted in specific traditions of duty, are authentic aspects of morality and identity and that the most significant of these are rooted in commitments that have become joined to religious loyalties. Something precious would be lost or betrayed if these were denied.

But these critics are only partly correct. They are also partly wrong when they view the matter as a situation where we must turn *either* to first principles of an abstract, universalistic kind *or* to concrete networks of culturally, historically, and biographically gained commitments, loyalties, and expectations that shape our senses of responsibility, especially if that is how they view the highest level of religious or theological truth. In fact, most ethical issues, including those of human rights, require a synthetic judgment, one in which we must join normative first principles to the concrete matrices of experience by which we know events and read the existing ethos of our lives — that particular networks of events, traditions, relationships, commitments, and specific blends of connectedness and alienation which shape the "values" of daily experience and our senses of obligation. The classic traditions of case study, codified in the *responsa* literature and in classic casuistry, as well as the modern structures of court procedure, exemplify this joining: they require both a finding of law, which involves critical reflection on juristic first principles behind the law, *and* a finding of "fact," which requires reliance on the experience-gained wisdom, often having to argue before a jury of peers. Moreover, they require an assessment of the consequences of various courses of action implied by a judgment about the interaction of principle and fact.

Indeed, it is theologically paradigmatic that following the accounts of the Decalogue in both Exodus and Deuteronomy, surely prime examples of universalistic abstract principles, the next several chapters are repositories of the casuistic results of the blending of the implications of those principles with the situations that people experienced concretely in their ethos. That joining of principle and fact rendered judgments that are held to contribute to the well-being of the common life and to the development of a morally righteous people. Similarly, much in the prophetic tradition makes the case against the infidelities of the people or the people in power by identifying the enduring principles in the covenants of old, the experience of social history in the present, and the prospects for a bleak, or a redeemed, future according to human deserts and divine mercy. And, for Christians specifically, to deny that any absolute universal can be connected to the realities of concrete historical experience in ways that lead to a redeemed future, is in fact a denial of the deepest insight of our faith: that Christ was both fully God and fully human, and that his life both fulfilled the commands of God, was concretely lived in

35

the midst of a specific ethos, and nevertheless pointed to an ultimate future that we could not otherwise obtain.

This should be our first lesson in understanding the bases of human rights. They foster specific kinds of pluralism first of all because theologically based moral judgments are, in principle, demanding of a universalistic reference point, but are simultaneously pluralistic in their internal structure. They demand critical reflection on the first principles of right and wrong, plus both the repeated analysis of the actual events and experiences of life as they occur in particular contexts, and a vision of the ultimate future — one that anticipates a more final assessment of what is right, judges what is wrong, and affirms what is already good as we live toward the future.[13] The philosophies and politics of "either/or" are inevitably lopsided.

The first implications of this brief excursus about "abstractions" for our question are these: Do not trust theologians, philosophers, or social critics who repudiate first principles or advocate positions or policies that encourage humanity to ignore them in favor of a view that accents only the concreteness of historical experience. Similarly, do not trust those philosophers or religious leaders who do not take into account the complex matrices of experience that people have in the concrete contexts of life. Moreover, we should place both under scrutiny on the question of whether their proposals regarding the prospects for the ultimate future are a horizon in which we shall be able to discern an assessment of our proximate synthetic judgments.

Not only do I want to argue that the affirmation of such "universal absolutes" as those stated in the Ten Commandments and less perfectly embodied in human rights provisions of our historic constitutions and such documents as the Universal Declaration are compatible with, and in fact seen most profoundly by, certain strands of the deeper theological heritage, I want to claim that without the impetus of theological insight, human rights concepts would not have come to their current widespread recognition, and that they are likely to fade over time if they are not anchored in a universal, context-transcending metaphysical reality.

The Individual and Soul Sovereignty

In addition I want to suggest that there is another way in which "abstraction" is required by the best of Christian and ethical views. At the practical level, persons are sometimes abstracted from their concrete historical situations and need the protection of abstract laws and rules and procedures of enforcement that say, "This person may already be alienated from his or her context of ordinary moral relationships, but the dismantling of this person's integrity must not proceed beyond specifiable limits; it is 'indivisible.' Thou shalt not torture, abuse, violate, exploit, or wantonly execute even the most miserable and guilty specimen of a human being!" We can see this when we are dealing with someone accused of a crime, imprisoned, subjected to slavery or forced labor, victimized by rape or torture, forced to submit to arranged marriages or liaisons, or denied the ability to participate by voice or vote in familial, political, or economic institutions that decide their fate. In these imposed situations, persons are functionally alone, abstracted, as they face a dominating power they cannot control and to which they do not give honest assent. Without knowing what the race, sex, nationality, cultural background, social location, political preferences, character, or network of friends of a person are, we must say, abstractly, "some things ought never to be done to them." And if persons need help in order to live and sustain some shred of dignity in the midst of some one or other of such situations, "some things ought to be done for them," as Michael Perry has put it.[14] This implies that other people and institutions must limit their powers, and not define the whole of the meaning of a person by the communities, traditions, and habits in which they are embedded. This means also that, in some ways, a profound individualism, in the sense of the moral inviolability of each person, in contrast only to communitarian regard, is required.

At other points, people abstract themselves from the matrices of life in which they ordinarily dwell when they choose to leave home, get married (especially if the partner is one whom the parents do not approve for reasons, say, of ethnicity or religion), seek access to a profession other than that of the "station in life" into which they were born, decide to have or not to have a child by the use of pregnancy technology, and, most critical for our discussions, decide whether to follow the faith in which they were born and raised with dedication and devotion, or turn to another by overt rejection or positive conversion — that is, by joining the inchoate company of atheists or agnostics or joining another community of faith. Here, in quite a different way than in some humanly imposed violation of personhood, one stands as an individual before the deepest levels of his or her own soul and before God or the emptiness of nothingness. People may be informed by another's advice, arguments, or threats, and a person's community of origin may have rules and regulations about such things, but in the final analysis the individual person stands sociologically alone in such moments. All the current debates about proselytism and hence freedom of religion at the personal level are at stake here.[15] Moreover, this fact of personal freedom implies the necessary right of people of the same "chosen" faith to associate and form "voluntary associations" on religious grounds, to engage in free speech, and to attempt to persuade others to voluntarily join their faith.[16] In these two instances, when people are under coercion that alienates them from their communities of life, or when they choose to leave their community of origin to join an association of conscientious, committed orientation, they must have the right to do so. Of course, no one is sovereign over God, but in regard to human conventions, these two examples illustrate a certain "soul sovereignty" with regard to individual human rights that, if denied, leads to the dehumanization of humanity. From a normative Christian point of view, not always recognized by all in the tradition, each person must be free from the miseries of oppression and the threat of arbitrary destruction, and must have, at least, the basic rights to form families, to find a calling, and to convert to a worldview or religion that is in accord with a personal understanding of the "best light." Christians hold that these matters should not be matters of coercion, and that the use of it in these instances to force or restrict a person's decisions results in a lie in the soul and the corruption of society. In this regard, a second level of pluralism is fundamentally affirmed and advocated by this tradition.

Christians and many Jews hold this view of "soul sovereignty" because we believe that each person is made in the "image of God." That is, we have some residual capacity to reason, to will, and to love that is given to us as an endowment that we did not achieve by our own efforts. And while every one of these areas of human life is imperfect, often distorted by sin, obscured by false desires or corrupted by exterior influences in sinful circumstances, the dignity conferred on us by the gift of the *imago* demands both an individual regard for each person and a constant drive to form and sustain those sociopolitical arrangements that protect the relative capacities to reason, to choose, and to love that are given with this gift. Moreover, Christians hold that each person is called into particular networks of relationships in which he or she may exercise these capacities, and that the Christian is to order these networks with justice. We believe that in Christ, we learn how God wants us to re-order — sacramentally, as some say, or as others say, covenantally — the institutions of the common life that are necessary to preserve humanity, and how to make them and ourselves more nearly approximate to the redemptive purposes God has for the world. Those Christians who know the history of the development of the social and ethical implications of their faith believe that the historical and normative defense of human rights derives from precisely these roots and that this particular tradition has, in principle, in spite of many betrayals of it by Christians, disclosed to humanity something universally valid with regard to human nature and the necessities of just social existence.[17]

Social Embodiment: The Christian Church

Still a third implication of this tradition for pluralism and human rights is signaled by the direct mention of the term "church." The formation of the Christian church, anticipated in certain sociological ways, of course, in the older traditions of the synagogues and, to a degree, in the ancient Mediterranean mystery cults, was a decisive influence in the formation of pluralistic democracy and in the generation of civil society with the legal protection of the rights of free association.[18] I shall not speak extensively about these matters here, except to state that I think that one of the greatest revolutions in the history of humanity was the formation of institutions differentiated from both familial, tribal, and ethnic identity as well as from political authority (as under the Caesars, Kaisers, and Czars of history), as happened in early Christianity by slowly making the claim stick that the church was the Body of Christ with an inviolable, divine sovereignty of its own. This was gradually made more actual by those now obscure, ancient struggles between pope and emperor, bishop and king, and preacher and prince, and again, more fully, in the modern Protestant, especially Puritan and Pietist, demanding the right to form congregations outside of state authorization, and in the struggles for tolerance. These developments have generated a social fabric where multiple independent institutions can flourish.[19] This has not only generated a diversified society in which colleges and universities, multiple political parties, a variety of economic corporations, and a mass of self-governing charitable and advocacy groups flourish, it has established the legitimacy of their claims to rights as associations with their own purposes. Indeed, it has made those parts of the world where these influences are most pronounced the safest havens for non-established and non-majoritarian religions, including non-Christian ones. The empirical consequence is that the Christian faith and its concrete social embodiment, for all the ambiguities, foibles, and outright betrayals of Christianity's own best principles (this faith did not abolish original sin, after all), has opened the door to the development of dynamic pluralistic democratic polities that are both protected *by* human rights ideals and laws and provide the organizational infrastructure for the protection *of* human rights of both persons and groups.

Two related problems in this area confront us as we face a global future. One is the basic question as to whether we can form a global civil society that does not have a theologically based inner moral architecture at its core. Historically, no society has ever existed without a religion at its center and no complex civilization capable of including many peoples and subcultures within it has endured without a profound and subtle religiously oriented philosophy or theology at its core. Yet some civilizations seem to have been repeatedly renewed by the development of doctrines and innovative social institutions based in their deepest heritage while others seem incapable of perpetual self-reformation. The present worldwide rhetoric and legal agenda of human rights, with its several "generations" of rights, is, I believe, most deeply grounded in a highly refined critical appropriation of the biblical traditions; but many of the current activists on behalf of human rights have little place for religion or theology in their conception of what they advocate. Can it endure without attention to its roots and ultimate legitimations? Doubtful!

If, however, human rights are universal in principle and the biblical, theological, and social legacies here identified provide a strong, possibly the only, grounds for recognizing and enacting them in the midst of a highly ambiguous social history, as I have suggested, we still have to ask what this means for those religions, philosophies, and cultures not shaped by this legacy. I am personally convinced of the fact that the theological motifs here discussed are, in this area of thought and action, scripted into the deepest levels of the human soul, even if they are overlaid by other obscuring doctrines, dogmas, practices, and habitual ways of thinking in many of the traditions of the world's religions, including some branches of Judaism and Christianity. Thus our task is to identify where, in the depths of all these traditions, that residual capacity to recognize and further refine the truth and justice of human rights insights lies, for this is necessary in order to overcome what otherwise is likely to be a "clash of civilizations." And if, God willing, we are able to survive such a clash, should it come, it is these that could, more than any other option known to me, at least provide a model for a just reconstruction of a global civil society.

2 Human Rights and Modern Western Faith: An Orthodox Christian Assessment

VIGEN GUROIAN

The philosopher Richard Rorty dismisses biblical faith as myth and illusion and spends untold pages of nice speech punching holes in Enlightenment theories that were leaky from the start. For these and other sleights of hand, he has become one of the most talked-about philosophers of our generation. As is evident, I am no admirer of Professor Rorty, but when he aims his criticisms at human rights doctrine and theories of an ahistorical human nature, I admit it, my ears perk up. I suppose I, too, am inclined to swing an ax at some of the larger trees of the Enlightenment wood.

In other philosophical and theological quarters, similar judgments have been tendered about the Enlightenment legacy and human rights, most notably by Alasdair MacIntyre and Stanley Hauerwas. MacIntyre argues that "the possession of rights [presupposes] the existence of a socially established set of rules" and that therefore "the existence of particular types of social institution or practice is a necessary condition for . . . a claim to a possession of a right . . . [to be] an intelligible type of human performance."[1] I take this to mean that the only real rights are norms of human conduct that are articulated in the customs and laws of particular historical communities, and that is pretty much where I stand on human rights.

I part company with all three writers, however, when they reject the notion of a normative human nature or deny the knowability of it. I want to distance myself from philosophical and theological positivism regarding our

This essay was originally published as "Human Rights and Western Faith: An Orthodox Christian Assessment," *Journal of Religious Ethics* 26, no. 2 (1998): 241-47. This slightly modified and reedited version appears here by permission of the author and Blackwell Publishing.

humanum. Rorty, in particular, has gone into the ghost-busting business outright. This is a man who protests too much that he is a reasonable fellow, while being positively spooked by metaphysical and epistemological specters that I am not at all sure lurk even in his dark wood of the Enlightenment. I am left in complete wonderment at his utter confidence that "most people — especially people relatively untouched by the European Enlightenment — simply do not think of themselves, as first and foremost, a human being." For if, as Rorty claims, these people think of themselves "as a certain *good* sort of human being — a sort defined by explicit opposition to a particularly bad sort,"[2] that very judgment surely must imply an intuition, if not a concept, of a common human nature which belongs to good as well as bad sorts of walking and talking bipeds.

Are we really supposed to take this kind of loose talk seriously? I do not think Rorty has got his history right or his facts straight when he makes generalizations like these — and he virtually assaults us with them all the time. Most Orthodox Christians, who do not live in the West, fit Rorty's category of persons relatively unaffected by the Enlightenment, yet they possess a strong concept of a common humanity, and we know where they got that idea. The same might be said of Muslims. The Enlightenment did not invent the concept of a universal human nature or the notion of a universal moral law, nor did Immanuel Kant or St. Thomas Aquinas or St. Augustine. What the Enlightenment did was to conjure up certain ghostly and disembodied notions of human nature and an accompanying doctrine of the "rights of man," which is a principal source of much of contemporary human rights thinking. Rorty, MacIntyre, and Hauerwas, each in his own manner, have shown us how this is so. But they risk throwing the baby out with the bath water. In their rejection of human rights, they all but dismiss the notion of a human nature and its norms. None of these writers comes at his critique of human rights in the manner that an Orthodox theologian is bound to do. Human rights thinking is alien to Orthodoxy; however, the notion that a normative human nature is concretely manifested in every human individual who comes into existence is central to Orthodox anthropology and theology.

Having set down these preliminary remarks, permit me to sketch out what amounts to only the most *preliminary* of clarifications. My contention is that Orthodox christology and the vision of redemption in Orthodox theology identify what is normatively human and necessary for the freedom and flourishing of human beings in a way that is very different from that of modern human rights theory. Orthodox christology and anthropology do not support theories of autonomous and secular human rights such as those that have emerged even within Western Christian thought.

On Christology and Human Rights

First, regarding christology, I am persuaded that a strongly dyophysitic accent in mainstream Protestant and Roman Catholic christology has contributed to what are now deeply embedded notions of human autonomy and rights in Western thought. These notions contradict Orthodoxy's insistence upon the theonomous nature of humanity revealed by the divine Word's incarnate existence. From an Orthodox point of view, what is normatively human must be defined in strict accord with the creature's relationship to the divine acts of creation and incarnation. The humanity that the Creator Word assumed is now and forever more united with his divinity: Jesus Christ was resurrected in his body and has taken that body to his Father. This answers any doubt as to whether the good and the *telos* of the human being, who is created in the image and likeness of God, may be considered apart from participation in and communion with the Divine Life itself (2 Peter 1:4). No temporal human good exists apart from a movement either toward or away from holiness and the company of the saints.

I am personally persuaded that the deepest inspiration of the doctrine of human rights has roots in Christian convictions. God is a person, and so are human beings who are created in God's image and likeness. Every human *hypostasis* has needs and makes legitimate claims to certain advantages that are necessary for human flourishing. *Hypostasis* is, of course, the Greek word that was adopted by the theologians of the Council of Nicaea to designate personal existence. It permitted the Council to draw the distinction between human, angelic, and divine being, while also attributing personhood to all three.

My own Armenian tradition with its Cyrillian monophysitism — represented in the dogmatic statement, "one nature, and that incarnate, of the divine Word" — has understood, from the outset of the great christological debates of the fifth and sixth centuries, the hazards of speaking of natures or essences in the abstract, whether pertaining to the divinity or the humanity of Jesus. The Council of Nicaea had employed the term *ousia* to connote concrete existence. God is one *ousia,* one being and nature. The Son is of the same being and nature as the Father. This is how the council interpreted Jesus' words in John's Gospel, "Whoever has seen me has seen the Father. . . . I am in the Father and the Father is in me" (John 14:9-10 NRSV). The theologians of Nicaea employed the term "nature" in a sense analogous to what modern physics means by a "solid." A solid, like a diamond or an ice cube, is a discrete substance that cannot be mixed into another solid in the way that one liquid or gas might be mixed with or emulsified in another.

When, at the Council of Chalcedon in 451, discussion shifted to a sharp distinction between *ousia* and *hypostasis* that entailed a language of two natures in reference to Christ, Armenians balked. This was reminiscent of Nestorianism, especially as the language of two natures appeared in Pope Leo's Tome. How could it be said, as Leo did, that "the Word performs what pertains to the Word, the flesh what pertains to the flesh" without dividing Christ in two? How could Christ be two "solids," two natures, Armenians asked, except he be two and not one? For Cyril of Alexandria, it was possible to say in the abstract that there is a *oneness* of two natures in Christ, but Leo's language suggested the impossible: a *unification* of two abstract natures in the concrete. Ultimately, my church rejected this "two natures" doctrine because it wanted to honor and safeguard the ancient teaching of "one Lord, one faith, one baptism" (Eph. 4:5 NRSV).

What, one might ask, does this curious piece of the history of Christian doctrine have to do with how one stands on human rights? My answer is that from the standpoint of Armenian Christianity, the legacy of Western dyophysitism extends into the Enlightenment in two essentially Christian heresies: deism and the rights of man. In deism, God is removed from his creation, and the incarnation is denied, implicitly if not explicitly. In the concept of the rights of man, humanity gains an autonomy that a consistently incarnational faith will not permit. From the religious point of view, human freedom is not autonomy, that is, pure self-determination; rather, it is *autexousion*, a graced capacity to achieve full ethical personhood and mystical participation in the life of God. There is always a synergy of nature and grace.

Deism and the rights of man are late secularistic developments of a nature and grace dichotomy that crops up in the West well back in the medieval period and forward into our own time. The Gelasian doctrine of the two swords, the eucharistic theology of transubstantiation, Kant's epistemology and his categorical imperative, the God of the gaps, the disembodied moral absolutes of the God of the idealists, the quest for the historical Jesus, and Rudolf Bultmann's demythologized kerygma are all expressions of this dichotomy of nature and grace.

Thus, while I respect the fact that contemporary human rights theory is not uniform — that it ranges from highly secularized interpretations to Roman Catholic Thomist teaching — from the perspective of Orthodoxy, and especially from an Armenian standpoint, the doctrine in all its varieties expresses a flawed understanding of the relation of nature and grace and God and persons in Jesus Christ.

In his *Ethics,* Dietrich Bonhoeffer states,

The Church's word to the world can be no other than God's word to the world. This word is Jesus Christ and salvation in His name. It is in Jesus Christ that God's relation to the world is defined. . . . In other words, the proper relation of the Church to the world cannot be deduced from natural law or rational law or from universal human rights, but *only* from the gospel of Jesus Christ.[3]

I agree. But permit me to reformulate this Reformed language into Orthodox speech. Human beings are not autonomous but theonomous: this is testified in the God-man, Jesus Christ, who is no less God than human and in whom all human reality finds its being, its norm, and its fulfillment.

On Redemption and Human Rights

The Orthodox understanding of redemption contrasts sharply with the strongly juridical and legalistic understandings of redemption that have predominated in Roman Catholic and Protestant traditions. I am referring especially to the notion of atonement as satisfaction given to God, which often carries a strong penal meaning. I can only begin to suggest the profound difference it makes for a Christian social ethics whether one holds primarily to the physicalist Orthodox vision of redemption as cure of sin and death that takes place *within* the creature or whether one adopts Western understandings of redemption as earned or imputed righteousness in which an inward change is not as significant as the claim to a change of the creature's *position* in relation to God.

I am painting with a broad brush. I am aware that much detail work would be expected of a fuller treatment. Yet it does seem to me logical and perhaps inevitable that a civilization in which the latter views of redemption prevailed would turn to a "solution" to human suffering in which justice *(jus)* and law supplant holiness and righteousness as the supreme objects of Christian striving. Nevertheless, as the Russian religious philosopher Nicholas Berdyaev rightly observed, "Redemption is . . . not [first of all] the reconciliation between God and man." It is, rather, the destruction "of the roots of sin and evil" in the heart of being.[4] Redemption is not first about human or divine justice but about cure of sin and victory over death; against death and sin combined, an ethics of law alone is quite impotent.

Accordingly, in Orthodox theology and ethics, the social imperative that stems from redemption in Jesus Christ is not initially a call to political or legal action but the much more radical call to repentance and self-limitation.

Repentance is the principal evidence of a deep inner conversion of heart, of *metanoia*. Humility (in Hebrew *'anah* and in Greek *tapeinos*), not justice (*jus*), is the highest virtue of Orthodox ethics. Humility born out of repentance combats self-love and is the balm that heals wounded pride. The counterpart of humility in political ethics is the magnanimity that curbs vengeance and the ever-present will to power.

Father Alexander Men was a Russian Orthodox priest martyred for his faith. In his sermons and writings, Men applied this Orthodox understanding of redemption as conversion and cure to his profound social concerns. He made it the cornerstone of his social gospel. Were space not limited here, I would try to demonstrate the full effect of this underlying theological vision in his social gospel, but we must be content with the following excerpt from an interview that Father Men gave shortly before he was brutally murdered with an ax in 1990. He said,

> I believe that just as in previous ages, people emerged to lead the world out of its spiritual dead end, so in our times too the right people will be found. And as regards repentance, the good news of Christ was preceded by a call to repentance; this is what John the Baptist called people to. And the very first word of Jesus' teaching was "Repent." And remember that in Hebrew this word means "turn around," "turn away from the wrong road." While in the Greek text of the Gospels, it is rendered by an even more resonant word, *metanoeite*, in other words *rethink* your life. This is the beginning of healing. Repentance is not a sterile "grubbing around in one's soul," not some masochistic self-humiliation, but a re-evaluation leading to action, the action John the Baptist called "the fruits of repentance."
>
> That's why there is so much hope in the numerous attempts now being made to rethink our recent history, to "change our minds." The abscess must be lanced, otherwise there will be no more cure.[5]

Alexander Solzhenitsyn also speaks out of this Orthodox Christian vision of redemption:

> "Human rights" are a fine thing, but [the difficult question is] how can we ourselves make sure that our rights do not expand at the expense of the rights of others. A society with unlimited rights is incapable of standing to adversity. If we do not wish to be ruled by a coercive authority, then each of us must rein himself in. . . . A stable society [and world] is achieved not by balancing opposing forces but by conscious self-

limitation: by the principle that we are always duty-bound to defer to the sense of moral justice.[6]

Solzhenitsyn rarely makes mention of human rights, and when he does, he is usually addressing Western ears or Western concerns; more often than not, what he means by "human rights" are civil rights and liberties protected by law. The questions he raises, however, about the use of the rhetoric of human rights issue a challenge. If the sin and woundedness that are in each one of us are not first cured, if healing has not begun, then human rights rhetoric will do little good. If repentance and forgiveness do not fill the brittle shell of this ethical and legal formalism, how can sinful human beings resist turning their claims to human rights into swords of vengeance or into injurious pretexts for self-aggrandizement? What is to prevent even the championing of the rights of the oppressed from becoming an exercise in self-righteous self-magnification?

These are some of the weaknesses and hazards that Orthodoxy finds in a doctrine of human rights. The limitations of this essay do not allow a complete critique. One last word, however, about the question that serves as the title for this volume. "Does human rights need God?" is a subcategory of the question "Does humankind need God?" Both versions reflect a legacy of secular humanism and rationalism that flirts with or even affirms the idea of autonomous human existence, whereas Orthodoxy starts from the premise that everything human is in "need" of, is dependent upon, God. As I stated earlier, our *humanum* is grounded in the being and act of God. Human existence is by origin and nature theonomous. Humanity that claims autonomy or is atheistic is fallen, sinful, and incomplete. Belief in the incarnation is belief not only that God exists as God but that God is human. Jesus Christ is "the Lamb slain from the foundation of the world" (Rev. 13:8 KJV). The *imago dei* includes the humanity of God. The Incarnate Divine Word is the measure of the fullness of our humanity (Eph. 4:13). He leads humankind to complete participation in the divine life (2 Peter 1:3-4). And this communion with the life of the triune Deity *is* the supreme human good and *telos*.

In a short space, I have endeavored to set down the important reasons why Eastern Orthodoxy does not invest much of its theological or moral capital in modern doctrines of human rights. I have ventured this argument knowing full well that for many who read this essay it is virtually a matter of dogma that a commitment to human rights necessarily follows from Christian belief. To this I am bound to respond, "Sisters and brothers, it simply is not so."

3 God and Human Rights in a Secular Society: A Biblical-Talmudic Perspective

DAVID NOVAK

God, Human Rights, and Democracy

The concept of human rights is endemic to democracy. Indeed, its acceptance is what distinguishes a democracy from "ordered brutality," to borrow the words of a leading democratic legal philosopher.[1] To be sure, some democratic theorists have argued that there is an overemphasis on human rights, but that is when human rights are reduced to individual claims on society at the expense of individual responsibilities to society.[2] Nevertheless, it is hard to find any such conservative critic of the overemphasis of human rights who would argue in principle for the value of a societal system that affirmed no human rights at all and only enforced acts that are duties to itself. And, as it turns out in fact, human rights seem to be affirmed only in democratic societies. Non-democratic societies, such as those run according to fascist, communist, or clerical (wrongly called "theocratic") ideologies, are notorious for their denial of any human right that could challenge the absolute authority presumed by those who have power in these nondemocratic societies.[3] So, these other forms of society are not only nondemocratic in principle, they are almost always anti-democratic in practice as evidenced by their contempt for human rights, even their contempt for the concept of human rights.

There is a great difference, though, between religious members of a democracy and its secularist members, especially in the ways they affirm human rights and even in the way they determine what some of these rights are. Also, even when religious people and secularists agree about a certain human right in practice, they frequently differ as to who are the actual subjects of this right. By "religious members" of a democracy, I mean those who publicly affirm their relationship with a god (most often, for them, *the God*) and who assert that their relationship with God has bearing on their political commitments, especially their commitment to human rights. By "secularist members," I mean those who deny that anyone's relationship with a god should have political significance. (Such secularists are not necessarily atheists in their private lives, but it seems that most of them whom I know have no god even in their private lives.) The religious members of a democratic society assume that public affirmation of human rights needs an affirmation of God. (But, as we shall see, that "need" is philosophical, not political.) Secularist members of a democratic society deny that such an affirmation of God is needed, let alone desirable.

Religious members of a democratic society should be prepared to publicly argue why their affirmation of human rights needs a prior affirmation of God, and suggest why this need is not just theirs. Nevertheless, they should do this without requiring any such prior affirmation of God from those who do not believe in God as the price for admission to philosophical discourse with believers, especially discourse about human rights in secular society. Indeed, to require any prior religious affirmation for admission to political discourse in civil society would be most undemocratic in any democracy that also affirms religious liberty, which is the liberty to affirm some religion or to deny any religion at all. Moreover, in debates about the foundations of human rights, religious members of a democratic society need only show why their religious affirmation of human rights provides a stronger foundation for these rights than do the various secularist alternatives, not that these secularist alternatives have no plausibility at all. Secularists, on the other hand, should show why they do not regard a religious affirmation of human rights to be inherently anti-democratic. Indeed, if they do regard such affirmations to be anti-democratic (as some of them certainly have done), then their logic should also lead them to move for outlawing religion in public. But that would be as anti-democratic as requiring citizens in a democracy to have one particular religion or even any religion at all.

Since I am a religious member of a democratic society (actually, two such societies, the United States and Canada), I can make only a religious case for human rights in good faith. Secularists should make their own arguments by themselves, and I am always prepared to listen to them carefully since I want to live in peace with them in civil society. Nevertheless, secularists should be able to do so without denying me the right to connect my religious belief to my political advocacy just as I should be able to do so without denying them their right to connect their nonbelief to their political advocacy. This type of reciprocal tolerance clearly recognizes that no one comes to political advocacy from nowhere, that all of us, believers and nonbelievers alike, come to our respective political positions from pre-political commitments.[4] For most people, at least in the democracies of the United States and Canada, their pre-political commitment is religious. Yet there are people whose pre-political commitment lies elsewhere. It is important for this secularist minority to locate for the rest of us more explicitly just where they are coming from. Religious people, on the other hand, should realize that no human coercion, whether legal or moral, should ever be employed to make secularists affirm any sort of religious commitment. Thus I do not deny anyone's right to argue his or her affirmation of human rights in public, even when I also think their original reasons for such affirmation are wrong or insufficient. I ask for the same right from those who think my original reasons are wrong or insufficient.

Biblical Precedents[5]

Let us now tentatively define human rights to be those justified claims a human individual makes upon the human collective among whom he or she lives, that is, his or her society. And, in a society where the moral authority of God is recognized, all such claims are clearly justifiable insofar as they refer to God's moral authority. By "God's moral authority," I mean God as the original source of moral law, and God as the judge who ultimately enforces that moral law. As a Jew, let me now cite the Hebrew Bible and bring in some talmudic comments for a few illustrations of how God's authority operates in both grounding human rights and enforcing them. But, as I shall argue later, none of these biblical illustrations is limited to the context of a particular covenanted community; that is, one does not have to be Jewish or believe in Judaism or in any particular religion in order to invoke them in his or her moral-political reasoning. Thus they can be cogently invoked in a secular society.

By "secular society" I mean a society that does not look to any particular historical revelation to justify its political existence and its legal authority. Thus a secular reason is one that does not look to any revelation as its moral source, but that does not mean God cannot be cogently invoked when making a moral or political argument in a secular context. Accordingly, one need not be a secularist to speak and act secularly. One can very much be a religious advocate of secularity; in fact, I think a better advocate of secularity.

The first illustration of the relation of human rights to God is the statement of an actual biblical norm.

Any widow or orphan you shall not oppress. If you do wrong them, when one does complain [*tsaʿoq yitsʿaq*] to Me, I shall listen to his complaint.

Then My anger shall burn and I shall kill you [*etkhem*] by sword; thus your wives will become widows and your sons orphans. (Exod. 22:22-24)

This clearly refers to an individual who has a legitimate claim on his or her society. The language of Scripture indicates that the victim is an individual person: *a* widow *(almanah)* or *an* orphan *(yatom)*. The use of the plural "you" and "your" indicates that it is a collective that is victimizing these individuals who are, no doubt, taken to be the most obvious examples of a larger class of those who are socially and economically vulnerable, and who are usually without powerful advocates on their behalf.[6] The presentation of this norm in the sequence of the biblical narrative, however, seems to assume that the reader is already familiar with the way injustice and its rectification have been described earlier in that narrative.

The language in Exodus is very reminiscent of two previous instances of rights violations and their rectifications by God in Genesis. Indeed, it is God whose original rights have been violated in the person of those created in his image, and it is God who will ultimately vindicate the innocent and punish the criminal. The key term is the term for "cry" *(tsa'aqah)*, which is the appeal of the innocent victims of crime for justice to be done, both justice for themselves and justice to those who have so victimized them. To whom do they cry for justice, originally and ultimately?

The first example comes from the first rights conflict in the Bible's presentation of human history: The conflict between Cain and Abel, a conflict that led to the first murder. There an original appeal is made to God to enforce a human right, in this case the human right to have one's murder avenged. Thus God says to Cain immediately after he has murdered his brother Abel, "What you have done! Your brother's blood is crying [*tso'aqim*] to Me from the ground" (Gen. 4:10).[7]

In the Cain and Abel story, Abel has a claim upon Cain: Do not kill me! Why? Because God takes personal interest in every human person who has been created in the divine image. In fact, that is very likely what it means to say that all humankind is made to "resemble [*bi-demut*] God" (Gen. 5:1), namely, God and humans are interested in each other insofar as they share some commonality, a commonality not found in God's relations with the rest of creation. "And the Lord God said that humans are like one of us [*k'ahad mimennu*], knowing good and bad" (Gen. 3:22).[8] As such, an assault on any other human being is taken to be an assault on God himself; in fact, one's ultimate reason for assaulting another human being might be because this is the closest one can come to assaulting God. Let it be remembered that Cain was still angry with God for having rejected his sacrifice (Gen. 4:4-7) just before we read that "when they were in the field, Cain rose up against Abel his brother, and killed him" (Gen. 4:8). Killing his brother Abel, whom God had favored, might well have been his attempt to take revenge on God.

Yet the very fact that it is Cain who initiates religion by being the first to offer "a gift to the Lord" (Gen. 4:3) shows that Cain himself surely believed that God takes a personal interest in him and his brother who joined him in this act of worship (the two of whom at that point in history constitute humankind). One brings a gift only when one has an intuition that it will be welcomed, even expected, by the one to whom it is being given. Cain is surely familiar with God when God asks him, "Where is Abel your brother?" (Gen. 4:9). So, because it is assumed that God takes a personal interest in every human person created in his image, we can thereby infer that God prohibits one human from harming another and that God will not allow one who harms someone else to escape retribution for his or her crime. Because of that personal interest, both in the experience of the victim and in the act of the victimizer, God will not allow any crime between human persons to go unnoticed without proper response to the moral situation of both persons so involved, whether victim or assailant.

The difference between the account of Cain and Abel, which we have just examined, and the proscription of injustice against the vulnerable and the promise of divine retribution in Exodus, which was brought as the prescriptive example of God's involvement in human rights, concerns who is the victimizer, not who is the victim. In both accounts the rights of a vulnerable human individual are being violated, whether that victim be one's younger (and presumably weaker) brother, or a widow, or an orphan. But, whereas in the Cain and Abel story we have only two individuals — there being no organized society until Cain "builds a city" (Gen. 4:17) — in the Exodus account there is an organized society. It is the society of the Israelites who have just accepted God's offer to be "a holy nation" (*goi qadosh* — Exod. 19:6), which means they were already a nation that was now to become a holy nation especially covenanted with God. The fact that they were already a nation even before being covenanted with God is evidenced by their already having a system of laws by which cases of injustice were being adjudicated. Even before the revelation of the Torah (beginning with the Ten Commandments) at Mount Sinai, a court system was already in place (Exod. 18:20-24).[9] The purpose of that court system was to protect the human rights of those who had been wronged by others.[10]

Since there was no society at the time of Cain and Abel, Abel can only appeal directly to God for justice. There is no one else to avenge his death. In the Exodus account, however, there are two possibilities. One, a victim of crime can appeal to the social collective to enforce his or her God-given right not to be harmed; or two, a victim can appeal directly to God to enforce that same God-given human right.

It seems that a victim would appeal to his or her society for justice when he or she could be harmed or when he or she has already been harmed by another individual member of that same society. It also seems that such an appeal to society would be made in a society that considers its prime duty to be the protection of the human rights of its members, first and foremost their right to be protected from injustice and their right to have injustices committed against them by fellow members of that society avenged. A society which recognizes that the rights it is enforcing are inalienable divine endowments rather than its own revocable entitlements will be able to perform its social duty with maximum cogency because it has earned the rightful trust of its members. As such, that society can in good faith call upon its members to "rightly pursue justice" (Deut. 16:20). According to one rabbinic opinion, it is wrong for a victim to appeal directly to God for justice when there is just human authority already present in his or her society.[11] In such a case, God has delegated the immediate enforcement of justice to the authorities in society, who are to act *in loco Dei* because they understand that "justice is God's" (Deut. 1:17). Nevertheless, those having political power may not assume that because of their collective status they are thereby exempt from the moral obligation to do justice to others, which is what God has already required of individual persons. No person, not even an official of society having collective authority, is above God's law or above God's judgment.

But it is unlikely that a victim would appeal to his or her society for justice if the very injustice being committed is being committed by the society itself through its positive laws and public policies. To be sure, if that society is committed to the enforcement of human rights as being mandated by divine law, then it is still possible that the social injustice being committed can be shown to be inconsistent with the fundamental principles of the political-legal system itself. Here internal rectification of the system itself is still possible, at least in principle. Nevertheless, what if those having political and legal power are in fact unwilling to rectify their own unjust victimization of the innocent and the vulnerable? In that case, the cries of the victims of social injustice will fall on deaf ears, the same deaf ears upon which Abel's cry to Cain for justice (before his being murdered by Cain) no doubt fell.[12] One's only recourse, then, is to seek justice from God. Indeed, a victim of injustice at the hands of society ought to complain to God about what has wrongfully been done to him or her rather than sink into political despair.

Belief in the God of justice *(mishpat),* the God who is "the Judge

[*shophet*] of the whole earth" (Gen. 18:25), gives the victims of injustice the as-
surance that in the ultimate scheme of things they do not have to "settle" for
the injustice done to them or to anybody else, that all injustice will be recti-
fied when God "will rightly [*be-tsedeq*] judge the world" (Ps. 96:13). And it
also means that the victims of injustice may not themselves violate the rights
of others by cynically assuming that the harm done to them proves that there
is no justice ever, for if so, what difference does it make whether one harms
someone else or not? Either the victims assume the idea of justice itself is an
illusion, or they assume justice is an ideal having no consequences in any real
world.[13] In fact, very often the experience of injustice leads its victims to imi-
tate their victimizers by finding their own victims: "Those to whom evil is
done, do evil in return," in the memorable words of the poet W. H. Auden.[14]

One can see true opposition to this type of moral or political cynicism
in the instruction, "A sojourner [*ger*] you shall not oppress," the reason being
given: "because you know what the life of the sojourner [*ha-ger*] is, since you
were sojourners [*gerim*] in the land of Egypt" (Exod. 23:9). The noun "sojourner" or "resident-alien" is used three times here and has three different
referents: (1) a Gentile individual living in Israel, (2) the state of being a
resident-alien in general, and (3) the people of Israel who had been resident-
aliens in Egypt. It is the concept of "resident-alienhood" in general that enables the Israelites to identify with those living under their own rule. So, instead of concluding that one may do the evil done to oneself to someone else,
Scripture concludes that from the negative we derive the positive.[15] From the
injustice done to the Israelites by the Egyptians when they were sojourners in
their land we learn the justice the Israelites are to do for the sojourner who
lives in their land. "There shall be one justice [*mishpat ehad*] for the sojourner
and the native-born" (Lev. 24:22). Neither justice nor the God of justice died
in Egypt, or even in Auschwitz.

Both the Egyptians and the Israelites are expected to already know what
are the human rights of sojourners in their respective societies. The Israelites
are to respect the rights of their sojourners contrary to the way the Egyptians
violated the rights of the Israelite sojourners: "What is hateful to you, do not
do to someone else," which the Talmud assumes is the fundamental basic
moral precept common to both Jews and Gentiles.[16] Respect for the right not
to be harmed and to be protected by society, and the corresponding duty not
to harm but protect the rights of others, are not just a civil right and a civil
duty but, rather, a human right and a human duty. Neither the right nor the
duty is to be violated anywhere by anyone, whether that individual is func-
tioning individually or collectively.

The situation of human rights is even worse in a society where basic injustice is built into the very political and legal institutions of the society itself. This comes out in the biblical account of the destruction of the cities of Sodom and Gomorrah, whose citizens are described as being "exceedingly wicked and sinful toward the Lord" (Gen. 13:13). Their evil and sinfulness comes to a head when God announces to Abraham that he plans to investigate "the cry [*za'aqat*] of Sodom and Gomorrah because it is excessive." According to rabbinic interpretation, the "cry" of the two evil cities is not the cry of the citizenry protesting their innocence before the divine Judge. It seems their society had already determined that "there is no law [*din*] and there is no judge [*dayyan*]," which is the rabbinic term for practical atheism.[17] The citizens themselves, being beyond any sense of social guilt, would not have known how to protest their innocence. Instead, the cry is the cry of the innocent people who have been persecuted by that very citizenry of Sodom and Gomorrah, a persecution that had been sanctioned by the political and legal institutions of those cities.[18]

The injustice here is more than the work of individual criminals. Were that the case, the officials of that society could be called upon to properly punish those individuals who have violated the laws of that society. Indeed, the injustice here is more than the work of officeholders who have abused their office. Were that the case, one could call attention to the fact that these officeholders are in violation of the laws of that society, even though in that case, there is often no one more powerful than these officeholders to actually call them to task. That is why, in ancient Israel, it took a prophet to remind kings of their violation of God's law that protected the rights of weaker members of their society. One sees that in the prophet Nathan's rebuke of King David for violating the rights of Uriah (2 Sam. 12:7-10), and in the prophet Elijah's rebuke of King Ahab for violating the rights of Naboth (1 Kings 21:17-22). Both Nathan's rebuke and Elijah's rebuke were taken seriously because David and even Ahab were rulers of Israelite societies that still recognized God's law and God's judgment.[19] One can even assume that is why the Israelite prophet Jonah was able to call the people of the gentile city of Nineveh to repentance by commanding them to turn away from "the violence which was in their hands" (Jonah 3:8); this was possible because "the people of Nineveh believed in the God of justice [*elohim*]" (Jonah 3:5). Thus one sees that, for the Bible, the seriousness with which the moral admonition of prophets was taken is not something confined to Israel. Israel is not the only nation that considers itself answerable to God's law and God's judgment. Furthermore, prophetic moral admonition itself is not confined to Israel. It does not seem that the people of Nineveh listened to Jonah because he was an Israelite prophet telling them to follow the law of Israel; rather, they listened to him because he reminded them to follow God's law as they knew it from their own cultural experience.[20]

Nineveh could be saved from its own sins, especially its collective ones, because the people there still recognized God's law within their own tradition. But Sodom and Gomorrah were beyond such salvation since their own tradition had already lost any recognition of a divine law that instituted human rights and specified them. In addition, they had already lost any recognition of divine judgment. In talmudic language, they had collectively forgotten both the moral admonition and the moral penalty.[21] Sending a prophet to admonish them would have been futile. Thus when Lot, the nephew of the prophet Abraham, admonishes the men of Sodom not to violate the strangers who have taken shelter in his house as sojourners, they revile him by reminding him that he himself is "this one who has come to sojourn [and who] is now acting as a judge!" (Gen. 19:9).[22]

Sodom and Gomorrah become, for the Bible, the epitome of social and political depravity that deserves the most severe divine punishment.[23] Their being "exceedingly wicked and sinful toward the Lord" (Gen. 13:13) is primarily their violation of basic human rights: a fundamental breach of morality. If so, why is their sin referred to God? The answer seems to be that "one who reviles the poor despises his Maker" (Prov. 17:5).[24] While one is not to abuse any of God's creatures, it seems that this verse refers to God as the maker of every human, whether male or female, rich or poor, "in his image" (Gen. 1:27; 5:1-2; 9:6). In the case of Sodom and Gomorrah, the violation of human rights is so endemic to the social system itself that there is no longer any recourse to either uncorrupted public officials or the traditions of the society itself. Thus there is only recourse to God himself to destroy the cities that have so fundamentally violated his moral law, the law that irrevocably entitles human beings to dwell in safety anywhere on earth, which God "has created to be a dwelling" (Isa. 45:18).

Theological-Political Argumentation in a Secular Society

I submit that everything represented above, which is only a small sample of biblical-talmudic discussions of God's connection to human rights, is germane to the great debates about human rights now being conducted in the secular societies of the United States and Canada. The founding document of the American republic, the Declaration of Independence of 1776, asserts that all humans "are endowed by their creator with certain inalienable rights." The Canadian Charter of Rights and Responsibilities of 1982 asserts, "Whereas

Canada is founded on principles that recognize the supremacy of God and the rule of law." (My interpretation of "the supremacy of God and the rule of law" is not that these are two separate assertions but, rather, that they are two terms in apposition. That is, *the supremacy of God is the rule of God's law.*[25] That is what "supremacy of God" as distinct from the more vague "existence of God" means.) The separation of church and state asserted in the bill of rights of both nations only means that there is to be no official national religion and that there are to be no religious requirements for citizenship or the holding of public office. It also implies that one cannot make a public argument, intended to bring others into agreement with oneself, whose basic premise is "because the Bible says so." Therefore, in public discussions of matters of law and right, one may not make an argument that presupposes the authority of any particular historical revelation such as the Torah from Sinai, the Sermon on the Mount, or the word of the Qur'an. But one can certainly quote Scripture to illustrate and clarify moral principles that can be argued for rationally rather than just authoritatively. Accordingly, one can definitely make an argument from a divine law that one can show is perceivable by human reason and affirmed in many different traditions, both religious and secular (for example, in English Common Law, which can still be invoked as precedent in American and Canadian courts). Religious people who understand this fundamental distinction will be able to make very cogent arguments in secular society for human rights, rights which are originally *from* God and finally vindicated *by* God. By so doing, they can "find grace and good favor in the eyes of God and of man" (Prov. 3:4).

4 Islam and the Challenge of Democratic Commitment

KHALED ABOU EL FADL

The question I deal with here is whether concurrent and simultaneous moral and normative commitments to Islam and to a democratic form of government are reconcilable or whether they are mutually exclusive. I will argue in this essay that it is indeed possible to reconcile Islam with a commitment in favor of democracy. I will do so by presenting a systematic exploration of Islamic theology and law as it relates to a democratic system of government, and, in this context, I will address the various elements within Islamic belief and practice that promote, challenge, or hinder the emergence of an ideological commitment in favor of democracy.

In many ways, the basic and fundamental objective of this chapter is to investigate whether the Islamic faith is consistent or reconcilable with a democratic faith. As I will address below, both Islam and democracy represent a set of comprehensive and normative moral commitments and beliefs about, among other things, the worth and entitlements of human beings. The challenging issue is to understand the ways in which the Islamic and democratic systems of convictions and moral commitments could undermine and negate, or validate and support, each other. At the outset of this essay, I make no apologies for my conviction that separate and independent commitments in favor of Islam and in favor of democracy are morally desirable and normatively good. The problem is to facilitate the coexistence of both of these desir-

This essay was originally published as "Islam and the Challenge of Democratic Commitment," *Fordham International Law Journal* 27, 4 (2003): 4-71. The current version, slightly modified and reedited for a more general audience, is substantially the same as the Fordham essay. I am grateful to my wife Grace for her invaluable feedback and assistance. I thank Naheed Fakoor, my executive assistant, and Omar Fadel, my faculty assistant, for their invaluable contributions to this project.

able moral commitments and, to the extent possible, to guard against a situation in which the one challenges and negates the other. In my view, reconciliation, and perhaps cooperation, between Islam and democracy is challenging but absolutely necessary.

When exploring this subject, the first issue that ought to be addressed is the ideal form of government in Islam. A jurist writing a number of centuries ago on the subject of Islam and systems of government, such as the well-known Muslim historian and sociologist Ibn Khaldun (d. 784[1]/1382), would have commenced his treatise by separating all political systems into three broad types. He would have described the first as a natural system — a system that approximates a primitive state of nature. This is an uncivilized system of lawlessness and anarchy in which the most powerful in society dominate and tyrannize the rest. In such a system, instead of law, there would be custom, and instead of government, there would be tribal elders who are respected and obeyed only as long as they remain the strongest and the most physically able. The second system would be described as dynastic, and dynastic systems, according to Muslim jurists, are tyrannical as well. Such systems are based not on custom but on laws issued by a king or prince. According to Muslim jurists, such systems are also illegitimate; because the king or prince is the source of the law, the system is considered baseless, whimsical, and capricious. In such a system, people obey laws out of necessity or compulsion, but the laws themselves are illegitimate and tyrannical. The third system, and the most superior, is the caliphate, which is based on Shariʿah law, the body of Muslim religious law founded on the Qurʾan and the conduct and statements of the Prophet. Shariʿah law, according to Muslim jurists, fulfills the criteria of justice and legitimacy, and binds the governed and governor alike. Because the government is bound by a higher law that may not be altered or changed, and because the government may not act whimsically or outside the pale of law, the caliphate system was considered superior to any other.

Many Muslim scholars, like Ibn Khaldun, consistently made the same assumption: The Islamic political system was considered to be a challenge to the world. While all other polities have individualistic and whimsical laws, and are doomed to despotic governance, the caliphate system of governance is superior because it is based on the rule of law.[2] Whether as a matter of historical practice this assumption was justified or not, the material point was that classical Muslim jurists exhibited a distinct aversion to whimsical or unrestrained government. A government bound by Shariʿah was considered meritorious in part because it is a government where human beings do not have unfettered authority over other human beings, and there are limits on the reach of power. So, for instance, a Sunni jurist such as Abu al-Faraj Ibn al-

Jawzi (d. 597/1200) asserted that a caliph who tries to alter God's laws for politically expedient reasons is implicitly accusing the Shari'ah of imperfection. Ibn al-Jawzi elaborated upon this by contending that, without the rule of Shari'ah, under the guise of political expediency or interests, a ruler may justify the murder of innocent Muslims. In reality, he argued, no political interest could ever justify the killing of a Muslim without legitimate legal cause, and it is this type of restraint that demonstrates the superiority of a Shari'ah system over the other two alternative systems of governance.

This classical debate is rather fascinating for several reasons. It is fair to say that in the contemporary age, the challenge of good governance is posed most aptly by a democratic system of government, and not simply by limited or restrained government. In espousing the principle of limited government and the rule of law, classical Muslim scholars were, in fact, asserting principles that are at the core of all democratic practices in the modern world. But it is important to recognize that the idea of limited government is no longer in this day and age, by itself, sufficient for proving the merit of a particular system of governance. Today, the system of government that has the strongest and most compelling claim to legitimacy, and moral virtue, is a democracy. The mere fact that, with very few exceptions, every despotic regime in the world today claims to be more democratic, and less authoritarian, is powerful evidence of the challenge democracies pose to the world. Most authoritarian governments claim to be popular with the people they rule over, and attempt to conceal the appearance of despotism and arbitrariness, but in doing so they also tacitly affirm the primacy and moral superiority of the democratic paradigm in the modern age.

Although limited government and the rule of law are necessary for the establishment of a democratic order, these are not the elements that give a democracy its moral and persuasive power. The legitimacy of a democratic order is founded on the idea that the citizens of a nation are the sovereign, and that a democratic government gives effect to the will of that sovereign through representation. As such, the people are the source of the law, and the law is founded on the basis of fundamental rights that protect the basic well-being and interests of the individual members of the sovereign. Whether there is a written constitution or not, according to democratic theory, there must be a process through which the sovereign may guard and protect its rights and also shape the law. As far as Islam is concerned, democratic theory poses a formidable challenge. Put simply, if Muslim jurists considered law derived from a sovereign monarch to be inherently illegitimate and whimsical, what is the legitimacy of a system in which the law is derived from a sovereign, but the sovereign are the citizens of a nation? The brunt of the challenge to Islam is this: If God is the only sovereign and source of law in Islam, is it meaningful to speak of a democracy within Islam, or even of Islam within a democracy, and can an Islamic system of government ever be reconciled with democratic governance?

Struggling to answer this question is an endeavor fraught with conceptual and political pitfalls. On the one hand, arguing that constitutionalism and Islamic political doctrines are compatible immediately raises the problem of historical and cultural anachronism. How can a modern concept reflecting values that evolved over centuries within a particular cultural context be sought in a remarkably different context? In many ways, democracy cannot be theorized, but must be practiced through a culture that is tolerant of the other, open to disagreement, amenable to change, and that values the process, quite often regardless of the results it generates. On the other hand, denying that Islamic political doctrines could support a democratic order implies that Muslims are doomed to suffer despotism, unless they either abandon or materially alter their traditions. Furthermore, culture can be reconstructed and reinvented partly through the power of ideas, and if ideas are lacking, there is really never a possibility of a systematic or directed cultural change.

Therefore, anytime one portends to discuss whether Islam and democracy are compatible, one is also taking an implicit normative stance. This is so because both Islam and democracy are conceptual frameworks anchored in systems of commitment and belief. Both require conviction and conscientious dedication, without which they cannot really exist. In the same way that it is possible to perform Islamic rituals without ever being a believing Muslim, it is also possible to have all the trappings and processes of a democracy without ever creating a democracy. It is possible for a country to have a constitution, parliament, judiciary, elections, and other institutions of democracy without being democratic.[3] Similarly, it is possible for a government to implement the rules and regulations of Islamic law without being, in any real sense, Islamic.[4] What defines either a democracy or Islam are the moral values that one associates with either one of these systems of belief, and the attitudinal commitments of their adherents. I say this because, in my view, the broad tradition of Islamic political thought contains ideas and institutions that could potentially support or undermine a democratic order. There are trajectories or potentialities found in historical Islamic doctrines that could be utilized to promote or oppose a democratic system of governance. Saying this, however, is akin to asserting that there are raw materials that could be utilized to manufacture finished products. But without the willpower, inspired vision, and moral commitment, these raw materials remain of little use. Similarly, regardless of the doctrinal potentialities found in the Islamic tradition, without the necessary moral commitment, and conscientious understanding, there can be no democracy in Islam. At least Muslims, for whom Islam is the authoritative frame of reference, must develop a conviction that democracy is an ethical good, and that the pursuit of this good does not constitute an abandonment of Islam.

Islam and the Moral Commitment to Democracy

Should Muslims strive toward a democratic system of government, and if so, why? Any honest approach to the issue should start with these basic questions. Arguably, Muslims might legitimately prefer a system of government that submits to the divine will instead of abiding by the vagaries of human whimsies. Arguably, conceding sovereignty to God is more virtuous than accepting the sovereignty of human beings, and in fact the very idea of human sovereignty smacks of self-idolatry. In addition, one might even contend that the only reason that some Muslims seek to establish a democratic system of governance is because of their infatuation with everything Western, and that they should instead hold steadfast to what is legitimately and authentically Islamic.

These are formidable questions, but I believe they are also the wrong ones. The Qur'an did not specify a particular form of government, but it did identify social and political values that are central to a Muslim polity, and it urged Muslims to pursue and fulfill these values. Among such Qur'anically ordained values are the promotion of social cooperation and mutual assistance in pursuit of justice (Qur'an 49:13; 11:119), the establishment of a consultative and non-autocratic method of governance,[5] and the institutionalization of mercy and compassion in social interactions (Qur'an 6:12, 54; 21:107; 27:77; 29:51; 45:20). Therefore, it would stand to reason that Muslims ought to adopt the system of government that is the most effective in helping Muslims promote the pertinent moral values, and, in this regard, it could be plausibly argued that democracy is the most effective system for doing so. If Muslims are convinced that democracy is the best available means for serving the moral purposes of their religion, it hardly seems relevant whether democracy is a Western or non-Western idea. What is relevant is the existence of a conviction and belief in the merits of a democratic system, as opposed to any other possible system, and a commitment to the fostering and promotion of such a system through the moral venues facilitated by Islamic law and ethics.

In my view, there are several reasons that commend democracy, and especially a constitutional democracy, as the system most capable of promoting the ethical and moral imperatives of Islam. These reasons are elaborated upon below, but in essence I would argue that a democracy offers the greatest *potential* for promoting justice and protecting human dignity, without making God responsible for human injustice or the infliction of degradation by human beings upon one another. As I have argued elsewhere, authoritarianism, if inflicted in the name of religion, is a transgression upon the bounds of God. Authoritarianism allows despots to usurp the divine prerogative by empowering some human beings to play the role of God.[6] In order to avoid having a small group of people appointing themselves as the voice of God, and speaking in God's name, there are two options. Either we ought to deny everyone the authority to speak on God's behalf, or we endow everyone with that authority — either we allow no human being to be vested with the divine power, or we vest everyone with such a power. The former option is problematic because the Qur'an provides that God has vested all of humanity with divinity by making all human beings the viceroys of God on this earth; the latter is problematic because a person who does good cannot be morally equated with a person who does evil — for instance, a saint does not have the same moral worth as a serial killer. A constitutional democracy avoids the problem by enshrining some basic moral standards in a constitutional document; thus, it guarantees some discernment and differentiation, but at the same time it ensures that no single person or group becomes the infallible representative of divinity. In addition, a democratic system offers the greatest possibility for accountability, and for resistance to the tendency of the powerful to render themselves immune from judgment. This is consistent with the imperative of justice in Islam. If in a political system there are no institutional mechanisms to prevent the unjust from rendering themselves above judgment, then the system is itself unjust, regardless of whether injustice is actually committed or not. For instance, if there is a system in which there is no punishment for rape, this system is unjust, quite apart from whether that crime is ever committed or not. A democracy, through the institutions of the vote, separation and division of power, and guarantee of pluralism, at least offers the possibility of redress, and that, in and of itself, is a moral good.

There are several other reasons for commending a constitutional democracy as the system most consistent with Islamic moral imperatives, and I will explore them below, but first it is important to acknowledge that regardless of the practical merits identified, there are serious conceptual challenges that stand as obstacles to a democratic commitment in Islam, namely, the religious law of Shari'ah, and the idea that the people in a democracy, as the sovereign, can be free to flout or violate Shari'ah law. This challenge requires that we delve into the epistemology of Shari'ah and the meaning of God's sovereignty.

The problem has been that in contemporary Islam, there has not been a serious and systematic effort to evaluate either the concept of sovereignty or that of Shari'ah, as each may relate to modern political systems. The dominant Muslim responses to the challenge of democracy have tended to be either apologetic and defensive or nationalistic and rejectionist, but both responses have remained largely reactive. Muslim apologists, primarily as a means of emphasizing the compatibility of Islam with modernity, tended to claim, first, that democracy already exists in Islam. Typically, they maintained that the Qur'an is the functional equivalent of a constitution, and they also tended to recast the early history of Islam as if it were an ideal democratic experience. Apologists defended the public image of Islam by indulging in anachronisms, often pretending that the Prophet was sent to humanity in order to teach it the art of democratic governance. Therefore, they would declare the fundamental compatibility between Islam and democracy as a conclusion to be accepted as a matter of faith and belief, rather than as a proposition to be argued and proven. It is important to note, however, that this assumption was not the product of a moral commitment to democracy, but rather was the result of a keen interest in power. A democratic Islam was simply the vehicle by which they sought to empower themselves against the onslaught of various competing political forces, and Islam was also the means by which they sought to bid for domination over others. This is why we find that many of the apologists, for instance, were affiliated with the Muslim Brotherhood movement in Egypt, or with some other religio-political movement in the Muslim world. This is also why we find that the political practices of the apologists do not reflect the type of ethical virtues associated with democratic thought, such as tolerance of dissent, or valuing intellectual and cultural diversity. For example, we find that many of the American Muslim organizations which consistently affirm the compatibility of Islam with democracy are, in fact, quite despotic both in their internal dynamics and in the type of theology to which they adhere. This is because, for these organizations, democracy is affirmed politically, but not believed or internalized ethically.[7]

The second main response in modern Islam has been to insist that the Islamic political system is different and unique, and to argue that such a system might overlap with a democracy in some regards and might depart on others. The main emphasis of this approach is on cultural or intellectual independence and autonomy, and therefore any attempt to commit to a democratic system of governance is seen as a sign of surrender to what is called the Western intellectual or cultural invasion of the Muslim world. For instance, the Pakistani propagandist Abu al-A'la al-Mawdudi contended that the Islamic system of government is a theo-democracy, which, he insisted, is very different from either a theocracy or a democracy.[8] In addition, adherents of this approach frequently proclaim that the political system of Islam is a *shura* government, which they claim has nothing to do with a democratic system of government. Like the apologist approach, this trend is largely reactive in the sense that it defines itself solely by reference to the perceived "other." According to this orientation, an Islamic system cannot be democratic simply because the West is. But, rather inconsistently, the partisans of this approach often spend a considerable amount of energy trying to prove that Western democracies are hypocritical, and that they are not democracies at all. It is as if they see the merits of a democracy, but out of a blind sense of nationalistic tribalism they insist that the West does not really have it, and Muslims ought not pursue it. Importantly, however, what the adherents of this approach claim to be of essence to an Islamic political system is as alien, or indigenous, to Islam as is a democratic system of government. In other words, the adherents of this approach construct a reactive symbolism of what an Islamic system ought to be, but such symbolism is not necessarily derived from any genuine and authentic Islamic historical experience. It is wholly and completely derived from what they believe the "other" is not, and, consequently, that derived construct is as much of a historical anachronism as is a democratic vision of the Prophet and his companions' polity. It is fair to say that the adherents of this orientation are far more anti-Western than they are pro-Islamic.

The dominance of the apologetic or rejectionist orientations throughout the colonial and post-colonial eras in Islam has resulted in the stunting of the Islamic creative impulse toward the challenge of democracy. Is Islam compatible with a democracy? The response can only be that it depends on whether there are a sufficient number of Muslims willing to commit to the democratic ideal, and willing to undertake the type of critical reappraisal of Islamic theology and law necessary to give full effect to this commitment. Thus far, most of the efforts at achieving this have been on largely functionalist and opportunistic grounds that, if anything, ultimately discredit the very idea of reform within Islam. Overwhelmingly, contemporary Muslim reformers have attempted to justify a democracy in Islam solely on the grounds of *maslaha* (public interest). Typically, such reformers are satisfied with asserting that most of Islamic law may be changed to serve the public interests of Muslims, and jump from that assertion to the conclusion that the adoption of democracy ought not pose any serious obstacles because of the primacy of deference to public interest in Islamic jurisprudence. The fact is that such reformers have also tended to come from the ranks of people who have nothing more than the most superficial familiarity with the epistemology and methodology of Islamic jurisprudence. In addition, the logic of public interest is like a harlot; it offers its services to democrats and despots alike. Between the often opportunistic logic of reformers, the obstinacy of rejectionists, and the insincerity of apologists, the possibilities for a democracy within Islam have not been seriously explored. The balance of this essay will focus on the possibilities offered by the intellectual heritage of Islam, and also point out the issues that pose the greatest challenge to Muslims willing to make a commitment to democracy.

God As the Sovereign

I will discuss the issue of political representation below, but at this point it is important to start exploring the idea of God as the sovereign lawmaker in an Islamic state, and whether such a paradigm is inconsistent with a democratic system of government. Interestingly, early in Islamic history, the issue of God's dominion or sovereignty in the political sphere *(hakimiyyat Allah)* was raised by a group known as the Haruriyya (later known as the Khawarij) when they rebelled against the fourth Rightly-Guided Caliph ʿAli Ibn Abi Talib (d. 40/661). Initially, the Haruriyya were firm supporters of ʿAli, but they rebelled against him when he agreed to arbitrate his political dispute with a competing political faction led by a man named Muʿawiya. Ultimately, the effort at reaching a peaceful resolution to the political conflict was a failure, and, after ʿAli's death, Muʿawiya was able to seize power and establish himself as the first caliph of the Umayyad Dynasty. At the time of the arbitration, however, the Khawarij, who were pious, puritan, and fanatic, believed that God's law clearly supported ʿAli and, therefore, an arbitration or any negotiated settlement was inherently unlawful. The Khawarij maintained that the Shariʿah clearly and unequivocally supported ʿAli's claim to power, and that any attempt at a negotiated settlement, in effect, challenged the rule of God (and thus God's sovereignty or dominion) and therefore, by definition, was illegitimate. Ironically, ʿAli himself had agreed to the arbitration on the condition that the arbitrators be bound by the Qurʾan, and that they would give full consideration to the supremacy of the Shariʿah; but to ʿAli's mind, this did not necessarily preclude the possibility of a negotiated settlement, let alone the lawfulness of resorting to arbitration as a way of resolving the dispute. In the view of the Khawarij, by accepting the principle of arbitration and by accepting the notion that legality could be negotiated, ʿAli himself had lost his claim to legitimacy because he transferred God's dominion to human beings. ʿAli's behavior, according to the Khawarij, had shown that he was willing to compromise God's supremacy by transferring decision-making to human actors instead of faithfully applying the law of God. Not surprisingly, the Khawarij declared 'Ali a traitor to God, rebelled against him, and eventually succeeded in assassinating him.

It is notable that the Khawarij's rallying cry of "dominion belongs to God" or "the Qur'an is the judge" *(la hukma illa li'llah* or *al-hukmu li'l-Qur'an)* is nearly identical to the slogans invoked by contemporary fundamentalist groups.[9] But considering the historical context, the Khawarij's sloganeering was initially a call for the symbolism of legality and the supremacy of law.[10] This search for legality quickly descended into an unequivocal radicalized call for clear lines of demarcation between what is lawful and unlawful. The anecdotal reports about the debates between 'Ali and the Khawarij regarding this matter reflect an unmistakable tension about the meaning of legality and the implications of the rule of law. In one such report, members of the Khawarij accused 'Ali of accepting the judgment and dominion *(hakimiyya)* of human beings instead of abiding by the dominion of God's law. Upon hearing of this accusation, 'Ali called upon the people to gather around him, and brought a large copy of the Qur'an. 'Ali touched the Qur'an while instructing it to speak to the people and to inform them about God's law. Surprised, the people gathered around 'Ali exclaimed, "What are you doing! The Qur'an cannot speak, for it is not a human being." Upon hearing this, 'Ali exclaimed that this was exactly the point he was trying to make! The Qur'an, 'Ali explained, is but ink and paper, and it does not speak for itself. Instead, it is human beings who give effect to it according to their limited personal judgments and opinions.[11]

Anecdotal stories such as these not only relate to the role of human agency in interpreting the divine word, but also symbolize a search for the fundamental moral values of society. In thinking about these moral values, it is important to differentiate between issues that are subject to political negotiation and expedience, and issues that constitute unwavering matters of principle and are strictly governed by law. Furthermore, one can discern in such reports a search for the proper legal limits that may be placed upon a ruler's range of discretion. But more important, they also point to the dogmatic superficiality of proclamations of God's dominion or sovereignty in order to legitimate and empower what are fundamentally human determinations. For a believer, God is thought of as all-powerful and as the ultimate owner of the heavens and earth, but what are the implications of this claim for human agency in understanding and implementing the law in a political system?

As I argue below, arguments claiming that God is the sole legislator and only source of law engage in a fatal fiction that is not defensible from the point of view of Islamic theology. Such arguments pretend that human agents could possibly have perfect and unfettered access to the will of God, and that human beings could possibly become the mere executors of the divine will, without inserting their own human subjectivities in the process. Furthermore, and more important, claims about God's sovereignty assume that there is a divine legislative will that seeks to regulate all human interactions. This is always stated as an assumption, instead of a proposition that needs to be argued and proven. As discussed later, it is possible that God does not seek to regulate all human affairs. It is also as possible that God leaves it to human beings to regulate their own affairs as long as they observe certain minimal standards of moral conduct, and that such standards include the preservation and promotion of human dignity and well-being.

According to the Qur'an, human beings are the vicegerents of God and the inheritors of the earth, and are the most valued invention in God's creation. In the Qur'anic discourse, God commanded creation to honor human beings because of the miracle of the human intellect, which is the microcosm of the abilities of the divine itself. Arguably, the fact that God honored the miracle of the human intellect, and also honored the human being as a symbol of divinity, is sufficient in and of itself to justify a moral commitment to the values that are necessary for protecting and preserving the integrity and dignity of that symbol of divinity.[12] As I argue below, the fact that God is sovereign and creation is God's dominion cannot be used as an excuse to escape the burdens of human agency. Seen from a different perspective, the notion of God's sovereignty can easily be exploited to overcome and marginalize the agency of most human beings in conducting the affairs of their polity. Invariably, however, this will only mean that an elite will rule in God's name while pretending to implement the divine will. This is fundamentally at odds with the epistemology and methodologies of classical Islamic jurisprudence. As is argued later, God's sovereignty is honored in the search for the ways that human beings may be able to approximate the beauty and justice of God. It is also honored in the attempt to preserve and safeguard the moral values that reflect the attributes of the sublimity of the divine. If God's sovereignty is used to argue that the only legitimate source of law is the divine text, and that human experience and intellect are irrelevant and immaterial to the pursuit of the divine will, however, then the idea of divine sovereignty will always stand as an instrument of authoritarianism, and as an obstacle to democracy.[13] I will further develop this argument below, but in order to make this argument more accessible, I will first lay a broader foundation for Islamic legal and political doctrines.

The Powers of the Ruler

If, as many Muslim fundamentalists and Western orientalists contend, God's dominion or sovereignty means that God is the sole legislator, then one would expect that a caliph or Muslim ruler would be treated as God's agent or representative. If God is the only sovereign within a political system, then the ruler ought to be appointed by the divine sovereign and serve at his pleasure. But in the same way that the meaning and implications of God's sovereignty were the subject of an intense debate in pre-modern Islam, so was the topic of the powers and capacity of the ruler.

It is well established, at least in Sunni Islam, that the Prophet died without naming a successor to lead the Muslim community. The Prophet intentionally left the choice of leadership to the Muslim nation as a whole. A statement attributed to the Rightly Guided Caliph Abu Bakr asserts, "God has left people to manage their own affairs so that they will choose a leader who will serve their interests."[14] The word *khalifa* (caliph), the title given to the Muslim leader, literally means the successor or deputy. Early on, Muslims debated whether it was appropriate to name the leader "the Caliph of God" *(khalifat Allah),* but most scholars preferred the designation "the Caliph of the Prophet of God" *(khalifat rasul Allah).* Hence, the well-known jurist al-Mawardi (d. 450/1058) stated,

> And, he is called Caliph because he succeeded the Prophet [in leading] the nation *[ummah].* So it is proper to call him the caliph of the Prophet [successor of the Prophet]. The scholars disagreed over whether it is proper to call him the Caliph of God. Some allowed it because he [the leader] fulfills the rights of God in His people . . . but the majority of the jurists disallowed it . . . because succession can only be in the rights of one who is dead or absent, and God is never absent or dead.[15]

Nevertheless, the caliph's source of legitimacy and parameters of his powers remained ambiguous. Whether the caliph was considered the Prophet's successor or God's deputy, from a theological point of view the caliph did not enjoy the authority of either the Prophet or God. Theologically speaking, God and his Prophet cannot be equated with any other, and their powers of legislation, revelation, absolution, and punishment cannot be delegated to any other. Yet, the exact nature and extent of the caliph's powers remained contested. This is partly due to the fact that the divine law provides a nexus to the powers and authority of both God and his Prophet. In principle, the application of God's law implies giving effect to the divine will, which, in turn, implicates the authority of the divine. Therefore, Ibn al-Jawzi, for example, states, "The Caliph is God's deputy over God's followers and lands, and [the caliphate entails] applying His orders and laws. [This function] was performed by His Prophets and the Caliph performs that role after them [the Prophets]."[16]

Even if one assumes that the caliph cannot be considered the moral equivalent of God or the Prophet, the question remains: how much of the Prophet's legislative and executive authority does the caliph enjoy? According to the prominent jurist Ibn Taymiyya (d. 728/1328), the word "caliph" simply means the physical or historical act of ruling after the Prophet, but it does not connote the transference of the Prophet's authority or power. The caliph is the historical, not the moral, successor of the Prophet, and thus the moral and legal authority of the Prophet (or God) does not vest in a person carrying the title of caliph.[17] At one point, Ibn Taymiyya stated,

> He [the caliph] is not the people's Lord so that he could possibly do without [their assistance]; and he is not God's Prophet, acting as their agent to God. But he and the people are partners who [must] cooperate for the welfare [of the people] in this earthly life and the Hereafter. They [the people] must help him, and he must help them.[18]

Ibn Taymiyya's conception of the relationship between the ruler and the ruled is egalitarian, but it does not help in understanding the source of the caliph's powers or in delineating the nature of the relationship between the ruler and his people. Ideally, the ruler and the ruled should cooperate in order to maximize the best interests of the community, but the question remains: What is the exact nature of the caliph's powers vis-à-vis his subjects?

The jurist al-Baqillani (d. 403/1013) is more explicit in differentiating between the authority of the caliph and that of God or the Prophet. He argues the following:

> The *imam* [leader] is chosen to apply the laws expounded by the Prophet and recognized by the nation, and he, in all that he does, is the nation's trustee and representative; and it [the nation] is behind him, correcting him and reminding him . . . and removing him and replacing him when he does what calls for his removal.[19]

In al-Baqillani's conception of the caliphate, the ruler is the people's duly delegated agent who is charged with the obligation of implementing God's law. This brings us closer to the idea of a representative government, and to a government of limited powers — arguably, the limitations are imposed by the people, who act as overseers, ensuring compliance with God's law. The imperative of acting as overseers is performed pursuant to the religious obligation to enjoin the good and forbid the evil *(al-amr bi'l ma'ruf wa al-nahy 'an al-munkar)*. According to Islamic law, Muslims are commanded to enjoin the good and forbid the evil, which includes the obligation to prevent the government from violating the Shari'ah.[20] Significantly, according to the classical theory, the caliph's charge is not necessarily to give effect to the will of the people, but to give effect to God's will, as exemplified by God's law.[21] But this brings us full circle, once again, to the issue of the boundaries set by the divine law, and to the extent that Shari'ah law provides limits on the discretion and power of the ruler.

But aside from the issue of the exact limits placed upon the ruler's powers, it is imperative that it be recognized that wedding the notion of the caliphate to the divine law creates an intimate connection between the caliph and the divine will, and that the divine will is not as discernible as some would like to believe. Whether the caliph is considered God's deputy or the Prophet's deputy, the question is this: To whom does the caliph answer? If the caliph's primary obligation is to implement the divine law, then, arguably, the caliph answers only to God. Since God's law is not always discernible, as long as the caliph's actions are plausible interpretations of the mandates of God's law, then such interpretations must be accepted. But the idea that the caliph's primary charge is to give effect to God's law, and the associated idea that the caliph answers only to God, creates a symbolic privity or, at least, the appearance of a special relationship between the caliph and God. It is not so much that the caliph becomes the representative of the divine will, but that the caliph comes to be perceived as having a symbolic association or connection with God, as the guardian and protector of God's will and law. Often, this is manifested simply in a presumption of deference to the caliph.

Al-Baqillani's discourse itself reflects this symbolic connection when he discusses whether a ruler may name a successor to the caliphate. Al-Baqillani argues that, in fact, it is permissible for the caliph to do so, and that the people should accept his nomination. His justification is the most interesting part of his discussion; he argues that the people should accept the caliph's decision because there is a legal presumption that the caliph always acts in the best interest of his people. According to al-Baqillani, for people to believe otherwise is a sin that calls for repentance.[22] This type of presumption is coherent only if the ruler represents the divine will, and not the will of the people, and only if the ruler answers to God, and not the people. If the ruler discharges the duties of piety by giving effect to God's law, however God's law is defined, he has fulfilled his duties toward the people, and the quality or genuineness of his intentions is assessed only by God. As a result of this type of paradigm, most Sunni jurists argued that a ruler is not removable from power unless he commits a clear, visible, and major infraction against God (in other words, a major sin).[23]

Muslim jurists, however, did not completely sever the connection between the ruler and the people. In Sunni theory, the caliphate must be based on a contract *('aqd)* between the caliph and *ahl al-hall wa al-'aqd* (the people who have the power of contract; also known as *ahl al-ikhtiyar* or the people who choose), who give their *bay'a* (allegiance or consent to the caliph). In the classical theory, a person who fulfills certain conditions *(mustawfi al-shurut)* must come to power through a contract entered into with *ahl al-'aqd,* pursuant to which the caliph is to receive the *bay'a* in return for his promise to discharge the terms of the contract. The terms of the contract were not extensively discussed in Islamic sources. Typically, jurists would write a list of terms that included the obligation to apply God's law and the obligation to protect Muslims and the territory of Islam, and in return the ruler was promised the people's support and obedience. There is no precedent in Islamic discourses for a negotiated contract of the caliphate. The jurists seemed to treat the contract as a contract of implied terms, but there is no explicit rejection of the notion of a contract of negotiated terms. The extent to which the contract of the caliphate is subject to the principle of freedom of contract and permissibility of negotiation remains unexplored in Islamic thinking. Thus far, it has been assumed that Shari'ah law defines the terms of the contract.

Who are the people that have the power to choose and remove the ruler? According to some, like the Mu'tazili[24] scholar Abu Bakr al-Asam (d. 200/816), it is the public, at large, that constitutes this group. Therefore, according to this view, there must be a general consensus over the ruler, and each person must individually give his vote of allegiance to the ruler.[25] The vast majority of Muslim jurists disagreed with this position and adopted a more pragmatic approach to power. They argued that *ahl al-'aqd* are those who possess the necessary *shawka* (power or strength) to ensure the obedience or, in the alternative, the consent of the public. Although it does make a material difference whether the people who possess this *shawka* represent the consent of the governed or the ability to yield a sufficient amount of power to ensure the obedience of the public, this issue remained unclear.

The idea of the consent of the governed ought not to be equated, however, with conceptions of delegated powers or government by the people. The consent of which some jurists speak does not seem to mean the existence of a representative government that seeks to give effect to the will of the people.

Rather, consent in pre-modern Muslim discourses appears to be the equivalent of acquiescence. Typically, Muslim jurists assert that *ahl al-ʿaqd* must be people who fulfill certain conditions such as decency, probity, knowledge, and wisdom. Beyond these qualifications, the jurists assert that the group with the power to choose must consist of a certain number of the notables of society *(shurafaʾ al-umma)* or the prominent jurists. There is considerable disagreement about how many individuals would be sufficient to form such a group. Some, such as the jurist al-Juwayni, argued that the exact number is immaterial; the group that chooses the caliph could be a single person or a hundred as long as the consent of this group represents the consent of the majority of the people.[26]

It is important to note that pre-modern Muslim scholars exhibited a certain amount of distrust toward the laity *(al-ʿamma)*. For example, the Muʿtazili scholar al-Jahiz (d. 255/868-869), describing the laity, wrote, "They [the laity] tend to float with every ebb and flow, and maybe [the laity] will be more content with choosing [to the caliphate] the wrong-doers instead of the righteous [rulers]. . . ."[27] This type of attitude was widespread among Muslim jurists, and considering the historical period in which they wrote, it is not surprising. But this also meant that although many of the concepts employed in political discourse came close to affirming the idea of government through representation, they never in fact did so. It is as if Muslim jurists generated legal concepts that were derived from the historical practices of the early Muslims, but never developed these concepts and utilized them toward a theory of representation. For example, Muslim jurists struggled with the conceptual nature of the contract of the caliphate. Various Muslim jurists maintained that this political contract is akin to an employment contract, sale contract, or marriage contract in trying to figure out the jurisprudence that should apply to this unique form of contractual relationship.[28] The political contract had rather clear historical origins — it was initiated and practiced by the Companions after the death of the Prophet. The Prophet himself was keen on taking the *bayʿa* of his followers on several occasions. Even more, when the Prophet became the ruler of Medina, he drafted what is now known as the Constitution of Medina *(wathiqat al-Madina)*. The Constitution of Medina does not read like a modern constitutional document — rather, it reads more like a contract or a corporate organizational document. These historical precedents must have persisted into the practices of the early Muslim community. So, although the historical origin was clear, the theoretical justifications for the doctrines of a political contract, consent, and the pledge of allegiance remained ambiguous. Significantly, as the jurists formed a socially and professionally recognizable class of experts, they reasoned that the purpose of the contract is to uphold God's law. The notion of political representation, how-ever, remained undeveloped, at best. The overwhelming majority of Muslim jurists do not contend that the purpose of the caliphate's contract is to repre-sent the will of the governed. Instead, these jurists thought of the contract as essentially a promise to uphold God's law. The consent of the people is needed because the contract is premised on a cooperative relationship be-tween the governor and governed, with the purpose of guarding and protect-ing the righteous religion and Shari'ah. Even though, as we will see below, there are glimpses of the notion of representation on behalf of the people, the dominant paradigm is one in which both the ruler and ruled act as God's duly delegated agents *(khulafa' Allah)* in implementing the divine law.

Particularly after the age of *mihna* (inquisition — 218-234/833-848) the 'ulama (religious scholars or jurists) were able to establish themselves as the exclusive interpreters and articulators of the divine law. Toward the end of the reign of the 'Abbasid Caliph al-Ma'mun (r. 198-218/813-833), the caliph adopted the Mu'tazili doctrine of the createdness of the Qur'an, and insti-tuted an inquisition against those jurists who refused to adhere to this doc-trine. Although ostensibly about a theological dispute concerning whether the Qur'an was created or eternal (uncreated), in reality the inquisition was a concerted effort by the state to control the juristic class and the method by which Shari'ah law was generated. Ultimately, however, the inquisition failed and, at least until the modern age, the jurists retained a near exclusive mo-nopoly over the right to interpret the divine law.[29] Thus, in order for a caliph and community to attain and continue enjoying Islamic legitimacy, they would have to dedicate themselves to upholding the will of God as articulated by the jurists. In a sense, we end up with a tri-polar dynamic with the ruler and governors at one pole, the jurists at another, and the lay public at the third. But one would have to consider the possibility that between the inter-pretive and legislative tasks of the jurists and the executory duties of the ruler, the common people do not play a major role in the negotiative process be-tween the three social poles. This possibility is quite clear in a statement by the jurist Ibn al-Qayyim, who states,

> Properly speaking, the rulers *[al-umara']* are obeyed [only to the extent] that their commands are consistent with the [determinations] of the reli-gious sciences *[al-'ilm]*. Hence, the duty to obey them [the rulers] derives from the duty to obey the jurists *[fa ta'atuhum tab'an li ta'at al-'ulama]*. [This is because] obedience is due only in what is good *[ma'ruf]*, and what is required by the religious sciences *[wa ma awjabahu al-'ilm]*. Since the duty to obey the jurists is derived from the duty to obey the Prophet,

then the duty to obey the rulers is derived from the duty to obey the jurists [who are the experts on the religious sciences]. Furthermore, since Islam is protected and upheld by the rulers and the jurists alike, this means that the laity must follow [and obey] these two [i.e., the rulers and jurists].[30]

This type of statement generates the impression that the Islamic system of government is a theocracy or, at least, a legalistic technocracy, and in fact inspired by passages such as this, modern fundamentalist groups do treat it as such. But understood within their proper historical contexts, statements such as the one quoted above would be read more as an aspirational moral exhortation than a constitutional delineation of the authority of the jurists. The absence of a singular authority conclusively and authoritatively defining the divine law, and the remarkable diversity of opinions and approaches within Islamic legal practices, have formed a barrier against the formation of a central church that could rule in God's name. In addition, no church could provide a jurist with the insignia of investiture and render him authoritative regardless of his relationship to the laity. There were seminaries that trained Muslim jurists, but the amount of influence and authoritativeness that a jurist would enjoy depended on his ability to convince various strata within society of his sincerity, knowledge, and integrity. In the pre-modern age, the epistemology of Islamic jurisprudence, and the processes that formed the juristic class, contained popularistic elements. In fact, the idea of government bound by law was the symbolic field where, while armed with the divine sanctity of Shari'ah law, Muslim jurists were able to play the role of the representatives and the mediators on behalf of the government and the governed. In order to better understand this process, it is necessary to disentangle several layers of meaning in the debates surrounding the concept of a government bound by Shari'ah.

A Government Bound by Law or a Government of Laws

As noted above, pre-modern and modern scholars often repeat that the quintessential characteristic of a legitimate Islamic government is that it is a government subject to and limited by Shari'ah law. Although this concept does tend to offer support for the principles of limited government and the rule of law, we must distinguish between the idea of the supremacy of law and the idea of the supremacy of legal rules. The two are quite distinct, and each concept has the potential of producing very different orientations toward the relationship between law and power. In asserting the supremacy of Shari'ah, Muslim scholars were not arguing that there ought to be a process that guards core legal values and that this process is binding upon the government. Rather, they were arguing that the positive commandments of Shari'ah, such as punishment for adultery or the drinking of alcohol, ought to be honored and implemented by the government.

The problem, however, is that it is possible for a government to declare its intention to abide by all the positive commandments of Shari'ah but otherwise manipulate the interpretation and application of the rules in order to obtain desired results. As is the practice in several contemporary Islamist states, nothing prevents the government from implementing a process that rubber-stamps whatever the government deems desirable. Unless there are institutional mechanisms, and procedural guarantees safeguarding the implementation of law, the fact that a government is committed to implementing a particular set of rulings does not amount to the supremacy of law, or the establishment of the rule of law.

The problem in this regard is that the juristic conception of a government limited by Shari'ah amounted to a notion that the government is acting lawfully if it is implementing the legal rulings of Shari'ah. Nevertheless, a government, for instance, could implement Shari'ah criminal penalties, prohibit usury, dictate rules of modesty, and so on, and yet remain a government of unlimited powers not subject to the rule of law. This is because Shari'ah is a general term for a multitude of legal methodologies and a remarkably diverse set of interpretive determinations.[31] Unless the conception of government is founded around core moral values about the normative purpose of Shari'ah, and unless there is a process that limits the ability of the government to violate those core moral values, the idea of a government bound by Shari'ah remains hopelessly vague. It is quite possible for a government to faithfully implement the main technical rules of Shari'ah but otherwise flout the rule of law. In fact, using the implementation of the technicalities of Shari'ah as an excuse could allow the government unrestrained powers. For instance, under the pretense of guarding public modesty, the government could pass arbitrary laws forbidding many forms of public assembly; under the guise of protection of orthodoxy, the government could pass arbitrary laws punishing creative expression; under the guise of protecting individuals from slander, the government could punish many forms of political and social criticism; and a government could imprison or execute political dissenters while claiming that the dissenters are sowing *fitnah* (discord and social turmoil). Arguably, all these governmental actions are Shari'ah-compliant unless there is a clear sense about the limits imposed upon the ability of the government to service and promote even the Shari'ah. Put differently, the rules of law cannot be used as an excuse to flout the rule of law, and the state cannot be allowed to usurp the process by which Shari'ah law is identified or determined. The rule of law does not mean the existence of a government bound by law as much as it means a government bound by the process that produces the law. More importantly, it also means that the processes of law, themselves, are bound by fundamental and unwavering moral commitments that ensure that the law is not used as an instrument of tyranny and oppression.

In pre-modern juristic literature, the issue of limits to be placed on the lawmaking power of the state was discussed, in part, under the rubric of public interest *(al-masalih al-mursalah)* and blocking the means to illegality *(sadd al-dhari'ah)*. Both jurisprudential concepts, although technically different, enabled the state to extend its lawmaking powers in order to fulfill a good or avoid an evil. For instance, pursuant to the principle of blocking the means, the lawmaker could claim that behavior that is lawful ought to be considered unlawful because it leads to the commission of illegal acts. In essence, both public interests and blocking the means were enabling devices that provided the law with considerable flexibility and adaptive ability. They were also double-edged concepts, however. They could be employed to respond to social demands, but they could also be used to expand the law and augment its intrusiveness at the expense of individual autonomy. Muslim jurists disagreed sharply on the permissibility and scope of these legal methodologies because a considerable number of jurists worried that these concepts were limitless and that they could be utilized to create a wide range of temporal law not based on Shari'ah.[32] The concept of blocking the means to evil, in particular, is founded on the idea of preventive or precautionary measures *(al-ihtiyat)*, and it is this aggressive reactionary nature that could be exploited to expand the power of the state under the guise of protecting the Shari'ah. For instance, the claim of precautionary measures has been used in Saudi Arabia to justify a wide range of restrictive laws against women, including the prohibition against driving cars. In many instances, this amounted to the use of Shari'ah to undermine Shari'ah.[33] This type of dynamic can be avoided not only through the adoption of procedural guarantees, but more importantly, through basic commitments to the dignity and freedoms of human beings, which the Shari'ah can be utilized to justify but cannot be allowed to undermine.

An important dimension to the challenge of establishing the rule of law is the complex, and often ambiguous, relationship between Shari'ah law and what may be called the administrative practices of the state or expediency laws *(al-ahkam al-siyasiyyah)*. As noted earlier, by the fourth/tenth century Muslim jurists had established themselves as the legitimate and exclusive authority empowered to expound the law of God. Only the jurists were deemed to possess the requisite level of technical competence and learning that would qualify them to investigate and interpret the divine will. While in the first two centuries of Islam it was possible to find jurists citing the practices of the state as a normative precedent, this became increasingly rare.[34]

This did not mean that the practice of the state was considered illegitimate or without justification, but rather that the determinations of the jurists were considered to be of prescriptive value, and the state was expected to play the role of enforcer, and not the maker, of divine laws. Only the juristic law could enjoy the seal of divinity, while state laws were considered temporal and, therefore, primarily the product of functional necessities rather than an interpretation of the divine will. But pursuant to the powers derived from its role as the enforcer of divine laws, the state was granted a broad range of discretion over what were considered matters of public interest (known as the field of al-siyasah al-Shar'iyyah). The state's rule-making activity in the exercise of this discretion was considered to be akin to regulatory administrative rules that have temporal weight but that are not a part of binding precedents of Shari'ah law. State regulations were lawful and enforceable as long as they did not contravene the divine law, as expounded by the jurists, and as long as they did not constitute an abusive use of discretion (al-ta'assuf fi masa'il al-khiyar). This is the reason that jurisprudential works meticulously documented the determinations of jurists, but did not document state regulations. State regulations were documented in texts written by state functionaries composing works on the administrative practices of the state.

The differentiation between temporal, or perhaps secular, state regulations and juristic Shari'ah law in Islamic history is subtle and often quite complex. It also raises serious questions about Muslim conceptions of state power and ideas of sovereignty. But it has not been sufficiently explored in modern scholarship, and, therefore, it is difficult to draw any firm conclusions from the little that we do know about these classical discourses.[35] Nevertheless, it is rather clear that the classical jurists did not consider Shari'ah as existing in conflict or even in tension with administrative law. What was described as al-ahkam al-Sultaniyyah or al-siyasah al-shar'iyyah was expected to guard and help fulfill the aims of Shari'ah. The administrative regulations of the state were considered a function of public policy or politics, but in the dictum of Muslim jurists, Shari'ah is considered the foundation of law, and politics is its protector.[36] Shari'ah was expected to play the dual role of enabling and limiting the regulatory powers of the state. In theory, the Shari'ah lends legitimacy to the regulatory powers of the state, but, in turn, such regulations are not supposed to contravene the Shari'ah. This paradigm, however, ended full circle with the core problem of clearly delineating the limits to the government's assertion of state power. To what extent can the government extend the reach of its laws under the guise of guarding or properly fulfilling the purposes of Shari'ah?

Concerns about the reach of the government's power under Shari'ah have antecedents in Islamic history, and so, by the standards of the modern age, this is not an entirely novel issue. The Maliki jurist al-Qarafi (d. 684/1285) attempted to articulate a theory defining the legal jurisdiction of caliphs, judges, and juris-consuls.[37] There is also historic anecdotal evidence expressing concern about the ability of contending parties to manipulate the interpretation of the Shari'ah to achieve certain aims. For instance, a report was attributed to the Prophet in which he says, "If you lay siege to a fortress, do not accept the surrender of the fortress on the condition that you will apply God's law, for you do not know [what] God's law requires. Rather, have them surrender on the condition that you will apply your own judgment."[38] Reports such as this reflect a nascent concern with the nature of the constraints that the broad concept of Shari'ah may have on the actual process of adjudication or resolution of disputes. The invocation of Shari'ah or the Qur'an and Sunna in confrontations with authority, however, was often used as a symbolic point referring to legitimacy or legality in the management of the social order. For example, in another anecdotal report that reflects this dynamic, the first Umayyad caliph Mu'awiya (r. 40-60/661-680) asked Hujr b. 'Adi al-Kindi (d. 51/671) for his allegiance *(bay'a)*. Al-Kindi reportedly agreed to give his allegiance but only on the condition that Mu'awiya abide by the Qur'an and Sunna. Mu'awiya refused, arguing that a conditional allegiance is ineffective, and, hence, al-Kindi refused to give his oath of allegiance.[39]

The difficulty, however, is that these types of concerns that led to the differentiation between the divine law of the jurists and the temporal laws of the state are nearly entirely absent from the framework of contemporary Islamists. To date, Islamist models, whether in Iran, Saudi Arabia, or Pakistan, have endowed the state with legislative power over the divine law. This is a relatively novel invention in Islamic state practices. Traditionally, Muslim jurists insisted that the rulers ought to consult with the jurists on all matters related to law, but the jurists, themselves, never demanded the right to rule the Islamic state directly. In fact, until recently, neither Sunni nor Shi'i jurists ever assumed direct rule in the political sphere.[40] Throughout Islamic history, the jurists *('ulama)* performed a wide range of economic, political, and administrative functions, but, most important, they acted as negotiative mediators between the ruling classes and the laity. As Afaf Marsot states, "[The *'ulama]* were the purveyors of Islam, the guardians of its tradition, the depository of

ancestral wisdom, and the moral tutors of the population."[41] While they le-
gitimated and often explained the rulers to the ruled, the jurists also used
their moral weight to thwart tyrannous measures and, at times, led or legiti-
mated rebellions against the ruling classes.[42] As Marsot points out, "[t]o both
rulers and ruled they were an objective haven which contending factions
could turn to in times of stress."[43] Modernity, however, through a complex
dynamic, turned the *ulama* from "vociferous spokesmen of the masses" into
salaried state functionaries that play a primarily conservative, legitimist role
for the ruling regimes in the Islamic world.[44] The disintegration of the role of
the *ulama* and their co-optation by the modern praetorian state, with its hy-
brid practices of secularism, has opened the door for the state to become the
maker and enforcer of divine law, and in doing so, the state acquired a formidable power that only served to further engrain the practice of authoritarianism in various Islamic states.

The Ideal of a Consultative Government

The Qur'an instructs the Prophet to consult regularly with Muslims on all
significant matters, and also indicates that a society that conducts its affairs
through some form of deliberative process is considered praiseworthy in the
eyes of God (3:159, 42:38). There are many historical reports indicating that
the Prophet regularly consulted with his Companions regarding the affairs of
the state. In addition, shortly after the death of the Prophet, the concept of
shura (consultative deliberations) became a symbol signifying participatory
politics and legitimacy. There are a variety of early Islamic historical narratives that indicate that the Qur'anic discourse on a consultative and deliberative sociopolitical order had captured the imagination of early Muslims. The
failure to enforce or adhere to *shura* became a common theme invoked in
narratives of oppression and rebellion. For example, it is reported that the
Prophet's cousin 'Ali reproached Umar b. al-Khattab, the second caliph, and
Abu Bakr, the first caliph, for not respecting the *shura* by nominating Abu
Bakr to the caliphate in the absence of the Prophet's family.[45] The opposition
to 'Uthman b. 'Affan (r. 23-35/644-656), the third Rightly Guided Caliph, accused him of destroying the rule of *shura* because of his alleged nepotistic
and autocratic policies. The pretender to the caliphate, Ibn al-Zubayr (r. 60-
73/680-692), justified his rebellion by accusing the Umayyads of destroying
the *shura* and undermining the rights of the people *(huquq al-nas).*

Although the precise meaning of *shura* in these historical narratives is
unclear, most certainly the concept did not refer to the mere act of a ruler so-

liciting the opinions of some notables in society. The term seemed to signify the opposite of autocracy, government by force, or oppression. This is consistent with the juristic attitude toward despotism *(al-istibdad)* and whimsical and autocratic governance *(al-hukm bi'l hawa wa al-tasallut)* — realities that they considered as repulsive and evil. Even when Muslim jurists prohibited rebellions against despotic rulers, they tolerated despotism not as a desirable good but as a necessary evil.

After the third/ninth century, the concept of *shura* took an institutional shape in the discourses of Muslim jurists. *Shura* became the formal act of consulting *ahl al-shura* (the people of consultation), who, according to the juristic sources, are the same group of people who constitute *ahl al-'aqd* (the people who choose the ruler). Sunni jurists debated whether the results of the consultative process are binding *(shura mulzima)* or nonbinding *(ghayr mulzima)*. If the *shura* is binding, then the ruler must abide by the determinations made by *ahl al-shura*. The majority of the jurists, however, concluded that the determinations of *ahl al-shura* are advisory, not compulsory. But, rather inconsistently, many jurists asserted that, after consultation, the ruler must follow the opinion that is most consistent with the Qur'an, Sunnah, and the consensus of jurists. In effect, while these jurists were not willing to argue that the ruler ought to be free to ignore the opinions that are the most consistent with the Qur'an, Sunnah, and consensus of the jurists, they did not go as far as advocating a mandatory duty upon the ruler to follow such opinions. Interestingly, some jurists, such as Ibn Taymiyya, maintained that the ruler should attempt to ascertain the general consensus of Muslims, and not simply the consensus of jurists, and follow it.[46] Most jurists, however, left the matter open-ended by limiting themselves to the argument that even if the caliph is knowledgeable in law, he should not rule on any problem that involves Shari'ah without first consulting the jurists.[47] As al-Ghazali asserted in this context, "Despotic, non-consultative decision-making, even if from a wise and learned person, is objectionable and unacceptable."[48]

Modern reformists have seized upon the ideal of a consultative government as a way of arguing for the basic compatibility between Islam and democracy. There is no doubt that the imperative of *shura* is an important participatory ethic in the Islamic intellectual heritage. This is so irrespective of how this ethic was used or misused in Islamic history because, as a normative ideal, it could be co-opted and utilized in the furtherance of a democratic commitment. But even if the ethic of *shura* is expanded into a broader concept of a participatory government, no less important than the process are the moral commitments that inform the process. If the purpose of consultation is to find a correct answer that is derived from the divine will, one might end up with the awkward situation where divinity is not represented by a single ruler but by a consultative or legislative body. Instead of a ruling autocrat being capable of speaking on God's behalf, the authority is transferred to a council-like body that is empowered with the voice of God. This is problematic because such a body can be used to inflict a tyranny of the majority against a discrete minority, suppress dissent, and limit diversity. Thus, even if *shura* is transformed into an instrument of participatory representation, this instrument must itself be limited by a scheme of private and individual rights that serve an overriding moral goal such as justice. In other words, *shura* must be valued not because of the results it produces but because it represents a moral value in itself. As a result, regardless of the utility or disutility caused by the existence of dissenting views, dissent would be tolerated because doing so is seen as a basic part of the mandate of justice.

Justice and the Islamic Polity

Muslim political thought dealt extensively with the purpose of government. The statement of Imam al-Haramayn al-Juwayni (d. 478/1085) is fairly representative of the argument of Muslim jurists. Al-Juwayni states,

> The *imama* [government] is a total governorship and general leadership that relates to the special and common in the affairs of religion and this earthly life. It includes guarding the land and protecting the subjects, and the spread of the message [of Islam] by the word and sword. It includes the correcting of deviation and the redressing of injustice, the aiding of the wronged against the wrongdoer, and taking the right from the obstinate and giving it to those who are entitled to it.[49]

The essential idea conveyed here is that government is a functional necessity put in place to resolve conflict, protect religion, and uphold justice. In some formulations, justice is the core value that justifies the existence of government. Ibn al-Qayyim (d. 751/1350), for example, makes this point explicit when he asserts the following:

> God sent His message and His Books to lead people with justice. . . . Therefore, if a just leadership is established, through any means, then therein is the Way of God. . . . In fact, the purpose of God's Way is the establishment of righteousness and justice . . . so any road that establishes what is right and just is the road [Muslims] should follow.[50]

This argument is rooted in a methodical debate among pre-modern scholars about the nature of people if left without a government. This debate is remarkably similar to the seventeenth-century Western discourse on the state of nature or the original condition of human beings. The Islamic debate focused on the original, so-to-speak uncorrupted, nature of human beings, and how that nature affects the role and purpose of government. Some scholars, such as Ibn Khaldun (d. 784/1382) and al-Ghazali (d. 505/1111), argued that human beings are by nature fractious, contentious, and not inclined toward cooperation. Al-Ghazali, in particular, added that human beings are prone to misunderstandings and conflicts. If one observes the affairs of people, he noted, one will notice that married couples and even parents and children fight, and refuse to cooperate in mutually beneficial endeavors. Therefore, he and others argued, government is necessary to force people to cooperate with each other. Government, in a paternalistic fashion, must force people to act contrary to their fractious and contentious natures, and in everyone's general best interest.[51]

Another school of thought exemplified by al-Mawardi (d. 450/1058) and Ibn Abi al-Rabi' (d. 656/1258) argued that people, by their nature, have a tendency to cooperate for physical and spiritual reasons. In fact, God created human beings weak and in need of cooperation with others in order to limit the ability of human beings to commit injustice. Although this school of thought did not elaborate upon the meaning of justice, its adherents asserted that without cooperation, human beings will not be able to overcome injustice *(zulm)* or establish justice *('adl)*; instead, the strong will violate the rights *(huquq)* of the weak and injustice will become widespread. By cooperating with each other, human beings will be able to restrain the strong and safeguard the rights of the weak. Furthermore, God created human beings diverse and different from each other so that they would need each other. This need invites human beings to further augment their natural tendency to assemble and cooperate in order to establish justice. Importantly, human beings, by nature, desire justice, and will tend to cooperate in order to fulfill it. If human beings exploit the divine gift of intellect and the guidance of the law of God, through cooperation they are bound to reach a greater level of justice and moral fulfillment. The ruler, this school of thought argued, ascends to power through a contract with the people pursuant to which he undertakes to further the cooperation of the people, with the ultimate goal of achieving a just society or, at least, maximizing the potential for justice.[52]

This juristic discourse offers formidable normative possibilities for democratic thought in modern Islam. In the Qur'anic discourse, justice is asserted as an obligation owed to God, and also owed by human beings to one another. In addition, the imperative of justice is tied to the obligations of enjoining the good and forbidding the evil, and the necessity of bearing witness on God's behalf. Although the Qur'an does not define the constituent elements of justice, and in fact seems to treat it as intuitively recognizable, the Qur'an emphasizes the ability to achieve justice as a unique human charge and necessity.[53] In essence, the Qur'an requires a commitment to a moral imperative that is vague but that is recognizable through intuition, reason, or human experience.

It is important here to consider more carefully the juristic argument on the importance of human diversity for the cooperative efforts at seeking justice. This juristic discourse is partly based on the Qur'anic statement that God created people different, and made them into nations and tribes so that they will come to know one another. Muslim jurists reasoned that the expression "come to know one another" indicates the need for social cooperation and mutual assistance in order to achieve justice (49:13). Although the premodern jurists did not emphasize this point, the Qur'an also notes that God made people different, and that they will remain different until the end of human existence. Further, the Qur'an states that the reality of human diversity is part of the divine wisdom, and an intentional purpose of creation (11:119).

The Qur'anic celebration and sanctification of human diversity, in addition to the juristic incorporation of the notion of human diversity into a purposeful pursuit of justice, creates various possibilities for a pluralistic commitment in Islam. This could also be developed into an ethic that respects dissent and honors the right of human beings to be different, including the right to adhere to different religious or nonreligious convictions. Furthermore, the debate regarding the original condition and the proclivity of human beings toward justice could be appropriated into a normative stance that considers justice and diversity to be core values that a democratic constitutional order is bound to protect. This discourse could then be appropriated into a notion of delegated powers in which the ruler is entrusted to serve the core value of justice in light of systematic principles that promote the right of assembly and cooperation, and the right to dissent in order to enhance the fulfillment of this core value. Even more, a notion of limits could be developed that would restrain the government from derailing the quest for justice or from hampering the right of the people to cooperate, or dissent, in this quest. If the government fails to discharge the obligations of its covenant, then it loses its legitimate claim to power.

This, however, is wishful thinking because there are several factors that militate against the fulfillment of these possibilities in modern Islam. First, modern Muslims, themselves, are hardly aware of the Islamic interpretive tradition on justice. Both the apologetic and the puritan orientations, which are the two predominant trends in modern Islam, have largely ignored the paradigm of human diversity and difference as a necessary means to the fulfillment of the imperative of justice. Second, as discussed above, the conception and role of the government or caliphate remained rather vague in Islamic practice. The third factor, and the most important one, is that even if modern Muslims reclaim the interpretive traditions of the past on justice, the fact remains that, at the conceptual level, the constituent elements of justice were not explored in Islamic doctrine. Justice, as a moral value, has an intuitive appeal, but it is also a vague concept.

The question in this regard is this: If one demands justice, what specific conditions is one demanding? The possibilities are many; they could include a restoration of rights pursuant to a particular vision of rights, equality of entitlements, equality of opportunities, a proportional balance between duties and rights, and so on. In order for the demand for justice to have any specific meaning, it is necessary to investigate the particular factors that are material to a state of justice. But there is a tension between the obligation of implementing the divine law and the demands for justice, and that is the tension produced by the process of definition. To put it bluntly, does the divine law define justice or does justice define the divine law? If it is the former, then whatever one concludes is the divine law, therein is justice. If it is the latter, then whatever justice demands is, in fact, the demand of the Divine.

Put differently, if the organizing principle of society is the divine law, the risk is that the subjectively determined divine law becomes the embodiment of justice. Under this paradigm, there is no point in investigating the constituent elements of justice — there is no point in investigating whether justice means equality of opportunities or results, or whether it means maximizing the potential for personal autonomy, or, perhaps, the maximization of individual and collective utility, or the guarding of basic human dignity, or even the simple resolution of conflict and the maintenance of stability, or any other conception that might provide substance to a general conception of justice. There is no point in engaging in this investigation because divine law preempts any such inquiry. Divine law provides particularized positive enactments that exemplify, but do not analytically explore, the notion of justice. Conceptually, the organized society is no longer about the right to assembly, cooperation, or the right to explore the means to justice, but simply about the implementation of divine law. This brings us full circle to the problem identified above, which is that the implementation of divine law does not necessarily amount to the existence of limited government, rule of law, or even the protection of basic individual rights.

It is important to note, however, that, considering the primacy of justice in the Qur'anic discourse is coupled with the notions of human vicegerency, and that the divine charge of justice has been delegated to humanity at large, it is plausible to maintain that justice is what ought to control and guide all human interpretive efforts at understanding the law. This requires a serious paradigm shift in Islamic thinking. In my view, justice, and whatever is necessary to achieve justice, is a divine imperative, and is what represents the supremacy and sovereignty of the divine. God describes God's self as inherently just, and the Qur'an asserts that God has decreed mercy upon God's self (6:12, 54). Furthermore, the very purpose of entrusting the divine message to the Prophet Muhammad was as a gift of mercy to human beings.[54] In Qur'anic discourse, mercy is not simply forgiveness, or the willingness to ignore the faults and sins of people.[55] Mercy is a state in which the individual is able to be just with himself or herself, and with others, by giving each their due. Fundamentally, mercy is tied to a state of true and genuine perception; that is why, in the Qur'an, mercy is coupled with the need for human beings to be patient and tolerant with each other.[56] Most significantly, diversity and differences among human beings are claimed in the Qur'anic discourse as a merciful divine gift to humankind (11:119).[57] Genuine perception that enables persons to understand and appreciate, and become enriched by the diversity of humanity, is one of the constituent elements for the founding of a just society, and for the achievement of justice. The divine charge to human beings at large, and Muslims in particular, is, as the Qur'an puts it, "to know one another," and utilize this genuine knowledge in an effort to pursue justice.

This, in my view, means that the divine mandate for a Muslim polity is to pursue the fulfillment of justice through the adherence to the need for mercy. Although coexistence is a basic necessity for mercy, in order to pursue a state of real knowledge of the other and to aspire to a state of justice, it is imperative that human beings cooperate in seeking the good and beautiful, and that they do so by engaging in purposeful moral discourse. The more the good and beautiful is approached, the closer a polity comes to a state of divinity.

Significantly, however, implementing legalistic rules, even if such rules are the product of the interpretation of divine texts, is not sufficient for the achievement of genuine perception of the other, mercy, or, ultimately, justice. The paradigm shift of which I speak requires that the principles of mercy and justice become the primary divine charge. In this paradigm, God's sovereignty lies in the fact that God is the source and authority that delegated to human beings the charge to achieve justice on earth by fulfilling the virtues that are approximations of divinity.[58] Far from negating human subjectivities through the mechanical enforcement of rules, such subjectivities are accommodated and even promoted to the extent that they contribute to the fulfillment of justice. Significantly, according to the juristic discourses, it is not possible to achieve justice unless every possessor of a right *(haqq)* is granted his or her right. As discussed below, God has certain rights, humans have rights, and both God and humans share some rights. The challenge of vicegerency is to first recognize that a right exists, then to understand who is the possessor of such a right, and, ultimately, to allow the possessor of a right the enjoyment of the prescribed right. A society that fails to do so, regardless of the deluge of rules it might apply, is not a merciful or just society.[59] This puts us in a position to explore the possibility of individual rights in Islam.

The Rights of the People in Islam

All constitutional democracies afford protection to a particular set of individual interests, such as freedom of speech and assembly, equality before the law, right to property, and due process of law, but which exact rights ought to be protected, and to what extent, is subject to a large measure of variation in theory and practice. There is also a considerable amount of debate in democratic societies about the sources and nature of individual rights, as well as about whether there are inherent and absolute individual rights or presumptive individual entitlements that could be outweighed by countervailing considerations.[60] In this essay, for the most part, by individual rights I do not mean entitlements but qualified immunities — the idea that particular interests related to the well-being of an individual ought to be protected from infringements whether perpetrated by the state or other members of the social order, and that such interests should not be sacrificed unless for an overwhelming necessity. But I doubt very much that there is an objective means of quantifying an overwhelming necessity, and thus I believe that some individual interests ought to be unassailable under any circumstances. These unassailable interests are the ones that, if violated, are bound to communicate to the individual in question a sense of worthlessness, and that, if violated, tend to destroy the faculty of a human being to comprehend the necessary elements for a dignified existence. Therefore, for instance, under my conception of rights, the use of torture and the denial of food or shelter or the means for sustenance, such as employment, under any circumstances, would be violations of an individual's rights.

It is fair to say, however, that the pre-modern juristic tradition did not articulate a notion of individual rights as privileges, entitlements, or immunities. Nonetheless, the juristic tradition did articulate a conception of protected interests that accrue to the benefit of the individual. In order to better understand the idea of protected interests in Islamic law, it is important to note that the purpose of Shari'ah in jurisprudential theory is to fulfill the welfare of the people *(tahqiq masalih al-'ibad)*. Typically, Muslim jurists divided the interests of the welfare of the people into three categories: the necessities *(daruriyyat)*, the needs *(hajiyyat)*, and the luxuries *(kamaliyyat or tahsiniyyat)*. According to Muslim jurists, the law and political policies of the government must fulfill these interests, in descending order of importance — first, the necessities, then the needs, and then the luxuries. The necessities are further divided into five basic values, *al-daruriyyat al-khamsah:* religion, life, intellect, lineage or honor, and property. But Muslim jurists did not develop the five basic values as conceptual categories and then explore the theoretical implications of each value; rather, they pursued what can be described as an extreme positivistic approach to these rights. Muslim jurists examined the existing positive legal injunctions that arguably can be said to serve each of these values, and concluded that by giving effect to these specific legal injunctions, the five values have been sufficiently served. So, for example, Muslim jurists contended that the prohibition of murder in Islamic law served the basic value of life, the law of apostasy protected religion, the prohibition of intoxicants protected the intellect, the prohibition of fornication and adultery protected lineage, and the right of compensation protected the right to property. It is important for modern Muslims to concede that limiting the protection of the intellect to the prohibition against the consumption of alcohol or the protection of life to the prohibition of murder is hardly a very thorough protection of either intellect or life. At most, these laws are partial protections to a limited conception of values, and, in any case, cannot be asserted as the equivalent of individual rights because they are not asserted as immunities to be retained by the individual against the world. Unfortunately, one is forced to conclude that the way the juristic tradition treated these five values amounted to denying them any theoretical social and political content, and that these values were reduced to technical legalistic objectives. This, of course, does not preclude the possibility that the basic five values could act as a foundation for a systematic theory of individual rights in the modern age.[61]

To argue that the juristic tradition did not develop the idea of fundamental or basic individual rights does not mean that that tradition was oblivious to the notion. In fact, the juristic tradition tended to sympathize with individuals who were unjustly executed for their beliefs or those who died fighting against injustice. Jurists typically described such acts as a death of *musabara,* a term that carried positive or commendable connotations. In addition, Muslim jurists produced an impressive discourse condemning the imposition of unjust taxes and the usurpation of private property by the government. In fact, the majority of Muslim jurists refused to condemn or criminalize the behavior of rebels who revolted because of the imposition of oppressive taxes or who resisted a tyrannical government. In addition, the juristic tradition articulated a wealth of positions that exhibit humanitarian or compassionate orientations. I will mention here only some of these positions. For instance, Muslim jurists developed the idea of presumption of innocence in all criminal and civil proceedings, and argued that the accuser always carries the burden of proof *(al-bayyina 'ala man idda'a)*. In matters related to heresy, jurists repeatedly argued that it is better to let a thousand heretics go free than to wrongfully punish a single, sincere Muslim. The same principle was applied to criminal cases; the jurists argued that it is always better to release a guilty person than to run the risk of punishing an innocent person. Moreover, many jurists condemned the practice of detaining or incarcerating heterodox groups even when such groups openly advocated and proselytized their heterodoxy (such as the Khawarij), and argued that such groups may not be harassed or molested until they carry arms and form a clear intent to rebel against the government. Muslim jurists also condemned the use of torture, arguing that the Prophet forbade the use of *muthla* (the use of mutilations) in all situations,[62] and opposed the use of coerced confessions in all legal and political matters.[63] In fact, a large number of jurists articulated a doctrine similar to the American exculpatory doctrine — confessions or evidence obtained under coercion are inadmissible at trial. Interestingly, some jurists even asserted that judges who rely on a coerced confession in a criminal conviction are to be held liable for the wrongful conviction. Most argued that the defendant, or his family, may bring an action for compensation against the judge, individually, and against the caliph and his representatives, generally, because the government is deemed to be vicariously liable for the unlawful behavior of its judges.

But perhaps the most intriguing discourse on the subject in the juristic tradition is that which relates to the rights of God and the rights of people. The rights of God *(huquq Allah)* are rights retained by God, as God's own through an explicit designation to that effect.[64] These rights belong to God in the sense that only God can say how the violation of these rights may be punished and only God has the right to forgive such violations. These rights are, so to speak, subject to the exclusive jurisdiction and dominion of God, and human beings have no choice but to follow the explicit and detailed rules that God set out for the handling of acts that fall in God's jurisdiction. In addition, in the juristic theory, all rights not explicitly retained by God accrue to the benefit of human beings. In other words, any right *(haqq)* that is not specifically and clearly retained by God becomes a right retained by people. While violations of God's rights are forgiven by God only through adequate acts of repentance on our part, the rights of people may be forgiven only by the people. For instance, according to the juristic tradition, a right to compensation is retained individually by a human being and may be forgiven only by the aggrieved individual. The government, or even God, does not have the right to forgive or compromise such a right of compensation if it is designated as part of the rights of human beings. Therefore, the Maliki jurist Ibn al-ʿArabi (d. 543/1148) states,

> The rights of human beings are not forgiven by God unless the human being concerned forgives them first, and the claims for such rights are not dismissed [by God] unless they are dismissed by the person concerned. . . . The rights of a Muslim cannot be abandoned except by the possessor of the right. Even the *imam* [ruler] does not have the right to demand [or abandon] such rights. This is because the *imam* is not empowered to act as the agent for a specific set of individuals over their specific rights. Rather, the *imam* only represents people, generally, over their general and unspecified rights.[65]

Most of these discourses occur in the context of addressing personal monetary and property rights, but they have not been extended to other civil rights, such as the right to due process or the right to listen, to reflect, and to study, which may not be violated by the government under any circumstances. This is not because the range of the rights of people was narrow — quite to the contrary; it is because the range of these rights was too broad. It should be recalled that people retain any rights not explicitly reserved by God. Effectively, since the rights retained by God are quite narrow, the rights accruing to the benefit of the people are numerous. The juristic practice has tended to focus on narrow legal claims that may be addressed through the processes of law rather than on broad theoretical categories that were perceived as nonjusticiable before a court. As such, the jurists tended to focus on tangible property rights or rights for compensation instead of focusing on moral claims. So, for instance, if someone burns another person's books, that person may seek compensation for destruction of property, but he could not bring an action for injunctive relief preventing the burning of the books in the first place. Despite this limitation, the juristic tradition did, in fact, develop a notion of individual claims that are immune from governmental or social limitation or alienation.

There is one other important aspect that needs to be explored in this context. Muslim jurists asserted the rather surprising position that if the rights of God and the rights of people (mixed rights) overlap, in most cases the rights of people should prevail. The justification for this was that humans need their rights, and need to vindicate those rights on earth. God, on the other hand, asserts God's rights only for the benefit of human beings, and, in all cases, God can vindicate God's rights in the hereafter if need be.

As to the rights of people, Muslim jurists did not imagine a set of unwavering and generalizable rights that are to be held by each individual at all times. Rather, they thought of individual rights as arising from a legal cause brought about by the suffering of a legal wrong. A person does not possess a right until he or she has been wronged and, as a result, obtains a claim for retribution or compensation. To shift paradigms would require the transformation of traditional conceptions of rights to a notion of immunities and entitlements, so that rights become the property of individual holders, before there arises a specific grievance and regardless of whether there is a legal cause of action. The set of rights that are recognized as immutable and invariable are those that are necessary to achieve a just society while promoting the element of mercy. In my view, these must be the rights that guarantee the physical safety and moral dignity of a human being.

It is quite possible that the relevant individual rights are those five values mentioned above, but this issue needs to be re-thought and re-analyzed in light of the current diversity and particularity of human existence. The fact that the rights of people take priority over the rights of God, on this earth, necessarily means that a claimed right of God may not be used to violate the rights of human beings. God is capable of vindicating whichever rights God wishes to vindicate in the hereafter. On this earth, we concern ourselves only with discovering and establishing the rights that are needed to enable human beings to achieve a just life while, to the extent possible, honoring the asserted rights of God.[66] In this context, the commitment to human rights does not signify a lack of commitment to God, or a lack of willingness to obey God. Rather, human rights become a necessary part of celebrating human diversity, honoring the vicegerents of God, achieving mercy, and pursuing the ultimate goal of justice.

Interestingly enough, it is not the pre-modern juristic tradition that poses the greatest barrier to the development of individual rights in Islam. Rather, the most serious obstacle comes from modern Muslims themselves. Especially in the last half of the past century, a considerable number of Muslims have made the unfounded assumption that Islamic law is concerned primarily with duties, and not rights, and that the Islamic conception of rights is collectivist, not individualistic.[67] Both assumptions, however, are based only

on cultural assumptions about the non-Western "other." It is as if these interpreters fixed on a Judeo-Christian or perhaps Western conception of rights
and assumed that Islam must be different.

In the 1950s and 1960s, most Muslim countries, as underdeveloped nations, were heavily influenced by socialist and national development ideologies, which tended to emphasize collectivist and duty-oriented conceptions of
rights. Therefore, many Muslim commentators claimed that the Islamic tradition necessarily supports the aspirations and hopes of what is called the
Third World. But such claims are as negotiative, reconstructive, and inventive
of the Islamic tradition as any particular contemporaneous vision of rights.
The reality is that claims about both individual rights and collectivist rights
are largely anachronistic. Pre-modern Muslim jurists did not assert a collectivist vision of rights or an individualistic vision. They did speak of al-haqq
al-'amm (public rights), and often asserted that public rights ought to be
given preference over private entitlements. But as a matter of juristic determination, this amounted to no more than an assertion that the many should not
be made to suffer for the entitlements of the few. For instance, as a legal
maxim, this was utilized to justify the notion of public takings or the right to
public easements over private property. This principle was also utilized in
prohibiting unqualified doctors from practicing medicine.[68] But, as noted
above, Muslim jurists did not, for instance, justify the killing or the torture of
individuals in order to promote the welfare of the state or the public interest.
Even with regard to public takings or easements, the vast majority of Muslim
jurists maintained that the individuals affected are entitled by the state to
compensation equal to the fair market value of the property taken. In addition, pursuant to a justice perspective, one can argue that a commitment to
individual rights, taken as a whole, will accrue to the benefit of the many (the
private citizens) over the few (the members of ruling government).

I do believe that the common good is greatly enhanced, and not ham-
pered, by the assertion of individual rights, but this point needs to be developed in a more systematic way in a separate study.[69] My point here, however,
is that the juristic notion of public rights does not necessarily support what is
often described as a collectivist view of rights.[70] Likewise, the idea of duties
(wajibat) is as well established in the Islamic tradition as the notion of rights
(huquq) — the Islamic juristic tradition does not show a proclivity toward
one more than the other. In fact, some pre-modern jurists have asserted that
to every duty there is a reciprocal right, and vice versa.[71] It is true that many
jurists claimed that the ruler is owed a duty of obedience, but ideally they also
expected the ruler to safeguard the well-being and interests of the ruled. The
fact that the jurists did not hinge the duty to obey on the obligation to respect

the individual rights of citizens does not mean that they were, as a matter of principle, opposed to affording the ruled certain immunities against the state. In some situations, Muslim jurists even asserted that if the state fails to protect the well-being of the ruled, and is unjust toward them, the ruled no longer owe the state either obedience or support.

Perhaps the widespread rhetoric regarding the primacy of collectivist and duty-based perspectives in Islam points to the reactive nature of much of the discourse on Islamic law in the contemporary age. From a theological perspective, the notion of individual rights is easier to justify in Islam than a collectivist orientation. God created human beings as individuals, and their liability in the hereafter is individually determined as well. To commit oneself to safeguarding and protecting the well-being of the individual is to take God's creation seriously. Each individual embodies a virtual universe of divine miracles — in body, soul, and mind. Why should a Muslim commit himself or herself to the rights and well-being of a fellow human being? Because God has already made such a commitment when God invested so much of Godself in each and every person. This is why the Qur'an asserts that if a person kills a fellow human being unjustly, it is as if he or she has murdered all of humanity — it is as if the killer has murdered the divine sanctity, and defiled the very meaning of divinity (Qur'an 5:32).

Moreover, the Qur'an does not differentiate between the sanctity of a Muslim and that of a non-Muslim.[72] As the Qur'an repeatedly asserts, no human being can limit the divine mercy in any way, or even regulate who is entitled to it (2:105, 3:74, 35:2, 38:9, 39:38, 40:7, 43:32). I take this to mean that non-Muslims, as well as Muslims, could be the recipients and the givers of divine mercy. The measure of moral virtue on this earth is who is able to come closer to divinity through justice, not who carries the correct religious label. The measure in the hereafter is a different matter, but it is a matter that is in the purview of God's exclusive jurisdiction. God will most certainly vindicate God's rights in the hereafter in the fashion that God deems most fitting, but on this earth, our primary moral responsibility is the vindication of the rights of human beings. Put this way, perhaps it becomes all too obvious that a commitment in favor of human rights is a commitment in favor of God's creation and, ultimately, a commitment in favor of God.

The Promise of Individual Rights

What are the possible sources of individual rights in Islam? In natural law theory, certain rights, derived through reason or intuition, are considered innate and fundamental. These rights are not subject to violation by majoritarian determinations and are retained against society and state. It is important to note that the natural law tradition emerged from a thoroughly religious, especially Christian, paradigm, and that the retreat of natural law before positivist theories of law occurred only after natural law became secularized and alienated from its religious foundations. This, however, has become an extremely complicated issue ever since the so-called secularized natural law has, thanks to the efforts of people like John Finnis, experienced a powerful resurgence in the past thirty years or so, and also after the very meaning and connotations of secularism have become highly contested in Western democracies.

Nevertheless, at a minimum, and contrary to the assumptions of some secularists, a belief in fundamental individual rights does not necessarily need to be based on the exclusion of God from public life. Even more, a commitment to a paradigm of individual rights does not need to detract from God's supremacy or dominion on this earth. The integrity, honor, and dominion of the Divine need not be compromised or equivocated in any fashion in order for the accountability of human beings for their agency to be given full recognition. The rights of human beings are simply a basic component of recognizing the direct accountability of individual agents to God rather than to other human beings. If the individual agent does not have rights that safeguard his *ability* to discharge his obligations toward God, then the integrity of the agency itself is compromised, and the whole logic of individual accountability cannot be sustained in any serious fashion. The integrity of the agency, and the individual accountability of the agent, mandates that the agent be free to deny his agency, and even God, and that the agent be able to declare his willingness to take full responsibility for this individual decision before God in the hereafter. Forcing individuals to discharge the obligations of their agency toward God renders the agency, itself, meaningless because it presumes that one agent can take responsibility for the agency of another, which is something that the Qur'an, quite clearly and explicitly, rejects.[73]

In the Islamic context, however, the most challenging issue pertaining to individual rights is not the conceptual origins of rights but the role of the text in relation to any claim of rights. In Islam, the real question remains, Is it possible to develop a conception of rights as fundamental and inalienable, of rights that are not subject to waiver or compromise through legal interpretation, even if it is the interpretation of the divine text? This question recalls the classical debate on the nature of *husn* (what is good or beautiful) and *qubh* (what is bad or ugly). Like the debates on the nature of justice, the issue here was whether good and bad have an inherent essence that exists separate from the divine will, or whether they are entirely determined by God. So, for instance, is a particular value good or bad because the divine text says it is, or is it so because good and bad have an inherent or natural essence to them?[74] If moral values such as goodness, justice, and mercy are created and determined by the divine will, then, arguably, these values are contingent, and not natural, because they do not have an objective essence.

In the classical period, the main argument against the idea of natural essence or inherent values was that it conflicts with the immutability of God. If moral values have not been generated by an act of divine creation, then this would mean that there is creation outside of God. Furthermore, if God is bound or obliged to respect certain inherent moral values, this would seem to challenge the absoluteness of God's will and power. Although the idea that an immutable God cannot be bound or limited by moral values seems plausible, it does confront considerable difficulties. The text of the Qur'an itself uses words such as "justice," "mercy," and "goodness" as if they have an objectively discernible quality. The Qur'an does not attempt to define any of these moral values, but it does refer to them as if they are inherently recognizable by human beings. It consistently calls upon people endowed with a healthy intuition *(yatadhakurun)* or balanced rationality *(ya'qilun)* to recognize the existence of such moral values, and to strive to implement them.

But is God bound by the values that God advocates? For instance, when the Qur'an states, "God has prescribed mercy upon Himself" (6:12, 54), does this mean that mercy, as a concept, existed separate and apart from God, and then God chose to bind himself by it? Alternatively, does it mean that God created a moral value, such as mercy, as binding upon his creatures, but then decided to abide by it himself? But the verse also implies that God had the choice either to be merciful or not, and that God has chosen to be merciful. This verse, however, could have various possible connotations, all of which are not necessarily conclusive as to the issue of natural rights. For instance, it could be argued that God decreed mercy upon himself because God recognized that to do otherwise would be immoral.

The classical debate on this issue focused on whether it is possible for God to commit ugliness, the implication being that if God is bound by moral values, then so are human beings. But I do think that the issue, for the most part, is resolved by the fact that the Qur'an consistently describes God as endowed with moral values such as beauty, justice, compassion, and mercy. The issue, in my view, is not whether God is bound by moral values, for God is the embodiment of moral values.[75] If God embodies moral values, then exploring and seeking to understand the objective reality of morality is part of understanding the objective reality of God. This is an issue of crucial importance, and so it deserves to be restated and emphasized. God, in my view, is not bound by moral virtue; God is the embodiment of moral virtue. Beauty and moral virtues are what God is, and moral virtues are inherent to the very concept of divinity. If God describes Godself as just or merciful, then this is what God is. In my view, God's moralities and virtues are inseparable from God, and they are unalterable because God is unalterable. As such, God's morality is binding on all, in the same way that God is present for all. Divinity is approached, in my view, through studying the divine moral imperatives rather than the rules of law, because morality is prior to law, in the same way that God is prior to anything, including the text or law.[76] Therefore, I would argue that inalienable human rights exist not in a state of nature, but by the fact or reality of divinity of creation. In other words, such rights are derived not from the law of nature but from the law of creation, which is the product of the divine design. By asserting, for instance, that God is merciful and compassionate, the text can and does help human beings understand the law of creation, but there is no reason to assume that it is the only means for attaining such a comprehension. In fact, the Qur'anic text, by urging people to reflect upon creation, and by inviting them to utilize their rational faculties, clearly recognizes that the text is not the only means for understanding creation or divinity.

It is important to understand that the text is a part, and not the whole, of creation, and that the part cannot be treated as if it can abrogate or render the whole irrelevant.[77] Humans' instincts, intuitions, and reasoning processes, as well as the objectively observable laws of nature, are all a part of the divine creation as well, and there is no reason to grant the text a decisive and exclusive veto power over all other means to comprehending creation. Doing so assumes that the text, which is realizable only through subjective interpretation, is necessarily a more reliable means to realizing the divine or understanding creation. As far as the text is concerned, it is of crucial significance to differentiate between texts that explain creation and those that attempt to organize creation. The former inform the seeker about the nature of divinity and educate on the laws of creation, while the latter administrate an aspect of creation within time and space limitations. For instance, foundational texts educating human beings on dignity, mercy, diversity, and justice as divine natures and moral imperatives are quite different from organizational texts that specify what ought to be done in a case of divorce or in a situation involving commercial contracts. The first set of texts elucidate the laws of creation, while the second set of texts explain the laws of society within a particular time and space dimension. In addition, the first set of texts is subject to a process of moral interpretation, while the second set of texts is subject to legal interpretations. It is reasonable to argue that legal interpretations must fulfill and further, not negate, moral interpretation.

In this sense, interpretations of the law of creation, in which the rights of individuals are found, are prior to interpretations of the laws of organization, and ought to be the standard by which legal interpretations are evaluated, rejected, or adopted. According to this conceptual framework, the inherent and fundamental rights of human beings that cannot be waived or denied through legal interpretation, even if based on a text, are those immunities and entitlements that, after reflecting upon divinity, creation, and foundational texts, human rational faculties are able to conclude are mandated by the very act of creation, the need to investigate creation, and the necessity of bearing full responsibility for one's agency before God. Pursuant to this paradigm, I do not think it would be difficult to defend the right to think and study, the right to believe and speak, the right to be free from molestation or assault, and right to shelter and food as basic and fundamental Islamic human and individual rights.

Democracy and the Islamic State

In the modern age, a large number of commentators have grown comfortable with the habit of producing a laundry list of concepts such as *shura*, the contract of the caliphate, the idea of *bay'a*, and the supremacy of Shari'ah, and then concluding that Islam is compatible with democracy. In my view, these vacuous approaches are the product of intellectual torpor induced by the rather abysmal fortunes of the Islamic heritage in the modern age. Islamists who have pursued this superficial and apologetic method of dealing with the challenge of democracy in the modern age have done so largely in reaction to internal calls for the full-fledged adoption of secularism in Muslim societies. For these Islamists, secularism has come to symbolize a misguided belief in the supremacy of rationalism over faith, and a sense of hostility to religion as a source of guidance in the public sphere. In fact, secularism is seen as originating with Westernized intellectuals who were themselves not religious, and who sought to minimize the role of Islam in public life. As such, secularism, known as *'ilmaniyya*, is often treated as a part of the Western intellectual invasion of the Muslim world, in the periods of both colonialism and post-colonialism — an invasion that is more insidious and dangerous than the Christian Crusades.

While I disagree with these reactive accusations against the secularist paradigm, I do agree that secularism has become an unworkable and unhelpful symbolic construct. To the extent that the secular paradigm relies on a be-

lief in the guidance-value of reason as a means for achieving utilitarian fulfillment or justice, it is founded on a conviction that is not empirically or
morally verifiable. One could plausibly believe that religion is an equally valid
means of knowing or discovering the means to happiness or justice. In addition, given the rhetorical choice between allegiance to the Shari'ah and allegiance to a secular democratic state, quite understandably most devout Muslims will make the equally rhetorical decision to ally themselves with
Shari'ah. But beyond the issue of symbolism, as noted earlier, there is considerable variation in the practice of secularism. It is entirely unclear to what extent the practice of secularism requires a separation of church and state, especially in light of the fact that there is no institutional church in Islam. Put
differently, to what extent does the practice of secularism mandate the exclusion of religion from the public domain, including the exclusion of religion as
a source of law?

The fact that "secularism" is a word laden with unhelpful connotations
in the Islamic context, however, should not blind us to the seriousness of the
concerns that secularists have about a political order in which Shari'ah is
given deference or made supreme. Shari'ah enables human beings to speak in
God's name and effectively empowers human agency with the voice of God.
This is a formidable power that is easily abused, and therefore, it is argued,
secularism is necessary to avoid the hegemony and abuse of those who pretend to speak for God. The challenge this poses for a democratic order is considerable because Shari'ah is a construct of limitless reach and power, and any
institution that can attach itself to that construct becomes similarly empowered. Yet Islamists, and secularists, often ignore the historical fact that the
'ulama, until the modern age, never assumed power directly, and that Islamic
law was centralized and codified only when it came under the influence of the
French civil law system. Until the Ottoman Empire, no state succeeded in
adopting a particular school of law as the law of the state, and even after the
Ottomans adopted Hanafism as the official school of the state, they never
managed to enforce this school to the exclusion of the others. The very idea of
a centralized and codified Shari'ah law was instigated by jurists, educated in
the civil law system, who sought to reform and modernize Islamic law by
making it more adaptable to the needs of the modern nation-state. But it is
important to realize that Shari'ah law, as a codified, state-sponsored set of
positive commands, is a serious break with tradition and a radical departure
from the classical epistemology of Islamic law.

In order to engage in a more nuanced discourse on the dynamics between Shari'ah and the state, it is necessary that we develop a more sophisticated understanding of Shari'ah itself. I reserved this issue to the end because

it was necessary that we lay a sufficient foundation before engaging this topic. As part of this foundation, it is important to appreciate the centrality of Shari'ah to Muslim life. The pre-modern jurist Ibn Qayyim appropriately captures this sentiment in the following statement describing Shari'ah:

> The Shari'ah is God's justice among His servants and His mercy among His creatures. It is God's shadow on this earth. It is His wisdom which leads to Him in the most exact way and the most exact affirmation of the truthfulness of His Prophet. It is His light which enlightens the seekers and His guidance for the rightly guided. It is the absolute cure for all ills and the straight path which if followed will lead to righteousness. . . . It is life and nutrition, the medicine, the light, the cure and the safeguard. Every good in this life is derived from it and achieved through it, and every deficiency in existence results from its dissipation. If it had not been for the fact that some of its prescriptions remain [in this world], this world would become corrupted and the universe would be dissipated. . . . If God would wish to destroy the world and dissolve existence, He would void whatever remains of its injunctions. For the Shari'ah which was sent to His Prophet . . . is the pillar of existence and the key to success in this world and the Hereafter.[78]

Shari'ah is God's way; it is represented by a set of normative principles, methodologies for the production of legal injunctions, and a set of positive legal rules. As is well known, Shari'ah encompasses a variety of schools of thought and approaches, all of which are equally valid and equally orthodox.[79] Nevertheless, Shari'ah as a whole, with all its schools and variant points of view, remains the way and law of God. The Shari'ah, for the most part, is not explicitly dictated by God. Rather, Shari'ah relies on the interpretive act of the human agent for its production and execution. Paradoxically, however, Shari'ah is the core value that society must serve. The paradox here is exemplified in the fact that there is a pronounced tension between the obligation to live by God's law and the fact that this law is manifested only through subjective interpretive determinations. Even if there is a unified realization that a particular positive command does express the divine law, there is still a vast array of possible subjective executions and applications. This dilemma was resolved, somewhat, in Islamic discourses by distinguishing between Shari'ah and *fiqh*. Shari'ah, it was argued, is the divine ideal, standing as if suspended in midair, unaffected and uncorrupted by the vagaries of life. The *fiqh* is the human attempt to understand and apply the ideal. Therefore, Shari'ah is immutable, immaculate, and flawless — *fiqh* is not.[80]

As part of the doctrinal foundations for this discourse, Sunni jurists focused on the tradition attributed to the Prophet, stating, "Every *mujtahid* [ju-
rist who strives to find the correct answer] is correct" or "Every *mujtahid* will
be [justly] rewarded." This implied that there could be more than a single correct answer to the same exact question. For Sunni jurists, this raised the issue
of the purpose or the motivation behind the search for the divine will. What
is the divine purpose behind setting out indicators to the divine law and then
requiring that human beings engage in a search? If the divine wants human
beings to reach *the* correct understanding, then how could every interpreter
or jurist be correct? The juristic discourse focused on whether or not the
Shari'ah had a determinable result or demand in all cases, and if there is such
a determinable result, are Muslims obligated to find it? Put differently, is there
a correct legal response to all legal problems, and are Muslims charged with
the legal obligation of finding that response?

The overwhelming majority of Sunni jurists agreed that good faith diligence in searching for the divine will is sufficient to protect a researcher from
liability before God. As long as the reader exercises due diligence in the
search, he will not be held liable nor incur a sin regardless of the result. Beyond this, the jurists were divided into two main camps. The first school,
known as the *mukhatti'ah*, argued that ultimately there is a correct answer to
every legal problem. Only God knows, however, what the correct response is,
and the truth will not be revealed until the final day. Human beings, for the
most part, cannot conclusively know whether they have found that correct response. In this sense, every *mujtahid* is correct in trying to find the answer,
but one reader might reach the truth while the others might mistake it. God,
on the final day, will inform all readers who was right and who was wrong.
Correctness here means that the *mujtahid* is to be commended for putting in
the effort, but it does not mean that all responses are equally valid.

The second school, known as the *musawwibah*, argued that there is no
specific and correct answer *(hukm mu'ayyan)* that God wants human beings
to discover — in part because, if there were a correct answer, God would have
made the evidence indicating a divine rule conclusive and clear. God cannot
charge human beings with the duty to find the correct answer when there is
no objective means to discovering the correctness of a textual or legal problem. If there were an objective truth to everything, God would have made
such a truth ascertainable in this life. Legal truth, or correctness, in most circumstances, depends on belief and evidence, and the validity of a legal rule or
act is often contingent on the rules of recognition that provide for its existence. Human beings are not charged with the obligation of finding some abstract or inaccessible legally correct result. Rather, they are charged with the

duty to diligently investigate a problem and then follow the results of their own *ijtihad*. Al-Juwayni explains this point by asserting,

> The most a *mujtahid* would claim is a preponderance of belief *[ghalabat al-zann]* and the balancing of the evidence. However, certainty was never claimed by any of them [the early jurists]. . . . If we were charged with finding [the truth] we would not have been forgiven for failing to find it.[81]

According to al-Juwayni, what God wants or intends is for human beings to search — to live a life fully and thoroughly engaged with the divine. Al-Juwayni explains: "it is as if God has said to human beings, 'My command to My servants is in accordance with the preponderance of their beliefs. So whoever preponderantly believes that they are obligated to do something, acting upon it becomes My command.'"[82] God's command to human beings is to diligently search, and God's law is suspended until a human being forms a preponderance of belief about the law. At the point that a preponderance of belief is formed, God's law becomes in accordance with the preponderance of belief formed by that particular individual. In summary, if a person honestly and sincerely believes that such and such is the law of God, then, to that person it is in fact God's law.

The position of the second school *(musawwibah)*, in particular, raises difficult questions about the application of the Shari'ah in society. This position implies that God's law is to search for God's law, otherwise the legal charge *(taklif)* is entirely dependent on the subjectivity and sincerity of belief. The first school *(mukhatti'ah)* indicates that whatever law is applied is potentially God's law, but not necessarily so.[83] In my view, this raises the question: Is it possible for any state-enforced law to be God's law? Under the first school of thought, whatever law the state applies, that law is only potentially the law of God, but we will not find out until the final day. Under the second school of thought, any law applied by the state is not the law of God unless the person to whom the law applies believes the law to be God's will and command. The first school suspends knowledge until we are done living, and the second school hinges knowledge on the validity of the process and the ultimate sincerity of belief.

Building upon this intellectual heritage, I would suggest that Shari'ah ought to stand in an Islamic polity as a symbolic construct for the divine perfection that is unreachable by human effort. As Ibn Qayyim stated, it is the epitome of justice, goodness, and beauty as conceived and retained by God. Its perfection is preserved, so to speak, in the mind of God, but anything that is channeled through human agency is necessarily marred by human imperfection. Put differently, Shari'ah as conceived by God is flawless, but as understood by human beings Shari'ah is imperfect and contingent. Jurists ought to continue exploring the ideal of Shari'ah, and ought to continue expounding their imperfect attempts at understanding God's perfection. As long as the argument constructed is normative, it is an unfulfilled potential for reaching the divine will. Significantly, any law applied is necessarily a potential unrealized. Shari'ah is not simply a collection of *ahkam* (a set of positive rules) but also a set of principles, methodology, and a discursive process that searches for the divine ideals. As such, Shari'ah is a work in progress that is never complete.

To put it more concretely, a juristic argument about what God commands is only potentially God's law, either because in the final day we will discover its correctness (the first school) or because its correctness is contingent on the sincerity of belief of the person who decides to follow it (the second school). If a legal opinion is adopted and enforced by the state, it cannot be said to be God's law. By passing through the determinative and enforcement processes of the state, the legal opinion is no longer simply a potential — it has become an actual law, applied and enforced. But what has been applied and enforced is not God's law — it is the state's law. Effectively, a religious state law is a contradiction in terms. Either the law belongs to the state or it belongs to God, and as long as a law relies on the subjective agency of the state for its articulation and enforcement, it is necessarily not God's law. Otherwise, we must be willing to admit that the failure of the law of the state is, in fact, the failure of God's law and, ultimately, of God himself. In Islamic theology, this possibility cannot be entertained.[84]

Of course, the most formidable challenge to this position is the argument that God and his Prophet have set out clear legal injunctions that cannot be ignored. Arguably, God provided unambiguous laws precisely because God wished to limit the role of human agency and foreclose the possibility of innovations. There is, however, a two-part response to this argument. Regardless of how clear and precise the statement of the Qur'an and Sunna, the meaning derived from these sources is negotiated through human agency. For example, the Qur'an states, "As to the thief, male or female, cut off *[faqta'u]* their hands as a recompense for that which they committed, a punishment from God, and God is all-powerful and all-wise" (5:38). Although the legal import of the verse seems to be clear, at a minimum it requires that human agents struggle with the meaning of "thief," "cut off," "hands," and "recompense." The Qur'an uses the expression *iqta'u*, from the root word *qata'a*, which could mean to sever or cut off, but it could also mean to deal firmly, to bring to an end, to restrain, or to distance oneself from. Whatever the meaning generated from the text, then, can the human agent claim with absolute certainty that the determination reached is identical to God's? And even assuming the issue of meaning is resolved, can the law be enforced in such a fashion that one can claim that the result belongs to God? God's knowledge and justice are perfect, but it is impossible for human beings to determine or enforce the law in such a fashion that the possibility of a wrongful result is entirely excluded. This does not mean that the exploration of God's law is pointless; it only means that the interpretations of jurists are potential fulfillments of the divine will, but the laws as codified and implemented by the state cannot be considered as the actual fulfillment of these potentialities.

Institutionally, it is consistent with the Islamic experience that the *'ulama* can and do play the role of the interpreters of the divine word, the custodians of the moral conscience of the community, and the curators reminding and pointing the nation toward the ideal that is God.[85] But the law of the state, regardless of its origins or basis, belongs to the state. It bears emphasis that under this conception there are no religious laws that can or may be enforced by the state. The state may enforce the prevailing subjective commitments of the community (the second school), or it may enforce what the majority believes to be closer to the divine ideal (the first school). But it bears emphasis: in either case, what is being enforced is not God's law. This means that all laws articulated and applied in a state are thoroughly human, and should be treated as such. Any codification of Shari'ah law produces a set of laws that are thoroughly human. These laws are a part of Shari'ah law only to the extent that any set of human legal opinions can be said to be a part of Shari'ah. A code, even if inspired by Shari'ah, is not Shari'ah — a code is simply a set of positive commandments that were informed by an ideal but do not represent the ideal. Put differently, creation, with all its textual and nontextual richness, can and should produce foundational rights, and organizational laws that honor and promote the foundational rights, but the rights and laws do not mirror the perfection of divine creation. According to this paradigm, democracy is an appropriate system for Islam because it denies the state the pretense of divinity. Moral educators have a serious role to play because they must be vigilant in urging society to approximate God, but not even the will of the majority can come to embody the full majesty of God. Under the worst circumstances, if the majority is not persuaded and insists on turning away from God, as long as they respect the fundamental rights of individuals, including the right to ponder creation and call to the way of God, those individuals who constituted the majority will have to answer, in the hereafter, only to God.

5 Enduring Change: Confucianism and the Prospect of Human Rights

ANTHONY C. YU

That which is above physical form we call the way; that which is below physical form we call instrument. That which transforms and regulates [things] we call change. To deduce [such principles] and act on them we call connection. To take up [such principles] and install them among the people of the world we call service and enterprise.[1]

From the beginning, this essay will attempt both a critique of Chinese Confucianism as it is traditionally conceived and a reinterpretation of certain Confucian concepts that may provide the basis for the formulation — perhaps even the advocacy — of universal human rights. Instead of arguing for the cultivation of virtues and the exaltation of "communal values" favored by

---

This essay began as an invited lecture in a year-long series in 1998 on "The Souls of Nations and the Prospect for Democracy" sponsored by the John M. Olin Center for Inquiry into the Theory and Practice of Democracy at the University of Chicago. I acknowledge with gratitude the generosity and kindness of my colleagues, Professors Nathan Tarcov and Joseph Cropsey, directors of the Center. The essay has also benefited from the discerning comments of my colleagues and friends — Professors Alan Gewirth, Jean Bethke Elshtain, Franklin Gamwell, Bruce Lincoln, Victor Mair, Henry Rosemont, and Lisa Raphals. The first version of the essay, with full citations of the Chinese texts in the original, was published by *Lingnan Journal of Chinese Studies,* new series, no. 2 (October 2000): 27-70. Translated into Chinese, the essay also appeared in *Newsletter of the Institute of Chinese Literature and Philosophy,* Academia Sinica 11, no. 3 (September 2001): 1-52. A slightly revised English version without Chinese citations was subsequently published in *Human Rights Review* 3, no. 3 (April-June 2002): 65-99. The current version, slightly modified and re-edited, is substantially the same as the *HRR* essay, and it is published here by permission from both *Lingnan Journal of Chinese Studies* and *HRR.*

many contemporary revivalists of Confucianism, the essay focuses on the important but neglected notion of desire *(yu)* pervasively discussed by ancient Chinese philosophers, including Confucius himself. According to these thinkers of the period encompassing the five centuries before the Common Era, the basis of both virtue and vice is nothing if not human desire. It is the defining feature of our common humanity, because whether we love the good sufficiently to seek it and do it or not determines who we are. As such, it is also one vital symptom of agency that constitutes the human subject as an individual, for no one can love virtue or vice on behalf of someone else.

The so-called Negative Golden Rule promulgated by Confucius himself — "What you yourself do not desire, do not impose on others" (*Analects* 12.2; 15.24; cf. also 5.12) — thus affirms both the reality and the limit of desire, no less than the importance of the self. An eighteenth-century Chinese commentator's elaboration on this insight, as I will argue in the concluding section of my essay, may serve further to develop a discourse on the irreducible worth and significance of the individual that must presuppose any advocacy of universal rights.

Relative to the question posed in the title of this volume, my essay's argument makes no appeal to assumptions of theistic transcendence. My silence on this point is not intended to slight the undeniable contributions that theistic religions have made to modern Western theories of rights; it is, rather, occasioned by both topical and historical considerations. Whether Confucianism can be regarded as a religion, and whether theism alone defines religion, are two complex questions that have divided scholarship through the centuries. Even without taking up such issues, which cannot be easily and briefly addressed, I hope that what follows demonstrates how certain Confucian tenets may be critically retrieved for contemporary reflection, thereby also honoring cultural particularity within a comparative and pluralistic context.

Continuity and Change: A Linguistic Parable

Whether there is such a thing as the "essence" or "soul" of China and whether it can change over time are questions that I'd like to examine on this occasion. Even for a single individual, the questions of the subject and personal identity — who am I and in what sense is the "I" of today the same as the "I" of yesterday — are questions of great complexity and much discussion.[2] To extend such a discussion to the most populous nation on earth (its onsite population is now estimated to be nearly 1.3 billion, with several hundred millions more in diaspora) may seem a hopelessly quixotic and benighted undertaking, not to mention an arrogant exercise in writing "essentialism" despised by many quarters of contemporary scholarship. Nevertheless, to study the subject that I have assigned myself, I find I cannot avoid treating the difficult topic of cultural identity and the prospect for its change.

To note the difficulty inherent in my project does not mean that students of China have been reluctant to debate the peculiar or distinctive characteristics of that civilization. Indeed, throughout the long course of China's existence, interested observers both past and present, native and foreign, have not hesitated in making pronouncements about that culture's spirit and content — declarations that are most affirmative or most critical, wildly errant or astutely percipient. Adjudicating between markedly conflicting visions or "sightings" (as Jonathan Spence calls them in his 1998 book, *The Chan's Great Continent: China in Western Mind*) regarding any reputedly defining feature of China is not only hazardous, however, but must also turn on further debate and interpretation. "Our understanding of Chineseness," according to the wise suggestion of historian Wang Gungwu, "must recognize the following: it is living and changeable; it is also the product of a shared historical experience whose record has continually influenced its growth; it has become increasingly a self-conscious matter for China; and it should be related to what appears to be, or to have been, Chinese in the eyes of the non-Chinese."[3]

Take, for example, the matter of the Chinese language which, particularly in its scriptural form, may certainly be considered an enduring bequest of Chinese culture. Enjoying a virtually unparalleled history of longevity and continuous development over several thousand years, the language has exerted incalculable influence on every major aspect of Chinese civilization.[4] What is enduring, however, is not synonymous with the unchanging. For example, the technological advance in the form of the personal computer during the last decade has wrought a revolution in the use and dissemination of Chinese that is wholly without precedent. For native and foreign users alike, the computer's alphabetical keyboard has, perhaps unintentionally, abetted the language reform measures pioneered by the People's Republic of China (PRC) when it first introduced the Pinyin system. This system, which has been severely criticized and resisted (by even myself), has suddenly been transformed into a virtually universal practice. Assisted by the computer, the Pinyin system has succeeded in providing an irresistible link between script and sound, through the enforced adoption of an alphabetical syllabary. For the first time in their long history, the users of the Chinese language are compelled to confront a *phonological* method of comprehending, retaining, and reproducing their language; that is, to match script to phonological representations that are completely conventionalized, hence standardized. The Pinyin system is fashioned entirely by the English alphabet. This is the crucial difference. Although the alphabetization of Chinese phonemes by the PRC reformers was at first intended primarily for facilitating uniform vocalization and easy comprehension, the introduction of the computer changed the picture radically by joining this phonetic representation of the language to the effective reproduction of the script. Not only does Pinyin grant immediate utility to the keyboard, but it also directly assimilates into the language — and thus domesticates — symbolic elements once thought to be completely alien.[5]

The computer also ironically assists the other salient plank of the PRC's linguistic reform platform. The composition of the Chinese word (traditionally made up of both logographic and, frequently, phonographic elements) now becomes correspondingly less important. The PRC's systematic proposal to simplify the graphic complexity of the characters and to promote, whenever context allows, the interchangeable use of homonyms is thus undeniably a logical extension of the decision to privilege sound and speaking over the writing system.[6] Whether this kind of development must eventuate in the gross distortion and impoverishment of the Chinese language, as many critics once charged, and how will it affect the long-term preservation and modification of Chinese, are questions not relevant to the present inquiry. Nevertheless, one paradox — the changeability of the culturally permanent — has become certain, for language as part of the quintessentially Chinese, because of the computer, has been touched and transformed by some element essentially foreign and alien. The non-Indo-European has become in part Indo-European.

Is this kind of development also possible in other domains of Chinese civilization such as the Chinese "soul"? This is the question underlying the remaining portions of my essay, where I turn to explore the perennially controversial issue of individual vs. community or group in Chinese. The issue will be focalized here as an examination of classical Confucianism and its compatibility with the modern advocacy of human rights. I have chosen to frame my inquiry along this line not merely because, as one scholar has put the matter, "the problem of human rights lies at the heart of modern political discourse."[7] Just as importantly, the discussion of the individual's role and significance in Chinese culture inevitably encroaches on the central tenets of Confucian ethics and politics. For more than two millennia, the powerful and pervasive ideology sustaining imperial governance, kinship structures, social values, familial morality, and the formal educational system has been irrefutably Confucian. This cultural dominance has cast its long shadow even into contemporary China, as a passing journalistic remark today can still refer, justly, to

Confucianism and Communism as that nation's "sustaining [albeit collaps-ing] value systems."[8] Abroad the tradition continues its influence on diaspora Chinese communities the world over. Even more impressively, attempts at the rehabilitation and retrieval of the Confucian tradition, among certain edu-cated elites also enjoying apparent support from state and local governments, have been steadily escalating in China itself during the post-Mao era that be-gan in the seventies.[9] An exercise such as the one I'm trying to conduct here, therefore, cannot avoid querying the persistent relevance of the Confucian tra-dition for Chinese communities looking toward the next millennium.

The Weight of Ancestors

In his thoughtful essay significantly titled "Early Civilization in China: Re-flections on How It Became Chinese,"[10] historian David Keightley enumer-ates many factors that helped to answer his titular question. These include hi-erarchical social distinctions, massive mobilization of labor, an emphasis on ritual in all dimensions of life including the early institutionalization of an-cestor worship, an emphasis on formal boundaries and models, an ethic of service, obligation, and emulation, little sense of tragedy or irony, the lack of significant foreign invasions, and the absence of any pluralistic national tra-ditions in China, from the Neolithic to the early imperial age.[11] Another dis-tinctive aspect of early Chinese civilization, "an emphasis on the group rather than the individual," finds striking illustration in Keightley's comparison of a fifth-century kylix vase by the Penthesileia Painter with a *hu* wine vase dated to the Eastern Zhou period (late sixth to fifth century). Whereas the lone fig-ures of Achilles and the Amazon queen occupy virtually the entire surface of the Greek vase, the decor of the Chinese vessel displays scenes of group activi-ties — battles by land and sea, banquets, hunting, and the picking of mul-berry leaves. Because these scenes are "stereotypical silhouettes" of nameless hordes, "the overwhelming impression conveyed by these tableaux is one of contemporaneous, regimented, mass activity."[12]

Keightley's observation that the prevalence of the group is already man-ifest in early China seems to me to be keen and unerring. From preserved ma-terial inscriptions of the Neolithic to the formal writings of the early Han, a culture that displays so voluminous a record and so large a vocabulary of an-cestral gradation and ranking, lineage, and kinship structures must be, even on a *prima facie* basis, interested in the life in and of the group. Similarly, the documents on rituals all center on court, clan, and household duties and ac-tivities, and they hardly qualify as prescriptions for personal ethics or individual behavior.[13] Ritual events inscribed on bronze vessels, ritual behavior attributed to a practitioner like Confucius (for example, *Analects* 10), and ritual patterns codified in various classic texts (*Zhou Li, Yi Li, Liji*) are not writings intended to induce proper behavior based on sound knowledge and critical judgment of a single individual (note Ἕκαστος), the starting point of Aristotle's *Nicomachean Ethics* (1094a26-1095a12). They provide, rather, the purpose and plan of action already selected, established, and judged as worthy of persons or various kinds of person; the meaning of an individual's very existence is, at the same time, unalterably defined by social status.[14]

In a well-known passage where Duke Jing of the state of Qi asked the Master about government,

> Confucius answered, "Let the ruler be a ruler, the subject a subject, the father a father, the son a son."
> The Duke said, "Splendid! Truly, if the ruler be not a ruler, the subject not a subject, the father not a father, the son not a son, then even if there be grain, would I get to eat it?"[15]

The marvelous feature of this dialogue is its purposive opacity. Neither the sage nor his interlocutor feels obliged to explain what letting a subject be a subject means. In the immediate context of the anecdote both men seem to know exactly, well beforehand, the practical content implied in Confucius's dicta, no less than the serious consequences of the success or failure of action on the part of persons thus classified. The punch clause of the Duke's utterance is especially illuminating in this regard. The force of his rhetorical question is premised on his belief (and by extension, his listener's as well) that agricultural success ("if there be grain") can guarantee neither biological gratification (a human like him must eat) nor entitled benefit (as ruler and father, he might expect filial sharing of food from sons or tributes of grain from subjects). Rather, the Duke's enjoyment of sustenance in the taxonomic ideal depends on each differentiated class of persons in the social order, including the Duke himself, fulfilling the unspecified but understood moral obligations.

There should be no mistake, however, that the implied rank and status of the persons thus classified already express concretely a set of unequal relations. In the biological realm, the son within the context of his own household may eventually attain the rank and status of a father. In the political sphere, on the other hand, the subject, unless he happens to be one who eventually overthrows the ruler, will likely remain forever a subject. It is the asymmetry of such relations, later to be permanently codified by Confucian disciples into the so-called Five or even Ten Relations *(wu lun, shi lun)*, that makes the meaning of the individual person in traditional Chinese culture not easily reconcilable with the basic presuppositions informing the Western discourse on human and civil rights.

If one were to pose at this juncture the question as to what is the most significant and representative feature of Chinese social thought that has endured through the centuries, my own reply would point to the intimate homology that countless writers and thinkers have drawn between the state *(guo)* and the family *(jia)*. Furthermore, the single social practice that offers both compelling illustration and underpinning of such a homology is also one that has rendered Chinese culture extremely distinctive, if not entirely unique, in the long course of its history. Long antedating the time of Confucius, ancestor worship has found ample documentation in the Shang oracle bones inscriptions. This familiar cultural practice within the affairs of the Shang state played a "central, institutionalized role" because, as Keightley has astutely observed, it "promoted the dead to higher levels of authority and impersonality with the passage of generations, encouraged the genesis of hierarchical, protobureaucratic conceptions, and . . . enhanced the value of these conceptions as more secular forms of government replaced the Bronze Age theocracy."[16]

The decisive contribution of Shang ancestral worship was precisely this union in itself of the three realms of power that determine and constrain human existence: the sacral, the biological, and the political. In contrast to the Greek concern for questions of origins, "first causes," or "first principles," the more social and biological conception of identity among the Chinese, says Keightley, led to a corresponding concern for "genealogy and history. A hierarchy of ancestors leading back to a dimly perceived founding ancestor or ancestress was answer enough because it satisfied the kinds of questions that were being asked."[17] Although classic Chinese texts did not raise the questions of origin or first cause in the same abstract manner as those of Greek antiquity, there should be no doubt that the name and status of ancestor belong to the realm of the sacred, because their act of procreation was thought to possess primordial significance. Keightley's insight is, in fact, confirmed by a passage in the section on "Special Livestock for Suburban Sacrifice [*Jiaotesheng*]" in the Han anthology *Record of Rites*. This passage declares that because "all things originate from Heaven [and] humans originate from the ancestor, this is why one offers food and drink to the Exalted *Di*. The Suburban Sacrifice magnifies the repayment of origin and the return to the beginning."[18]

Notice that this statement aligns Heaven *(Di)* and ancestor all in a continuum of power. This power is by definition religious or sacral because it has to do with one's ultimate origin, the *archē* of the individual and the community. To dishonor or betray one's parents and ancestors is to spurn or transgress one's origin.[19] Conversely, because ancestors and Heaven are functional equals in this formula, the sacral significance of parents is enormous, for they are always on their way to becoming ancestors *(zu)*. Hence filial acts, as acts of "repayment of origin and return to origin," are always sanctioned by Heaven, whereas a statement such as that by Jesus in Matthew 10:34-39 on the cost of discipleship becomes virtually incomprehensible to this day for many Chinese.[20]

Although the date of the *Liji (Record of Rites)* as a Han anthology, incontestably and thoroughly Confucian in its outlook and authorship, may be separated from the Shang period by close to a thousand years, the interpretation of the royal sacrifice and its reference to *shangdi* may well have articulated an archaic ideal that would far outlive its initial, genetic impact to shape and influence subsequently vast stretches of imperial culture. Keightley's words, this time from another source, must be cited one more time:

> Shang religion was inextricably involved in the genesis and legitimation of the Shang state. It was believed that Ti [Di], the high god, conferred fruitful harvest and divine assistance in battle, that the king's ancestors were able to intercede with Ti, and that the king could communicate with his ancestors. Worship of the Shang ancestors, therefore, provided powerful psychological and ideological support for the political dominance of the Shang kings. The king's ability to determine through divination, and influence through prayer and sacrifice, the will of the ancestral spirits legitimized the concentration of political power in his person. All power emanated from the theocrat because he was the channel, "the one man," who could appeal for the ancestral blessings, or dissipate the ancestral curses, which affected the commonality.[21]

Keightley's observation calls attention to the pivotal role of the political leader or sovereign in mediating religious meaning and participation in religious activities as an integral function of his political authority. Such a function, we must emphasize, has remained constant in all of Chinese imperial history, for the emperor or sovereign was never exempted from the duty to offer appropriate sacrifices, to ancestors and to other related transcendent powers variously conceived, that were deemed crucial for the state's health and well-being.

The most significant development in respect to the union of religion, politics, and kinship structures in China's imperial history — the phenomenon which some scholars have termed "institutionally diffuse religion"[22] —

came at the moment when the first emperor of China took for his dynastic title the name of Qin Shihuangdi or the First August Emperor of Qin in 221 BCE. The word for "emperor" here is indeed *di*, frequently translated as "God" in the scholarship on Shang religion and chosen by Mateo Ricci centuries later as the appropriate nomenclature for the Christian deity. Vatican rejection in the Rites controversy led to Ricci's eventual choice of the term *tianzhu* [literally, Lord of Heaven], but *di* was revived by Protestant missionaries in the nineteenth century, and the term *shangdi* since has existed for nearly two centuries in their biblical translation as an accepted name for God. Even more significant for our discussion here is the fact that the term *di* may, as a number of scholars have argued, etymologically connote the sense of ancestor.[23] When, therefore, the first emperor who united China assumed this title for himself, that single name would weave together in itself the related strands of Chinese conceptions of transcendent origin, paternity, authority, and power.

As if fearing that this single term would be insufficient to make apparent the symbolic significance of the ruler, the word *zu*, a much more common term for ancestor, was incorporated into the dynastic title of the first emperor of the Han. Henceforth, in the different appellations of individual reigns since 206 BCE, the ruler named as *di* or *zu* could mean quite literally that the ruler was a "god of martial prowess [*wudi*]" or "high ancestor [*gaozu*]," as many of them were called. Still later in the opening years of the Tang, the dynastic title of the second emperor was established as *taizong* or supreme ancestor. With this string of names forever canonized in the official annals of imperial history, as one can see, transcendence has been nominally rendered immanent and made familiar as kin, but such appellations also purport to indicate unambiguously that the ruler's power and authority remain godlike and, therefore, absolute. Moreover, they are meant to facilitate the venerable understanding obtaining even in Confucius's time that between state and family there exists a complete and practicable homology.[24] If the ruler, king, or emperor is, in fact, the grand ancestor of his subjects, political virtues must find their expression in kinship terms, much as the household patriarch will be enabled by such discursive propping to rule with impunity as god and ruler within his family and clan.

The Homology of Virtues

To be fair to the historical Confucius (551-479 BCE), his teachings have little to say about ancestors as such, but we must remember as well that they never dispute the important necessity of sacrifices *(ji)*, including those established for ancestors (for example, *Analects* 2.5, 24). Although there are only a few remarks about parents *(fumu)* scattered throughout the *Analects,* it cannot be denied that his observations on filial piety *(xiao)* in conjunction with how to serve one's parents (*shi fumu:* for example, *Analects* 1.7; 4.18) and how to serve one's ruler (*shi jun; Analects* 1.7; 3.18-19; 11.12; 14.22) are more abundant throughout his collected sayings.

Significant in this regard is the homologous relationship already drawn by Confucius between service to one's family and that to the state. When queried by someone why he was not taking part in government, Confucius replied,

> The *Book of History* says, "Oh! Simply by being a good son and friendly to his brothers a man can exert an influence upon government." In so doing a man is, in fact, taking part in government. How can there by any question of his having actively to "take part in government"?[25]

Herein lies the seed for his famous doctrine adumbrated in the *Great Learning* that the state's proper governance (*zhi guo)* must be a direct consequence of one's success in regulating one's family *(qi jia)* and the cultivation of oneself *(xiu shen).* The putative commentary on this doctrine by his disciple Zeng Shen, with a pointed allusion to the *Analects* text cited above, makes the connection even more taut and explicit:

> What is meant by "in order rightly to govern the State, it is necessary first to regulate the family," is this: — It is not possible for one to teach others, while he cannot teach his own family. *Therefore, the gentleman, without going beyond his household, completes the lessons for the State.* There is filial piety: — therewith the sovereign should be served. There is fraternal submission: — therewith elders and superiors should be served. There is kindness: — therewith the multitude should be treated.[26]

This comment indicates clearly the appropriation of an essentially family virtue, *xiao* or filial piety, and its direct application to the political realm, all as part of the gradation of ethical obligations in accordance with social rankings. In another instance, the Han *Record of Rites* will grandly argue how altruism and administration of justice are directly dependent on the proper filial regard for clan ancestors and kin. In the section titled "Great Commentary [*Da zhuan]*" we find this remarkable summation that deserves full citation:

> Now kinship is the bond of connection. Where the starting point is affection, one begins with the father and ascends by rank to the ancestor;

where the starting point is rightness, one begins with the ancestor and descends in natural order to the deceased father [note how hierarchy privileges the distant over the recent]. Thus the way of humans is to love one's parents *(shi gu rendao qinqin ye)*. Because one loves one's parents, one honors the ancestors; honoring one's ancestors, one also reveres the clan. Because one honors the clan, one also keeps together the members of the family branches. Keeping together these members dignifies the ancestral shrine; dignifying the ancestral shrine, one attaches great importance to the altars of land and grain. Valuing the altars, one therefore loves the hundred names [the metaphor for the people], and when one loves the people, there will be the accurate administration of punishment and penalty. When punishment and penalty are accurate, the ordinary people will find security, and when people are secure, resources and expenditures will both suffice.[27]

Since the anthology defines the clan as those who share in the patrilineal name *(tong xing cong zong)*,[28] this passage makes plain that the needs and aspirations of the basic family unit, whether the king's household or the commoner's, must be satisfied before attention may be directed to other units. The crucial turn in this line of argument comes in the somewhat puzzling contention that love of people would derive from the regard for the altars of land and grain. In the context of Confucian writings, however, one point seems evident: altruism is thought to be motivated primarily through the concerns of self-preservation, concretely expressed in the attempt to maintain sufficient sustenance for proper sacrifices to one's ancestors. Distributive justice in the Confucian view thus cannot be premised on the equal provision of justice for the constituent members of society, irrespective of kinship affiliations. In principle, what is due the people (the hundred names or *baixing*) is meted out in a centrifugal movement from the family or clan as the anchoring unit of that society. If that fundamental unit fails in its filial obligations, according to the logic of the passage I cited above, the rest of society cannot hope to find security or even the proper administration of retributive justice (punishment and penalty).

Such an understanding of altruism will accord with how the cardinal virtue of *ren* has been glossed and developed by Confucius and his follower. Antedating, in fact, the Confucians, an ancient source like the *Classic of Documents* already hints at the intimate association between *ren* — a word that has been variously rendered in English as benevolence, humaneness, human-heartedness, and even sublime generosity of the soul — and virtues valorized in clan rules and ethics *(zongfa lunli)*. In the scribal prayer preserved in the section titled "Metal Bond [*Jinteng*]," the clause "we are kindly as well as filial [*yu ren ruo kao = xiao*]" has been read by a modern authority as "we are obedient to the will of our ancestors."[29] The observation by Fan Wenzi recorded in the *Zuo Commentary* also asserts that "not forgetting one's origin is *ren*."[30] Again, the words of Liji set down in the "Jinyu" section of the *Guoyu* [Discourses of the States] declare that "for those who practice benevolence, loving one's parents is called *ren*."[31] Finally, we have included, with obvious approbation in the *Analects* itself, the statement by the philosopher Youzi or You Ruo that "being a filial son and an obedient brother is the root of *ren*."[32] As we shall see momentarily, this conclusion makes sense only in the context of the rationale structured in the entire assertion of the philosopher.

Read together with the declarations cited, the gloss preserved in the *Doctrine of the Mean*, 20, is both illuminating and instructive. "*Ren* is people," declares the text, "but loving one's parents is its greatest [manifestation]." This explicit exegesis provided by the second clause finds repeated and sympathetic echoes in someone like Mencius, who reiterates the same definition in 7A.15: "Loving one's parents is benevolence [*qinqin, ren ye*]." For him, *ren* is an affect that obtains primarily and most fully between parent and child, in such a special way, in fact, that one may regard it as something natural or decreed. (Cf. 7B.24: "the way benevolence pertains to the relation between father and son . . . is the Decree, but therein also lies human nature.") In another passage (7A.45), Mencius differentiates the proper affect toward kin and nonrelations with this striking gradation:

> Towards living creatures a gentleman would be sparing but show them no benevolence; towards the people he would show benevolence but not love. When he loves his parents he would show benevolence to the people. When he shows people benevolence he would be sparing towards the living creatures.[33]

The logic of Mencius and the compilers of the Han anthology on rites, as we can see, remains consistent because, according to them, one cannot even show benevolence to the people *(ren min)* without first loving one's parents *(qinqin)*.

Confucians have consistently maintained that what I have called here the homology of virtues is the most intimate affect appropriate to a kinship environment (the home, the household, the clan), and the ethical actions thus motivated are literally and equally applicable outside that environment. Since in imperial principle there is no space "under Heaven that is not the ruler's territory," the domain of the state both encircles and encompasses the domestic one. United, moreover, in symbolic significance in the person of the patriarch are the figures of the sovereign and the father, and it is this equation that grants viability and authority to the ethical homology. According to the Confucian formula set forth in the *Xiaojing* [Classic of filial piety],

> when we take that by which we serve the father to serve the mother, the love is the same. When we take that by which we serve the father to serve the ruler, the reverence is the same. Thus the mother takes one's love, whereas the ruler takes one's reverence. He who takes both is the father. Therefore, when one uses filial piety to serve one's ruler, he will be loyal.[34]

Notice that the logic implied in the above passage is what enables the Confucian to posit that the obverse of such prescriptive behavior is equally true: that is to say, when one serves the ruler with loyalty, the person must be a filial son. It is in the light of such reasoning that one can grasp more fully the powerful argument of You Ruo's full assertion preserved so prominently in *Analects* 1.2:

> For a man who is both filial and obedient as a younger brother, it is rare that such a person would love to affront his superiors *(fan shang)*. In fact, there has never been such a person who, being disinclined to affront his superiors, is still fond of inciting a rebellion *(zuo luan)*. A gentleman works at his roots; once the roots are established, the Way will grow therefrom. Are not filial piety and being obedient as a brother the roots of humaneness *(ren)?*[35]

Filial piety, a practice of personal rectitude, is now decisively recognized for its true worth — an apposite model for public political virtue — because its attitudinal assumptions and behavioral manifestations ("the roots") can benefit not merely parents and kin, but also supremely those in power and authority.

The Confucian discourse, moreover, does not emphasize this homology of virtue merely to shore up the formulated claims of personal and domestic ethics. In its writing of the state and history, this line of teaching serves as one linchpin of its overall world-regulating *(jingshi)* intent and design, as when the phrase *qinqin* is expanded from the basic meaning of loving one's parents to the love or regard for one's blood kin within a primarily political context. Witness the pronouncement on the defeat of Earl Xi by Duke Zheng: Among the several causes mentioned that would seal the former's destruction, the historian-commentator included the observation that Xi did not cherish kin relations *(bu qinqin)*, for his feuding with Zheng represented a repudiation of the fact that they had the same surname.[36] Even in *Realpolitik,* apparently, the obligations and demands of kinship retain their normative force. Why such a construct of human relations conjoining ancestry, paternity, rulership, and ethics succeeds in such a compelling and lasting fashion has been well summarized by a contemporary scholar:

> It was the ancestors who created the human species, and while all humans were "born equal," they were "equal" in the sense of being equally human and different from animals. Moreover, only humans could recognize ancestors. Thus ancestors took precedence over nature. Thus also filial piety quite rapidly became a core value in the Chinese web of interpersonal relationships, an axis linking the individual human being, his family, and his society. By the Han dynasty, filial piety had already become institutionalized as a criterion for selection of persons into officialdom.[37]

In the light of Youzi's observation, that criterion could not be more appropriate!

The Contemporary Debate

Certain scholars who would like to reconcile classical Confucian teachings with the liberal political thought of the West and the contemporary promotion of human rights frequently attempt to do so on the supposed basis that "the true person [in the Chinese tradition] is construed as a thoroughly social being."[38] This anthropological concept is in turn construed usually as an epitome of the desirable emphasis on moral duties and obligations. For many observers of China, the Confucian exaltation of group over individual is not even simply a legacy of a single culture. To the extent that historical Confucianism has been a known cultural export over the centuries, East and South Asian societies deeply influenced by such traffic are also indisputably implicated. The extent of Confucian impact in a particular society, whether as a result of conscious promotion (Korea, *Tokugawa* Japan, contemporary Singapore, Nationalist China on Taiwan) or as lingering habits of thought and action in diaspora communities, may be variously measured. The effect of its undeniable presence, however, has often been praised, for the principal emphasis on state and family over the individual person is routinely touted as a core element of the so-called "Asian values" that would effectively curb what are perceived as the corrosive excesses of Western individualism. In a much quoted interview, Singapore's Lee Kuan Yew declares that

Eastern societies believe that the individual exists in the context of his family. He is not pristine and separate. The family is part of the extended family, and then friends and the wider society. The ruler or the government does not try to provide for a person what the family best provides.[39]

Sharpening the polemical tone of the debate, Ian Buruma, in his review of the recent book by Hong Kong's last governor, Christopher Patten, has this observation:

> Patten's experience in Hong Kong made him reexamine his political instincts. And he concluded that his taste for free market economics, the rule of law, and the universality of liberal ideas was more than a matter of instinct. These *were* big ideas. And the propaganda for "Asian values," putting loyalty to the state above individual liberty, and duty and obedience above democratic rights, was a challenge to the Big Ideas: Lee Kuan Yew versus Locke, Mahathir versus Adam Smith. Was the "Asian" combination of capitalist economics and authoritarian rule exceptional?[40]

Possible answers to Buruma's rhetorical question divide even further those scholars interested in accommodating or reconciling the so-called Asian reality with both contemporary economics and contemporary politics. In the view of Hong Kong's Ambrose King, who thinks that "the East Asian experience demonstrates that democracy and modernity are not necessarily inseparable from individualism," the ideal would be the development of a "democratically Confucian political system or society" in which human rights are to be defined in "communal" or "social" terms.[41] For King as for others sympathetic to the accentuation of "communitarian" values, the Confucian tradition seems a rich and viable cultural resource for instilling and reinforcing such values. Thus, according to Sumner B. Twiss, "human rights in general are compatible in principle not only with cultural traditions that emphasize the importance of individuals within community (which is a more apt characterization of western liberalism) but also with cultural traditions that may emphasize the primacy of community and the way that individuals contribute to it — that is, *both* more liberal individualist *and* more communitarian traditions."[42]

Such a line of argument dwelling on "communitarian values" and the human person as a "social being," regrettably, tends to overlook the fact that in Confucian teachings, different social groups have different ethical and political claims on that "social being." It tends to forget as well that in the Confucian state, groups, communities, classes, and stratifications that constitute and define all those relations *(lun)* are no more equal than the individual. On the other hand, as one historian in the very first volume of *The Cambridge History of China* has observed, already discernible among the trends characteristic of intellectual development from the period of the Warring States (403-221 BCE) to the Han and beyond would be an "emphasis on the ideal of social harmony, *albeit a harmony based on inequality.* In other words, the emphasis is on the readiness of each individual to accept his particular place in a structured hierarchy, and to perform to the best of his ability the social duties that pertain to that place."[43]

It need hardly be said that such an emphasis would find the staunchest support and the most eloquent exposition in the Confucian elite, who at every opportunity seem ready to draw on the state-family homology to buttress the cardinal principles of rulership. Thus in the chapter on "Governing the Family [*zhijia*]" in his pioneering *Manual for Family Instruction* or *Jiaxun* that became the model for countless subsequent imitations, the Sui official Yan Zhitui (531-591) bluntly declares,

> when the anger expressed by the cane is abolished in one's house, the faults of the rebellious son immediately appear. When punishment and penalty are inaccurate, the people have no basis even to lift their hands and feet. Leniency and severity in governing one's house are the same as those in the state.[44]

And, even if Confucius himself did not initiate the practice of ancestor worship, this ancient ritual and its correlative ideal of filial piety, as we have seen, were already deftly appropriated by his first- and second-generation disciples as decisive expressions of domestic propriety, itself deemed indispensable for political order. Under the impact of Neo-Confucian revivalism of the Song Dynasty onward, in fact, not only would the ancestral cult and its rituals crowd the pages of the popular genre of family instruction manuals, but the design and erection of the family shrine, a custom increasingly adopted by Song elite officials, would come to dominate even domestic architecture.[45]

The Confucian insistence on the priority of sociopolitical relations embedding the individual and their immutable claims on that person has not been spared from fierce critique by a wide group of Chinese intellectuals early in the twentieth century. When one examines, for example, the content of the polemics that made famous the early republican iconoclast Chen Duxiu (Ch'en Tu-hsiu, 1879-1942), one can readily discern that his attack of Confucian ideals and practices was based squarely on the charge that they had historically deprived major social groups like "sons and wives" of their "personal individuality" and "personal property."[46] Although Chen was to become eventually one of the leading theoreticians for the Chinese Communist Party, which succeeded in building probably the most totalitarian state known in Chinese history, it should be remembered as well that his early contributions to the intellectual ferment of his time stemmed from the conviction, shared by many of the so-called May Fourth thinkers, that the new and modern needed in China was a revolutionary discovery and appreciation of the individual.[47]

Among sinological savants working outside of China, there are those who would advocate the retention and possibly the revival of Confucianism by contending that its principal tenets may even have anticipated certain aspects of Western liberalism and that the Confucian insistence on the priority of sociopolitical relations embedding the individual may not be incompatible with the Western discourse of human rights. Thus in his thoughtful essay of 1979, Wang Gungwu had already anticipated much of the rhetoric and tactics employed by contemporary Confucian loyalists by trying to link "the idea of reciprocity" with "idea of implicit rights." Adducing from various prescriptions in the *Analects*, the *Zuo Commentary*, and *Mencius* for the ideal behavior appropriate to various social ranks (for example, "the ruler should treat the subject with propriety, the subject should serve the ruler with loyalty"), Wang would argue that these duties and obligations might well be thought of as a form of rights, in the sense of reciprocal obligations categorically demanded of the sovereign, the subject, the father, the son, and the spouses.[47] Similar arguments have also been repeatedly advanced by Tu Weiming and W. Theodore de Bary.

According to the latter, the long line of elite officials studding Chinese imperial history and nurtured in both the letter and spirit of Confucian orthodoxy could be seen to have among its ranks a number of thinkers whose political philosophy seemed to promise transcendence over its own cultural ethos and limitation. Noted late medieval figures like Wang Fuzhi (1619-92), Huan Zongxi (1610-95), and Tang Zhen (1630-1704) could be gathered in what might be called "the liberal tradition" of China, because they clung to the Confucian insistence of the subject's duty of fearless remonstrance and advocated in their writings various forms of "egalitarianism."[49] It is this tradition, in the view of de Bary and other like-minded colleagues, that may even help explain how a certain phrase of Confucian rhetoric, first proposed by the then existent Republic of China, came to find adoption in the Universal Declaration of Human Rights ratified by members of the United Nations in 1948.[50]

Humane and persuasive as such a line of argument may seem, the problem lies in its failure to confront squarely the issue that the concept of reciprocity in Confucian thinking refers to "differentiated but mutual and shared" obligations. They are for that very reason not equal claims or obligations. De Bary is fond of citing the Mencian passage in 3A.4 where different obligations are spelled out for different classes of people: for example, affection between parent and child, rightness between ruler and ministers, distinctive duties for spouses, gradation for old and young, and trustworthiness between friends.[51] This schematization, unfortunately, is always upheld without the concomitant but necessary acknowledgment that even these five relations and their idealized obligations themselves embody an inherent hierarchical preference. Since our debate involves the consideration of textualized tradition and historical reality, we must again refer to the *Record of Rites*, in which the section on "Jitong [Summary of Sacrificial Principles]" declares that,

> In sacrifices are ten relations which may be seen in the way of serving the ghosts and spirits, in the obligations between ruler and subject, in the relation between father and son, in the ranks dividing the noble and the lowly, in the distance separating the kin, in the bestowal of title and reward, in the distinction of duties between husband and wife, in the impartiality of governmental affairs, in the observance of order between old and young, and in the boundaries set between high and low.[52]

This statement has elicited in turn from Fei Xiaotong (Hsiao-t'ung), the father of sociology in modern China, the observation that "*Lun* [relations] is order based on classifications" conceived on the very commingling of "concrete social relationships" with "abstract positional types [for example, noble and lowly, high and low]." According to him, "the basic character of traditional Chinese social structure rests precisely on such hierarchical differentiations. . . . Therefore, the key to understanding networks of human relationships is to recognize that such distinctions create the very patterns of Chinese social organization." Because "the framework of social structure" confuses the symmetric and asymmetric models of the social and remains "unchangeable"[53] unless the very categories for its construction are dismantled or reconceived, the thesis of contemporary Confucian revivalists — that the ideal of moral reciprocity prescribed for those relations would provide an adequate analogue to the concept of right — becomes highly questionable.

Since the Confucian notion of reciprocity always embodies preference and priority, it must perforce enjoin unequal sanctions against disparate social ranks in the event of legal infraction, a notion directly contradicting the modern Western conception of equality before the law. Because humans cannot avoid or escape moral failures, the question that Confucianism must confront is not about the necessity to inculcate and practice virtue, or even about the possibility of "self-renewal [*zixin*]" and "self-correction [*gaiguo*]."[54] In the public realm of society, it has to do, rather, with what happens when virtue fails and how those in power will be held accountable. Subjects, wives, children, and inquisitive journalists may be swiftly penalized if they err, but who will effectively censure, curb, or bring to justice the transgressive emperor, the patriarch, the judge, the senior minister, or the members of the ruling party? The question of human rights, in this context, is not about mutual kindness, assistance, and cooperation, however noble such acts may be in themselves. Rather, it is about the lower and lowest levels of human society and what recourse they have and do not have when they are abused and ill-treated. Must they rely merely on the "fearless remonstrance of loyal ministers" that de Bary's books exalt repeatedly? Are exile, imprisonment, or remonstration till execution — the three supreme examples of benevolence *(ren)* in the Shang singled out for praise by Confucius in *Analects* 18.1 — the only viable alternatives when rulers and subjects disagree in a contemporary Asian society?

The question of how the ruling classes are to be judged, in fact, finds an illuminating discussion in a well-known passage of *Mencius.* When a subject fails in his duties, according to Confucian doctrine, he may be killed after the ruler has made a thorough investigation of the matter (*Mencius* 1B.7). On the other hand, even a tyrant as famous as the last king of the Shang could not induce Mencius to permit regicide as a general principle. Since, however, Mencius could not alter recorded history, his justification for killing Zhou, the last king of Shang, was ingenious: The latter had degraded himself so badly by his immoral despotism that he could no longer be classified as king, but merely "a fellow [*yi fu*]." Hermeneutics had thereby saved both official history and morality, for then Mencius could declare resoundingly: "I have heard that a fellow Zhou had been executed, but I have not heard that a sovereign had been executed" (1B.8).

History, however, may prove to be more stubbornly intractable than this brilliant piece of sophistry. Despite Mencius's unambiguous and repeated counsel that the people and the officials have what seems a right to leave and abandon an unprincipled or evil ruler, thereby depriving him of his so-called legitimacy (4B.4),[55] what is recorded in history presents a wholly different picture. In the long annals of the Chinese tradition, there has not been a single change of dynastic power without violence and bloodshed. On the contrary, even the infra-household competition for power between, say, a crown prince and his rival siblings or cousins more often than not begins and ends in the sword, the rope, or the poisonous cup. The only accounts of peaceful transmission of rulership are those attributed to the reigns of the sage kings,

Yao, Shun, and Yu, but their mythic status at the dawn of Chinese history should also warn us that their examples betoken more of Chinese desire than veracity.

This irrefutable phenomenon of Chinese history, I would argue, indicates something more than the unavoidable clash "between ideal values and their implementation in historical practice,"[56] a judgment that smacks more of romantic hermeneutics pervasive of certain phases of scholarship treating Buddhist and Christian histories than of a sound conclusion. In that view, the founding ideals of these two traditions are allegedly so rarefied and pure that they were almost immediately misunderstood by their followers; they can be recovered only by the sympathetic perspicacity of modern interpreters. For me, rather, the basis for doubting the Confucian tradition and its modern viability must center on something more fundamental: namely, the essentially biological model of the patriarchal family and its use as a luminous mirror of the state that Confucians had extolled from the beginning. One may well ask whether the family, even at the level of a large, extended household of the clan, can justly reflect the complexity and the necessity of impersonal arbitration that must obtain in the political body of a contemporary nation. Can such a family model provide adequate underpinning for the ideals of social equality and minimal human rights? I suspect not, not because the Chinese do not or cannot envision such ideals as desirable ends, as some advocates of cultural particularism have erroneously argued, but because the model itself long cherished and defended by the Confucian discourse is not conducive to the establishment of these ends.[57]

Even in extremely liberal societies today, families are not thought to be organized around a scripted and contracted system of rights but fundamentally by an unspoken or loosely specified code of duties, obligations, and expectations that are posited as the proper behavior of kinship. This is the reason why there is growing vexation in the United States today, in the courts no less than in social commentary, as to when and how the impersonal state should intervene when the fundamental rights of citizens as household members are violated or denied by other members of the same household.[58] By contrast, Confucius and his disciples, as I have tried to show, have articulated a meticulously specified code that directly grounds political virtues on familial ones. The logical question that must be asked at every formulation of Confucian social and personal ethics is this: What recourse does a Chinese have when such prescribed norms are not observed or abused, that is, when reciprocity is withheld or rejected? Confucius was forthright in answering a disciple's query by declaring, "The ruler should employ his subject according to the rules of propriety; the subject should serve his ruler with loyalty." But the question the disciple failed to bring up next is, What happens when the ruler fails the rules of propriety? As we have seen already in the Mencian discussion of tyranny, that ruler's failure has enormous consequence because the philosopher recognizes clearly the possibility that "innocent people" could be killed by such a person (*Mencius*, 4B.4). Here the classic Confucian homology of the state and family breaks down.

On the one hand, parents and children in any society and at any time may inflict on each other unspeakable cruelty and abuse, but their relations would not necessarily dissolve even after such atrocity, nor would they be likely to depose parents or disown ancestors in the name of the "Mandate of Heaven." Politics may abound in any family, but the biological relations of humans, now even certifiable across the centuries by DNA testing (as in the recent case of Thomas Jefferson's descendents), are thus not exactly the same as the essentially social nature of state governance. On the other hand, therefore, when government and rulers prove oppressive and tyrannous, the inevitable remedy must focus on accountability and change, preferably by peaceful means. We need to hear again the lesson given at the side of Mount Tai, where Confucius inquired of a grievously weeping woman by several graves. Queried by Confucius as to why she did not quit her region after her father-in-law, her husband, and her son were all devoured by tigers, she gave this decisive reply: "There's no harsh government here." Whereupon Confucius was moved to say to his disciples: "Remember this, little ones. Harsh government is worse than tigers!"[59]

This enlightened insight, alas, yielded no further reflection for possible change in the fundamental form of governance, for both Confucius and Mencius could only counsel withholding of service or withdrawal from the territorial state entirely when the ruler was without the *dao*. Even under dire circumstances, the Confucians throughout China's imperial history never bothered to examine whether the state-family homology could truly withstand scrutiny from the perspective of either the origin of these two different forms of community or the basis of their possible dissolution. Because the foundation of the Confucian social order is the teleology of the group, the charge, so frequently voiced by academicians committed to Asian cultures and values, that the philosophy of human rights promotes individualism seems to me a premise begging the crucial point of this modern and still emergent philosophy. As I see the matter, the philosophy of human rights cannot be simply interested in "communitarian values," as most contemporary Confucian advocates would have it, because those values may not be sufficient substitutes for rights. At the level of fundamental principles in social organization and civic governance, a community that can be injurious, whether by accident or design, to some members of the community hardly qualifies as a desirable community for all. For that reason, the bottom line of the theory of human rights must concern itself with individuals, indeed in principle with every single human being, because "the justified interests in question," as Alan Gewirth has articulated the matter so incisively, "are distributively common to all human beings."[60] Before those "interests in question," some principles must be established whereby both ruler and commoner would exist only as two individuals who may lay equal claim to those interests, and that claim should not be jeopardized by any prevenient hierarchical ordering.

Concluding Reflection: Revising Confucianism

Since much contemporary discussion of the theories of human rights and the Confucian tradition is premised on the alleged conflict between "communitarian values" and the Western concern for the single person, does this mean that the advocacy of any form of human rights must presuppose an understanding of an individual who is "unassailable," "anarchic," and obsessed with "radical autonomy"? Put in the most succinct manner and the bluntest terms, is there any strand of Confucian thinking that places greater value on the individual, on what may properly belong to a single human being — whether life, possession, freedom of belief, or choice — that the community, whether familial or sociopolitical, cannot alter, co-opt, or remove without just cause? The answer to this last question may register serious pessimism if one invokes and clings to such a form of hierarchical authoritarianism as enshrined in the popular, proverbial saying, "When a sovereign requests a subject to die and he does not, he is disloyal; when a father wants a son to perish and he does not, he is unfilial."[61] On the other hand, there may be hope for mitigating such pessimism if one takes into consideration certain strands of the Confucian discourse since the seventeenth century that began to query received orthodoxy on rulership. If such a movement might not quite measure up to a "liberal tradition" thus named by contemporary scholarship, nevertheless, some Confucian elite did seem to respond to some liberalizing impulses, and, in hindsight, their ideas might have begun to "individualize [*gerenhua*]," "privatize [*sirenhua*]," and "quotidianize [*riyong changxing hua*]" Confucian values and practices.[62] Not only did thinkers such as Li Zhi (1527-1602), Huang Zongxi (1610-1695), and Gu Yanwu (1613-1682) begin an escalating questioning of the concept of the sovereign as absolute inherited power, but the widening discussion of what constituted the public and the private *(gong, si)* increasingly focused attention on the meaning of the solitary person's moral worth along with its obligations.[63]

In the light of this development, some words of Dai Zhen (1723-1777) may be regarded as taking on unanticipated significance, as when he declares that "one person's desires are the same desires of all persons under Heaven."[64] Taken from Dai's famous expository commentary on certain key concepts of Mencius, this statement in its context is merely one expanding on the commonality of origin and similarity of response in the genesis and manifestation of desires as adumbrated in an ancient text like the *Record of Music* (*Yueji*). Indeed, Dai's expansive discourse on nature, affect/disposition, and desire (*xing, qing, yu*), undeniably creative and synthetic, still appears largely as yet another attempt at reconciling the sometime conflictive observations of Mencius and Xunzi with those of Song Neo-Confucians on these venerable categories.[65] What is noteworthy is the new object of desire that Dai posits for moral disposition and action:

> In human life, there is nothing worse than the inability to fulfill one's life. Desiring to fulfill one's life while also fulfilling the lives of others, this is humaneness. Desiring to fulfill one's life to the extent of injuring without regard for the lives of others, this is inhumanity.[66]

Later (p. 198), Dai further clarifies the first part of his assertion with the formulation: "Humaneness is the virtue of life productive of life [literally, the hard-to-translate phrase *shengsheng* has the tautological force of making life alive]. . . . When one person fulfills one's own life and infers from this principle to help all under Heaven to fulfill their lives, this is humaneness."[67]

The Mencian overtones of Dai's assertions become audible if we recall the famous discussion on competitive desires recorded in *Mencius* 6A.10. That ancient thinker's acknowledged fondness for both fish and bear's palm serves on that occasion as a pretext for differentiating desires with far weightier consequence. Declaring that life and dutifulness are both objects of his desire (*yu*), Mencius proceeds to make the grand claim that he would forsake life because he desires dutifulness more. Immediately realizing, however, that such nobility may not be common, Mencius attempts valiantly to make universal the virtue of choosing virtuously by specifying how one's acceptance of food, an indisputable necessity of life, depends on the condition of its provision. If food is given with abuse, according to Mencius, "even a traveler would not receive it." Such an attitude (*xin*) is allegedly common to all (*ren jie you zhi*), but immediately Mencius feels obliged to equivocate: it's just that the worthy person is able not to lose this alleged fundamental disposition of benevolence. This distinction between attitude and ability, unfortunately, revises and limits the intended scope of the Mencian claim.

In contrast to his master's text, what is new in Dai Zhen's formulation is precisely how his view of the human condition and the supreme good of humaneness or benevolence *(ren)* is based on the universality of desire and its object without further qualification. For a reader conscious of Western social thought, it is difficult to read Dai's first sentence without noticing its remarkable affinity with Aristotelian premises. Just as the Greek philosopher has sought to ground his systematic investigation of ethics and politics on "the good life," "doing well," and "happiness or well-being" *(eu zēn, eu prattein, eudaimonia)* as synonyms for the supreme good that all humans seek *(Nicomachean Ethics* 1094b), Dai Zhen's singular notion of "life fulfillment [*suisheng*]" is no less all-encompassing a foundation for his claims. The drive to fulfill one's life, let us notice here, has nothing to do with human relations, because it is not dictated by kinship ties, or occasioned by culturally prescribed social position, or dependent on sanction by a particular community. Because they are common to all humans — from the highest ruler to the lowliest peasant — the desire and its object as universals possess the condition of equality as both phenomenon and quality. One can no more say that only some people have such a desire than assert that a peasant ought to aim at a lesser degree of self-fulfillment than a prime minister.

Precisely because it is fundamental to humanity as such, the desire's life- and thus self-affirming potency perforce must carry with it a negative possibility. Just as the quest for one's own well-being and happiness can be undertaken at the expense of the other, the drive toward life fulfillment can also hurt others. Like the antecedent Aristotle, who had hardly begun his monumental treatise before he felt obliged to mention the notion of self-restraint, Dai Zhen's remark also immediately proceeds to forestall the possible negative consequence of such a desire. By setting the reckless injury of another life *(qiang ren zhi sheng er bu gu)* as the limit of this desire, the Chinese thinker, it may plausibly be argued, has put his finger on one crucial issue animating the debates of ethics and politics in different civilizations down through the ages: how to reconcile the most essential values cherished by an individual with those values of other individuals.

Dai Zhen, to be sure, did not think or write in a vocabulary of rights as developed and used in the post-Enlightenment discourse on the subject. No student of Chinese history and thought, however, would deny that the concept of humaneness or benevolence *(ren)* has functioned as virtually a categorical imperative for the history of Confucian thought. It is to Dai's credit, I believe, that his definition of virtue as life productive of life *(shengsheng zhi de)* has succeeded in injecting new content into the familiar concept of *ren*. Though Dai's notion may be interpreted as having stemmed from such a familiar source as Confucius's dictum in *Analects* 12.10 — "to love someone is to want the person to live [*ai zhi yu qi sheng*]" — Dai's innovation and strength, I would argue, lie exactly in detaching the content of *ren* from the altruistic but kinship-based implications of the Confucian injunctions to "love people [*ai ren*]" scattered in the *Analects* (for example, 1.5-6; 12.22) and in the *Mencius* (4B.28).[68] Dai's idea, when coupled with the concept of the desire for self-fulfillment *(yu sui qi sheng)*, bears the enormous importance of recognizing, and thereby legitimating with greater clarity and force, the reality of self-affirmation and thus self-love, self-interest, and self-preservation. We should remember that already in *Mencius* 6A.14, there seems to be the recognition that a person's self-love is unitary because, according to that thinker, there is no self-discrimination of bodily parts. Hardly has he finished with this observation, however, when Mencius proceeds to offer his own self-contradictory hierarchy of preferences by claiming that "the parts of a person differ in value and importance." Thus, "a man who takes care of one finger to the detriment of his shoulder and back without realizing his mistake is a muddled man."[69]

In contrast to Mencius again, Dai Zhen's definition of humaneness or benevolence as "the virtue of life productive of life" avoids precisely this sort of inconsistent account of desire. The first verb of the punning binome *shengsheng*, though acknowledged by Dai to bear the meaning of cosmic procreation when linked with the consideration of Heaven or Nature (p. 199: *zai tian wei qihua zhi shengsheng*), hardly refers to mere biological reproduction when it relates to the human *(zai ren)*. Instead, it has the reflexive sense of making or keeping life alive, and thus the definition directly involves the maintenance and preservation of life, for self and for others.[70] If life productive of life is truly the quintessential content of *ren*, any violation of life through destruction or injury, whether on the individual or communal level, is potentially as well as actually a violation of the supreme ideal. Both the affirmation of the universal desire for self-fulfillment and the correlative injunction to avoid reckless destruction of other lives in quest of the same fulfillment thus provide a firm basis for true egalitarianism. Could not such an idea serve also as a seed or seminal motif in developing a Confucian understanding of human rights that attends to the irreducible worth and dignity of the life of the individual? Could Chinese culture be led to recognize that the moral obligation of the state or body politic, no less than that of the individual, must be dedicated to "join all [people] under Heaven to fulfill together their lives [*yu tianxia gong sui qi sheng*]"?

Such a focus on the individual, let it be emphatically stated here, is not synonymous with the espousal of individualism, and one should point out that the opposition between "individualism" and "communitarian values" so often central to the present topic is typically drawn in a manner far too crude to formulate what is at stake. To affirm the individual in the sense implied by the concept of universal human rights is not necessarily to affirm individualism in the sense that one's fulfillment is privatized or defined independently of his or her communal relatedness and participation. Conversely, to affirm communitarian values is not necessarily to subscribe to the traditional values of a given community in the sense that a person's fulfillment depends on his or her participation in the community so defined.

Pondered in the light of our contemporary debate on rights, the striking quality of Dai's words may well be their potential for self-transcending implication and application, because in those remarks I cited, the single person and the community ("all under Heaven") are indissolubly and dialectically related. Although the phrase "under Heaven [*tianxia*]" in context undoubtedly means the imperial empire, in principle its significance may surely be so developed that it transcends its local or national delimitation. "When one person fulfills one's own life and infers from this principle to help all under Heaven to fulfill their lives" — does not such a statement carry an ideal germinal and germane to honoring universal humanity without dismissal or sacrifice of the individual? If one's quest for self-fulfillment must not be carried out to the extent of injuring another who, in principle, is engaging in the selfsame quest, does not the community act as a check and limit on the individual's anarchic or antinomian impulse? To fashion a conception of the individual's inviolable dignity and worth from the thought of a Qing philosopher, or, for that matter, from any other source, Chinese or otherwise, need not therefore be taken as a total repudiation of the so-called "communitarian values." How could one disagree with any injunction for those in power to treat subjects and citizens with respect, kindness, and trustworthiness, as Confucian teachings had done for millennia? What modern advocates of Confucianism need to realize is that even the noble prescription for reciprocity among various social strata is itself conditioned by that very unequal stratification. Once the imperial system of governance has been dismantled, and the republican revolution of 1911 is an irreversible fact of history, the same fate has also been handed to its undergirding system of social organization. How could one continue to invoke, for example, the relations between sovereign and subjects *(jun chen)* as part of the basis for morality and action? Exiled from the imperial society, Confucian teachings have become, in the poignant phrase of Yu Yingshi, "wandering souls [*you hun*]."[71] Such spirits may be retained in the collective memory of the Chinese people, but they need to embody modified content or restructured substance if they are to address realistically and effectively the altered social contexts.

If not all Confucian values are in principle antithetic or inimical to the modern advocacy of human rights, it must be acknowledged that that advocacy does presuppose a radically different evaluation of the person and the group. From the latter perspective, the rulers and the state are no more moral or virtuous than the ordinary individual, and this belief directly contradicts the notion, held in a large part of the Confucian tradition, that the sovereign or the collective governing body, by virtue of power, must be superior even in morality. The belief, perhaps first articulated in Mencius's pointed lesson for Prince Xuan of Qi, that the "failure to become a true King is due to a refusal to act, not to an inability to act,"[72] remains a stubborn legacy. I thus agree with Lucian Pye's criticism of Zhao Fusan, once the vice president of the Chinese Academy of Social Sciences, who reversed the insight enshrined in the title of American theologian Reinhold Niebuhr's well-known text, *Moral Man and Immoral Society*, with his remark that in China's cultural tradition, "individuals have never been placed above society, and the values of individuals have always been unified with the responsibilities of society."[73] The question posed by human rights and their advocacy concerns precisely what happens when society or its governing persons fail in goodwill and virtue. What recourse does a powerless person have, not merely to redress grievance or injustice, but also to protect his or her life from arbitrary injury, detention, or destruction? What safeguard or limit does a society possess that prohibits and prevents the group from the abuse of power? It is to such questions that Reinhold Niebuhr's sagacious aphorism holds the greatest relevance: "man's capacity for justice makes democracy possible; but man's inclination to injustice makes democracy necessary."[74]

On the assumption that leadership may fail on an individual or corporate level, the advocacy of rights, of participatory democracy and the rule of law from which no official is ever exempt, may in principle be taken as a rejection of a notion, long cherished by the Chinese, that we should "use people to govern the state [*yi ren zhi guo*]." In reply to Zhao Fusan's contention, we may say that human rights, properly articulated and implemented, do not place the individual above society so much as attempt to respect and do justice to the well-being of both individual and civil society. The advocacy of rights represents, even in minimalist expectations, an advocacy for both individual and community forms of safeguard that derive from the establishment of more viable and soundly conceived institutions. Those institutions are desirable and necessary because, in a larger context, the political question posed by human rights is not even exhausted by the prevention of injustice or the abuse of power. What Dai Zhen might not have realized when he wrote those interesting words is a sense — now felt and embraced by so many communities globally — that equal participation in the exercise of political power must be a necessary condition for the full realization of human capacities. Democracy, an independent, effective judiciary, and a free press thus not only protect against the invasion or harm of each individual's fundamental dignity; they also enable communal participation constitutive of human fulfillment *(sui ren zhi sheng)*. It should quickly be added, of course, that better conceptions (theory) or even better institutions do not guarantee a more perfect society in the sense of a flawless realization of exalted ideals. The advocacy of rights, therefore, ought not to be construed as a blind endorsement of Western societies and their values. In the United States alone, the problems stemming from entrenched racism leading to unmitigated violence, through corporate greed, corruption, and wastefulness, to bias, sloth, and ignorance that miscarry the law, and to state secrecy and duplicity, will form a litany of imperfections that truly shocks and dismays.[75] After more than two centuries, the republic that is the United States of America is still grappling daily to live up to the better ideals inscribed in its founding Constitution.

I began this study by referring to Professor Wang Gungwu's appeal to a "shared historical experience" of the Chinese to help us understand what Chineseness means at any particular moment. A quick glance at part of that shared historical experience now may render moot some of the scholarly controversies that I have hitherto reviewed. In the world we know today, ancestor worship exists in a much reduced scale and scope among most Chinese communities, and the large, clannish households for most families are virtually a thing of the past. Nearly a century has transpired since China's last emperor was deposed. Only a so-called "dictatorship of the proletariat" remains in the world's most populous nation, but even that government is changing as it struggles to cope with the imperatives of change. China, I'm pleased to note, had signed two crucial treaties — the "International Covenant on Economic, Social and Cultural Rights" in 1997 and the "International Covenant on Civil and Political Rights" in 1998 — although it continued to insist on the sole legitimacy of the Chinese Communist Party. Its recent practice of brutal suppression of the followers of Falun Gong may also indicate a tenacious clinging to the long-held conviction in historical China that the state itself must be the final arbiter of what constitutes legitimate religious practice and belief. Whatever official justification for its current policy and action the PRC government may offer, and however small and insignificant a group the Falun dissenters may appear at the moment, they should not lead us to concur with the sentiment that China is somehow not yet ready for human rights because of its particular social and political condition. Apparently the tens of thousands who congregated in Tiananmen Square in 1989 already thought otherwise, and the thousands that have continued to assemble and march in Hong Kong in commemoration of June 4 seem also to be of the same mind and conviction. In addition to its formal signatures on the two international covenants, the Chinese government since 1991 has issued a series of lengthy and detailed papers concerning its evolving understanding of human rights and related problems.[76] Such public efforts may represent, minimally speaking, the PRC's serious effort to come to grips with many of the issues pertinent to the subject of rights and thereby renders terribly ironic and even anachronistic the Confucian revivalist point of view. Despite the skillful apologetics for Asian authoritarianism exploited by the likes of Lee Kuan Yew and Mohamad Mahathir, the people of South Korea and Taiwan are firmly and steadily implementing a rule of law and a comprehensive participatory democracy. The surprising result of Taiwan's March 2000 election, in fact, should give the lie to the contention of cultural and regional particularism that somehow Asian Chinese are not receptive to political and social practices that presume a lofty view of the individual. Ought not this kind of "shared historical experience" count, too, in the contemporary debate on human rights? Perhaps the time has come when revolutionary changes in the culture of politics will occur as swiftly (though perhaps not as painlessly and surreptitiously) as those in the Chinese language with the alphabetization of the computer keyboard.

Let me close by citing Long Yingtai, an activist of Taiwan who, as a widely read author and respected cultural critic, was appointed to head Taipei's Bureau of Culture for the last few years. With a doctorate in English from the University of Kansas, she caused considerable stir in the early eighties by writing scathing critiques of the autocratic KMT (Nationalist) government. She persisted in her publications despite repeated threats of arrest and incarceration, winning eventual recognition as one of the handful of writers who played a major role in the liberalization of that island community. Asked to reflect on her experience of the past decade, she ended a recent article with this conclusion:

> One who has lived through the eighties in Taiwan has to be an individualist through and through: someone who will continue to dream about the dawn while confronting the deepest personal darkness. Never blink![77]

These are words of enduring change because they teach us the difficult but rewarding lesson that the change that must be endured is the change that endures.

PART II

SECULAR RESPONSES

6 Natural Law and Human Rights:
A Conversation

ROBERT P. GEORGE

The editors posed a series of questions to Professor George, seeking to discover how natural law theory might respond to the question, "Does human rights need God?" and to put his contribution into dialogue with the themes raised by other essays in this volume. The editors opted for a question-and-answer format for this contribution to reflect George's position as one of the leading proponents of natural law theory. In his work George frequently finds himself confronted by individuals perplexed by or opposed to natural law philosophy. George is keen to enter into such debates, which allow both interlocutors to reason through the issues presented. The conversational format of the following thus offers a medium that highlights and exemplifies key components of George's thought. Our conversation is presented below in the original interview format.

As a natural law thinker, how do you understand human nature and human rights?

A natural law theory is, in essence, a critical reflective account of the constitutive aspects of the well-being and fulfillment of human persons and the communities they form. Such a theory will propose to identify principles of right action — moral principles — specifying the first and most general principle of morality, namely, that one should choose to act in ways that are compatible with a will toward integral human fulfillment. Among these principles are respect for the rights people possess simply by virtue of their humanity — rights which, as a matter of justice, others are bound to respect, and governments are bound not only to respect but, to the extent possible, protect.

Natural law theorists understand human fulfillment — the human good — as variegated. There are many irreducible dimensions of human well-being and fulfillment. This is not to deny that human nature is determinate. It is to affirm that our nature, though determinate, is complex. We are animals, but rational. Our integral good does include our bodily well-being, but also our intellectual, moral, and spiritual well-being. We are individuals, but friendship and sociability are constitutive fundamental aspects of our flourishing. In ways that are highly relevant to moral reflection and judgment, man truly is a social animal.

By reflecting on the basic goods of human nature, especially those most immediately pertaining to social and political life, natural law theorists propose to arrive at a sound understanding of principles of justice, including those principles we call human rights. In light of what I've already said about how natural law theorists understand human nature and the human good, it should be no surprise to learn that most natural law theorists reject both strict individualism and collectivism. Individualism overlooks the intrinsic value of human sociability and tends mistakenly to view human beings atomistically. Collectivism compromises the dignity of human beings by tending to instrumentalize and subordinate their well-being to the interests of the larger social units of society. Individualists and collectivists both have theories of justice and human rights, but they are, as I see it, highly unsatisfactory. They are rooted in important misunderstandings of human nature and the human good. Neither can do justice to the concept of a human *person,* that is, a rational animal who is a locus of intrinsic value (and, as such, an end-in-himself who may never legitimately be treated as a mere means to others' ends), but whose well-being intrinsically includes relationships with others and membership in communities (beginning with the family) in which he or she has, as a matter of justice, both rights and responsibilities.

Are human rights hard-wired into our nature?

I fear the metaphor "hard-wired into our nature" is more likely to mislead than to illuminate. Human rights exist if it is the case that there are principles of practical reason directing us to act or abstain from acting in certain ways out of respect for the well-being and the dignity of persons whose legitimate interests may be affected by what we do. I certainly believe that there are such principles. They cannot be overridden by considerations of utility. At a very general level, they direct us, in Kant's phrase, to treat human beings always as ends and never as means only. When we begin to specify this general norm, we identify important negative duties, such as the duty to refrain from enslaving people. Although we need not put the matter in terms of "rights," it is perfectly reasonable, and I believe helpful, to speak of a right against being enslaved, and to speak of slavery as a violation of human rights. It is a right that people have, not by virtue of being members of a certain race, sex, class, or ethnic group, but simply by virtue of our humanity. In that sense, it is a *human* right.

But there are, in addition to negative duties and their corresponding rights, certain positive duties. And these, too, can be articulated in the language of rights, though here it is especially important that we be clear about by whom and how a given right is to be honored. Sometimes it is said, for example, that education, food, or health care is a human right. It is certainly not unreasonable to speak this way; but much more needs to be said if it is to be a meaningful statement. Who is supposed to provide education, food, or health care to whom? Why should those persons or institutions be the providers? What place should the provision of education, food, or health care occupy on the list of social and political priorities? Is it better for education, food, and health care to be provided by governments under socialized systems or by private providers in markets? These questions go beyond the application of moral principles. They require prudential judgment in light of the contingent circumstances people face in a given society. Often there is not a single, uniquely correct answer. The answer to each question can lead to further questions; and the problems can be extremely complex, far more complex than the issue of slavery, where once a right has been identified its universality and the basic terms of its application are fairly clear. Everybody has a moral right not to be enslaved *and* an obligation as a matter of strict justice to refrain from enslaving others; governments have a moral obligation to respect and protect the right and, correspondingly, to enforce the obligation.

Is there a set of nonnegotiable rights recognized by natural law, and how might these rights differ from what others might call human rights?

You asked about the "set" of "nonnegotiable" human rights. What I've said so far will provide a pretty good idea of how I think we ought to go about identifying the members of the set. But in each case the argument would have to be made, and in many cases there are complexities to the argument. One basic human right that almost all natural law theorists would say belongs in the set is the right of an innocent person not to be directly killed or maimed. This is a right that is violated when someone makes the death or injury of another person the precise object of his action. It is the right that grounds the norm against targeting noncombatants, even in justified wars, and against abortion, euthanasia, the killing of hostages, and so forth. Of course, in the case of abortion, some people argue that human beings in the embryonic or fetal stages of development do not yet qualify as persons and so do not possess human rights; and in the case of euthanasia, some argue that permanently comatose or severely retarded or demented people do not (or no longer) qualify as rights-bearers. I think that these claims are mistaken, but I won't here go into my reasons for holding that the moral status of a human being does not depend on his or her age, size, stage of development, or condition of dependency. I've presented this argument in great detail in my other writings.[1] Here I will say only that people who do not share my view that human beings in early stages of development and in severely debilitated conditions are rights-bearing persons may nevertheless agree that *whoever* qualifies as a person is protected by the norm against direct killing of the innocent.

Your understanding of human rights is closely linked to human dignity. Can you articulate for us your account of human dignity?

It seems to me that the natural human capacities for reason and freedom are fundamental to the dignity of human beings — the dignity that is protected by human rights. The basic goods of human nature are the goods of a rational creature — a creature who, unless impaired or prevented from doing so, naturally develops and exercises capacities for deliberation, judgment, and choice. These capacities are truly God-like (albeit, of course, in a limited way). In fact, from a theological vantage point they constitute a certain sharing — limited, to be sure, but real — in divine power. This is what is meant, I believe, by the otherwise extraordinarily puzzling biblical teaching that man is made in the very image and likeness of God. But whether or not one recognizes biblical authority or believes in a personal God, it is true that human beings possess a power traditionally ascribed to divinity — namely, the power to be an uncaused causing. This is the power to envisage a possible state of affairs, to grasp the value of bringing it into being, and then to act by choice (and not merely by impulse or instinct) to bring it into being. That state of affairs may be anything from a work of art to a marriage. Its moral or cultural significance may be great or comparatively minor. What matters in view of the question you've put to me is that it is a product of human reason and freedom. It is the fruit of deliberation, judgment, and choice. We may, if we like, consider as a further matter whether beings capable of such powers could exist apart from a divine source and ground of their being. But I don't think it makes sense to deny that beings whose nature is to develop and exercise such powers are lacking in dignity and human rights and may therefore be treated as mere objects, instruments, or property.

If reason is fundamental to human dignity and human rights, what are the sources of authority for moral reasoning according to natural law?

Natural law theorists are interested in the intelligible reasons people have for their choices and actions. We are particularly interested in reasons that can be identified without appeal to any authority apart from the authority of reason itself. This is not to deny that it is often reasonable to recognize and submit to religious or secular (for example, legal) authority in deciding what to do and not do. Indeed, natural law theorists have made important contributions to understanding why and how people can sometimes be morally bound to submit to, and be guided in their actions by, authority of various types. But even here, the special concern of natural law theorists is with the *reasons* people have for recognizing and honoring claims to authority. We do not simply appeal to authority to justify authority.

One might then ask whether human beings are in fact rational. Can we discern any intelligible reasons for human choices and actions? Everybody recognizes that some ends or purposes pursued through human action are intelligible at least insofar as they provide means to other ends. For example, people work to earn money, and their doing so is perfectly rational. Money is a valuable means to a great many important ends. No one doubts its instrumental value. So even skeptics do not deny that there are instrumental goods. The question is whether some ends or purposes are intelligible as providing *more than merely instrumental* reasons for acting. Are there intrinsic, as well as instrumental, goods? Skeptics deny that there are intelligible ends or purposes that make possible rationally *motivated* action. Natural law theorists, by contrast, hold that friendship, knowledge, virtue, aesthetic appreciation, and certain other ends or purposes are intrinsically valuable. They are intelligibly "choice-worthy," not simply as means to other ends but as ends-in-themselves. They cannot be reduced to, nor can their intelligible appeal be accounted for exclusively in terms of, emotion, feeling, desire, or other subrational motivating factors. These "basic human goods" are constitutive aspects of the well-being and fulfillment of human persons and the communities they form, and they thereby provide the foundations of moral judgments, including our judgments pertaining to justice and human rights.

Of course, there are plenty of people today who embrace philosophical or ideological doctrines that deny the human capacities I maintain are at the core of human dignity. They adopt a purely instrumental view of practical reason (for example, Hume's view that reason is nothing more than "the slave of the passions") and argue that the human experience of deliberation, judgment, and choice is illusory. If they are right, then the entire business of ethics is a charade, and human dignity is a myth. But I don't think they are right. Indeed, I don't think that they can give any account of the norms of rationality to which they must appeal in making the case against reason and freedom that is consistent with the denial that people are capable of more-than-merely-instrumental rationality and true freedom of choice. My colleagues

Germain Grisez and Joseph Boyle, together with the late Olaf Tollefsen, make a powerful argument along these lines against skepticism and the denial of free will in a book entitled *Free Choice: A Self-Referential Argument.*

If human reason is the ultimate ground of human rights, how can we explain or understand widespread failures to recognize and respect human rights in others, even if we demand them for ourselves?

As human beings, we are rational animals; but we are imperfectly rational. We are prone to making intellectual and moral mistakes and capable of behaving grossly unreasonably — especially when deflected by powerful emotions that run contrary to the demands of reasonableness. Even when following our consciences, as we are morally bound to do, we can go wrong. A conscientious judgment may nevertheless be erroneous. Some of the greatest thinkers who ever lived failed to recognize the human right to religious liberty. Their failure, I believe, was rooted in a set of intellectual errors about what such a right presupposes and entails. The people who made these errors were neither fools nor knaves. The errors were not obvious, and it was only with a great deal of reflection and debate that the matter was clarified. Of course, sometimes people fail to recognize and respect human rights because they have self-interested motives for doing so. In most cases of exploitation, for example, the fundamental failing is moral, not intellectual. In some cases, though, intellectual and moral failures are closely connected. Selfishness, prejudice, partisanship, vanity, avarice, lust, ill-will, and other moral delinquencies can, in ways that are sometimes quite subtle, impede sound ethical judgments, including judgments pertaining to human rights. Whole cultures or subcultures can be infected with moral failings that blind large numbers of people to truths about justice and human rights; and ideologies hostile to these truths will almost always be both causes and effects of these failings. Consider, for example, the case of slavery in the antebellum American south. The ideology of white supremacy was both a cause of many people's blindness to the wickedness of slavery and an effect of the exploitation and degradation of its victims.

What is the role of religion and/or God in your understanding of natural law?

Most, but not all, natural law theorists are theists. They believe that the moral order, like every other order in human experience, is what it is because God creates and sustains it as such. In accounting for the intelligibility of the created order, they infer the existence of a free and creative intelligence — a personal God. Indeed, they typically argue that God's creative free choice provides the only ultimately satisfactory account of the existence of the intelligibilities humans grasp in every domain of inquiry.

Natural law theorists do not deny that God can reveal moral truths and most believe that God has chosen to reveal many such truths. Natural law theorists also affirm, however, that many moral truths, including some that are revealed, can also be grasped by ethical reflection apart from revelation. They assert, with St. Paul, that there is a law "written on the hearts" even of the Gentiles who did not know the law of Moses. So the basic norms against murder and theft, though revealed in the Decalogue, are knowable even apart from God's special revelation. The natural law can be known by us, and we can conform our conduct to its terms, by virtue of our natural human capacities for deliberation, judgment, and choice. The absence of a divine source of the natural law would be a puzzling thing, but only in the sense that the absence of a divine source of any and every other intelligible order in human experience would be a puzzling thing. Our puzzlement might well cause us to reconsider the idea that there is no divine source of the order we perceive and understand in the universe. It is far less likely to cause us to conclude that our perception is illusory or that our understanding is a sham.

Given the above analysis, can natural law provide the basis for an international human rights regime without consensus on the nature of God and the role of God in human affairs?

Anybody who acknowledges the human capacities for reason and freedom has good grounds for affirming human dignity and basic human rights. These grounds remain in place whether or not one adverts to the question, "Is there a divine source of the moral order whose tenets we discern in inquiry regarding natural law and natural rights?" I happen to think that the answer to this question is "yes," and that we should be open to the possibility that God has revealed himself in ways that reinforce and supplement what can be known by unaided reason. But we do not need agreement on the answer, so long as we agree about the truths that give rise to the question, namely, that human beings, possessing the God-like powers of reason and freedom, are possessors of a profound dignity that is protected by certain basic rights.

So, if there is a set of moral norms, including norms of justice and human rights, that can be known by rational inquiry, understanding, and judgment even apart from any special revelation, then these norms of natural law can provide the basis for an international regime of human rights. Of course, we should not expect consensus. There are moral skeptics who deny that there are moral truths. There are religious fideists who hold that moral truths cannot be known apart from God's special revelation. And even among those who believe in natural law, there will be differences of opinion about its precise content and implications for certain issues. So it is, I believe, our permanent condition to discuss and debate these issues, both as a matter of abstract philosophy and as a matter of practical politics.

You are considered a leading expert in the New Natural Law Theory. Can you explain for us what is "new" about this school of thought? In other words, do you understand New Natural Law to be a revival of a historic phenomenon or is there something particularly modern that is added? Does the latter imply human rights that were not recognized by "old" natural law thinkers?

There is little that is fundamentally new about what some call the New Natural Law Theory. Most of what Germain Grisez, John Finnis, Joseph Boyle, and I say at the level of fundamental moral theory is present, at least implicitly, in the writings of Aristotle, Thomas Aquinas, and other ancient, medieval, and early modern thinkers. Some think what we say is fundamentally new (and wrongheaded) because we are resolute about respecting the distinction between description and prescription and avoiding the fallacy of proposing to derive normative judgments from purely factual premises describing human nature. An example of the fallacy is the putative inference of the value of knowledge from the fact that human beings are naturally curious and desire to know. But here we are being faithful to the methodological insights and strictures of Aristotle and Aquinas. Contrary to what is sometimes supposed, they recognized that what would later come to be called "the naturalistic fallacy" is indeed a fallacy, and they (especially Aquinas) were stricter about avoiding it even than was David Hume, who is sometimes credited with "discovering" it.

If, standing on the shoulders of Aristotle and Aquinas, we have been able to contribute anything significant to the tradition of natural law theorizing, it is founded on Professor Grisez's work showing how what he calls "modes of responsibility" follow as implications of the integral directiveness of the most basic principles of practical reason — principles that direct human action toward basic human goods and away from their privations. The modes of responsibility are intermediate in their generality between the first and most general principle of morality ("always choose in a way that is compatible with a will toward integral human fulfillment") and fully specified moral norms that govern particular choices. The modes include the Golden Rule of fairness and the Pauline Principle that evil may not be done, even for the sake of good. They begin to specify what it means to act (or to fail to act) in ways that are compatible with a will toward the fulfillment of all human beings in all the respects in which humans can flourish. John Finnis, in the fifth chapter of his book *Natural Law and Natural Rights,* provides an excellent analysis of the content of the modes of responsibility (which he calls "principles of practical reasonableness") and the ways in which they function in moral deliberation to exclude unvirtuous choices and actions

You asked whether New Natural Law theorists claim that there are human rights that were not known to natural law thinkers of the past. Contemporary natural law theorists of various descriptions — not only those associated with Grisez, Finnis, and myself — defend a basic human right to religious liberty. This right was not widely acknowledged in the past, and was even denied by some prominent natural law theorists. They wrongly believed that such a right presupposed religious relativism or indifferentism, or entailed that religious vows were immoral or nonbinding. It is interesting that when the Catholic church put itself on record firmly in support of the right to religious freedom in the document *Dignitatis Humanae* of the Second Vatican Council, it presented both a natural law argument and an argument from specifically theological sources. The natural law argument for religious liberty is founded on the obligation of each person to pursue the truth about religious matters and to live in conformity with his conscientious judgments. This obligation is, in turn, rooted in the proposition that religion — considered as conscientious truth-seeking regarding the ultimate sources of meaning and value — is a crucial dimension of human well-being and fulfillment. The right to religious liberty follows from the dignity of man as a conscientious truth-seeker.

What do you understand to be (1) the greatest threat and (2) the greatest hope for improving the current human rights situation?

As I see it, the greatest threats are from ideologies hostile to a sound understanding of human dignity and the rights protecting it. In some parts of the world, these ideologies are religious in form. Religious freedom and other basic human rights are denied in the name of theological truth. In other parts of the world, the threats are from secularist ideologies. Here, rights are often denied in the name of rights. An overarching right to "autonomy" or "radical individualism" is asserted to justify choices and actions that harm others and compromise the common good. In both cases, moral failings conspire with intellectual errors to sustain humanly destructive bodies of ideas. In a certain sense, the moral failings are at opposite extremes: fanaticism and selfishness. Interestingly, extremists on the opposing sides make valid criticisms of each other. Radical Islamists, for example, harshly condemn the decadent features of cultures in which the ideology of "autonomy" flourishes. Expressive individualists denounce the subjugation of women and the oppression of religious dissenters where fundamentalist Islam holds sway. Of course, most Muslims are not radical Islamists. And the majority of Westerners have not embraced the doctrines of expressive individualism. But that does not mean that we have no reason to worry about the influence and spread of these ideologies. Even as minority positions, they do great harm. For the sake of human dignity and human rights we should be prepared to engage the ideological struggle, opposing doctrines at either extreme with resolution and unfailing moral and intellectual seriousness. Threats exist because all of us, as human beings, are imperfectly reasonable and imperfectly moral. We can go off the rails. Hope exists because we really do possess the capacities for reasonableness and virtue; truth — including moral truth — is accessible to us and has its own splendor and powerful appeal. We will never, in this vale of tears, grasp the truth completely or in a way that is entirely free from errors. Nor will we fully live up to the moral truths we grasp. But just as we made progress by abolishing the evil of slavery, by ending legally sanctioned racial segregation, and by recognizing the right to religious freedom, I'm confident that we can make progress, and reverse declines, in other areas.

7 Religion, Religions, and Human Rights

LOUIS HENKIN

The fiftieth anniversary of the United Nations Universal Declaration of Human Rights of 1948 (the "Universal Declaration") surely deserved celebration. Celebration also provides an occasion for reflection, and I have been asked to reflect on the vexed relationship between religion and human rights. I do so as a human rights scholar and as an observer of religious practices, not a student of religion or religions or religious ethics.

I speak of religions in the plural. Religions are particular, concrete, historical communities with members, practices, and boundaries. If we ask why religions have been slow to embrace the human rights idea, the answer often lies in the nature of these particular, concrete, historical communities — in the exigencies of identity, social function, and group survival. Theologians, philosophers, and other academics properly distinguish "religion" from "religions," but in that distinction, "religion" is abstracted, and the claims that are made about it are claims about an abstraction. In the public mind, "religion" does not exist; there are only "religions." Surely, in the political universe in which human rights are played out and matter, "religion" cannot avoid identification with "religions," with every — any — particular religion. And, unhappy as this is to say, every religion at some time, in some respect, has had to answer to the human rights idea for human rights violations, many of them unspeakable. Moreover, theoreticians dealing with the relation of "religion" and human rights make their task too easy, dismissing the actual practices of actual "religions" as perhaps aberrant, certainly as less telling than their gen-

---

This essay was originally published as "Religion, Religions, and Human Rights," *Journal of Religious Ethics* 26, no. 2 (1998): 229-38. This slightly modified and reedited version appears here by permission of the author and Blackwell Publishing.

eralized abstract construct. But religions cannot escape from the sins of their various "fundamentalisms" when they become oppressive or affiliated with terrorism, by being distilled by academics into "religion." Nor will such distillation cleanse religions of the tarnish of association with political repression, or excuse particular communities for their patterns of distinction and discrimination on grounds of race, or sex — or even religion.

When I explore the possibility of cooperation, of convergence between religion and human rights, I mean to consider the possibility of conciliation between real communities with long-standing reasons for mutual suspicion, not the possibility of displaying the theoretical compatibility of abstract ideas.

Ideological Differences

The idea and the morality of religions differ from the idea and ideology of human rights in their sources and in the bases of their authority; in the forms in which their respective moral codes are given expression; and, to some extent, in elements of their respective moral codes.

First, as to the source and authority of their respective morality: Religion and religions — surely, the principal religions — see their moral code as part of a total cosmic order and as emanating from a Supreme Legislator. The Supreme Legislator, directly or through authorized representatives, has prescribed a moral code of human behavior in an authoritative text. All human beings, and their communities, leaders, and political institutions, are bound by that moral code.

For the Western monotheistic religions, that morality might derive from, be implicit in, or find support in the received story of creation and its traditional elaborations. According to this familiar narrative, persons are created in the image of God; some consider Adam the single ancestor of all humankind, and God the father of us all. That has important implications: All human beings are not merely distant cousins, but siblings, brothers or sisters; morality rests on a foundation of equality; and justice, truth, fairness, and love are central moral precepts. The moral implications and consequences of that story are understood to be set forth, in principle and in some detail, in holy text, as elaborated in tradition.

By contrast, in its contemporary articulation, the human rights ideology, aiming at universality (and developed during years when half the political world was committed to atheism), has eschewed invoking any theistic authority.[1] It has avoided rooting itself in any story of human origins, or even in "natural" law or "natural" rights. The human rights ideology does not see human

146

rights as integral to a cosmic order. It does not derive from any sacred text. Its sources are human, deriving from contemporary human life in human society. Human rights is a political idea and ideology that claims to reflect a universal contemporary moral intuition. Human institutions have adopted the idea to serve the purposes of the good life within national political societies in an international political system — the cause of freedom, justice, peace.

The human rights idea and ideology begin with an *ur* value or principle (derived perhaps from Immanuel Kant), the principle of *human dignity.* Human rights discourse has rooted itself entirely in human dignity and finds its complete justification in that idea. The content of human rights is defined by what is required by human dignity — nothing less, perhaps nothing more. (Some advocates for human rights may derive their commitment to human dignity from religious ideas or assumptions — for example, from the creation of persons by God in the image of God — but the human rights idea itself does not posit any religious basis for human dignity.)

To be sure, religions also accept human dignity as a cardinal theme and motif. One finds hints of it in the principal Western religions.[2] But the contours of the religious morality developed around this concept are not congruent with the implications of human dignity as commonly conceived in the domain of human rights.[3] Brief consideration of particular contemporary interests and concerns may illuminate the differences:

Freedom of Religion and Religious Choice

The Human Rights code declares freedom of conscience and religious choice to be a human right. Religions, however, reject at least some religious choice: Religions reject atheism. In the past, religions condemned idolatry (and killed idolaters). Religions generally continue to condemn apostasy and resist the proselytizing of their constituents by other religions. Religious anti-Semitism (or anti-Semitism supported or tolerated by religions) has not been unknown.

Equality and Nondiscrimination

For the contemporary human rights ideology, human dignity requires equality and nondiscrimination, including nondiscrimination on grounds of religion or nonreligion. Religions, in contrast, have accepted — indeed mandated — distinctions on the basis of religion, permitting (requiring) distinctions between one religion and other religions, between the faithful and the infidel.

Gender Distinctions

The principal religions have established distinctions between the genders. Religions may insist that not only men but women also find their human dignity in such distinctions. For the human rights idea and its ideology, on the other hand, many gender distinctions are unacceptable relics of an earlier social context and are inconsistent with human dignity today.

Capital Punishment

The Bible prescribes principles and norms of justice — procedural justice, criminal justice, and distributive justice; but its criminal justice calls for capital punishment for many offenses. (In Judaism, later generations had to mitigate the rigors of capital punishment by setting up nearly insuperable procedural and evidentiary obstacles to convicting the accused.) The human rights ideology, though it has not wholly outlawed capital punishment, clearly aims at its abolition because it derogates from human dignity — the dignity of the person executed, as well as the dignity of the members of the society that executes. (It does not accept the argument that the human dignity of the victims of crime requires or justifies capital punishment.)

Historical-Political Tensions

Philosophical and theological differences aside, the relation of "the religious world" to the human rights idea has not been simple, has not been consistent, has not always been even comprehensible.

Some years ago, I characterized religion as an alternative ideology, indeed, as a competing ideology, and a source of resistance to the ideas of human rights.[4] Permit me to explain, with some impressionistic observations, as an observer, not an expert.

Religions — however defined or denoted — have not always welcomed the human rights idea, or recognized its kinship, or sought its cooperation. Religions are much older than the human rights idea and have seen no need for that idea. Religions laid claim to conceptions of the good, of the good society, long ago, without any idea of rights. The Bible — and the Qur'an, too, I think — knew not rights but duties. The Bible — to take the best-known example — mandates a duty upon me to love my neighbor; but it does not present my neighbor as having a right to be loved by me; he or she, one might say, is only a third-party beneficiary of my duty to God.

Religions have not been wholly comfortable with the idea of human rights. They do not welcome the ideological independence of human rights, its insistence on nontheistic supports for the idea, its resistance to the higher law of society and even to divine law. Religions have not had confidence in an ideology that does not claim divine origin or inspiration and has no essential place for the Deity. Spokesmen for religion have declared secular foundations for human rights to be weak, unstable, and doomed to fail and pass away. Some religions resist what they see as the concentration on, indeed the apotheosis of, the individual and the exaltation of individual autonomy and freedom. The emphasis of religion, of religions, was not upon the individual but upon the community — the People of Israel, Christendom, Islam, on the cosmic or the social order.

The human rights idea — for John Locke, for Thomas Jefferson — begins instead with liberty, an essential element in their political philosophy, with political society maintained by freedom of contract, and with social contract the basis for legitimate political authority. Religion, though recognizing freedom of will, makes no virtue of liberty, which it often equates with anarchy. The religious ideal has not been individual liberty, autonomy, but conformity to God's will and to divine law. The human rights idea today is part of an ideology of constitutionalism, which includes commitments to the rule of law, popular sovereignty, and representative democracy. Religions have not often been committed to democracy, or to universal suffrage, or to representative government. The authority of the majority is supported in the Bible, but not as a political ideology. Religion was for a long time closely identified with the divine right of kings, not with universal suffrage. In other times, religions have sometimes identified with totalitarian repressive regimes.

For the human rights movement, universal human rights cannot rest on theistic foundations. Such supports are not available, or acceptable, to those who cannot share theistic assumptions — as was, of course, the case for a good part of the world's population during the forty years of the Cold War. Theistic support for human rights is not a comfortable stance even for societies such as the United States, which are committed to separation of church and state, and where political actors avoid wearing their religion and their religious commitment on their political shields — even though their members are largely "religious." Theistic foundations for human rights are rejected also by those who, taking their own particular religion very seriously, are uncomfortable under the umbrella of generic *religion,* which also shelters many whose religions and religious views are anathema. Some religious people refuse to have their religion and its principles reduced — or distilled — or vaporized — into an abstraction that is perhaps dear to some academics but is devoid of content.

In the end, and at bottom, for the human rights movement insistence on the nontheistic foundations of the contemporary human rights idea reflects a quest for universal acceptance and universal commitment to a common moral intuition articulated in specific agreed-upon terms. The Universal Declaration is not anti-religious; it is not even nonreligious. It is — many believe — a magnificent articulation of our common morality, and an essential support for religion, for religions, for humankind, in the troubled, hopeful world at the new millennium.

Abiding Affinities

Today, religions are not unaware of the degree to which their interests are or could be advanced by the human rights idea, its bill of rights, its legal authority, its political consequence. In a real sense, all the rights recognized in the Universal Declaration are of deep religious interest and significance — rights that relate to the integrity of the person (as by freedom from torture), to a just criminal system, to protection of the family and of marriage, to freedom of expression and association, to education.

All religions are concerned for the rights of their constituents to enjoy all their human rights free from discrimination on the basis of religion; they are concerned also for the equal protection of the laws, for equal treatment for their constituents, and for freedom from discrimination in the protection of the laws. Some rights are specific to religions. Article 18 is of particular importance: "Everyone has the right to freedom of thought, conscience and religion; this right includes freedom to change his religion or belief, and freedom, either alone or in community with others and in public or private, to manifest his religion or belief in teaching, practice, worship and observance." Of course, all religions are concerned for the right to freedom of thought, conscience, and religion for their own constituents, but they cannot afford to care less for such rights for others.[5]

In the years ahead, religions are likely to be concerned for freedoms for minority religions, for rights to associate, to acquire property and to maintain it in the face of the state's power of eminent domain.

Yet despite these obvious points of convergence between religion and human rights, many have noted, and some have decried, the distance between the churches and other religious institutions, on the one hand, and the nongovernmental human rights universe, on the other. Few denominations have had human rights programs of general applicability. Minority churches — and in many countries (for example, the United States) every church is a minority — have been vigilant to protect their own freedoms, but they have been less alert to the rights of others. Where particular issues have inspired cooperation, cooperation has tended to be limited to the national scene, there being notably less concern for the freedoms (even the freedom of religion) of others in other countries. In the United States, *with exceptions,* religious bodies have concentrated on domestic constitutional issues, not on international human rights. Ecumenical action in support of human rights has not seemed to come naturally.

At one time, noninvolvement in international human rights may have been rooted in unfamiliarity, or in skepticism; at one time, it may have been dictated by overriding political considerations, as during the Cold War. Noninvolvement by religious bodies in international human rights may have been dictated in part by the need to make hard choices in the allocation of resources, material and spiritual. Perhaps reticence was induced by a concern for *correctness,* a desire not to intrude into what seemed to be primarily the affairs of other countries and other religions.

The attitudinal divide between religion and human rights has not been one-sided. The human rights community has not reached out to religions or sought their embrace. It has sought secular underpinnings or links for human dignity; it has seen no need for theistic roots or links for human dignity. The human rights idea has valued autonomy and individual freedom, sometimes above order and community. Political-social relations with religion have often been frosty. From the human rights perspective, religions have often achieved order at the cost of repression, of inequalities, of limitations on individual liberty and on individual development. The human rights movement has noted too many instances of religion linked to tyrannical caesars associated with repression and injustice, even with murder and genocide.

Recent Embrace

Recently, however, religions seem to have come to terms with human rights. In new and diverse political-societal contests, religious thought has had to address the idea of rights as part of a general development of a theory of God, the individual, and society. Religion generally — and every particular religion — has had to develop attitudes toward modern society and modern political authority, if only in self-defense. Some religions are the established religion in some states, allied with political authority, and they have had to define an ideological attitude toward the human rights claims of the country's inhabitants. Every religion is a minority religion in some states, and it has had to adapt to minority status. Every religion has had to respond to the needs of its members in large, impersonal, developed (or developing), urban, industrial societies.

Religions seem to have overcome (or suppressed) earlier discomfort with the human rights idea. As religions have defined themselves as nearly identical with morality, as ideological differences have thinned and narrowed, human rights have become religiously acceptable, even welcomed. As human rights have become the political idea and ideology of our times, religions have come to embrace it.

Indeed, some religions have begun to claim to be the source and the foundation, the progenitors, of the human rights idea, of the idea of human dignity that underlies it, of the commitment to justice that pervades it, of the bulk of its content. They have come to see human rights as natural rights rooted in natural law, natural law religiously inspired. The ancestors of the human rights idea, we are reminded, were religious Christians (Locke, Kant) — or at least deists (Jefferson).[6] Religions have begun to welcome, and claim, human dignity as a religious principle implicit in teachings concerning the *imago dei*, the fatherhood of God, the responsibility for the neighbor. They have claimed as their own the concept of justice and its specifics: criminal justice, procedural justice, distributive justice, justice as fairness; some religions include economic and social rights as religious obligations. The law of some religions has provided ingredients for particular human rights: for example, the right to privacy.

From our contemporary perspective, ideologically and usually in practice, religion in the past provided the good life and the good society for the believer, not for the infidel; for the resident, not the stranger; for men, not women; for masters, not slaves. Now, religions — at least some religions — increasingly recognize that the idea of human rights requires them to reexamine ancient practices that may, in fact, be less a matter of theological doctrine or other enduring values than relics of the arrangements and practices of societies long gone. It is not farfetched to suggest that in some cases religions are in the process of joining with the human rights movement to make religions — if you will — more religious and to assure that religions, polities, societies, and communities all respect and ensure our common morality.

I regret to have to say that the recent openness of religions to the discourse of human rights is hardly universal. Old patterns persist and are, in some places, even exaggerated. The end of the Cold War removed official atheism as a world force and formally "liberated" religion, religions, and churches in formerly repressive countries, but the news for human rights is not everywhere good. In different countries in different measure, churches have come into power, but liberation and political power have not invariably meant responsibility. These newly powerful churches exhibit no apparent interest in human rights generally. They rarely cooperate with human rights organizations in support of the human rights of their own country's population, not even in support of the specifically religious rights of other religious bodies and their adherents. They have shown little concern for human rights generally in other countries. In parts of the world, "fundamentalist" movements are manifestly intolerant of other denominations within their own religion, as well as of other religions, and, seizing or joining with political power, they are disposed toward oppression of human rights generally. In other places, religions have joined the banners of "cultural relativism," deviating from the mainstream of the international human rights movement and its accepted norms.

Even in the United States there continues to be no essential sustained cooperation between the world of religion and the human rights movement. Religious bodies have supported legislation and policies to bring pressure on foreign governments in support of freedom of religion, but some of these movements are limited to religions for which they have particular affinity; few of them exert the same influence against violations of other human rights. Human rights bodies still tend to see religions as sensitive and alert only to threats to their own denomination, their own believers and institutional arrangements — or, at most, to threats to the religious rights of others, but not to other rights, to freedom of expression, or to political dissidence. The human rights movement still tends to associate religion with fundamentalist intolerance, with indifference to individual autonomy and freedom, with the subordination of women. For its part, the human rights movement has sometimes neglected violations of the freedom of religion at home and abroad, perhaps assuming that the religious world is itself sufficiently alert and equipped to attend to those freedoms.[7]

Approchement in the Future

Despite abiding differences, convergence, *approchement* of religion and human rights, is not an idle dream but a justifiable hope. It will not include

153

theological-ideological homogenization. Human rights are not, and cannot be, grounded in religious conviction. Such a contention is factually and historically mistaken, and it is conceptually imperialistic. The human rights ideology is a fully secular and rational ideology whose very promise of success as a universal ideology depends on its secularity and rationality. No one can expect merger or full comfortable cooperation between religious and human rights organizations. Not so long ago, the Year of Human Rights — 1998 — found even Western religions to be still less than wholly comfortable with the human rights ideology and found the human rights movement reluctant to accept any religious commitment to human rights that insists that religion is indispensable to the idea.

Yet too much can be made of these differences. Whether speaking from the perspective of religions or of human rights, people often note their differences rather than their common ground. It is important, therefore, to recognize and to affirm that the two worlds have, on the whole, a common commitment to a moral code, even if not to its source.[8] There is a common commitment to an economic and social agenda, even if for religion it may entail not rights but charity (which, as I recall, is, for major religions, not an act of grace but a religious obligation). A common agenda for action is not yet on the horizon, though, and there is an urgent need for dedicated men and women in both camps to enlarge the "agenda-overlap" and to join forces in its pursuit. This will be possible, however, only if both communities can give up their claims to provide a total and exclusive ideology.

Human rights may have become the idea of our time in part because ours is the age of development, industrialization, urbanization, which in many parts of the world have helped undermine what religion and tradition long offered the individual, while these have appeared as obstacles to development in a hurry. In fact, however, the idea of rights is not, and does not claim to be, a complete, all-embracing ideology. It is not, in fact, in competition with other ideologies. Religion explains and comforts; tradition supports; development builds. The human rights idea does none of these. In today's world — and tomorrow's — there may be no less need for what religions and traditions have always promised and provided.

Representatives of religion have been right to reject any claims for human rights as a total ideology. Human rights — cold rights — do not provide warmth, belonging, fitting, significance, do not exclude the need for love, friendship, family, charity, sympathy, devotion, sanctity, or for expiation, atonement, forgiveness. But if human rights may not be sufficient, they are at least necessary. If they do not bring kindness to the familiar, they bring — as religions have often failed to do — respect for the stranger. Human rights are not a complete, alternative ideology, but are a *floor*, necessary to allow other values — including religions — to flourish. Human rights not only protect religions but have come to serve religious ethics in respects and contexts where religion itself has sometimes proved insufficient. Human rights are, at least, a supplemental "theology" for pluralistic, urban, secular societies. There, religions can accept if not adopt the human rights idea as an affirmation of their own values, and can devote themselves to the larger, deeper areas beyond the common denominator of human rights. Religions can provide, as the human rights idea does not adequately provide, for the tensions between rights and responsibilities, between individual and community, between the material and the spirit.

Although there is no agreement between the secular and the theological, or between traditional and modern perspectives on human beings and on the universe, there is now a working consensus that every man and woman, between birth and death, counts, and has a claim to an irreducible core of integrity and dignity. In that consensus, in the world we have and are shaping, the idea of human rights is an essential idea, and religions should support it fully, in every way, everywhere.

8 The Challenge of Religious Fundamentalism to the Liberty and Equality Rights of Women: An Analysis under the United Nations Charter

COURTNEY W. HOWLAND

I. Introduction

Religions have traditionally promoted, or even required, differentiated roles for women and men. It may well be argued that any separation of gender spheres is detrimental to women's equality. There is no need, however, to address this broad question in the context of religious fundamentalism, whose rise in all major religions has been accompanied by a vigorous promotion and enforcement of gender roles whose explicit intent entails the subordination and disempowerment of women.

Religious fundamentalism poses the most acute problems for women's equality, but many conservative religious groups share substantial areas of doctrine with the fundamentalists. The two groups are often differentiated solely by the political activism of fundamentalists rather than by significantly different religious beliefs. This political activism throws into sharp relief the conflicts between rights of religious freedom and women's rights of liberty and equality.

In Part II of this essay, I define "religious fundamentalism" and discuss the contemporary rise of religious fundamentalism in Buddhism, Christianity, Hinduism, Islam, and Judaism. A common goal of these movements is to pass state laws that reflect religious laws. There is a special concern with family laws and personal status laws, which have a particularly strong impact on women.

This essay was originally published as "The Challenge of Religious Fundamentalism to the Liberty and Equality Rights of Women: An Analysis under the United Nations Charter," 35 *Colum. J. Transnat'l Law* 271 (1997): 271-377. The author is especially grateful to Michael Singer, who read drafts of this essay. His extensive comments and invaluable insights are reflected at main points throughout the text. This slightly reedited version appears here by permission of the author and Columbia University.

In Part III, I focus on a particular doctrine of fundamentalists common to the five religions that well illustrates their goal of subordinating women: a wife is required to submit to the authority of her husband. This doctrine requires, either explicitly or implicitly, that a wife is to be obedient to her husband. The obedience rule legitimates the husband's discipline of his wife and thus makes women vulnerable to physical abuse. Fundamentalist modesty codes help to reinforce the oppressive aspect of the obedience law. Moreover, the obedience law, subordinating in and of itself, also serves as a basic norm justifying a variety of religion-specific discriminatory rules.

In Part IV, I analyze religious fundamentalist laws under the United Nations Charter ("Charter")[1] and the Universal Declaration of Human Rights ("Universal Declaration").[2] The Charter is the foundational treaty for international law and provides a paradigm for the analysis of the conflicts within international human rights laws raised by religious fundamentalist laws. I argue that the text of the Charter itself makes clear that the entitlement to human rights is not to be determined by any religious law and that race, sex, and religious discrimination must be treated equally. I further demonstrate that the international community has already resolved the conflict between racial discrimination and religious freedom under the Charter, and also under the Universal Declaration, and that the same standard must apply to the conflict between sex discrimination and religious freedom. In addition, I apply these arguments to a completely new area and argue that states violate the Charter by asserting religious fundamentalist doctrine as a basis for entering general reservations to provisions in human rights treaties that uphold women's rights. I conclude that a state that enacts into its legal system religious laws that subordinate women, or that creates under state law a zone of autonomy for religion to impose such religious laws upon women, is in violation of the Charter. I suggest how the international community should treat states in violation of the Charter.

II. Contemporary Religious Fundamentalism

The use of the term "fundamentalism" to describe a religious movement evokes high emotion.[3] Whatever the preferred term, however, the movement thus identified is an important reality recognized by women from many diverse backgrounds and religions throughout the world. The term "religious fundamentalism" is particularly meaningful for many religious women as representing a movement within religion that they understand to be oppressive of women.[4] Women have recognized the phenomenon and movement of fundamentalism and have formed groups around the world specifically to fight fundamentalism.[5] For example, Women Against Fundamentalism is a group composed of Catholics, Protestants, Hindus, Sikhs, Muslims, and Jews, all of various origins (Afro-Caribbean, English, Asian, Indian, Iranian, Irish, and others) whose activities are aimed at curbing fundamentalism across a wide range of religions and countries.[6]

Acting in a quite different context, academic scholars too have observed the modern phenomenon defined as religious fundamentalism. Some scholars have expressed concern or given apologias about defining the phenomenon of fundamentalism cross-culturally or using the term "fundamentalism" itself (instead preferring other terms[7]). Nonetheless, there has developed an extensive academic discipline that uses the term, even if uneasily, because these scholars have "felt the cumulative force of a series of 'family resemblances' as [they] move from one militantly antimodern religious group to another, tradition by tradition, and culture by culture."[8] These family resemblances have prompted scholars to endeavor to set out definitional criteria[9] and determine the various sociological causes and effects of the phenomenon.[10] These scholars come from a variety of religions, races, and nations[11] and work in various disciplines.[12]

Although these two groups (religious women engaged in political struggle and academic scholars) are not always explicit or precise in defining fundamentalism, my analysis of their work shows plainly that the two groups generally agree on the broad criteria that define a religious group as fundamentalist. These are that the group believes that the group and society need to be rescued from the secular state;[13] rejects Enlightenment norms, particularly individual rights and secularism;[14] is committed to the authority of ancient Scripture;[15] holds a total worldview such that religious beliefs are inseparable from politics, law, and culture;[16] relies on an idealized past;[17] is selective in drawing from the past for religious traditions and orthodox practice;[18] centers that idealized past in a patriarchal framework mandating separate gender spheres and a "pristine morality";[19] rejects outsiders and the concept of pluralism;[20] and is committed to activism and fighting for changed social, political, and legal order.[21]

Fundamentalism thus defined exists within many religions, ethnic groups, and countries, and takes different forms within these various contexts.[22] Nevertheless, these fundamentalist movements share in common the feature that they are effecting political, legal, and social changes that are highly detrimental to women's rights. For most academic writers, this is merely one aspect of the general political activism that characterizes the movement. However, women, and especially religious women, engaged in po-

litical struggle against the movement emphasize that the central aim of its social and political activism is to restrict women to a narrowly defined role and
exercise control over them within the patriarchal family structure.[23] They
also see fundamentalism's militant activism in changing social and legal
structures of society as inextricably linked with its appeal to selected traditional beliefs encompassing separate-spheres ideology for men and women.

It might be argued that a definition of fundamentalism that focuses on
the group's reliance on historical patriarchal doctrine fails to distinguish fundamentalism from "conservative" religion, and even from religion in general.
The major religions emerged and developed in patriarchally structured societies, and their texts and traditions are imbued with patriarchy and with
treating women unequally in various contexts.[24] Although this argument has
intuitive and logical appeal, it ignores the experience of many religious
women who have suffered under fundamentalism and fought to resist it. Fundamentalism is real and has meaning for numbers of religious women from
different religions and countries who experience it as a very real threat to
their freedom and often their lives. These women perceive themselves to be
religious despite their resistance to fundamentalist trends within their religion, and may perceive themselves to be feminists despite the intensity of
their religious belief.[25]

Scholars generally rely on the militant activism of fundamentalism to
distinguish it from "conservative" or "traditional" religion. Fundamentalists
fight in and against society for political, social, and legal changes, through the
legal and political system or by means of violence, whereas traditional conservative groups appear more passive in accepting the political and legal
structures of society.[26] Indeed, fundamentalists have often critiqued the traditional conservatives of their respective religions for not being sufficiently
involved in activist political ideology and militant action.[27] Nonetheless,
there will be groups that are difficult to characterize clearly as fundamentalist
or conservative.[28] To avoid this problem I discuss groups in each religion that
are generally agreed to be fundamentalist rather than merely conservative.
The fact that the groups are clearly fundamentalist does not prevent their legal doctrine overlapping with the doctrine of conservative groups, however.

Throughout this essay I discuss fundamentalist doctrine and the legal
and political acts that fundamentalists perform. I do not attempt to interpret
or rely on any of the primary religious texts, revelatory texts, or sacred myths
of the religions as religious theology.[29] Nonfundamentalist religious groups
may argue that fundamentalism misinterprets the religious texts or doctrines,
or even that it wrongly asserts nonreligious views as religious doctrine, but
these internal theological disputations are irrelevant to my analysis. The

point is that religious fundamentalists believe in and assert their interpretations as religious doctrine, and raise claims of religious freedom for their actions based upon these doctrines.

III. Religious Fundamentalist Laws
Requiring the Obedience of Women

In this Part, I focus on a particular religious fundamentalist legal norm that I call the obedience rule. This states that a wife is required to submit to the authority of her husband — to be obedient to her husband. In addition to being subordinating in and of itself, this rule serves as a basic general norm justifying a variety of religious rules that limit women's independence and autonomy, and ensure women's subordinate position to men.

I focus on this rule of obedience for two main reasons: first, the rule is such a gross manifestation of the subordination of women that there can be little good-faith argument that the rule promotes the equality of women; and second, the effect of the rule on women's lives is profound since it ramifies into laws regarding education and employment. Thus, the obedience rule serves as a clear example of a rule designed to maintain women in a subordinate position, and as such it brings the conflict between rights of religious freedom and women's rights of equality and liberty into sharp relief.

In Section A of this Part, I discuss in general the subordinating aspect of a relationship founded on obedience. Section B is divided into five sections discussing fundamentalism within five major religions: Buddhism, Christianity, Hinduism, Islam, and Judaism.

A. Women's Religious Duty of
Submission and Obedience to Men

In this section, I discuss the background to the obedience rule and explore how subordination inevitably follows from a relationship based on obedience. I also consider religious fundamentalists' rationalizations for such subordination.

Religious fundamentalist legal structures regard women's sexuality as potentially evil and destructive of men.[30] The legal structures of fundamentalist marriage and divorce and modesty codes[31] serve as enforcement mechanisms to maintain women's chastity and control their sexuality. The principle underlying these structures is that women are to be submissive to men in general, and in particular that a wife must submit and be obedient to her husband.

In a fundamentalist regime, girls first learn obedience to their fathers[32] and marriages may be arranged for them at a young age in order to protect their chastity.[33] The marriage ceremony or marriage contract gives the husband the right to his wife's submission and obedience.[34] Moreover, her obligation to submit and obey is also regarded as her own duty of religious practice and worship. If she disobeys her husband, she is thus guilty of a double violation: of her husband's right to her obedience and of her own religious duties.

The obedience rule means that a husband has the right of sexual access to his wife at any time, the final say in reproductive decisions, the right to forbid his wife to work, and the right to forbid his wife to continue her education. A wife's submission to her husband has no time limit, but continues through the rest of her life. Moreover, it is generally legitimate for men to enforce the obedience rule through physical punishment. As a result, women may be subject to beatings and physical violence for disobedience. The obedience rule places a crippling physical burden on women. Under religious fundamentalist doctrine there is general insistence on hierarchical relations between women and men, with men having a divine mandate to exercise authority over women with little restriction.

Fundamentalists do not deny that women have fewer rights than men under the obedience rule. Some argue that this structure is appropriate because women are inferior.[35] Others, often in response to international disapproval of a doctrine of inferiority of women and to claims of religious women that religious fundamentalism is not treating them equally, have argued that women and men are equal before the deity but have natural and different — rather than unequal — rights and duties under religious law.[36] According to this latter argument, the entire religious fundamentalist social structure justifies women having fewer rights in certain areas, including under the obedience rule. Thus, fundamentalists claim that a wife's duty of submission and obedience is an equal exchange for the duty of "protection" that her husband owes to her, in the form of an obligation to provide basic material and financial support: food, shelter, and clothing.[37] Wives are assigned the role of having children and caring for them in the private sphere of home, while the public sphere of employment and government belongs to men.

This "protection," however, does not alleviate the wife's subordination but rather enhances it by increasing her financial dependence on her husband, making her more vulnerable in the event of divorce or widowhood. This is particularly dangerous in this fundamentalist context, where it is generally much easier for a husband than a wife to obtain a divorce.[38] In addition, the wife may lose her right to maintenance during marriage or be divorced if she is disobedient or "rebellious."[39] Thus, if women do not obey their husbands' wishes, their very survival is in danger.[40] The wife is particularly vulnerable in the event of the husband's death, as she is unlikely to have accumulated any property during her child-bearing years because of her dependence upon her husband, and is also unlikely to have any training to be able to earn wages. Some fundamentalist structures will not permit her to work in any event. If she is lucky, she may become dependent upon a son or other male relative, to whom she now owes her duty of submission.

Fundamentalists' substantive arguments fail to provide a credible defense for the obedience rule, and fail to demonstrate that the obedience rule supports women's equality or is necessary for women's equality. It is thus difficult to credit these ad hoc different-but-equal arguments with good faith since they support the same hierarchy of relations between the sexes as is supported by traditional fundamentalist (and conservative) religious doctrines that, in turn, are explicitly based on the natural inferiority of women.[41]

B. Five Major Religions

The following five sections deal with the respective religious contexts of Buddhism, Christianity, Hinduism, Islam, and Judaism. In each section, the first part identifies the fundamentalist religious-legal doctrine concerning the obedience rule and the second part reviews the success of the political activity of fundamentalists in conforming the law in their respective states to their religious-legal doctrine.

1. Buddhism

Buddhist fundamentalism is found in several parts of the Buddhist world.[42] This section deals primarily with fundamentalist movements in Theravada Buddhism[43] in Sri Lanka[44] and Thailand,[45] and in the New Religions of Japan.[46]

a. The Religious-Legal Doctrine Various fundamentalist groups support notions of a traditional family and morality that, in turn, serve as the basis for separate roles and spheres of activities for women and men.[47] A central doctrine underlying separate-spheres ideology is that women are unable to control their dangerous sexuality, which is potentially destructive of men.[48] To deal with this problem, marriages are arranged for women at young ages before their chastity is in danger,[49] at which point they enter the realm of their husband's authority. According to traditional doctrine, embraced in Theravada movements, every woman must bear three kinds of subordination: "to her father when young, to her husband while married, and to her son when old."[50] In the New Religions of Japan, "women are urged to be meek and submissive and to build up the husband's ego by performing elaborate gestures of deference and respect, simultaneously indicating self-effacement and humility on their part."[51] Thus, being a good wife and mother is not only the proper role for women, but is imbued with religious significance.[52] The New Religions unabashedly assert men's superiority over women: "it's men who are superior, and the women who are behind all the trouble in the world."[53] Modesty codes also require that a woman have humility in all things, particularly in relation to men.[54]

The doctrine of a woman's submission and obedience to her husband goes beyond rhetoric; it is enforced by the threat and reality of sanctions. A woman who does not conform to this approved role may experience stigmatization and devaluation. Moreover, violence to enforce obedience to the husband is also a constant threat. In Thailand, for example, where many people consider that "a husband is entitled to 'discipline' his wife," battered women often believe that their situation is due to bad "karma," in accordance with the Buddhist belief that the accumulation of good or bad deeds in the past may influence one's present life.[55] Fundamentalists are also concerned that as a woman's economic independence increases, she will be less committed to the patriarchal family.[56] Consequently, they regard employment outside the home as interfering with her role as wife and mother. Thus, the requirement that wives submit to husbands has the additional impact of limiting a woman's earning possibilities.

b. Political Activity to Conform State Law to Religious-Legal Doctrine

A great deal of fundamentalist political activity is devoted to maintaining and enlarging the requirement of women's submission. A number of the Japanese New Religions are lobbying to bring back the *"ie"* model of patriarchal family life by reinstating the relevant parts of the prewar Meiji Civil Code.[57] The *ie* model of family consisted of the "househead, wife-of-househead, successor, successor's wife, and the unmarried children of the successor generation."[58] The eldest male was the head of the family, and normally he was succeeded by his eldest son. The househead had authority over all *ie* property.[59] Women could not own real property other than in very exceptional circumstances, and any other property a woman brought to the marriage belonged to her husband for him to dispose of without her consent.[60] Men could divorce women for, among other reasons, adultery or failure to produce a male child, and the divorced wife had no automatic entitlement to financial assistance.[61] Women could initiate divorce only under rare circumstances (not including adultery).[62] The husband obtained custody of children as members of his *ie*.[63] The Meiji Civil Code also strictly forbade contraception and education about contraception.[64] The repeal of the Meiji Civil Code brought many legal reforms for women in the areas of marriage, divorce, and property, and consequently increased their power in postwar Japan.[65] A number of the New Religions desire to reverse these reforms.[66]

2. Christianity

Fundamentalisms in Christianity exist in traditional branches such as the Roman Catholic Church (RCC), the Orthodox Church, and Protestantism, and have also developed in other Christian sects or offshoots.[67] The vast array of Christian fundamentalist groups is spread over strikingly diverse geographic locations: from the United States to Latin and Central America, and from Britain to India.[68] I draw examples from this wide range of Christian fundamentalist groups with particular emphasis on fundamentalist groups within American Protestantism[69] such as sect fundamentalists[70] and Reconstructionists,[71] and from fundamentalist groups within the RCC.[72] The RCC groups rely heavily on traditional conservative doctrine, with some groups fully endorsing RCC interpretations of doctrine.[73]

a. The Religious-Legal Doctrine Many of these various Christian fundamentalist groups perceive Western culture to be in a desperate state as a result of the decline of what they perceive to be the basic unit of society, the "traditional family."[74] They regard women's sexuality as potentially dangerous and destructive of men.[75] Fundamentalists look back with nostalgia to the nineteenth-century construct of a middle-class family[76] or even to a seventeenth-century construct.[77] Fundamentalists define "traditional" family to mean a legally married man and woman with children, where the man is the head of the family and preferably is the sole financial supporter of the group.[78] They strongly support a separate spheres gender ideology,[79] which they base on a religious requirement that women be submissive and subordinate to men. Some read the Scriptures as calling for the headship of man and the subordination of woman.[80] Others, steeped in the belief that the Bible is infallible and that it condones women's subordination, come to view the hierarchy of men over women as somehow "natural."[81] All agree that a girl grows up subject to the authority of her father, who then delivers her in marriage to her husband's authority.[82] The father, as leader of the family,[83] exercises discipline with absolute authority over his wife and children.[84] He is the chief, if not sole, breadwinner and the protector of and provider for his wife and family.[85] In return, the wife is to submit to her husband and serve the needs of her husband and children.[86] She is also subject to a modesty code in matters of behavior and dress.[87]

Fundamentalist Protestants' model for marriage is thus based on an exchange of protection for obedience and submission. A wife who does not obey is termed "rebellious," and she is admonished to treat her husband as a "high priest and prophet of God."[88] This is particularly oppressive since modern studies show a high incidence of spousal abuse in fundamentalist Christian homes.[89] "Where wives are taught to submit blindly to their husbands' every word and deed, . . such teachings provide a good covering for abuse under the guise of bringing one's wife 'into subjection.' Thus the batterer does not consider his actions abusive; he is simply fulfilling his God-given responsibilities."[90] Many women whose husbands enforce obedience through physical violence are counseled by Christian religious advisors to stay in these battering relationships, and convinced that they themselves are in the wrong.[91]

The requirement of submission and obedience detracts from the possibility of a woman achieving any economic independence or autonomy, since her husband may exercise his authority by limiting or forbidding her from working outside the home. Fundamentalists regard a woman's economic independence as undesirable since it will reduce her commitment to patriarchy.[92]

b. Political Activity to Conform State Law to Religious-Legal Doctrine

Christian fundamentalists are increasingly active in the political arena to enact their vision of Christian society into law.[93] For example, in the United States, they hope to pose a direct threat to the secular state and to establish the United States as a Christian country.[94] Not surprisingly, their particular goal is to establish the legal structure of the patriarchal family and women's subordinate role in it. Thus, Christian fundamentalists strongly opposed the Equal Rights Amendment to the U.S. Constitution[95] as preventing women from serving their proper submissive role as wives and mothers,[96] and are credited with its defeat.[97] They have also worked to prevent passage of statutes or to repeal already enacted statutes that protect abused children and abused wives because the statutes interfere with the husband's disciplinary rights to enforce obedience.[98]

Catholic fundamentalist groups have also politically supported "traditional" family laws and opposed laws that did not fit the patriarchal family model.[99] The RCC itself is always heavily involved in political activity, including the political lobbying of individual states.[100] A recent Vatican success was lobbying China to ban reformist Catholic groups from the 1995 United Nations Conference on Women's Rights in Beijing.[101] Thus, these groups, which have long fought for women's equality, were excluded from the debate on formulating international legal policy on women's equality, whereas the Vatican, which has historically and consistently opposed women's equality, even including women's fight for suffrage, participated in the debate.[102]

3. Hinduism

There are several Hindu fundamentalist movements, with the main movements located in India and focused on making India a Hindu state.[103] The most important is Rashtriya Swayamsevak Sangh (RSS),[104] a combined religious and cultural organization whose political manifestation is the Bharatiya Janata Party (BJP) (The Indian People's Party)[105] and whose affiliate Vishva Hindu Parishad (VHP) (World Hindu Society) is responsible for promoting religious and cultural aspects of Hindu fundamentalism.[106]

a. The Religious-Legal Doctrine The RSS-VHP-BJP ideology embraces selected traditional and conservative practices of Hinduism that correspond to its view of an idealized past, particularly the glory of India and the glorification of male warriors.[107] Its rhetoric centers on certain mythological epics of Hinduism that it seeks to make relevant to contemporary times.[108] It vigorously promotes the epic *Ramayana* as grounded in historical fact, representative of Hindu truths, and providing a moral foundation for contemporary India.[109] The epic is the story of Lord Rama, the human incarnation of the god Vishnu, and his wife, Sita.[110] Sita sacrifices her life to prove her chastity to her doubting husband and thereby uphold his honor.[111] Throughout Hindu fundamentalism in India, Rama is considered admirable and represents the ideal Hindu man, a warrior, while Sita is considered to be the ideal wife, chaste, obedient, and self-sacrificing.[112] These role models reinforce strong gender ideologies that require separate and distinct roles for each sex.[113]

Hindu fundamentalism reaffirms these divine role models in another epic myth that constitutes important rhetoric for the movement: the story of the god Siva and his consort, the goddess Sati, whose name means chastity or virginity.[114] Like Sita, Sati sacrifices herself to save the honor of her husband.[115] Along with Sita, Sati represents the Hindu ideal woman,[116] whose devotion to her husband constitutes "the fire of her inner truth *(sat)* . . . [that] bursts forth in flames" and consumes her.[117] *Sati* is thus the name given to a woman who is burned to death on her husband's funeral pyre, with this ultimate sacrifice for her husband's honor representing the ideal of virtuous and honorable womanhood.[118] The RSS holds strongly to the view that women are best able to serve the Hindu nation by following this deepest tradition of the role of women in Hindu society as manifested by Sita and Sati.[119]

Thus, the primary religious role for Hindu women as promoted by the RSS family of organizations is to be a devoted wife and mother.[120] Hinduism, however, views women as possessed of a dangerous sexuality that constantly threatens to destroy their virtue, and that they cannot themselves control.[121] Consequently, women must be subject to external controls to maintain their virtue.[122] The girl or young woman is first controlled by her father or male guardian.[123] If, despite this control, she loses, or is perceived to have lost, her virtue, she disgraces her family and her male relatives are therefore "obliged to execute her."[124]

The woman's marriage reduces her potential to disgrace her family.[125] Consequently, a family is always anxious to marry off daughters, and will pay for the privilege in the form of dowry.[126] Dowry as practiced in Hinduism reinforces the view of women as objects that men control and dispose of like chattels,[127] and this is sufficient reason to justify the Indian government's prohibition of dowry.[128]

Marriage transfers the woman from the control of her father to the control of her husband. "After her marriage, her husband is for her in the position of god. . . . The husband of a married woman is her 'lord' and master. . . ."[129] The highest religious duty of a woman is to be "devotional and conjugal" to this her personal god.[130] This role requires her absolute obedience,[131] and indeed the RSS describes the duty of absolute obedience that RSS members owe to the leader as that found in an "ideal Hindu family."[132]

Hindu fundamentalists prescribe or legitimate a number of social mechanisms for ensuring the wife's obedience and maintaining the husband's control. The religious modesty laws of *purdah* require a woman to stay indoors and segregated from men, effectively keeping women isolated and submissive.[133]

It is also accepted practice that the husband may enforce his wife's duty of obedience by beatings and other violence.[134] Since he is the sole judge of whether she is obedient, this further condones his being violent if she displeases him in any way. His displeasure commonly finds expression in complaints of inadequate dowry that escalate into beatings, torture, and murder. Such murders are known as "dowry deaths" or "bride-burnings" and, despite their illegality, they occur frequently and regularly in Hindu society in India, and are on the increase.[135] Most dowry deaths take the form of the husband setting the wife on fire and then claiming that the burning was a kitchen acci-dent or that the wife committed suicide in a good derivation of the *sati* tradi-tion.[136] As a result, the police often classify dowry deaths as accidents or sui-cides, and consequently there are few prosecutions.[137] Some wives, in the Sita and Sati tradition, do commit suicide, often as a result of great harassment, beatings, and torture from their husbands.[138]

The greatest and most spectacular demonstration of loyalty, obedience, and submission is made by the wife who becomes a *sati* for her husband's benefit.[139] The religious practice of becoming a *sati* was outlawed by the Brit-ish in 1829 and has remained illegal, although it has continued to occur.[140] It was not until Roop Kanwar became a *sati* in 1987, however, that the religious practice created a furor in India.[141] The eighteen-year-old Roop Kanwar had been married eight months to a twenty-four-year-old man when he died.[142] Some eyewitnesses said that she mounted his funeral pyre voluntarily, whereas others claimed that she was drugged by her in-laws, tried neverthe-less to escape, but was pushed back onto the pyre to burn.[143]

This *sati* prompted Hindu fundamentalists, including the Hindu reli-gious political parties such as the BJP, to rally to support the institution and practice of becoming a *sati*, particularly against government law.[144] All the major actors in this movement were men: men served in the religious roles of the *sati sthal*, men ran the committee for defending the *sati*, men organized the rallies to support the *sati*, men gave the speeches to support the *sati*, and men have been combing the religious and historical texts to justify the *sati*.[145] These fundamentalist men ignored the fact that not every *sati* acts volun-tarily, however; many are pushed onto the pyre.[146] Even without immediate physical coercion, a widow in Indian Hindu society is regarded as so inauspi-cious and burdensome and faces such a bleak prospect that she may well yield to social pressure to become a *sati* as the path of least resistance.[147]

In 1974 the Indian government Committee on the Status of Women is-sued a report, *Towards Equality,* which concluded that Hinduism was one of the critical determinants in women's inferior status in India.[148] The report observed that a woman in orthodox Hinduism "is called fickle-minded, sen-sual, seducer of men; given to falsehood, trickery, folly, greed, impurity and thoughtless action; root of all evil; inconsistent and cruel. . . . In childhood a woman must be subject to her father, in youth to her husband, and when her lord is dead to her sons. A woman must never be independent."[149] But despite legal reforms in the last twenty years since *Towards Equality,* the rise of Hindu fundamentalism has brought an increase in dowry deaths, an increased ac-ceptance of *purdah* and *sati,* and an increase in the general dependency of women.[150]

b. Political Activity to Conform State Law to Religious-Legal Doctrine
The RSS-VHP-BJP family, flush with power from its 1996 electoral gains, continues its intense political activity pushing for legal reforms that correspond to its notion of a Hindu state. In furtherance of this goal, Hindu fundamentalists call for repeal of the Hindu Marriage Act of 1955 and the Hindu Succession Act of 1956[151] that reformed Hindu religious practices by giving women more rights in marriage, banning polygamy, allowing for widow remarriage, giving women statutory bases for divorce, and giving women some rights in inheritance where they formerly had none.[152] Their nationalist aim for a Hindu state is enhanced by cutting back on women's rights, as was already clear at the time of the passage of the Hindu Marriage Act and Hindu Succession Act when fundamentalist opponents of the bills called them "anti-Hindu and anti-Indian" and declared that they would put "religion in danger."[153]

4. Islam

In Islam, fundamentalist groups are found among both the Sunni and the Shi'ite Muslims in a broad range of geographic locations. I draw examples from a wide variety of groups with particular emphasis on three representative groups: the Muslim Brotherhood;[154] the Jama'at-i-Islami;[155] and the Ayatollah Khomeini's Islamic movement in Iran and its related groups.[156] Despite great diversity within Muslim fundamentalism and with regard to the interpretation of orthodox practices, the movements are strikingly similar in certain doctrines and goals.[157]

a. The Religious-Legal Doctrine   A central doctrine throughout Muslim fundamentalism is that women harbor the seeds of destruction of all society and that to avoid this they and their sexuality must be carefully controlled.[158] Fundamentalists blame women's uncontrolled sexuality for the modern Western sensate culture, represented by selfishness, greed, and immorality.[159] Unless women adhere strongly to their "natural" role as childbearers they will become unchaste and immoral and bring down the rest of society.[160] To avoid these consequences, Muslim fundamentalists support traditional notions of morality with emphasis on separate gender spheres.[161] Their separate-spheres ideology requires segregation of the sexes so that women's alluring sexuality does not morally undermine men. Under this ideology, the place for the woman is confined at home caring for her family, of which the man is indisputably head.[162] A man must be head of the family in order to maintain control over the dangerous sexuality of the women in the family, and because women are considered unsuited to any role of authority by virtue of their submissive nature and periodic instability.[163]

Indeed, a number of Islamic fundamentalists explicitly declare men to be superior to women,[164] which places men in control of women and requires that women be obedient to men.[165] The requirement of obedience to the male head of household extends through every woman's entire life,[166] but is particularly compelling for a married woman in respect of her husband.[167] Obedience requires submission to her husband in all things, including sexual and social matters.[168] Furthermore, fundamentalist doctrine allows men to enforce this duty of obedience through violence. If a wife is disobedient, a proper husband is first to "appeal to her good sense, and if she does not improve, then he may abandon her in her marital bed. Thereafter, it is permissible for him to give her a good, but gentle, beating."[169]

Muslim fundamentalists also utilize the modesty doctrine of *hejab* for ensuring the wife's obedience and reinforcing the husband's control, particularly his economic control. *Hejab* (as interpreted by fundamentalists) requires segregation of women and men and dictates that women are not to leave their houses unless absolutely necessary, and if they do go out, they should be fully covered, often including veiling the face.[170] *Hejab* sets up barriers against a woman working outside the home, and makes it very difficult for her to achieve economic independence. This accords with fundamentalist doctrine disallowing a woman to earn money like a man[171] and forbidding her to work without her husband's permission.[172] Fundamentalists disfavor any economic independence for a woman because it would "ma[k]e her free of the authority of the father and husband."[173] A woman's inheritance rights are also very limited.[174] A woman who nevertheless succeeds in living outside male control is regarded as a threat to the good morality of society, and as such is in constant mortal danger.[175]

b. Political Activity to Conform State Law to Religious-Legal Doctrine

Fundamentalist political activity has pressed for enactment of family and personal status laws as part of state legal systems, and this has succeeded in a number of states.[176] In most cases, fundamentalists owe this success not to any vote of confidence in their viewpoint but rather to their use of violence to intimidate people into silent compliance with their actions, which is especially effective where the populace is already intimidated by corrupt, oppressive, and undemocratic government.[177]

Fundamentalist success is reflected in the enactment of state laws requiring the obedience of women: marriage and divorce laws, and *hejab*.[178] The marriage laws of various Islamic states provide that marriage transfers a woman from the control of her father to the protection and control of her husband.[179] As a wife, her duty of obedience to her husband may be statutorily explicit[180] or implicit through the concept of *nashiz*. A *nashiz* is a disobedient or rebellious wife,[181] and this may include a woman who acts superior to her husband, disobeys his orders, leaves her marital home without legitimate reason or her husband's permission, works outside the home without his permission, or uses contraception without permission.[182] For example, Shi'ite Muslim fundamentalists specifically define a *nashiz* to include a wife who denies her husband his conjugal rights, even temporarily, and a wife who borrows money without the permission of a judge or of her husband.[183]

A *nashiz* loses her right to protection under the marriage contract for as long as she is disobedient.[184] This protection is the right to maintenance — food, clothing, and housing — as long as "she places or offers to place herself in the husband's power so as to allow him free access to herself at all lawful times . . . and . . . obeys all his lawful commands for the duration of the marriage."[185] This is a serious threat to a woman who is made financially dependent on the husband and may not work without his permission.[186] Moreover, a husband may obtain an obedience order from a court against his wife, and "if she still persists, he is entitled to divorce her and, because she has violated his rights, he is under no obligation whatsoever to provide maintenance for her."[187]

The ultimate act of disobedience by a wife is adultery.[188] In 1990 Iraq decreed that according to its fundamentalist ideology, men were allowed to kill their womenfolk for adultery.[189] Since the killing is based on the husband's (not a court's) assessment of the situation, it may easily occur if the adultery is merely feared or suspected rather than real. Kurdistan has recently passed a law absolving a man for murder of his wife if he can prove she was morally disobedient.[190]

A further threat is that a man may divorce his wife at will or whim.[191] After a divorce an ex-wife is entitled to maintenance in some circumstances during the three-month period of *iddat,* which is intended to determine whether she is pregnant.[192] After this she is not entitled to maintenance regardless of the number of years of marriage and her financial dependence on her husband. The fear of unilateral divorce and no financial support strongly encourages obedience. It is also important to note that during the period of *iddat* the husband may unilaterally revoke the divorce,[193] and is thereupon entitled to "resume the conjugal relationship with the wife without her consent."[194]

Finally, fundamentalists have succeeded in enforcing their interpretation of *hejab* by public laws specifically requiring the dress of *hejab*. In Sudan the fundamentalist military regime has required that "women should dress in loose long dresses and cover their heads,"[195] and when their dress is inappropriate they are now subject to amputation of hands and feet, hanging, stoning to death, or hanging followed by crucifixion of the body.[196] Khomeini's Islamic regime quickly passed a law making it mandatory for women to wear the "Islamic veil" in public.[197] Violation brings a woman seventy-four lashes and internment for rehabilitation, with her family being compelled to pay her internment expenses.[198] In Iran, police may now beat women on the streets and otherwise harass them if they are not veiled,[199] and women have been tried and even executed for failure to observe *hejab.*[200] *Hejab* also serves to justify other limitations on women. For example, in Iran and Saudi Arabia, women are not allowed to drive; in Kuwait, women do not have the right to vote; and in Algeria, fundamentalist law has now delegated women's right to vote to men.[201]

This treatment of women under state laws is designed to make them submissive and obedient. The violence inflicted by husbands, religious men in the streets, and Shariʿate jurists is designed to keep women in their subordinate place, obedient and dependent. Indeed, the success of Islamization throughout the Muslim world has primarily been measured in terms of either the repeal of laws that granted women more rights or the codification of the fundamentalist interpretation of Shariʿah personal status and family laws that support the institution of the patriarchal family.[202]

5. Judaism

I draw examples of Jewish fundamentalism from a wide variety of groups, with particular emphasis on groups known as *haredim* (Ultra-Orthodox Jews),[203] who are primarily anti-Zionist,[204] and the Zionist group Gush Emunim (GE).[205] Each group follows its own interpretation of Jewish religious laws *(halakhah),* but their interpretations are quite similar in certain doctrines as a result of their sharing many Ultra-Orthodox norms.

a. The Religious-Legal Doctrine   Jewish fundamentalists reject modernity, which for them means decadent contemporary Western culture.[206] They see the sexual licentiousness of modernity as a consequence of women straying from their proper role as wife and mother, and their ideology strongly endorses separate gender spheres and segregation of the sexes.[207] All of the groups require a degree of submissiveness and obedience of women to men, most particularly in marriage.[208]

Although fundamentalist Judaism does not explicitly declare that a wife must be submissive and obedient to her husband, the overall structure of marriage and divorce laws delegates such a degree of authority and power to the husband as to allow him effectively to coerce his wife's obedience.[209] The assumption is "that authority over her was transferred from her father to her husband."[210] Fundamentalist norms of marriage oblige the husband to provide for the wife's basic physical needs, and normally impose on him a financial obligation in the event of divorce.[211] In return, the wife is obliged to care for the home and children.[212] In this context, the husband's coercive power is established by three fundamentalist *halakhah* norms: first, during the life of the marriage, the husband has rights to his wife's earnings, the produce of all property she owned prior to the marriage, and inheritance of her property upon her death;[213] second, the husband retains the exclusive power of divorce;[214] and third, the husband may obtain a divorce on the ground of the wife being "rebellious."[215]

Under fundamentalist law, no divorce may take place unless the husband consents and gives his wife a divorce writ *(get)*.[216] Until he does so the marriage continues in existence and he continues to exercise control over her earnings and income from her property. Thus, she remains economically dependent on the marriage and without financial resources to leave. His price for agreeing to end the marriage may be a beneficial financial settlement.[217] The husband's unilateral power with respect to divorce is further enhanced by the concept of the rebellious wife *(moredet)*, which may serve him as a ground for divorce.[218] If a wife refuses sexual relations or fails to do housework without valid reason, her husband may deem her rebellious and divorce her, whereupon she forfeits her divorce settlement.[219] In Israel, there have been cases of women being declared "rebellious" for refusing to sew buttons on their husband's shirts or to perform other domestic chores, and in consequence being denied maintenance in the divorce.[220]

By vesting these powers in the husband, fundamentalist Judaism gives him coercive force to ensure that his wife is submissive and obedient and behaves as he wishes. Jewish fundamentalists, however, are not clear as to whether a husband may beat his wife. Some rabbis interpret the *halakhah* as giving the wife grounds for divorce if she is beaten, although of course the divorce still requires her husband's consent.[221] Under other interpretations of the *halakhah* a wife who leaves her husband because of a beating may be termed rebellious and thereby made to forfeit the divorce settlement.[222] In any event, physical abuse of the wife in fundamentalist families, by her sons as well as her husband, is a serious problem.[223]

The *halakhah* norms of modesty reinforce a woman's dependency on men, particularly her husband. The purpose of the modesty laws is to guard women's chastity and to prevent women from "tempting" men into adultery.[224] The modesty laws require segregation of the sexes in all public areas: at the synagogue, at school, in government, and in entertainment.[225] The rules restrict women's dress, movement, employment, and independence.[226] Modesty laws also require women to be generally quiet because a woman's voice is regarded as seductive.[227] They further require that a woman should stay in her home if possible, and in any event within the confines of her fundamentalist community.[228] Some sects do not allow women to drive.[229]

The modesty laws operate as gatekeepers. By confining women to their homes, performing housework and childcare, these laws generally aid in legitimating women's submission to the authority of their husbands. By confining women to their community, these laws ensure that women do not hear new ideas that might allow them to reevaluate their subordinate position. By preventing women from working outside the house, these laws ensure women's economic dependency.[230] In sum, under fundamentalist legal structures, the modesty, marriage, and divorce laws ensure women's obedience to their husbands and confine them to the role of wife and mother.

b. Political Activity to Conform State Law to Religious-Legal Doctrine

Jewish fundamentalists are politically active in Israel. Many a fundamentalist group has its own political party, while other fundamentalist groups join together for political representation.[231] The resulting small parties wield great influence in Israel because neither of the two major political parties is generally able to form a government without forming an alliance with these religious parties.[232] As a result, these religious parties have a history of being able to extract concessions and financial benefits from the Israeli government. Some fundamentalist political effort is directed at maintaining and extending the force of their doctrine within their own communities.[233] Other political efforts are aimed at replacing the secular state with a religious state that acknowledges the *halakhah* as its exclusive law.[234] For example, GE has a "Proposed Torah Constitution for the State of Israel" and seeks to "institute the ancient system of law and justice" of the *halakhah*.[235]

Fundamentalists have succeeded in making *halakhah* norms part of state law in several crucial areas. The religious courts have exclusive jurisdiction in marriage, divorce, and ancillary matters,[236] and concurrent jurisdiction (with consent of the parties) in personal status and property disputes between spouses.[237] Other religious norms have been enacted as Israeli law.[238] Moreover, fundamentalists fight to broaden Rabbinate jurisdiction in general,[239] and specifically to empower the religious courts to nullify marriage or divorce proceedings outside Israel.[240] The fundamentalist focus on marriage and divorce and modesty laws is of particular concern to women because of the disproportionately negative impact that these laws have on women. Jewish fundamentalists are engaged in political activity aimed to ensure that the laws of the state implement their vision of woman's proper role as wife and mother, and to make sure that women occupy no legitimate place in the public life of the polity.[241]

IV. The International Legal Framework

In Part III, I demonstrated that religious fundamentalist laws systematically treat women differently from men. The marriage and divorce laws and modesty codes require women to submit to the authority of their husbands and obey them, resulting in a great disparity of power between men and women. This disparity subjects women to physical abuse and economic dependence, and limits their educational and employment opportunities. Fundamentalists are trying to make these religious laws part of state legal systems and have already succeeded in a number of instances. Such laws discriminate on their face and deny women the rights to equality and liberty provided under international human rights treaties. These religious fundamentalist laws, however, may themselves claim protection under these same human rights instruments as manifestations of religious belief. Thus, religious fundamentalism presents clearly an acute conflict between international human rights that promote equality and liberty for women and human rights that promote the freedom of religion or belief.[242]

In this Part, I analyze religious fundamentalist laws under the United Nations Charter and the Universal Declaration.[243] The Charter is the foundational treaty of contemporary international law and prevails over all other international obligations.[244] It provides the overall legal framework for relations between states and constitutes the primary source for legal guidance with respect to the challenge posed by religious fundamentalism to women's rights. The Universal Declaration, as an authoritative interpretation of the human rights guaranteed in the Charter, provides further guidance. I thus work out a resolution to the challenge posed by religious fundamentalism as provided by the Charter and the Universal Declaration.

As with any international treaty, analysis must be based squarely on the text.[245] Where the text provides standards and guidance for resolving conflicts, it is inappropriate to resort prematurely to a balancing approach.[246] This is especially true with regard to the Charter and the major human rights instruments, where the parties have already identified and negotiated which factors are important, and agreed to a final text which reflects the balance acceptable to all parties. Focusing on the text is particularly important in areas of cultural sensitivity, where the parties have compromised in a specific way in order to resolve potential conflicts. Given the diversity of cultures of the state parties to the Charter, cultural sensitivity requires an acknowledgment that the agreed language in the documents already represents the balance that states desired to strike among themselves to harmonize their potentially conflicting cultures and religions.

Analysis under the Charter requires an evaluation of the substantive content of human rights covered by the Charter, which itself offers guidance as to how its broad language may be given more specific content. The Universal Declaration also provides an interpretive framework for discerning the substantive content of the human rights implicated under the Charter. Analysis of the Universal Declaration raises further issues such as the extent to which it is a legal obligation at all, what substantive rights it protects, and which states are bound by this determination.

In Section A, I discuss the human rights standards under the Charter and the Universal Declaration. In Section B, I evaluate religious fundamentalist laws under these instruments. In Section C, I address state accountability in order to ascertain whether religious laws or the activities of nonstate religious actors may be attributed to the state. In Section D, I argue that reservations made to human rights treaties on the basis of religious fundamentalist principles are themselves violations of the Charter. Finally, in Section E, I suggest the appropriate consequences for states in violation of the Charter.

A. The United Nations Charter and the Universal Declaration

Almost all states are members of the United Nations and are thus bound by the minimum standards set by the Charter.[247] The promotion of women's liberty and equality appears in the preamble of the Charter, alongside the promotion of peace, security, and tolerance among nations.[248] The preamble makes no reference to religion. Rather, the underlying premise is that the dignity of each human being and equal rights among humans (and specifically between men and women) are of paramount importance.

The Charter affirms the broader purposes of the United Nations in article 1(3), including "promoting and encouraging respect for human rights and for fundamental freedoms for all without distinction as to race, sex, language, or religion. . . ."[249] Furthermore, in article 56, all members "pledge themselves to take joint and separate action in cooperation with the Organization for the achievement of the purposes set forth in article 55,"[250] specifically, the promotion of "universal respect for, and observance of, human rights and fundamental freedoms for all without distinction as to race, sex, language, or religion" as guaranteed by article 55(c).[251]

1. Implications of the Language of the Charter

This language of articles 55(c) and 56 carries several important implications. First, under article 56 member states have a twofold legal duty with respect to article 55(c).[252] The article 56 pledge constitutes an affirmative obligation to cooperate with the work of the United Nations in observing and promoting human rights.[253] Moreover, "an undertaking to cooperate in the promotion of human rights certainly does not leave a State free to suppress or even to remain indifferent to those rights."[254] Member states must not put themselves in the position of being incapable of cooperating as this would undermine the object and purpose of the Charter.[255] The language of these articles is at once binding and aspirational, and both qualities demand that member states take no action to prevent or undermine the development and understanding of human rights in accordance with the Charter. This twofold duty — the duty of cooperation and the obligation not to undermine — exists for each UN member state, regardless of whether it is a party to any other human rights treaty.

I would also argue that the duty of each state to cooperate and not to undermine now extends to a direct obligation of the state to promote and observe human rights, including those that relate to the state's internal affairs. The United Nations has already acted extensively in the area of human rights by setting standards for promotion and observance of human rights and by establishing goals for the achievement of respect for human rights. This activity is of such breadth and depth that the affirmative obligations of states to cooperate and not to undermine may only be understood to mean that states have an individual affirmative duty to promote and observe human rights. Thus, the nature of a member state's affirmative obligation, as delineated under article 55(c), is to observe the rules of human rights and fundamental freedoms and to promote their observance.[256]

Second, the language of the Charter makes clear that human rights under the Charter are not dependent upon religion, nor is any particular religion their source.[257] The Charter contains provisions in favor of religion, but these are simply one manifestation of the principle of nondistinction.[258] The Charter establishes the principle of nondistinction by explicitly listing those characteristics of human beings that may not be used as a basis for denying human rights and fundamental freedoms. These characteristics — race, sex, language, and religion — are listed as separate and independent characteristics. Religion is not privileged in protection over any other characteristic, and moreover, the prohibition of distinction based on religion means that no religion is privileged over any other religion. By direct implication, the language of the nondistinction provision establishes that the entitlement to human rights and fundamental freedoms under the Charter is not to be determined or evaluated by any religious law.[259]

A third important implication of this Charter language is that it recognizes and anticipates the potential for denying human rights and fundamental freedoms on the basis of the specified characteristics. Moreover, it is clear that groups of the very types that article 55 protects may be the source of unlawful distinctions against other such groups. For example, the prohibited distinctions made on the basis of race will generally be made by another race, and the prohibited distinctions on the basis of religion will generally be those made by a different religion. The Charter language presupposes that restrictions may need to be imposed on the very groups that article 55 protects. Therefore, with the protections of human rights and fundamental freedoms based on a particular group identity come corollary duties of these same groups to respect the liberty and the equal protections afforded to the other protected groups.

Fourth, the Charter's command that human rights and fundamental freedoms are to be enjoyed "without distinction"[260] sets a minimum standard of conduct required of all members. Thus, the International Court of Justice (ICJ) has held that "without distinction" certainly prohibited South Africa's establishing and enforcing "distinctions, exclusions, restrictions and limitations exclusively based on grounds of race . . . which constitute a denial of fundamental human rights . . . a flagrant violation of the purposes and principles of the Charter."[261] Thus, provisions that on their face either impose unequal burdens or grant unequal favors are obvious barriers to equal enjoyment of human rights and fundamental freedoms.

Fifth, the "without distinction" language establishes the principle that the distinctions are themselves of equal importance. There is no notion of any hierarchy among these distinctions that might privilege one prohibited distinction over another. The explicit language of article 55 does not differentiate between distinctions on the basis of race, distinctions on the basis of sex, and distinctions on the basis of religion. Thus, not only are these distinctions equally prohibited, but the standard for evaluating whether there is a violation of the "without distinction" language must be the same.

Sixth, in addition to the right to be free from illegal distinctions, the Charter protects substantive "human rights and fundamental freedoms."[262]

Scholars differ as to the meaning of "human rights and fundamental freedoms."[263] Nonetheless, merely because the international community is unable to agree exactly which human rights and fundamental freedoms are covered by article 55 does not transform it into a "procedural" statute such that if there are rights, then article 55 prohibits certain distinctions, but if there are no rights, then article 55 does not supply them. The preamble of the Charter particularly reaffirms a faith in fundamental rights and the dignity and worth of the person.[264] The Charter thus presumes the existence of fundamental rights and freedoms and article 55 reaffirms this presumption along with the substantive prohibition of distinction.

2. The Human Rights and Fundamental Freedoms Protected Directly by the Charter

There are several approaches for determining which human rights and fundamental freedoms the Charter substantively protects. Starting with the narrowest interpretation of article 55, it refers, at a minimum, to those fundamental rights and freedoms that are *jus cogens*.[265] If, however, the "human rights and fundamental freedoms" of article 55 include only *jus cogens* norms, article 55 would appear to be superfluous, since all states are bound by *jus cogens* even in absence of the Charter. A possible response is that article 55 is merely declarative of what all states agreed as *jus cogens*. But under this interpretation the nondistinction principle of article 55 becomes redundant.[266] Thus, this narrow interpretation of article 55 is quite strained, and the article should be read as indicating that there are additional human rights and fundamental freedoms which may not be denied on a discriminatory basis.

The second argument is that article 55, in addition to incorporating *jus cogens* norms, incorporates or parallels customary international law of human rights and fundamental freedoms, including those not necessarily at the level of *jus cogens*.[267] This suggests a reciprocal effect: article 55 helps to determine what is customary law, and customary law helps to flesh out what article 55 means. This reciprocal effect must be explored in the context of the process of development of customary international law. A new rule of customary international law is recognized where there is, first, evidence of sufficient state practice and, second, a determination that states conceive themselves as acting under a legal obligation *(opinio juris)*.[268] State practice requires substantial "uniformity" and "generality" of practice by the states whose interests are affected.[269] The recognition of a rule of customary law does not require absolute or universal practice. It is "sufficient that the conduct of States should, in general, be consistent with such rules, and that instances of State conduct inconsistent with a given rule, should generally have been treated as breaches of that rule, not as indications of the recognition of a new rule."[270] Evidence of state practice and *opinio juris* is found in, *inter alia,* the decisions of international tribunals, the actions and opinions of organs and representatives of international organizations, particularly the United Nations, the actions and expressed views of states, including the decisions of national tribunals, and scholarly writings.[271]

International and national courts, and commentators, have identified a minimum list of customary international human rights which substantially overlaps with *jus cogens* norms.[272] The list is somewhat greater, however, and it is acknowledged that the general principles of equality and nondiscrimination form part of customary law.[273] Prohibition of systematic discrimination on the basis of race is considered customary law, and also meets the burden of proof of being *jus cogens.*[274] Commentators, although absolute and insistent about the status of systematic racial discrimination under customary law, have been surprisingly less emphatic in their declarations concerning the status of systematic sex discrimination.[275] Some, nonetheless, are willing to acknowledge that the prohibition of state sex discrimination "may already be a principle of customary international law."[276] This acknowledgment is supported by *opinio juris* and state practice; ample evidence exists over the last twenty-five years of pronouncements of the international community at United Nations conferences,[277] of member states reaffirming their commitment to women's equality in numerous human rights treaties,[278] and of national legislatures and courts enforcing equality for women.[279] The fact that some states still practice discrimination and distinction on the basis of sex should be treated as noncompliance with the norm rather than as evidence of a new rule.[280]

These customary norms of nondiscrimination that have developed since the Charter help to elucidate the Charter, and, in this manner, articles 55 and 56 incorporate customary international law, and subsequent state practice and *opinio juris* help set the standards with regard to human rights and fundamental freedoms. But customary norms must also be interpreted in conformity with the Charter. The Charter is more than just a treaty; "it prevails expressly over all other treaties, and implicitly over all laws, anywhere in the world."[281]

Since the Charter requires that the standards for "without distinction" be the same for race, sex, and religion, then the customary norm of the prohibition against systematic race discrimination sets the standard for prohibition of discrimination with respect to sex and religion. The Charter's principle of equality between nondistinctions controls in this setting. Thus, if states develop and uphold a standard with respect to the prohibition of systematic racial discrimination regarding fundamental rights, states must apply the same standard with respect to sex and religious discrimination. For example, if states conclude that it is impermissible to disallow voting on the basis of race, then it is equally impermissible to disallow voting on the basis of sex or religion. Systematic discrimination on the basis of sex or religion must be a violation of customary international law as long as discrimination on the basis of race is treated as such. Moreover, the standards set in one area may not be used to shift the balance already set between the prohibited distinctions under the Charter. The Charter disallows a hierarchy in the prohibitions of discriminations which would elevate the prohibition of one distinction as more important than the prohibition of another. For example, the very recognition of a customary norm of nondiscrimination based on religion, but not on sex, shifts the delicate balance of human rights between competing interests that the Charter achieves. It would open up the possibility of privileging religious rights of freedom at the expense of women's equality and liberty rights and allowing for exactly the odious distinctions that article 55 forbids. Thus, the Charter disallows an imbalance to be created in the development of customary law, and a customary norm in conflict with the Charter cannot exist.

If articles 55 and 56 are understood to cover, in addition to the *jus cogens* norms, these additional customary norms of nondiscrimination, then these customary norms appear to add little to the Charter's explicit language of nondistinction. In fact, it would appear that the reciprocal effect of the Charter determining customary law is more evident in this instance than that of customary norms illuminating the Charter.[282] These customary norms prohibit discriminating about underlying rights and freedoms, but their standards give us little clear guidance as to the nature of the underlying human rights and fundamental freedoms. The Charter itself, on the other hand, does give such guidance. The ICJ, for example, found that South Africa's systematic racial discrimination violated the Charter, and the Court made specific reference to the underlying rights and freedoms that were being denied on this basis.[283] Thus, the implication of article 55 is that there are underlying rights and freedoms that article 55 also protects, in addition to the right to be free from discrimination.

It should now be clear that the Charter must cover a range of substantive rights and freedoms in order for articles 55 and 56 to make comprehensive sense when read in light of its object and purpose.[284] Many commentators have argued that the Universal Declaration[285] provides the obvious answer as to what rights and freedoms are covered in the Charter. The argument that the Universal Declaration explicates articles 55 and 56 in the Charter takes various forms, with some arguments interweaving with others. Some commentators argue that although declarations by the General Assembly are not technically binding,[286] they nonetheless have legal effect as evidence of customary law.[287] Others agree that the Universal Declaration has such legal effect, but attribute this effect to the General Assembly having quasi-legislative status.[288] Another group of commentators finds that the Universal Declaration is an "authoritative interpretation" of the human rights referred to in the Charter, and that the derivation from the binding authority of the Charter gives obligatory force to the Universal Declaration,[289] such that "the Declaration, as an authoritative listing of human rights, has become a basic component of international customary law, binding on all states, not only on members of the United Nations."[290] Thus, "members can no longer contend that they do not know what human rights they promised in the Charter to promote,"[291] and nonmembers as well are bound by the human rights Charter provisions as explicated by the Universal Declaration since these provisions have entered into customary international law.[292] The Universal Declaration thus gives shape to articles 55 and 56 of the Charter. Like the Charter, the Universal Declaration also has aspirational goals, and members are expected to work toward those goals in accordance with article 56.[293]

3. The Human Rights and Fundamental Freedoms Protected by the Universal Declaration under the Charter

The Universal Declaration provides that all persons are entitled to the rights and freedoms in the Universal Declaration without discrimination of any kind, including that based on race, sex, or religion.[294] As with the Charter's nondistinction language, the implication of this nondiscrimination language is that no particular religious law is the source for human rights nor may be determinative of international human rights standards.[295]

If there is any doubt concerning this implication of the nondiscrimination language, the preparatory work of the Universal Declaration makes clear that no particular religion was to be deemed the foundation for human rights.[296] For example, in drafting the Universal Declaration the issue was raised as to whether to include some reference to a deity in the preamble and in article 1, such that article 1 would read that "human beings are created in the image of God .. [and] are endowed by nature with reason and conscience."[297] The drafters deliberately rejected any references to a deity or to the immortal destiny of human beings so as not to impose the philosophical concepts of natural law (which derives from one particular religion) on countries to which it was alien and also not to impose it on nonbelievers.[298] This refusal to introduce particular religious reference supports the interpretation of the nondiscrimination language of the Universal Declaration as rejecting any particular religion as a preferred foundation of international human rights.[299]

Moreover, article 18, which protects the right to freedom of thought, conscience, and religion,[300] was the subject of much discussion because it was considered to include the right to change one's religion or belief.[301] Saudi Arabia opposed the right to change one's religion because the right conflicted with Saudi Arabia's interpretation of the Qur'an, and also might favor proselytizing missionaries.[302] Afghanistan, Iraq, Pakistan, and Syria joined Saudi Arabia's rejection of this right during Committee discussions.[303] The right was adopted by the Committee, however, and later the Pakistani representative prepared a speech arguing that the right was not inconsistent with the Qur'an.[304] All Muslim member states except Saudi Arabia voted for the Universal Declaration after being on notice as to the meaning of article 18 and of the intentional rejection of making any particular religion the determinative source for human rights.[305] Therefore, the Universal Declaration must be seen as the agreed balance that member states fairly struck between their different religions and cultures, and thus the introduction of subsequent factors to that balance should be avoided.[306]

Article 18 also guarantees the right to freedom of thought, conscience, and religion and the manifestation of religion or belief in practices and observance.[307] The right to nonreligious beliefs is of equal status with the right to religious beliefs, and different religious beliefs are of equal status with each other. The Universal Declaration also guarantees the right to education, whose aim is the full development of the individual and the promotion of tolerance and friendship among all nations, racial groups, and religious groups.[308]

With respect to discrimination on the basis of sex, the Universal Declaration states that men and women "are entitled to equal rights as to marriage, during marriage and at its dissolution."[309] Analyses of equality in international law do not require identical treatment in every case.[310] Nonetheless, only distinctions that are reasonable or just, based on objective criteria, and proportionate to the justification are allowed.[311] A finding of unjust or unreasonable discrimination may be made without regard to intention or motive, "whether the motive be bona fide or mala fide."[312]

Given that there is great potential for conflict between these various rights and freedoms, the Universal Declaration allows for certain limitations on them. The methodology suggested by the language of the Universal Declaration is as follows: first, there needs to be a determination of whether a particular law or act attributable to the state fails to safeguard a substantive right in the Universal Declaration.[313] If so, there needs to be a corresponding determination of whether the law or act itself represents the exercise of a protected freedom or right. If it does, then there is a clear case of conflict between rights, and the question is whether the law or act constitutes a permissible limitation under article 29.

Article 29 deals with the permissible limitations allowed for all rights under the Universal Declaration. Such limitations are to be "solely for the purpose of securing due recognition and respect for the rights and freedoms of others and of meeting the just requirements of morality, public order and the general welfare of a democratic society."[314] This suggests a two-prong approach to discerning whether limitations are allowable. The "due recognition" standard allows that if the exercise of a right by one individual results in failure to acknowledge a right that is clearly owed to another individual, then the former right may be limited. The "just requirements" standard allows a society to limit rights to the extent necessary to maintain a democratic form of government.[315] The terms "morality" and "public order" are thus limited to meaning public order and morality in the context of democratic principles. These terms of article 29(2) should also be read in light of the requirement of article 29(3) that "rights and freedoms may not be exercised contrary to the purposes and principles of the United Nations."[316] Democratic principles, therefore, may not be interpreted in such a way as to subvert the rights and freedoms recognized by the Charter, and which the United Nations promotes under article 55.

The "due recognition" and "just requirements" standards are standards determined by international law. Thus, national law or religious law may not be the source for either of these standards.[317] Furthermore, article 29 requires the same treatment for all rights, and thus corresponding situations must be treated symmetrically. For example, if a state enacts a law protecting religion to the detriment of women, a determination must be made as to whether such limitations on the rights of women are necessary for the due recognition of the religion and the just requirements of a democratic society. This must be symmetric to the case of a state that enacts a law protecting women against religious pressures and a determination must be made as to whether the limitation on religion is necessary for the due recognition of the rights of women and the just requirements of a democratic society. The determination of "due recognition" in each case needs to establish the same level of respect between the rights of women and religion in both cases. Thus, by symmetry, "due recognition" of religion cannot be determined in isolation from concerns of "due recognition" of the rights of women or other groups. This implies that "due recognition" requires at a minimum a respecting of the basic norms of human dignity and freedom.[318] This approach treats the two different discriminations (on the basis of sex and religion) equally and according to the methodology suggested by the language itself.

Finally, article 30 allows a state to impose limitations on rights or freedoms if "any states, groups or person . . . engage in any activity or perform any act aimed at the destruction of any of the rights and freedoms set forth herein."[319] Article 30 is thus concerned with not only the actions of states but the actions of private individuals as well.[320]

B. Religious Fundamentalism Evaluated under International Standards

This section first analyzes religious fundamentalist laws[321] directly under the Charter according to the minimal standards applicable to all states without taking the Universal Declaration into account. Second, the section analyzes religious fundamentalist laws under the Universal Declaration.

1. Religious Fundamentalist Laws Analyzed Directly under the Charter

Assuming that articles 55 and 56 cover only *jus cogens* norms, it is nonetheless clear that some religious fundamentalist laws violate these norms. For example, a *jus cogens* norm prohibits state murders as arbitrary and extra-legal.[322] These murders are "defined as killings committed outside the judicial process by, or with the consent of, public officials, other than necessary measures of law enforcement to protect life or as acts of armed conflict."[323] If a state explicitly delegates to a husband the right to kill his wife for adultery,[324] it has consented to his acting as a prosecutor, judge, and summary executioner. The result is arbitrary deprivation of life by extra-legal killing in violation of the *jus cogens* norm. Thus, a state's passage of this type of law violates its Charter duty under articles 55 and 56.[325]

The second suggested minimum standard under the Charter is that articles 55 and 56 are informed by at least the customary law of nondiscrimination in addition to *jus cogens* norms. As discussed, these customary norms must develop in conformity with the Charter's principle of equality in the treatment of prohibited distinctions.[326] The best guidance is offered by the ICJ in its Advisory Opinion in the *Namibia* case, which sets forth the standards for racial nondiscrimination, which would be applicable to all prohibited distinctions under the Charter, and which implicitly rejects any religious justification of systematic racial discrimination and apartheid.[327] The apartheid system in South Africa (and consequently Namibia) was founded on the Afrikaners' Old Testament Christianity of Calvinist origin.[328] Afrikaners believed that they were the chosen people with a divine mission to rule over all others, and from this followed their belief in white supremacy and a policy of racial segregation and discrimination.[329] The ICJ refused to allow South Africa to present factual evidence to prove both South Africa's "good faith" concerning apartheid and its intention to promote the well-being and progress of the inhabitants.[330] Instead the ICJ found as a matter of law that the government's intent and motives concerning its systematic discrimination were irrelevant and that it was not necessary to determine the effects of apartheid.[331] Thus, it would not have been relevant if South Africa had argued any of the following: that its intent concerning apartheid was in "good faith" because it was protecting the (Afrikaner) populace's right to religious freedom; that its good intent was clear because it was fulfilling the divine plan for Afrikaners; that Afrikaners' freedom of religious belief would be deeply infringed if they were not able to assert their divinely ordained supremacy over Africans; or that the divine plan was clear about the natural role for whites and blacks and this was reflected in the policy of apartheid. The Court found that no motive or intent, whatever the source, could justify such systematic discrimination and denial of human rights under the Charter. Furthermore, evidence that the apartheid system worked well — such as testimony by Africans that the system of apartheid promoted their well-being and progress — was also irrelevant. By refusing to hear evidence on either intent or the beneficial quality of apartheid the Court was essentially finding systematic discrimination per se illegal and without any possible justification under the Charter.

Although South Africa did not raise the religious arguments, the ICJ must have been aware of them. The Court specifically noted that the policy of apartheid, and its related laws and decrees, were a matter of public record of which the Court was cognizant.[332] Thus, the Court did not need to be informed of the Afrikaners' religious beliefs because those beliefs were evidenced in all the past laws and decrees as a matter of public record from the early *Voortrekker* republics to contemporary South Africa and Namibia.[333] Such knowledge did not persuade the Court that religious beliefs could justify apartheid policy or be evidence of "good faith" with respect to the policy.

These arguments justifying systematic racial discrimination and apartheid on the basis of religious belief are superfluous now. There is no chance that the international community would accept that religious belief justifies systematic racial discrimination. Thus, even to the extent that the Court did not have the religious justification arguments in mind in the opinion, it is clear that international law would not now accept freedom of religious belief as justification for systematic racial discrimination. In this context of racial discrimination, the ICJ established the standard for nondiscrimination under the Charter: the Charter prohibits establishing and enforcing distinctions, exclusions, restrictions, and limitations exclusively on the ground of race.[334]

As discussed, the "without distinction" language of the Charter does not distinguish between the prohibited distinctions, and thus this standard for nondiscrimination in the context of race discrimination and religious freedom is applicable to the context of sex discrimination and religious freedom.[335] Systematic discrimination on the basis of sex under religious fundamentalist laws is not permissible as a manifestation of the freedom of religious belief under the Charter any more than South Africa's system of apartheid was permissible. Both violate the Charter.

2. Religious Fundamentalist Laws
Analyzed under the Universal Declaration

Assuming that the Universal Declaration is an authoritative interpretation of the human rights in the Charter or is itself customary international law, then it becomes clear that a number of religious fundamentalist laws conflict with guarantees under the Universal Declaration. As we have seen, many religious fundamentalist systems of marriage and divorce require women to submit to their husbands, and even obey their husbands. These laws conflict with two areas of protection in the Universal Declaration: liberty rights and equality rights. Evaluation of liberty rights first requires an inquiry into what articles of the Universal Declaration are apparently violated by the laws. Then, if there are apparent violations and thus a conflict between women's rights and the right to freedom of religion, the analysis proceeds to consider whether these laws constitute permissible limitations on women's rights in accordance with the methodology of article 29.[336] Evaluation of equality rights first requires an inquiry as to whether the laws differentiate between men and women, and, if so, then whether the differentiation constitutes discrimination under international legal standards. If the laws discriminate, then there is a conflict between women's rights and the right to freedom of religion, and the issue becomes whether the laws are permissible limitations on women's rights under the methodology of article 29. Thus, the equality analysis requires an extra step to determine if the differentiations are discriminatory *before* turning to article 29, at which point the analysis proceeds exactly as for the liberty issues.

It is important to note that the Universal Declaration mandates that article 29 is the sole method for dealing with a conflict between rights. Thus, it is only at the article 29 stage of analysis that the primary religious fundamentalist justification for these laws — that they constitute the exercise or manifestation of religious belief — may be considered.[337] The religious-belief justification may not be presented at an earlier stage of the analysis because it would subvert and avoid the Universal Declaration's standard for how conflicts between rights must be resolved. The earlier stages of both the equality and liberty analyses are for the purpose of determining whether women's rights are impinged upon and limited by religious fundamentalist laws such that a conflict is presented between women's rights and the right to religious freedom. The earlier stages of both analyses do not consider the argument that these laws are based on religious freedom because that claim is, and must be, dealt with by the analysis under article 29. This section therefore first discusses the equality and discrimination analysis, then the liberty issues, and finally evaluates both under the article 29 methodology.

a. Equality Analysis   The first stage in the equality analysis — whether there is differentiation — is straightforward. Religious fundamentalist laws differentiate on their face with respect to marriage, divorce, and modesty. The differentiation places obvious burdens on women: submissive status, physical abuse, economic dependence, limitations on travel in their own community and abroad, and limitations on their ability to work and seek education. The laws place women in an inferior position to men and demand that women have less power than men, granting men the final say in all matters as the heads of families.

The second stage in the equality analysis is to determine whether the distinctions amount to what would be discrimination against women under international standards if there were no issues of exercise or manifestation of religious belief to be considered (these issues are, of course, considered under the article 29 analysis). Although international standards do not require identical treatment of men and women similarly situated, they nonetheless do require the distinctions to be reasonable or just, based on objective criteria, and to be proportionate to the justification.[338] The justifications that religious fundamentalist groups give, explicitly or implicitly, are generally that women are inferior, women's sexuality needs external controls (as provided for in these laws), that women should be economically dependent upon men, and that the man is the proper head of the household and the family.[339] Religious fundamentalists may base these justifications on religious norms or on stereotypes. Religious norms are considered below under the article 29 methodology dealing with the conflict between religious belief and women's rights. For the present stage of the analysis, it should be recalled that the language of the Charter and the Universal Declaration disallows any religious norms to determine international standards of equality and human rights, so that no religious norm may determine the definition of what constitutes discrimination against women under the Charter and the Universal Declaration.[340] Moreover, stereotypes are not considered reasonable justifications for the systematic denial of equality in general, nor for specific discriminatory treatment under the marriage and divorce laws.[341] Consequently, the justifications given by religious fundamentalists do not satisfy the requirements of being reasonable or just, and based on objective criteria. Finally, even if it is alleged that the laws do not intend to discriminate, lack of intent is irrelevant under international standards.[342] Thus, under international standards of nondiscrimination, the systematic quality of the sex discrimination of religious fundamentalist laws violates article 16(1) (dealing specifically with marriage and divorce) and the general prohibition of nondiscrimination under article 2. A clear conflict is thus presented between women's equality rights and religious freedom, which must be analyzed under article 29.

b. Liberty Analysis   The obedience and modesty laws impinge on the liberty rights of women, particularly those relating to security of the person, participation in a democratic society, and religious freedom and belief. Article 3 guarantees everyone the right to life, liberty, and the security of the person.[343] Explicitly or implicitly authorizing husbands to discipline their wives results in the physical abuse of women and violates their article 3 right to security of the person.[344] Moreover, article 8 guarantees everyone the right to an effective judicial remedy for violations of human rights guaranteed under law.[345] Thus, the state's failure to provide a woman with effective remedies for assault and battery by her husband violates a woman's article 8 right to effective remedies.

Requiring wives to be obedient to their husbands also interferes directly with their liberty rights associated with participation in a democratic society, thus violating articles 18-21. These rights include the right to freedom of thought and conscience (article 18),[346] the right to freedom of opinion and expression (article 19),[347] the right to freedom of assembly (article 20),[348] and the right to take part in government including the right to vote (article 21).[349] There are no limitations on what the husband may require under the obedience rule, and for this reason, the need for his permission is a direct interference with a woman's rights under these articles.[350]

The article 18 guarantee of the freedom of thought encompasses political thought. The right to political belief is also bolstered by article 19, which guarantees everyone the right to freedom of opinion and expression, and "this right includes freedom to hold opinions without interference and to seek, receive and impart information and ideas through any media and regardless of frontiers."[351] The obedience rule and modesty rules directly impinge on these rights since a woman may not seek, receive, or impart information without her husband's permission. In some cases, she is not supposed to leave her own house unless absolutely necessary and with her husband's permission, and she is not allowed to leave the country without his permission. The result is that she has no public place to express her political opinion and belief and no forum in which to exchange ideas. Thus, she is subjected to interference in her freedom to hold opinions and her ability to receive information on which to base her opinions.

Even if a woman is confined to her home, she continues to have rights under articles 18 and 19. Her expression of these rights within her home can be little more than an expression of opposition to the requirement of obedience. Thus, her acts of civil protest must take place within her home. Acts of disobedience may be interpreted as reflecting her general political belief in the equality of women or a more specific political belief that women should not be in submission to their husbands. In any event, it is quite clear that her political belief does not have to amount to a comprehensive political theory in order to qualify as an article 18 or 19 right. In the contexts of political asylum and refugee applications,[352] courts are recognizing that a woman's opposition to the subservient role imposed on her by her husband and societal norms is the expression of political belief, and that mandating her to conform to those roles is repression of her political belief.[353] Feminism itself has been recognized as a political opinion and is entitled to the same protection as other political opinions.[354] Furthermore, courts are recognizing that the physical abuse a woman receives from her husband may serve as a reprisal for her political views and for her failure to conform to a subservient role. For example, an immigration judge granted political asylum in the United States to a Jordanian woman who had suffered severe, sustained abuse by her husband for years, finding a direct nexus between her expression of political opinion and the abuse she received.[355] In cases where the state authorizes the husband to be the head of the family or fails to protect women who suffer abuse at the hands of their husbands,[356] courts have found that domestic abuse may serve as the means by which a state persecutes a woman for her political beliefs, and thus she may properly be regarded as a victim of state political repression.[357]

Article 20 provides the right to freedom of peaceful assembly and association. Obedience rules and modesty codes directly impinge on this political right since a woman may not join any assembly without her husband's permission, and may also be subject to modesty code penalties if she joins a public assembly. Article 21 gives everyone the right to vote, to take part in the conduct of public affairs, or to be elected to government.[358] Plainly, religious fundamentalist laws of modesty and obedience that restrict women's voting rights are a direct infringement of article 21 rights.[359] In addition, obedience rules operate as restrictions on rights in that they entitle a husband to require his wife to vote a certain way, forbid her to run for election, and even forbid her to obtain information about political parties. Even if a wife obtains her husband's permission to run for election, the modesty code prohibitions on her appearing and speaking in public may make this impossible in practice.[360] The requirements of obedience and modesty codes thus are a direct infringement of a woman's article 21 rights.

Furthermore, the combination of modesty codes and obedience rules foreclose a woman's participation in the democratic process of society because she has no opportunity to lobby or work for the change of the very laws that repress her political rights. It is fair to conclude that these religious fundamentalist laws do not reflect the result of democratic process since there is no evidence that women have had any opportunity to participate in the passage of these laws which subject them to a submissive status backed up by sanctions.[361] Thus, these obedience and modesty laws, enforced by physical violence, repress a woman's political beliefs and their expression.

The obedience and modesty laws also conflict with a woman's freedom of religious belief guaranteed under article 18. A wife's disobedient act may well arise out of a religious belief concerning appropriate behavior that differs from her husband's belief. Even a wife who remains obedient for fear of reprisal may nonetheless believe that her religious duty should not be to submit to her husband's authority. In either case, the result is suppression of her religious belief and its manifestation. Thus, obedience rules and modesty codes clearly impinge on the religious beliefs of women who believe that obedience and submission are not required. The groups of religious women fighting fundamentalism in many different countries are representatives of such women.[362] This is particularly true of those women who have had to go into exile for their religious and political beliefs because their society has become unsafe for them as a result of incitement of hatred for their beliefs.[363] The obedience and modesty laws conflict with these women's rights to freedom of religious belief and its manifestation.[364]

Furthermore, religious fundamentalist state laws that require a husband's permission for his wife to work impinge on the rights guaranteed under both articles 19 (right to freedom of association) and 23 (right to work).[365] The legal requirement that a wife needs her husband's permission to travel also conflicts with the article 13 guarantee of freedom of movement within one's own state and the right to leave one's own state.[366] Finally, the obedience and modesty laws will in many cases interfere with the right to education under article 26(1) and the right to full development of the personality under article 26(2).

It is clear that the obedience and modesty laws conflict with a multitude of the articles of the Universal Declaration, involving both equality and fundamental liberties, and constitute a substantial and systematic invasion of women's rights. At this stage, it is necessary to acknowledge that the obedience and modesty laws also are manifestations of religious belief (of at least part of the citizenry of a state). Thus, there is a conflict in rights, and an analysis under article 29 is necessary.

c. Article 29 Analysis   The methodology for application of article 29 requires a determination as to whether the obedience laws and modesty codes, as manifestations of religious fundamentalist belief, operate as permissible limitations on the international legal rights of women. Such an invasion of women's rights is allowable only for the purpose of securing "due recognition" of the right to religious belief or the "just requirements" of a democratic society.[367] The standard of "due recognition" is an international standard and has been developed in international law.[368] First, the standard may not depend upon the tenets of a particular religion and may not be determined by any particular religion, no matter how passionate its desire to discriminate as part of religious belief.[369] Second, the international community accepts certain activities as core and integral to the right of religious belief and manifestation of religious belief.[370] These activities include the right to worship, to maintain places of worship, and to choose religious leaders.[371] It has not been suggested that the obedience laws and modesty codes fall within the core activities of religion. Arguably it follows from this that religion can make no claim for due recognition of obedience laws and modesty codes, and that consequently international law tolerates no intrusion by these codes into the rights guaranteed to women. Even if this is not entirely accepted, it nonetheless remains the case that all religious activities, core or otherwise, are subject to the due recognition standard of article 29. The implementation of this standard is best explored in the context of the conflict between the manifestation of religious belief and the prohibition of racial discrimination, as discussed next.

Third, international jurisprudence has worked out the limits beyond which recognition of a religion is not due, in the context of racial discrimination. The major jurisprudential developments have taken place in the international approaches to slavery and apartheid.[372] In these contexts, gross and systematic discrimination was not accepted for the sake of giving due recognition to religion. As discussed, this demonstrates that the standard of due recognition for religion may not be interpreted without consideration of the due recognition of minimum basic norms of human dignity and freedom of other protected groups.[373]

The major religions historically supported and justified slavery, with the three religions that rely on the Old Testament finding justification within it.[374] Religious justification supported the Christian and Islamic role in the North Atlantic slave trade and slavery in the New World.[375] The New World Christian doctrine preached to slaves was that slaves should accept their servile position as part of the divine plan; that they were spiritually equal even if not equal in the world; that their religious duty was one of obedience to their master; that they should feel happy and content with their position; and that they should accept discipline and correction since it was for their sins, and in any event their reward for bearing their punishments patiently was to be in heaven.[376] Moreover, "Christianizing" slaves was regarded as good practice since it would increase the likelihood of their being obedient to their masters.[377] Despite some Christian sects' change in the nineteenth century to a new theological position mandating the abolition of slavery, other Christians continued to justify slavery on the basis of the Old Testament and fought its abolition.[378] Moreover, the underlying doctrine that Christianity was good for black African heathens served to feed ideologies of racial inferiority that justified institutionalizing racial discrimination into law long after slavery was abolished in the New World, and indeed such ideologies survive to the present day.[379]

The international community gradually became opposed to slavery. By 1919 the Allies had signed conventions which contained, *inter alia*, a brief clause committing them to the suppression of slavery, and the covenant of the League of Nations had also determined that slavery and the slave trade should be suppressed.[380] Nevertheless, slavery was not outlawed in Saudi Arabia until 1962 and in Oman until 1970.[381] Furthermore, certain Christian sects still justify the institution of slavery,[382] and Muslim religious fundamentalists still argue that the enslavement of infidels is justified.[383] Regardless of religious doctrine in Christianity and Islam, international mores and law did not, and do not, hold that "due recognition" requires that these religious sects be allowed to determine the issue of slavery for themselves or to practice slavery. Slavery, particularly slavery based on belonging to a particular racial group, constitutes gross systematic discrimination and fails to give "due recognition" to the rights and freedoms of the group suffering discrimination. It is in this fashion that international law has rendered the standard of "due recognition" for religious rights consistent with the standard of "due recognition" for the rights of a racial group.[384]

Given the equal treatment of race and sex discrimination under the Charter and Universal Declaration,[385] the international standard of "due recognition" of religious rights would thus not require that religious fundamentalist groups be allowed to determine the issue of the equality of women for themselves and to practice systematic sex discrimination. Comparison may be drawn between slavery on the basis of race as it has been justified under religious rhetoric and women's inferior position as it is currently justified under religious fundamentalist rhetoric.[386] Both rhetorics regard the roles of women and slaves as part of a divine plan, where spiritual equality may be neatly separated from earthly hierarchies.[387] Contemporary religious fundamentalism (of all religions) promotes doctrine to women very similar to Christian doctrine preached to slaves: wives should accept their servile position as part of the divine plan; they are spiritually equal even if not equal in the world; their religious duty is one of obedience to their husbands; they should feel happy and content with their positions; and they should accept discipline and correction since it is for their sins, and in any event their reward for bearing their punishments patiently is in heaven or in rebirth.[388]

The second example of international consensus demonstrating that due recognition for religion nevertheless allows suppression of a religious manifestation is in the case of systematic racial discrimination and apartheid in South Africa and territories under South Africa's control. The Dutch settlers (Boers or Afrikaners) of South Africa practiced slavery and justified it on similar religious grounds to those used in the New World.[389] After Britain took over South Africa in the early 1800s and enacted laws liberating Africans from many restrictions, the Boers reacted in a mass organized migration away from British rule.[390] The participants in this migration, the *Voortrekkers,* took their inspiration from Old Testament Christianity of Calvinist origin.[391] With the Bible as their guide, they asserted their dominance over nonwhites as based on Ham's curse, and regarded them as "not actually human."[392] The crucial event of the Great Trek was the Afrikaners' victory over the Zulus in the battle of Blood River in 1838 in which they not only won territories but, crucially, were reassured in their belief that God had chosen them for the divine mission of preserving the rule of the Afrikaner white race.[393] In 1848 further British territorial annexations pressed the *Voortrekkers* to trek again to establish new republics that would protect their religious theory and practice of white supremacy.[394] They established the Orange Free State and Transvaal

(South African Republic) as Christian societies whose laws explicitly prohibited "equality between coloured people and the white inhabitants of the country either in Church or state."[395] But the British annexed Transvaal in 1877, and under Paul Kruger Afrikaners' resistance to British rule culminated in the Anglo-Boer wars.[396] Kruger's nationalism was based on the Calvinism of the Afrikaner churches and the sacred history of the Great Trek and Blood River.[397] His Calvinist mission is the foundation for the Afrikaner nationalist apartheid policies a half century later.[398] By 1948, the Afrikaner Nationalist Party was elected on a platform of apartheid, a policy which was regarded as a requirement of "Divine Will" since "Blood River was, after all, a proof that God favored white civilization, or at least white Afrikaners."[399] The *Voortrekkers*' belief in being the chosen people with a calling to protect and defend their white civilization was fully expressed when South Africa became an independent republic in 1961.[400] Afrikaners had finally managed to merge completely their religious beliefs with their own political state, thereby creating the ideal religious fundamentalist state.

Despite the religious underpinnings of apartheid, international opinion had turned against it by the early 1970s.[401] The international community did not consider manifestation of religious belief as taking precedence over freedom from systematic racial discrimination and thereby constituting a defense of apartheid.[402] Indeed, the international community did not even take seriously the idea that a certain Christian sect's ideology could determine the standards for discrimination or practice it. It was self-evident that systematic racial discrimination was a gross violation of the Charter and the Universal Declaration,[403] and that "due recognition" of the right to religious freedom did not require the allowance of systematic discrimination as a manifestation of religious belief.

As previously discussed, under the language of the Charter and the Universal Declaration, these standards of the prohibition of discrimination apply equally to sex discrimination, and no religious sect may set these standards for international law.[404] Article 29 of the Universal Declaration does not require under international legal standards that recognition is "due" for white supremacy and male supremacy simply because these are manifestations of religious belief. Thus, according to these standards, manifestations of religious beliefs in the form of systematic sex discrimination, affecting most, if not all, of women's civil and political rights, should not be accorded "due recognition." This does not amount to a destruction of religious rights. But if "due recognition" were understood to allow religious fundamentalist laws as permissible limitations on women's rights, the result would be the wholesale destruction of women's equality and liberty rights. In this context, parallel recognition of a basic minimum of women's equality and liberty rights is due.[405]

Article 29 also requires a second inquiry as to whether the obedience laws and modesty codes are permissible limitations on women's rights because they are needed to advance the "just requirements" of a democratic society.[406] As already discussed, the contrary is clearly the case. The marital submission and modesty laws for women grossly interfere with women's involvement in the creation and maintenance of a democratic society. Religious fundamentalist laws of marriage, divorce, and modesty present a system that is intrinsically repressive of divergent political views.[407] Thus, these religious fundamentalist laws are not necessary to advance the "just requirements" of a democratic society; indeed, they positively undermine the democratic process by limiting the participation of half the population in democratic government.[408]

Therefore, under article 29, religious fundamentalist laws of obedience and modesty do not constitute permissible limitations on women's rights as they are not for the sole purpose of securing "due recognition" of the right to religious belief or for the just requirements of a democratic society. These laws, if attributable to the state, are thus in violation of the Universal Declaration.

Finally, article 30 permits a state to restrict groups or individuals that aim to destroy the rights of others. Religious fundamentalists would appear to be exactly the type of destructive group that article 30 contemplates: a group that aims to destroy the rights and freedoms of women. Religious fundamentalists' destructive tendencies are evidenced by their discriminatory legal systems, their political activity that targets women's rights, and their reservations to treaties that particularly implicate women's rights.[409] Restrictions on religious fundamentalist laws are warranted to the extent the laws destroy the rights of women.[410]

C. The Accountability of States for Religious Fundamentalist Laws

In this section, I evaluate state accountability for religious fundamentalist laws that conflict with guarantees under the Charter and the Universal Declaration. Section IV.B determined that religious fundamentalist laws of obedience and modesty conflict with the guarantees of articles 55 and 56 of the Charter and numerous articles of the Universal Declaration. There is, however, no violation of these instruments unless states are accountable for the religious fundamentalist legal systems in question. A state is accountable in three kinds of situations: first, when the state acts directly by enacting state laws and by enforcing laws administratively and judicially; second, when the state enforces laws in a discriminatory fashion such that the state is complicit in the violations of private actors; and third, under certain circumstances, when the state is complicit in violations by private individuals by failing in its duty to provide any effective remedy for the violations.[411]

The first type of state accountability is generally manifest in practice: a state is accountable for laws it has enacted or enforced, and if the laws deny guarantees under the Charter and Universal Declaration, then the state is in violation of these instruments.[412] This means that religious fundamentalist states which have enacted and enforced laws that discriminate against women — such as Algeria, Bangladesh, Iran, Iraq, Pakistan, and Sudan[413] — are contravening the Charter and the Universal Declaration. Israel[414] and India[415] also directly contravene the Charter and the Universal Declaration by their enforcement of discriminatory religious laws through their jurisdictional delegation to religious courts. The enactment and enforcement of these laws violates international obligations under the Charter, and states should vigilantly resist the temptation to enact such laws despite the often intense religious fundamentalist pressure to do so.

The second type of state accountability is found where the state has facially nondiscriminatory laws but enforces them on a discriminatory basis. This involves state action in that as a matter of state policy (explicit or otherwise) state police or prosecutors ignore certain crimes. Thus, even a state which has not enacted religious fundamentalist laws would be complicit if it enforced law on a discriminatory basis, thereby violating its international obligations. For example, the state might criminalize general physical assault but defer to societal norms of religious fundamentalism that permit a husband to discipline his wife. If in consequence the state fails to prosecute battering husbands under this general law, it is discriminating on the basis of sex in enforcement of the law.[416] Such discrimination in enforcement may be prevalent in society as a whole when religious fundamentalist pressure is strong, or may be applied particularly within religious fundamentalist communities that are separate from the main society.

The third type of state accountability applies when a state systematically fails to provide an effective remedy for violations of human rights or fundamental freedoms. Article 8 of the Universal Declaration specifically guarantees everyone the right of an effective judicial remedy for such violations.[417] It applies to all states, including those whose laws are nondiscriminatory both facially and in application, and thus imposes an affirmative obligation on states to provide effective remedies. This affirmative obligation requires the state to restrict nonstate actors from violative acts.

State accountability for private actions is particularly applicable with regard to violations of the right to security of the person in article 3 of the Universal Declaration. In the parallel context of the ICCPR's guarantee of the security of the person, the Human Rights Committee, in *Delgado Páez v. Colombia,* found that the state's failure to protect Delgado from anonymous threats and an attack by an unknown person violated his right to security of the person.[418] It was not sufficient protective state action that Delgado could use the Colombian court system or could report the threats and attack to the police; the state should have done more.[419]

The most compelling case of a state's accountability for failing to prevent or punish private acts is in the battering and murder of women that occur systematically under religious fundamentalist laws. Thus, a state's failure to act in these types of abuse cases makes the state complicit not only because the enforcement may be discriminatory as discussed above but because the state has failed to provide an effective remedy for the systematic violation of human rights. States that have not enacted religious fundamentalist laws still have an affirmative obligation to provide effective protection and effective remedies to women who are abused under the obedience laws of the fundamentalist communities. The state's affirmative duty to provide effective legal remedies may require more than providing a legal remedy for physical assault. Mere provision of legal remedies may not be sufficient in the religious fundamentalist context because women are often limited in their contact with outside sources of information and thus may not even be aware that such remedies exist. Thus, the affirmative duty of the state may require it to inform women about legal remedies, and to do so in such a way as to ensure that women are not subject to reprisals by men in the community.

States' affirmative duty may also oblige them to take additional action, particularly in light of the systematic and wide-ranging violations of civil and political rights by religious fundamentalist discriminatory laws.[420] A state would be permitted, and indeed may have a duty, to outlaw religious practices that are systematically violative of women's liberty and equal rights.[421] Under this approach, it is arguable that states with strong religious fundamentalist movements, including, for example, Japan, Italy, Sri Lanka, and the United States, may have a duty to pass laws prohibiting the practice of requiring wives to be obedient.[422] Such laws would reach religious fundamentalist communities and also send a broader message to society that the submission of women is unacceptable. Determining the parameters of such a law to meet international law concerns is, however, worthy of an essay in itself.

D. Religious Fundamentalist Reservations
to Treaties Also Violate the Charter

In this section I consider state actions with respect to reservations to human rights treaties on the basis of religious fundamentalist laws, and argue that these reservations themselves constitute violations of the Charter.

Religious fundamentalism is premised on the notion that religious law takes precedence over all other law and defines, *inter alia,* relations between different religions and between men and women. Thus, some states have argued, in the context of human rights treaties, that religious law takes precedence over international human rights law even when the state has not entered reservations to the treaty on this basis.[423] A state that justifies its violation of a treaty on the basis that its particular religious law pre-empts international law is obviously in violation of the core principle of international law that a state may not use municipal law to justify its failure to comply with international legal obligations.[424] This principle applies to religious municipal law just as it applies to secular municipal law.[425]

Other states have asserted that religious law takes precedence over international law human rights standards when they have entered reservations to treaties on that basis.[426] For example, Egypt's reservation to article 16 of CEAFDAW (concerning equality of men and women in all matters relating to family life) states that the "Islamic Sharia's provisions whereby women are accorded rights equivalent to those of their spouses . . . *may not be called in question*."[427] In response, other states have argued that the reservations are in bad faith since they undermine the object and purpose of a particular treaty, while others have argued that the reservations are invalid or must be construed narrowly.[128]

These assertions of a religious fundamentalist position in both declarations in response to accusations of a treaty violation and reservations to treaties should not, however, be viewed merely in the context of the particular treaty in question. Rather, these assertions should be considered in light of the state's twofold obligation under articles 55 and 56 of the Charter to cooperate with the United Nations in promoting equal rights for women and men and not to undermine the object and purpose of the Charter by putting themselves in a position of incapacity to cooperate with such promotion.[429] States also have a general duty to perform their obligations under the Charter in good faith according to the principle of *pacta sunt servanda.*[430]

A state's act of making a reservation is a public international act equivalent to the issuance of *opinio juris.* States which assert the supremacy of a particular religious law in determining issues of sex distinction (by the very act of claiming not to be bound on the basis of that particular religious law) are taking a position in direct conflict with articles 55 and 56.[431] The Charter specifically eschews religious law as the source for human rights, and, thus, any particular religious law may not determine the standards for the "without distinction" language.[432] Furthermore, these assertions conflict with article 55's requirement of equality between the prohibitions of distinctions and threaten to upset the delicate balance that the Charter achieves between these different types of distinctions. Thus, these declarative statements and reservations represent the state taking a public position which is contrary to the Charter. Public statements contrary to the Charter demonstrate bad faith and violate the state's twofold duty to cooperate and not to undermine. Thus, these states, by making these assertions, are in violation of their legal obligations under articles 55 and 56.[433]

E. The Consequences for Violation of the Charter

In previous sections, I have determined that states which protect religious fundamentalist norms over international human rights norms are in violation of the Charter and the Universal Declaration.[434] These violations take the form of gross and systematic sex discrimination. The international community has already dealt with systematic discrimination as a Charter violation in the context of racial discrimination as a manifestation of religious belief, and the same standards and compliance mechanisms must apply to sex discrimination.[435]

The international community expressed condemnation of South Africa's system of racial discrimination through various enforcement techniques, mainly relating to South African membership in the United Nations and other international organizations. Under the Charter, the Security Council may suspend a state's membership in the United Nations;[436] or the General Assembly, upon recommendation of the Security Council, may expel the state for consistent violation of the principles of the Charter.[437] In the early 1970s the United Nations gave serious consideration to expelling South Africa because its systematic racial discrimination violated the Charter. Those arguing for expulsion in the Security Council emphasized that under apartheid there were classifications of citizens solely on the basis of race with the result that blacks had highly unequal property rights, and suffered barriers to free movement, denial of the right to assemble freely, denial of voting rights, unequal educational opportunities, and cruel and degrading treatment by the state authorities.[438] The argument was that these practices violated the UN Charter as well as the Universal Declaration.[439] These limits on rights are directly parallel to the limits that women experience under religious fundamentalist laws: classification on the basis of sex resulting in denial of employment opportunities and property rights; denial of free voting; denial of the right of assembly; denial of free movement; unequal educational opportunities; cruel and degrading treatment by authorities in their act of enforcing obedience and modesty codes; and physical abuse by husbands in which the state is complicit through its failure to provide effective remedies.[440]

On October 30, 1974, France, the United Kingdom, and the United States vetoed a proposed resolution in the Security Council to expel South Africa, primarily on the basis that expelling South Africa would reduce any influence the United Nations might have over changing South Africa's policies.[441] The General Assembly then took the matter into its own hands and refused to accept the credentials of the South African delegation, noting that South Africa's policy of apartheid was a constant violation of the principles of the Charter and the Universal Declaration.[442] The General Assembly's rejection of the credentials of South Africa was a use of the credentials process to question the legitimacy of the government of South Africa and, in practical effect, to suspend South Africa's membership in the United Nations.[443]

This same procedural process of rejecting credentials should be used with respect to states enforcing religious fundamentalist laws that establish a system of sex discrimination. This procedure is preferable to outright expulsion for two reasons. First, as a practical matter, the Security Council would not expel any member because of some states' belief that expulsion will limit international influence on a pariah state. Second, the procedural process of rejecting credentials has a strong coercive effect by shaming the state before the international community while at the same time allowing for the state to regain membership if it reforms. Other enforcement actions that should be taken against these states — again, parallel to the case of South Africa — include suspension and expulsion from various international organizations, particularly specialized UN organizations.[444] Censure by international organizations can also be particularly effective.[445]

These various measures to enforce the prohibition of systematic discrimination and subsequent denial of human rights are excellent precedents for the appropriate treatment of states that engage in systematic sex discrimination through religious fundamentalist legal systems. All enforcement mechanisms at the community's disposal should be used to coerce these pariah states to cease violating articles 55 and 56. It is time for the international community to live up to the standards of the Charter and the Universal Declaration.

PART III

REGIONAL EXPERIENCES

9 The Israeli-Palestinian Conflict of Rights: Is God the Only Problem?

SARI NUSSEIBEH

Perhaps there is no place on earth more in need of an answer to the question "Does human rights need God?" than Palestine-Israel ("Palest-El"), a land in which Muslim and Jewish blood spills daily in the name of the same almighty, loving, and vengeful God. But this land and its struggles yield no easy answers, only more questions. In this essay I highlight the complexity and difficulty of talking about God and human rights in Palest-El, and how conflicting edicts and laws form a complex puzzle that challenges human reason. The questions I raise involve the idea of sacred space and spiritual claims of exclusive authority to safeguard locations imbued with religious significance. These questions are not limited to land rights, however, but touch on the most fundamental questions of religious authority, including the role of human reason in interpreting and applying divine messages and edicts and the ability of human creativity to transcend seemingly insurmountable conflicts and construct meaningful and enduring solutions.

Children of Abraham

Islam looks upon itself as the spiritual inheritor of the Abrahamic message. Indeed, the Qur'an clearly states that Abraham was the first Muslim — something which may come as a surprise to those who associate the birth of Islam with Muhammad. But this Abrahamic association is not a reference to the genealogical line, which links Ishmael to the Arabs (the term "Arab" in any case has in the scholarship tradition a much wider application). It is a reference, rather, to the monotheistic message purportedly carried by Abraham. More specifically, it is also a reference to the meaning of Islam as a religion that epitomizes the submission or surrender of the human will to God. The idea of total surrender to God's will is embodied in the story of the sacrifice — Abraham's submission to God's order to slaughter his beloved son. This is regarded as the ultimate test of faith, the total surrender of oneself, of one's most prized human feelings, to God's will. To this day, Islam's major annual festival celebrates God's merciful interjection at the last minute, when the test of submission to faith by Abraham had been duly passed, and Abraham was instructed to sacrifice the lamb instead.

The question of who is the proper spiritual inheritor of the message of Abraham is not merely an abstract historical, theological dispute for academics to debate. The Abrahamic spiritual pervasion of Judaism (which in the biblical tradition is a predominant feature) and of Islam (which in that same biblical tradition is less known) finds expression in present-day existential contentions over divine space and status in the context of the Israeli-Palestinian conflict. To whom does Abraham (and thus his burial place in Hebron) belong, Jews or Arab-Muslims? Are Jews simply performing a divine edict as they settle in and around Hebron, to the chagrin of its Arab inhabitants? Did Abraham indeed intend to perform his sacrificial act on that holy rock now enveloped by one of Islam's oldest-standing architectural marvels — the Dome of the Rock? Is that location, thus, Judaism's holiest shrine, which was later celebrated in the construction of the two temples, and the safekeeping of the holy tablets brought over from Mount Sinai? Is it, rather, an Abrahamic, and thus an *Islamic,* shrine, especially given the original event of the sacrifice with which the holy rock is associated?

To further complicate these conflicting claims over possession of this holy site, one may ask if in fact it is *less* Islamic given Islam's nonrecognition of that site as the site of the sacrifice — indeed, Islam's association of the sacrifice with Mecca rather than with Jerusalem. In fact, in the present day, Islam associates the sacrifice with Ishmael, Abraham's firstborn, rather than with Isaac, son of Abraham and Sarah. Other than this Abrahamic connection, what does the Dome of the Rock celebrate for Muslims in the first place? Muslims believe the rock to be the site of Muhammad's ascension to heaven. But why was Muhammad called upon to perform that holy ascension from that particular spot, not from Mecca or Medina? What *prior* religious significance did Islam assign to that site, to give meaning to the selection of that spot? Indeed, why were the Muslims called upon to direct their prayers to that spot long before Mecca came to replace it as the site of pilgrimage, and long before the journey of ascension? Is there significance to the tradition that Muhammad chose to tie his winged horse, al-Buraq, specifically to that western wall called the al-Buraq Wall, and otherwise known as the Wailing or Western Wall? Did the tying of the winged horse to that wall confer a religious value to the wall, or did the wall's pre-existing religious value determine where the horse was to be tied? Did the Qur'an and the later Islamic tradition look upon the land of the "Furtherest Mosque — al-Aqsa" as being holy for some reason other than and prior to the journey of ascension? Specifically, is not the reference to it as holy made in association with Moses? Is there, in other words, a historical mystery binding Jews and Muslims in one faith that needs to be unraveled? Would unraveling such a mystery help bring about religious reconciliation? Or are there two totally distinct religions, whose shared traditions need to be separated further? Are Arab-Muslims justified in regarding themselves as exclusive safekeepers of the Holy Land against all intruders, as the prophetic tradition tells them? Are Jews justified in regarding themselves as its rightful inheritors, called upon to gather in it, in preparation for the coming of the Messiah? Can two rights, dispensed by the same Author, conflict? And over and above Abraham, and beyond him, what does God have to say about all this? Does God have his own story to tell? And indeed, how does archeological rather than biblical or religious history figure in all this? Does truth matter?

God's Faithful

Clearly, conflicts of this nature would be simpler to understand if there were two gods. Indeed, they may not arise at all if those gods operated in geographically far apart provinces. If they were to operate within the same province, however, we could understand why there was a conflict: One god could have dispensed the order to X to rule over Z, while the second god could have dispensed the conflicting order to Y of ruling over that same space, Z. If, however, only one and the same God dispenses conflicting orders to X and Y, then logically there are three possible conclusions: (1) God does that in his wisdom, and X and Y are justified in fighting each other to death in fulfillment of his purpose (death being an inevitable conclusion to fighting, however one tries to soften or civilize the exhibition of one's firepower); (2) God's wisdom is to put X and Y to that contrary and anti-Abrahamic test of making them submit his edicts to *their* reason; or (3) they should simply know better than to fight each other, regardless of God or his edicts. Literalists (Jewish or Muslim, but also Christian) normally opt for the first option: that is, to carry out his edict however much pain and misery it unleashes, or however much "commonplace" injustice is caused to "the other." But as they go about doing this, in general they cannot conceive of a divine "double-track" strategy, or that their enemies are also acting by a contrary edict of the same God. It is simpler to assume either that, if their enemies really do think they are acting on behalf of God, he is a lesser god than theirs; or that, if he is the same God, then their enemies have simply misunderstood or misinterpreted him, such that each side believes that they alone are the legitimate and rightful spokesmen on his behalf in addition to their being his rightful heirs. This creates a fundamental conflict between God and human rights.

It is difficult in this latter type of situation to think of "the other," to use a Charles Taylor concept, as having equal worth, and as being entitled, therefore, to the same rights as yourself. More fundamentally, it may even be difficult simply *to think* of the other. Typically, a soldier on the frontline aiming to shoot simply seeks *to see* his target, not to think about him. A premeditated act of murder might require serious thinking, involving the conscious effort to develop a rationale for singling that person out. But an act of killing perpetrated in the context of a collective, self-righteous, and, especially, divinely justified confrontation would seem to involve or require a process of *abstraction* from others rather than a process of *cognition* of them. The celebration of self-worth in this kind of context implies blindness to the other.

"A Prayer to God," written by Mark Twain at the turn of the twentieth century, in the context of the American-Philippino war, elegantly and simply reflects the total blindness to the other, or unconsciousness of them implied by one side's supplication to its Lord in preparation for a military engagement with the enemy: praying that your own father return safely to his children is to pray that the other's children be orphaned; to pray that your country be protected from the horrors that may be visited upon it by its enemy is to pray that horrors be visited upon their country; to pray that your loved ones be rejoined together is to pray that theirs be forever torn asunder. There is no escaping this repellent hypocrisy of a prayer to your God for war. Palest-El is a place where one is justified in asking, If Man created God, is it high time that he undo this "miscreation"?

You may indeed be "civil" about carrying out God's mission or espousing his message. You may gently try to persuade your contender that you do not specifically mean *him* any harm. Indeed, *he* is just incidental in the grand design. After all, you are simply trying to act out God's will on earth. What moral argument can be stronger? You are not, after all, maliciously or avariciously seeking to deprive him of a home or property, or to replace or rule over him. Yours is not a common *earthly* project. God wants you, expects you, to fulfill his design by creating your own state, rebuilding your temple, preparing for the coming of the Messiah. Who are we, whether instrument or object, to stand in his way? Or, if yours is the other message from that God, and you are exhorted to protect his land, then none of your earthly leaders has the right to bargain with any part of it, and any such bargain must be deemed null and void. Yours would simply be the fulfillment of his command that this be his state, in keeping with his laws. You will certainly not mistreat your subjects if they are not of your own ilk, or unduly discriminate against them once your government is established. Yours, after all, is a tolerant religion, the last and best. Meantime, however, you have to fight against him who stands in your way of fulfilling this divine mission. If killing is required, and the suffering of death, then so be it, not because you revel in blood or despise life but because life and suffering are to you but fleeting human conditions, and you seek reality itself beyond earthly life, a divine existence which liberates you from humanity, a reunion with the Creator, and blissful immortality itself.

Are such literalists *right*, justified, in choosing to carry out divine edicts without question? Is their choice *rational?* Do they in fact exercise a choice at all, whether it is the right choice, or the rational choice, or are they conditioned to believe and act as they do? Is the demand that a moral choice be rational in this context, itself rational? Or are moral choices, and specifically those that derive their justification from a heavenly edict, not in need of being rational — rationality being, after all, but an earthly and human condition?

As an example of the literalist approach to applying divine edicts to earthly situations, I am reminded of the following encounter. Sitting in a cafe on the Mount of Olives overlooking the walled Old City of Jerusalem one day, a Christian pilgrim explained to me, using her fingers to point in the air and at the city before us as she proceeded to describe a time in the future, how the Golden Jerusalem would one day descend from the heavens unto earth. But what about the people and the streets and the houses already there, I asked her, feeling somewhat agitated at the prospect. Totally oblivious, unperturbed, she replied: Oh, they would all be gone, replaced by the divine beings of the golden city. Did she imagine herself to be one of them, reborn and spiritually flown from her future grave faraway in some Christian land, now descending upon and transplanting the earthly city of flesh and blood which I happen to call "home"? It was difficult for me to decide whether this friendly pilgrim was schizophrenic. How could she be, if she were simply sharing a belief held in common by many others? How can a belief be irrational if it is commonly held by otherwise normally rational people, and if it is institutionalized and reinforced in authoritative literature, religious establishments, and traditions? And even if it were a humanly irrational belief, what difference would that make to its being divinely *true*, or to its *worth?* Surely, the ultimate test of faith is to submit one's will, as well as one's reason, to edicts and theories one cannot fully fathom. Dare one challenge such edicts and theories with one's reason?

Faith and Reason

Dare one subject a divine edict to the test of human reason? It may have happened before, but with dire consequences, when God ordered the angels, constituted of that divine existential fiber, to bow to Adam, who was but an earthly creature, made of lowly material. "How can that make sense?" asked one of the bewildered angels. An early Muslim historian, al-Shahrastani, recounts how this impudent question, followed by an enactment of its rational conclusion, that he shall not bow, set forth Satan's saga, and that of the school of rationalism. Clearly, according to this mainstream Muslim author, not only does faith require a surrender of one's most burning human emotions, such as the love one has for one's child, but it requires a surrender of one's most reliable guide for action, namely, one's own reason. Not only should one not adhere to the principles of reason in such sensitive matters: one should also be warned of the Devil himself, the progenitor of rationalism. How else would one understand a mother's celebration of her son's death at the hands of enemy soldiers, or in the process of blowing to smithereens himself and tens of enemy citizens around him, regardless of age or sex? Is this a primordial celebration of revenge, of many heads for one? Or is it a celebration of faith, of an Abrahamic reenactment of Islam's quintessential article of belief? How else would one understand the brazen high-noon robbery of someone else's property, or someone else's basic human rights?

In the well-known Arabic medieval treatise, *The Decisive Treatise Outlining the Relationship between Faith and Reason,* Averroes tries to save the role of human reason in a literalist environment of religious edicts. Clearly, he argues, faith and reason cannot contradict one another, for God is behind both. But if they seem to, then this must be due to some ambiguity in the language expressing the articles of faith. In this kind of situation, this language should be subjected to a scholarly interpretation. Such an interpretation will either lead to a reformulation of the edict/article in question in terms of other edicts/articles which pose no contradiction, or, if the contradiction persists, then we should adhere to the dictates of reason on this matter. In this treatise Averroes draws upon the Qur'an to defend his argument that God has given precedence to reason in such matters, by demonstrating how this text extols us to use reason to understand the world. His cry, however, is a cry in the wilderness. Indeed, he did not fare much better than many other thinkers who began to challenge traditions, both religious and "scientific," in the Western world during the Dark Ages, and even through the Enlightenment years. His books, like many of those before him and after him, were burned. Reason is fine, his opponents would say. But reason is a human faculty, and is thus frail.

How can we rationally pit reason against the edicts of he who created man? If something does not make sense, using frail human reason, then that is only because we try to apply reason's low standards to a higher, indeed, to a supreme order or design, which by definition we cannot fathom.

A rationalist group of theologians called the Mu'tazilites appeared in early Islam. Theirs was sometimes referred to as the "School of Justice and Unity." They were accused of being rationally radical, and disputations arose between their followers and the more "rationally sedate" theologians. Among the disputes was whether God can throw an innocent child into the fires of hell. The Qur'an does not envisage limitations on God's omnipotence. God can do anything. But by throwing an innocent child into the fires of hell, would God not be acting unjustly? And is God, whose quintessence is justice, capable of being unjust? Surely, his justness restricts his omnipotence. This is not a matter of whether God would, in fact, *act* unjustly, because clearly he wouldn't. It is a matter of whether he *can* act unjustly. The opponents argued that God can act as he pleases. But since punishing the innocent would not please him, he would clearly not act in this manner. This disputation extended over the field of ethics more generally, and in particular over the field of action and responsibility: if agents are not answerable for their actions in a direct and inevitable way, or if reward and punishment are not organically tied to these actions, and God *can* dispense reward and punishment as he pleases, in what sense could we then hold agents responsible for their actions? Indeed, a discourse leading into the same thicket of disputation has to do with how *free* agents are in the first place, in an order already predetermined to the minutest detail, a detail God already *knows* even before an agent is born. Needless to say, the radical rationalists had a limited life span in the Islamic milieu. Logically, they needn't have, and argumentation could have been sponsored and encouraged under the Abrahamic umbrella, as it has been in the Jewish and Shi'ite traditions. But mainstream Muslim theology, once allowed to raise its head, managed to dominate the entire Sunni landscape, preventing the free evolution and development of exegesis, and laying out the path that a reenactment of the past is the only direction for religious progress.

An Ethos of Suffering

The area of human rights involves many layers of law, international, national, and local. The situation in Palest-El is more complicated still. The country is almost like a cross-laws puzzle. Divine, human, and natural laws and values

cross each other. It is but a world of shadows, where "life" has only an imperfect manifestation. Real life is in the hereafter. "Death" has only an imperfect
manifestation, for there is no death in the hereafter, but a continuity of reward
or punishment. And if death or self-annihilation can thus be celebrated as a
virtuous act of martyrdom, an assured step toward true life, *suffering* can also
come to be measured by standards of the hereafter, rather than by human standards of the here and now. Indeed, we know how suffering is *celebrated,* even
idolized, in the Christian tradition. Christians believe that God Almighty, incarnate in Jesus of Nazareth, chose to suffer for humanity. The event is immor-
talized in literature and art. It constitutes an essential creed of that religion.
For human beings generally, whether Christian or not, the creed is subcon-
sciously pervasive. It is not only a question of whether one can *suffer* suffering
if the cause is divine. It is also a matter of one being imbibed with or suffused
by a supreme, mystical sense of self-righteousness as one endures, even pro-
longs, the experience, against all earthly common sense, against reason.

Israelis and Palestinians prefer to endure suffering for their divine
cause, in various forms and degrees, rather than allow themselves to choose
mundane solutions. Relinquishing absolute values, or self-perceived rights
and divine edicts, for mundane benefits or interests seems to be essentially
anti-Abrahamic to the core. There are situations, of course, where suffering is
inescapable, but only because there are no mundane solutions except exclusivist ones. In such circumstances, suffering is seen as less evil than perishing
altogether. But there are also situations where suffering is preferred to a less-
than-absolute solution. It is situations like these that cause one to ponder.

Dispersed primarily throughout the Arab world, there are currently
over two million Palestinian refugees living in camps in Lebanon, Syria, and
Jordan. Their plight originating in the 1948 *al-Nakba,* when Israel was born, a
third generation of dispossessed and mostly disenfranchised Palestinians is
now filling the over-crowded camps. Many still keep the keys to their old
homes in what since became Israel. They harbor a collective dream. They
dream of being able to return home. They dream of turning the clock back, of
returning to a place and a time from which they were forcefully ejected. They
cannot fathom justice being carried out without the fulfillment of their
dream. Israel's reality, for them, is fleeting, temporary. Their dream is absolute, immortal. They will not exchange it for a tangible substitute. Better to
hold on to the dream than to accept reality, however far-fetched the possibility of making their dream come true. There are over a half-million Israelis
now implanted in the areas occupied by Israel in 1967. They look upon themselves as enacting the divine command to gather together in the Holy Land.
They re-create biblical place-names where they believe their ancestors lived

before the injustice done to them, and the diaspora they were made to suffer. But now, three thousand years later, they are back, and can impose their settlement by force. As they look around them, however, they sense they are in the midst of a hostile environment. They may be shot at as they drive around in their cars to work; the school bus carrying their children home may be ambushed. Their loved ones may be killed. But they choose to suffer, because it is suffering for a divine cause. The hard-core religious settlers will cling to these places by force rather than accept a less-than-absolute solution. Better to suffer hostility — even impose a diaspora on "the other" — than to suffer compromise.

Palest-El is a land of absolutes. A land awaiting the Armageddon. Absolutists from faraway cheer on the protagonists. God's design must unfold itself as the ingathering proceeds, and the unchosen ones continue to suffer, or begin to fade away. It is not for the love of literalist Jews that the literalist Christians support the suffocation of Palestinians. It is in anticipation of the great recall, when the misguided will, in one Messianic fell swoop, return unto the true Christian fold. Can this be an Age of Reason, an age of human values and human rights? What would reason and rationally grounded morality dictate? Can we imagine the country now under Israel's control being truly democratic, that is to say, allowing all its residents equal rights as human beings under the same law, even extending its law of return to Palestinians as to Jews? Would such a country seem uncivilized? Its one major principle would be the requirement to treat all its citizens as equal human beings. But such a country would fulfill neither the Zionist or Judaic project, nor the Arab nationalist or Muslim one. It would be neither a Jewish state nor a Muslim one; neither an Israeli state nor a Palestinian one. It may be a rational as well as a humanitarian solution, but in the circumstances it is a rejected one, fulfilling neither the religious nor the nationalist imperatives motivating the two sides.

Thus it is that Palest-El is under compulsion of the irrational and the amoral, that the two sides seek to deal with each other mostly through force and confrontation. Their respective religious beliefs seem to outweigh basic common sense and basic moral values. Can we imagine that same country being geographically divided between two states? Under the parochial religious and nationalist circumstances mentioned, such a solution might seem more practical, addressing both rational as well as moral principles though in a less-than-absolute way. But even such a compromise, in its nature, aggravates large segments of the populations on the two sides. It is, nonetheless, a compromise that has been in the works at least for the past decade. So far, it has proven difficult to implement as its implementation goes against the grain. The commitment to it, where it exists, seems half-hearted. Its shape and outline seem shamefully utilitarian, shamefully antithetic to the divine design. A true soldier of God would surely fight it to the death.

Tribalism vs. Humanism

So it is that humanity seems to be being challenged by God. Neither can human rationalism or human values compete to reign supreme. A religious *tribalism* seems to prevail. This is a structure in which closed systems compete with each other for status and space. Equality may obtain among individuals within each closed system, but it neither obtains between systems nor yet between individuals belonging to different systems. Terms such as "injustice" or "aggression" have a meaningful application within one system. They lose their significance and even acquire opposite meanings when applied to the other system. Occupation is liberation. Resistance is terrorism. Terrorism is justified. Racism is democracy. Democracy is segregation. Equality is benign rule. The chosen are the traitors.

It is a world of conceptual chaos. An equal allocation of water among Israelis would seem self-evidently appropriate. Nobody could conceive that any other allocation would be permissible, or just. But unequal allocations between Israeli settlers and Palestinian villagers is not even frowned upon, let alone legally or morally challenged by the purported upholders of democracy and equal rights. Indeed, the usurpation of water resources by settlers is ignored; it does not merit any attention or acknowledgment. Injustice grinds its way into daily routine so long as a mentality of tribalism prevails. The indiscriminate taking of human life is abhorrent. But news of the blowing up of Israeli children or Holocaust survivors gathered for a Pesach dinner at some restaurant is gleefully received by one side. News of the death of Palestinian women and children does not merit even a slight moral stir from the other. Indeed, the very idea of compassion with other human beings is summarily dismissed. Excuses for tribal attitudes can always be found. God is the excuse of last resort, if all other excuses fail. God is the excuse that human beings do not have equal worth.

Thus, it seems, Palest-El is a country where one is justified in asking, Is God the obstacle to human rights — above all, to the right of equality between men? The appeal to God may cause a problem in understanding rights, but it is difficult to reconcile different rights, or claims of rights, quite independent of God. Even if the Jews were not God's chosen race, and were not fulfilling a divine destiny in forcefully ensconcing themselves in someone else's home, making it their own, do they not nonetheless have a right in having a home — in particular, even if only a psychological safe house in the aftermath of the Holocaust? Can a Palestinian (or any other people, for that matter) *morally* respond: Maybe, but let it be somewhere else. Let it be in Nigeria, for example, as the Zionist elders once considered, or anywhere else, so long as it is not on Palestinian soil. Would this be a moral response, or would this just be a legalistic defense of one's own property rights, a way of passing the buck? True, Palestinians are rightly aggravated by the old Zionist dictum, "A land without a people for a people without a land," a principle of action used to justify Israel's many years of conscious blindness to the people from whom the land was robbed. But justified aggravation aside, as well as definitions of "empty land," wouldn't the Palestinian response be tribal rather than moral, and self-centered rather than altruistic or humanitarian? And wouldn't it, alas, be typical? Could any country or people tolerate another people's move to slice off a piece of what they regard as their land for themselves, regardless of their consent, and against their will? Surely, you will say, someone homeless stepping into your house and forcefully settling himself in one or more of its rooms is an infringement on your legal property rights. Would the Turks have a right in declaring independence or autonomy in Germany, or the Maltese in Italy, or the Algerians in France, or the Cubans in Florida? Would it make a difference whether such a declaration was reached as the fruition of a willful plan, or whether it evolved slowly and naturally as a need of an already established migrant group? Indeed, what would have been the British reaction had the Balfour Declaration promised the Jewish people a homeland in Britain rather than in Palestine in the first place?

On the one hand, allowing ourselves to question the moral foundation of what is a typical, tribal response might open the door to absolute chaos. On the other hand, chaos does not of itself seem to be a state of injustice. On the contrary, order implies injustice, insofar as it is based upon tribal, rather than humanitarian, values and directives. And if reason favors order rather than chaos, history tells us that morality is not the preferred option of peoples and governments.

A legalistic or typical response to a homeless claimant might be that though they certainly have no right in or over your property, they certainly cannot be denied the right to *some* property. The neatness of this answer does not stand to the challenge of reality, however. Thus, let us suppose that a certain place contains a certain number of properties, and an equal number of owners, plus one. In this case, one can neither place the claimant (or *wildcard*) in any one of the properties without infringing on some pre-existing owner, nor can one pretend the wildcard is not part of the game. There simply is no other property for the wildcard. Left to the owners, the simplest way to deal with the threat is to throw the extra card out. Each owner might feel more comfortable thinking that the wildcard could find a home in someone else's property. Indeed, if the wildcard were to strike first at the neighbor's property, other owners might think it in their interest to *stabilize* this intrusion, as a means of maintaining order and safeguarding their own home. Considered in advance and from behind a Rawlsian sort of veil of ignorance, however, the property owners might individually decide that it is more prudent to act preemptively by *outlawing* the intrusion of the wildcard into any one of the properties, and they might hence collectively agree to the introduction of a convention at once affirming their rights to their respective properties while denying that right to the wildcard. Let the wildcard be homeless, the convention would imply, rather than allowing for an infringement of rights, or for the breakdown of order. Our convention, the owners would say, does not deny the wildcard an equal right to the right we have allocated to ourselves. On the contrary, it accords him that right in the same way that right is accorded to us. Too bad that the wildcard cannot fend for himself the way we do. But clearly, this is a tribal rather than a human convention.

Tribal War

Tribalistic thinking unfortunately may lead to more dire consequences than leaving the wildcard homeless, to fend for himself. "Terrorism" is a term which is in common use in Palest-El. Israelis accuse Palestinians of being terrorists, and vice versa. Actually, both sides practice terrorism as a matter of course. Terrorism is an instrument of coercion by fear and force. Bin Laden may be one of very few "honest" terrorists. His use of terrorism is blunt, and he does not shy of calling it by its name. Seasoned terrorists are not so transparent. They camouflage their terrorism with interpretations and concepts that are meant to present it as the right of the innocent and the victims to defend themselves. In response to being called terrorist, Palestinians say that occupation itself is the embodiment of terrorism.

Is occupation truly a form of terrorism? Occupation (for the occupied) is not a democratic choice. It does not come by invitation. It is conceived by force. It exists by force and fear. It does not have lapses, weekends, or holidays. It is a continuously running affair. If you are under occupation, then you are so whatever you do. You make love to your wife and beget children under occupation. You dream under occupation. As you watch the rain beginning to fall in winter, you do so under occupation. Occupation, like God, is everywhere and always. Occupation knows no rest. Occupation watches every step you take, every word you write, every thought you think. Occupation is all-powerful, and its vengeful wrath insuperable. Occupation dispenses rewards and punishments. It can wreak havoc on a household, a village, ravaging its stone structures to the ground. Or it can link up the village to the electricity grid, or provide the means of sustenance to one of its obedient servants. It raises men as it pleases, and can crush them inside its prison cells as it pleases. Occupation can crush a human being from inside as well as from outside. It can connive to compromise an innocent young virgin, and then use this to blackmail her into becoming a spy on her family and friends. Or it can simply and bluntly put an end to a young man's life. Occupation can assume different shapes. Once it can appear in the form of a civilized officer dropping by to chat and have some tea. Another time it can appear in the form of tanks and armored vehicles that rumble their way threateningly through the center of your small village. Occupation can uproot your ancestral olive trees from under your nose, or carve off a piece of your land, under the protection of the gun. Occupation can imprison you inside your home for days and weeks on end, sometimes making you unable to step out into the balcony, or to look out through your window, at pain of aggravating armed soldiers brandishing their guns. Occupation provides you with work, and takes it away. It allows you to travel to the next town, or turns you back. Occupation scrutinizes your papers, belongings, and appearance at roadblocks. You are in the grip of a soldier's whim. Will you be able to go about your business that day? Only the Occupation knows. Only the Occupation decides. Will your children return home safely from school that day? Only the Occupation knows. Only the Occupation decides. Occupation is a beast that feeds off force and spreads fear to maintain its grip on the people's will.

Palestinians were first called terrorists soon after the occupation began. The literal translation of the Hebrew word used is "spoilers," that is, someone who, typically, violently spoils the general run of things. Soon, however, all kinds of people became spoilers of sorts, subject to arrest, prison terms, or other forms of punitive measures. Someone associating himself with a nationalist group, though totally uninvolved with the use of weapons, could be sentenced to a long prison term. Someone caught trying to hang up a Palestinian flag, or writing a nationalist slogan on the wall, could risk getting shot. Indeed, the term "Palestinian" was considered anathema, totally blotted out in all references in official Israeli media to "the Arabs" of Judea and Samaria. "The Arabs of Judea and Samaria" continued to be portrayed as an extra package of assorted individuals and groups, a *special* variety, who happened to be aimlessly roaming in the Land of Israel, taking advantage of the absence of its true landlords. The proper *home* of this species was somewhere else, in those vast expanses of desert that naturally fit them, and where their brethren lived. To call them by the collective national name they use to call themselves was to succumb to a dangerously conflicting narrative of what has been happening in the Holy Land for the preceding fifty years. It was to succumb to the horrifying reality of the bloody birth of Israel, to its non-Immaculate conception. It was to be awoken to the harsh reality that the birth, or rebirth, of a people had come at the expense of another people, a human group with collective or national claims to that property at least as valid as theirs. Thus, the denial of Palestinian national identity, and the occupation's vicious war against all nationalists.

Resistance against occupation, even by military means, is enshrined in international law as a natural right. But do international laws uphold a system of military power rather than, or more than, a system of moral values? I can understand a person *dying* in the defense of a cause, Gandhi once said, but I cannot understand a person *killing* for it. His moral exhortation is totally lost in a world of human passion, natural rights, divine edicts, and international law. And where all these rights and laws are jumbled up in a cross-laws puzzle, double standards are not the exception but the rule. All such standards derive from an exclusivist self-worth. Otherwise, by what human right can one justify stabbing to death in the back a ninety-year-old Rabbi inching his way painstakingly into the Damascus Gate of the Old City on his way to the Western Wall on the Shabbat? Or randomly shooting at a medical doctor driving from a settlement on his way to work in an Israeli hospital, and killing him? Or blowing up a night club or a restaurant in the middle of town, tearing to shreds the flesh and lives of countless civilians? Are the targets in these cases *human* or simply organisms belonging to a different *special* variety? Wherein lies the supposed source of justification for performing such "inhuman" acts? Is it derivable from a *preceding* sense of injustice, or do its roots lie in some compelling *future* just cause? Surely, a preceding sense of pain may *explain* a humanly ugly act, but it can never *justify* it. And a compelling just cause may similarly *clarify* the intention behind a specific act of violence, but it can hardly justify it. What value is there in a State that has been built on the ruins and suffering of another people? What *right* is there in killing another person's brother just because he killed yours? Is revenge or rage a human right? Or is it, at best, a *tribal* right, or a right in the *de facto* sense of its being a natural impulse in the abyss of the jungle, rather than in the aspired-to sense of its belonging to the realm of human values? In what sense can I justify my moral outrage when one of my own kinsmen is killed, if my natural impulse is to kill the kinsman of another? I can certainly and honestly say I am outraged. But to claim morality is surely to be equally outraged at the killing of my loved one as at my own impulse to kill another's in rage or revenge, or in the pursuit of my goal.

Israel's creation, from a Palestinian perspective, constituted an act of aggression. From an Israeli point of view, it constituted a long-awaited and rightful conception. But abstracted from who was right in acting as they did, and abstracted from tribal passion, does a people not shirk moral responsibility if and when they reject hosting a homeless claimant? Forgetting for an instance legal arguments for the establishment of rights and claims, and regardless of their validity, is not an argument for sharing the land, for hosting the homeless, perfectly rational and moral? Is it so unreasonable to hope for human, rather than for tribal, sympathy? Clearly, this principle would work both ways, applying now to Palestinians as it did earlier to Jews.

Let us consider the problem of the wildcard from another perspective. Suppose one day a brother to you is born and your parents place his crib in your bedroom. Clearly, you were neither consulted beforehand nor did you provide your consent to the new arrangement. Indeed, you might even have protested the only way you know how, by screaming and making a mess. You feel that your space has been threatened. He squeaks and squeals, and you observe to your horror that his presence spreads in your previously private space like an unsolicited cobweb, each day reducing your margin of free movement even further. You can no longer leap in your imagination to that corner in your bedroom over there, because your mother has already filled it with the newborn's crib-toy. You are shunned from this space by his scream, his things, his smell. You are no longer alone, no longer king, no longer master, no longer sovereign. Were your parents right in giving birth to him? Does he have a right to the space he has come to permeate? Do you have a right to jump out of your crib, and, with one fell swoop, to kill him? And, if you both have a natural right to your respective cribs, is there a way, once that right is granted, to share that common space ever after? Is there a virtual border in that space delineating between what is rightfully yours, and what his? Or is there no space in that bedroom but for you, no ownership, property, or precedence right but that which is yours? Do you say, sympathetically, that you have nothing against his being born, only that he could have been born somewhere else, by some other parents? Is such sympathy a reflection of a true sense of morality?

One's sympathy with one's brother is surely familial, with one's kinsmen tribal, with one's compatriots national. But in human terms, surely Jews and Arabs are brothers. Perhaps that kinship is even more profound, as Palest-El is a country whose peoples, according to a recent genome survey undertaken by the Hebrew University, share more in common than with races abroad. Just as the common brotherhood of humanity is unrealized between individuals, however, surely so it is among nations and groups. Yet, do we fail to treat each other as brothers because our morals or our passions dictate that we prefer certain individuals and interests over others? And, if it is our passions that are to blame, do we not thereafter groom our reason so as to best service this passion? For a long period, Israelis and Palestinians simply refused to recognize each other as coherent entities with individuated identities. There was simply a denial of the other. Palestinians claimed that the Jews are not a people (therefore deserving of a state), and the Israelis refused to recognize the Palestinians as a people (therefore also deserving of a state). Once the first hurdle of mutual recognition was crossed, however, the second hurdle of deciding how and where such states should exist was reached. But it is not moral values that guide the process of delineating space as that hurdle is being crossed; rather, it is the balance of power, an order conceived in the image of a caste system separating the more powerful, and accordingly more worthy, from the less powerful, and less worthy.

Whose Rights: Individual vs. Collective Rights

Clearly, we must not allow tribal passions to masquerade as moral imperatives, even when reason conflicts with moral values, since tribal passions cause chaos. Rather, we must maintain a clear moral lens through which to make our judgments, and we must face up to our tribal passions, recognizing them for what they are. We must also face up to our conflicting rights-claims. The problem of conflicting rights is not simply confined to conflicts between groups, as for example between Israelis and Palestinians; or to that between an individual and the group to which that individual belongs, as the debate between liberal and communitarian philosophies; or to a conflict between the summation of individual rights and the *general* right of that collective sum of individuals. Rights can also and annoyingly conflict in reference to the same entity or individual. Take the rights, for example, of return and of statehood for the Palestinians. Let us not dwell on the question whether Palestinians have the right of return, whether as enshrined in divine, international, or natural principles. Let us also not dwell on the question whether the Palestinians have a collective right to freedom. Let us assume they have both. But let us assume also that these two rights cannot be simultaneously fulfilled. Would this be a heinous oddity in human affairs? And would it be a heinous crime to suggest, since both cannot be simultaneously fulfilled, that one be preferred to the other? Do rights, in other words, make sense as rights only if they can *all* be, indeed, must be, justifiably pursued, or should rights rather be viewed as occurring in an order of priority, the fulfillment of one justifiably preempting or foreclosing the search for the fulfillment of another right, lower on the list? Why not view the matter of preferring statehood over return simply as the matter of choosing to accept one university's acceptance offer over another's — with the difference, of course, that in one case both offers tangibly exist while in the other both are but a projected aim or desire? It makes perfectly good sense to argue that, in the pursuit of one right, one often forecloses the option of pursuing the other. Indeed, can't one argue that *in order* to be able to fulfill one right it is, by definition, necessary that one forego even seeking the fulfillment of the other? Clearly, if a case can be argued for such a prioritization at the level of the individual, it can analogously be argued at the level of the collective or group. It is in the very nature of group decisions that priorities have to be made, and some (rightful) scenarios have to be chosen at the expense of others. A collective Palestinian decision to forgo the right of return in favor of the right to statehood or to forgo the right of statehood in favor of the right of return is thus a common, rather than a unique, situation.

The problem, however, arises when one has to balance between a collective and an individual choice. For suppose, as it is sometimes argued, that some or all Palestinian refugees decide that they will pursue the right of return as individuals, since they indeed have the right to do this in spite of any decision taken by any representative claimant on their behalf. Let us also suppose that refugees constitute a hefty bulk of the total population. How can the matter of conflicting aims, as well as acts, be settled? Are we to assume that individual rights in this case are overriding? Do individual rights *always* override a contrary collective right? Are there cases where a collective right can *justifiably* override individual rights? Let us assume, at least for the sake of this stage of the argument, that the representative authority in question is truly representative, having been duly elected by the entire group of people it claims to represent. Let us further assume that such an authority, backed by a majority, decides in favor of statehood. In what sense can we claim that its decisions are therefore *binding* on those who voted (justifiably) against? Surely, if the question involved simply had to do with a *preference* (for example, joining the common market), the very meaning of democracy would imply that the majority decision has to be binding. Our example, however, has to do not simply with a preference for an altogether new state of affairs; rather, it has to do with rightful claims that have hitherto been forcefully denied. Can a majority decision be so construed as to justify a total closure on those rightful claims? I believe the answer has to be a cautious yes. Cautious, because one has to guard against arguing in favor of totalitarianism in the course of pursuing a collective right. And yes, because many cases can be construed where it is indeed and clearly justifiable to pursue such a course.

Let us thus hypothesize an extreme case where a highway thief happens to lure you into stopping your family-packed car in an isolated spot, and proceeds to rob your family members of their belongings under the threat of a gun. You glimpse a rare opportunity as his attention, after he has robbed your wife of her jewelry, is momentarily distracted by his greedy inspection of a particular diamond ring she had just turned over to him. If you quickly turn the engine on and press the gas pedal, there might just be a chance of saving the other belongings, including your mother-in-law's even more precious jewelry. A quick scan of the faces of people in the car tells you that your companions have read your mind and that, with the exception of your horrified wife, who still hopes you will bravely manhandle the robber and return her jewelry, all of them are begging for you to take the chance and drive speedily off. You make your calculations instantaneously. Your wife has a right to stay put and fight the robber to get her jewelry back. Her mother, as well as each one of the family members in the car, has a right to save their own jewelry and money from being robbed. It makes no sense to drop your wife off and leave, partly because you know that doing this would make you lose the opportunity to drive safely off, and partly because you worry what might happen to her if you did manage to leave. Your wife has a rightful claim to the jewelry she was just robbed of. But you decide that, viewed as a whole, it is better to save the lot than to risk finding your entire family penniless on a deserted sidewalk. The sudden sound of the roaring engine is totally overwhelmed by the sound of your wife's outraged screams. Have you, acting on behalf of yourself and your companions, acted prudently? Was the preference of the majority a blatant violation of the rights of one individual? Were you justified in acting as you did, even as you foreclosed the ability of your wife to pursue her rightful claims? On the whole, one would assume that a common-sense answer to these questions will be one where you will be commended for acting as you did. Your children, at least, were spared a possible life-threatening situation.

Conclusion

In addition to questions of conflict between individual and group rights, there is the issue of *sympathy*, or *solidarity*. Palestinians might believe they have a right to statehood, and might realize that the fulfillment of this right implies foregoing the right of return, but they might nonetheless feel defused of motivation for statehood because of the sympathy they feel to their right of return. In such a case, a rational assessment points one way, while their sense of sympathy points another. Palestinians can become petrified, unable to move forward as summoned by reason, but unable also to wind the clock back as summoned by their romanticized dream. Their situation can thus become more complex by the day. Their lifeline seems to be ruled by forces which, though initially created by them, are now totally out of their control.

Israelis are in a parallel bind. On the one hand reason summons them to divest themselves of a property inhabited primarily by members of another nation, who might eventually pose a dilemma between democracy and nationalism. Sentiments summon them to stay put, stuck to a territory breeding bipeds of a different ilk. It is a petrified situation. Neither can a Jewish Israel be democratic, nor a democratic Israel be Jewish. Can Israel pull back, against its sentiments? Can it maintain its hold of this territory, against reason? Unable to decide, Israel's situation becomes more complex by the day. Its lifeline seems to be ruled by forces which, though initially created by it, are also now totally out of its control.

In an ideal world, a world still of chaos but where humanity prevails over tribalism, Israelis and Palestinians would share the land, under a political system where rights are distributed equally among individuals. In a less-than-ideal world, a world of reason, they would divide the land, each side living under a separate political system. But the world Israelis and Palestinians inhabit is unfortunately neither ideal nor less-than-ideal. It is a cross-laws puzzle world where ideals and values are turned upside down, with divine, natural, and conventional imperatives fusing one another where they touch.

This place, Palest-El, is the site where earth meets heaven and hell. There is a tradition that relates that when Adam first set foot on earth it was on the holy rock, now enveloped by that architectural jewel, the Dome of the Rock. Muhammad's journey of ascension, we are told, took place from that site. Early Caananite and Philistine gods had their abodes there. Further up on the Mount of Olives, a medieval church marks the spot where Jesus is said to have ascended to heaven. Below the mount used for threshing flour, where David is said to have bought a spot of land from Arnan the Jebusite to build a place of worship for his god, a pretty valley swerves and gently runs to the Dead Sea, some thirty kilometers away. Along its route, one or two monasteries still retain the preserved skulls of ancient monks, together with some icons. But where it is closest to the revered Rock, the valley goes by the name of Gehenna, a burning sacrificial site of death where bodies were thrown to the ever-raging flames. Its biblical name resonates in the Arabic term for hell, *Gehannam*. Condensed within a kilometer radius are situated both the abodes of heavenly immortals and the damned gates of hell. This is one inimitable powerhouse. It is the contact point of the earthly and the divine. Not more than half a kilometer away the body of Christ himself is said to have been laid to rest. His path of pain, the Via Dolorosa, with its painstakingly archived stations, runs from the same mount to his crucifixion and burial site. Everything that is here, is at once here and not here. It is earthly, and not earthly; it is one and three; it is buried and not dead; it is subject to physical laws and totally impervious to them. It is the past and the future. It is the site of suffering and of redemption. A thin rope is said to run across the valley. On the day of resurrection, men shall walk it. Those whose works please God shall cross it safely into heaven. Those whose works displease him will fall into hell. This world unfortunately goes by the name of God's Holy Land.

But one has a right to wonder whether God is the cause, or the excuse, for the human tragedy that blights this hallowed place. One has a further and overriding right, as a human being, and especially in this *Terra Sancta,* to continue to seek an ideal world in the here and now, and not only in the hereafter.

10 God, the Devil, and Human Rights: A South African Perspective

CHARLES VILLA-VICENCIO

The overt support for human rights by the Religions of the Book is a recent phenomenon. Religious leaders had hitherto, with few exceptions, condemned such rights as humanistic nonsense. Some within these traditions viewed human rights to be of the Devil, while those who early on made the link between John Locke's secular doctrine of human rights and the affirmation of human dignity in the Scriptures (a dignity which coexists with textual sanction of human subjugation) were voices crying in the wilderness. It was a cry without the support of the church, mosque, temple, or synagogue. Perhaps it is because institutional religion failed so dismally in its humanizing task that God raised up a prophet within secular humanism to promote human rights. This secular tradition in time reminded religious institutions of a dimension of their own traditions that had hitherto lain essentially fallow.

The South African human rights crisis in theological and related debate was thrust into the public arena partly through a rather crude intervention by J. M. Potgieter, a Professor of Private Law at the University of South Africa in the late 1980s.[1] Dismissing any notion of the general population having inalienable rights, he suggested that the restoration of humanity could only happen through conversion to Christ — an argument that enjoyed the tacit support of many within the established churches. The argument was, of course, but a small step from the reactionary kind of apartheid theology that located rights and privileges in the hands of whites as carriers of the gospel and civilization. Right-wing Christians picked up on the argument, contending that "an honest person needs no special rights in order to associate, disassociate, assemble, read, speak, perform, or travel." They argued that "the rights [demanded by human rights groups] for the arrested, accused and convicted were aimed primarily at limiting the power of the police."[2]

The most significant critique of this position came through the publication of a small group of Afrikaner academics who argued that it is precisely because of human sin, which gives rise to an inflated sense of self-perception, that a declaration of human rights is a necessary basis for recognizing the rights of others.[3] The cautious wording and careful presentation of the argument in this declaration, at the same time, bears testimony to the sensitivity of the debate on human rights in church circles, including the Dutch Reformed Church, as recently as the late 1980s.

Ecumenical and global theological debate on human rights was more forthright than what was offered by the Dutch Reformed theologians. The debate on human rights was, at the same time, a cautious and late development. It was not until Vatican II that the Roman Catholic Church gave official sanction to human rights, while at least some of the Protestant churches made their first tentative step in this direction a few years earlier. The inaugural assembly of the World Council of Churches in Amsterdam issued a declaration on religious liberty and the importance of the churches' work for human rights on the eve of the adoption of the Universal Declaration of Human Rights (the "Universal Declaration") in December 1948. It was not, however, until 1979 that the major Protestant denominations, the Vatican, and the Pan-Orthodox Council sought to coordinate efforts to promote human rights. Suffice it to say, ecclesial support for human rights came late, and when it came it was cautious.

Judaism's historic focus was also not on human rights. David Novak has shown elsewhere that Judaic ethical teaching is primarily grounded in the relationship that human beings have with God — rather than in *human* rights per se.[4] In Goitein's words, Jewish philosophers and thinkers were primarily concerned with "God, not man," resulting in the passive acceptance and promotion of human inequality and abuse.[5] Essentially it took the Holocaust to awaken Jews to the resources within their own tradition that affirm the fundamental rights of human beings.[6]

Islam, in turn, felt doubly alienated from the notion of human rights, which it viewed as transmitted by a dominant Christian church and as an instrument of both Western cultural and political domination. The Shari'ah, incorporating law, ethics, ritual, cultural practices, hygiene, good manners, and religious belief, prescribed a divinely ordained way of life. As the West engaged the East, militarily, politically, and culturally, and the church encountered Islam through evangelism and conflict, it was but a short step for Muslims to resist all that was seen to be a manifestation of Western hostility. This included a rejection of the emergence of a Western, secular notion of human rights. Rejecting any notion of the Universal Declaration as *universal*, Riffat Hassan particularly rejects its secular nature as at least unwise to the extent that "human rights become meaningful only when placed within the framework of their belief-system."[7] In Abdullahi An-Na'im's words, "The most serious objection to secularism as the foundation of the universality of human rights is its inability to inspire or motivate believers, who are the vast majority of the world."[8] As is the case with Christianity and Judaism, the contemporary affirmation of Qur'anic principles of human rights is a recent phenomenon. And, argues Hassan, it is an alternative to the Universal Declaration, "actualizing the Qur'anic version of human destiny."[9]

Today, of course, most thoughtful religious people claim that human rights are a God-given right. If religious organizations put their institutional foot down to protect their own self-interest by shunning human rights in the past, most have since lifted that foot to support human rights in a changing political milieu — perhaps again partially out of self-interest. Cynicism apart, from a human rights perspective this is good news. I simply suggest that it took the secular human rights awakening — characterized in the post–World War II rejection of the kind of barbarism that made human dignity dependent on race, creed, breeding, and ideology — for this to happen.

The normal rejoinder to this argument is to show that the seeds of human rights ideas can, at least, be discerned in those dimensions of the world religions that emphasize human dignity, good neighborliness, and social justice. This said, unless the intervention of the world's religions into rights talk and practice can add new insights or a new incentive to human rights, it would be reasonable to conclude that religion can, at best, merely be attributed with certain general historical, ethical ideas that contribute to human rights thinking.[10]

In this essay I first provide a comment on the context out of which the human rights agenda emerged in South Africa. This contextual comment will serve as background out of which I suggest arises an ambiguity within the South African human rights struggle. This ambiguity gives rise to a sense of transcendence amidst what is the secular humanist quest for moral and political renewal. It is here that secular and theological languages often merge, providing space for talking of God in a secular state. I conclude by arguing that human rights are most potent when contextually grounded in the ethos of a given society.

Human Rights in South Africa

Max Horkheimer, an early exponent of the critical theory of the Frankfurt Institute for Social Research, and an existentialist and atheist, suggested that "behind every genuine human endeavour stands a theology." He argues that a political and ethical paradigm that "does not preserve a theological moment in itself, no matter how skilful, in the last analysis is mere business."[11] My hypothesis is that, carefully considered, *this* sense of the theological, a restlessness and a lure that draws humanity beyond itself, is readily discerned in the ambiguities of the struggle for human rights in South Africa. In the next section of this essay, I address the nature of this transcendence more explicitly.

The battle for human rights in South Africa has essentially been a struggle for the vote, for land, and for survival — all issues of human rights, although not always pursued as such and often not articulated as such by many of those engaged in this struggle. A brief oversight of the South African struggle for a constitutional state is important to discern the human transcendence that I suggest is both "more than secular" and "less than religious" in the Horkheimerian sense. It also shows that any notion of a Bill of Rights, constitutionally protecting the rights of citizens, is a very recent development in South African politics.

Indeed, the franchise debate in South Africa was such that it countered the argument in favor of a Bill of Rights. The vote, it was argued, was sufficient to protect the rights of the citizens. The British notion of parliamentary sovereignty was imposed in the colonial period and, in a moot way, continues to influence political thinking in South Africa even in this day and age.

Sir William Blackstone's famous affirmation of the supremacy of parliament in 1765 was to leave an indelible mark on British colonies around the world. "To set judicial power above that of the legislature," he argued, "would be subversive of all governments." For him, the power of parliament was "absolute and without control."[12] The context was, of course, the English Glorious Revolution of 1688 and hard-won parliamentary democracy over the divine right of kings that saw William and Mary (with trimmed royal prerogatives) succeed James II, the last of the notorious Stuarts. Transposed into a colonial context, however, it meant the exclusion of those whom the colonial masters deemed to be unworthy of the vote. It meant racism and the subjugation of the native population.

And when the Boers trekked north in 1835 to escape the imposition of English rule in South Africa, they too resisted any thought of subjecting their newly won freedom in the South African Republic (Transvaal) in any way. Any thought to the contrary was bluntly dealt with when, in 1895, Chief Justice J. G. Kotze found certain *besluiten* (informal decisions) by the *Volksraad* (parliament) to be contrary to the *Grondwet* (constitution). President Kruger summarily dismissed Kotze from his post, insisting that "the testing right is a principle of the devil."[13] Boer sovereignty was attributed to divine providence. Anything, including *human* rights, which was seen to question or violate *divine* sovereignty, was of the devil.

When the Union of South Africa was established in 1910, incorporating the Cape Colony, Natal, and the two former Boer Republics (Transvaal and Orange Free State), any thought of limiting the will of the people (read *white* people) as expressed through parliament was regarded as unnecessary, unwarranted, and undemocratic. The Union of South Africa Act was a decidedly racist document. It denied the vote to the vast majority of black South Africans. At the same time, it stated that no person registered or capable of registering to vote in the Cape, according to pre-Union franchise qualifications, could be deprived of the vote, despite race or color.[14] The Act required that this entrenched clause could be amended only on the basis of a two-thirds majority vote at a joint sitting of both Houses of Parliament.

Although the 1865 Colonial Laws Validity Act stipulated further that any act repugnant to an act of the British Parliament was to be regarded as null and void, this obstacle was removed by the Statute of Westminster Act of 1931, which resulted in South Africa becoming an independent state within the British Commonwealth of Nations. South Africa was quick to follow up on this development by enacting the Representation of Natives Act in 1936, which removed black African voters from the common voter's roll. When the National Party came to power in 1948, it also set its mind to finding a way of removing the "coloureds" from the common voter's roll. Prime Minister D. F. Malan reiterated the position of President Kruger in dismissing any limitation of the sovereignty of parliament.[15] Legislation designed to gerrymander numbers in parliament ensured that "coloureds" lost the vote.[16] When white South Africans elected to become a Republic in 1961, the new Republican constitution again entrenched the supremacy of parliament. The 1983 Constitution further entrenched white supremacy, this time locating maximum power not in parliament but in the white executive branch of a white government. In the words of Frederik Van Zyl Slabbert, leader of the opposition in parliament at the time, this was "white dictatorial rule."[17]

Given the heritage that characterized generations of colonialism and fifty years of apartheid rule, it is ironic, and yet understandable, that the black majority chose a liberal constitution with a Bill of Rights that ultimately breached the established South African pattern of electoral majoritarianism. Ironic, because they stood to benefit if free from constitutional restraints and a Bill of Rights that guaranteed their former oppressors a set of rights they had themselves been denied for so long. Understandable, because they sensed the long-term corrosive effects of exploitation on the exploiter as well as the exploited. The factors that persuaded the African National Congress (ANC) to promote and ultimately adopt a liberal constitution with a Bill of Rights and affirm an international human rights agenda are, of course, many and varied. In order to attract Western support, the emerging new black-majority government was obliged, for example, to abandon any thought of not affirming individual property rights (despite the fact that most whites, either directly or indirectly, had acquired the title deeds to property as a result of apartheid privilege). It was similarly obliged to turn away from any earlier thought of nationalizing the commanding heights of the economy. Evidence also shows, however, that human rights values underpinned the history of the various struggles in South Africa from the earliest days of colonialism. This was not an alien concept imposed on South Africans by the Western world. It was latently there in early forms of resistance to colonialism, anti-slavery agitation, and the struggle for the freedom of the press as far back as the 1820s. It was seen in the anti-war sentiments of Olive Schreiner, in Emily Hobhouse's campaigns against the treatment of Boer women and children in British concentration camps during the Anglo-Boer or South African War, in trade union struggles, and in passive resistance campaigns. It was there in the adoption of the Freedom Charter in 1955 and in the anti-apartheid movement that resulted in the ultimate collapse of the apartheid regime and the birth of South African democracy in 1994.

Faith communities were, of course, an important part of the broad national anti-apartheid movement. This was an inclusive movement that bore neither the imprint of religion nor that of anti-religious secularism. There are many personalities in South African history — religious, secular, and atheist — of whom contemporary human rights activists can justifiably be proud: John Pringle, Mahatma Gandhi, Abdul Abdurahman, Emily Hobhouse, Olive Schreiner, Sol Plaatjies, Albert Luthuli, Lilian Ngoyi, Braam Fischer, Alan Paton, Ruth First, Beyers Naudé, Steve Biko, Robert Sobukwe, Nelson Mandela, Desmond Tutu, and others — many of whom are unknown and unsung. Obviously not all espoused the values enshrined in the Universal Declaration, the battery of subsequent UNO human rights instruments, or the essential teachings of Amnesty International, Human Rights Watch, or the about-to-be-born International Criminal Court (ICC). Each, however, made a significant contribution to the South African struggle for a culture of human rights.

The point has already been made that the South African struggle was essentially about the vote, land, and survival, a process that inevitably saw more than a few human rights violations. This human quest for freedom and the demand for human dignity overcame the law of the conqueror, colonial custom, racist political obduracy, and the barrel of the gun. This quest manifests itself not in the revengeful pursuit of power as an end in itself, but in the birth of something better — something captured in the heart of human rights culture. The Freedom Charter (which is at least one manifestation of this early quest) is not the Universal Declaration. It is, however, a vitally important contextual affirmation of human dignity in a harsh and brutal period of South African history. Today, the staunchest supporters of the Freedom Charter have, for the most part, transcended its essential teaching, and yet it endures as a significant human rights symbol that helped usher in the human rights dispensation that unfolded in 1994.

Two significant contemporary human rights developments were born within this tradition.[18] In 1986, the ANC committed itself to a justifiable Bill of Rights, designed to protect the fundamental rights and liberties of all individuals in the country. This was followed by the publication of the organization's Constitutional Guidelines,[19] which again affirmed the place of a Bill of Rights in the total constitutional process. The South African government, at the same time, referred the question of a Bill of Rights to the Law Commission for response.[20] The areas of agreement between the proposals of the ANC and the government of the day were significant, while the equally significant differences were items on the agenda for debate that would eventually result in the Bill of Rights that is the cornerstone of South African democracy.

South Africans boast of a constitution that is among the most progressive and human-rights friendly in the world. Its Bill of Rights is commonly regarded as an instrument worthy of emulation. And yet, any new beginning can only emerge from the circumstances that constitute the past. These circumstances include both resentment and hope. The resentment comes from those who no longer enjoy the unjust privileges of the past. It also comes from those who continue to experience poverty and exclusion and who sometimes question the generosity of a Constitution and Bill of Rights that protects and confers essential rights on those very people who denied them their essential rights for so long. This said, the government that enjoys significant electoral support, essentially from the poor and excluded, has resisted temptations to tamper with the Constitution. The Constitutional Court has ruled against the executive branch of government, and the executive has accepted the ruling. The press has harshly criticized the government's handling of HIV/AIDS, President Mbeki's stance on Zimbabwe, and state expenditure on arms, without serious threat of censure. The populace has accepted election results at national, regional, and local levels. To adapt Chinua Achebe's celebrated phrase,[21] the constitutional state is still in the morning of the first day of creation. And yet it has demonstrated a resolve to honor its birthright of human rights, freedom, and mutual respect in the wake of apartheid abuse.

The willingness of South Africans, including those who suffered most at the hands of colonialism and apartheid, to seek a way beyond both prosecutions and amnesia through the Truth and Reconciliation Commission continues to confound many. It suggests a level of humanity (of *ubuntu*),[22] compassion, and restoration that bespeaks the quest for a way of transcending past conflicts in a rugged, less than ideal process that has offended many human rights advocated by allowing some human rights abuses to escape punishment. The ultimate goal of this checkered, controversial, and contested process is at the same time an end that few, even in their uneasiness, find difficult to dismiss.

The sustainability of this process may, of course, in the long run yet be tested as the impact of poverty, unemployment, crime, and HIV/AIDS and related problems test the resolve of everyone involved to play by the rules of the Constitution and Bill of Rights. Only time will tell whether the nation has the capacity to endure. It is too early to tell. The indications are that to succeed, a creative tension needs to be maintained between what the nation can deliver at any given time and the expectations of those whose needs were legitimately stimulated and energized by the dawn of democracy in 1994. I return in the final section of this essay to the hermeneutics of this task, but first in the following section I address the question of transcendence.

God and the Secular State

How does one account for this home-grown South African tradition of human rights, which, I suggest, reveals a "more than secular" and "less than religious" built-in sense of theological openness? It is an openness that is frequently bedeviled by that which is hegemonically theological.

My assigned topic is, Where does God fit into the process? Indeed, is there a place for God in a nation that strives to overcome human subjugation and to honor human rights in a context where religion has been slow and hesitant in promoting such rights — until, of course, it was popular and expedient to do so? Specifically, this is a context in which black theology, the Kairos theology, and contextual theology were most articulate in renouncing apartheid, and yet did not enjoy the support of the mainline churches. Of course, there were voices within the churches that supported these theologies. But it was a "church within the church" rather than the church itself that carried the flame of human rights, human liberation, and human dignity. How then does one talk with integrity of God in a context where religion has discredited itself?

Perhaps one way is by talking of the human condition, which includes a deep anthropological refusal to submit to subjugation. The history of social thought suggests that there is in humankind an impulse to be free, to reach beyond the confines of control — whether political, intellectual, or spiritual. "Do you not believe," asks St. Augustine, "that there is a 'deep' so profound as to be hidden even to that person in whom it is?"[23] The need to plumb this deep is the essence of human spirituality. It is for the believer the place where the human soul encounters the divine. For others, it is the place where questions about the meaning of life are asked, if not answered. Whether religion or belief in God is a neurosis, a projection, or a response to "something" beyond or within oneself, it is a human phenomenon that has throughout history disturbed, challenged, and often annoyed not only born-again atheists and reassured religionists alike, but also those whom William James called the "once born" and "healthy minded."[24]

Intrigued by an array of South Africans returning to the public domain after President de Klerk's momentous decision in February 1990 to remove the ban on political organizations, release political prisoners, and invite exiles to return home, I took it upon myself to interview some returning exiles and persons who were hitherto banned or imprisoned, wanting to know what drove them to pay the incredible price that so many of them paid in the struggle against apartheid.[25] Among those whom I interviewed was Joe Slovo, celebrated atheist, head of the South African Communist Party, demonized by the former regime as an anarchist and enemy of the state. He described himself as a "believing unbeliever." "I believe in the roots of faith and understand its driving energy . . . but reject the metaphysics that constitutes part of the dominant religions of the West," he said. He recalled being asked by Johan Heyns, the former moderator of the Dutch Reformed Church, "if you do not believe, if you do not have faith, if you have no God hypothesis, what is the source of your morality?" Slovo referred to the Crusades, the conquest of the Americas by the conquistadors, and Kaiser Wilhelm's troops marching into World War I with *"Gott Mit Uns"* emblazoned on their buttons. A mild-mannered man, he refrained from reminding Heyns that the very church to which he belonged had for decades provided theological legitimization for apartheid. "I believe in the greatness of the human spirit," Slovo said, "[in] the ability of humanity to build a paradise on earth. . . . I am an unrehabilitated utopian, and intend remaining one until the day I die. If the human race is to conquer the dehumanizing aspects of life, a utopian or eschatological vision of what society can and must become is imperative." What is important for him is that people committed to the "humanizing process" find one another in praxis if not in metaphysics.[26]

When I spoke to Nelson Mandela about such things, he thoughtfully suggested that "speaking of God is a matter beyond articulation." He said that it is an experience he did not fully comprehend. "Religion is about mutual love and respect for one another and for life itself. It is about dignity and the equality of humankind made in the image of God."[27]

Ruth Mompati, a tough and remarkable veteran of the struggle, spoke of the power of an inner spirit, *Seriti* in Tswana, which has its origin in *Modimo* or God. In near Augustinian terms, she suggested that "human beings are awakened by this presence within them. It has to do with us ultimately not being able to deny being human." For her, the imperative to be fully human is the incentive to create "a just and peaceful future for our children."[28]

A final word from Cheryl Carolus, a Cape Town–based activist who was in and out of jail prior to the South African transition. She recently completed a term as South African ambassador to St. James' Court in London. Speaking in 1991, she said, "I am both secular and religious in a spiritual rather than institutional sense." Her concern was to create "a correlation between what I do and what I believe." "There is a deep longing inside us for a place in the sun," she told me. "That 'place in the sun' includes material things, make no mistake about that," she insisted. "Human beings, however, need more than that. We need bread to stay alive, but we do not live by bread alone. We are in restless quest for human fulfilment."[29]

These voices from political prisoners and exiles, located somewhere between the spiritual and the secular, the religious and the material, are representative of a spirit of renewal that has characterized the shift in South Africa from an overtly Christian state to a constitutional and secular state. It is a shift, argues Lourens du Plessis, that warrants the support of Christians for the new South African Constitution, despite (perhaps *because*) it no longer contains the explicit theological imperatives of earlier constitutions. "The prime object of South Africa's sovereign Constitution," he suggests, "ties in with the Christian quest for a government bound by higher norms and values founded on the conviction that no moral ruler can have absolute power because God has ultimate authority in heaven and on earth."[30] The point is this: the ideals of renewal, aimed at ensuring such norms and values that protect the rights of all South Africans, are entrenched in a "nonreligious" theological openness, rather than an explicitly Christian constitution that is ultimately deeply anti-theological.

The racially defined 1983 Constitution is framed "In humble submission to almighty God." It pledges the nation to "uphold Christian values and civilized norms."[31] The preamble to the 1996 Constitution begins with the words, "We, the people of South Africa, Recognize the injustices of the past; Honour those who suffered for justice and freedom in our land; Respect those who have worked to build and develop the country; and Believe that South Africa belongs to all who live in it, united in diversity." The preamble ends with the words,

> May God protect our people.
> *Nkosi Sikelel' iAfrika. Morena boloka setjhaba sa heso.*
> *God seen Suid-Afrika.* God bless South Africa.
> *Mudzimu fhatutshedza Afurika. Hosi ketekisa Afrika.*[32]

Some Christians, including many who never thought of taking to the streets in opposition to apartheid, marched on Parliament to express their misgivings concerning the secular character of the new Constitution, which they saw as undermining the Christian values entrenched in earlier constitutions. The irony escapes few. The difficulty of speaking about God with integrity in a situation where words and deeds clash is a concern with which thoughtful South Africans will wrestle for years to come.

Whatever else the Scriptures of the world's great religions may be, they include stories of people learning little by little, with difficulty and sometimes with reluctance, the meaning and referent of the word "God." The God of the Hebrew Scriptures, suggests Cornelius van Peursen, is "an ever new and always surprising recognition of a liberating presence."[33] Differently put, the Hebrew notion of God is *experienced* and *acknowledged* rather than defined or even articulated. Indeed, in the early Hebrew religious tradition, the name of God was regarded as so sacred that it remained beyond mention. Event-language predates the language of being in the Bible.

At the height of the South African struggle, the South African Dominican theologian Albert Nolan wrote an important book that proved to be among the most controversial of the apartheid era, entitled *God in South Africa: The Challenge of the Gospel.*[34] Arguing that the gospel needs to be contextually understood and discerned, he spoke of the anger of God being directed against the demonic, oppressive, and dehumanizing system of apartheid. He similarly spoke of the struggle against apartheid as a manifestation of the gospel. Briefly put, he interpreted the South African struggle as a disclosure of God as event. Similarly, it could be argued that the human rights struggle is a disclosure of God's presence. For some, his categorization of who are the saints and sinners was too political — even simplistic, lacking in careful analysis. This aside, the biblical sense of God as event within which the human quest for dignity, rights, and respect is enacted suggests the need for a mediating, self-correcting dialectic between theological talk and human rights talk. An-Na'im's thoughtful essay on the synergy and independence of human rights, religion, and secularism is helpful in this regard.[35] The ambiguity of the South African human rights struggle gives implicit contextual expression to An-Na'im's quest for a self-correcting, complementary culture of human rights. A more careful methodological grappling with his quest for synergy and interdependence can be particularly useful within emerging democracies such as South Africa, where the dangers and hope of change are still fresh and pliable. In such situations, the ambiguities of hegemony and freedom are often still blurred, and yet the possibilities of continuing renewal are perhaps greater than in established societies where routinization and control are entrenched.

Does human rights need God in such a situation to ensure renewal? Bluntly stated, it depends on your God. The God of H. F. Verwoerd (the architect of apartheid), the God of Archbishop Tutu, and the God beyond the comprehension of Nelson Mandela are not all the same. So let us be discerning and cautious in making the link between God and human rights. Julian Huxley thought that any notion of a God "out there" was no more than "the last fading smile of a cosmic Cheshire Cat."[36] And yet he saw a place for what he called a "religion of life," which creates new options and possibilities for humanity. In this tradition, Martin Heidegger thought that to live religiously is not necessarily to be a Christian, a Muslim, or a Jew. It is "to dwell poetically."[37] Paul Tillich spoke of the "God beyond God" and the need to "transcend theism."[38] Jacques Derrida, in turn, speaks of "religion without religion."[39] His dreams, desires, prayers, and tears are a passion, suggests John Caputo,[40] for more than what is tangibly present; it is for "the unimaginable, un-foreseeable, un-believable, absolute surprise."[41] This quest for the totally other is, at the same time, in response to what is embedded in the present.[42] It is to be discerned through engagement with the world and with one's neighbor. In Levinas's words, it is encountered in the eye of the other person, who makes an ethical claim that, once encountered, cannot be dismissed or walked away from.[43] It is this intersubjectivity which distinguishes the insights of Derrida and Levinas from those whom Barth saw as promoting an individualistic, anthropological, human-centered religion. Barth considers such religion a rebellion against God — giving rise to the deification of self and the notion of the super*man*. Barth therefore warned that God "must never be identified with anything which we name or experience or conceive or worship as God."[44] Indeed, it is conceivable that the thinking of Barth has more in common with the thinking of Derrida, Levinas, and others who locate themselves outside of the conventional theological paradigms, than is often realized.[45] What unites them is more than a quest for some Greco-rational-ontological conceptualization of what it is that lures humanity beyond the prevailing situation. It is the recognition of the need for an ethical-political alternative that shatters the complacency of the status quo.

An-Na'im suggests secularism is incapable of inspiring this vision.[46] I am suggesting that any attempted institutionalization or control of God carries with it the danger of a similar kind — that of destroying a sense of the transcendent. Any notion of God, the unique and omniscient One, is necessarily metaphor. Doxology, liturgy, poetry, and song (including the freedom songs of those who struggle against evil) are the most appropriate ways to acknowledge the Other, the Divine — indeed God. If this sense of the Other is what we refer to when we ask whether human rights needs God, then, "yes indeed, human rights needs God." We need an ideal beyond ourselves. But we should not fret too much about defining, naming, or protecting this God from those who do not sense God or define God as some of us do. Don Cupitt's *Long-Legged Fly* is helpful. Theology and what he calls the "its objects" should be viewed historically and not as timeless entities, he maintains. Recognizing that "the faith once given" is mediated through classical texts grounded in the culture of the day, any thoughtful contemporary notion of transcendence or God needs to take contemporary language, culture, and experience into account. Cupitt speaks of the need for a "continual construction" — indeed, a "reinventing" of belief.[47] Like the long-legged fly upon the stream, the religious pursuit of transcendence must be "light, resourceful and fast-moving."[48] This, I suggest, is the essence of the kind of religion that can be understood and instrumentally useful in a post-apartheid, secular age — within which scars and memories of those who cried, "Lord, Lord" but failed to do the will of the Father still persist.

The theological implications of what I have said are immense. Suffice it to say, I am dabbling in the tradition of Kierkegaardian subjectivity and Bonhoeffer's sensed need for a "religionless" Christianity[49] — a tradition that has been left largely unassimilated and undeveloped by Bonhoeffer and others. My quest is to understand the "reaching-out for something" in the space between belief and nonbelief of Slovo, Mandela, Mompati, Carolus, and many, many others in South Africa and around the world who sense the incentive to reach beyond "what is" to "what ought to be."

Does human rights need that kind of God, imminent within the struggle to be human? Yes. But not everyone names "seeking to grasp what is ultimately beyond our comprehension and grasp" as God. This God is experienced, not defined; encountered, not named; celebrated and sometimes cursed; but never owned.

Allow me to contextualize my comments: I was asked while working in the Truth and Reconciliation Commission whether my theological career had in any way equipped me to do the work I was doing (as national research director) in the Commission. I pointed out that I rarely spoke a theological word or used a theological symbol, and yet it was the most theological job I had ever engaged in. The South African quest for renewal reminds us that human beings cannot renounce being human. They ultimately rise against what oppresses, what seduces, and what renders us less than human. It is not a process of unmitigated progress. The outcome is not inevitable. And yet, when the process begins there is no way of going back. To be part of this process in South Africa, Bosnia, Serbia, Rwanda, Sierra Leone, the Middle East, or the United States of America is to experience the incentive to be more than we are, or our nations have achieved, at any given time. Those of us who stand in a religious tradition acknowledge this as the call of God. Given the tardy involvement of the historic religions in the struggle for human rights we would, however, be most insensitive not to look also for the call of God deep within the secular quest for wholeness.

Many within situations of despair in South Africa and elsewhere have, at the same time, been sustained in their quest for human rights by a vision and incentive that is neither named nor fully understood. Perhaps to name it is to restrain it. It is to limit the force and the lure of what Dag Hammarskjöld called "a wind from the unknown."[50] This is why the Hebrew Bible favors event-language over the language of being — which frequently involves political compromise, moral restraint, and spiritual confusion. The task of hermeneutics is to rediscover what Luther once called the Word within the Word. Johan Baptist Metz referred to this as the "dangerous memory"[51] hidden within the Bible (and surely other texts) — dangerous because it has the capacity to overthrow the alliance between religion and power that has come to characterize most dominant forms of religion.

Contextuality and the Hermeneutics of Human Rights

The pursuit of freedom and human rights is captured in many different symbols, affirmations, and creeds — both religious and secular. Chief among these is the Universal Declaration and the many human rights instruments spawned by it. It is the task of people committed to the pursuit of the common good to concretize and promote this freedom, as well as the rights and responsibilities captured within these instruments, in relation to the needs and challenges of a particular context. The goal is to enable the universal to become particular — the word to become flesh.

This is a complex task. It is here that human rights take root and grow. If they fail to do so, the danger is that they become little more than an abstract idea. For this concretization to happen, it is necessary to move beyond pledges and the waving of banners, to the gradual implementation and practice of human rights. The huge and daunting questions of poverty, crime, unemployment, HIV/AIDS, child abuse, women's rights, and related concerns facing South Africa and other African countries can begin to be tackled only piecemeal. Any hope for a quick eschatological overcoming of such challenges is not only naive, it is also dangerous.

Herein lies the hermeneutical task. It involves posing the inevitable question concerning the meaning of a specific human right in a particular place at a particular time. It is a problem, I suggest, that involves three interrelated tensions: the *universal* and the *particular,* the *ideal* and the *possible,* the *static* (or symbol) and the *dynamic* (or application). In this final section of this essay I reflect, only by implication, on each of these tensions. I do so in seeking to affirm the importance of a *universal* set of values — an *ideal,* a *universal symbol,* in *dynamic* pursuit of what is actually *possible* in a *particular* context at any given time. This involves an exercise in uncovering the latent and surplus meaning of the classic text. This meaning needs to be carefully discerned. It often takes time to emerge. And when it does, it is often no more than a first tentative step in a long journey toward the ideal. Indeed, so tentative is it that those who run and those who are impatient to reach their goal fail to see it.

It is this that makes transitional justice such a contested terrain. It is a terrain within which the first tentative steps toward a culture of human rights are questioned, challenged, and frequently rejected as both insufficient and without promise. The South African transition is a celebrated case. It offers no easy answers to complex questions. It provides no human rights guarantees for the future. It offers only a small beginning.

At the same time, the South African example poses a host of questions. For example, not all negotiated transitions will always promote human rights. Questions about the duty to prosecute will continue to be debated. When and under what circumstances should the United Nations or the International Criminal Court overrule a peacemaking initiative in, say, South Africa, Sierra Leone, Burundi, the Democratic Republic of the Congo, or anywhere else? The advent of the International Criminal Court is probably the most important human rights development of recent years. At the same time, it presents the world with a host of questions that can perhaps only be addressed once the work of the Court is established. The words of Secretary-General Kofi

Annan both anticipate and provide a tentative way forward. He points out that the ICC is intended to "ensure that mass-murderers and other arch-criminals cannot shelter behind a state run by themselves or their cronies, or take advantage of the breakdown of law and order." He continues, "It is inconceivable that, in such a case, the Court would seek to substitute its judgement for that of a whole nation which is seeking the best way to put a traumatic past behind it and build a better future."[52]

His words provide focus for tensions in hermeneutical practice referred to above — in addressing the needs of a particular situation, where the ideal may need to be suspended to ensure the beginning of the reform process, within which the rule of law and a culture of human rights is affirmed. To return to the South African settlement, a failure to have offered conditional amnesty for gross violation of human rights would clearly have resulted in the apartheid generals having refused to agree to the settlement, to allow the birth of democracy, and to protect the new constitution. Since amnesty was adopted by a democratically elected government that has committed itself to comply with other human rights obligations, the world has (with concern by some) generally accepted that conditional amnesty was an acceptable price to be paid for peace. And it can presumably be morally justified on the basis of the cessation of war and the beginning of peace, which is in every sense a fundamental human right. This involves not so much a suspension of the right of the victims to pursue prosecution and the obligation of the state to prosecute those guilty of gross violation of human rights, as a *choice* between prosecution and the right to give peace a chance. Again the questions abound: Who should be prosecuted and who not? Can some crimes be subject to amnesty and others not? Are perpetrators of genocide more worthy of prosecution than those, say, in South Africa who were guilty of promoting a system of discrimination decreed by United Nations Security Council Resolution 556 of 1984 as being a crime against humanity?

There are no easy answers to such questions. Politically, amnesty, reconciliation, and truth are becoming part of the political instruments of government. They are here to stay, unless we want to suggest that in some situations *righteous war* needs to be fought to the bitter end, despite the cost of many innocent lives. Frederik van Zyl Slabbert, a leader of the opposition in a former white South African parliament until he resigned his position as a way of extracting himself from exclusive white politics, and one of South Africa's most astute political commentators, suggests that amnesty is perhaps the most powerful political instrument available to governments seeking to create a new order out of the past conflict. "This," he argues, "will not be amnesty through confession, dialogue, and reconciliation, but amnesty based on calculating the political benefits that may flow from it being conferred. Of course, it can contribute to tolerance, reconciliation, and commonality of purpose. But then again, it may polarise and embitter. May those who have the power to give it, be blessed with the Wisdom of Solomon."[53]

I suggest that in situations of enduring conflict, the process leading to an affirmation of the highest echelons of human rights is usually attained through the calculation of political benefit within a broad culture of human rights, rather than through the rigid imposition of the "do's and don't's" of human rights purists. The people locked in the worst kind of conflict have a right to explore the possibility of peace that does not fulfill the human rights demands made by those thousands of miles away in the Hague, Geneva, or elsewhere, where theory, idealism, and legal dogmatism sometimes reign supreme.

The African notion of *ubuntu* is a deeply human, profoundly moral, and passionately compassionate philosophy. It knows neither the dogmatism of Western legal systems nor the rigidity of many human rights idealists. Its aim is healing, restoration, and reconciliation rather than retribution, revenge, and exclusion. An exchange between Churchill Mxenge, the brother of Griffiths Mxenge (an anti-apartheid lawyer and activist murdered by the South African security police) and Archbishop Tutu provides an important insight into the notion of *ubuntu*. "Tutu is a man of the cloth, a man who believes in miracles," says Mxenge. "But I cannot see him being able overnight to cause people who are hurt and bleeding simply to forget about their wounds and forget about justice." Tutu responds by suggesting that "retribution is largely Western. The African understanding is far more restorative — not so much to punish as to redress or restore a balance that has been knocked askew. The justice we hope for is restorative of the dignity of people." *Ubuntu*, says Tutu, involves the essential belief that "no one can be healthy when the community is sick."[54]

The quest for human rights within the context of *ubuntu* places reconciliation, inclusivity, compromise, and cooperation at the center of the human rights debate. The Armageddon anticipated by many in the 1980s did not happen. The showdown between good and evil, in the sense of one side winning and the other being annihilated, simply did not occur. The negotiated settlement, the new Constitution and the Truth and Reconciliation Commission, did not seek revenge. The quest was for a different kind of victory — a victory over revenge, aimed at overcoming the *causes* of the conflict. It encapsulates the ideals of the international human rights agenda, involving a society of people living at peace and in harmony with itself. And yet it is prepared to compromise on how to get there. The do's and don't's of human rights idealists are not embraced as ends in themselves. South Africa's biggest human rights challenge is the creation of a social platform where former ene-mies learn to live together, as a basis for creating a fountainhead and the nec-essary social energy out of which a new sense of moral imagination can emerge to address the ravages of the past and avoid the potential landmines of the future.

Donald Shriver argues that there is "nothing more 'natural' in human relations than revenge, and nothing less political."[55] The pursuit of human rights is a possibility only within the context of a political settlement. We need to think strategically, in that sense politically, in order to create the space within which the high ideals of human rights can be achieved. To create this space, the competing claims of opposing groups in any conflict need to be ac-commodated. Johan Degenaar argues that "rights should never be viewed in terms of an ideal of justice conceived as an ahistorical standard. Rights and justice are constructed in historical contexts of struggle in which politically contested claims are made."[56] For Degenaar, the attainment of rights in a conflictual and diverse society comes through dialogue in which moral agents communicate their most essential fears, needs, and aspirations to one an-other, finding the necessary compromise that enables them to live together. This involves finding the latent and surplus meaning of the classic texts within the human rights debate. It involves applying the universal within the particular. It involves settling for what is reasonably possible as the next pos-sible and logical step. Speaking theologically, it involves a cautious human re-sponse to a gracious and restoring God who is beyond our ability to name or control and who continually calls us beyond ourselves and beyond our dogma.

Dag Hammarskjöld showed a profound theological understanding of this God:

I am being driven forward
Into an unknown land.
The pass grows steeper,
The air colder and sharper.
A wind from my unknown goal
Stirs the strings
Of expectation
Still the question
Shall I ever get there?
There where life resounds,
A clear pure note.
In the silence.[57]

11 What Kind of God Does Human Rights Require?

MARTIN PALOUŠ

For as I went through the city and looked carefully at the objects of your worship, I found among them an altar with the inscription, "To an unknown god." What therefore you worship as unknown, this I proclaim to you. (Acts 17:23)

The organizing question of this volume — "Does human rights need God?" — can be reversed: "Does God need human rights?" The matter is the relationship between God and man; the problem of whether respect for human rights — generally recognized as a *conditio sine qua non* of any form of democratic governance and politics — can be used as a kind of proof of God's existence, proving that despite modern secularism and all the atheistic inclinations of our "enlightened" times, the realm of the divine and the realm of the human, in any open society, belong essentially together.

I have organized my reflections on the issue of God and human rights into four parts. In the first two parts, I remind us of two fundamental distinctions, or rather tensions, that must be recognized in any attempt to explore what Aristotle called *philosophia peri ta anthrōpina,* to inquire into the philosophical foundations of our "human condition." First, I look at the distinction between two elementary *modi* of human existence, the *vita activa* and the *vita contemplativa;* and second, I examine the polar relationship arising within human existence between its finiteness and historicity on the one hand, and its openness toward transcendence or eternity on the other. In the third section of the essay, I mention the classical political "virtues" — such as self-control, respect for common sense, generosity, moderation, and so on — and I use Cicero as an outstanding example of a moderate politician. I argue that the Ciceronian attitude toward public matters, the Ciceronian moderate state of mind, should be recommended as the point of departure in our contemporary debate concerning politics, God, and human rights. In my fourth and final remark, I try to apply the previous points to our present situation. I comment briefly on the current perception of human rights issues in Central Europe — influenced by the Central European experiences with totalitarianism in the twentieth century, and tested today against sometimes odd realities of post-communist transitions. I would like to use this case as a concrete illustration of how the *vita contemplativa* can eventually inform and shape the *vita activa*. I want to emphasize the healing power of "common sense" and the importance of Ciceronian "moderation" in our current spiritual and political crisis. I conclude by raising the question of the possible role of "divine" transcendence in the process of "globalization" that has accelerated since the fall of Communism in 1989, and has become the main characteristic of our human situation in the world in the beginning of the twenty-first century. Thanks to this trend — which is perceived as necessary and unavoidable on our current historical crossroads — all members of the human species, living in historically, culturally, and religiously heterogeneous communities, have been brought closer together than ever before and have been made, despite the plurality and diversity that belongs to our human condition, a part of one planetary mankind.

I

Let us start from the Aristotelian distinction between two fundamental ways of human life, *vita activa* and *vita contemplativa*, so powerfully and creatively used in the political thought of Hannah Arendt.[1] On the one hand, there is our being in the world we share — engaged in three fundamental human activities, "labor, work, and action"[2] — with the plurality of others. On the other hand, there are the noetic activities of man, taking place in the "soul," in the *interior domus* of one's "self," that is to say, in that inner space where each of us can temporarily withdraw from the common world of appearances.[3] As humans — belonging to the species *zoion logon echōn, animal rationale*, according to the Aristotelian taxonomy[4] — we are able to interrupt temporarily all activities we have been busy with and to "think," that is, to see our own situation in the world as if from a distance.[5] In the fleeting moment of contemplation we are able to discover the abyss lurking behind and beyond *ta phainomena*, the appearances of things around us, things given to us in our experience. The fundamental, and always awe- and wonder-evoking, difference between Being and Nothingness (between "is" and "is not") not only reveals the nature of things experienced but also makes us aware of our own finite existence in time, of our life that will pass away in the moment of our death and still cannot be lived well without being directed by the *nous* or reason; without being informed by knowledge that is permanently tested against the horizon of the divine eternity.[6]

The importance of this distinction cannot be overestimated. Its discovery, whose history can be traced back to the origins of "politics" and "philosophy" in ancient Greece, brought into existence European (Western) civilization with its "open" political culture (whose very essence is human freedom) and its "rationalistic" concept of science. It is obvious, however, that what is at stake here is not just a matter for historians, professional philosophers, or other experts interested in the past lives of Western philosophical or political ideas. The discovery of "self" that enables a person to share the public space with the plurality of others, and at the same time to put his own opinions and beliefs under the test of reason, is an event to be understood originally on the elementary, existential level of human life. Here we are confronted with a fundamental question that is tied to our own pursuit of self-understanding. And this is a hermeneutical problem that cannot be tackled properly by any of our modern historical, social, legal, or political sciences, a problem that must be approached in the way the classical political thinkers of ancient Greece employed when leading their dialogues with contemporary politicians and studying *more Socratico*, the political ideas and practical politics of their own times.

Is it not here — in the context of the question of who we are — that the concepts whose relations are to be analyzed in this volume, God and human rights, should first be approached and rediscovered? Is it not true that all other contexts in which they are commonly used and should be studied — the theological context for the former and legal/political context for the latter — are derivative? Is it not true that without careful clarification of how these terms are constituted on the existential level, all answers to the question "What kind of God does human rights require?" could lead us astray and leave us lost in all sorts of metaphysical fallacies and perplexities?

II

Bringing the problem of relationship between God and human rights to the existential level, we have obtained a basic clue in our inquiry: The relation of a person to the transcendent pole beyond his own activities cannot be separated from his relationship to himself, to his own finite existence in the human world. The bond between man and God is essentially anthropomorphic. We cannot move forward in our efforts to answer the question, "What kind of God does human rights require?" unless we are able to understand that there is a kind of mirror linkage here — in other words, unless we are able to grasp our own human existence in the light of our experience with the divine. With that in mind, we can make the second step. The conflict between *vita activa* and *vita contemplativa,* the never-ending quest for the meaning of finite human life, does not take place in a vacuum but, rather, always is a matter of concrete human beings finding themselves in concrete places and in concrete times. The context to which we have to pay attention when reflecting on the relation between humans and God is the open field of human history. Here we are touching upon an essential and important problem. The human openness toward transcendence and eternity introduces the element of movement into the human world. It is in the conflict between *vita activa* and *vita contemplativa* itself that human history in fact begins.[7]

The consequences of the fact that not only we mortals but also the world into which we were born and are going to leave at the moment of death is not stable, but ever-changing, are enormous. The ever-present element of divine transcendence in it cannot be separated from our finiteness and must be treated as a historical problem. Both human rights and God are concepts that have their own history. Both God and human rights, by their very nature, transcend our finite being-in-the-world,[8] "are not from this world," but both at the same time represent historical phenomena. "All men are created equal," in the famous words of the American Declaration of Independence, and, indeed, "they are endowed by their Creator with certain inalienable rights." At the same time, such a statement could not have been pronounced except under very specific historical circumstances, for a very clear purpose, and with very significant political implications. On the one hand one can say that human rights needs God in order to be declared "inalienable"; to gain the status of a principle that transcends the field of current *Realpolitik* and the existing rule of man; to help to form a government that accepts the finiteness of human existence or nature and institutionalizes human freedom. On the other hand, the answer to the question why human rights "needed" God in the particular case of American colonies revolting — to justify why it became necessary to dissolve the "political bands" which had tied them to the British Crown — is presented in the form of "facts" to "be submitted to a candid world" and demonstrating that "the history of the present King of Great Britain is a history of repeated injuries and usurpations."[9]

In this sense even our current inquiry cannot be conceived from the position of a detached observer but must be conscious of its own historical context. It should be driven first of all by our own inner need to seek truth about ourselves, as well as our need to act in such a way as to ensure that our concrete, historically conditioned society will remain free and open. It is certainly true that human rights, as we know and recognize them today, were discovered and declared under the unique circumstances of great revolutions: English, French, and American. It is also true that these three history-making events of the seventeenth and eighteenth centuries indeed became "turning points" and started the transition from the Middle Ages to modernity. Our own current situation, in the beginning of the twenty-first century, however, is also "revolutionary." The central position of Europe and European civilization in the context of universal human history is not taken for granted any more as it used to be. The fundamental fact today is that all nations living on the Earth have become parts of one globalized humanity. All of us, whether we like it or not, whether we live somewhere in the "center" or on a distant and isolated periphery, are finding ourselves in one interconnected, interdependent, multicultural, and multireligious "postmodern" world. What about the future of the monotheism we have gotten used to within our Western, predominantly Christian tradition? How should we accept the highly unpleasant and puzzling fact that even our faith in one God has to struggle today with the problem of plurality? Is our concept of human rights — as we perceive, discuss, and use it today — really completely "inalienable," or are we doomed to rethink it again and again, forced by unpredictable historical events, such as the fall of Communism in 1989 or the tragedy of 9/11?

To understand the "essence" of our current human rights discourse and politics requires more than reminding ourselves of the spirit of great modern revolutions. In order to know "who we are" today, we also need to go back to the crucial moment at the beginning of Western history, to the emergence of the Greek city-state. The very concept of human rights and its relation to God cannot be properly understood without taking into consideration the ethos and experience of the *polis,* historically the first state that was based on the principle of equality of its citizens and ruled not by the will of a deified emperor or pharaoh but by "law." Again it is Aristotle who provides us with the most analytical and most systematic account of Greek politics.

"The observation tells us," reads the first sentence of Aristotle's *Politics,* "that every state [*polis*] is an association [*koinōnia*], and that every association is formed with a view to some good purpose [*agathou tinos heneken*]."[10] And a little further: the *polis* must be conceived as "the final association" (*koinōnia teleios*).[11] With its creation, "for all practical purposes the process is now complete; self-sufficiency [*autarkeia*] has been reached and while the state came about as a means of securing life itself [*tou biou heneken*], it continues in being to secure the good life [*tou eu zēn*]."[12] On the individual level, *eu zēn*, to lead a "good life," means to commit oneself, consciously and voluntarily, to the service of "practical wisdom and virtue" *(phronēsei kai aretē)*. On the level of state, it means to guard "law" *(nomos)* and to serve "justice" *(dikē):* "for justice is the arrangement of the political association [*politikēs koinōnias taxis*], and a sense of justice decides what is just [*hē de dikaiosynē tou dikaiou krisis*]."[13]

Obviously it is impossible to discuss here the whole corpus of Aristotle's political thought. Nonetheless, the lines quoted from the first book of *Politics* illustrate my point more than clearly. In *Politics*, Aristotle put himself consciously into the position of unbiased observer of political matters. Nonetheless, the way he deals with the topic shows the underlying Greek political experience and the Greek spirit that were born with the emergence of the *polis*. The *polis* came into existence in the moment when those who managed their "private" households *(oikiai)* as autocratic despots decided to create a common space to deal with common matters. Transferred from the possession of one, the rule *(archē)* was put "into the midst of people" *(en meson toi dēmoi)*.[14] The might of emperor or pharaoh, so far the only recognized ultimate source of order in the human world, was to be replaced by law *(nomos)*. A "final human association" *(koinōnia teleios)*, in Aristotle's terms, came into existence. It was the *polis*, a community not ordered hierarchically, as was the case of all previous state bodies — "empires with complicated hierarchies and bureaucracies, and yet . . . essentially no more than a giant household or aggregate of households gathered around the central cell of the royal house"[15] — but horizontally, based on the plurality of free and equal men. *Isonomia*, equality before the law, conferred freedom on the citizens of the *polis*, gave them the right to act and to speak freely before the assembly of their peers, and shielded them against the excessive and arbitrary uses of state power.[16]

Citizens should have felt themselves free of the risk of being killed, imprisoned, enslaved, or otherwise harmed in their daily lives by the actual ruler. The elementary intention of the "rule of law" was to give them freedom and to protect them against willful tyrants and usurpers, those inclined to overstep their human lot and to seek their own aggrandizement. Conflicts and disputes in the *polis* could not be resolved by intervention of absolute power from above, but only strictly within the limits of political justice *(politikon dikaion)*. Binding decisions in all disputed matters could be taken only by the proper judicial organ of the *polis* in "due process." With freedom and equality in the sphere of justice, members of the *polis* had the right to submit accusations and, when sued, were entitled to a fair and public trial.

Elected jurors sat in judgment on their fellow citizens, sworn to listen impartially to both sides and to vote strictly on the issue at hand.

Aristotle, observing the political processes throughout *Graecia Magna,* was of course well aware of the difference between the ideal and reality, between the perfect constitution of state *(politeia aristē)* and the constitutions of various concrete city-states of the past and the present, often in the hands of bad rulers and finding themselves in the constant process of change. What is crucial for him, however, is the ability to make such a distinction and to be aware of the underlying distinction between the state as "a means of securing life itself," and the state that achieves "self-sufficiency" *(autarkeia)* and "continues in being to secure the good life" — the distinction between the state organized as a grand household and a *polis;* between autocratic and non-autocratic forms of government; between the bad political regime, where the ruler seizes power just to promote his self-interests and to satisfy his *libido dominandi,* and the good one where the ruler promotes the common interest *(to koinē symphereon)* and acts strictly as "a guardian of what is just and hence of what is equal."[17]

As we have seen, Aristotelian political thought is based on concepts of "political justice," "common interest," "equality," "the rule of law,"[18] and, moreover, on the underlying conviction that "the good life" of the *polis* is, in spite of all the uncertainty and danger connected with its freedom, preferable to the life lived just for the "continuous preservation of life through work and production."[19] Nonetheless, it seems, at first sight, that Aristotle was unable to address satisfactorily the question that is topical for our inquiry concerning the relation between God and human rights. So far we have talked about the *polis* from the perspective of citizens — free men and privileged holders of "civil rights" — those few within any concrete *koinōnia* of ancient Greeks who were distinguished from all others by their "participation in giving judgment and holding office."[20] (A *polis* is "a number of such persons large enough to secure a self-sufficient life."[21]) But what about all other "inhabitants" of a "city-state," women, children, old people, craftsmen, slaves, foreigners who were permanent residents, and so on? What is their situation within a *polis,* which is "an association of free men?"[22] Do they have (or can they hope to achieve) a legal status that would confer on them at least some rights? Can they hope that their inferior position will one day end, and that they too will be free and equal?

It is important to note that Aristotle is quite ambivalent or even fuzzy at this point. On the one hand, he is inclined to say that women and slaves are unsuited by nature to become citizens. Therefore, they do not and cannot belong to the *polis,* and their natural place is within households or villages[23] on its territory.[24] On the other hand, when we take into consideration the whole corpus of Aristotle's anthropology *(philosophia peri ta anthrōpina)*[25] — and one has to read his *Politics* in this context — it is evident that it aims toward a different concept of human nature. "*All men* aim at happiness and the good life,"[26] says Aristotle later in the *Politics* (Book VII) when discussing the conditions within an ideal or perfect state. And again, "*all men* by nature desire to know"[27] reads the famous opening sentence of his *Metaphysics*. Already these formulations indicate that his ethical teaching — which represents the basis of his political thought — introducing the distinction between "virtue of character" and "virtue of thought"[28] has a strong noetic component. And as such, it is not "elitist," "racist," "sexist," or in any other way "supremacist," to use expressions from our current political vocabulary, but essentially "egalitarian," "nondiscriminatory," and "democratic."

First of all, one has to take into consideration that Aristotle is an "empiricist." The concepts (mostly his own creations) used by him describe the social and/or political reality observed. The Aristotelian descriptions, however, are far from being "value-free" in our modern sense, but are inseparably connected to his ethical point of departure — with his underlying conviction that the human "good" and the freedom of the *polis* belong essentially together; that the recognition of a distinction between "life for life" and a "good life" is the origin of the *polis* and all political. It is this conviction that inspired Aristotle to give his account of human associations (pre-political and political), forms of constitutions, citizenship, regime changes, state education, and so on. What one should keep in mind is the fact that the Greek *poleis,* which as "associations of free men" enjoying their "civil rights" were formed by a tiny minority of the overall population, were preceded and surrounded by grand empires managed as "aggregates of households" where all were in the position of slaves. No "rule of law" was recognized, and only the divine ruler could be considered free. Furthermore, what can be observed in the Greek world — and Aristotle gives great attention to this phenomenon — is what we would call in our modern terminology the process of "emancipation." More and more individuals were liberated to enter the public space and become citizens. The domination of pre-political gentilitian structures *(genē)* based on blood relationships — each having its own cult-places, priesthood, assembly house, common treasury, and, of course, ruler as a head executive *(anax or archōn)*[29] — was step-by-step broken and replaced by the political power stemming from the new administrative units of the emerging *polis.*[30] This "emancipation," which brought sometimes hardly manageable dynamism into the Greek political life, had, nonetheless, its cultural and historical limits. As Eric Voegelin clearly states, "The individual never gained the personal status in his political unit which, under the influence of the Christian idea of man, characterized the political formations of Western civilization; it always remained in a status of mediation throughout the fictitious tribal and blood-relationships within the *polis*."[31] He continues, "[T]he pathos of the polis was the pathos of a dynamic participation of the people in the culture that originated in the aristocratic society. The dynamics were on the side of the 'people.'"[32]

We must also remind ourselves in this context of the Aristotelian distinction between *vita activa* and *vita contemplativa,* which we discussed in the previous section. "Philosophy and the spirit of polis are closely linked," states Czech philosopher Jan Patočka in the context of his explorations of the beginning of European history.[33] It is this link on which one has to focus in order to understand what is the real source of dynamism so evident in the patterns of Athenian constitutional history; this problem is connected with the Aristotelian concept of human nature.

"For it is owing to their wonder that men both now begin and at first began to philosophize,"[34] reads the famous dictum from Aristotle's *Metaphysics* about the origin of philosophy. The impulse to set out on a journey "to know for the sake of knowing,"[35] "in order to know and not for any utilitarian end,"[36] is that awesome and shocking moment when "a man who is puzzled and wonders thinks himself ignorant,"[37] desires "to escape from ignorance."[38] It is exactly this moment when the philosopher is born. Because we already said that all men by nature desire to know — in order "to escape from ignorance" that they are aware of — it is obvious that the opportunity to think freely and to pursue "this as the only free science"[39] is open to everybody. The possibility of *vita contemplativa* must be conceived as universal. To be a philosopher is a matter of "quality" of individual noetic life, and it depends neither on aristocratic origin nor on the current status one has within the *polis* — whose institutions were, as we have seen, still decisively influenced by the gentilitian traditional spirit of Greek society, by the fact that Greek egalitarian political culture originated in the milieu of aristocratic society.

It must be always emphasized: Such an act of liberation is not and has never been an easy thing. It requires courage and determination because, as a free thinker, man finds himself by definition in the situation of one standing against many. "Aristotle," says Patočka, when arguing that philosophy and *polis* have a common origin, "to be sure, also tells us that the lover of myths is also a philosopher in a way;[40] though he will be one only if he seeks to awaken a sense of wonder or awe over what *actually* is; the wonder of being is no fable, it manifests itself only to those who dare come to the boundary of night and day into the gate to which *dikē* holds the key, and such a daring one is at the same time *eidos phos,* the human being who knows."[41]

To summarize: The *polis* was brought into being as a body whose members were not only endowed with certain rights and privileges, but also had a duty to participate actively in the maintenance and protection of its order. The *conditio sine qua non* for the *polis*'s survival was the existence of citizens determined not only to mind their private business but also to be actively involved in public matters; to let the law *(nomos)* emerge in the never-ending process of lawgiving. It was not the law in books or in stone but exactly this collective legislative activity which made citizens *(politēs)* free and equal. The *polis* consciously turned away from the aspirations of previous divine rulers to secure to the "state" they were administering the status of immortality. It based its original social contract, distinguishing between the good life of free men and the life focused fully on its maintenance and self-preservation, on the acceptance of the tough reality of human finiteness and the historicity of the human world.

It was the resulting tension between the condition of plurality characterizing the life of citizens in the public space of the *polis,* and the requirement, imposed separately on each of them, to achieve personal integrity through the thinking activities taking place inside the "soul," which preoccupied the *polis* and set it into permanent motion. And it was this tension, whose purest articulation was the conflict between the *polis* and the philosopher, that burst out in the world of the ancient Greeks, bringing European culture into existence and pushing it on the path of its universal history. Once more we can refer here to the *Heretical Essays in the Philosophy of History* of Jan Patočka:

> [T]he Athenian *polis* is something that crystallizes gradually in conflicts with its neighbors, as well as in the struggles of political parties in which *tyrannis,* opposed to the spirit of the *polis,* plays anything but a minor role. Yet, [it is precisely because of] the circumstances [in which] the *polis* arises and sustains itself amid international and external struggles, that [the] long-sought word of Hellenic life [comes to characterize] the new formation and new form of life. Here, in very specific conflicts on a modest territory and with minimal material means is born not only the Western world and its spirit, but perhaps world history as such. The Western spirit and world history are bound together in their origins: it is the spirit of free meaning bestowal, it is the shaking of life as simply accepted with all its certainties, and at the same time the origin of new possibilities of life in that shaken situation, that is of philosophy. Since, however, philos-

ophy and the spirit of *polis* are closely linked so that the spirit of *polis* survives ultimately always in the form of philosophy, this particular event, the emergence of *polis,* has a universal significance.[42]

What does all this have to do with our question concerning the relation between God and human rights? In my view, three preliminary conclusions here must be taken into further consideration.

First, what must be clarified in this debate is the relation between its substance and its political context. This tension becomes obvious whenever we want to speak, for instance, about human versus civil rights. It is the existence of a *polis* with its ideals of the "good life" and the "rule of law" that allows this question. The *polis,* the first body in world history whose inhabitants had the courage to institutionalize freedom as the substance and purpose of their "good life," was certainly not able even remotely to realize our standard of human rights. At the same time, without this Greek "origin" the question of human rights could never be raised and would be devoid of any meaning.

Second, the question of human rights is not solely inseparable from its concrete political context. Pointing to the more fundamental problem of human nature, it seems to represent the major dynamic factor dismantling all static structures produced in the flow of human history and bringing about the historical change. What we can observe from the empirical Aristotelian perspective in the classical world of the Greek *polis* is the series of reform steps whose aim was to amend existing constitutional frameworks to keep pace with the process of liberating more and more individuals from the shackles of servitude and bringing them into the *polis* — in our modern language the process of social and political emancipation. We should never forget this dynamism when we try to understand and bring into the debate of God and human rights the Aristotelian political and ethical thought, the whole corpus of *philosophia peri ta anthrōpina.*

And third comes the impact of conflict between the *polis* and the philosopher. It is the realm of *vita contemplativa,* the realm we enter when we think, which generates the most powerful impulse for our liberation, which is the strongest equalizer as far as our human nature is concerned. It is the Socratic turn from the fascination with the "power and glory" of his great and beloved city to the "care about the greatest improvement of the soul"[43] that can help in the moment of decay and crisis. The question of human nature acquires different and not only empirical meaning here, and we can discover all implications that human rights are indeed universal; we can reflect on what it means that all humans — belonging to different *poleis* in different times and places, but always under God — are equally endowed with their natural and inalienable rights.

III

In our efforts to analyze the relationship between God and human rights, we have departed from the distinction between our *vita activa* and our *vita contemplativa*. As a tension experienced between who we are in the external world and our interiority, this distinction does not seem to be conditioned by or tied to any specific culture or civilization but rather seems to belong to our human existence as such, to our human nature. At the same time, it is true that the most distinct and observable materialization of this aspect of the human condition belongs to European (or Western) civilization, where it has gained the form of irreconcilable conflict between *polis* and philosophy. It is this conflict, actually, where European history as such — or Europe's historicity — has its origin, according to Jan Patočka. It is here that the never-ending search for order in human society has begun, striving to counteract all forces destabilizing and disordering any historical human community. *Epimeleia tēs psychēs*, the care for the soul — the appeal to obey first that inner "oracle" *(daimonion)* that Socrates, according to his own testimony, had since he was a child,[44] and that each of us can discover within ourself thanks to our human nature — was offered by classical philosophers as the only available cure for all the diseases of the "good" but open and therefore unsecured life of the *polis*.

This appeal of classical philosophers undoubtedly represents the strongest possible *moral* argument why all men and women, created equal, should be guaranteed the fundamental right to have rights and to take care for the soul. At the same time, the outcome of the trial of Socrates and all the following lessons that classical philosophers learned from their interactions within the political sphere illustrate clearly the depth of the problem that emerged for any future political body that came into existence in the course of European history. The very existence of "lovers of knowledge" after the conviction of Socrates by his fellow-citizens and their primary preoccupation with invisible things and that "mysterious good," to be sought primarily not in politics but "in Academic philosophy,"[45] betrays clearly a new danger to which the identity of the free citizen is exposed, especially in the moments of political crisis: the separation of the realm of thought from the realm of action; the depoliticization of philosophy, and the elimination of philosophy from politics; a situation in which humans caring for souls hope to achieve inner unity with themselves by withdrawing from public matters and finding themselves in their relation to the external world in a state of alienation.[46]

One can rightly object that the classical philosophers themselves were well aware of this split and that not only Socrates himself but both his greatest disciples, Plato and Aristotle, considered the achievement of balance between *vita activa* and *vita contemplativa* to be one of the major tasks, maybe the major task, of their thought. For reasons that will become clear in a moment, let us follow in the next step of our analysis the example of a man who introduced the basic Greek concepts into his own Roman environment and was at the same time a great and accomplished statesman: Marcus Tullius Cicero.[47] To be sure, he is certainly not the only one who belongs in this category. Nonetheless, his moderate, generous, open-minded, but at the same time realistic, approach to the problem of the link between the requirements imposed on us by philosophy, and the responsibilities we have to the political order, which guarantees our freedom, including the freedom of thought and the freedom of expression, is definitely worthy of our attention.

Whereas the efforts of Socrates to save the spirit of the *polis* from the forces of disorder and disintegration did not succeed — and it was the unstoppable decline of Greek *poleis* that brought the Greek philosophers into the state of alienation — the Roman republic in the time of Cicero (106-43 B.C.) was still on the ascent to world supremacy. In this sense, Cicero's primary source of inspiration was the historian Polybius (205-123 B.C.),[48] who, unlike his predecessor Thucydides, did not need to cope with "the greatest movement yet known in history," which destroyed from within Hellenic civilization through the deadly conflict of Peloponnesian War.[49] Polybius was "seeking an explanation for the extremely rapid, almost unprecedented expansion of Roman power."[50] The might and political success of a state that once was just a poverty-stricken village on the periphery of the civilized world; the fact that its mixed regime (combining in a judicious mixture the elements of monarchy, aristocracy, and democracy) passed successfully the test of time; the Roman sophisticated law, which grew gradually from the rustic customs of ancestors and amalgamated into the balanced composite of old and new legal norms — all these observations of Polybius were adopted by Cicero and became the firm, indubitable point of departure for his own philosophical reasoning and argumentation in the political realm.

Whereas for the great majority of philosophers in the post-classical period — for Academic Skeptics or Epicureans, for instance — the *vita contemplativa* gained absolute supremacy, Cicero, who is considered by many "a dilettante rather than a serious student of philosophy,"[51] belongs among those few thinkers who were firmly convinced of the opposite. For mainstream Western political thought, the phenomena linked to the *vita activa* can be rightly understood only when observed from a distance by an impartial, safely disengaged observer, who simply "left aside," as Hannah Arendt remarked, the fundamental aspect of the political realm — "the condition of plurality."[52] Cicero, on the contrary, set for himself the task of restoring the primacy of the political sphere in Roman political thought and firmly believed that "the practical life ought to be preferred to the contemplative life."[53] He was very well aware that Greek thought was perceived as an alien element in Rome and was treated, especially because of its speculative tendencies, by the pragmatic Roman spirit with a certain disdain and suspicion. But in spite of that, he was deeply convinced that it was of key importance for the healthy development of Roman culture, which needed to be open to Greek political ideas and insights made by the classical philosophers coming from the Socratic tradition.

As an Academic Skeptic, Cicero shared the fundamental Socratic view concerning the limited value of any particular human knowledge. He believed that it is the dialogue that must be recommended and intentionally cultivated as the principal tool of human cognition relevant in the public sphere. The dialogue as a literary form "lends itself to the presentation and examination of conflicting opinions, it permits the writer to focus on the relative merits of the positions being examined while at the same time suggesting, rather than revealing, the content and direction of his own thought. The form of dialogue permits the writer to guide the discussion, but places the burden of following the argument [to] its conclusion upon the reader."[54]

And it is exactly here where philosophy can, according to Cicero, render enormous service to the city. Even though the dialogue does not produce decisive evidence that is ultimately right or wrong, it can — while allowing each individual dialogue's reader to make up his or her mind — at least cultivate and humanize the public life and shed some light onto otherwise obscure, confusing, and necessarily conflicting situations. One does not need to add that such an instrument of public policy can obviously be especially useful in the moments of crisis, when the basic values and principles of a political order become questionable and are sometimes ruthlessly examined in public; when the whole political body has to reexamine its foundations and use its collective prudence and common sense to navigate safely through the narrow pass between the past and the future, between the Scylla of fundamentalism and the Charybdis of relativism, between the rule of iron fist and anarchy, both being deadly enemies of civic freedom.

As a realist, Cicero was well aware that not everybody in the state can become a philosopher, that not everybody can actively contribute to balanced judgment, addressing the open issues as they have been identified in the process of deliberation. So, he set for himself a kind of minimalist goal. He introduced the alien Greek philosophy to Rome, to inspire and strengthen within the city the group of decent, open-minded individuals. He promoted the Socratic culture of dialogue and never-ending search for the public good to give voice to the middle class, respecting and praising gentlemanly behavior, tolerating conflicting opinions, and recognizing the civic virtues Aristotle so eloquently analyzed in the context of his *philosophia peri ta anthrōpina:* to remain always sober, temperate, and self-reflexive in one's own words and actions; to be ready to lead others but never to forget that what makes a great leader is not his large ego or strong hand but his prudence and moderation; to know that what is just and right should be always looked for as a kind of middle term between two extremes.

Only where there is such a climate of ideas, *cultura animi,* which Cicero tried to evoke when inviting his readers to the environment of his philosophical friends (his contemporaries or the members of the older Scipionic circle[55]), is it possible to hope that the basic intention driving these conversations — "to promote the firm foundation of states, the strengthening the cities, and the curing of the ills of peoples"[56] — can be taken seriously, that the challenges connected with the historical existence of Western civilization can be tackled with good faith, and that they can have at least some hope for success. Only in this context, in my view, does it make sense to raise the question of to what extent Cicero's political ideas appeal to the specific experience of Rome or to what extent they could be generalized in such a way that they could be applicable for other political situations in different times and in other states or cities. Only in this context should one read the fascinating debates between the interlocutors of Cicero's dialogues, which offer very clear and classical formulas about the nature of law that might be seen as quite relevant in the later civil rights versus human rights debates. Is the law a man-made thing and justice just the product of this or that human society? Are all rights to be granted to the members of a political community nothing more than creations of legislative organs of the state? Or should we delegate the principal legislative initiative to Almighty God, in agreement with one of the participants of the three-day-long dialogue in *Republic:*

> True law is right reason in agreement with nature; it is of universal application, unchanging and everlasting; it summons to duty by its commands, and averts from wrongdoing by its prohibitions. And it does not lay its commands or prohibitions upon good men in vain, though neither have any effect on the wicked. It is a sin to try to alter this law, nor is it al-

lowable to attempt to repeal any part of it, and it is impossible to abolish it entirely. We cannot be freed from its obligations by senate or people, and we need not look outside ourselves for an expounder or interpreter of it. And there will not be different laws at Rome and at Athens, or different laws now and in the future, but one eternal and unchangeable law will be valid for all nations and all times, and there will be one master and ruler, that is God, over us all, for he is the author of this law, its promulgator and its enforcing judge.[57]

Let us leave all these questions open and let us try, in conclusion, to sum up the Ciceronian lesson. To what extent is his argument relevant for our own human rights dialogue or conversation?

When observing the contemporary political phenomena and trying to delimit the content and scope of our human rights discourse, we should be conscious of all dangers and ideological fallacies that can stem from the fact that many eloquent preachers or activists of this cause are voicing primarily their state of alienation. What must be identified as a great danger for any meaningful dialogue on this topic is the ongoing conflict between the requirements and appeals of *vita activa* and *vita contemplativa;* the loss of spiritual balance within our political culture; and the collapse of our common sense, which seems to be one of the most obvious warning symptoms of our current political crisis. And what should be recommended as the remedy for this deficiency, which is often lurking behind the abundance of goodwill and self-professed altruism of so many human rights activists and defenders? The Ciceronian courage and determination to revive in our messy situation in the contemporary world the tradition of Socratic philosophy; to enlighten our politics, absorbed in the daily factional power struggles, with a healthy dose of Aristotelian moderation. Is it not the case, even today, that the cause of human rights can be served well only in an environment of quiet generosity, gentlemanly behavior, and balanced judgment, an environment that can emerge only as a result of a productive conflict of different opinions brought together in dialogue? If there is a God who can be recognized and eulogized as the good patron and guardian of Ciceronian tradition in Western politics, is it not exactly he whom human rights does need?

IV

In the last section of this essay, I am going to return from the past to the present and comment briefly on some current originally Central European issues in the ongoing human rights debate. I will analyze here — using the example of Czechoslovak Charter 77 — the concept of human rights that emerged in the dissidents' struggle against totalitarianism. In conclusion, I plan to wrap up the arguments elaborated in the previous sections in the light of history we are making now, in the beginning of the twenty-first century, and summarize once more my answer to the central question of this volume.

In order to present the case of Charter 77, the Czechoslovak human rights movement active in the final stage of Communist rule over Central and Eastern Europe,[58] I have to start with a concise overview of some basic historical facts concerning Czechoslovakia and to make an attempt at their explanation. The fundamental problem of Czechoslovakia was that it came into existence as an independent state with "the help of nineteenth-century ideas" that informed, according to Patočka, "the explanations of the war of 1914/1918" and "proved incapable of explaining the central phenomenon of the twentieth century"[59] — the profound crisis of European civilization whose most visible and most destructive manifestation became the rise of totalitarianism.

"The history of Europe since the eighteenth century," wrote Masaryk, the founding father of the Czechoslovak state and its first president, in the book whose intention was to render an account of his foreign action during the war years, "proves that given democratic freedom, small peoples can gain independence. The World War was the climax of the movement begun by the French Revolution, a movement that liberated one oppressed nation after another, and now there is a chance for a democratic Europe and for freedom and independence of all her nations."[60]

This quotation shows clearly the conviction of its author that the world after World War I would be moving in the same direction as it had been before, during "the Golden Age of Europe" of the nineteenth century; that all dominant modernization trends of this era — the gradual increase of quality of life in all European societies, the dramatic enhancement of their possibilities with the help of all sorts of scientific discoveries and technical innovations — would continue; that in spite of all possible regressive movements, temporal troubles, and aberrations, European civilization, guided by reason and filled with the "ideals of humanity," would keep marching on the path of progress. The Czechoslovak democratic "nation-state" was supposed to take its place next to other free and democratically ruled nation-states, to become part of a new, "progressive" political architecture, shaped by the newly emerging democratic spirit, more integrative approaches, and the development of a peaceful international legal order, which would eliminate war from the realm of international politics.

Masaryk was well aware that the nation whose cause he tried to promote was small; that international politics, in spite of all Wilsonian ideals gaining at least temporary predominance in the world of the day, was primarily a domain of power. He realized that Czech smallness did not mean only the lack of resources, the disadvantage that results from small numbers and the fragile geo-strategic position of Central Europe, being sandwiched between Germany and Russia. He knew that it was also a kind of "quality" connected with parochialism and often pusillanimity of current Czech society, reflecting the spirit of "liberated servants," which characterized its rebirth from the oblivion of its "dark times" (that had started with the debacle in the Battle on White Mountain in the early seventeenth century)[61] into its enlightened modern existence.[62] Masaryk's greatness as a thinker and his statesmanship were based on his personal courage to address and challenge this endemic smallness in a conscious, straightforward manner. Already in the 1890s, he tried to challenge his fellow-citizens and formulate the Czech question in worldly terms ("as a world question," as he himself put it).[63] World War I offered him a unique opportunity to make a great step forward in his efforts to shake modern Czechs out of their "shells." The gaining of political independence was supposed to be just the beginning of a further process of national maturation, to be accomplished — after the struggle between "reactionary" theocracies and "progressive" democracies was decisively won by the latter — in the next forty to fifty years.

Masaryk's great political vision, based on his belief in progress and the power of human reason, however, was nothing but a great illusion. The twentieth century turned out to be not just an extension of the previous period, a continuation of processes initiated by the Enlightenment and liberating "one oppressed nation after another." The ideas of the nineteenth century were insufficient to offer clear guidance and spiritual orientation in the new situation. Given the international constellation that arose after the war and the both spiritual and political crisis that became more and more manifest all around Europe in the 1930s, Masaryk could only dream and pray that history would give his newly independent country a break to grow and to mature in peace, but he simply could not get it.

The rise of Hitler to power in Germany and the ambitions of his Nazi movement to gain world supremacy first destroyed Czechoslovakia. Then the German Reich unleashed World War II. Liberation in May of 1945 brought only temporary relief and evoked false illusions. Only ten months later, Churchill announced in his famous Fulton speech that he saw the iron curtain falling down in Europe. In February of 1948, the Communist Party, backed by Stalin's Soviet Union, came into power. Germany and Europe seemed to be divided irreversibly, and Czechoslovakia became part of the "Eastern bloc" building its "radiant socialist futures" under the total control of Moscow, a control that should remain in place, as the propagandists of new regime liked to repeat again and again, "forever."

The society of Czechs and Slovaks had to endure and survive all sorts of methods and social experiments designed to bring them under the control of totalitarian leaders and force them to comply with the blueprints of their ideology. First came the 1950s with their unlimited, merciless rein of Stalinistic terror, which executed its opponents, sent thousands of free-minded individuals to jails or concentration camps, organized regularly all sorts of witch-hunts and "party purges," pursued the draconian process of nationalization and collectivization, and destroyed systematically all nonconformist social and civic institutions and replaced them with the web of Potemkin villages and totalitarian "façade organizations."

Then came the "golden sixties." They brought, under the label of de-Stalinization and the policies of "peaceful coexistence of the countries with different social systems," undoubtedly at least some relief. Most of the surviving political prisoners were released. The people experienced a certain "thaw," enjoyed the fresh air coming into the poisoned and stuffy environment of the "socialist system of government," and started to slowly raise their heads again and cherish hope that the Soviet iron grip could be at least loosened and that socialism might be "reformable." Prague Spring of 1968, an attempt to endow the existing totalitarian system with a "human face," arose with the greatest possible expectations of this kind and opened at least temporarily the door to the West. Nonetheless, the Soviet-led invasion of Czechoslovakia on the twenty-first of August sent a clear message not only to the Czechs and Slovaks but to all Central Europeans: Their hopes for a more open future were futile. Their region was not only under the full control of the Soviet Union, but abandoned by the West, in the name of Cold War stability and political realism. This was exactly the moment when things really turned around for us. What happened was not only the deepest crisis endangering the socialist system of government, as it was later put by the ideologues of the "normalization era" that followed immediately, but it was also our own crisis. Central Europeans had to realize that their future depended not only on the lot prepared for them by others but also on their own judgment.

Here is how the transition of totalitarianism from its "young years" to its "advanced stage" — to the situation in the period of "normalization," when the Communist Party tried to consolidate again its shaken power in the 1970s — is described by Václav Havel, undoubtedly the brightest Czech analyst of the normalization regime and the most consistent critic of the totalitarian state of mind. Because Havel's approach to this indeed peculiar metamorphosis of totalitarian rule is in my view unrivalled and has become classic, I dare to quote from him at unusual length:

> The past twenty years [this essay was written in April of 1987] can almost serve as a textbook illustration of how an advanced or late totalitarian system works. Revolutionary ethos and terror were replaced by dull inertia, pretext-ridden caution, bureaucratic anonymity, and mindless, stereotypical behavior, all of which aim exclusively at becoming more and more what they already are.
>
> The songs of zealots and the cries of the tortured are no longer heard; lawlessness has put on kid gloves and moved from the torture chambers into the upholstered offices of faceless bureaucrats. If the President of the Republic is seen in the streets at all, he is behind the bulletproof glass of his limousine as it roars off to the airport, surrounded by the police escort, to meet colonel Qadaffi.
>
> The advanced totalitarian system depends on manipulatory devices so refined, complex, and powerful that it no longer needs murderers and victims. Even less does it need fierce Utopia builders, spreading discontent with dreams of a better future. The epithet "Real Socialism," which this era coined to describe itself, points a finger at those [for] whom it has no room: the dreamers.[64]

No surprise that the Czech population's most common reaction to the normalization practices imposed on them from above corresponded to their deeply rooted political habits and "traditions." Masaryk's statues re-erected in 1968 were removed again. Masaryk's spirit was quickly dumped and forgotten. Czechs rediscovered once more their infamous Svejkish qualities: opportunism beyond the grave; readiness to play with serious faces, but duplicitous thoughts; all the games proposed by totalitarian rulers who were ready to offer to the ruled a smart "social contract" — a relatively undisturbed private life and even some personal benefits in exchange for loyalty to the "normalization regime."

Nonetheless, one should not be surprised either that this situation — when nothing or almost nothing wrong was visible on the surface, but the "normalized" society was day after day disintegrating and demoralized by an endless chain of lies and deception — was diagnosed by people like Václav Havel as leading into a serious spiritual and political crisis.[65] If Central Europe was not to accept her lot, to which Milan Kundera tried to draw attention when he published his famous article about its "tragedy,"[66] the 1970s in

Czechoslovakia was certainly the moment that called for a kind of Socratic action. And it was Charter 77, originally a group of 242 individuals, who decided to step into the public space, to speak up and to accept this uneasy and in all sorts of ways risky role.

There are two key moments that inspired the creation of Charter 77 and in fact served as the legal basis of its argument with Czechoslovak authorities — the adoption of the Final Act of Conference on Security and Cooperation in Europe on August 1, 1975, which launched the so-called Helsinki Process, and the entry into force in Czechoslovakia of two major human rights instruments of the United Nations on March 23, 1976.[67] In a moment, I will touch upon this aspect of the international environment in which Charter 77 came into existence and pursued its activities. First, I suggest we examine briefly the primary motives that made the vast majority of signatories of this document get on board, and examine the experience they started as soon as they became a part of this quite unusual human rights adventure. And these are the questions we must keep in mind: Do not Charter 77 and similar cases of resistance against totalitarianism demonstrate that any substantive human rights debate needs more than a focus on valid law, both domestic and international, more than a rigorous examination of whether the states in their legal actions — administrative, civil, or relating to the questions of criminal justice — comply with their human rights obligations? Is not the very concept of human rights of such a nature that it is very difficult or almost impossible to separate it from its original (extralegal) existential basis?

According to its declaration from January 1, 1977, Charter 77 was a "free, informal, open community of people of different convictions, different faiths and different professions united by the will to strive, individually and collectively, for the respect of civic and human rights,"[68] both in Czechoslovakia and in the world. Coming from all walks of life — Christians of all denominations, Jews, Marxists and expelled Communists, freethinkers, independent liberal intellectuals, and quite often just sheer eccentrics and adventurers — those who decided to sign the Charter 77 document were sending to the authorities and to the general public one single but all-important message. They found it impossible to keep silent any more in a situation when hypocrisy had become a generally recognized social norm, all basic human rights existed "regrettably on paper only," and a large number of people became "victims of a virtual apartheid." To challenge that situation they did not create an organization for the oppositional political activity. They got together only to adopt a clear, unambiguous moral stance in public matters.

The vast majority of people may have found this type of behavior quixotic or even silly. What, however, was immediately obvious to everybody who had the ears to hear and the capability to listen, was that with Charter 77 the Czechoslovak society regained not only the voice of conscience and freedom but also the voice of common sense. The human rights dialogue with the government, suggested in the original declaration, never started and most likely never could because of the nature of a totalitarian regime. The deadening silence of normalization was nevertheless broken, and there were many other and maybe more valuable candidates to enter the proposed public debate, to exchange opinion on relevant matters, both in Czechoslovakia and abroad. The whole new discourse became a social reality whose aim was to start to ask meaningful questions again; to reexamine who we really were, who we had become in our current situation; to document cases of the unjustly persecuted and express solidarity with them and with their families; to search for the truth in the whole range of public issues, whose treatment was for decades dominated by all sorts of ideological distortions, bureaucratic mindlessness, opportunistic manipulations, and very often sheer lies.

The way in which Charter 77 launched its human rights initiative re-opened, under the conditions of an "advanced and stabilized totalitarian system,"[69] the central question of classical political philosophy: What is the highest good that should be the ultimate aim of our actions? All Socratic philosophers in Charter 77's ranks certainly gained an excellent opportunity to re-read the texts of old classics in the light of their own experience. What was at stake here was indeed the matter of personal integrity in the political environment poisoned by what Cicero described as *morbus animi,* the spiritual disease caused by the *aspernatio rationis,* the contempt of reason.[70] The question was the existence of the man of reason — who does not have the truth in his possession but lives with the Platonic problem of "care for the soul" — in the *polis* struck by a totalitarian plague. In other words, such circumstances called into question the potency of reason under such a regime.

At the same time, however, there was another important thing that those who decided to devote themselves to *vita contemplativa* had to accept as a part of their bold philosophical exercise within Charter 77: The argument of plurality as the elementary condition of *vita activa,* with which Hannah Arendt entered into the dialogue about Western political thought. There were not only individuals with their lonely heroic internal struggles to live according to the Socratic appeal, in unity with themselves; but others were here too, who shared the same experience, who had to endure the same harassment from the side of authorities, who were exposed to the same type of questions and existential tensions, who were ready to express in concert their solidarity. The participants in Charter 77, seeking "general public interest," were not only contributing to the restoration of the moral consciousness of society, but also were recreating and rediscovering its absent, and for so long paralyzed, public space. It was due to the emergence of what was called the dissidents' "parallel *polis*"[71] that the totalitarian regime lost a substantive part of its magic after the Declaration of Charter 77 was published; this was why the cause of human rights was not perceived only as a strong moral appeal coming from lonely voices calling from the desert, but became in the course of time a political matter of great importance and also got the necessary visibility and recognition on both domestic and international fronts.

My reference to the Socratic philosophers participating in Charter 77 may have raised some eyebrows or awakened a smile on the readers' lips, but there was one among Charter 77's founding fathers who was undoubtedly worthy of this name: one of its first three spokepersons, who died only two months after its pronouncement (in March of 1977), one of the last students of Edmund Husserl — Jan Patočka. He published in the last weeks of his life a short but important text, "What Charter 77 Is and What It Is Not (Why Right Is on Its Side and No Slander or Forcible Measures Can Shake It)."[72] It seems to me quite appropriate to conclude the debate on the philosophical significance of Charter 77 with his thoughts.

The central theme of this text is morality as a necessary condition of human existence, something which escapes by its very nature any state control, no matter how much power and control a state has. "No society," warns Patočka, "no matter how good is its technical foundation, can function without moral foundation, without conviction that has nothing to do with opportunism, circumstance, and expected advantage. Morality, however, does not exist just to allow society to function, but simply to allow human beings to be human. Man does not define morality, according to the caprice of his needs, wishes, tendencies and craving; it is morality that defines man."[73]

The respect for human rights is, according to Patočka, nothing else than just recognition of this plain truth: "The idea of human rights is . . . the conviction that even states, even society as a whole, are subject to the sovereignty of moral sentiment: that they recognize something unconditional, that is higher than they are, something that is binding even on them, sacred, inviolable, and that in their power to establish and maintain a rule of law, they seek to express this recognition."[74]

Patočka's explanations and conclusions give away the solid dose of Socratic irony. The fact that the governments, including the government of socialist Czechoslovakia, are concluding and signing international agreements on human rights, that international human rights conventions are becoming now a part of their legal order, marks the beginning of a new era in the history of mankind in which the governments subordinate their own sovereign authority to the claims and dictates of morality. They confirm by these acts that *"a higher authority does exist,"*[75] to which all citizens "are obliged, individually, in their conscience, and to which states are bound by their signatures on important international covenants; that they are bound not by the expediency, according to the rules of political advantage and disadvantage, but that their signatures there mean that they accept the rule that *politics are indeed subject to law and that law is not subject to politics."*[76] Charter 77 is, according to Patočka, nothing else but an outgrowth of this conviction. It is an expression of joy of Czechoslovak citizens that their government has decided to recognize and participate in this epochal change. It is their positive response, their solemn and public "yes" approving that decision. It is, indeed, a great and very welcome thing, Patočka concludes, that motivations for human actions "need no longer be exclusively, or for the most part, grounded in fear or personal advantage, but rather in respect for what is highest in man, in his understanding of his obligations and of the common weal, of the need to take upon oneself even some discomfort, misunderstanding, and a certain risk."[77]

For the reader who is experienced in international law and politics it is immediately evident that the author of this text is not a lawyer but a philosopher. Yet, it is Patočka's argument that brings me back to the legal context within which the initiative of Charter 77 emerged. The question was whether international obligations of state — be it just political commitments, such as to participate in the Helsinki process, or legal obligations created by the signed and ratified international conventions, whose fulfillment could be required and violations sanctioned under international law — could be recognized as a new source of rights of individual citizens. The moral reasoning of Patočka emphasized the existential basis of human rights discourse and highlighted the fact that its current participants — the signatories of Charter 77, whose spokesperson he became — were ready to take upon themselves "even some discomfort, misunderstanding, and a certain risk"; it was not a particularly strong legal argument and could hardly convince the biblical scribes and pharisees nor contemporary experts on international law. What does it actually say about the nature of human rights that the patient endurance of inhabitants of the "parallel *polis*" managed to convince in the end even these experts, that it was the dissidents, and not their opponents, who were right and won decisively their extraordinary legal case?

Patočka's philosophical contribution to our human rights debate in the seventies had another important consequence. It was developed in the context of his philosophy of history and offered a new perspective on the Czech political program, partly continuing in Masaryk's tradition, partly departing from it, exactly in those aspects where Masaryk — as the Czech experience in the twentieth century demonstrated — failed. Patočka agreed with Masaryk that Czech parochialism and smallness must be constantly challenged by powerful universal ideas; that the Czech question must always be thought through and conceived as "a world question." On the other hand, he did not agree with Masaryk's progressivist concept of world history. He realized that the European superiority in global matters ended with the totalitarian horrors of the twentieth century; that after the European path of progress to the radiant future collapsed, humanity was in need of "a new political principle," which Hannah Arendt was calling for in the preface to her *Origins of Totalitarianism*: "a new law on the earth, whose validity this time must comprehend the whole of humanity, while its power must remain strictly limited, rooted in and controlled by newly defined territorial entities."[78]

Patočka distinguished between two legacies: first, the European civilization left to the emerging post-European world, with its imperial, self-assured, and assertive way of conquest whose most powerful weapon is the instrumental, scientific reason of the Modern Age; and second, the much older and by definition more uncertain way of internal transformation, whose guiding principle is the "care for the soul," the never-ending quest for inner truthfulness, a really human — always finite and never complete — wisdom or knowledge (*hē anthrōpine sophia* of old Socrates). And there is no doubt that the cause of human freedom and human rights, threatened maybe more than ever before in the post-European — multicultural, multireligious, and more and more interconnected — world, exhorts us to set out on the second path, to accept its Socratic principle with all implied challenges and difficulties.

The miraculous change of 1989 brought Central Europe back on the map of the Western world. The short twentieth century ended with the collapse of Communism, and in the period that followed, first our region, then the whole of Europe, and now even the whole world have been undergoing a profound transformation. With the beginning of the twenty-first century, and especially after 9/11, a new era is clearly announcing itself, the age of planetary mankind and globalization. What is the burden we are carrying with us from the past? How do we protect our freedom, which seems to be endangered again, when totalitarianism does not reside any more in well-defined states or other clearly distinguishable territorial entities and has acquired a new form of loose, fuzzy, and seemingly invisible international terrorist networks? What kind of God does human rights need in our current situation?

I tried to offer at least some answers to this question throughout this essay, based mainly on my Central European experience. So let me conclude by praying to this God, who has, to be sure — if he or she exists at all — many different faces and speaks in many different languages, and asking him for what Hannah Arendt, one of the greatest Central Europeans of the twentieth century, had in mind when she wrote,

> the old prayer which King Solomon, who certainly knew something of political action, addressed to God — for the gift of an "understanding heart," the greatest gift a man could receive and desire — might still hold for us. As far removed from sentimentality as it is from paper work, the human heart is the only thing in the world that will take upon itself the burden that the divine gift of action, of being a beginning and therefore being able to make a beginning, has placed upon us. Solomon prayed for this particular gift because he was a king and knew that only an "understanding heart," and not mere reflection or mere feeling, makes it bearable for us to live with other people, strangers forever, in the same world, and makes it possible for them to bear with us.[79]

12 Religious Freedom: A Legacy to Reclaim

AMBASSADOR ROBERT A. SEIPLE

An important dimension of the relationship between human rights and religion is the right to religious freedom. This chapter demonstrates the importance of religious freedom to the development of this country and its foreign policy. Religious freedom was an important value for many of the American founders, particularly Roger Williams and William Penn (founders of the Rhode Island and Pennsylvania colonies, respectively). Indeed, a very important incident in Roger Williams's life helped shape how the issue of religious liberty would be framed in the national consciousness. When Williams was still in Massachusetts, his ideas about religious freedom so provoked the establishment that the authorities decided to banish him from the colony and deport him to England. Before he could be captured, however, Governor Winthrop, who was part of the council that voted to banish Williams, warned him of the imminent arrest and allowed Williams to escape to Rhode Island. In the words of Williams, "that ever-honored governor, Mr. Winthrop, privately wrote to me to steer my course to Narragansett Bay and to the Indians. . . ." With this preemptive act, Winthrop demonstrated a grace that speaks to tolerance and says a great deal concerning his quiet respect for Williams. This value — the best of tolerance leading to respect — became foundational to how the American forefathers approached, morally and pragmatically, the issue of religious liberty.

Roger Williams's contemporary, William Penn, made a similarly foundational contribution to institutionalizing freedom of conscience. In Penn's words, "Because it is most reasonable for a man to believe according to his own conscience and not according to another man's conscience [therefore] it is unrighteous to persecute a man for not maintaining that religion which in his conscience he believes to be false."[1]

Further, as Mary Dunn, a Penn biographer, points out, "William Penn was well aware that the major obstacle to religious freedom did not consist in moral and theological issues, but in the notion that religious uniformity was a necessary, a basic element to political stability."[2] Both the ideal of freedom of conscience and the pragmatics of religious pluralism anchored Penn's approach to this issue.

And then this insight from Dane Shelly, Research Associate at the Institute for Global Engagement, commenting on Roger Williams: "Rather than weakening the government and Church, Williams believed that freedom of conscience would strengthen those ideas and institutions which were grounded in truth. In effect, true Christianity would be strengthened when it was tested, right government when it was debated."[3] Clearly, the linked components of political stability and security were seen as a logical outgrowth of religious freedom.

More poetically, Williams's friend John Milton argued for this freedom in his classic apology for freedom of conscience, *Areopagitica*:

> And though all the winds of doctrine were let loose to play upon the earth, so Truth be in the field, we do injuriously, by licensing and prohibiting, to misdoubt her strength. Let her and Falsehood grapple; who ever knew Truth put to the worse, in a free and open encounter?[4]

Milton argues for a level playing field, realizing that truth will ultimately carry the day. Perhaps we also see the unspoken intimation here that there would be problems if one faith — either through legislation or the abuse of majority rule — were elevated over another, exacerbating the differences between and thereby driving wedges between different faiths.

Over time, as the colonies sought to form themselves into states of a unified nation, other noted individuals also weighed in. James Madison, in an address to the General Assembly of the Commonwealth of Virginia, 1785, spoke out against coercive force in the assimilation of religion. It is, said Madison, a fundamental and undeniable truth

> That religion or the duty which we owe to our creator and the manner of discharging it can be directed only by reason and conviction, not by force or violence. The religion, then, of every man must be left to the conviction and conscience of every man; and it is the right of every man to exercise it as these may dictate.[5]

Thomas Jefferson always referred to religious liberty as the "First Freedom," demonstrating his own understanding that if the mind and the heart are not free, nothing else really matters. A stable, secure civil society cannot be built without this freedom because, without it, none of the other rights such as freedom of the press, freedom of speech, and freedom of association will ever be credible or legitimate. Just as the true test of a government's commitment to liberal democracy is tolerance for opposition parties, the true test of commitment to civil society is religious freedom.

This brings us to a key understanding inherent in the thinking of the American forefathers. Consider the following from the Rhode Island Charter from England, a document written in 1663. Seeking to avoid the oppressive theocracy from which they fled, and a similar oppression from the Massachusetts Colony, the Rhode Island Colony stated their feelings clearly:

> [T]hey have ffreely declared, that it is much on their hearts . . . to hold forth a livlie experiment, that a most flourishing civill state may stand and best bee maintained . . . with a full libertie in religious concernements; and that true pietye rightly grounded upon gospell principles, will give the best and greatest security to sovereignetye, and will lay in the hearts of men the strongest obligations to true loyalty. (Original Old English text)[6]

Very simply, a nexus point between religious freedom and security was assumed. Religious freedom promotes security through the captured loyalty of its citizens.

These components of religious freedom — pluralism, freedom of conscience, the free embrace of faith, tolerance and respect, individual security, and institutional stability — became signature themes in our earliest history. More than just words, they were offered with passion and commitment. Historian Paul Johnson comments further: "[America's] first Christian inhabitants were only too anxious to explain what they were doing and why . . . in a way, the first American settlers were like the ancient Israelites. They saw themselves as active agents of divine providence."[7]

Thankfully, these "radical" ideas of religious freedom have now been woven deeply into the fabric of American life. But more gratifying, these ideas have taken root internationally. Is this development *solely* a legacy of the deep yearnings of the American colonists toward the issue of religious liberty? Certainly not. Penn, Williams, and those who came later were simply speaking for that common cry for freedom that emanates from all of humanity. Human dignity, sanctity of life, the knowledge that each has been created in God's image, created with free will — these are the commonly held universal principles that speak to every individual's best instincts and highest values.

The philosophical and theological underpinnings are strong. But the pragmatics, especially those that concretely relate to a values-based civil society, are just as enduring. In that vein, consider the admonition of the International Crisis Group in its report of 1 March 2001, a report that speaks to increasing religious persecution in Central Asia: "Treat religious freedom as a security issue, not just a human rights issue, and advocate unequivocally that regional security can only be assured if religious freedom is guaranteed and the legitimate activities of groups and individuals are not suppressed."

Today we see this as a profound insight. For what was commonly understood, even assumed, in the seventeenth century was ironically lost and seemingly forgotten in the stability that resulted from tolerance. Today, in the shadow of 9/11 and the first religious war of the twenty-first century, Americans are rediscovering — and, one hopes, recapturing — the best elements of their own legacy of religious liberty. The bold echo of the Rhode Island Charter of 1663 is being heard ever more.

Legislating Freedom

It is certainly no accident, then, that religious freedom legislation would eventually emerge from the United States. To be sure, America was not the first entity to spawn such thinking in the modern age. The need was obviously felt coming out of World War II, and it was met in a rather extraordinary document, the Universal Declaration of Human Rights (the "Universal Declaration"), an international covenant that continues to influence global behavior regarding human rights and, by extension, the practice of religion (Article 18). By the 1990s, however, with over 600 million people worldwide being persecuted for what they believe, or in whom they believe, the U.S. government felt compelled to put its enormous shoulder to the wheel of religious rights internationally. That effort would translate into formal legislation.

The International Religious Freedom Act of 1998 (IRFA) ultimately received approval by overwhelming margins in both houses of Congress. On the one hand, given the fact that at the time Americans were still slogging through the culture wars with the worst of partisan politics, a bipartisan vote of this magnitude was nothing less than amazing. This surface unanimity, however, was not indicative of the long eighteen-month struggle between two very different methodological approaches to the issue of religious freedom. The acrimonious debate (the State Department, for example, was actively opposed to this legislation, and only dropped its resistance when congressional unanimity seemed certain) biased the international perception of this bill, even though there was an enormous difference between initial drafts and the final outcome. Given the fact that implementation methodology was ultimately at stake, an understanding of that debate is essential.

The legislative process began in May 1997, when Congressman Frank Wolf of Virginia introduced a bill entitled "The Freedom from Religious Persecution Act." A year later, after being studied and revised by no fewer than five House committees, the Wolf-Specter Bill, as it was now called (Senator Arlen Specter of Pennsylvania simultaneously introduced the bill in the Senate), passed the House overwhelmingly, 375-41. Behind the scenes, Christian denominations and faith-based, nongovernmental organizations were being solicited for support.

Still, many were uneasy. The rationale behind the bill seemed to focus on persecuted Christians alone. Many thoughtful Christians worried that such an emphasis would exacerbate differences between various religions, effectively driving wedges between faiths, a divisiveness that spoke to the worst of religion rather than the best of the faith. The Christian emphasis, for some, also diminished the moral and theological strength of the faith. Did Christianity need a legislative "edge" to compete? Whatever happened to Milton's level playing field? In the international marketplace of ideals, was it really necessary to give Christianity a boost? Many thought not.

The second major point in the debate centered on punishment — what to do with the persecutors. There was no mistaking this emphasis. It was seen in the aggressive language of denunciation, the assumption that punishment was the only way to change bad behavior, the focus on force and pressure to rectify past wrongs. Sanctions, the blunt instrument of a powerful nation, would underscore our sense of moral rectitude as we imposed our will on others. The attitude of many activists regarding American economic power was in-your-face: "We have it, you need it, look out, world, here we come."

Many winced. Jeremy Gunn, an astute observer of this legislative process and a superb lawyer for religious freedom internationally, sums up the feelings of many: "By enacting a law to promote international religious freedom, the United States understandably raises the suspicions of observers, both at home and abroad, as to its motives and its actions."[8] He then goes on to note the point of real tension:

> Critics can thus portray the adoption of IRFA as an example of the United States pandering to conservative Christians, acting unilaterally, ignoring the greater human rights discussion, foisting its own ideology of church and state, and using sanctions to force others to adopt its peculiar priorities in the human rights agenda.[9]

Unfortunately we are still faced with the residue of that perception, a perception that became a lasting reality even with the very significant degree of nuance added to the legislation as it was transformed from the original Wolf-Specter iteration into the much more complex and flexible Act that is IRFA.

As the debate over Wolf-Specter played out in the House, a small number of congressional staffers quietly began to frame a much different bill. The overwhelming House vote notwithstanding, these new drafters knew that the House bill had absolutely no chance in the Senate. In March of 1998, Senator Don Nichols of Oklahoma introduced this alternative bill, the bill that would eventually become IRFA.

It took over twelve thousand words to capture the complexity of religious freedom, but the purpose of the legislation is stated very simply: to "condemn violations of religious freedom, and to promote, and to assist other governments in the promotion of, the fundamental right of freedom of religion."[10] With these words, the ideological battle was almost over. *Promotion* was lifted up, *punishment* was pushed to the background. Not surprisingly, the tone of the legislation changed. Theological arrogance and secular hubris gave way to universal values and protection for all peoples. Gunn provides an excellent summary:

> The unsuccessful Wolf-Specter Bill and the successful Nichols IRFA Bill revealed two strikingly different approaches to the goal of promoting religious freedom. The Wolf-Specter approach was characterized by its focusing on the more egregious cases of "religious persecution" (as it would be defined in U.S. law), its emphasizing persecution of Christians, its suspicion of the Clinton administration and the diplomacy of the U.S. State Department, and its choice of automatic sanctions as the best means to force offending regimes to alter their behavior. The Nichols IRFA approach emphasized, to the contrary, support for all people who suffer from violations of religious liberty as defined by international standards, diplomacy rather than sanctions, and providing better information on the status of religious freedom worldwide.[11]

A further summary demonstrates just what was at stake in the debate:

> These contrasting viewpoints perhaps exemplify something more than America's contradictory attitudes about freedom of religion or even human rights generally. They perhaps exemplify two different strands of American thinking about the role of the United States in the world. Both strands understand the need for American engagement in the world, but

the terms of that engagement are quite different. The first believes that the United States and its government know best what should be done, and the question is whether the government has the courage and fortitude to push, pull, cajole, and sanction other countries until the American objective is accomplished. The second viewpoint, although fully wishing to engage the United States in an effort to improve the lives of those who suffer for their religious beliefs, nevertheless understands that the United States leads best when it leads by a genuine, informed, and sincere commitment to promoting all human rights.[12]

Lighting Candles and Cursing the Darkness

In the final version of IRFA, the State Department was made the primary implementer of the legislation (amazingly, the State Department was totally bypassed in the Wolf-Specter Bill). The promotion of religious freedom was now a component of the foreign policy of the United States. There would be an Ambassador-at-Large at State who would oversee implementation of the Act. An annual report would be issued on the status of religious freedom worldwide. The President was given a smorgasbord of options for dealing with recalcitrant behavior (from a diplomatic démarche to the imposition of economic sanctions). The Act also established a quasi-independent U.S. Commission on International Religious Freedom. This nine-member commission was created to provide accountability for the implementation of the Act, both by reviewing actions taken by the State Department and by making its own recommendations to the President and Congress.

Given the primary role of the State Department for religious freedom issues, the presence of an independent commission might seem to be redundant. In fact, the commission was a relatively late addition to the legislative process. One can argue the facts surrounding the creation of the commission and its attendant rationale. This writer, however, was present at the commission's first meeting, when the mission for this entity was discussed. A key member mused, "Are we to light a candle or curse the darkness?" There was silence for a moment, and then the member answered his own question, "I guess we ought to curse the darkness." No one corrected the answer. Although the language of the final bill clearly comes down on the side of "promotion" — thereby providing a positive bias to the implementation strategy — the punishment stick of the original Wolf-Specter Bill was not to be discarded. It was now in the hands of the commission, but more important, its use would become a measuring rod for the commission's effectiveness.

The final bill, either because of or in spite of the contentious debate, emerged with considerable strengths. In addition to what was previously mentioned, note the following themes inherent in the legislation.

Inherent Strengths

One theme inherent in the legislation is the concept of universality. Any protection of freedom needs a sustaining rationale based on human dignity and the sanctity of all life. An imposition of Western values, for example, would only increase the suspicions regarding the intentions of the U.S. Both language and rationale needed to transcend ideologies, cultures, histories, and governmental systems. IRFA wisely incorporates the language of the international covenants that have come before it, beginning with the Universal Declaration.[13]

Of course, the concept of universality is still being questioned. The Universal Declaration, quite frankly, would inspire a massive debate, with an outcome in doubt, if it had to be recreated today. The original document achieved success only when the drafting commission agreed on the right to, though not necessarily the rationale for, human dignity. The French theologian Jacques Maritain, commenting on the difficulty of the process, said, "We agree on these rights, providing we are not asked why. With the 'why,' the dispute begins."[14] So, agreement was reached on the principle of human dignity without requiring consensus as to the basis.[15] This is not simply a rhetorical slight of hand, but a practical approach to what Paul Brink calls the "middle ground," an appropriate goal "that preserves particularity even as it promotes public civility."[16]

Make no mistake, the language of universality is absolutely essential in a document like the IRFA. Implementation would be impossible without it. Inherent in all of these preceding international covenants is the assumption of mutual accountability. Why can an American ambassador call on the Chinese head of the Religious Affairs Bureau — even though China is a country with a different history, culture, and organizing principles — and feel comfortable in raising the issue of religious freedom? Is this not the latest guise for preaching American values to the rest of the world? Absolutely not. The universality of human dignity is a transcendent assumption and the international covenants that are based on these values allow, even demand, mutual accountability.[17] Quite simply, the intentionality behind the language and the preamble of the IRFA provides the freedom and the comfort level to speak boldly and directly on this issue, in any capital of the world.

A second fact to note is that the IRFA is an inclusive bill. It is international in its scope. It targets no one particular region or one particular religion. The bill underscores the nonnegotiable freedom of "thought, conscience, and belief" — upholding the right not to believe in a religion as much as the right to believe. No one is left out. The freedom of conscience, and the right to act on the basis of conscience, is guaranteed and protected for all.

The third strength is the obvious demand for justice inherent in the Act. IRFA gives voice to those 600 million, mostly nameless, individuals who are enduring persecution this day. The Act confirms that Americans will stand with them, establishing a voice for those who have no voice, lifting up the marginalized, the victimized, the powerless, and the vulnerable of our world. On one level, the IRFA was designed to make things right for those who were being denied their basic freedoms, suffering under the boot of the more powerful and the more privileged.

IRFA helps send important messages about the importance of justice (and not just narrow "national interest") in international affairs. Justice demands that sin has consequence. The "evil that men do" can be recorded, targeted, attacked, and defeated; the proper application of power and authority can be employed to right wrongs and correct grievances. An environment of impunity will not always be allowed to exist. The ongoing, systemic, egregious acts of governments and individuals alike will be put under the glare of this legislation — a strong statement of purpose emanating from "the last remaining superpower."

This suggests a fourth strength: hope. "Hope" is a future-oriented word that gains its legitimacy and credibility through tangible manifestations in the *present*. Positive signs need to be observed *today*, which point toward a better, more hopeful, *tomorrow*. When the U.S. Congress voted unanimously for IRFA, a powerful signal was sent to the persecuted religionists of the world. In the corridors of power, the plight of the persecuted was being discussed. The last remaining superpower was making a statement for the vulnerable of the world. They would now have a full partner. The considerable strength of the United States would come alongside the religiously oppressed, standing with them, taking their part. This point cannot be overstated. The emergence of IRFA provided a huge dosage of hope for all of those throughout the world who were experiencing suffering because of their faith.

The Report: Institutionalizing Religious Freedom

In discussing IRFA's strengths, it is more than appropriate to spend a moment on the Annual Report on International Religious Freedom, mandated by the

Act. It has been said that the beginning of wisdom is calling something by its proper name. A good report is designed to do just that. This, then, can become a primary communication tool among governments, nongovernmental organizations (NGOs), and the human rights community at large. The issue of religious freedom has had a need for honest communication for some time. Indeed, the Achilles' heel for this issue has been the fragile combination of great passion supported by limited anecdotal research. Factual reporting from a reputable source is an absolute must if this issue is to be credibly maintained in the public eye.

Literally hundreds of Foreign Service Officers are involved in the State Department's Annual Report on International Religious Freedom. Putting a report out on 194 countries is a mammoth endeavor. The good news, and perhaps an unintended consequence of the report, is that this exercise, more than anything else, institutionalized the issue of religious freedom in the State Department and, by extension, in the foreign policy of the United States.

The mantra employed in the formulation of the report is "truth without surprise." Inputs are available from a variety of sources: American embassies, international NGOs, the human rights community, and religious groups both here and abroad. Compiling all of the source material normally produces a picture of remarkable clarity. Only in the most closed societies (North Korea, for example) has there been difficulty in collecting enough data to tell the whole story. Following the issuing of the report, the State Department Office begins immediately to work with the information available to it, briefing appropriate State Department officials even while beginning the more difficult task of ameliorating some of the conditions abroad. If progress is made in resolving a difficult situation for religious freedom in a certain country, the next report notes that progress. The report, then, can be used as a very effective leveraging device to encourage positive change in a country's religious freedom record.

With respect to the specific layout of the report, there is a preface where the philosophical underpinnings of this issue are highlighted. Next there is an "executive summary," which mentions every country where some violation of religious freedom took place within the last year. The countries are usually grouped together according to the perceived total impact of the violations. The specific country reports then follow with the factual data gleaned from the multiple inputs mentioned previously. This data is nuanced in a number of ways: Government oppression is distinguished from individual acts. A distinction is also noted between actual government engagement and government's response to group action within a country. An environment of impunity fostered by the government is ultimately just as dangerous as government-led violations and is so noted. The report considers whether the violations were "ongoing" or whether they simply represent a single occurrence. Were they intentional ("systemic") or just an unfortunate happening? Were the violations pervasive or an aberration? And, most important to the issue of designating a country as a "country of particular concern" (the language of the Act), were the violations "egregious," namely, did persecution take place? Persecution is a very specific term, suggesting that some form of physical mayhem has occurred, such as torture, rape, killing, kidnapping, or prolonged detention without cause. And, finally, this persecution needs to be specifically linked to religious freedom. There is a great deal of abhorrent behavior initiated by governments around the world, much of it a reflection of a felt need for security by those in power. If religious freedom is not a substantial element in this dynamic, however, the report might not even mention the incidents. It is fair to say that these judgments are often difficult to make, and a great deal of discernment is necessary to find the proper balance.

The report does not draw conclusions. If one is familiar with the language of the international covenants and the specifics of the International Religious Freedom Act of 1998, those conclusions are fairly easy to reach. The report is not meant to be a moral judgment on a country, but again, those judgments can easily be made by the reader. Finally, the report does not offer "next steps" for those countries engaged in violations of religious freedom. This is not a major shortcoming given the obvious intent of the United States, namely, advocating for religious freedom worldwide. Ultimately, any attempt to ameliorate religious oppression in the world should be judged by how those suffering for their faith are helped by the action taken. Is there a greater measure of justice for those who have no voice? Is there legitimate and credible hope for those marginalized by the powers arrayed against them? Might there be a better future for those individuals and countries represented negatively in this year's report? The beginning of wisdom, and the first steps in bringing relief to people of faith around the world, is calling something by its proper name. The State Department's Report on International Religious Freedom does just that.

The Final Product: Reporting on the Report

IRFA, of course, is not without its shortcomings. This report that has done so much good in institutionalizing the issue of religious freedom within the U.S. government has two obvious problems. First, since it is an annual record, only a relatively small period of time is highlighted. The ability to view long-term historical trends is limited, as is the possibility of applauding small but positive progress that might be taking place. A yearly report, like a yearly budget, places some artificial analytical restraints, especially since solving the problems of religious freedom around the world is a very long-term exercise. A second problematic issue with the report is that the United States is not one of the countries reported on. America is judging, in effect, everybody but itself. This intentional absence of an American record, and the unintended hubris it portrays to the rest of the world, produces some of the negative blowback that we are still experiencing today.

In accordance with IRFA, the report must produce the specifics that will allow the president (in reality, his delegated official, the secretary of state) to designate those countries that are engaged in "ongoing, systemic, and egregious" violations of religious freedom as "countries of particular concern" ("CPCs"), with the possibility of U.S. sanctions to follow. Quite frankly, this exercise gets most of the media attention associated with the report, and ultimately might be the biggest distraction to long-term, enduring solutions to religious freedom problems around the world. It is my personal experience that the CPC list is about 5 percent of the total exercise of putting together an annual report but receives 95 percent of media's attention. To date, the report as a whole has been largely ignored in the media and by human rights groups alike, in favor of this more titillating item of designation and sanctions. Certainly the human dynamic at work is understandable, but this emphasis unfairly trivializes the report and, by extension, trivializes the issue of religious freedom. Sanctions, especially unilateral sanctions, have a checkered career at best, and can create additional problems for those who need to be served, those who are suffering in various parts of the world today because of their faith.

Since the inception of this Act, there has always been tremendous pressure to increase the number of countries on "The List." The United States presently sanctions more countries than any five other countries combined, with little noticeable long-term affect. It is hard to see this diplomatic "tool" having much viability in the future. Moreover, since 9/11, the utility of sanctions has been largely compromised by geopolitical realities. Security concerns are at the top of our hierarchy of values, and any country that is providing the United States any help at all in the battle against terrorism probably will escape sanctions, regardless of religious freedom violations.[18]

The U.S. Commission for International Religious Freedom set up by IRFA is another area of concern. Established to provide accountability, the commission, nevertheless, was created from a negative impulse; namely, a number of legislators did not believe that the State Department would handle this issue properly without an independent force looking over its shoulder. This structure has created a certain redundancy as well as a need to "be against" State Department initiatives. The commission, perhaps understandably, has struggled with its own identity and has yet to develop a clear complementary role to the Office of International Religious Freedom at the State Department.

A "watchdog" role is not the way that one creates positive synergy. As a result, we have seen a "yes, but" reaction to many of the positive changes in religious freedom around the world. In Laos, for example, a combined effort of the Lao Ambassador and the State Department managed to free virtually all of the Christians who were in jail during the summer of 2000. The commission reacted with its "yes, but" and suggested that Laos be one of the next countries designated as a country of particular concern with sanctions to follow because of additional issues yet to be corrected. "Cursing the darkness" does not allow for applauding the small, positive steps a country might be taking. The public watchdog role works against good private diplomacy.

Similarly, the State Department also has its infrastructure challenges with regard to the implementation of IRFA. This is still a relatively new office at State, fleshed out in additional detail through the legislation but with no additional funding from Congress.[19] In a department where budget and staff are always a problem endemic to existing issues, it is difficult to create an ongoing critical mass with such a new office like religious freedom. Given these realities, a redundancy between State and the commission is probably not affordable. Additionally, the resultant energy loss (instead of a positive supporting synergy) works against an issue that is still relatively new within the federal government.

Finally, for all of its strengths, IRFA, at the end of the day, is only working on the symptoms of the problem. Very little is done to change the underlying causes of religious persecution. A world not safe for diversity because political cultures do not teach people how to deal with deep differences, pervasive superficiality in understanding real religious faith (both "our" faith and that of "the other"), abusive governmental power, unsophisticated missionary activity where the message is undermined by inappropriate methodologies — these are all issues that will have to be addressed before there is any realistic hope of global solutions that endure. A longer view is most certainly necessary, even though the legislation, as mentioned before, unintentionally works against such a timeline. Many of the countries of concern are also confronted with mass illiteracy, deeply ingrained poverty, border skirmishes from leftover wars, and dependency on international aid; in general, they are a long way from the kind of sustainable solutions that the world ultimately requires. Patience, and the importance of applauding small steps, cannot be overstated. It has taken America over 225 years to reach its present level of imperfection. Realism is imperative, and large candles a necessity.

Weaving the Fabric of Foreign Policy

So how do we reclaim the richness of our religious freedom heritage while ameliorating the negative challenges inherent in a complex world? How do we effectively integrate the historical rhetoric with our present reality, creating a coherent and consistent foreign policy context for religious liberty?

At the outset, we need to resist the simplistic dichotomy of moral imperative and *Realpolitik*. The so-called "soft" issues, like religious freedom, have a profound influence on the "hard" issues — the pragmatics of governing, assuring a nation's place within the global community, maintaining economic and military security, and so on. After all, good people can negotiate the "hard" issues. But it is the "soft" issues that people die for. The beginning of the twenty-first century clearly demonstrates the indivisible nature of these components. The first war of the twenty-first century (begun on 9/11) is a religious war. Afghanistan and Iraq cannot be understood without the religious component. Each country has secured a brighter future, to some extent, through the alleviation of religious persecution. We now have a "new" component in the geopolitical dynamic: religion. Many people are prepared to die for it. Even more are prepared to kill for it. We neglect this issue at our considerable peril.

Religious freedom and security are inextricably linked. Thomas Jefferson certainly understood this when he declared religious freedom to be the "First Freedom." Personal security cannot possibly exist when the mind and heart are shackled. Notice this linkage in the statements made by two of the more interesting individuals of this century. Sheik Mohammed Sayed Tantawi, a respected Sunni Muslim leader from al-Azhar Mosque in Cairo, says this: "If I force you to become a Muslim, I destroy Islam and I destroy myself. What you must have to come to the truth is freedom."[20] And then this, from Iranian President Khatami, in an extraordinary statement designed to challenge the power of hardliners in his country: "The best, most secure and legal option for this country is Islamic democracy, where both religion and freedom are respected."[21]

On the one hand, religious freedom protects the individual from improper force leading to self-destruction. On the other, this freedom contributes to a "most secure . . . option" for a country. The moral imperative and

Realpolitik are mutually accountable. Religious freedom and security are complementary components of a stable civil society. Where this is understood, one finds highly developed nations, properly anchored by moral imperatives, individually secure and institutionally stable.

When this linkage is not understood, or devalued by a country, both components are diminished. In China, for example, the party-state appears to have an acute fear of any social force whatsoever that it cannot understand or that it finds impossible to control through the usual tools of manipulation and intimidation. Religion falls into this category. House churches are suppressed, because of their growth. The Falon Gong has been hounded, because of its visibility. Buddhism in Tibet and Islam in the northwest autonomous region experience crackdowns because the Chinese government, always worried about its borders, overreacts to "forces" it does not understand.

The irony in all of this is that China, in the name of security, has created a very insecure situation. An attack on the moral imperative makes for a much weakened *Realpolitik*. It is almost impossible to define national security when citizen security is denied because of a person's core beliefs.

Uzbekistan provides another example with similar principles involved. On February 16, 1999, a small terrorist group attempted to assassinate President Islam Karimov by bombing a major government building. Had the president been there just a few minutes earlier than his actual arrival, that assassination would have been successful. Uzbekistan's security was attacked, and the government of Uzbekistan had every right, indeed, obligation, to respond. The response, however, was an overreaction, and it has proven to be immensely counterproductive. Although the known terrorists were relatively few in number (some sources say fewer than twelve), President Karimov proceeded to fill the jails with tens of thousands of innocent people — in this case, pious Muslims. This classic overreach had the effect of taking moderate Muslims and radicalizing them. Their core identity was now under attack and, in what psychologists call "frustration aggression," the resistance within Uzbekistan solidified against the government.

Even paranoids have real enemies — especially when the paranoia leads to persecution. The reactionary paranoia of the Uzbek crackdown has had the tragically ironic effect of transforming benign elements into real enemies. Uzbekistan's citizens no longer feel secure. They feel oppressed, and they resist. This "push-back" has made Uzbekistan less secure. Once the moral imperative — religious liberty for pious Muslims — was denigrated, the practical side of government was greatly weakened as well.

America, unwittingly, has also contributed to this unfortunate dichotomy. Following the events of 9/11, security, understandably, became the top priority. The U.S. was under attack, individually and corporately. It had every right to take military action; indeed, responsible government demanded nothing less. For a comprehensive response, however, we needed additional military staging areas, fly-over rights, shared intelligence, and, in some cases, joint military operations. But in order to secure governmental permission from other nations we apparently felt the need to suspend human rights obligations from those same countries. Indeed, some of them who were egregious persecutors of religious freedom were given a "pass" on their violations in exchange for helping us meet a security concern.

Designating countries and sanctioning them for religious freedom violations, as mentioned previously, is an imprecise exercise, often of dubious value, where those we seek to serve sometimes get hurt in the "blowback." But to take these violations of religious freedom "off the table," in favor of better security, demonstrates a profound misunderstanding of both components. We have mistakenly broken the nexus point between religious freedom and security and, in the long run if not immediately, weakened a relationship that is foundational to the building of stable societies.

Interests and Values

The unwitting wedge that periodically appears in this nexus of religious freedom and security also is evident in the unfortunate conflict between national values and national interests. Once again, a false dichotomy is created that can result in very real, and disastrous, consequences. Values represent the "soft" issues, the moral imperatives that we would like to think anchor our identities, the way we see ourselves and the way we hope the world sees us. Religious freedom is one such value. Human rights in general accurately define our values. Tolerance, respect for diversity, and religious pluralism all contribute to what we hope is a true sense of self. An earthquake response in Iran, feeding starving children in North Korea, upholding sanctions that fight apartheid in South Africa — these are all representative values, and history has shown that we take them seriously.

But we also have national interests. No surprises here: Much of our national interest revolves around our military security and economic might. We need trade to be free, markets to be open, and pricing that favors profits. We man military bases around the world, at least in part, in order to ensure these favorable trade conditions. We are capable of making difficult decisions periodically to ensure cheap oil, productive manufacturing plants, and profitable bottom lines.

We want to work with other countries when we can, but we will "go it alone" when we must. We pay United Nations dues when international policies please us. We withhold money when our "national interests" are being challenged. History has shown that we are capable of shrugging off UN resolutions when we want to (such as those regarding Israeli-Palestinian relations) but hold fast to them when it fits our national interests. We are powerful enough to go to war alone. As Vietnam and Somalia have shown, we are also powerful enough to leave on our own timetable.

Like true schizophrenics, we don't know when we are being inconsistent. Our values prompt an IRFA, partially implemented via a report that evaluates every nation on the face of the planet *except* the United States — a classic case of inconsistency that seemingly doesn't cause Americans to lose any sleep. America rhetorically embraces national values while blithely indulging national interests, and only periodically wonders why these are not one and the same.

Some worry. Chalmers Johnson, in his book appropriately called *Blowback,* is very direct: "An excessive reliance on a militarized foreign policy and an indifference to the distinction between national interests and national values in deciding where the United States should intervene abroad have actually made the country less secure in ways that will become only more apparent in the years to come."[22]

Perhaps none of this would matter if America were small, weak, nonthreatening, with little to envy. But this is not the case. Writing in the provocative book *Why Do People Hate America?* Ziauddin Sardar and Merryl Wyn Davies do not pull punches: "America is what we have termed a 'hyperpower' — a nation so powerful that it affects the lives of people everywhere. Yet, Americans are shielded from knowledge and debate about the actual consequences of U.S. engagement with the rest of the world."[23] A further slap: "America has the power and resources to refuse self-reflection. More pointedly, it is a nation that has developed a tradition of being oblivious to self-reflection."[24] Our schizophrenia seen in the difference between national values and national interests has created for others "the authentic rogue state . . . a rogue state of colossal military and economic might."[25]

The impact on American foreign policy, at least in the eyes of these authors, is frightening:

> With the U.S. you get a standardised theory and practice in its dealings with the world. The theory is always about 'our values', which are placed on a global pedestal: justice, democracy, human rights, freedom, civic concerns, compassion, resolve, responsibility — all the great virtues of

Western civilization. But the practice consistently contradicts these values. In other words, politically, America relates to the rest of the world in terms of double standards. This is one of the most common complaints about America; and a fundamental reason why America is hated in the world.[26]

Fear, of course, is always mixed with envy: "America is not just the lone hyperpower — it has become the *defining* power of the world. America defines what is democracy, justice, freedom; what are human rights and what is multiculturalism; who is a 'fundamentalist', a 'terrorist', or simply 'evil'. In short, what it means to be human."[27]

One can certainly argue that nothing more is happening here than axes being ground with rhetorical flourish. Assumptions can be challenged, examples may be flawed, and biases are clearly in evidence. But there is still much about these two books that cannot be dismissed.

Johnson chose his title, *Blowback,* and then defined it as "reaping what we sow." Interestingly, unlike *Why do People Hate America?* this book was written before 9/11. The prescience thus attached gives it more credibility than merely a breast-beating blast of impassioned rhetoric. Both books, however, call America to account for its double standard, a contradiction between values and interests. The Achilles' heel of human rights is inconsistency. Even the greatest power in the history of the world will wear thin under the eroding forces of inconsistency. The moral imperative will be irreparably damaged if our interests are allowed to become so wildly discordant with our values. To date, we have been inconsistent and powerful enough to get away with it, but large parts of the world are angry with America. More important, this dynamic will always saddle our foreign policy with a great deal of unnecessary suspicion.

Cautious Discourse

In response to the organizing question of this volume — "Does human rights need God?" — there is no doubt that a higher comfort level with and a deeper understanding of religion will ameliorate many of the problems I have sketched. Sad to say, this will not be easily accomplished. Unlike the ease with which the our forefathers discussed and publicly lived out core beliefs, America today has adopted a cultural bias against such conversations. We are quick to trumpet the "wall of separation" between church and state, defending a principle that has dramatically changed over the last 225 years. No longer is religion to be protected from state. The emphasis today is a shielding of state from religion. Senator Joe Lieberman had all of three days, in the 2000 presidential election, to give the country a refreshing view of the role that faith had played in his life. Then the liberal establishment began to wince. Quietly but firmly, the personal discourse on faith commitments was shut down, never to be heard again in the campaign.

In the name of good governance, America has separated church from state. Unfortunately, this has taken place at the expense of good analysis. We are hard-pressed to see the role that religion can exercise in the geopolitical dynamic. We are surprised to know that virtually all the non-NATO world (and even a good portion of the NATO world) would never think to create such a separation, a fact that has major implications for nation-building, writing new constitutions, establishing rule of law, and the like. But we are different. In the words of Stephen Carter, "In our sensible zeal to keep religion from dominating our politics, we have created a political and legal culture that presses the religiously faithful to be other than themselves, to act publicly, and sometimes privately as well, as though their faith does not matter to them."[28]

Tom Farr, longtime director of the International Religious Freedom Office at the State Department, weighs in with these words:

> The contemporary understanding of the role of religion, with its axioms of personal autonomy, privacy, and government neutrality between religion and irreligion (the liberal version of "separation of church and state"), has dominated U.S. foreign policy approaches to religion-based behavior. It has meant that, with few exceptions, American foreign policy has been ill equipped to understand and appreciate the spiritual basis for political and moral action. . . . American strategists are often hamstrung by a tendency to analyze human behavior in exclusively political and economic terms. Some have also concluded that religious persecution is a "soft" human rights issue, and a low priority in realistic approaches to protecting American interests. What has resulted from all of these assumptions is a 'compartmentalizing' of religion and religious behavior, leading to a dangerous indifference which played a key role in America's unpreparedness for many of the traumas of the late 20th century, including the 1979 revolution in Iran, the explosion of the Balkans in the 1990s, and the continuing intransigence of the Israeli-Palestinian issue.
>
> The attacks of September 11, 2001, the war against religion-based terrorism, and the American attempts to demilitarize and stabilize terror-supporting nations like Afghanistan and Iraq have raised the stakes significantly for American foreign policy. The need to understand the

sources and consequences of religion-based behavior has never been greater.[29]

Religion in the public square is an absolute necessity, and the discourse around the subject needs to be intentionally increased. This may require a periodic shifting of the "wall" of separation, that major icon of the left. Or, to be less radical, a slight change in the metaphor itself. Again, the words of Stephen Carter: "[I]n order to make the Founder's vision compatible with the structure and needs of modern society, the wall has to have a few doors in it."[30]

A greater intentionality toward religious discourse could also alleviate the present curse of superficiality. Thoughtful reflection, a commitment to respect, unbiased scholarship — all are critically important here. At the Institute for Global Engagement, our mantra has been consistently clear: "Understand your faith at its deepest and richest best, and enough about your neighbor's to show it respect." What are the eternal verities, the historic orthodoxy, the heroes, the giants of the faith? Why, in the words of Pascal, do "good men believe it to be true?" What does it say about community, the "other" in our midst, our neighbor? The days of "drive-by" religion, "ready-fire-aim" methodologies, and lighter-than-air theologies need to be put aside. Religion has always demanded more. Now our world is making similar demands as well.

Most of the language in the International Covenants on Religious Freedom stops with the word "tolerance." We can do better. Tolerance is a limp form of grace generally applied to people we don't especially care for. It is an open-ended concept, taking us from "easy ecumenism" to a universality that ceases to acknowledge legitimate differences. Carter has a wonderful word to offer on this subject:

> Tolerance without respect means little; if I tolerate you but do not respect you, the message of my tolerance, day after day, is that it is *my* forbearance, not *your* right, and certainly not the *nation's* commitment to equality, that frees you to practice your religion. You do it by my sufferance, but not with my approval. And since I merely tolerate, but neither respect nor approve, I might at any time kick away the props, and bring the puny structure of your freedom down around your ears.[31]

Respect speaks to a celebration of what we have in common. The undergirding rationale for all of human rights is the fact that each of us has been created in the image of God. Such a profound reality, an identity with the Divine, an acknowledgment of the sanctity and sacredness of all humankind, demands a relationship with our neighbor that can be nothing less than respectful.

Deepening one's own faith, respecting the faith of the "other," if practiced universally, would eliminate sectarian violence as we know it today. It is the single largest contribution that an individual can make to homeland and global security and a world desperate for a peace that can be sustained.

The conflict seen in the world today bears witness to misunderstood faith, inappropriately applied, with no respect for another's core beliefs. Take Osama bin Laden: His gospel has been truncated from the best of Islam — essentially reduced to a jihad against the West. He has absolutely no respect for anyone else's beliefs. When this redacted gospel is placed into the hands of a religious zealot, worst-case scenarios become reality.

A word of caution is appropriate here. Religious leaders in the West tried to respond to the event of 9/11. In times of crises, the role of spiritual leaders is often elevated. The layperson wants answers, seeks a rationale, wants someone to make sense out of a terrible tragedy. Sometimes the leader is elevated to a role higher than his or her expertise would support. To be candid, many religious figures were unprepared to describe Islam, to see in Islam anything more than a monolithic faith, to provide a sophisticated and nuanced articulation of the best of Islam. Large categories were quickly formed. "One size fits all," a shortcut to stereotyping, was the order of the day. Once stereotyped, it was easy to demonize. And it is always easy to hate that which we have learned to demonize. Violence ofttimes completes this negative spiral.

In effect, some religious leaders in the West carried out, in principle though not in violent intent, the same superficial exercise that negatively characterized Osama bin Laden. A truncated gospel, a misunderstood gospel, an inappropriately applied gospel — all presented with impassioned zealotry. We must do better.

Next Steps

How might we bring the issue of religious freedom into the mainstream in such a way that our country and our world will see, understand, and take seriously the important role of religion in global affairs today? In this regard, there exists some low-hanging fruit.

Training could be both comprehensive and integrated at the Foreign Service Institute. Real-world lessons should inform syllabus creation. In the clear light of day, principles should be debated and assimilated and, ultimately, religion should get as much attention as economics. Values and interests should become more creatively interwoven in the minds of Foreign Service Officers.

Similarly, military chaplains could be given enhanced opportunities to provide religious meaning to global events affecting their charges. Religion, as a geopolitical component, must be encouraged from the top. Effectiveness would be measured by a chaplain's competency to connect the dots, to provide theological rationale, to answer the unspoken (and perhaps previously unasked) questions concerning individual understandings as well as corporate values. Respect for the "other" should become foundational to how the military understands global rules of engagement.

Congressional delegations should now be automatically briefed by the IRF office before departing abroad. Religious freedom issues could be woven into every trip agenda. Countries would never again be able to infer from an absent agenda item that that issue is no longer important. When warranted, American officials could begin bilateral discussions about the role and importance of religious freedom rather than tacking it on as an afterthought. Trade, intelligence gathering, and mutual security issues can share space with our nation's core values at the table of foreign policy.

The business community also needs to be educated on the issue of religious freedom, its complementary role with security, the relevance of rule of law, and the necessity for predictable outcomes. The business community will understand; they need the same components present before investments are made: Work together. Agree not to embarrass the "other." Preclude another celebration in Beijing commemorating fifty years of Communism, exchanging busts of Lincoln, suggesting that Chinese peasants need food more than freedom.[32] Enduring relationships can never be built on such sycophantic moments. We are capable of so much more.

Finally, we need to bring the issue of religious freedom, and religion in general, into the mainstream of the inter-agency process of our federal government. It will not be easy. Culture is very difficult to change, and for a long time now, government officials have been conditioned against religious discourse in public. But this is a different time, with different issues, and religion is dominant in many of the conflicted areas of our globe. We have all felt the gravitational tug toward the worst abuses of religion. It is now time to explain how the best of our faith commitments can help point the way to enduring solutions.

Consider just one recent example of the new nexus points of dialogue and collaboration that are now becoming possible. On the sixteenth of December, 2003, a small group gathered for a meeting in Washington, D.C. The invitation came from the Institute for Global Engagement and the Pew Forum on Religion and Public Life. The purpose of the meeting was to discuss the role of religion and how we might collectively embrace the issue in today's geopolitical equation. Individuals represented themselves, their own instincts and passions, their own desires to make a difference — to be relevant — in today's world. They came from the State Department and the Department of Homeland Security. There were academics and activists. The three Abrahamic faiths were represented by individuals who had spent lifetimes cultivating the best of their faiths. The intelligence community had a spokesperson. Social scientists, anthropologists, and international relations experts were all in evidence.

In a small, quiet way, a dialogue was begun. It is far too early to presume where it will go. At the very least, it is hoped that such a beginning will ultimately provide the metaphorical equivalent of the IRF Report, namely, an issue that has been institutionalized and made prominent again because we are willing to discuss, to reflect, to include, to respect religion — all in the interest of national (and global) values and interests.

One hopes that in all of this we will begin to see anew what our forefathers saw so clearly: A divine presence that provided the rationale for human dignity, religious beliefs that called us to our best instincts and highest values, a core identity that enhanced personal security and contributed to the security of the state through the loyalty of its citizens, the presence of hope as the cry for justice was answered, and legitimate diversity without the need for homogeneity — respectful tolerance *with integrity.* The balance was always healthy. A specific religion would never dominate this government; government, however, would be forever informed by the values that flow from the best of religion.

It is a wonderful history with a marvelous vision. It is time now to renew our claim to this enduring legacy.

Afterword

JEAN BETHKE ELSHTAIN

In 1998, fifty years after the adoption of the Universal Declaration of Human Rights, a vigorous debate ensued on the theme of what sort of legitimation or justification human rights required. Arguments and opinions varied. For some, God must be in the picture: how else to explain the premise of human dignity that underscores nearly all universalist evocations of human rights? If God did not grant all of his children an inviolable dignity, then who or what did? Are we to take the premise of human dignity as a Kiplingesque "just so" story? That doesn't seem a very sturdy foundation upon which to erect something as fundamental, powerful, and important as human rights.

There are other bases, critics responded, than the theistic one. Perhaps one might make recourse to nature and nature's laws, although here the post-Darwinian understanding of nature and the survival of the fittest does not seem the stuff out of which human rights is derived. Nature pre-Darwin could be appealed to in a strongly teleological sense. But nature post-Darwin seems a rather different sort of entity — far more likely to feed the fancies of authors of tomes arguing that pitying and trying to spare the weakest and least fit is womanish sentimentalism (though "womanish" would likely be avoided in a day and age when sensitivity about gender, if not about weakness, is pervasive). There are all sorts of ways to dress the thesis of survival of the fittest up in its Sunday-best, of course, so it sounds a good bit less harsh. We are more likely, therefore, to read about "evolutionary strategies" than about a harsh neo-Darwinism, but, one way or the other, it comes down to the conclusion that, if nature structures anything, it is the quest for survival. Although the new natural law thinkers, represented in this volume, are doing their best to revive the older notion of natural law as it indeed survives, especially in Thomistic philosophy and theology, theirs is often a lonely struggle.

Others, prescinding from both God and nature or natural law, make recourse to the notion of diffuse human sentiment as sufficiently sturdy to buttress and to ground human rights over the long haul, a kind of utilitarian version of the Golden Rule: As I would not like to feel pain, so I should not knowingly inflict it. But anyone familiar with the sordid history of much of the twentieth century understands full well that there are a good number of people in the world who enjoy inflicting pain and who are not in the least bothered by some Golden-Rule notion of reciprocity; or, better said, they anticipate reciprocity as a degraded form of payback. That is, they fully expect, should they ever fall into the hands of those they have tormented, to be tormented in turn. That's a chance worth taking, in the view of such ruthless operators.

As this debate continues, another, one that has been a feature of American academic life for at least fifteen years, proceeds apace. I refer to the jousting between the "universalists" and the "particularizers," or some variant on these. Anyone who believes there are cross-cultural and trans-national values, norms, and goods is perforce a universalist. Anyone who believes such notions are balderdash is something else. That "something else" takes a variety of forms. In its most extreme manifestation, that of radical postmodernism, one finds moral and cultural relativism that doesn't blink at the prospect of societies that practice human sacrifice, enforce the *suttee,* or think female genital sexual mutilation is just another cultural practice. Perhaps we don't "like it" but perhaps "they" do, so it is none of our business to criticize it or attempt to extirpate it. Any sensible person sees the nihilism embedded in such a view, and most sensible people also realize that it is possible to advance universal claims and aims without thereby running roughshod over people's individual and unique cultures and beliefs. Some *via media* is called for. Many defenders of human rights "properly understood" believe that human rights itself serves as one such decent "middle way."

The volume the reader holds in his or her hand has, as the reader by now recognizes, traversed the terrain of this debate. The aims of the volume were set forth admirably in the introduction by our able editors. To add more to the richness of each featured chapter is surely, at this point, superogatory. Let it simply be said that there is no more important project than to reflect on human rights, on why we need them, and on why they, in turn, need "something else," some legitimating force, some potent grounding, lest they fall victim to the radical relativizers who just don't "like" them.

The series in which this volume appears aims to make more sophisticated and nuanced our understanding of the complex interplays between religion and politics. Our task is not to add to that complexity; rather, it is to acknowledge it and to take its measure, thereby combating the "simplifiers" who take refuge in slogans about separationism or America as "God's country" rather than looking at the world around them and at the many intricate features of the interplay between our religions and our politics.

Endnotes

Notes to the Introduction

1. Jacques Maritain, *Man and the State* (Chicago: University of Chicago Press, 1951), p. 77.

2. The Universal Declaration of Human Rights, G.A. Res. 217A(III), UN GAOR, 3rd Sess., UN Doc. A/810 (1948), Preamble.

3. See, for example, Irene Bloom, J. Paul Martin, and Wayne Proudfoot, *Religious Diversity and Human Rights* (New York: Columbia University Press, 1996); Joseph Runzo, Nancy Martin, and Arvind Sharma, *Human Rights and Responsibilities in the World Religions* (Oxford: One World, 2003); Robert Traer, *Faith in Human Rights: Support in Religious Traditions for a Global Struggle* (Washington, D.C.: Georgetown University Press, 1991); and John Witte and Johan D. van der Vyver, *Religious Human Rights in Global Perspective* (The Hague: Martinus Nijhoff, 1996).

4. Witte and Van ver Vyver, *Religious Human Rights in Global Perspective,* p. xviii.

5. See, for example, Mark Hill, *Religious Liberty and Human Rights* (Cardiff: University of Wales Press, 2002), or Natan Lerner, *Religion, Beliefs, and International Human Rights* (New York: Orbis, 2000).

6. See, for example, Abdullahi Ahmed An-Na'im, *Human Rights in Cross-Cultural Perspectives* (Philadelphia: University of Pennsylvania Press, 1992), and Santiago Nino, *The Ethics of Human Rights* (Oxford: Clarendon, 1991).

7. Samuel Huntington, "A Clash of Civilizations?" *Foreign Affairs* 73, no. 3 (Summer 1993): 2-26.

8. See, for example, Joanne Bauer and Daniel Bell, *The East Asian Challenge for Human Rights* (Cambridge: Cambridge University Press, 1999); Daniel Bell, *East Meets West: Human Rights and Democracy in East Asia* (Princeton, N.J.: Princeton University Press, 2000); and James Hsiung, *Human Rights in East Asia,* (New York: Paragon House, 1985).

9. Vigen Guroian, p. 42 in this volume.

10. Anthony C. Yu, p. 127 in this volume.

11. Charles Villa-Vicencio, p. 233 in this volume.

12. Louis Henkin, p. 147 in this volume.

13. Guroian, p. 47 in this volume.

14. Khaled Abou El Fadl, p. 63 in this volume.

15. Max L. Stackhouse, p. 39 in this volume.

16. Stackhouse, p. 28 in this volume.

17. Yu, p. 130 in this volume.

18. Yu, p. 107 in this volume.

19. Villa-Vicencio, p. 238 in this volume.

20. Alfred North Whitehead, *Adventures of Ideas* (New York: Free Press, 1967), p. 42.

21. Sari Nusseibeh, p. 224 in this volume.

22. Henkin, p. 154 in this volume.

23. Henkin, p. 155 in this volume.

24. El Fadl, p. 86 in this volume (internal citations omitted).

25. Guroian, p. 47 in this volume.

26. Stackhouse, p. 36 in this volume.

27. Villa-Vicencio, pp. 238-39 in this volume.

Notes to Chapter 1

1. Although I was deeply engaged in the movement for civil rights in the 1960s, as led by Martin Luther King Jr., my experiences in India and the old East Germany in the 1970s forced the question to the level of human rights. The results of my explorations led to "Some Intellectual and Social Roots of Modern Human Rights Ideas," *Journal for Scientific Study of Religion* 20, no. 4 (1981): 301-9, then to *Creeds, Society, and Human Rights* (Grand Rapids: Eerdmans, 1984), and several related subsequent efforts.

2. Most Christians hold that this adoption or "baptism" of nonbiblical ideas that are compatible with the universalist moral and spiritual insights of the gospel is quite possible, is sometimes able to refine what the tradition held reflexively, and is anticipated in earlier portions of the Bible itself, especially in the Wisdom literature. It was extended in the traditions that developed after the fuller formation of Judaism and Christianity in the selective embrace of Greek philosophy, Roman law, and, later, certain insights from other cultures. It is being further extended today as people from many cultures bring other philosophical, moral, social, and religious insights with them into contemporary theological and ethical understanding. The famous passages in the book of Acts, which speak of all having "the law written on their hearts" and of those gathered from many regions understanding the preaching "each in his own language," are being reenacted.

3. For an argument that the roots of modern views of human rights are utterly dependent on Jewish roots and Christian developments see Georg Jellinek, *Die Erklärung der Menschen — und Bürgerrechte: Ein Beitrag zur modernen Verfassungsgeschichte* (Leipzig, 1895).

4. John Nurser, *For All Peoples and All Nations: The Ecumenical Church and Human Rights* (Washington, D.C.: Georgetown University Press, 2005), pp. 14ff. Cf. Mark Hill, ed., *Religious Liberty and Human Rights* (Cardiff: University of Wales Press, 2002), although some of these essays are less directly relevant to this topic.

5. Hans Küng, ed., "Parliament of World Religions' Global Ethic," *National Catholic*

Reporter, 24 Sept. 1993, pp. 11-12. See also his *Global Responsibility: In Search of a New World Ethic* (New York: Crossroad, 1991), and *A Global Ethic for Global Politics and Economics* (New York: Oxford, 1997). These are deeply related to his earlier works, one with Josef van Ess et al., *Christianity and the World Religions: Paths to Dialogue with Islam, Hinduism, and Buddhism* (New York: Doubleday, 1986), and another with Julia Ching, *Christianity and Chinese Religions* (New York: Doubleday, 1989). Similarly, the Millennium World Peace Summit of Religious and Spiritual Leaders, meeting in New York in 2000, declared that "Believers have a right to make their lives conform with their beliefs. But no one has a right to use their beliefs to take the lives or violate the rights of others. No religion allows for that" (worldpeacesummit@ruderfinn.com).

6. See, for example, John Witte Jr., "A Dickensian Era of Religious Rights: An Update on *Religious Human Rights in Global Perspective,*" *William and Mary Law Review* 42, no. 3 (2001): 707-70, and his "God's Joust, God's Justice: The Revelations of Legal History," *Princeton Seminary Bulletin* 20, no. 3 (1999): 295-313, which have informed views contained in this presentation at several points.

7. The problems remain in the old East Germany, and hostility to "guest workers" remains intense among the youth. And, in regard to India, the ENI (Ecumenical News Information, 16 Sept. 2002) reported that Dalits in India rejoiced when a UN Committee voted to classify "casteism" as "racism." In this, caste has been recognized as evil cross-culturally, but it has not been overcome. If anything, certain current movements under the flag of Hindutva, a virulent form of Hindu Nationalism, seem to be reinforcing caste consciousness and attempting to reestablish traditional roles for women.

8. A fascinating recent account is Mary Ann Glendon, *The World Made New: Eleanor Roosevelt and the Universal Declaration of Human Rights* (New York: Random House, 2001). She mentions the religious influences on the development of human rights at several points, with special reference to the contributions of the Lebanese Protestant Charles Malik and the French Catholic Jacques Maritain. Further, Paul Gordon Lauren, *The Evolution of Human Rights* (Philadelphia: University of Pennsylvania Press, 1998), offers a broader treatment of influences from other world religions. These studies contribute to a growing correction of an anti-religious bias in parts of the human rights community, deriving from the anti-Catholic Enlightenment tradition rooted in the French Revolution.

9. The idea of "natural law" and its relationship to theology has been debated for centuries and is subject to many interpretations as complicated as scientific views of the "laws of nature" that have no ethical content. I intend the use most common in jurisprudence, an appeal to universal principles of justice discernible by reason, a usage that leaves open the question of whether or not they, and the capacity to discern them, are given by God. Traditions of natural law that have given rise to concepts of human rights, however, are essentially theological in nature, as we see in Roman Catholic and Calvinist thought. See the cluster of books that came out to celebrate the fiftieth anniversary of the United Nations Declaration of Human Rights, for example: Brian Tierney, *The Idea of Natural Rights* (Atlanta: Scholars Press, 1997), Guenther Haas, *The Concept of Equity in Calvin's Ethic* (Waterloo, Canada: Wilfred Laurier University Press, 1997), Knud Haakonssen, *Natural Law and Moral Philosophy* (Melbourne: Cambridge University Press of Australia, 1996); and see the conversations on these traditions in Michael Cromartie, ed., *A Preserving Grace: Protestants, Catholics, and Natural Law* (Grand Rapids: Eerdmans, 1997).

10. Some of these objections to human rights are catalogued and critiqued in "Religion and Human Rights: A Discussion," with Louis Henkin, Vigen Guroian, John Langan, S.J., et al., *Journal of Religious Ethics* 26, no. 2 (1998): 229-71. I attempted to address some of the key objections in my response, "The Intellectual Crisis of a Good Idea," in the same issue of the *Journal of Religious Ethics*, as well as in "Religion and Human Rights: A Theological Apologetic," with S. Healey, in *Religious Human Rights in Global Perspective*, ed. J. Witte and J. van der Vyver (The Hague: Martinus Nijhoff, 1996), pp. 485-516; and in "Human Rights and Public Theology: The Basic Validation of Human Rights," *Religion and Human Rights: Competing Claims?* ed. Carrie Gustafson and Peter Juviler (New York: M. E. Sharp, 1999), pp. 12-30.

11. This view is argued by Alasdair MacIntyre, *After Virtue* (Notre Dame: University of Notre Dame Press, 1981), who after years advocating Hegel, Marx, and Nietzsche, attacks both Protestantism and the Enlightenment, especially Kant, which he says generated the modernity that led to the terrors of the twentieth century (ignoring the fact that the statism of imperial Germany, which Hegel approved, the socialism of Marx, and the nihilism of Nietzsche all sought to dismantle the Christian and Enlightenment defenses of human rights against these forces of terror). Other noted critics of the rights traditions are Michael Sandel (vs. John Rawls), Selya Benhabib (vs. Jürgen Habermas), and Stanley Hauerwas (vs. Reinhold Niebuhr). Certain parallel discussions appear in Asian philosophy — see, for example, William Theodore de Bary and Tu Weiming, eds., *Confucianism and Human Rights* (New York: Columbia University Press, 1998) — and in perspectives from other parts of the world. See Gustafson and Juviler, eds., *Religion and Human Rights: Competing Claims?*

12. John Kelsey and Sumner Twiss, eds., *Religion and Human Rights* (New York: Project on Religion and Human Rights, 1994), p. 38.

13. This "ethical trinity" of moral judgment is one of the basic themes of my teaching and writing, and is most recently presented in the "General Introduction" to *God and Globalization*, vol. 1 (Harrisburg: Trinity Press International, 2000).

14. I draw from Michael Perry's masterful treatment of the ethical implications of policies and judgments based on human rights and their religious foundations, summarized as "Some things ought not to be done to anyone, and some things should be done for everyone" (which implies "anyone"), in *Religion and Human Rights: Four Inquiries* (New York: Oxford University Press, 1999). See also the forum on this work, *Journal of Law and Religion* 14, no. 1 (1999-2000): 1-120.

15. John Witte Jr. and R. C. Martin, eds., have collected a remarkable series of essays on this issue from Jewish, Christian, and Islamic perspectives: *Sharing the Book: Religious Perspectives on the Rights and Wrongs of Proselytism* (Maryknoll, N.Y.: Orbis, 1999).

16. I leave aside, for the moment, the question of whether humans ever make an unaided decision on these points, for whether one advocates "predestination," "prevenient grace," or "free will" the social implications are comparable. A useful collection of essays showing these public consequences and implications for the present can be found in R. C. White and A. G. Zimmerman, eds., *An Unsettled Arena: Religion and the Bill of Rights* (Grand Rapids: Eerdmans, 1989). I think that the evidence is convincing that the entire First Amendment to the United States Constitution, and not only the so-called "establish-

ment" and "free exercise" clauses, derive from this theological view of human rights with these implications.

17. The anti-church policies of the French Revolution, with its "Declaration of the Rights of Man" asserted on anti-theological, positive law grounds, in contrast to some dominant theocratic views of Christianity of the time, prompted the established churches in Europe to resist human rights arguments for several centuries, with disastrous results. But the longer and deeper legacy of the tradition has reasserted itself, as mentioned above. The major Christian traditions, however, have recovered and recast the legacy of their deeper insights in a series of teachings and authoritative statements: Walter Abbot and Joseph Gallagher, *Dignitatis Humanae* (Vatican Declaration on Human Freedom, 1965); see also George Weigel and Robert Royal, *A Century of Catholic Social Thought* (Washington: Ethics and Public Policy Center, 1991); David Hollenbach, *Claims in Conflict: Retrieving and Renewing the Catholic Human Rights Tradition* (New York: Paulist, 1991); World Council of Churches, *Human Rights and Christian Responsibility* (Geneva: World Council of Churches, 1976); Allen O. Miller, ed., *A Christian Declaration of Human Rights: Theological Studies of the World Alliance of Reformed Churches* (Grand Rapids: Eerdmans, 1977); Lutheran World Federation, *Theological Studies of Human Rights* (Minneapolis: Fortress, 1978).

18. For example, "Piety, Polity, and Policy," in *Religious Beliefs, Human Rights, and the Moral Foundations of Western Democracy,* ed. C. Esbeck (Columbia: University of Missouri Press, 1987), pp. 13-26; and "Christianity, Civil Society, and the State: A Christian Perspective," in *Civil Society and Government,* Ethikon Series, vol. 5, ed. Nancy Rosenblum and Robert Post (Princteon, N.J.: Princeton University Press, 2002), pp. 255-65.

19. For primary documents see A. S. P. Woodhouse, *Puritanism and Liberty* (London: J. M. Dent, 1938). Cf. also Michael Walzer, *The Revolution of the Saints* (New York: Athenium, 1968), and Robert Bellah et al., *Christianity and Civil Society: Boston Theological Institute,* ed. R. L. Peterson (Maryknoll, N.Y.: Orbis, 1995).

Notes to Chapter 2

1. Alasdair MacIntyre, *After Virtue,* second ed. (Notre Dame: University of Notre Dame Press, 1984), p. 67.

2. Richard Rorty, "Human Rights, Rationality, and Sentimentality," in *On Human Rights,* ed. Stephen Shute and Susan Hurley (New York: Basic, 1993), p. 126.

3. Dietrich Bonhoeffer, *Ethics,* German original 1949, trans. Neville Horton Smith (New York: Macmillan, 1965), p. 357.

4. Nicholas Berdyaev, *The Destiny of Man,* Russian original 1931, trans. Natalie Duddington (New York: Harper and Row, 1960), pp. 103-4.

5. Alexander Men, *Christianity for the Twenty-First Century* (New York: Continuum, 1996), p. 142.

6. Alexander Solzhenitsyn, *Rebuilding Russia* (New York: Farrar, Straus, and Giroux, 1991), p. 54.

Notes to Chapter 3

1. Ronald Dworkin, *Taking Rights Seriously* (Cambridge: Harvard University Press, 1978), p. 205.

2. See Mary Ann Glendon, *Rights Talk* (New York: Free Press, 1991), pp. 47-89.

3. The term "theocracy" (literally, "the rule of God") was coined by the first-century-C.E. Jewish historian Josephus, who said it means "placing all sovereignty [*archē*] and authority in the hands of God" (*Against Apion,* 2.167, trans. H. St.-John Thackeray [Cambridge: Harvard University Press, 1926], 1:358-59). Josephus is referring to a Jewish society ruled according to revealed law. Yet, even in such a society, one can recognize the two features of democracy most of us hold dear, namely, popularly chosen government and human rights. Moreover, as I shall argue later, even secular societies like the United States and Canada, which are not governed by revealed law, might be considered "theocracies" inasmuch as they recognize in their founding documents that all rights, including the right of popularly chosen government, are from God. Unfortunately, though, the term "theocracy" is now frequently used to designate such anti-democratic states as Iran and Saudi Arabia, which are governed by an oligarchy of clerics.

4. See David Novak, *The Jewish Social Contract: An Essay in Political Theology* (Princeton: Princeton University Press, 2005).

5. Unless otherwise noted, all biblical quotations in English are my own translation from the traditional (Masoretic) texts: *Biblia Hebraica,* seventh ed., ed. R. Kittel (Stuttgart, 1951).

6. *Mekhilta:* Neziqin, trans. J. Z. Lauterbach (Philadelphia: Jewish Publication Society of America, 1935), 3:141.

7. I translate the first sentence in the vocative voice rather than in the interrogative voice (as in most of the English translations), following Martin Buber and Franz Rosenzweig's German translation: *Was hast du getan! (Die Fünf Bücher der Weisung)* (Cologne: Jakob Hegner, 1954), p. 18.

8. See David Novak, *Halakhah in a Theological Dimension* (Chico, Calif.: Scholars Press, 1985), pp. 96-101; also, David Novak, *Natural Law in Judaism* (Cambridge: Cambridge University Press, 1998), pp. 167-73.

9. See *Babylonian Talmud:* Zevahim 116a (the view of Rabbi Joshua).

10. See *Babylonian Talmud:* Baba Kama 99b-100a re Exod. 18:20, where the practice of equity is prescribed in cases where following the strict sense of positive law would lead to great injustice in fact. See, for example, *Babylonian Talmud:* Baba Metsia 83a re Prov. 2:20.

11. *Babylonian Talmud:* Baba Kama 93a re Gen. 16:5 and Tosafot, s.v. "d'eeka" thereon; also, Nahmanides, *Commentary on the Torah:* Exod. 22:22.

12. In *Midrash ha-Gadol:* Genesis, ed. M. Margulies (Jerusalem: Mosad ha-Rav Kook, 1947), p. 119, it is Cain who, during a fight with his brother, pleads for his life from Abel, but when Abel releases him, he then treacherously turns on Abel and kills him on the spot. The implication here is that Abel would also have pleaded with Cain for his life if he had had the chance to do so. Cf. Louis Ginzberg, *The Legends of the Jews* (Philadelphia: Jewish Publication Society of America, 1909), 1:109.

13. See David Novak, *Jewish Social Ethics* (New York: Oxford University Press, 1992), pp. 163-65.

14. "September 1, 1939," in *Seven Centuries of Verse: English and American,* second revised ed., ed. A. J. M. Smith (New York: Charles Scribner's Sons, 1957), p. 686.

15. See *Babylonian Talmud:* Nedarim 11a and parallels.

16. *Babylonian Talmud:* Shabbat 31a.

17. This fundamental denial is put in the mouth of Cain by the rabbis. See *Targum Yerushalmi:* Gen. 4:8; also, *Palestinian Talmud:* Kiddushin 4.1/65b.

18. See *Babylonian Talmud:* Sanhedrin 109a-b; also, Ginzberg, *The Legends of the Jews,* 1:245-50.

19. See *Palestinian Talmud:* Sanhedrin 2.3/20a re Ps. 17:2.

20. See *Babylonian Talmud:* Taanit 16a re Jonah 3:8; also, Ginzberg, *The Legends of the Jews,* 4:250-53.

21. See *Babylonian Talmud:* Sanhedrin 54a.

22. Cf. Exod. 2:14.

23. See, for example, Deut. 29:22-23; Isa. 1:9.

24. *Tosefta:* Sanhedrin 13.8.

25. See David Novak, "Law: Religious or Secular?" *Virginia Law Review* 86 (2000): 569-96.

Notes to Chapter 4

1. The first date provided is from the *Hijri* or Islamic calendar which, as a purely lunar calendar, is consistently shorter than the Christian calendar. The *Hijri* calendar year is abbreviated AH.

2. See, for example, Ann Lambton, *State and Government in Medieval Islam: An Introduction to the Study of Islamic Political Theory: The Jurists* (Oxford: Oxford University Press, 1981), p. 19; W. Montgomery Watt, *Islamic Political Thought: The Basic Concepts* (Edinburgh: Edinburgh University Press, 1968), pp. 102-3; Hanna Mikhail, *Politics and Revelation: Mawardi and After* (Edinburgh: Edinburgh University Press, 1995), pp. 20-21; H. A. R. Gibb, "Constitutional Organization," in *Law in the Middle East,* vol. 1: *Origin and Development of Islamic Law,* ed. Majid Khadduri and Herbert J. Liebesny (Washington, D.C.: Middle East Institute, 1955), pp. 3-27, 9, 12; and Khaled Abou El Fadl, *Rebellion and Violence in Islamic Law* (Cambridge: Cambridge University Press, 2001).

3. Cases in point would be many Third World countries that have all the formal trappings of democracies but do not lead a democratic life.

4. In my view, a case in point would be Saudi Arabia, where many purported Islamic laws are in effect, but the government fails to embody most Islamic virtues or moralities.

5. I am here referring to the concept of government through *shura,* which is discussed later.

6. On this, see Khaled Abou El Fadl, *And God Knows the Soldiers: The Authoritative and Authoritarian in Islamic Discourses* (Lanham, Md.: University Press of America, 2001); Khaled Abou El Fadl, *Speaking in God's Name: Islamic Law, Authority and Women* (Oxford: Oneworld Publications, 2001).

7. For instance, after I had written a regular column in an Islamic magazine for many years, my column was suddenly terminated and my work banned because I disagreed with the leadership of the organization that publishes this magazine. Not surprisingly, this organization tirelessly proclaims the democratic nature of Islam, and even claims that the Prophet was a philosopher of democracy. But apologetic stances such as this often translate into a hypocritical despotism in actual practice.

8. See his main work on the subject, Abu al-A'la al-Mawdudi, *al-Khilafa wa al-Mulk*, trans. Ahmad Idris (Kuwait: Dar al-Qalam, 1978), pp. 13-21.

9. Ironically, Shi'i and Sunni fundamentalist groups detest the Khawarij and consider them heretics, but this is not because these modern groups disagree with the Khawarij's political slogans, but because the Khawarij murdered 'Ali, the cousin of the Prophet.

10. Of course, I realize that this claim is quite controversial for Muslims and non-Muslims alike. Nevertheless, I believe that this argument is supported by the fact that the rebellion of the Khawarij took place in the context of an overall search for legitimacy and legality after the death of the Prophet. Furthermore, the research of some scholars on the dogma and symbolism of the early rebellions lends support to this argument. See Hisham Ja'it, *al-Fitnah: Jadaliyyat al-Din wa al-Siyasah fi al-Islam al-Mubakkir* (Beirut: Dar all-Tali'ah, 1989).

11. Muhammad b. 'Ali b. Muhammad al-Shawkani, *Nayl al-Awtar Sharh Muntaqa al-Akhbar* (Cairo: Dar al-Hadith, n.d.), 7:166; Shihab al-Din Ibn Hajar al-'Asqalani, *Fath al-Bari bi Sharh Sahih al-Bukhari* (Beirut: Dar al-Fikr, 1993), 14:303.

12. According to the Qur'an, as a symbol of the honor due to human beings, God commanded the angels, who are incapable of sin, to prostrate before Adam. The angels protested that God was commanding them to honor a being that is capable of committing evil and causing mischief. God conceded as much, but explained that the miracle of the intellect, in and of itself, deserves to be honored, and that God has made human beings the vicegerents of divinity. On this, see Fazlur Rahman, *Major Themes of the Qur'an* (Minneapolis: Bibliotheca Islamica, 1994), pp. 17-36.

13. Among the most important, but also one of the most neglected, treatises was written by a former chairman of the Muslim Brotherhood organization in Egypt, where he effectively refutes Mawdudi's arguments on *hakimiyya*. Rather tellingly, the author's arguments, despite their liberal implications, would have been far more persuasive to medieval Muslim jurists than contemporary fundamentalist publicists. See Hasan Isma'il al-Hudaybi, *Du'ah la Qudah* (Cairo: Dar al-Nashr al-Islamiyya, 1977).

14. 'Abd Allah b. Muslim b. Qutayba (attributed), *al-Imama wa al-Siyasa*, ed. Zini Taha (Cairo: Mu'assasat al-Halabi, 1967), p. 21. This book is traditionally known as *Ta'rikh al-Khulafa*'.

15. 'Ali b. Muhammad al-Mawardi, *al-Ahkam al-Sultaniyya* (Cairo: Mustafa al-Halabi, 1966), p. 15.

16. Abu al-Faraj al-Baghdadi Ibn al-Jawzi, *al-Shifa' fi Mawa'iz al-Muluk wa al-Khulafa*', ed. Fu'ad Ahmad (Alexandria: Dar al-Da'wa, 1985), 1:93.

17. Qamar al-Din Khan, *Ibn Taymiyya*, trans. Mubarak al-Baghdadi (Kuwait: Maktabat al-Falah, 1973), pp. 102-22.

18. Khan, *Ibn Taymiyya*, p. 178.

19. Al-Baqillani, "al-Tawhid fi al-Radd," in Yusuf Ibish's *Nusus al-Fikr al-Siyasi al-Islami: al-Imama 'ind al-Sunna* (Beirut: Dar al-Tali'ah, 1966), p. 56. On Baqillani's political thought, see Yusuf Ibish, *The Political Doctrine of al-Baqillani* (Beirut: American University of Beirut, 1996).

20. On the duty of enjoining the good and forbidding the evil, see the masterful study by Michael Cook, *Commanding the Right and Forbidding the Wrong in Islamic Thought* (Cambridge: Cambridge University Press, 2000). On the assertion of this duty against the government, see Abou El Fadl, *Rebellion and Violence*, pp. 123, 180-82, 194-96, 273-74, 304-6. Typically, Sunni jurists differentiated between the duty of enjoining the good and forbidding the evil in matters involving the rights of God *(huquq Allah)* as opposed to matters involving the rights of human beings *(huquq al-'ibad* or *huquq al-adamiyyin)*. Sunni jurists also distinguished a third category of rights, which they called the mixed rights of God and human beings *(al-huquq al-mukhtalatah)*. The rights of human beings were further divided into private and public rights *(al-huquq al-'ammah wa al-huquq al-khassah)*. Each category of rights necessitated different rules of jurisdiction and methods of enjoining the good and forbidding the evil. The emphasis was primarily juristic: the classical jurists discussed which categories required the intervention of the *al-shurtah* (the police), the *muhtasib* (the market inspector), or the judiciary. In this context, nongovernmental interveners or private activists were called *al-mutatawwi'un* (volunteers). Especially as to the rights of people and private rights, although Sunni jurists did envision a role to be played by private nongovernmental individuals in enjoining the good and forbidding the evil, for the most part they were opposed to forcible self-help. See al-Mawardi, *al-Ahkam*, pp. 303-22; al-Qadi Abu Ya'la al-Farra', *al-Ahkam al-Sultaniyya* (Beirut: Dar al-Kutub al-'Ilmiyya, 1983), pp. 284-308. Nevertheless, this is among the areas of Islamic thought that remains poorly studied in modern scholarship, and therefore it is difficult to understand the full implications of this juristic discourse.

21. Ibish, *Political Doctrine*, p. 99.

22. Al-Baqillani, "al-Tawhid," p. 76.

23. Watt, *Islamic Political Thought*, p. 58; Lambton, *State and Government*, pp. 19, 37.

24. The Mu'tazilah was a theological school of thought whose adherents called themselves *ahl al-'adl wa al-tawhid* (the people of justice and unity). The school traces its origins to the thought of Wasil b. 'Ata' (d. 131/748) in Basra. The Mu'tazilah are often described as rationalists for their emphasis on rational theology. They also considered justice and enjoining the good and forbidding the evil to be among the five basic principles of faith. The Mu'tazilah's five principles of faith were (1) *tawhid* (believing in the unity and singularity of God); (2) *'adl* (justice); (3) *al-wa'd wa al-wa'id* (the promise of reward and threat of punishment); (4) *al-manzilah bayna al-manzilatayn* (those who commit a major sin are neither believers nor nonbelievers); (5) *al-amr bi al-ma'ruf wa al-nahy 'an al-munkar* (commanding the good and prohibiting the evil).

25. Citing the precedent of the Prophet in Medina, al-Asam maintained that this included free Muslim women, but not non-Muslims or slaves. Reportedly, upon migrating to Medina, the Prophet took the *bay'a* from a number of native women as well as men. Muhammad 'Imara, *al-Islam wa Falsafat al-Hukm* (Beirut: n.p., 1979), pp. 431-32.

26. Abu Ma'ali al-Juwayni, *Ghiyath al-Umam fi Iltiyath al-Zulam*, ed. Mustafa Hilmi and Fu'ad Ahmad (Alexandria: Dar al-Da'wa, 1978), pp. 55-57. Also see al-Baqillani, "al-

Tawhid," pp. 48-49; 'Imara, *al-Islam*, p. 439; 'Abd al-Qadir al-Baghdadi, "Kitab Usul al-Din," in *Nusus*, pp. 132-33.

27. 'Imara, *al-Islam*, p. 435.

28. For instance, see al-Baghdadi, "Kitab," pp. 132-33; Lambton, *State and Government*, p. 18.

29. Abou El Fadl, *Rebellion and Violence*, pp. 90-96; A. J. Wensinck, "Mihna," in *Shorter Encyclopedia of Islam*, ed. H. A. R. Gibb and J. H. Kramers (Leiden: E. J. Brill, 1991), pp. 377-78.

30. Shams al-Din Abu Bakr Ibn Qayyim al-Jawziyya, *I'lam al-Muwaqqi'in 'an Rabb al-'Alamin*, ed. 'Abd al-Rahman al-Wakil (Cairo: Maktabat Ibn Taymiyya, n.d.), 1:10.

31. Structurally, Shari'ah is comprised of the Qur'an, *Sunna*, and *fiqh* (juristic interpretive efforts). Substantively, the Shari'ah refers to three different matters: (1) general principles of law and morality; (2) methodologies for extracting and formulating the law; and (3) the *ahkam*, which are the specific positive rules of law. In the contemporary Muslim world, there is a tendency to focus on the *ahkam* at the expense of the general principles and methodology. It is entirely possible to be Shari'ah-compliant, in the sense of respecting the *ahkam*, but to ignore or violate the principles and methodologies of Shari'ah.

32. On these concepts, see Mohammad Hashim Kamali, *Principles of Islamic Jurisprudence*, rev. ed. (Cambridge: Islamic Texts Society, 1991), pp. 267-81, 310-20.

33. On the prohibition against women driving automobiles, see Abou El Fadl, *Speaking in God's Name*, pp. 235, 272-73, 278-80.

34. On the emergence of these historical developments, see Abou El Fadl, *Rebellion and Violence*, pp. 90-99.

35. Examining this issue, some scholars reached the premature conclusion that Shari'ah law was primarily theoretical and unenforceable throughout Islamic history. They argued that the state relied on administrative regulations and, for the most part, ignored Shari'ah law. For example, see Noel J. Coulson, *A History of Islamic Law* (Edinburgh: Edinburgh University Press, 1964), pp. 120-34; Joseph Schacht, *An Introduction to Islamic Law* (Oxford: Clarendon, 1964), pp. 49-56. This conclusion, however, oversimplifies the legal dynamics and process in Islamic history. At this point, it is fair to say that the arguments of scholars such as Coulson and Schacht perpetuate unhelpful historical mythology.

36. For instance, see al-Mawardi, *al-Ahkam*, p. 18; Taqi al-Din Ibn Taymiyyah, *al-Siyasah al-Shar'iyyah* (Beirut: Dar al-Afaq al-Jadidah, 1983), p. 142. Similarly, Muslim jurists often would assert that religion is the foundation and the political authorities are its protector.

37. Sherman Jackson, *Islamic Law and the State: The Constitutional Jurisprudence of Shihab al-Din al-Qarafi* (Leiden: E. J. Brill, 1996); Sherman Jackson, "From Prophetic Action to Constitutional Theory: A Novel Chapter in Medieval Muslim Jurisprudence," *International Journal of Middle East Studies* 25 (1993): 71-90. In addition, there is a considerable juristic discourse on the proper jurisdiction of the police and market inspectors as opposed to judges. In summary, the police and market inspectors have no jurisdiction over any issue that involves competing factual or legal contentions. These issues must be referred to the judge. See 'Abd al-Rahman b. Nasr al-Shayzari, *The Book of the Islamic Market*

Inspector (Nihayat al-Rutba fi Talab al-Hisba), trans. R. P. Buckley (Oxford: Oxford University Press, 1999), p. 28 n. 1; al-Mawardi, *al-Ahkam*, p. 100.

38. Shams al-Din Muhammad b. Ahmad b. 'Uthman al-Dhahabi, *Siyar A'lam al-Nubala'*, fourth ed. (Beirut: Mu'assasat al-Risalah, 1986), pp. 19, 190.

39. Abu Muhammad 'Ali b. Sa'id b. Hazm, *Jamharat Ansab al-'Arab*, ed. E. Levi Provencal (Cairo: Dar al-Ma'arif, 1948), p. 401.

40. After the evacuation of the French in Egypt in 1801, 'Umar Makram with the assistance of the jurists overthrew the French agent left behind. Instead of assuming power directly, the jurists offered the government to the Egyptianized Albanian Muhammad 'Ali. See Afaf Lutfi al-Sayyid Marsot, "The Ulama of Cairo in the Eighteenth and Nineteenth Century," in *Scholars, Saints, and Sufis*, ed. Nikki Keddi (Berkeley: University of California Press, 1972), pp. 149-65, 162-63.

41. Marsot, "The Ulama," p. 149.

42. Marsot, "The Ulama," p. 150.

43. Marsot, "The Ulama," p. 159.

44. Daniel Crecelius, "Egyptian Ulama and Modernization," in *Scholars, Saints, and Sufis*, pp. 167-209, 168. Crecelius makes this point about the *'ulama* of Egypt in the modern age. Of course, there are notable exceptions in the contemporary Islamic practice. Many clerics have become prominent opponents of the present Muslim regimes and suffer enormously for their troubles.

45. Jalal al-Din al-Suyuti, *Ta'rikh al-Khulafa'*, ed. Ibrahim Abu al-Fadl (Cairo: Dar al-Nahda, 1976), p. 109.

46. Ibn Taymiyya, *al-Siyasa al-Shar'iyya*, p. 136.

47. Abu Hamid al-Ghazali, *Fada'ih al-Batiniyya*, ed. 'Abd al-Rahman Badawi (Cairo: Dar al-Qawmiyya, 1964), pp. 191, 193; Muhammad Jalal Sharaf and 'Ali 'Abd al-Mu'ti Muhammad, *al-Fikr al-Siyasi fi al-Islam: Shakhsiyyat wa Madhahib* (Alexandria: Dar al-Jami'at al-Misriyya, 1978), pp. 399-403.

48. Al-Ghazali, *Fada'ih*, pp. 186, 191; Sharaf and Muhammad, *al-Fikr al-Siyasi*, pp. 399-403.

49. al Juwayni, *Ghiyath al-Umam*, p. 15.

50. Ibn Qayyim al-Jawziyyah, *I'lam al-Muwaqqi'in*, 4:452.

51. Nizam Barakat, *Muqaddima fi al-Fikr al-Siyasi al-Islami* (Riyadh: Jami'at al-Malik Su'ud, 1985), p. 116; Sharaf and Muhammad, *al-Fikr al-Siyasi*, pp. 377, 380-81, 514-15; Abu Hamid al-Ghazali, *al-Iqtisad fi al-I'tiqad* (Cairo: n.p., 1320 AH), p. 106.

52. Sharaf and Muhammad, *al-Fikr al-Siyasi*, pp. 209, 212; Barakat, *Muqaddima*, p. 107; Ridwan al-Sayyid, *al-Umma wa al-Jama'a wa al-Sultah* (Beirut: n.p., 1984), pp. 207-8; 'Ali b. Muhammad al-Mawardi, *Adab al-Dunya*, pp. 116-27.

53. On the obligation of justice in the Qur'an, see Rahman, *Major Themes of the Qur'an*, pp. 42-43; Toshihiko Izutsu, *The Structure of Ethical Terms in the Qur'an* (Chicago: ABC International Group, 2000), pp. 205-61. On the various Muslim theories of justice, see Majid Khadduri, *The Islamic Conception of Justice* (Baltimore: Johns Hopkins University Press, 1984).

54. Qur'an 21:107, which addressing the Prophet states, "We have not sent you except as a mercy to human beings." Also see Qur'an 16:89. In fact, the Qur'an describes the whole of the Islamic message as based on mercy and compassion. Islam was sent to teach and es-

tablish these virtues among human beings. I believe that as to Muslims, as opposed to Islam, this creates a normative imperative of teaching mercy. Qur'an 27:77, 29:51, 45:20. But to teach mercy is impossible unless one learns it, and such knowledge cannot be limited to text. It is *ta'aruf* (the knowledge of the other), which is premised on an ethic of care that opens the door to learning mercy, and in turn teaches it.

55. In Qur'anic terms, *rahma* (mercy) is not limited to *maghfira* (forgiveness).

56. The Qur'an explicitly commands human beings to deal with one another with patience and mercy (90:17) and not to transgress their bounds by presuming to know who deserves God's mercy and who does not (43:32). Islamic moral theory focused on mercy as a virtue will overlap with the ethic of care developed in Western moral theory. See Joan C. Tronto, *Moral Boundaries: A Political Argument for an Ethic of Care* (London: Routledge, 1994), pp. 101-55.

57. This idea is also exemplified in a tradition attributed to the Prophet asserting that the disagreement and diversity of opinion of the *umma* (Muslim nation) is a source of divine mercy for Muslims. See Isma'il al-Jirahi, *Kashf al-Khafa' wa Muzil al-Ilbas* (Beirut: Mu'assasat al-Risala, 1983), 1:66-68. Whether the Prophet actually made this statement or this statement is part of the received wisdom that guided the diverse and often competing interpretive traditions within Islam is beside the point. The point is that this tradition, Prophetic or not, was used to justify an enormous amount of diversity within the Islamic juristic tradition, and it played an important role in preventing the emergence of a single voice of authority within the Islamic tradition. On this issue, see Abou El Fadl, *And God Knows the Soldiers*, pp. 23-36.

58. Of course, approximating the divine does not mean aspiring to become divine. Approximating the divine means visualizing the beauty and virtue of the divine, and striving to internalize as much as possible of this beauty and virtue. I start with the theological assumption that God cannot be comprehended or understood by the human mind. God, however, teaches moral virtues that emanate from the divine nature, and that are also reflected in creation. By imagining the possible magnitude of beauty and of its nature, human beings can better relate to the divine. The more humans are able to relate to the ultimate sense of goodness, justice, mercy, and balance, which embody divinity, the more they are able to visualize or imagine the nature of divinity, and the more they are able to model their own sense of beauty and virtue as approximations of divinity.

59. Debates on individual rights raise questions about the nature, foundations, and universality of such rights. The historical discontinuities of individual rights suggest that, despite the absolutist-moral overtones of some rights-talk, individual rights are the product of complex historical processes. See Austin Sarat and Thomas R. Kearns, eds., *Legal Rights: Historical and Philosophical Perspectives* (Ann Arbor: University of Michigan Press, 1997); Louis Henkin, *The Age of Rights* (New York: Columbia University Press, 1990); S. I. Benn and R. S. Peters, *The Principles of Political Thought: Social Foundations of the Democratic State* (New York: Free Press, 1966 [1959]), pp. 101-20; Carl Wellman, *A Theory of Rights: Persons Under the Laws, Institutions, and Morals* (Totowa, N.J.: Rowman and Allanheld, 1985).

60. I would argue that the protection of religion should be developed to mean protecting the freedom of religious belief; the protection of life should mean that the taking of life must be for a just cause and the result of a just process; the protection of the intellect

should mean the right to free thinking, expression, and belief; the protection of honor should mean the protecting of the dignity of a human being; and the protection of property should mean the right to compensation for the taking of property.

61. Muslim jurists, however, did not consider the severing of hands or feet as punishment for theft and banditry to be mutilation.

62. A considerable number of jurists in Islamic history were persecuted and murdered for holding that a political endorsement *(bay'a)* obtained under duress is invalid. Muslim jurists described the death of these scholars under such circumstances as a death of *musabara*. This had become an important discourse because caliphs were in the habit of either bribing or threatening notables and jurists to obtain their *bay'a*. See Abou El Fadl, *Rebellion and Violence*, pp. 86-87.

63. Classical jurists would normally list most acts of worship, and Qur'anically prescribed criminal punishments, as part of the rights of God. Accordingly, fasting during the month of Ramadan, praying five times a day, or punishment for adultery, for example, are parts of the rights of God. The punishment for theft was often designated as a mixed right. Another important distinction in the classical sources was the differentiation between acts of *'ibadat* (worship) and *mu'amalat* (conduct involving social interaction). *'Ibadat*, in most occasions, were designated as implicating the rights of God, while most *mu'amalat* were designated as implicating the rights of people. While *'ibadat* were considered unchangeable and personal between the individual and God, *mu'amalat* were considered changeable, negotiable, and within the realm of human discretion. Significantly, modern-day puritans have tried to blur the distinction between the two categories, claiming that all conduct, including social interactions, fall within the realm of *'ibadat*, and then claiming that the state is responsible for enforcing the rights of God on this earth, and that the rights of God take priority over the rights of people. This is quite a shift from the traditional categories of Islamic law because it effectively injects the state into the relationship between individuals and God. In my opinion, it even amounts to the dethroning of God, as the state comes to sit in God's place.

64. Abu Bakr Muhammad b. 'Abd Allah b. al-'Arabi, *Ahkam al-Qur'an*, ed. 'Ali Muhammad al-Bajawi (Beirut: Dar al-Ma'rifah, n.d.), 2:603; Khaled Abou El Fadl, *Conference of the Books* (Lanham, Md.: United Press of America, 2001), pp. 105-8.

65. This idea is reflected in the well-known tradition attributed to the Prophet that whenever God commands humans to do something, then they should do of it as much as they can. This tradition represents further recognition of the contingent and aspirational nature of human ability, and that while humans may strive for perfection, God is perfection, itself.

66. For this often-repeated claim, see Lawrence Rosen, *The Justice of Islam* (Oxford: Oxford University Press, 2000), pp. 7, 79-80, 156-57; Bernard G. Weiss, *The Spirit of Islamic Law* (Athens: University of Georgia Press, 1998), pp. 145-85; Rhoda Howard, *Human Rights and the Search for Community* (Boulder, Colo.: Westview, 1995), pp. 92-104.

67. Muslim jurists also asserted that specific rights and duties should be given priority over general rights and duties. But, again, this was a legal principle that applied to laws of agency and trust. Although the principle could be expanded and developed to support individual rights in the modern age, historically it was given a far more technical and legalistic connotation.

68. On this, see Yves René Marie Simon, *The Tradition of Natural Law: A Philosopher's Reflections,* ed. Vukan Kuic (New York: Fordham University Press, 1992 [1965]), pp. 86-109; Alan Gewirth, *Human Rights: Essays on Justification and Applications* (Chicago: University of Chicago Press, 1982), pp. 218-33; John Finnis, *Natural Law and Natural Rights* (Oxford: Clarendon, 1980), pp. 205-18.

69. Someone might want to argue that collectivist rights schemes are superior to individual rights schemes. But a collectivist rights scheme would need to be justified on Islamic grounds as much as an individualist rights scheme. Both types of rights schemes are equally alien, or familiar, to the Islamic tradition. In addition, I do not dispute either the morality of some collectivist rights, such as the rights of indigenous people and the right to culture, or that these rights could be justified on Islamic grounds. But from an Islamic perspective, it is much harder to justify the sacrificing of the safety or well-being of individuals in pursuit of a collective right. It seems to me that the collectivist rights mentioned above are justifiable largely when a collectivity is trying to protect its individuals and collective interests from aggression coming from outside the collectivity. In other words, it is justifiable when a community of people, sharing common interests, are trying to protect themselves from external dangers. But it seems far less justifiable when the community is turning inward, and trying to target individuals within its own membership, under the auspices of protecting the character of the collectivity against the dangers of dissent. On this issue, see James Crawford, ed., *The Rights of Peoples* (Oxford: Clarendon, 1995); Alexandra Xanthaki, ed., "Collective Rights: The Case of Indigenous Peoples," in *Human Rights in Philosophy and Practice,* ed. Burton Leiser and Tom Campbell (Burlington, Vt.: Ashgate, 2001), pp. 303-13; Emily R. Gill, "Autonomy, Diversity, and the Right to Culture," pp. 285-300 in the same source.

70. On the relationship between duty and right in Roman law, and the subsequent Western legal tradition, see Finnis, *Natural Law,* pp. 205-10. The dynamic that Finnis describes is very similar to that which took place in classical Islamic law. Also see on rights and responsibilities: Lloyd L. Weinreb, "Natural Law and Rights," in *Natural Law Theory: Contemporary Essays,* ed. Robert P. George (Oxford: Clarendon, 1992), pp. 278-305.

71. Some pre-modern jurists did differentiate between Muslim and non-Muslim especially in matters pertaining to criminal liability and compensation for torts.

72. The Qur'an seems to treat religious compulsion as an act that compromises the integrity and self-evident autonomy of the truth of God (see 2:256; 10:99). The Qur'an also repeatedly affirms the principle that no human can bear responsibility for the accountability of the other (see 6:164; 17:15; 35:18; 39:7; 53:38).

73. On this debate, see Abou El Fadl, *Speaking in God's Name,* pp. 160-61, 168. The Mu'tazila argued that good and bad are inherent and recognized, but not created, by the divine text. Good and bad are realizable by reason as well as by revelation.

74. I would argue that moral values, whether one considers them characteristics or as part of the essence of God, are inseparable from the manifestation of godliness. In order to understand God, one must understand the moral values that are either at the essence of God or that characterize God. Put differently, to know morality is to know God. The law as found in the divine text is one possible manifestation of God, but it is not all-inclusive of the reality of God. Therefore, an inquiry into moral values — an inquiry into the reality of

God — cannot be limited to the divine text, which is an important, but partial, manifestation of God.

75. In my view, the primary commitment of a Muslim should be to God and God's moral essence, and not to the specific rules of law. Therefore, if there is a conflict between the morality of a legal rule and our moral conception of God, it is the latter that must take priority.

76. I am assuming that textual law is always a product of interpretation. In other words, I am assuming that the text, divine or not, never speaks for itself — the text always manifests meaning through the negotiative agency of the reader of the text.

77. The literature on the history, theory, and practices of secularism is vast. Most theoretical treatments understandably have remained wedded to the Western historical experience. See Blandine Kriegel, *The State and the Rule of Law* (Princeton, N.J.: Princeton University Press, 1995), pp. 123-34; Horace M. Kallen, *Secularism Is the Will of God: An Essay in the Social Philosophy of Democracy and Religion* (New York: Twayne, 1954); Harvey Cox, *The Secular City: Secularization and Urbanization in Theological Perspective* (New York: Macmillan, 1965); Daniel Callahan, ed., *The Secular City Debate* (New York: Macmillan, 1966).

78. Ibn Qayyim, *I'lam al-Muwaqqi'in*, vol. 3, 3.

79. The four surviving Sunni schools of law and legal thought are the Hanafi, Maliki, Shafi'I, and Hanbali schools.

80. I am simplifying this sophisticated doctrine in order to make a point. Muslim jurists engaged in lengthy attempts to differentiate between the two concepts of *Shari'ah* and *fiqh*. See, for example, Weiss, *Spirit of Islamic Law*, pp. 119-21.

81. Al-Juwayni, *Kitab al-Ijtihad*, pp. 50-51.

82. Al-Juwayni, *Kitab al-Ijtihad*, p. 61.

83. I am ignoring in this context the role of *ijma'* (consensus) because of the complexity of the subject. Some modern Muslims have argued that the doctrine of consensus is the normative equivalent of majority rule. I think this is a gross oversimplification, and, in any case, majority rule is not the same as a constitutional democracy that defers to majority determinations unless they violate fundamental rights.

84. Contemporary Islamic discourses suffer from a certain amount of hypocrisy in this regard. Often, Muslims confront an existential crisis if the enforced, so-called Islamic laws result in social suffering and misery. In order to solve this crisis, Muslims will often claim that there has been a failure in the circumstances of implementation. This indulgence in embarrassing apologetics could be avoided if Muslims would abandon the incoherent idea of Shari'ah state law.

85. In order for the *'ulama* to play a meaningful role in civil society, however, they must first regain their institutional and moral independence.

Notes to Chapter 5

1. *The Classic of Change,* "Commentary on the Appended Phases," 1, 12 (my translation).

2. See, for example, Paul Ricoeur, *Oneself As Another,* trans. Kathleen Blamey (Chicago: University of Chicago Press, 1992).

3. Wang Gungwu, *The Chineseness of China: Selected Essays* (Hong Kong: Oxford University Press, 1991), p. 2.

4. See, for example, Jerry Norman, *Chinese* (Cambridge: Cambridge University Press, 1988), p. 1: "Few language names are as all-encompassing as that of Chinese. It is made to serve at once for the archaic inscriptions of the oracle bones, the literary language of the Zhou dynasty sages, the language of Tang and Song poetry and the early vernacular language of the classical novels, as well as the modern language in both its standard and dialectal forms." Also Christoph Harbsmeier in *Science and Civilisation in China*, vol. 7, pt. 1, "Language and Logic," ed. Joseph Needham (Cambridge: Cambridge University Press, 1998), p. xxi: "there is only one culture in the world which has developed systematic logical definitions and reflections on its own and on the basis of non–Indo-European language. This is the Chinese culture. The history of logical reflection in China is therefore of extraordinary interest for any global history of logic and hence for any global history of the foundations of science."

5. One consequence of this development, though not yet fully understood, is precisely this necessity of thinking phonetically when using the computer. Whereas in the pre-computer days a person writing in Chinese might well have reproduced a number of graphs on the page without knowing their precise or "correct" vocalization in the dominant vernacular, and this situation applies to even the clumsy Chinese typewriters, the current student taught to be reliant on the alphabet keyboard and a particular phonological system of representation must master the proper phonemes that delimit the range of this individual's working vocabulary. Wrong pronunciation or misvocalization while using a computer may mean complete stoppage of writing until the correct sound (i.e., correctly spelled phoneme) is ascertained. With this critical constraint, not only a tradition of several thousand years in acquiring, retaining, and reproducing a graphic — hence essentially imagistic — language has been drastically modified, but the very nature of that language itself may have been irreversibly altered. Since keyboard usage enforces strict reliance on mastery of a particular dialectal form of the language, "the limitations of speech and hearing" (to quote Wang Gungwu) are reimposed to a significant degree in the communicative process. On the other hand, the global familiarity of the English alphabet and the speed of the computer join to provide unprecedented rapidity in the use and dissemination of the Chinese script.

Seen in this light, what the PRC began as a programmatic reform to help educate its vast population by opting to adopt Pinyin, a syllabary constructed out of the English letters, is now immeasurably aided and made irreversible by the computer. In its global use, a resolutely non-alphabetical language has forever been alphabetized at least in its vocalized mode. Confronted by the recurring phenomenon on the computer that the phoneme *ma* may actually betoken eighteen graphs and as many or even more meanings, the student may be led by habit to valorize a sonic unit constructed in an alphabetical syllabary as a sort of stable, if not superior, semantic unit over against the individualized characters.

6. I have noticed an increased tendency in myself, in colleagues and students, and even occasionally in Hong Kong and Taiwan journalism to use the "wrong" homonyms, typographical errors most likely generated by computer-based word-processing or typesetting. For an eloquent but somewhat uncritical eulogy of the alphabet, see Ivan Illich, *In*

the *Vineyard of the Text: A Commentary to Hugh's "Didascalicon"* (Chicago: University of Chicago Press, 1993), pp. 39-40.

7. Ann Kent, *Between Freedom and Subsistence: China and Human Rights* (Hong Kong: Oxford University Press, 1993), p. 5.

8. *The New York Times,* Wednesday, November 17, 1999, p. A15.

9. Witness the series of conferences devoted to Confucius and his teachings that were held in Hangzhou, 1980, in Beijing, 1989 (an international symposium to celebrate the sage's 2,540th birthday anniversary), and again in Beijing, 1994, during which gathering Lee Kuan Yew was the keynote speaker. On September 26, 1999, the celebration for the 2,550th birthday anniversary was held with great fanfare at Confucius's birthplace, Qufu of Shandong Province, and it coincided with the completion of the first phase of construction of a sizeable Research Institute of Confucius. See *Shijie ribao* [The World Journal], Monday, September 27, 1999, p. 2.

10. David N. Keightley, "Early Civilization in China: Reflections on How It Became Chinese," in *Heritage of China: Contemporary Perspectives on Chinese Civilization,* ed. Paul S. Ropp (Berkeley: University of California Press, 1990), pp. 15-54.

11. Keightley, "Early Civilization in China," pp. 31, 48-53.

12. Keightley, "Early Civilization in China," p. 17. This treatment of early Greek civilization by Keightley, to be sure, is vulnerable to criticism because he has concentrated exclusively on one depiction of archaic heroism and ignores completely both geometric pottery and the all-important implications of *polis* (city) and *domos* (house) that have been present even in Homeric epics, not to mention later philosophers, dramatists, and historians. Whatever decorative motif might have been preferred by early Greek pottery, a culture showing little concern for communitarian values, however defined, could hardly be expected to produce Plato's *Republic,* Thucydides' *History of the Peloponnesian War,* and Aristotle's *Politics.*

13. The classic work of modern scholarship that decisively links the early Chinese kinship system to ritual performance is, of course, Claude Lévy-Strauss, *The Elementary Structures of Kinship,* rev. ed., trans. James Harle Bell et al. (Boston: Beacon, 1969), pp. 311-92. It is another irony of Chinese history that owing to rapid modernization, dual career families (conditions obtaining both in China and in Hong Kong, Taiwan, and other diaspora Chinese communities), and the one-child policy officially implemented in 1981 on the mainland, the massive vocabulary of extended kin relations may become progressively lost to children of current and future generations.

14. Just as it is unthinkable for the ordinary plebeian to behave like a minister, for that would indicate inordinate insolence, so a father is considered perverse if he engages in actions deemed appropriate only for his children, a sure sign of moral weakness. It is the recognition of this feature of ancient Chinese society, in fact, that must presuppose any discussions of the relations of the individual to the group by Confucius and followers, a period that spans the sixth century BCE to the Common Era.

15. Confucius, *The Analects,* trans. D. C. Lau (Hong Kong: Chinese University Press, 1992), XII, 11, p. 113.

16. Keightley, "Early Civilization in China," p. 31.

17. Keightley, "Early Civilization in China," p. 35.

18. *Liji zhuzi suoyin* [Text and Concordance to the *Record of Rites*], ed. D. C. Lau and

Chen Fong Ching (Hong Kong: Commercial Press, 1992), 11.20, p. 71. Among the many formal sacrifices associated with the state and the ruler, according to the Han Confucian official Dong Zhongshu (?179-?104 BCE), "none is more important than the Suburban Sacrifice." See *Chunqiu fanlu* [Luxuriant Dew of the *Spring and Autumn Annals*] (SBBY edition) 15.7a.

19. For this reason the most dreaded form of punishment, developed later for the most severe offense against family and clan and administered by the community and not by the government, is the removal of one's name from the ancestral shrine (e.g., the scene in the contemporary film *Ju Dou*).

20. "Do not think that I have come to bring peace on earth; I have not come to bring peace, but a sword. For I have come to set a man against his father, and a daughter against her mother, and a daughter-in-law against her mother-in-law; and a man's foes will be those of his own household. He who loves father or mother more than me is not worthy of me; and he who loves son or daughter more than me is not worthy of me; and he who does not take his cross and follow me is not worthy of me" (Revised Standard Version).

21. David N. Keightley, "The Religious Commitment: Shang Theology and the Genesis of Chinese Political Culture," *History of Religions* 17 (1978): 12-13.

22. See, for example, C. K. Yang, *Religion in Chinese Society: A Study of Contemporary Social Functions of Religion and Some of Their Historical Factors* (Berkeley: University of California Press, 1961); Robert P. Weller, *Unities and Diversities in Chinese Religion* (Seattle: University of Washington Press, 1987).

23. For a succinct argument based on thorough review of pertinent scholarship, see Robert Eno, "Was There a High God Ti in Shang Religion," *Early China* 15 (1990): 1-26; and also Xu Zhuoyun, *Xi Zhou shi* [History of the Western Zhou] (Taipei: Lianjing, 1984), pp. 95-106. For a dissenting and somewhat reactionary view, see Xu Fuguan, *Zhongguo sixiangshi lunji xubian* [Additional Essays on the History of Chinese Thought] (Taipei: Shibao chubanshe, 1982), pp. 239-44.

24. I use this term in a sense analogous to how it is used in the biological sciences: structural similarity of two parts of one organism based on a common developmental origin.

25. Confucius, *Analects* ii.21, p. 17 (Lau's translation).

26. Zeng Shen, *The Great Learning* in *The Chinese Classics,* trans. James Legge, second rev. ed. (Taipei: Wenshijie chubanshe, 1972), vol. 1, p. 370. Emphasis added.

27. *Liji* 16.12, p. 92.

28. *Liji* 16.3, p. 91.

29. For the clause, see *Shangshu jinzhu jinyi* [A Contemporary Critical Edition of *The Book of Documents*], annotated and trans. Qu Wanli (Taipei: Commercial Press, 1969), p. 85. For the reading, see Feng Youlan, *Zhongguo zhexueshi xinbian* [A History of Chinese Philosophy, new ed.] (Beijing: Renmin chubanshe, 1980), vol. 1, chap. 4.

30. See *Zuo Commentary,* Duke Cheng, ninth year.

31. *Guoyu* 7.10a (SBBY).

32. Confucius, *Analects* 1.2 (my translation). D. C. Lau, following Qian Daxin, the Qing philologian, emends *ren* (benevolence) to *ren* (humans). Accordingly, Lau's translation of the last part of the statement reads, "the root of a man's character." See *The Analects,* trans. Lau, p. 3.

33. My translation here follows D. C. Lau's rendering of *ai* as "sparing." See *Mencius* (Hong Kong: Chinese University Press, 1984), vol. 2, p. 285.

34. *Xinyi Xiaojing duben* [The Classic of Filial Piety, with a new contemporary translation], ed. and annotated by Lai Yanyuan and Huang Junlang (Taipei: Sanmin shuju, 1992), p. 31 (chap. 5).

35. Confucius, *Analects* 1.2 (my translation).

36. *Zuozhuan,* Duke Yin, 11: "Thus the Gentlemen knew that Earl Xi was about to perish . . . for he did not love his kin [*bu qinqin*]."

37. D. W. Y. Kwok, "On the Rites and Rights of Being Human," in *Confucianism and Human Rights,* ed. William Theodore de Bary and Tu Weiming (New York: Columbia University Press, 1998), p. 85.

38. Sumner B. Twiss, "A Constructive Framework for Discussing Confucianism and Human Rights," in *Confucianism and Human Rights,* ed. de Bary and Weiming, p. 32.

39. In Fareed Zakaria, "Culture Is Destiny: A Conversation with Lee Kuan Yew," *Foreign Affairs* 73, no. 2 (March/April 1994): 113.

40. Ian Buruma reviewing Christopher Patten, *East and West: China, Power, and the Future of Asia,* in *The New York Review of Books* 45, no. 14 (September 1998): 18.

41. Ambrose C. Y. King, "Confucianism, Modernity and Asian Democracy," in *Justice and Democracy: Cross-Cultural Perspectives,* ed. Ron Hontekeo and Marietta Stephaniants (Honolulu: University of Hawaii Press, 1997), pp. 174, 175.

42. Twiss, "A Constructive Framework for Discussing Confucianism and Human Rights," p. 34.

43. Derk Bodde, "The State and Empire of Ch'in," in *The Cambridge History of China,* vol. 1: *The Ch'in and Han Empires, 221 B.C.–A.D. 220,* ed. Denis Twitchett and Michael Loewe (Cambridge: Cambridge University Press, 1986), p. 30. Emphasis added.

44. Yan Zhitui, *Yanshi jiaxun jijie* [Yan's Manual for Family Instruction, with multiple commentaries], annotated by Wang Liqi (Beijing: Guji, 1980), p. 54.

45. For a recent and stimulating discussion of the "text" of the Chinese house and related topics, see Francesca Bray, *Technology and Gender: Fabrics of Power in Late Imperial China* (Berkeley: University of California Press, 1997), esp. chaps. 1-3 on "the construction of Chinese social space."

46. See Ch'en Tu-hsiu, "The Way of Confucius and Modern Life," in *Sources of Chinese Tradition,* comp. William Theodore de Bary, Wing-tsit Chan, and Chester Tan, vol. 2 (New York: Columbia University Press, 1960), pp. 153-56. A hint of editorial bias is apparent when the introductory notes of this entry declare, "Ch'en directs his fire at social customs and abuses which *seemed* to have Confucian sanction but had no place in the modern age" (emphasis mine). To this observation, Hamlet's words to his mother may seem an appropriate response: "Seems, madam? Nay, it is, I know not seems." As the Columbia editors themselves so meticulously demonstrate in their annotations, Ch'en's excerpted essay of no more than three pages (in English translation) cites the *Record of Rites* no fewer than seventeen times and the *Yi-li* (*I-li,* Anthology of Propriety and Ritual) once for documentation of these "customs and abuses." If more documentation is desired, one can simply turn to the bountiful pages of imaginative and anecdotal literatures of China's imperial past.

47. See Ch'en Tu-hsiu, "The True Meaning of Life," in *Sources of Chinese Tradition,* pp. 167-69. For an account of the critique of Confucianism during the early decades of this

century by Ch'en, Wu Yu, and others, see Chow Tse-tsung, *The May Fourth Movement: Intellectual Revolution in Modern China* (Cambridge, Mass.: Harvard University Press, 1960), pp. 300-313. Although it is true that there had not been many persons who "declared themselves anti-Confucian" resolutely during more than two millennia of Chinese imperial history, as Chow Tse-tsung has remarked (*The May Fourth Movement*, p. 300), the fortunes of Confucianism in the twentieth century, understandably more varied because of vast and cataclysmic change, have fluctuated between hostile opposition and arduous rehabilitation both on the mainland and in diaspora communities elsewhere. (See Gungwu, *Chineseness*, chaps. 11-12; Jing Wang, *High Culture Fever: Politics, Aesthetics, and Ideology in Deng's China* [Berkeley: University of California Press, 1996], pp. 64-117.) Thus, not only are the gyrating vicissitudes of Confucian reception in recent Chinese experience conducive to creating immense historical ironies, but those ironies themselves may also betoken the ongoing but halting efforts on the part of the Chinese to come to terms with part of their most cherished and stubborn cultural legacy. Within the People's Republic itself, at times sponsoring not merely virulent attacks on the person and ideals of the ancient sage but also brutal attempts to uproot virtually all traces of the tradition, there has been nonetheless in the post-Mao period some movement also to retrieve and revive a Confucius more compatible with its own understanding of national modernity. On the other hand, in an island nation like Taiwan which prides itself as the keeper and sustainer of genuine Confucian values in both government and society, the last two decades have witnessed the flowering of stringent critique, a discourse of *ressentiment* unsparing in both scope and severity against this venerable tradition even as the nation strives to become a full-fledged democracy enjoying unprecedented forms of freedom.

48. Wang Gungwu, "Power, Rights, and Duties in Chinese History," reprinted in *Chineseness*, pp. 165-87.

49. See William Theodore de Bary, *The Liberal Tradition in China* (Hong Kong: Chinese University Press, 1983; New York: Columbia University Press, 1983). The thesis of the book is briefly rehearsed and reemphasized in his more recent *Asian Values and Human Rights: A Confucian Communitarian Perspective* (Cambridge, Mass.: Harvard University Press, 1998), pp. 158-67. For a detailed critique of this book by de Bary, see my review article, "Which Values? Whose Perspective?" *Journal of Religion* (April 2000).

50. See three pieces in *Confucianism and Human Rights*, ed. de Bary and Weiming: William Theodore de Barry, "Introduction," p. 5; Twiss, "A Constructive Framework," p. 41 and n. 35; Irene Bloom, "Mencian Confucianism and Human Rights," pp. 96-97.

51. De Bary, *Asian Values and Human Rights*, pp. 17ff., quote on p. 18.

52. *Liji* 26.11, p. 131.

53. *From the Soil: The Foundations of Chinese Society*, a translation of Fei Xiaotong's *Xiangtu Zhongguo*, with an introduction and epilogue by Gary G. Hamilton and Wang Zheng (Berkeley: University of California Press, 1992), p. 66.

54. These are the concepts in the traditional Chinese juridical system singled out for praise by Heiner Roetz's thoughtful essay, "Confucianism and Some Questions of Human Rights," printed by the Institute Designate of Chinese Literature and Philosophy, Academia Sinica, July 1999, pp. 9-11. Assuredly, Confucian teachings advocate the importance of self-reform or mending one's behavior in face of mistakes or errors (*Analects* 1.8; 15.30).

The problem of what to do, however, remains when the supreme ruler does not practice such an ideal of self-correction.

55. De Bary, *Asian Values and Human Rights*, p. 8.

56. De Bary, *Asian Values and Human Rights*, p. 10.

57. For a recent critique of cultural particularism, see, for example, Bo Yang [Guo Libang], "Renquan nalai Zhongguo tese [How could human rights have special Chinese character]!" in *Central Daily News* (overseas edition), Monday, February 23, 1998, p. 5.

58. The *Chicago Tribune* of Saturday, May 9, 1998, bore the front-page, headlined story of a Chinese couple, resident immigrants to the United States, who had been threatened by the Cook County State's Attorney's office with the criminal charge of domestic battery and possible deportation for alleged physical abuse of their eight-year-old daughter (p. 1). The father in particular was accused by the state for "hitting his . . . daughter in the face, arms and legs" (p. 2) on account of her alleged loss of a ring. Believing that they were merely exercising their own right of meting out appropriate discipline for their errant child, the parents were bewildered by "the American way." Confronted by both outcries from the Asian communities and coverage by the media, the state eventually dropped the deportation threat and settled with the family by imposing on the father "a penalty of one year of court supervision" and "counseling" (p. 1). However one may interpret this story, the events of the episode may well serve as an ironic commentary on the quoted remark of Lee Kuang Yew that "the ruler or the government does not try to provide for a person what the family best provides." In pondering possible examples drawn from Chinese history, past and present, the issue confronting Mr. Lee is whether "what the family best provides" is always the best for the individual member.

59. *Liji* 4.45, p. 28.

60. See Alan Gewirth, "Common Morality and the Community of Rights," in *Prospects for a Common Morality*, ed. Gene Outka and John P. Reeder Jr. (Princeton, N.J.: Princeton University Press, 1993), p. 34.

61. To the best of my knowledge, there is no original source for this proverb, but one convenient textual embodiment may be found in chapter 78 of the novel *Xiyouji* (Beijing: Zuojia chubanshe, 1954). See p. 893 of this edition and also *The Journey to the West*, trans. and ed. Anthony C. Yu, 4 vols. (Chicago: University of Chicago Press, 1977-84), vol. 4, p. 43. My citation of this saying does not mean to ignore the fact that in the systems of military discipline maintained in even the "liberal, individualist West," there is the similar construal of a subject's refusal to die on command as a form of treason. What is much more heartening is the development in a place like Taiwan, where the dawning consciousness that alternative forms of service may substitute for the military draft has found recent legislative enactment. See the *Central Daily News* (overseas edition), January 17, 2000, p. 3.

62. This is the thesis of Yu Yingshi, *Xiandai ruxue lun* [On Contemporary Confucianism] (River Edge, N.J.: Global, 1996), pp. 1-59.

63. Yu Yingshi, *Xiandai ruxue lun* [On Contemporary Confucianism], pp. 23-24.

64. See *Mengzi ziyi shuzheng* [Expository Commentary on the Words of Mencius] in *Dai Zhen quanshu* [Complete Works of Dai Zhen], 5 vols. (Beijing: Qinghua daxue chubanshe, 1991), vol. 5, p. 152. An English version of the Commentary may be found in *Tai Chen on Mencius: Explorations in Words and Meaning*, trans. Ann-ping Chin and

Mansfield Freeman (New Haven: Yale University Press, 1990). The translations of Dai's text in this essay are my own.

65. See *Dai Zhen quanshu* [Complete Works of Dai Zhen], vol. 5, pp. 176-94.

66. *Dai Zhen quanshu* [Complete Works of Dai Zhen], vol. 5, p. 159.

67. *Dai Zhen quanshu* [Complete Works of Dai Zhen], vol. 5, p. 159.

68. The space of this essay precludes a detailed consideration of Zhao Jibin's provocative but controversial thesis that the meanings of *ren* (humans) and *min* (people, citizens) are sharply and consistently differentiated throughout the *Analects*. According to him, the former refers only to the aristocratic strata of society, whereas the latter term signifies the populace or common people. See his *Lunyu xintan* [New Explorations of the *Analects*] (Beijing: Renmin chubanshe, 1959), pp. 1-27.

69. *Mencius* 6A.14 (Lau, 2:239).

70. The binome *shengsheng* derives from the "Commentary of the Appended Phrases," 5, of the *Classic of Change*. Two lines of the received text read: "producing life is called change; completing [an] image is called the 'Key.'" The parallel construction makes it obvious that the second graph of both sentences must be read as nominals, objects of the antecedent verbal graphs "to produce/beget" and "to complete." The received text thus puts "greater emphasis on the generative capacity of the Way," as Edward Shaughnessy observes in his translation of the Mawangdui version of the classic. Instead of a binome, however, that version has only a single *sheng*, and the line's slightly different vocabulary also makes for a different reading: "giving life to [something] is called 'the image.'" See Edward L. Shaughnessy, trans., *I Ching: The Classic of Changes* (New York: Ballantine, 1996), pp. 192-93 for text and translation, and p. 327 for comment.

71. Yu Yingshi, *Xiandai ruxue lun* [On Contemporary Confucianism], p. 36.

72. *Mencius* 1A.7 (Lau, 1:13).

73. See Pye's "The State and the Individual: An Overview Interpretation," in *The Individual and the State in China*, ed. Brian Hook (Oxford: Clarendon, 1996), p. 20. To be fair to Zhao, such generalizations, as Pye recognizes, merely echo or repeat similar ideas held by someone like Lee Kuan Yew. Furthermore, one can hardly open a newspaper published in Taiwan for very long without reading pundits and educators who exalt the students to let society educate them. Moral Society and Immoral Man, indeed!

74. See Reinhold Niebuhr, *The Children of Light and the Children of Darkness: A Vindication of Democracy and a Critique of Its Traditional Defense* (New York: Charles Scribner's Sons, 1944), p. xiii.

75. For a recent example of unbridled racism that ends in open killing, see the story on one Buford Furrow in Los Angeles, who reported shooting a Filipino-American postal worker in cold blood simply on the ground that the latter was "non-white." The report may be found in the *Chicago Tribune*, Friday, August 13, 1999, sec. 1, p. 3. For a powerful critique of certain American values and practices in relation to the consideration of human rights, see Henry Rosemont Jr., "Human Rights: A Bill of Worries," in *Confucianism and Human Rights*, pp. 54-66.

76. For the white papers released by the State Council on the subject, one may cite the following: "Human Rights in China" (1991), "Criminal Reform in China" (1992), "Tibet — Its Ownership and Human Rights Situation" (1992), "The Situation of Chinese Women" (1994), "Family Planning in China" (1995), "The Progress of Human Rights in

China" (1995), "The Situation of Children in China" (1996)), "Progress in China's Human Rights Cause in 1996" (1997), "Freedom of Religious Belief in China" (1997). See Deng Yong and Waqng Feiling, *In the Eyes of the Dragon: China Views the World* (Lanham, Md.: Rowman and Littlefield, 1999). For a convenient anthology of writings on rights by various Chinese intellectuals, including dissidents, during the twentieth century, see Stephen C. Angle and Marina Svensson, eds., *The Chinese Human Rights Reader: Documents and Commentary 1900-2000* (Armonk, N.Y.: M. E. Sharpe, 2001).

77. See "Bashi niandai zheyang zouguo [This was the way we went past the eighties]," in *Zhongguo shibao* [China Times], Wednesday, August 12, 1998, p. 37.

Notes to Chapter 6

1. See, for example, Robert P. George, "Human Cloning and Embryo Research," *Journal of Theoretical Medicine and Bioethics* 25, no. 1 (2004): 3-20.

Notes to Chapter 7

1. The American Declaration of Independence, often invoked as an early expression of the human rights idea, declared that we are all endowed with rights by the Creator, but the reference, I believe, means only that God, by giving us life, gave us rights. (And Thomas Jefferson's rights, like John Locke's, included notably "liberty," which is not a prominent value in religious morality.) Moreover, the American Declaration cites only rights to life, liberty, and the pursuit of happiness; it does not otherwise identify any other rights or moral code with which human beings are endowed by the Creator. The Creator does not appear in contemporary twentieth-century international human rights instruments.

2. Judaism, for example, even derived normative principles — for example, privacy — from a concept much like human dignity.

3. Or, perhaps, religions have defined human dignity so that it will coincide with a morality rooted in particular theological foundations and in its historic-sociological manifestations over centuries of life in particular religious societies.

4. Louis Henkin, *The Age of Rights* (New York: Columbia University Press, 1990), epilogue.

5. The Universal Declaration is not explicit as to a right to proselytize, but that right may be protected by the freedom of expression; some religions may claim such a right as part of the right of their members to change their religion.

The Universal Declaration does not recognize an individual's right to have his or her religion "established," nor a right to be free from "establishment," to have the sort of wall of separation between church and state that characterizes the constitutional jurisprudence of the United States (a jurisprudence that is in some flux but is likely, I believe, to retain its essential character).

6. The first modern champions of human rights seem to have been the Levelers, who declared that God's law trumped the king's law.

7. Some human rights organizations have opposed recent measures by the United

States to press foreign governments in defense of freedom of some religions only, or even of freedom of religion, generally, but not human rights generally — on the ground that such measures give the message that the United States is not as concerned with other human rights violations, not even violations such as genocide, torture, or long-term arbitrary detention.

8. And even if not on "pro-choice" or "pro-life."

Notes to Chapter 8

1. United Nations Charter, 16 June 1945, 59 Stat. 1031, T.S. No. 993, 3 Bevans 1153 [hereinafter UN Charter].

2. The Universal Declaration of Human Rights, G.A. Res. 217A (III), UN GAOR, 3rd Sess., pt. 1, at 71, UN Doc. A/810 (1948) [hereinafter Universal Declaration].

3. The term has sometimes been used pejoratively to describe religious activism by some religious group other than the writer's group. See John S. Hawley and Wayne Proudfoot, "Introduction," in *Fundamentalism and Gender* (New York: Oxford University Press, 1994), pp. 1, 18, 19. It has particularly been used to fuel anti-Muslim sentiments. See Gita Sahgal and Nira Yuval-Davis, "Introduction: Fundamentalism, Multiculturalism and Women in Britain," in *Refusing Holy Orders*, ed. Gita Sahgal and Nira Yuval-Davis (London: Virago, 1992), pp. 1, 3.

4. Religious women fighting fundamentalism come from a wide variety of religions and races, and many of them lay stress on their cultural origins and attachments. Although an outsider's critique of a religion and culture may well be as valid as that of an insider, most of these religious women generally confine their critique to their own respective religion and culture and so do not raise the issue of outsider critique. Religious women may analyze fundamentalist groups as violating their own religious norms of dignity and respect as well as Western norms. Thus, it is improper to dismiss them (as some fundamentalists are wont to do) as representing only a Western, white, or Christian perspective. See *infra* notes 5, 6, 23, 25 and accompanying text. Indeed, a number of the women find themselves in the dilemma of wanting to fight both the West and fundamentalism. See *infra* notes 6, 23. The fact that women from different religions, perspectives, and a great variety of cultures recognize these religious movements as detrimental to women demonstrates that this recognition is cross-cultural, and supports the cross-cultural legitimacy of defining and critiquing fundamentalism.

5. See Sahgal and Yuval-Davis, *supra* note 3, pp. 8-9, 16-25 (discussing the strong link between fundamentalist movements and women's oppression which has caused women to establish organizations in many countries to fight fundamentalism).

6. The women who write for Women Against Fundamentalism include not only scholars but a school teacher, journalist, novelist, filmmaker, activist, and political exiles. See *Refusing Holy Orders*, *supra* note 3, pp. 16-25, 236-37. The group also includes many other women with whom these women have worked, and whom they include in their writings. Other such groups include Women Living Under Muslim Laws (WLUML), which is an international network linking women in different Muslim countries to exchange information and to fight against women's discrimination that has increased under fundamen-

talism, see Marie A. Hélie-Lucas, "Women Living Under Muslim Laws," in *Ours by Right,* ed. Joanna Kerr (London: Zed Books, 1993), pp. 52-64, and Jyoti Mhapasekara's group of drama activists in India, which takes a strong stand against religious fundamentalism, see Katherine K. Young, "Women in Hinduism," in *Today's Woman in World Religions,* ed. Arvind Sharma (New York: State University of New York Press, 1994), pp. 77, 91.

7. Some scholars and political leaders, from various religions, have proposed other terms, but these have their own drawbacks. Other terms that have been suggested include "obscurantism," "extremism," "renaissance," and "revivalism." "Obscurantism" and "extremism" seem inherently more pejorative than "fundamentalism," and are less exact ("obscurantism" does not suggest the militant anti-modern religious *activism* characteristic of fundamentalism, and "extremism" acknowledges the activism but not the religious ideology and political theory underpinning it). "Renaissance," on the other hand, aims to be an unqualified approving term of fundamentalism, and its usage usually demonstrates a desire to avoid any critical analysis. "Revivalism" fails to capture the substantive nature of *how* the religion is being "revived" in this contemporary phenomenon: by a backward historical glance to "fundamentals" expressed in simplified, easy-to-understand, easy-to-relate-to, easy-to-emote-about terms. Thus, as the editors of *The Fundamentalism Project* conclude, "[n]o other coordinating term was found to be as intelligible or serviceable. And attempts of particular essayists to provide distinctive but in the end confusing accurate alternatives led to the conclusion that they were describing something similar to what are here called fundamentalisms." Martin E. Marty and R. Scott Appleby, "Introduction: The Fundamentalism Project: A User's Guide," in 1 *The Fundamentalism Project: Fundamentalisms Observed* (Chicago: University of Chicago Press, paperback ed. 1944 [1991]), pp. vii, viii [hereinafter "Introduction," *Fundamentalisms Observed*]. For all these reasons, "fundamentalism" remains a preferable, if problematic, choice.

8. Hawley and Proudfoot, *supra* note 3, p. 5; see "Introduction," *Fundamentalisms Observed, supra* note 7, p. ix (discussing apologias of scholars and "family resemblances" of fundamentalisms).

9. Scholarly definitions derive from the first use of the term, by a branch of American Protestantism that emerged at the turn of the century to defend militantly the strict maintenance of traditional, orthodox beliefs against liberalizing trends. The group members referred to themselves as "fundamentalists" by virtue of their commitment to what they termed the "five fundamentals" of their religion. See Hawley and Proudfoot, *supra* note 3, pp. 11-15; Margaret L. Bedroth, *Fundamentalism and Gender: 1875 to the Present* (New Haven: Yale University Press, 1993), pp. 3-4; Sahgal and Yuval-Davis, *supra* note 3, p. 3. For a discussion of the criteria used by scholars to define religious fundamentalism, see *infra* notes 13-21 and accompanying text.

10. For examples, see Hawley and Proudfoot, *supra* note 3, pp. 19-35; "Introduction," *Fundamentalisms Observed, supra* note 7, pp. vii-x; Martin E. Marty and R. Scott Appleby, "Conclusion: An Interim Report on a Hypothetical Family," in 1 *The Fundamentalism Project: Fundamentalisms Observed, supra* note 7, pp. 814, 816 [hereinafter "Conclusion," *Fundamentalisms Observed*]; Bruce B. Lawrence, *Defenders of God: The Fundamentalist Revolt against the Modern Age* (San Francisco: Harper and Row, 1989), pp. 106-19; Lionel Caplan, ed., *Studies in Religious Fundamentalism* (Albany: State University of New York Press, 1987), pp. 14-20. Also, the individual essays and articles that comprise *The Funda-*

mentalism Project, and which are cited in this essay, discuss how the definition of fundamentalism is applied to specific religious groups.

11. For example, in most cases in the several volumes of *The Fundamentalism Project,* the author is from the nation or religious tradition about which he (or in a few cases, she) is writing, and some are in sympathy with fundamentalism. See Martin E. Marty and R. Scott Appleby, "Introduction," in 3 *The Fundamentalism Project: Fundamentalism and the State,* ed. Martin E. Marty and R. Scott Appleby (Chicago: University of Chicago Press, 1993), pp. 1, 5 [hereinafter "Introduction," *Fundamentalism and the State*]. The scholar may not be a fundamentalist, but that does not necessarily mean that the scholar's critique is wholly Western. Marty and Appleby thus have no basis for regarding the participants in *The Fundamentalism Project* as "resolutely of the Western Academy," see *ibid.,* p. 5 and n. 7. Possibly they are, incorrectly, assuming either that only the Western Academy is capable of tolerance or that any capacity within a culture for critique of its own norms must derive from Western Enlightenment thought.

12. The disciplines of the scholars writing for *The Fundamentalism Project* include, *inter alia,* anthropology, economics, history, philosophy, political science, sociology of religion and theology.

13. For this criterion as part of religious women's definition, see Sahgal and Yuval-Davis, *supra* note 3, pp. 7-8, and as part of academic definition, see Hawley and Proudfoot, *supra* note 3, pp. 16-17, 19.

14. For this criterion as part of religious women's definition, see Sahgal and Yuval-Davis, *supra* note 3, pp. 7-8, and, as part of academic definition, see Hawley and Proudfoot, *supra* note 3, p. 16; "Introduction," *Fundamentalisms Observed, supra* note 7, p. vii.

15. This criterion is of course applicable only within religious traditions based on Scripture. For this criterion as part of religious women's definition, see Sahgal and Yuval-Davis, *supra* note 3, pp. 3-5, and, as part of academic definition, see Hawley and Proudfoot, *supra* note 3, pp. 13, 14, 20-21; "Conclusion," *Fundamentalisms Observed, supra* note 10, p. 820; Lionel Caplan, "Introduction," in *Studies in Religious Fundamentalism, supra* note 10, pp. 14-20; Gideon Aran, "Jewish Zionist Fundamentalism, The Bloc of the Faithful in Israel (Gush Emunim)," in 1 *The Fundamentalism Project: Fundamentalisms Observed, supra* note 7, pp. 265, 305.

16. For this criterion as part of religious women's definition, see Sahgal and Yuval-Davis, *supra* note 3, pp. 4, 7; Hélie-Lucas, *supra* note 6, p. 53, and, as part of academic definition, see "Introduction," *Fundamentalisms Observed, supra* note 7, p. ix; Rhys H. Williams, "Movement Dynamics and Social Change: Transforming Fundamentalist Ideology and Organizations," in 4 *The Fundamentalism Project: Accounting for Fundamentalisms,* ed. Martin E. Marty and R. Scott Appleby (Chicago: University of Chicago Press, 1994), pp. 785, 793, 802; see also John H. Garvey, "Fundamentalism and American Law," in 3 *The Fundamentalism Project: Fundamentalisms and the State, supra* note 11, pp. 28, 38, 39.

17. This criterion falls within religious women's criteria of selectivity and reliance on the patriarchal framework. See *infra* notes 18, 19. For this criterion as part of academic definition, see Martin E. Marty and R. Scott Appleby, "Introduction," in 4 *The Fundamentalism Project: Accounting for Fundamentalisms, supra* note 16, p. 1 [hereinafter "Introduction," *Accounting for Fundamentalisms*]; Hawley and Proudfoot, *supra* note 3, p. 16; "Introduction," *Fundamentalisms Observed, supra* note 7, p. ix; see also Lawrence, *supra*

note 10, pp. 106-19; Robert E. Frykenberg, "Accounting for Fundamentalisms in South Asia: Ideologies and Institutions in Historical Perspective," in 4 *The Fundamentalism Project: Accounting for Fundamentalisms, supra* note 16, pp. 591, 594.

18. For this criterion as part of religious women's definition, see Sahgal and Yuval-Davis, *supra* note 3, pp. 3-4; Hélie-Lucas, *supra* note 6, p. 53; and as part of academic definition, see Hawley and Proudfoot, *supra* note 3, p. 13; "Introduction," *Accounting for Fundamentalisms, supra* note 17, p. 1; "Introduction," *Fundamentalisms Observed, supra* note 7, p. ix.

19. For this criterion as part of religious women's definition, see Sahgal and Yuval-Davis, *supra* note 3, p. 8, and, as part of academic definition, see Hawley and Proudfoot, *supra* note 3, pp. 25-35; Caplan, *supra* note 15, pp. 14-20; Hava Lazarus-Yafeh, "Contemporary Fundamentalism — Judaism, Christianity, Islam," *Jerusalem Q.* 47 (1988): 37. For noting fundamentalist endorsement of "pristine morality," see Hawley and Proudfoot, *supra* note 3, pp. 20, 26-35; "Introduction," *Fundamentalisms Observed, supra* note 7, p. ix; Caplan, *supra* note 15, pp. 14-20.

20. For this criterion as part of religious women's definition, see Sahgal and Yuval-Davis, *supra* note 3, p. 4, and as part of academic definition, see Hawley and Proudfoot, *supra* note 3, pp. 13, 19-20; see also "Introduction," *Fundamentalisms Observed, supra* note 7, p. x; Frykenberg, "Accounting for Fundamentalisms," *supra* note 17, pp. 594, 596; "Introduction," *Accounting for Fundamentalisms, supra* note 17, pp. 1-2; Jay M. Harris, "'Fundamentalism': Objections from a Modern Jewish Historian," in *Fundamentalism and Gender, supra* note 3, pp. 137, 138-40 (arguing against use of the term "fundamentalism" while acknowledging that a criterion of scholars' definition of the term is rejection of pluralism).

21. For this criterion as part of religious women's definition, see Sahgal and Yuval-Davis, *supra* note 3, p. 4, and as part of academic definition, see Hawley and Proudfoot, *supra* note 3, pp. 16, 20-21, 30; "Introduction," *Fundamentalism and the State, supra* note 11, p. 2; "Introduction," *Fundamentalisms Observed, supra* note 7, p. ix; Frykenberg, "Accounting for Fundamentalisms," *supra* note 17, p. 594. The aim is "to replace existing structures with a comprehensive system emanating from religious principles and embracing law, polity, society, economy and culture . . [and] contain[ing] within it a totalitarian impulse." "Conclusion," *Fundamentalisms Observed, supra* note 10, p. 824. Scholars may list additional criteria, but those criteria listed in the text are regarded as the most critical.

22. Thus, I do not claim the existence of some "pure" form of fundamentalism "totally differentiated from other forms of culture and independent of all social institutions." "Conclusion," *Fundamentalisms Observed, supra* note 10, p. 817.

23. See *supra* notes 4, 5, 21 and accompanying text; Lazarus-Yafeh, *supra* note 19, p. 37 (arguing that factors in definition of "fundamentalism" are fundamentalist attitudes about gender roles and fundamentalists' rejection of legal changes that would ensure equality of women); Sahgal and Yuval-Davis, *supra* note 3, p. 8; see also Hélie-Lucas, *supra* note 6, pp. 52-56. In Buddhism, see Helen Hardacre, "Japanese New Religions: Profiles in Gender," in *Fundamentalism and Gender, supra* note 3, pp. 111, 113, 129 (discussing how Japanese new religions hold the traditional patriarchal family as sacred and under attack). In Christianity, see Daphne Hampson, *Theology and Feminism* (Oxford: Blackwell, 1990), pp. 6, 9-11 (discussing how Christianity and Judaism are rooted in the patriarchal historical past). In Hinduism, see Gita Sahgal, "Secular Spaces: The Experience of Asian Women Organizing,"

in *Refusing Holy Orders, supra* note 3, pp. 163, 176-77, 180, 187-90 (discussing how Hindu fundamentalism draws nostalgically on historic epics of patriarchy). In Islam, see Hélie-Lucas, *supra* note 6, p. 54 (discussing how fundamentalist Islam is promoting a version of Islam based on a fourteen-centuries-old way of life that subordinates women). An Iranian woman in exile states, "Fundamentalism is about absolute control over the female body and mind. It is about segregation and exclusion of women. The regime in Iran is founded on sexual apartheid. . . ." Maryam Poya, "Double Exile: Iranian Women and Islamic Fundamentalism," in *Refusing Holy Orders, supra* note 3, pp. 141, 159 (quoting Alma Gharehdaghi). Iranian women are one of the largest group of political exiles living in Britain. These women worked against the regime of the Shah, but then needed to escape Iran after the fundamentalist regime attacked women's rights. See Sahgal and Yuval-Davis, *supra* note 3, pp. 1-4, 8-11, 18-25; Hélie-Lucas, *supra* note 6, pp. 52-54. In Judaism, see Pnina N. Levinson, "Women and Sexuality: Traditions and Progress," in *Women, Religion, and Sexuality,* ed. Jeanne Becher (Philadelphia: Trinity Press International, 1991), pp. 45, 46, 60 (discussing that for fundamentalist Jews religious values are based on historical tradition which upholds separate-spheres gender ideologies).

24. See Harris, *supra* note 20, pp. 163-64 (rejects the concept of fundamentalism in Judaism by implicitly arguing that women have always been subordinate in Judaism and so there is no difference between so-called fundamentalist Judaism and religious Judaism); Mary E. Becker, "The Politics of Women's Wrongs and the Bill of Rights: A Bicentennial Perspective," 59 *U. Chi. L. Rev.* 453 (1992): 458-79 (arguing that sexism and patriarchy pervade Christianity and Judaism, such that the Freedom of Religion clause as currently interpreted subordinates women); Nira Yuval-Davis, "Jewish Fundamentalism and Women's Empowerment," in *Refusing Holy Orders, supra* note 3, pp. 198, 223 (discussing Jewish feminist theologians, Judith Plaskow and Gail Chester, who argue that removing patriarchal bias from Judaism is impossible and that feminism is inherently incompatible with religion); Hampson, *supra* note 23, pp. 6, 9-11 (arguing that equality of women is incompatible with Christianity because Christianity is rooted in the patriarchal historical past, and since Christianity and Judaism share history, it is also incompatible with Judaism). Thus, no matter how much the religion is "reformed" it will retain its patriarchal bias as part of its defining ethos. See also Hampson, *supra* note 23, *passim.*

25. See Hampson, *supra* note 23, pp. 32-41 (arguing that the feminist Christian theologians' struggle for critical feminist re-readings of Scriptures operate as apologetics and the only justification must be that they want to remain and be named Christians); see, e.g., *Refusing Holy Orders, supra* note 3, *passim* (discussing how the majority of authors continue to be Catholic, Hindi, Jewish, Muslim, and Protestant, and are opposed to fundamentalism within their religions); Deniz Kandiyoti, "Women and Islam: What Are the Missing Terms?" in *Women Living Under Muslim Laws, Dossier 5/6* (Dec. 1988–May 1989), pp. 5, 8 (arguing that the critique of the inherent patriarchal nature of Islam is no longer a useful analytical tool when Islam varies so much, but that the aim should rather be to fight Islamic laws that subordinate women); Rajni Kothari, "Fundamentalism Is Not Essence of Hinduism," *Illustrated Weekly of India,* 7-13 Dec. 1986, p. 16 (arguing that Hinduism was complex network of interrelated groups and that the notion of a majoritarian fundamentalist group is alien to Hinduism); *The Jewish Woman: New Perspectives,* ed. Elizabeth Koltun (New York: Schocken Books, 1976), *passim* (all contributors to this work are reli-

gious and are attempting to reform Judaism to incorporate feminist principles); see also Becker, *supra* note 23, pp. 469-74 (discussing why women are attracted to Christianity and Judaism despite the sexism of both religious doctrines).

26. See Hawley and Proudfoot, *supra* note 3, p. 12; "Introduction," *Fundamentalisms Observed, supra* note 7, pp. ix-x.

27. For examples of fundamentalists taking this position, see Mumtaz Ahmad, "Islamic Fundamentalism in South Asia: The Jama'at-i-Islami and the Tablighi Jama'at of South Asia," in 1 *The Fundamentalism Project: Fundamentalisms Observed, supra* note 7, pp. 457, 463 (discussing Jama'at-i-Islami's criticisms of conservative *'ulama*); Aran, *supra* note 15, pp. 265, 314 (describing Gush Emunim's criticism of the religious establishment for not being sufficiently politically activist); William D. Dinges, "Roman Catholic Traditionalism and Activist Conservatism in the United States: 1. Roman Catholic Traditionalism," in 1 *The Fundamentalism Project: Fundamentalisms Observed, supra* note 7, pp. 66, 67, 72, 74-75 (describing Catholic fundamentalist movements and the political actions of CTM, ORCM and the Society of St. Pius X in their critique of Roman Catholicism's Second Vatican Council, which they perceive as promoting a loss of Catholic hegemony in the social and political sphere); James Hitchcock, "Roman Catholic Traditionalism and Activist Conservatism in the United States: 2. Catholic Activist Conservatism in the United States," in 1 *The Fundamentalism Project: Fundamentalisms Observed, supra* note 7, pp. 101, 103-9 (discussing how conservative Catholic activism — his term for fundamentalism — rejects supreme legislative authority of Second Vatican Council).

28. A group may shift from one category to the other. Scholars have noted how a conservative group may experience a sense of besetment and beleaguerment that propels it into political militant action, transforming it into a fundamentalist group. See Hawley and Proudfoot, *supra* note 3, pp. 21-23; "Introduction," *Fundamentalisms Observed, supra* note 7, at ix; cf. Harris, *supra* note 20, pp. 160-61. The group may still rely on conservative religious legal norms as the base for its political and social activism, however.

29. The sources for this essay are, first, the writings of fundamentalists; second, the writings of scholars who have studied fundamentalisms from different disciplinary perspectives including anthropology, economics, history, philosophy, political science, and sociology; third, religious women fighting fundamentalism who have experienced fundamentalism firsthand; and fourth, religious conservatives and reformers who are cognizant of fundamentalist positions on certain matters. Unfortunately, much fundamentalist writing is not available in translation or is difficult to obtain, forcing reliance on secondary sources. Despite this obstacle, such an overall survey is important in order to highlight the structural similarities of oppression between movements despite their very different contexts.

30. See *infra* notes 48 (Buddhism); 75 (Christianity); 121 (Hinduism); 158-60 (Islam); 207, 224 (Judaism).

31. Modesty codes require the segregation of women from men in general, and demand that women stay primarily in their homes, act modestly, and dress with their entire body covered. See *infra* notes 133 (Hinduism); 170, 178, 195-201 (Islam); 224-30 (Judaism); see also notes 54 (Buddhism); 87 (Christianity).

32. See *infra* notes 50 (Buddhism); 82 (Christianity); 123 (Hinduism); 166, 179 (Islam); 210 (Judaism) and accompanying text.

33. See *infra* notes 49 (Buddhism); 125 (Hinduism); 158 (Islam); 208 (Judaism) and

accompanying text; see also United Nations, Harmful Traditional Practices Affecting the Health of Women and Children, Fact Sheet No. 23 (Aug. 1995), p. 17.

34. See *infra* notes 50-51, 55 (Buddhism); 81-86, 88-90 (Christianity); 129-32, 134 (Hinduism); 164-69, 178-85 (Islam); 215-20 (Judaism) and accompanying text.

35. See, e.g., *infra* notes 53 (Buddhism); 80 (Christianity); 148-49 (Hinduism); 164 (Islam) and accompanying text.

36. See *infra* notes 81 (Christianity); 164 (Islam) and accompanying text; Khurshid Ahmad, *Family Life in Islam,* 6th printing (Sussex: New Era Publications, 1993 [1974]), pp. 17, 34-35 (Islam); Safia Iqbal, *Women and Islamic Law,* rev. ed. (Delhi: Meridien, 1991), pp. i-ii, viii, xi, 17-18, 98-134 (Islam); Yuval-Davis, *supra* note 24, pp. 213, 217 (Judaism); Frances Raday, "Israel: The Incorporation of Religious Patriarchy in a Modern State," in 4 *Int'l Rev. of Comp. Pub. Policy* 209 (1992): 211 (Judaism); Paula Hyman, "The Other Half: Women in the Jewish Tradition," in *The Jewish Woman, supra* note 25, pp. 105, 108-9 (Judaism).

37. See *infra* notes 57-61 (Buddhism); 78, 85-86 (Christianity); 112-14 (Hinduism); 184-85 (Islam); 211-12 (Judaism) and accompanying text.

38. See *infra* notes 61-62 (Buddhism); 93 (Christianity); 151-53 (Hinduism); 191 (Islam); 215-20 (Judaism) and accompanying text. In some fundamentalist regimes, divorce is simply not permitted. See *infra* notes 99-100 (some Christian groups) and accompanying text.

39. See *infra* notes 88 (Christianity); 181-90 (Islam); 215, 218-20 (Judaism); see also notes 61 (Buddhism); 134-38 (Hinduism) and accompanying text.

40. See Shahla Haeri, "Obedience versus Autonomy: Women and Fundamentalism in Iran and Pakistan," in 2 *The Fundamentalism Project: Fundamentalisms and Society,* ed. Martin E. Marty and R. Scott Appleby (Chicago: University of Chicago Press, 1993), pp. 181, 187.

41. For example, in Christianity, Thomas Aquinas, who is regarded by many as the normative theologian of the Roman Catholic Church, viewed women as inferior. See Rosemary R. Ruether, "Catholicism, Women, Body and Sexuality: A Response," in *Women, Religion, and Sexuality, supra* note 23, pp. 221, 222; Uta Ranke-Heinemann, *Eunuchs for the Kingdom of Heaven: Women, Sexuality and the Catholic Church,* trans. Peter Heinegg (New York: Doubleday, 1990), pp. 157, 183-84, 188-90. Aquinas taught that women were defective human beings, morally, mentally, and physically, supporting their subordination to men. Hampson, *supra* note 23, pp. 16-17; Ruether, *supra,* pp. 222-23; Ranke-Heinemann, *supra,* pp. 183-200. His clear doctrine of women's inferiority would now meet with international disapproval, but "present Catholic teaching attempts to retain the conclusions of Thomas's thought without his premises." Ruether, *supra,* p. 224; see *infra* notes 72, 81. In Islam, traditional fundamentalist rhetoric found women to be inferior because of their mental and physical inferiority (see *infra* notes 162-67 and accompanying text), and recent arguments that support the same roles for women as equal but different are also founded on women's physical and mental inferiority. See, e.g., Iqbal, *supra* note 36, pp. 98-134. In Judaism, see *infra* note 209.

42. Fundamentalist groups exist in Theravada Buddhism, Mahayana Buddhism, and the New Religions of Japan. The primary sources for Buddhist fundamentalism are generally limited, particularly because of the paucity of translations available. Further

links need to be established with women fighting Buddhist fundamentalism in order to publicize fundamentalist policies.

43. Theravada Buddhism takes different forms in various countries, but relies heavily on traditional conservative Buddhist doctrine. Modern Theravada groups in Thailand and Sri Lanka share characteristics which have led to the characterization of movements within those countries as fundamentalist. Donald K. Swearer, "Fundamentalistic Movements in Theravada Buddhism," in 1 *The Fundamentalism Project: Fundamentalisms Observed, supra* note 7, pp. 628, 633; see generally Richard H. Robinson and Willard L. Johnson, *The Buddhist Religion: A Historical Introduction,* third ed. (Belmont: Wadsworth, 1982 [1970]), p. 3 (discussing traditional Theravada Buddhism).

44. Sri Lanka's contemporary Buddhist fundamentalism finds its roots in an early-twentieth-century revival movement in reaction against British colonialism. Stanley J. Tambiah, "Buddhism, Politics, and Violence in Sri Lanka," in 3 *The Fundamentalism Project: Fundamentalisms and the State, supra* note 11, pp. 589, 590, 603-4; Swearer, *supra* note 43, pp. 636. The person mainly responsible for this movement, Dharmapala, reinterpreted Buddhist spiritual ideas into a program designed to restore Sinhalese pride and to emphasize a puritanical sexual morality and etiquette of family life. See Tambiah, *supra,* p. 590; Swearer, *supra* note 43, pp. 637, 649; see *Return to Righteousness: A Collection of Speeches, Essays and Letters of Anagarika Dharmapala,* ed. Ananda Guruge (Ceylon: Ministry of Education and Cultural Affairs, 1965), pp. 108-10, 227, 234, 317-22. He appealed selectively to the Pali Chronicles, which portray Sri Lanka as an island sanctified by Buddha himself and ruled by just kings who defended Buddhism against evil forces, particularly the Tamils. Swearer, *supra* note 43, p. 647; Tambiah, *supra,* p. 590; James Manor, "Organizational Weakness and the Rise of Sinhalese Buddhist Extremism," in 4 *The Fundamentalisms Project: Accounting for Fundamentalisms, supra* note 16, pp 770, 772. His support for a Sinhalese Buddhist state led him to reject the idea of a secular state or a pluralist state tolerating Christianity, Hinduism, and Islam. Dharmapala's ideas and rhetoric continue to form a major part of the foundation of Buddhist fundamentalism.

Buddhist fundamentalism in Sri Lanka is evident in the political activist group Janata Vimukti Peramuna (JVP), a Buddhist revival movement involved in the killings and violent conflicts with Tamil Hindus. Swearer, *supra* note 43, p. 645. The JVP was banned in Sri Lanka in 1983, but it continues to operate under the cover of other organizations and includes members of political parties, members of the *sangha* (Buddhist monks), and individual lay Buddhist activists. See Tambiah, *supra,* pp. 608, 611-12, 615.

45. An example of a Buddhist fundamentalist group in Thailand is the Thai Theravada Buddhist group of Wat Dhammakaya ("Dhammakaya"). See Swearer, *supra* note 43, pp. 666, 667; Charles F. Keyes, "Buddhist Economics and Buddhist Fundamentalism in Burma and Thailand," in 3 *The Fundamentalism Project: Fundamentalisms and the State, supra* note 11, pp. 367, 394. Dhammakaya is estimated to have more than a million adherents and continues to grow rapidly. Keyes, *supra,* p. 394. Dhammakaya intends to create a new unity between national, religious, and personal identity, thus renewing Thailand as a Buddhist state. Swearer, *supra* note 43, pp. 658, 660, 665-66; Keyes, *supra,* p. 394. The group manifests intolerance to other perspectives on Buddhism, see Keyes, *supra,* p. 395, and has been associated with the "militant, reactionary political group" the Red Guards, who jus-

tify the killing of communists because they are "less than human." See Swearer, *supra* note 43, p. 666; Keyes, *supra*, p. 393.

46. The New Religions of Japan are derived primarily from Buddhism and Shinto-ism and are estimated to include one-fourth to one-third of the Japanese people. Hardacre, "Japanese New Religions," *supra* note 23, pp. 113-14. There are over three thou-sand New Religions, but this section relies primarily on three particularly successful fun-damentalist groups that have roots in Buddhism: Soka Gakkai, Seicho no Ie, and Reiyukai Kyodan. See Hardacre, "Japanese New Religions," *supra* note 23, pp. 113-14; Winston Davis, "Fundamentalism in Japan: Religious and Political," in 1 *The Fundamentalism Project: Fundamentalisms Observed, supra* note 7, pp. 782, 797, 799, 801; see also Edwin O. Reischauer, *Japan: The Story of a Nation* (New York: Knopf, 1970), p. 309; William Dawkins, "Anti-Religious Crusade Holds Political Message," *Fin. Times,* 23/24 Sept. 1995, p. 3. The religions are significantly entwined with political parties and emphasize the con-vergence between national identity and religion. See Hardacre, "Japanese New Religions," *supra* note 23, pp. 127-32.

47. See *Return to Righteousness, supra* note 44, pp. 32, 180-81, 345, 346; Hardacre, "Japanese New Religions," *supra* note 23, pp. 118-22, 127.

48. Traditional Buddhism, as followed by fundamentalists, regards women as temptresses. See Diane Y. Paul, *Women in Buddhism: Images of the Feminine in Mahayana Tradition,* second ed. (Berkeley: Asian Humanities Press, 1985 [1981]), pp. 3-5, 51 n. 8, 52.

49. The New Religions of Japan "tend to favor arranged marriages." Helen Hardacre, *Kurozumikyo and the New Religions of Japan* (Princeton, N.J.: Princeton University Press, 1986), p. 190 [hereinafter Hardacre, *Kurozumikyo*]; see Hardacre, "Japanese New Reli-gions," *supra* note 23, pp. 111, 123-24 (finding that New Religions encourage women to marry at young age and have numerous children). In the new religion of Reiyukai, 69 per-cent of families are from arranged marriages. Helen Hardacre, *Lay Buddhism in Contem-porary Japan* (Princeton, N.J.: Princeton University Press, 1984), p. 60.

50. Rita M. Gross, *Buddhism After Patriarchy: A Feminist History, Analysis, and Re-construction of Buddhism* (Albany: State University of New York Press, 1993), p. 42 and n.*; Women's Information Centre, "Shelter for Battered Women in Thailand," in *Third World/ Second Sex,* ed. Miranda Davies, vol. 2 (London: Zed Books, 1987), pp. 205, 208.

51. Hardacre, *Lay Buddhism, supra* note 49, p. 47; see Hardacre, *Kurozumikyo, supra* note 49, p. 190 (noting that women are required, subject to censure, to defer to men).

52. Hardacre, "Japanese New Religions," *supra* note 23, p. 119.

53. *Ibid.,* p. 111 (quoting sermon of religious leader).

54. *Ibid.,* p. 119. Even in the few Buddhist sects which allow for nuns, the nuns must wear fivefold robes, while monks wear only three robes. Nancey J. Barnes, "Women in Buddhism," in *Today's Woman in World Religions, supra* note 6, pp. 137, 141.

55. Women's Information Centre, *supra* note 50, pp. 206-7. A random sampling of Bangkok women in 1985 found that half of them had experienced physical violence and abuse. *Ibid.,* p. 207.

56. See Hardacre, "Japanese New Religions," *supra* note 23, p. 124.

57. *Ibid.,* pp. 118-19, 131; Davis, *supra* note 46, pp. 794, 803.

58. See Hardacre, "Japanese New Religions," *supra* note 23, p. 121.

59. *Ibid.,* p. 120.

60. *Ibid.*, p. 121.

61. *Ibid.*, p. 121.

62. *Ibid.*, p. 121.

63. *Ibid.*, p. 121.

64. See *ibid.*, pp. 121, 129.

65. *Ibid.*, pp. 119-22.

66. *Ibid.*, pp. 118-19, 131.

67. For a discussion of Mormon fundamentalism, see D. Michael Quinn, "Plural Marriage and Mormon Fundamentalism," in 2 *The Fundamentalism Project: Fundamentalisms and Society, supra* note 40, p. 240. For a discussion of Pentecostals and Rastafarians, see Diane J. Austin-Broos, "Pentecostals and Rastafarians: Cultural, Political, and Gender Relations of Two Religious Movements," *Soc. and Econ. Stud.* 36, no. 4 (1987): 1.

68. See, e.g., David Stoll, "'Jesus is Lord of Guatemala': Evangelical Reform in a Death-Squad State," in 4 *The Fundamentalism Project: Accounting for Fundamentalisms, supra* note 16, p. 99; Jorge E. Maldonado, "Building 'Fundamentalism' from the Family in Latin America," in 2 *The Fundamentalism Project: Fundamentalisms and Society, supra* note 40, p. 214; Elaine Foster, "Women and the Inverted Pyramid of Black Churches in Britain," in *Refusing Holy Orders, supra* note 3, p. 45; Steve Bruce, "Fundamentalism, Ethnicity, and Enclave," in 3 *The Fundamentalism Project: Fundamentalisms and the State, supra* note 11, p. 50 (Northern Ireland); Susan Bayly, "Christians and Competing Fundamentalisms in South Indian Society," in 4 *The Fundamentalism Project: Accounting for Fundamentalisms, supra* note 16, p. 726.

69. Protestant fundamentalism has its roots in American Protestant groups that emerged at the turn of the century and identified themselves as fundamentalist. See *supra* note 9.

70. In the 1940s and 1950s American Protestant fundamentalism split, with one segment, led by Billy Graham, thereafter describing itself as "evangelical." The rest, led by such individuals as Carl McIntire and Bob Jones, continued to describe themselves as "fundamentalists." See Laurence R. Iannaccone, "Heirs to the Protestant Ethic? The Economics of American Fundamentalists," in 3 *The Fundamentalism Project: Fundamentalisms and the State, supra* note 11, pp. 342, 345; Nancy T. Ammerman, "North American Protestant Fundamentalism," in 1 *The Fundamentalism Project: Fundamentalisms Observed, supra* note 7, pp. 1, 4 [hereinafter Ammerman, "North American Protestant"]. I use the term "sect fundamentalism" to describe groups of Christians who define themselves as fundamentalists after the split, and follow the doctrine and beliefs (as evolved) of the original fundamentalists. (Correspondingly, the term "sect evangelical" describes groups that have evolved from evangelicals after the split.) The term "fundamentalism" without qualification is used as elsewhere in this essay, and subsumes the fundamentalisms of both sect evangelicals and sect fundamentalists. See Iannaccone, *supra*, pp. 343, 344 and n. 7; Robert Wuthnow and Matthew P. Lawson, "Sources of Christian Fundamentalism in the United States," in 4 *The Fundamentalism Project: Accounting for Fundamentalism, supra* note 16, pp. 18, 24.

An example of a sect fundamentalist group is Jerry Falwell's ministry and Moral Majority, Inc., organization. See Jerry Falwell, *Listen America!* 258 (1980); Ammerman, "North American Protestant," *supra*, p. 43. Although Falwell officially disbanded the Moral

Majority in 1989, it was absorbed into his Liberty Federation group. See Iannaccone, *supra,* p. 346, n. 19. Falwell identifies himself as a sect fundamentalist, and his groups and associated organizations all meet the definition of fundamentalism. See Iannaccone, *supra,* pp. 344, 346; Ammerman, "North American Protestant," *supra,* pp. 43-49; Wuthnow and Lawson, *supra,* p. 26; Garvey, *supra* note 16, pp. 28, 29, 32. These organizations (with other Christian fundamentalist groups too numerous to mention) are collectively referred to as the New Christian Right (NCR) of which Falwell is a major spokesman. See Ammerman, "North American Protestant," *supra,* pp. 43, 44; Iannaccone, *supra,* p. 346; see also Garvey, *supra* note 16, p. 32.

71. Reconstructionists clearly meet the definition of fundamentalism. See Ammerman, "North American Protestant," *supra* note 70, pp. 53-55; Iannaccone, *supra* note 70, p. 349; Wuthnow and Lawson, *supra* note 70, p. 46. The two main Reconstructionist leaders are Rousas Rushdoony and his son-in-law Gary North. See Ammerman, "North American Protestant," *supra* note 70, pp. 49-50; Iannaccone, *supra* note 70, p. 348. Their theological foundation is Calvinist, Ammerman, "North American Protestant," *supra* note 70, p. 50, and their central ideological claim is that "Christians are called by God to exercise dominion" and to spread their gospel to all nations. See Gary North, *The Theology of Christian Resistance* (Geneva: Geneva Divinity School Press, 1983), p. 60; Rousas John Rushdoony, *The Institute of Biblical Law* (Phillipsburg: P and R Publishing, 1973), p. 9. Reconstructionist "dominion" theory is filtering into the mainstream of the NCR, Pentecostal traditions, and sect fundamentalists, although these groups do not always want to be openly associated with Reconstructionists. See Ammerman, "North American Protestant," *supra* note 70, pp. 53-55; Iannaccone, *supra* note 70, p. 349; Wuthnow and Lawson, *supra* note 70, p. 46.

72. The Vatican remains very politically active throughout the world to institute Roman Catholicism as the state religion and to promote Roman Catholic laws and principles within secular societies. Because the Vatican has done exactly this for centuries, scholars are reluctant to call it "fundamentalist," although this conclusion is often hinted at or implied. See Hawley and Proudfoot, *supra* note 3, pp. 24-25 (noting how Vatican expressed solidarity with Muslim fundamentalists in the Salman Rushdie affair in the context of how fundamentalists engage in mutual support); Frances Kissling, "The Challenge of Christianity, 44 *American. U. L. Rev.* 1345 (1995): 1345-46 (discussing fundamentalist tendencies within all religions with particular emphasis on Vatican). Vatican fundamentalist tendencies are particularly manifest in groups to which it gives support. A representative such group, which meets the definition of fundamentalism, is the Comunione e Liberazione (CL). See Dario Zadra, "Comunione e Liberazione: A Fundamentalist Idea of Power," in 4 *The Fundamentalism Project: Accounting For Fundamentalisms, supra* note 16, pp. 124, 124-45. The CL, an organization founded in Italy, claims divine authority for the RCC and aims to bring back the "expelled Church" and papal state to Italy and reassert "Catholic hegemony." *Ibid.,* pp. 124, 126-28, 142. The CL rejects Enlightenment norms, particularly the notion of the secular state and freedom of the individual. *Ibid.,* pp. 126, 129, 130. The CL regards itself as speaking "for the Church and for its rights. . . . CL can point to approval from the hierarchy and significant support from the Vatican in backing that claim." *Ibid.,* pp. 126, 143. CL's political arm has been connected to the Christian Democrat Party in Italy and became increasingly influential during the early 1990s. See *ibid.,* pp. 134, 141. The CL

has produced an "echo effect" in the RCC world, legitimating RCC condemnations of Enlightenment theory as the traditional enemy, along with Humanism and Protestantism. See *ibid.,* pp. 143, 144. For discussions of other Catholic fundamentalist groups, see Dinges, *supra* note 27, pp. 66-101; Hitchcock, *supra* note 27, pp. 101-39.

73. See *supra* note 27, p. 72.

74. See Zadra, *supra* note 72, pp. 131, 141 (discussing CL views of the fall of Italian society as directly linked to modern "undermining" of traditional family life); see, e.g., Falwell, *supra* note 70, pp. 121-37 (discussing idea as sect fundamentalist); James D. Hunter, *Evangelicalism: The Coming Generation* (Chicago: University of Chicago Press, 1987), pp. 76-109 (discussing idea as sect evangelical).

75. See Bedroth, *supra* note 9, p. 69 (discussing that fundamentalist Protestants viewed women as having the matches to light the dynamite in men, and thus women must contain their sexuality and not cause men to fall morally); see also George H. Tavard, *Women in Christian Tradition* (Notre Dame: University of Notre Dame Press, 1973), p. 183 (finding that in Protestant tradition, woman was viewed as far more sexual than man).

76. See Helen Hardacre, "The Impact of Fundamentalism on Women, The Family, and Interpersonal Relations," in 2 *The Fundamentalism Project: Fundamentalisms and Society, supra* note 40, pp. 129, 133 [hereinafter Hardacre, "Impact"].

77. See Ammerman, "North American Protestant," *supra* note 70, p. 50 (discussing Reconstructionists' nostalgia for seventeenth century); see, e.g., Gary North, *Political Polytheism: The Myth of Pluralism* (Tyler: Institute for Christian Economics, 1989), pp. 242-45.

78. See Ammerman, "North American Protestant," *supra* note 70, p. 68; Garvey, *supra* note 16, p. 30; Hardacre, "Impact," *supra* note 76, pp. 131-32.

79. See Ammerman, "North American Protestant," *supra* note 70, pp. 8, 40; Garvey, *supra* note 16, p. 30; Hardacre, "Impact," *supra* note 76, pp. 132, 139; see, e.g., Falwell, *supra* note 70, p. 150; Rushdoony, *Biblical Law, supra* note 71, p. 344.

80. See Hampson, *supra* note 23, p. 14; Tavard, *supra* note 75, p. 181; Susan D. Rose, *Women Warriors: The Negotiation of Gender in a Charismatic Community,* Soc. Analysis 48 (1987): 245. Sects of the Orthodox Church also require women to be submissive, and because of their general inability and weakness therefore to be ruled by men. Anca-Lucia Manolache, "Orthodoxy and Women: A Romanian Perspective," in *Women, Religion and Sexuality, supra* note 23, pp. 172, 180.

81. With respect to Protestants, see Bedroth, *supra* note 9, pp. 98, 124; Hampson, *supra* note 23, p. 14. With respect to the RCC, see "The Vatican's Summary of Evangelium Vitae," reprinted in CNS Documentary Service, *Origins* 24, no. 42 (6 Apr. 1995): 730. ("A very special task is entrusted to women, who are particularly close to the mystery of life, who are called to be its guardians and to reveal its fruitfulness when that task matures into relationships marked by unselfish giving and *willing service . . . free from individualism";* emphasis supplied); John Paul II, "On the Dignity and Vocation of Women," reprinted in CNS Documentary Service, *Origins* 18, no. 17 (6 Oct. 1988): 281.

82. See North, *Polytheism, supra* note 77, p. 601.

83. See Falwell, *supra* note 70, pp. 128, 151; Hunter, *supra* note 74, p. 79; Gary North, *Victim's Rights: The Biblical View of Civil Justice* (Tyler: Institute for Christian Economics, 1990), p. 45; Rose, *supra* note 80, p. 246.

84. See Bedroth, *supra* note 9, pp. 103-4; Tavard, *supra* note 75, p. 181; Nancy T.

Ammerman, "Accounting for Christian Fundamentalisms: Social Dynamics and Rhetorical Strategies," in 4 *The Fundamentalism Project: Accounting for Fundamentalisms, supra* note 16, pp. 149, 154 [hereinafter Ammerman, "Accounting for Christian Fundamentalisms"]; see, e.g., Falwell, *supra* note 70, pp. 128-29, 151; Hunter, *supra* note 74, p. 79.

85. See Falwell, *supra* note 70, pp. 128-29; Hunter, *supra* note 74, p. 79.

86. Falwell, *supra* note 70, pp. 128-29, 151; Hunter, *supra* note 74, p. 79; Rushdoony, *Biblical Law, supra* note 71, pp. 347-53; see Bedroth, *supra* note 9, p. 109 (quoting Protestant evangelical who states that a Christian wife is to be obedient in all things); Randall Balmer, "American Fundamentalism: The Ideal of Femininity," in *Fundamentalism & Gender, supra* note 3, pp. 47, 52-55 (discussing the fundamentalist religious requirement of feminine submission and obedience); see also Ammerman, "Accounting for Christian Fundamentalisms," *supra* note 84, pp. 154, 159; Ammerman, "North American Protestant," *supra* note 70, pp. 8, 40-41; Garvey, *supra* note 16, p. 30; Rose, *supra* note 80, p. 245; see, e.g., Marabel Morgan, *The Total Woman* (Portland: Pocket, 1973), p. 55 ("A Total [Christian fundamentalist] Woman caters to her man's special quirks, whether it be salads, sex or sports.").

87. See Bedroth, *supra* note 9, pp. 69, 82, 114 (explaining that fundamentalist Christian women must adopt modest dress, be properly covered, with no display of themselves that may cause Christian men to sin); Foster, *supra* note 68, pp. 45, 49, 65 (noting that in fundamentalist English Christian Black churches, maintenance of moral and modest dress codes are important).

88. Bedroth, *supra* note 9, p. 103.

89. See Bedroth, *supra* note 9, p. 116; James Alsdurf and Phyllis Alsdurf, *Battered into Submission: The Tragedy of Wife Abuse in the Christian Home* (Downers Grove, Ill.: InterVarsity, 1989), pp. 10, 16-17. Christian fundamentalist (Protestant and Catholic) emphasis on women's self-sacrifice and the glorification of their suffering and victimization make women particularly vulnerable to accepting battering relationships. See Becker, *supra* note 24, p. 465. Generally, such abuse is common in families with rigid sex roles and gross inequities in power distribution. See Alsdurf and Alsdurf, *supra*, p. 17; David Finkelhor et al., ed., "Common Features of Family Abuse," in *The Dark Side of Families: Current Family Violence Research* (Beverly Hills: Sage Publications, 1983), pp. 17, 19.

90. Alsdurf and Alsdurf, *supra* note 89, p. 18.

91. Becker, *supra* note 24, p. 465; Bedroth, *supra* note 9, p. 116; Alsdurf and Alsdurf, *supra* note 89, pp. 16, 18, 23. Under traditional religious law of the Orthodox Church a husband had a right to beat his wife, but if a wife raised her hand against her husband she could be divorced. Manolache, *supra* note 80, pp. 179-80. Although civil law rather than religious law now applies, the religious attitudes are unchanged. See *ibid.*, p. 180.

92. See Falwell, *supra* note 70, pp. 124-25.

93. Since the 1970s, there has been a surge in Protestant fundamentalist activism. See Ammerman, "North American Protestant," *supra* note 70, p. 38; see generally Jeffrey K. Hadden, "Televangelism and Political Mobilization," in *American Evangelicals and the Mass Media* (Grand Rapids: Zondervan, 1990), pp. 215-29. In Catholicism, CL's political actions are often aimed at lobbying for legislation affecting the family and bringing back Catholic hegemony. See Zadra, *supra* note 72, pp. 131, 140.

Fundamentalists have also fought to retain unequal laws in the face of reform. For example, the Indian Christian community has its own marriage and divorce laws under the Indian Divorce Act of 1869 and the Indian Christian Marriage Act of 1872. Leslie J. Calman, *Toward Empowerment: Women and Movement Politics in India* (Boulder: Westview, 1992), pp. 150, 152 and n. 17; see also notes 152, 415 (discussing family laws in India, which are divided along religious lines, with Hindus covered by the civil Hindu laws and Muslims covered by their own respective religious laws). Fundamentalists fought to retain these laws, under which a Christian husband may obtain divorce if his wife commits adultery, but a "husband's adultery, however, is not sufficient grounds for a wife to seek divorce." *Ibid.*, p. 152. This law was challenged, and the Kerala High Court in India held in 1995 that Christian women may now seek dissolution on grounds of desertion, cruelty, and adultery. See IWRAW, *The Women's Watch* 9, no. 3 (Jan. 1996): 6-7. It remains to be seen if standards of proof are enforced equally.

94. Falwell's groups fight against secular or liberal humanism for the return of "Christian civilization" in the United States. See Falwell, *supra* note 70, pp. 17-18; Ammerman, "North American Protestant," supra note 70, pp. 46-47. The political party of these groups is the Republican party. Falwell has endorsed the "civil disobedience" of another fundamentalist group, Operation Rescue, which has engaged in violent direct action against abortion clinics and doctors, justifying its violence as being based on divine law rather than secular laws. See Faye Ginsburg, "Saving America's Souls: Operation Rescue's Crusade against Abortion," in 3 *The Fundamentalism Project: Fundamentalisms and the State, supra* note 11, pp. 557, 563, 567, 569, 573 (noting that it is disingenuous for Operation Rescue to distinguish its "direct action" from "violent activities" since its activities are designed to create "an atmosphere of chronic fear of physical and emotional assault for both personnel and clients" by verbally and physically accosting women entering the clinics, blocking access to the clinics, following women and tracing their license plates in order to harass them at home, picketing the homes of clinics' personnel and physicians who in addition receive threatening letters and phone calls); Ammerman, "North American Protestant," *supra* note 70, p. 45; Garvey, *supra* note 16, p. 32; Sara Maitland, "Biblicism: A Radical Rhetoric?" in *Refusing Holy Orders, supra* note 3, pp. 26, 34-35; see, e.g., Randall Terry, *Operation Rescue* (1988), p. 175 (explaining that Operation Rescue's fight against abortion is to establish a nation whose politics and judicial system are founded on Judeo-Christian "Higher Laws"). Reconstructionists also hope to establish a Christian nation. See North, *Polytheism, supra* note 77, pp. 4, 15, 28, 35, 84-85; Rousas J. Rushdoony, "Biblical Law and Western Civilization," *J. Christian Reconstruction* 2 (1975): 5; Ammerman, "North American Protestant," *supra* note 70, pp. 50, 51. Rushdoony has proposed a legal system based on the law of Hebrew Scripture. See Rushdoony, *Biblical Law, supra* note 71, *passim;* Ammerman, "North American Protestant," *supra* note 70, p. 52. Some of his suggestions for implementing Mosaic laws have met with controversy, particularly that habitually rebellious children be put to death. See, e.g., Rushdoony, *Biblical Law, supra* note 71, pp. 185-92. See Ammerman, "North American Protestant," *supra* note 70, p. 52.

95. See Rebecca E. Klatch, *Women of the New Right* (Philadelphia: Temple University Press, 1987), pp. 136-39; Garvey, *supra* note 16, p. 30; see, e.g., Falwell, *supra* note 70, pp. 150-51.

96. See Ammerman, "North American Protestant," *supra* note 70, pp. 40-41; Garvey, *supra* note 16, pp. 30, 37; see, e.g., Falwell, *supra* note 70, pp. 19, 150-64.

97. See Ammerman, "North American Protestant," *supra* note 70, pp. 44-45.

98. See Ammerman, "North American Protestant," *supra* note 70, p. 45; see also the Alan Guttmacher Institute, "Supremacy of Parental Authority: New Battlecry For Conservative Activists," *Washington Memo,* 21 Dec. 1995, p. 4 (discussing introduction of bill "Parental Rights and Responsibilities Act," which would prohibit any federal, state, or local government from usurping the right of a parent to, *inter alia,* discipline a child and would have a "chilling" effect on intervention in child abuse cases).

99. See Zadra, *supra* note 72, pp. 131, 140, 141 (discussing CL's promotion of traditional family legal structures and its lobbying against divorce and abortion); Dinges, *supra* note 27, p. 91; Hitchcock, *supra* note 27, p. 110.

100. For example, the Vatican recently negotiated with ex-President Walesa a concordat with Poland concerning contraception, abortion, and divorce, and giving the RCC the right to teach religion in the state schools and special tax concessions to its clergy. The governing coalition, however, declined to ratify the concordat until a new constitution was in place. Christopher Bobinski, "Walesa in Threat to Resign over Abortion Reform," *Fin. Times,* 6 Jul. 1994, p. 2. Walesa lost the elections in November 1995, and the RCC may well see its power in Poland checked as a result.

101. See Julia Preston, "U.N. Summit on Women Bars Groups: China, Vatican Block Opponents' Admission," *Wash. Post,* 17 Mar. 1995, p. A36.

102. See Ruether, *supra* note 41, p. 223. For discussion on the Vatican's historic opposition to women's equality, see generally Mary Daly, *The Church and the Second Sex,* with the feminist post-Christian introduction and new archaic afterwords by the author (Boston: Beacon, 1985).

103. Hindu fundamentalism began at the turn of the century with Dayananda Sarasvati, the primary leader of the group Arya Samaj, which aimed to revive Hinduism in India through the establishment of a self-conscious Hindu identity with Hindu collective goals. Daniel Gold, "Organized Hinduisms: From Vedic Truth to Hindu Nation," in 1 *The Fundamentalism Project: Fundamentalisms Observed, supra* note 7, pp. 531, 538-39; cf. Krishna Kumar, "Hindu Revivalism and Education in North-Central India," in 2 *The Fundamentalism Project: Fundamentalisms and Society, supra* note 40, pp. 536, 539 (discussing the importance of Arya Samaj in Hindu "revivalism"). Arya Samaj started the first religio-political group of Hindu communalism, which eventually became known as the Hindu Mahasabha. Gold, *supra,* p. 539. By the 1930s, Hindu Mahasabha was led by the author Vinayak Damodar Savarkar, who wrote one of the most influential works of Hindu fundamentalism, *Hindutva,* defining what it means to be Hindu and calling for Hindu unity. See Vinayak Damodar Savarkar, *Hindutva,* ed. Veer Savarkar Prakashan (Bombay: South Asia Books, 1969 [1923-24]), p. 1. Hindu Mahasabha provides the link between Arya Samaj tradition and the Rashtriya Swayamsevak Sangh (RSS), see *infra* note 104, which the Hindu Mahasabha nurtured as a youth group. Gold, *supra,* p. 539.

104. RSS's founder and first leader, Kesnav Baliram Hedgewar, devoted his life to restoring the sought-after unity of *Hindutva,* see *supra* note 103. He regarded the Muslim and Christian invaders as the enemies of the Hindu nation. See Ainslie T. Embree, "The Function of the Rashtriya Swayamsevak Sangh: To Define the Hindu Nation," in 4 *The Fundamentalism Project: Accounting for Fundamentalisms, supra* note 16, pp. 617, 624. Hedgewar developed the RSS as an organization for training cadres of young men in the

Sanskritic ideals of the warrior. Robert E. Frykenberg, "Hindu Fundamentalism and the Structural Stability of India," in 3 *The Fundamentalism Project: Fundamentalisms and the State, supra* note 11, pp. 233, 241 [hereinafter Frykenberg, "Hindu Fundamentalism"]. RSS's next leader, M. S. Golwalkar, gave the RSS a systematic ideology of extreme intolerance of other modes of life and religion that has been compared to Hitler fascism. Embree, *supra*, p. 627; Gold, *supra* note 103, p. 566; see Frykenberg, "Hindu Fundamentalism," *supra*, pp. 240-41; see, e.g., M. S. Golwalkar, *We or Our Nationhood Defined* (Nagpur City: Bharat, 1939), pp. 47-48.

The RSS has political and cultural affiliate organizations, but retains its religious base. Embree, *supra*, pp. 619, 629. Although RSS was ostensibly banned in January 1993 after the destruction of the mosque at Ayodhya, see *infra* note 106, the organization and its network of two and a half million dedicated members continue to operate effectively, Embree, *supra*, p. 649, as evidenced by the large political gains made by its political party, the BJP, see *infra* note 105.

105. RSS formed its first political party in 1951, the Bharatiya Jana Sangh, which drew on members of Arya Samaj, Hindu Mahasabha, and RSS itself. The Jana Sangh broke apart, and the new party became the Bharatiya Janata Party (BJP) in 1980. Frykenberg, "Hindu Fundamentalism," *supra* note 104, pp. 244-45; Gold, *supra* note 103, p. 572; Embree, *supra* note 104, p. 638; Deepak Lal, "The Economic Impact of Hindu Revivalism," in 3 *The Fundamentalism Project: Fundamentalisms and the State, supra* note 11, pp. 410, 411-12. The BJP opposes the current relatively secular Indian government and fights to make India a Hindu state. Frykenberg, "Hindu Fundamentalism," *supra* note 104, pp. 248-51. The RSS and BJP made large gains in the 1996 elections, and the BJP emerged as the biggest group in parliament. See Mark Nicholson, "Indian PM to Resign after Poll Rebuff," *Fin. Times,* 10 May 1996, p. 1.

106. See Gold, *supra* note 103, pp. 567, 572, 574; Frykenberg, "Hindu Fundamental ism," *supra* note 103, pp. 242-48; Peter van der Veer, "Hindu Nationalism and the Discourse of Modernity: The Vishva Hindu Parishad," in 4 *The Fundamentalism Project: Accounting for Fundamentalisms, supra* note 16, pp. 653, 653; Embree, *supra* note 104, pp. 632, 637 38. VHP was started by Golwalkar in 1964 for the purpose of creating a permanent Hindu religious establishment for all of India. Frykenberg, "Hindu Fundamentalism," *supra* note 104, p. 245; van der Veer, *supra*, p. 655. The VHP is primarily led by religious leaders, and its goal is to impose Hinduism as the national religion of India. See van der Veer, *supra*, pp. 653, 656. It has been particularly successful in staging mass events of religious-political ritual. The most famous of these campaigns involved destruction of the Muslim mosque at Ayodhya (argued to be the birthplace of the god-hero Rama, see *infra* notes 109-11 and accompanying text), which resulted in the deaths of thousands of people, mostly Muslims. See van der Veer, *supra*, pp. 656, 662; John S. Hawley, "Hinduism: Sati and Its Defenders," in *Fundamentalism & Gender, supra* note 3, pp. 79, 79-80; Embree, *supra* note 104, pp. 646-48; Sahgal, *supra* note 23, p. 172. The RSS and VHP also operate abroad. See Sahgal, *supra* note 23, pp. 163-97.

107. See Kumar, *supra* note 103, pp. 550-56; Lal, *supra* note 105, p. 412; Frykenberg, "Hindu Fundamentalism," *supra* note 104, pp. 251-53; Embree, *supra* note 104, pp. 628-33; see also Gold, *supra* note 103, pp. 551, 553-55.

108. See Kumar, *supra* note 103, pp. 550-56; Frykenberg, "Hindu Fundamentalism," *supra* note 104, pp. 234, 253.

109. See Embree, *supra* note 104, p. 632; Kumar, *supra* note 103, p. 554; Frykenberg, "Hindu Fundamentalism," *supra* note 104, pp. 246-47; van der Veer, *supra* note 106, pp. 662-63; Sahgal, *supra* note 23, pp. 189-90.

110. Hindu fundamentalists have promoted Lord Rama as a historical rather than a mythological figure. They claim his birthplace to be a real northern Indian town, Ayodhya, see Sahgal, *supra* note 23, p. 171, where VHP's *Ramayana* campaign resulted in the destruction of the mosque and widespread rioting and killing, see *supra* note 106.

111. In the *Ramayana*, a demon abducts Sita but refrains from raping her. Rama wages war and rescues Sita but doubts her chastity (for which she, although abducted, is plainly responsible) and publicly disowns her. Sita defends her virtue by a test of fire, and the god of fire rescues her and testifies to her virtue and chastity. Rama and Sita return home and live in peace until further rumors surface, questioning Sita's chastity during the abduction. As a result, Rama banishes the pregnant Sita, who soon thereafter gives birth to two sons. Rama then recalls her and requires her to undergo a second test of fire for his people. Sita chooses to defend her virtue by dying, announcing publicly that she will thereby remove Rama's grief, shame, and dishonor, and asserts her loyalty to him by stating that she hopes he will be her husband in her next rebirth. For an account of this epic as related here, see Leigh Minturn, *Sita's Daughters: Coming Out of Purdah* (New York: Oxford University Press, 1993), pp. 170-73; Gerald J. Larson, "Hinduism in India and in America," in *World Religions in America: An Introduction*, ed. Jacob Neusner (Louisville: Westminster John Knox Press, 1994), pp. 177, 186.

112. Minturn, *supra* note 111, p. 173; Sahgal, *supra* note 23, p. 189; Vasudha Narayanan, "Hindu Perceptions of Auspiciousness and Sexuality," in *Women, Religion and Sexuality*, *supra* note 23, pp. 64, 67. *Ramayana's* powerful effect on role models is particularly apparent during the marriage ceremony, where the groom is regarded as representing Lord Rama, and the bride, Sita. See Lina M. Fruzzetti, *The Gift of a Virgin: Women, Marriage and Ritual in Bengali Society* (New Brunswick: Rutgers University Press, 1982), p. 13.

113. Thus, the women's organization of the RSS, see *infra* note 120, finds that "the basic principles and philosophy of women's life in India are quite different from those of men." Embree, *supra* note 104, p. 641.

114. In the myth, Sati becomes an ascetic like Siva and thereby wins him in marriage. Sati's father, disapproving of Siva as an unkempt ascetic hermit, holds an important sacrifice to which he invites all the top divinities except Siva. Sati confronts her father about this insult but is ignored, and so she kills herself to protest the insult to her husband. For an account of this epic as related here, see Minturn, *supra* note 111, p. 168.

115. See Narayanan, *supra* note 112, p. 67.

116. See Narayanan, *supra* note 112, pp. 65-67.

117. See Hawley, *supra* note 106, p. 82 (paragraph break suppressed, footnote omitted).

118. See *ibid.*, p. 81; Minturn, *supra* note 111, pp. 168-69. In European languages, the word *sati* is generally used to denote the religious practice of widow immolation rather than the woman herself, as it is used in Hindi.

119. See Embree, *supra* note 104, p. 641; see also Swami Dayananda Saraswati, *OM:*

Light of Truth or English Translation of the Satyarth Prakesh, trans. Chiranjiva Bharadwaja (Delhi: Bharat Mudranalaya, 1975), pp. 124-25 [hereinafter Dayananda, *Om*] (asserting that a wife should be subject to her husband's control). Fundamentalists argue that Hinduism is not based on individual rights and personal freedoms, but on community responsibilities. Minturn, *supra* note 111, p. 169; Young, *supra* note 6, pp. 121-22. Thus, women who follow in Sita's or Sati's steps are oriented to the community, not selfishly concerned with their independent freedoms. Hindu fundamentalists consistently require self-sacrifice and selflessness primarily from women for the benefit of men, however, and not the other way around. In this way, even the attractive concept of community responsibility is mustered in support of subordinating women.

120. See Embree, *supra* note 104, p. 641. Accordingly, women cannot join the RSS because the Hindu tradition of segregating the sexes prohibits joint activities in this context. See *ibid.;* Gold, *supra* note 103, p. 568. There is, however, a separate women's organization related to the RSS, the Rashtra Sevika Samiti. It promotes the realization of true Hindu womanhood, emphasizing "woman's chastity, purity, boldness, affection and alertness." See Embree, *supra* note 104, p. 641. The group rejects equal rights and economic independence for women because "this unnatural change in the attitude of women might have led to the disintegration of the family." See *ibid.* (quoting Rashtra Sevika Samiti, *An Organization of Hindu Women* [Nagpur: Sevika Prakashan, n.d.], p. 13).

121. Hinduism regards women as being more sexual than men, and although women's sexuality has some positive aspects it is nonetheless viewed as a source of temptation. Hindu belief is that women have stronger sex drives and psychic power *(shakti)* than men. See Minturn, *supra* note 111, pp. 201-8 (noting that husbands must satisfy women's sex drive or wives will be unfaithful, and women's sex drive drains men such that "women are an incurable disease and a barrier to a man's virtue"); Julia Leslie, "Sri and Jyestha: Ambivalent Role Models for Women," in *Roles and Rituals for Hindu Women,* ed. Julia Leslie (London: Pinter, 1991), pp. 107, 126 ("In general terms, all women [in certain Hindu myths] are portrayed as inherently impure, innately weak and wicked."); Dayananda, *OM, supra* note 119, pp. 27, 48 (explaining that men by avoiding looking at women — which promotes male lust — gain in strength); see also Narayanan, *supra* note 112, pp. 73-78.

122. See Minturn, *supra* note 111, p. 221.

123. See Sanjukta Gupta, "Women in the Saiva/Sakta Ethos," in *Roles and Rituals for Hindu Women, supra* note 121, pp. 193, 194-95.

124. Minturn, *supra* note 111, p. 202 ("Nothing is punished more severely than dishonor in women.").

125. Marriages are arranged for daughters at young ages, preferably before menstruation, to prevent premarital affairs. See Minturn, *supra* note 111, pp. 46-47, 203, 230; see also Dayananda, *OM, supra* note 119, pp. 90-92 (referring to Laws of Manu as his source for ages of marriage). The Hindu Marriage Act 1955 and Hindu Minority and Guardianship Act 1956, which raised minimum marriage ages to eighteen for women and twenty-one for men, have generally been ignored. Calman, *supra* note 93, p. 152. As recently as 1986, the Health Minister of the state of Uttar Pradesh in India admitted that there were a number of villages in Uttar Pradesh where all the girls over age eight were married. See *ibid.*

126. Dowry is a gift of property from the bride's family. Although ostensibly made to the bride, it is in reality a payment to the groom and groom's family as a condition for performance of the marriage. Young, *supra* note 6, p. 118. The amount of dowry depends upon the relative value (or, rather, lack of value) placed upon the girl, with detriments in her looks, education, and age "outweighed by an unusually high dowry." See Fruzzetti, *supra* note 112, p. 35. Dowry was originally a Brahmanical religious practice. With the spread of fundamentalism and reaffirmation of Hindu values through "Sanskritization" and Brahmanical values, dowry has been reinforced as an appropriate religious practice, Young, *supra* note 6, pp. 115-18, and has expanded into more communities and castes. Calman, *supra* note 93, p. 128.

127. See Calman, *supra* note 93, p. 126.

128. The Dowry Prohibition Act of 1961 was amended in 1984 and made giving or receiving dowry a substantive offense. Young, *supra* note 6, p. 118; Kirti Singh, "Obstacles to Women's Rights in India," in *Human Rights of Women*, ed. Rebecca J. Cook (Philadelphia: University of Pennsylvania Press, 1994), pp. 375, 392; Madhu Kishwar, "Towards More Just Norms for Marriage: Continuing the Dowry Debate," *Manushi* 53 (1989): 2-9.

129. Gupta, *supra* note 123, pp. 194-95; see Fruzzetti, *supra* note 112, p. 13; see also Calman, *supra* note 93, p. 124 n. 13 (observing that traditional Hindu family structure concentrates unchecked power in the hands of men, particularly husbands and male elders).

130. See Fruzzetti, *supra* note 112, p. 13. There is no apparent exception for the wife, as devotee, to refuse sex. Some authors argue that wives should agree with husbands in sexuality, but they acknowledge that, in practice, if a wife refuses sexual relations her husband may beat her or the elder woman of the house may make sure the wife becomes more obedient and accessible to her husband. Minturn, *supra* note 111, pp. 209-11; Renuka Singh, *The Womb of the Mind* (New Delhi: Vikas Pub. House, 1990), pp. 198-99, 201-2 (stating that Hindu women have the marital duty to submit to their husbands sexually and may be beaten if they do not).

131. See Minturn, *supra* note 111, p. 221.

132. Embree, *supra* note 104, pp. 625-26; see Gold, *supra* note 103, pp. 560-61.

133. *Purdah* is the cloistering of women by high-caste Hindus, with some aspects now popularized among other classes by "Sanskritization" and fundamentalism. See Minturn, *supra* note 111, pp. 73-93. Strict *purdah* requires a woman to cover her face in front of her husband and older men. *Purdah* also restricts a woman's travel alone, which otherwise would "contaminate" her character. See Dayananda, *OM, supra* note 119, pp. 128-29.

134. See Singh, *supra* note 130, pp. 198-99, 201-2; see also *supra* note 124.

135. Calman, *supra* note 93, pp. 124, 127; Govind Kelkar, "Violence Against Women: An Understanding of Responsibility for Their Lives," in *Third World/Second Sex* (vol. 2), *supra* note 50, pp. 179, 184. The Dowry Prohibition Act of 1961 was amended in 1984 and 1986 to make dowry death illegal. Indian Penal Code 304B; see Singh, *supra* note 128, p. 392. But dowry deaths continue to increase year by year. Calman, *supra* note 93, pp. 127-28; see Kelkar, *supra*, pp. 181-82. A typical week's newspaper reports about eight deaths of women that the authorities have evidence to link with dowry. Three typical examples that Calman reprints are:

"Haryana official victim of dowry": Mrs . . . Dala, a senior officer of the Haryana Government, died of burns in her in-laws' house on Tuesday night. . . . Her husband . . . was arrested on a charge of abetment to suicide. In her dying declaration, she stated she had been tortured by her husband and in-laws for not bringing enough dowry. (*Statesman,* 6 June 1986).

"Commits Suicide": A 28-year-old woman allegedly burnt herself to death because she could not stand the harassment by her husband. . . . The police have registered a case of abetment to suicide against the husband, an employee of the New Delhi government. (*Times of India,* 6 June 1986).

"Burnt for a Refrigerator": A young life was lost because of the rapacity of the in-laws. It began when the newly married Nirmal (24 years old) was unable to bring a refrigerator as part of her dowry. Nirmal was burnt to death. (*Statesman,* 11 June 1986).

Calman, *supra* note 93, p. 123. The government now estimates that in the decade since Calman's report dowry deaths have increased 170 percent, with 6,200 recorded last year. Molly Moore, "Consumerism Fuels Dowry-Death Wave," *Wash. Post,* 17 Mar. 1995, p. A35.

136. Calman, *supra* note 93, pp. 123, 127-28; Kelkar, *supra* note 135, p. 184.

137. Kelkar, *supra* note 135, pp. 181-82. One researcher in the Greater Bombay area examined all the coroner's death and postmortem certificates for these accidental deaths due to burns and concluded that authorities were reluctant to call dowry deaths murder and that not one certificate gave a "hint" as to how these "accidents" could have occurred. Calman, *supra* note 93, p. 127 (quoting Malini Karkal, "How the Other Half Dies in Bombay," *EPW,* 24 Aug. 1985).

138. Calman, *supra* note 93, pp. 124, 127.

139. See *supra* notes 116-19 and accompanying text.

140. Hawley, *supra* note 106, p. 81. It is not known how widespread the practice is since not all *sati*s are reported, given that the practice is illegal.

141. *Ibid.,* p. 81.

142. *Ibid.,* p. 81.

143. *Ibid.,* pp. 81-85.

144. *Ibid.,* pp. 87-91; Young, *supra* note 6, pp. 119-23.

145. Hawley, *supra* note 106, p. 100; see also Young, *supra* note 6, p. 121 (discussing Hindu scholars reexamining the history of *sati* in order to legitimate the practice).

146. Hawley, *supra* note 106, p. 83; see Mary Daly, *Gyn/Ecology: The Metaphysics of Radical Feminism* (Boston: Beacon, 1978), pp. 113-33. There are economic reasons why a family might want its widowed daughter-in-law to become a *sati*. This prevents her from inheriting her husband's property, which used to be prohibited under religious law but is now allowed under civil law. Young, *supra* note 6, p. 122. Also, families make money from visitors to *sati* shrines. Hawley, *supra* note 106, p. 84.

147. A widow's lack of virtue is regarded as responsible for her husband's death, but she may expiate this bad karma by becoming a *sati*. Minturn, *supra* note 111, p. 230; Narayanan, *supra* note 112, pp. 81-85. A widow who does not become a *sati* (most women) is perceived as having no further role in life because, when her husband dies, her repro-

ductive power, sexuality, and femaleness are regarded as being permanently removed since she gave them irrevocably to him upon marriage. See Minturn, *supra* note 111, p. 229; Narayanan, *supra* note 112, pp. 81-85; Fruzzetti, *supra* note 112, p. 103. Her in-laws' greatest fear is that she may become unchaste and "pregnant, *casting a possible shadow on the legitimacy of any previous children.*" Minturn, *supra* note 111, p. 229 (citing D. K. Stein, "Women to Burn: Suttee as a Normative Institution," *Signs: J. Women in Culture and Soc.* 4, no. 2 [1978]: 253-68) (emphasis added). For this reason, widows were forbidden to remarry and were to shave their heads in order to make them ugly so that they would remain chaste. Narayanan, *supra* note 112, pp. 81, 85. Widow remarriage was made legal in India, but it is rare for widows to remarry because remarriage is still regarded as highly dubious. See Fruzzetti, *supra* note 112, p. 103; Narayanan, *supra* note 112, pp. 83, 85; Vinaya Saijwani, "The Personal Laws of Divorce in India with a comment on Chaudry v. Chaudry," 11 *Women's Rts. L. Rep.* (1989): 49. Ironically, this religious prohibition against remarriage to protect the woman's chastity and dead husband's honor has encouraged young widows into prostitution as their only economic source of survival. Narayanan, *supra* note 112, p. 83. Despite legal reforms concerning remarriage, widows' position in society has actually worsened in recent times. See Young, *supra* note 6, p. 114; Minturn, *supra* note 111, pp. 221-22. Widowers, however, suffer no detriment from their status and have always been expected to remarry. There is not even a Hindi word for a widowed man. Fruzzetti, *supra* note 112, p. 104.

148. See generally Government of India, Ministry of Education and Social Welfare, *Towards Equality: Report of the Committee on the Status of Women in India* (1974). The rhetoric of traditional Hinduism offers no apologetics for its derogatory images of women and its regard for women as inferior. "In many important respects orthodox [Hindu] religious law . . . equated women with the lowest class of men." Frederick M. Smith, "Indra's Curse, Varuna's Noose, and the Suppression of Women in the Vedic Strauta Ritual," in *Roles and Rituals for Hindu Women, supra* note 121, pp. 17, 18-19.

149. *Government of India, supra* note 148, pp. 40-41.

150. See Young, *supra* note 6, p. 115.

151. Young, *supra* note 6, pp. 114, 125.

152. See Singh, *supra* note 128, pp. 375, 380-82; Saijwani, *supra* note 147, p. 41. Family laws in India are divided along religious lines, with Hindus covered by the civil Hindu laws, and Muslims and Christians each covered by their own respective religious laws. See *supra* note 93; Singh, *supra* note 128, pp. 378-79.

153. See Young, *supra* note 6, p. 114; Singh, *supra* note 128, pp. 380-81.

154. In the Sunni Arab world, The Muslim Brotherhood, founded in Egypt in 1928 by Hasan al-Banna, is one of the largest and most widespread of Muslim fundamentalist groups. See John O. Voll, "Fundamentalism in the Sunni Arab World: Egypt and the Sudan," in 1 *The Fundamentalism Project: Fundamentalisms Observed, supra* note 7, pp. 345, 360. It has member groups in Egypt, Jordan, Syria, Sudan, Palestine, Saudi Arabia, Kuwait, Qatar, and the United Arab Emirates. Voll, *supra*, pp. 359, 366, 390; Gehad Auda, "The Normalization of the Islamic Movement in Egypt from the 1970s to the Early 1990s," in 4 *The Fundamentalism Project: Accounting for Fundamentalisms, supra* note 16, pp. 374, 380. The Brotherhood meets the definition of fundamentalism. See Auda, *supra*, pp. 375, 379-81, 382-83, 386-89; James Piscatori, "Accounting for Islamic Fundamentalisms," in 4 *The Funda-*

mentalism Project: Accounting for Fundamentalisms, supra note 16, pp. 361, 363-64; Abdel Azim Ramadan, "Fundamentalist Influence in Egypt: The Strategies of the Muslim Brotherhood and the Takfir Groups," in 3 *The Fundamentalism Project: Fundamentalisms and the State, supra* note 11, pp. 152, 153; Voll, *supra*, p. 366. Al-Banna rejected Enlightenment principles of individual and intellectual freedom and any division between religion and politics. See Voll, *supra*, p. 360; see, e.g., Hasan Al-Banna, *Five Tracts of Hasan Al-Banna (1906-1949)*, trans. Charles Wendell (Berkeley: University of California Press, 1978), pp. 28-29, 75 [hereinafter Al-Banna, *Five Tracts*]; *Memoirs of Hasan Al-Banna*, trans. M. N. Shaikh (Karachi: International Islamic Publishers, 1981). He demanded that Egyptian law be reformed according to the Shari'ah (body of Islamic law derived primarily from the Qur'an) and that militaries be strengthened for Islamic *jihads* against nonbelievers. Auda, *supra*, p. 386.

In the early 1960s, Sayyid Qutb gave the Brotherhood new inspiration. See Voll, *supra*, pp. 370-71. His ideology aims to "re-create" Islamic life in totality such that divine sovereignty is paramount and the Shari'ah is followed; thus, prevailing social orders and political regimes must be overturned in the name of true Islam, violently if necessary. See Sayyid Qutb, *Milestones*, trans. unnamed (Burr Ridge: Am. Trust Publications, 1990), pp. 15-17, 23, 34-35, 43-62, 80-84; Auda, *supra*, pp. 377-78; Voll, *supra*, p. 372; see also Al-Banna, *Five Tracts, supra*, pp. 80, 82, 133-61. Qutb drew many of his ideas from the Islamic Pakistani fundamentalist Abul A'la Maududi, see Ramadan, *supra*, p. 156, who is discussed in detail below, see *infra* note 155. Qutb was tried and executed under the Nasser government, but his ideology continues to provide a base for Islamic fundamentalist movements. See Voll, *supra*, pp. 370, 372.

The Muslim Brotherhood has had various connections to violent *jihad* movements including the Jihad Organization, see Auda, *supra*, p. 382; Voll, *supra*, pp. 383, 388, 389; Courtney W. Howland, "Scepticism over Brotherhood's Protestations," Letter, *Fin. Times*, 8 Dec. 1995, which is regarded as responsible for the assassination of President Sadat in 1981. Auda, *supra*, p. 379. Such militant groups manifest particularly strong anti-Semitism and very limited, if any, tolerance for Christians; see Andrea B. Rugh, "Reshaping Personal Relations in Egypt," in 2 *The Fundamentalism Project: Fundamentalisms and Society, supra* note 40, pp. 151, 166-67; Auda, *supra*, pp. 387, 389, and are involved in violent activities, including the bombing of Christian churches. See Voll, *supra*, p. 389; Rugh, *supra*, p. 153. The Brotherhood fully entered legal organized politics in the 1980s and joined forces with the New Wafd party, with whom it won a number of seats in parliament. See Auda, *supra*, p. 387. Although certain factions of the Brotherhood have been viewed in recent times as less extreme than other Islamic fundamentalist groups, the Brotherhood is still strongly campaigning against the government and engaging in extremist tactics triggering arrests and reprisals. See James Whittington, "Mubarak Cracks Down on Islamists," *Fin. Times*, 24 Nov. 1995, p. 8; John Lancaster, "Fundamentalists Jailed Before Egypt's Election," *Wash. Post*, 24 Nov. 1995, pp. A31-A32; "Egypt Releases Islamic Activist," *Wash. Post*, 2 Nov. 1995, p. A26.

155. The Jama'at-i-Islami is a major group clearly meeting the definition of fundamentalism. See Rafiuddin Ahmed, "Redefining Muslim Identity in South Asia: The Transformation of the Jama'at-i-Islami," in 4 *The Fundamentalism Project: Accounting for Fundamentalisms, supra* note 16, pp. 669, 669; Ahmad, *supra* note 27, p. 462; Sajeda Amin

and Sara Hossain, "Women's Reproductive Rights and the Politics of Fundamentalism: A View from Bangladesh," 44 *Am. Univ. L. Rev.* 1319 (1995): 1336. The group was founded by Abul A'la Maududi, whose extensive writings, translated into many languages, provide excellent examples of fundamentalist rhetoric and theory and are central to Islamic fundamentalism today. See Ahmad, *supra* note 27, p. 464; see, e.g., Riffat Hassan, "An Islamic Perspective," in *Women, Religion and Sexuality, supra* note 23, pp. 93, 107-10; Hugh Roberts, "From Radical Mission to Equivocal Ambition: The Expansion and Manipulation of Algerian Islamism, 1979-1992," in 4 *The Fundamentalism Project: Accounting for Fundamentalisms, supra* note 16, pp. 428, 440 (noting that Algerian fundamentalism relies upon doctrines of Maududi and Qutb). Maududi founded Jama'at to give institutional support to his ideas for constructing an Islamic society where all civil institutions and state authority would be subordinate to divine law of the Qur'an and the Shari'ah. See Ahmed, *supra,* p. 674; Ahmad, *supra* note 27, p. 470. Religious scholars would exercise authority over all legislation to ensure that laws and practices were in accordance with the Qur'an and the Sunnah. See Ahmad, *supra* note 27, pp. 459, 463, 469; Ann E. Mayer, *Islam and Human Rights: Tradition and Politics* (Boulder: Westview, 1991), p. 26.

The Jama'at launched strong political campaigns to found Pakistan as an Islamic state. In the 1960s, it campaigned against reforms in family law, birth control, and the "modernizing" of Islam through acceptance of Western practices and Western sexual permissiveness. See Haeri, *supra* note 40, pp. 201-2; Ahmad, *supra* note 27, p. 474. The Jama'at continues its drive today for further "Islamization" in Pakistan, Bangladesh, and India. See Ahmed, *supra,* pp. 688-95; Ahmad, *supra* note 27, pp. 501-7; Amin and Hossain, *supra,* pp. 1336-40. Although Jama'at's own constitution forswears violence, it has been involved in a number of violent activities, and Maududi believed that *jihad* could be used to wage war against the infidels, including apostates and reformers. See Ahmed, *supra,* pp. 678-95.

156. Fundamentalism in the Shi'ite Muslim world is represented by various movements from Ayatollah Khomeini's Islamic movement in Iran to The Islamic Call and Islamic Fighters in Iraq and Battalions of Lebanese Resistance (AMAL). See Abdulaziz A. Sachedina, "Activist Shi'ism in Iran, Iraq, and Lebanon," in 1 *The Fundamentalism Project: Fundamentalisms Observed, supra* note 7, pp. 403, 403-4, 442, 446.

The Iranian post-revolutionary regime is considered a fundamentalist government. See Mahnaz Afkhami, "Women in Post-Revolutionary Iran: Aoo Feminist Perspective," in *In the Eye of the Storm: Women in Post-Revolutionary Iran,* ed. Mahnaz Afkhami and Erika Friedl (Syracuse: Syracuse University Press, 1994), pp. 5, 12; Haeri, *supra* note 40, pp. 187-89; Poya, *supra* note 23, pp. 141, 141-62; Sachedina, *supra,* pp. 403-7, 429. Khomeini's and subsequent post-revolutionary governments incorporate a strong reaction against modernization, particularly in the form of Western secularism based on Enlightenment principles, which they see as responsible for displacing the Qur'an and the Sunnah as the proper framework for societal institutions and laws. See Sachedina, *supra,* p. 411. Khomeini regarded the Shah's policies, particularly those aimed at reforms in family law and women's rights, as inimical to an Islamic society and thus they were first on his agenda for repeal. See *infra* notes 158, 178; Haeri, *supra* note 40, pp. 188, 190-93.

157. Indeed, many of the various fundamentalist groups maintain contact with each other. For example, the Jama'at-i-Islami of Bangladesh, India, and Pakistan, see *supra* note

155, the groups Dar-ul-Islam in Indonesia and Parti Islam Se-Malaysia in Malaysia, see Ahmad, *supra* note 27, pp. 458-59, and the groups Hizb-i-Islami of Afghanistan, the Islamic Movement of Algeria, the Jamiyat-al-Islah of Bahrain, the Islamic Tendency Society of Tunis, and the Rafah party of Turkey have all met together for conferences. *Ibid.,* p. 457.

158. See Abul A'La Maududi, *Purdah and the Status of Woman in Islam,* ed. and trans. Al-Ash 'ari (Lahore: Islamic Publications, 1972 [1939]) [hereinafter Maududi, *Purdah*], p. 2 ("[When] woman is raised to prominence . . . a storm of immorality and licentiousness follows in her wake. . . . She is actually reduced to the position of the Devil's agent, and . . . starts the degeneration of Mankind in general."); see also Al-Banna, *Five Tracts, supra* note 154, p. 26.

Marriages are arranged for girls at young ages in order to protect their chastity and honor. In a number of Islamic law states, the minimum age for girls for marriage is on average about fifteen. Jamil J. Nasir, *The Status of Women Under Islamic Law and Under Modern Islamic Legislation,* second ed. (Boston: Graham and Trotman, 1994), pp. 7-10 [hereinafter Nasir, *Status of Women*]. One of the first acts of the post-revolutionary Iranian government was lowering the age for marriage for girls with the aim of protecting their chastity. See Mayer, *supra* note 155, p. 130; Jane I. Smith, "Women In Islam," in *Today's Woman in World Religions, supra* note 6, pp. 303, 314. In rural areas the average age of brides is between thirteen and fifteen, but in certain parts of Iran 80 percent of wives had been married between the ages of nine and sixteen. Nasir, *Status of Women, supra,* p. 9.

159. See Syed Abul A'la Maududi, *Birth Control,* ed. and trans. Khurshid Ahmad and Misbahul Islam Faruqi (Lahore: Islamic Publications, 1987 [1943]), p. 16; Maududi, *Purdah, supra* note 158, pp. 39-72; Qutb, *supra* note 154, p. 83; Hassan, *supra* note 155, pp. 103, 108-9.

160. See Qutb, *supra* note 154, pp. 83, 119; S. Abul A'la Maududi, *The Meaning of the Qur'an,* vol. 4 (Delhi: Markazi Maktaba Islami, n.d. [1976]), p. 16; see also Maududi, *Birth Control, supra* note 159, p. 18.

161. See Rugh, *supra* note 154, pp. 158, 169-73 (discussing the Muslim Brotherhood); Haeri, *supra* note 40, pp. 183, 186, 188-95, 199, 201-4 (discussing Jama'at-i-Islami and post-revolutionary Iran); Ahmad, *supra* note 27, pp. 471-74 (discussing Jama'at-i-Islami); Amin and Hossain, *supra* note 155, pp. 1336-42 (discussing Jama'at-i-Islami).

162. Maududi, *Purdah, supra* note 158, p. 121; Ahmad, *supra* note 36, p. 34 (Khurshid Ahmad has been a translator of Maududi's and is a contemporary follower in Maududi's tradition); cf. Iqbal, *supra* note 36, pp. 102-5 (noting that a woman may not be the head of a family, much less the leader of a state, since this is inconsistent with her duties to care for her children and home).

163. Maududi, *Purdah, supra* note 158, pp. 121-23 (noting that women are naturally "submissive and impressionable" and that "in order to maintain the family system and save it from confusion some one must be entrusted with necessary authority. . . . Such a one can only be the man. For the member whose mental and physical state becomes unstable time and again during menstruation and pregnancy cannot be expected to use such authority with wisdom and discretion. . . . To maintain this division [of labor between husband and wife] there must be some safeguards provided in the social system . . ."); see also Azizah Y. al-Hibri, "A Comparative Study of Certain Egyptian, Syrian, Moroccan and Tunisian Marriage Laws," 4 *Int'l Rev. of Comp. Pub. Pol'y* 227 (1992): 231.

164. Maududi, *Purdah, supra* note 158, p. 148; S. Abul A'la Maududi, *The Meaning of the Qur'an*, vol. 2 (Delhi: Markazi Maktaba Islami, 1971), p. 325 n. 57 [hereinafter Maududi, *The Meaning of the Qur'an* (vol. 2)]; Hassan, *supra* note 155, pp. 110, 114; see also Mayer, *supra* note 155, pp. 131-32 (discussing examples of inferior status assigned to women under Iranian regime of Khomeini). Contemporary writers try to avoid this rhetoric and instead declare that the issue of equality is not relevant to the Islamic context. See Ahmad, *supra* note 36, pp. 34-35.

165. See Maududi, *The Meaning of the Qur'an* (vol. 2), *supra* note 164, pp. 321, 325 nn. 56-59 ("Men are the managers of the affairs of women because Allah has made the one superior to the other. . . . Virtuous women are, therefore, obedient; they guard their rights carefully in their absence under the care and watch of Allah."); Maududi, *Purdah, supra* note 158, pp. 148-49; see Ahmad, *supra* note 36, p. 34.

166. See Maududi, *Purdah, supra* note 158, p. 153 ("Just as a married woman has to obey and be looked after by her husband, so an unmarried woman has to obey and be looked after by the responsible men of her family.").

167. See Iqbal, *supra* note 36, p. 100 ("If he orders, she obeys him."); Huda Khattab, *The Muslim Woman's Hand Book* (London: Ta-Ha, 1993), pp. 40-41; John L. Esposito, *Women in Muslim Family Law* (Syracuse: Syracuse University Press, 1982), p. 23; Maududi, *Purdah, supra* note 158, p. 153; Wael B. Hallaq, "Islamic Response to Contraception-Fact Pattern VI.B., Symposium on Religious Law: Roman Catholic, Islamic, and Jewish Treatment of Familial Issues, Including Education, Abortion, *In Vitro* Fertilization, Prenuptial Agreements, Contraception, and Marital Fraud," 16 *Loy. L.A. Int'l & Comp. L.J.* (1993): 79 ("[I]n matters as relate to family life, the husband's wishes override those of the wife.").

168. See Khattab, *supra* note 167, pp. 40-41; Esposito, *supra* note 167, p. 23; Hallaq, *supra* note 167, p. 79. According to Rugh, a study of correspondence to the Egyptian *Islamic Banner* demonstrates fundamentalist views "that husbands have indisputable right to sex in the marriage relation. A writer explained to a reader that the Qur'an says women are a tilth for you to cultivate, so go to your tilth as ye will; in sum it is forbidden for a man to copulate with his wife during menstruation, but apart from that it is his right and privilege to penetrate her as long as it occurs through the proper channel." Rugh, *supra* note 154, p. 171. For example, during any fast a woman must refuse her husband's sexual advances. Khattab, *supra* note 167, p. 5. Therefore, a married woman may not observe any of Islam's optional fasts without her husband's permission, since he may prefer to safeguard his right of sexual access to his wife and refuse her permission to fast. Maududi, *Purdah, supra* note 158, pp. 146-47; Khattab, *supra* note 167, pp. 5, 40-41.

169. Rugh, *supra* note 154, p. 170; Maududi, *The Meaning of the Qur'an* (vol. 2), *supra* note 164, p. 321 (footnotes omitted) ("As for those women whose defiance you have cause to fear, admonish them and keep them apart from your beds and beat them."). Maududi explains that "there are some women who do not mend their ways without a beating." Maududi, *The Meaning of the Qur'an* (vol. 2), *supra* note 164, p. 325 n. 59.

170. See Maududi, *Purdah, supra* note 158, pp. 163-216. (Maududi's book is translated from Urdu into English and Arabic. The Arabic term for *purdah* is *hejab*. *Purdah*, in fact, is the term for the segregation of women in Hinduism.) *Hejab* is justified as a "wide-ranging system which protects the family and closes those avenues that lead towards illicit sex or even indiscriminate contact between the sexes in society." Ahmad, *supra* note 36, p. 35.

Hejab restricts women far more severely than men, on the ground that women's sexuality presents the danger and must be controlled. See Hassan, *supra* note 155, pp. 118-22. Some Egyptian fundamentalists state that unattractive women need not cover themselves because they will not cause men immoral thoughts, whereas other Egyptian fundamentalists find that "the whole of a woman's body is a pudendum except her face and hands." Rugh, *supra* note 154, p. 172; see Khattab, *supra* note 167, pp. 14-16 (noting that "External" *hejab* requires that woman's dress cover whole head and body, including neck, forearms, ears, legs; clothing should be loose, thick enough to conceal skin, not perfumed, not resemble men's clothing, not bright colors, not similar to clothing of non-Muslims, not dress of vanity, not be an adornment that would attract men's attention); Iqbal, *supra* note 36, pp. 52-59. (*Hejab* requires total segregation of the sexes and requires that woman is completely covered and concealed if she leaves her house so as to deter anti-social elements and not to attract attention.)

171. See Maududi, *Purdah, supra* note 158, pp. 25, 120-22, 154, 161; Haleh Esfandiari, "The Majles and Women's Issues in the Islamic Republic of Iran," in *In the Eye of the Storm: Women in Post-Revolutionary Iran, supra* note 156, pp. 61, 71.

172. See Iqbal, *supra* note 36, p. 25; Nasir, *Status of Women, supra* note 158, pp. 66-67 (discussing Iraqi law that woman loses right to maintenance if she works without her husband's permission); Sima Pakzad, "Appendix I: The Legal Status of Women in the Family in Iran," in *In the Eye of the Storm: Women in Post-Revolutionary Iran, supra* note 156, pp. 169, 174 (noting that under Iranian Islamic law the husband may prevent his wife from working if he can prove that occupation is against family interests).

173. Maududi, *Purdah, supra* note 158, pp. 14-15, 68. "Why should a woman who wins her own bread, supports herself economically and does not depend on anyone for security and maintenance, remain faithfully attached to one man only for the sake of satisfying sexual desires? Why should she be prepared to subject herself to so many moral and legal curbs to shoulder the responsibilities of family life?" *Ibid.*, p. 14. For a similar attitude in Buddhist and Christian fundamentalism, see *supra* notes 56 (Buddhism) and 92 (Christianity) and accompanying text.

174. For example, a daughter inherits half the share of a son. Maududi, *Purdah, supra* note 158, p. 154 n. 1; Ahmad, *supra* note 36, p. 35.

175. See Khalida Messaoudi, for "Oum Ali," Algeria, in *Center for Women's Global Leadership, Testimonies of the Global Tribunal on Violations of Women's Human Rights at the United Nations World Conference on Human Rights, Vienna, June 1993* (1994), p. 76. Messaoudi, an Algerian, testified to the case of Oum Ali, who was too terrorized to testify in Vienna. Oum Ali was divorced, abandoned by her husband, and living with seven children in an Algerian town. The fundamentalists regarded her as a menace to the morality of the town, came into her home, threw heating oil on the bed, and set fire to it in order to purify the house. The house was burned down, and one child was burned to death. Twelve men were arrested, prompting demonstrations by fundamentalists demanding their release. They did not deny the crime, but "in their minds . . . , they have the right to persecute any person — particularly women who are alone, who they believe are representatives of Satan, representatives of danger and immorality." *Ibid.*, p. 77.

176. Fundamentalist interpretations of the Shari'ah are being increasingly imposed and enforced in a number of countries: Algeria, see Marie-Aimée Hélie-Lucas, "Bound

and Gagged by the Family Code," in *Third World/Second Sex* (vol. 2), *supra* note 50, pp. 3, 3-15; Bangladesh, see *supra* note 155; Egypt, see *supra* note 154; Iran, see *supra* note 156; Iraq, see Hélie-Lucas, *supra* note 6, pp. 55, 61; Pakistan, see *supra* note 155; Rashida Patel, "Challenges Facing Women in Pakistan," in *Ours by Right, supra* note 6, pp. 32, 32-39; Sudan, see Asma Mohamed Abdel Halim, "Challenges to the Application of International Women's Human Rights in the Sudan," in *Human Rights of Women, supra* note 128, pp. 397, 399-405. See also Ann E. Mayer, "The Fundamentalist Impact on Law, Politics, and Constitutions in Iran, Pakistan, and the Sudan," in 3 *The Fundamentalism Project: Fundamentalisms and the State, supra* note 11, pp. 110, 110-52; Hélie-Lucas, *supra* note 6, pp. 54-59 (discussing Islamization in several countries). This has been accomplished by either passing state laws or enforcing state laws through the incorporation of a fundamentalist interpretation of the Shari'ah. These interpretations may well echo conservative Islamic codes, see Ahmad, *supra* note 27, p. 463; al-Hibri, *supra* note 163, p. 239, which are difficult to reform due to fundamentalist pressure.

177. Violent activity ranges from Islamic fundamentalist groups smuggling "surface-to-air missiles, 80mm mortars, hand-held rocket launchers and M-16 rifles" into the Philippines from Pakistan for military raids on Christian towns in the south of the country, see Edward Luce, "Pakistan, Philippines to combat terrorism," *Fin. Times,* 29/30 Apr. 1995, p. 3, to violently harassing Muslim women who do not conform to their "natural" roles, see *supra* note 175 (burning down a single woman's house). Fundamentalist activity in Egypt is having a general intimidating effect. See Raymond Stock, "How Islamist Militants put Egypt on Trial," *Fin. Times,* 4/5 Mar. 1995, p. III (discussing fundamentalist violence in Egypt including the stabbing of Nobel prize–winning author, Naguib Mahfouz). At least twenty-nine women have been killed in Algeria for protesting laws placing limitations on women. IWRAW, *The Women's Watch* 8, no. 1 (June 1994): 2. Individual protests continue in Iran. Dr. Darabi was dismissed from her job as a physician for refusing to wear a veil, and continued to be harassed when she attempted to set up in private practice. Her husband refused to allow her to leave Iran. She set herself on fire in a public square in Tehran to protest oppression of women in Iran. IWRAW, *The Women's Watch* 8, no. 1 (June 1994): 2.

178. See *supra* notes 170-72 and accompanying text. In the context of obedience laws, fundamentalist doctrine overlaps with conservative doctrine. Fundamentalists, however, fight to prevent reform of conservative obedience laws, to strengthen such laws, or to repeal laws in conflict with the obedience laws. For example, in Iran, one of Khomeini's first acts was to nullify the Iranian Family Protection Act which had been a reform to improve women's status and rights during marriage and divorce. Mayer, *supra* note 155, p. 130.

179. The extent of the father's control is particularly clear in his role as marriage guardian *(wali)*. If the father is dead, another male relative, or, if there is none, a judge (who is male) becomes marriage guardian. Under guardianship laws, a woman cannot contract her own marriage, even if she possesses full legal capacity. Nasir, *Status of Women, supra* note 158, pp. 10-12 (discussing laws of Morocco, Algeria, Iraq, Jordan, and Syria); Halim, *supra* note 176, pp. 400-402 (discussing Sudan's Islamization and subsequent passage of Personal Law for Muslims Act of 1991 requiring *wali* for women).

180. See, e.g., Moroccan Code, Bk. 1, Title 6, art. 36, clause 2; Algerian Code, Bk. 1, title 1, Ch. 4, art. 39, Clause 1; Tunisian Code, art. 23; Jordanian Code, art. 32; Sudan Personal

Law for Muslims Act of 1991, in Halim, *supra* note 176, p. 402; see al-Hibri, *supra* note 163, pp. 238-39. Laws of obedience also apply in Iran and Pakistan. See Haeri, *supra* note 40, pp. 181, 185-86.

181. This concept of a "rebellious" wife is similar to the Christian concept, see *supra* note 88 and accompanying text, and the Jewish concept, see *infra* notes 215, 218-20. There are, however, greater legal ramifications and punishments for women based on the concept of a "rebellious" wife in present-day Islam and Judaism.

182. See, e.g., Nasir, *Status of Women, supra* note 158, pp. 66-70 (discussing laws of Iraq, Jordan, Syria, Egypt, Kuwait); Jamil J. Nasir, *The Islamic Law of Personal Status* (Boston: Graham and Trotman, 1990), pp. 129-30 [hereinafter Nasir, *Islamic Law of Personal Status*]; Sudan Personal Law for Muslims Act of 1991, in Halim, *supra* note 176, p. 402; Hallaq, *supra* note 167, p. 80. A wife loses her right to maintenance if she travels unaccompanied by her husband, and conversely is bound to travel with her husband to wherever he wishes as long as it is safe — otherwise she loses her maintenance. Nasir, *Status of Women, supra* note 158, p. 68 (citing Jordan art. 37; Iraq art. 2[3]; Syria art. 70; Kuwait art. 90).

183. See Pakzad, *supra* note 172, p. 172; Nasir, *Status of Women, supra* note 158, p. 67.

184. See Nasir, *Status of Women, supra* note 158, p. 68; Nasir, *Islamic Law of Personal Status, supra* note 182, pp. 129-30.

185. See Nasir, *Status of Women, supra* note 158, pp. 64-65, 66 (footnote omitted); Sudan Personal Law for Muslims Act of 1991, in Halim, *supra* note 176, p. 402. This is the law in countries which adopt Shari'ah by incorporation, such as Saudi Arabia, as it is in countries which have enacted the provision as statute, such as Egypt, Jordan, Iraq, Kuwait, and Syria. See, e.g., Nasir, *Status of Women, supra* note 158, p. 65 (citing Egypt 25/1920, art. 1; Jordan art. 67; Iraq art. 23; Kuwait art. 74; and Syria art. 72/1); Sudan Personal Law for Muslims Act of 1991, in Halim, *supra* note 176, p. 402.

186. See Nasir, *Status of Women, supra* note 158, pp. 66-67.

187. Hallaq, *supra* note 167, p. 80. For example, a wife who disobeys her husband by using contraceptives violates his right to her obedience and he may "legally enjoin" her from using contraceptives. *Ibid.* Happily, in Kuwait "no obedience order obtained by the husband against her shall be implemented using force, the only penalty of noncompliance thereto being the loss of her maintenance." Nasir, *Status of Women, supra* note 158, p. 68 (citing Kuwait art. 88).

188. Women's chastity is so important to men that some states even provide by statute the husband's "right" that the wife shall guard her chastity. See Nasir, *Status of Women, supra* note 158, p. 41 (discussing Moroccan law).

189. Hélie-Lucas, *supra* note 6, p. 55. Stoning to death is a punishment for women's adultery under fundamentalist interpretation of the *Hudd* punishments. See, e.g., Patel, *supra* note 176, pp. 32-33, 36-37 (discussing application of *Hudd* punishments for adultery in Pakistan); see also Hélie-Lucas, *supra* note 6, pp. 58-59. In Iran there is a law that regulates the size of the stone with which the woman is to be killed. Messaoudi, *supra* note 175, pp. 76, 78-79. It should not be too large because then she would be killed too quickly, nor too small because then she would not be killed. *Ibid.*, p. 79. Amnesty International reported on the stoning of Saraya in Iran: "Saraya was buried up to her shoulders. . . . The stones were flying, her head and her chest were reduced to raw flesh. Using all of his

strength, the man hits her skull many times, her brain is scattered on the ground, and a big cry of joy arises, 'Allah o Akbar.'" *Ibid.*, p. 78.

190. See IWRAW, *The Women's Watch* 8, no. 3 (Dec. 1994): 4 (noting that this law was passed by the "autonomous Kurdistan government" and that "550 women have been murdered since the establishment of the new government.").

191. In general, husbands may divorce their wives at will and without court order (the right of *talaq*). See Nasir, *Status of Women, supra* note 158, pp. 74-76; Hélie-Lucas, *supra* note 6, p. 59. *Talaq* is the unilateral declaration of a husband divorcing and repudiating his wife and can be performed by word of mouth or in writing. It is legally binding. For statutory enactment of *talaq*, see, e.g., Syria art. 87/2, Morocco art. 44, Jordan art. 87, Iraq art. 34, and Kuwait art. 104; Sudan Personal Law for Muslims Act of 1991, in Halim, *supra* note 176, p. 403. Other Muslim states incorporate Shari'ah law with its provisions of *talaq*. Fundamentalists have interpreted these to allow the husband to make an *unwitnessed* declaration of repudiation, with no evidence that he has repudiated other than his own word. See Nasir, *Status of Women, supra* note 158, p. 79 n. 7. If the woman divorced by unwitnessed repudiation now remarries, her ex-husband, either for revenge or financial reasons, may later deny he pronounced *talaq*, at which point the woman can be tried for adultery (with the new husband) for which she risks being stoned to death. See Hélie-Lucas, *supra* note 6, p. 59. For example, in Pakistan, the state allows the ex-husband to retain control over his ex-wife by granting him the sole responsibility of filing a divorce notice of *talaq* with the state. In a case where the husband had pronounced *talaq*, failed "allegedly purposefully" to file the divorce notice, and subsequently notified the police of his wife's remarriage, the court found the ex-wife and her new husband guilty of adultery and fornication and ordered them flogged and imprisoned for seven years. See *Shera v. State*, P.L.D. 1982 F.S.C. 229 (1982); see generally Mark C. Hulbert, *Islamization of the Law in Pakistan: Developments in Criminal Law and the Regulation of Banking* (unpublished paper on file with author).

A wife may be able to get a divorce if she can get her husband's consent by giving him consideration *(khula)* for her freedom. See Nasir, *Status of Women, supra* note 158, pp. 84-87. Often this amounts to the wife forfeiting the dowry due to her on marriage. See also *ibid.*, p. 87. Otherwise, the grounds of divorce for a wife are very narrow and limited. See Nasir, *Status of Women, supra* note 158, pp. 92-101; Sudan Personal Law for Muslims Act of 1991, in Halim, *supra* note 176, p. 403.

192. Nasir, *Status of Women, supra* note 158, pp. 108-11, 113. The wife is generally not entitled to maintenance at all if she is divorced for disobedience. *Ibid.*

193. The husband may make the *talaq* irrevocable by making his pronouncement of repudiation three times with three *iddat* periods. See Nasir, *Status of Women, supra* note 158, pp. 82-84 (citing Egypt Act No. 25/1929 art. 3; Sudan Sharia Circular no. 41/1935 art. 3; Syria art. 92; Morocco art. 51; Iraq art. 37/2; Jordan art. 85; Kuwaiti art. 109.)

194. Nasir, *Status of Women, supra* note 158, p. 112.

195. Halim, *supra* note 176, p. 401. The Muslim Brotherhood members of the Egyptian Parliament also demand the legal and universal imposition of fundamentalist Islamic dress on women. See Auda, *supra* note 154, pp. 387-88.

196. Amnesty International USA, "Sudan, Amnesty Action" (Winter 1995): 1, 3.

197. See Haeri, *supra* note 40, p. 188. Veiling in Iran should be understood in the con-

text of its political significance. Some Iranian middle-class women donned the veil during the Revolution to show solidarity with working-class women, see Nayereh Tohidi, "Gender and Islamic Fundamentalism: Feminist Politics in Iran," in *Third World Women and the Politics of Feminism*, ed. Chandra Mohanty et. al. (Bloomington: Indiana University Press, 1991), pp. 251, 251-52, as a reaction against Shah Reza Pahlavi's repressive regime, which had prohibited veiling. But recognizing the political and historical context of voluntary veiling should not obfuscate the structural oppression of women manifested by fundamentalist interpretations of *hejab* requiring mandatory veiling. See generally Afkhami, *supra* note 156, pp. 17-18 ("Western feminists . . . appear as self-deprecating defenders of atrociously anti-feminist conditions, when they explain away oppressive behavior in the developing world on grounds of cultural relativism.").

198. See Haeri, *supra* note 40, p. 190. The "veil" is defined differently by different Muslim fundamentalist groups, but Khomeini's regime interpreted it to mean at least a long overcoat, pants, and a dark-colored scarf. See *ibid.*, p. 188 n. 44.

199. See "Baha'is Calm in Centre of Storm," *Toronto Star*, 22 Jan. 1994, p. L15; U.S. State Department, *Country Reports on Human Rights Practices for 1992* (1993): 1001; United Nations Economic and Social Council, Commission on Human Rights, 48th Sess., *Question of the Violation of Human Rights and Fundamental Freedoms in Any Part of the World, with Particular Reference to Colonial and Other Dependent Countries and Territories: Report on the Human Rights Situation in the Islamic Republic of Iran by the Special Representative of the Commission on Human Rights, Mr. Reynaldo Galindo Pohl, Pursuant to Commission Resolution 1991/82*, UN Doc. E/CN. 4/1992/34, 2 Jan. 1992, ¶190, p. 34; U.S. State Department, *Country Reports on Human Rights Practices for 1990* (1991): 1454, 1457; U.S. State Department, *Country Reports on Human Rights Practices for 1987* (1988): 1168; see, e.g., *Fisher v. I.N.S.*, 37 F.3d 1371 (9th Cir. 1994) (involving Iranian woman stopped by police for some strands of her hair outside her veil). An Iranian woman fled to Canada as a refugee after being fired from her job and being punished with thirty-five lashes for not wearing a veil within the privacy of her own home. Joanna Kerr, "The Context and the Goal," in *Ours by Right*, *supra* note 6, pp. 3, 5.

200. Hélie-Lucas, *supra* note 6, p. 59.

201. *Ibid.*

202. See Ann E. Mayer, "Islam and the State," 12 *Cardozo L. Rev.* 1015 (1991): 1027; see also al-Hibri, *supra* note 163, p. 241.

203. The term *haredim* has come to denote essentially the radical segment of Orthodox Jews (Ultra-Orthodox), where "Orthodox" denotes Jews who observe the Torah and its commandments, and interpret those commandments to require a traditional way of life punctiliously attached to ritual. Samuel C. Heilman and Menachem Friedman, "Religious Fundamentalism and Religious Jews: The Case of the Haredim," in 1 *The Fundamentalism Project: Fundamentalisms Observed, supra* note 7, pp. 197-99; see Avishai Margalit, "Israel: The Rise of the Ultra-Orthodox," *N.Y. Rev. Books*, 9 Nov. 1989, p. 38. Orthodoxy primarily divides into two groups, Hasidim and Misnagdim. Heilman and Friedman, *supra*, p. 208. The Hasidim began as followers of a spiritual and mystical movement in Eastern Europe that emphasized the legal authority of particular rabbis. Heilman and Friedman, *supra*, pp. 206-7; Jacob Neusner, "Judaism in the World and in America," in *World Religions in America: An Introduction, supra* note 111, pp. 151, 168. The Misnagdim (Hebrew "opponents")

emphasized rabbinic law and Talmudic learning and opposed Hasidic practices and mysticism. Heilman and Friedman, *supra*, p. 209. The two groups developed in ways that now make them quite similar with respect to the outside world, however: They measure their religious commitment in terms of fidelity to Jewish law, *ibid.*, p. 217; they share "an animosity to the culture of the non-observant and assimilation-oriented Jews," *ibid.*, p. 211; and they believe that "Jewish life and tradition was a superior alternative to anything that non-Jewish contemporary culture could offer," *ibid.*, p. 213; see Margalit, *supra*, p. 38 (discussing "halakhic fundamentalists").

204. The Hasidim and Misnagdim oppose Zionism, the notion of a secular Jewish state. See Heilman and Friedman, *supra* note 203, p. 234; Izhak England, "The Relationship between Religion and State in Israel," in *Jewish Law in Ancient and Modern Israel*, ed. and intro. Haim H. Cohn (New York: Ktav Pub. House, 1971), pp. 168, 172, 174-75. These anti-Zionist *haredim* include such groups as the Lubovitch Hasidim (existing in Brooklyn and Israel) and other Hasidic and Misnagdim groups which meet the definition of fundamentalism. See Heilman and Friedman, *supra* note 203, pp. 204-5, 212, 216-18, 226, 232, 257; Yuval-Davis, *supra* note 24, pp. 206, 209-10; Charles S. Liebman, "Jewish Fundamentalism and the Israeli Polity," in 3 *The Fundamentalism Project: Fundamentalisms and the State, supra* note 11, pp. 68, 68-69; Ehud Sprinzak, "Three Models of Religious Violence: The Case of Jewish Fundamentalism in Israel," in 3 *The Fundamentalism Project: Fundamentalisms and the State, supra* note 11, pp. 462, 469, 463-69; Michael Rosenak, "Jewish Fundamentalism in Israeli Education," in 2 *The Fundamentalism Project: Fundamentalisms and Society, supra* note 40, pp. 374, 380-81; Ian Lustick, *For the Land and the Lord: Jewish Fundamentalism in Israel* (New York: Council on Foreign Relations Press, 1988); Lawrence, *supra* note 10, pp. 120-52; Margalit, *supra* note 203, p. 38; cf. Harris, *supra* note 20, pp. 142-66 (arguing that the term "fundamentalist" is inappropriate for these Jewish groups since they have always had these characteristics). Some *haredim* have more recently developed Zionist concerns and have served as a basis for yet more extreme groups, such as those associated with Rabin's assassination. See "Raised in a Pious Family, Rabin's Killer Was Soldier, Scholar," *Wash. Post,* 12 Nov. 1995, p. A30; Avi Machlis and Julian Ozanne, "Act Spotlights Growing Culture of Extremism," *Fin. Times,* 6 Nov. 1995, p. 2.

205. Gush Emunim (GE) meets the definition of fundamentalism. See Samuel C. Heilman, "Quiescent and Active Fundamentalisms: The Jewish Cases," in 4 *The Fundamentalism Project: Accounting for Fundamentalisms, supra* note 16, pp. 173, 174-75; Liebman, *supra* note 204, pp. 69, 82; Aran, *supra* note 15, pp. 265-344; Yuval-Davis, *supra* note 24, pp. 207-8; Sprinzak, *supra* note 204, pp. 469-77; but see Rosenak, *supra* note 204, p. 402 (arguing that although GE has strong fundamentalist tendencies, it is "questionable" to identify it as fundamentalist within Judaism). Zvi Yehuda Kook (Kook the Younger) was the founding religious ideologue for the movement, which in more recent times has been headed by Moshe Levinger. Aran, *supra* note 15, pp. 266, 268; Yuval-Davis, *supra* note 24, p. 207; see Sprinzak, *supra* note 204, p. 470. In contrast with the *haredim,* GE is Zionist, see Sprinzak, *supra* note 204, p. 470; Aran, *supra* note 15, p. 268; Yuval-Davis, *supra* note 24, p. 207, and supports the Israeli militia as a vital religious and spiritual obligation. Aran, *supra* note 15, p. 268 (citing Rabbi Zvi Yehuda Kook, "Psalm XIX to the State of Israel," in A. Ben-Ami, *Everything: The Book of the Whole Land of Israel* (Tel Aviv: ha-Tenu'ah le-ma'an Erets Yisra'el ha-shalema be-shituf 'im hotsa'at s. Fridman, 1977)). GE's goal is to in-

crease Israeli sovereignty over all the "Land of Israel within its maximum biblical boundaries (from the Euphrates River in Iraq to the Brook of Egypt)." Aran, *supra* note 15, p. 268; see Sprinzak, *supra* note 204, pp. 469-70. GE is notorious for its lawless activism, especially: its illegal activities in settlement in the occupied territories, see Sprinzak, *supra* note 204, pp. 469-71; Yuval-Davis, *supra* note 24, pp. 207-8; Aran, *supra* note 15, pp. 267-68; its acts of vandalism and harassment of the Arab population; see Sprinzak, *supra* note 204, pp. 472-73; Aran, *supra* note 15, p. 267 and n. 26; its killing of a significant number of Palestinians, see Aran, *supra* note 15, p. 285; and its resisting any peace accord with Arabs. Aran, *supra* note 15, p. 287 and n. 27. For an account of GE's violent activities, see Sprinzak, *supra* note 204, pp. 473-77.

206. See Rosenak, *supra* note 204, pp. 381, 389, 406; Heilman and Friedman, *supra* note 203, p. 198. With respect to GE, see Aran, *supra* note 15, pp. 277 and n. 19, 281, 336.

207. See Heilman and Friedman, *supra* note 203, pp. 216-17 (discussing *haredim*); see also Rosenak, *supra* note 204, pp. 387-88. For GE, preventing moral decay requires segregating the sexes in education and entertainment from early childhood. See Aran, *supra* note 15, pp. 306, 313. Fundamentalists have justified their attempts to block participation by women in local religious councils and in the electoral college (which designates the Ashkenazic Chief Rabbi) on the basis of the threat to their morality if they had "to sit in the same room and discuss things at the same table with females who were not their wives." Levinson, *supra* note 23, p. 60.

208. Although doctrine formally requires a woman's consent to marriage, see Haim H. Cohn, *Human Rights in Jewish Law* (New York: Ktav Pub. House, 1984), p. 170; Blu Greenberg, "Female Sexuality and Bodily Functions in the Jewish Tradition," in *Women, Religion and Sexuality, supra* note 23, pp. 1, 8, in practice most girls in fundamentalist communities have their marriages arranged at an early age. See Yuval-Davis, *supra* note 24, pp. 199, 217. Early arranged marriages help protect a girl's chastity. This concern is reflected in marriage contracts, which normally provide for higher alimony for a virgin bride than for a nonvirgin bride. Greenberg, *supra*, p. 36.

209. Fundamentalists tend to obfuscate the subordinate position of women in the fundamentalist legal system, see Yuval-Davis, *supra* note 24, pp. 213-20; see also Saul Berman, "The Status of Women in Halakhic Judaism," in *The Jewish Woman: New Perspectives, supra* note 25, pp. 114, 116 (describing the "attempt through homiletics and scholasticism to transform problems into solutions and to reinterpret discrimination to be beneficial"), but the underlying rhetoric stresses the "natural" differences between the sexes and insinuates that women are inferior. See Yuval-Davis, *supra* note 24, pp. 211-14, 217; Becker, *supra* note 24, p. 464; Levinson, *supra* note 23, p. 50; Berman, *supra*, pp. 115-17.

210. Greenberg, *supra* note 208, pp. 1, 9; see Harris, *supra* note 20, pp. 163-64.

211. See Irwin H. Haut, *Divorce in Jewish Law and Life* (New York: Sepher-Hermon Press, 1984), p. 6; Moshe Meiselman, *Jewish Woman in Jewish Law* (New York: Ktav Pub. House, 1978), p. 83; Greenberg, *supra* note 208, p. 9 n. 33. His obligations are spelled out in a marriage contract *(ketubah)*. See Haut, *supra*, p. 7; Meiselman, *supra*, p. 88. These fundamentalist norms of marriage and divorce and property rights are based on "traditional" Jewish law. See Harris, *supra* note 20, pp. 163-4, 165.

212. See Yuval-Davis, *supra* note 24, pp. 199-200, 214; Greenberg, *supra* note 208, p. 9 n. 33. In practice, the Jewish Israeli marriage pattern across cultural and social lines con-

forms to the religious one as childcare is almost exclusively the wife's concern, except for discipline of children, which is left to the husband; the husband, as head of the family, controls the family budget. See Lesley Hazleton, *Israeli Women* (New York: Simon and Schuster, 1977), p. 174.

213. Haut, *supra* note 211, p. 6; see Cohn, *supra* note 208, p. 169 (noting that all property of the wife vests in her husband during marriage). Meiselman argues that as a wife may waive certain benefits in order to be financially independent, criticism of inequality in this context is unwarranted. Meiselman, *supra* note 211, p. 82. This ignores, however, the power of the structural norm that the wife would have to opt out of, a norm based on her being financially dependent. Evidence of the strength of the structural norm is that the rabbinical courts in Israel continue to adjudicate certain matters in accordance with Jewish law, such as enforcing the husband's right to income from his wife's property during marriage, even though the High Court of Justice opines that the matters are no longer the law of Israel. See Ariel Rosen-Zvi, "Forum Shopping Between Religious and Secular Courts (and Its Impact on the Legal System)," 9 *Tel Aviv Univ. Stud. L.* 347 (1989): 356 and n. 28.

214. See *infra* notes 216-17 and accompanying text.

215. See *infra* notes 218-20 and accompanying text.

216. Cohn, *supra* note 208, pp. 171-72; see Philippa Strum, "Women and the Politics of Religion in Israel," 11 *Hum. Rts. Q.* 483 (1989): 492; Raday, *supra* note 36, pp. 211-12; see also Haut, *supra* note 211, pp. 17-21. Divorce requires a proceeding in a rabbinical court, which either party may initiate. See Greenberg, *supra* note 208, p. 10. If the court finds appropriate ground for divorce it will recommend that the marriage be terminated, and this gives the husband a right to give his wife a *get*. See Asher Maoz, "Enforcement of Rabbinical Court Judgments in Israel," *Diné Israel* XIII-XIV 7 (1986-88): 22. He has no obligation to give a *get*, however, even if the court recommended the divorce on one of the few grounds available for the wife. The husband generally has more grounds than his wife for divorce. For example, "[a] married woman commits adultery when she has sexual relations with any other man than her husband, while a married man is legally an adulterer only when he becomes sexually involved with another man's wife." Hyman, *supra* note 36, p. 110; see Cohn, *supra* note 208, p. 173; Greenberg, *supra* note 208, pp. 33-34. If a woman's marriage is dissolved because of her adultery, she is not allowed to be married either to her former partner or her partner in adultery, whereas a man may divorce his wife and marry his adulterous partner or remarry his wife. Cohn, *supra* note 208, p. 173; see Greenberg, *supra* note 208, p. 34. Occasionally, rabbinical courts in Israel have ordered a husband to give a *get*, and on rare occasions his failure then to do so has triggered civil penalties, even imprisonment. Current practice in Israeli rabbinical courts declines to issue such orders, however, on the ground that a *get* that a husband issues against his free will is of doubtful validity. See Raday, *supra* note 36, pp. 211-12; Mosheh Chigier, *Husband and Wife in Israeli Law* (Jerusalem: Harry Fischel Institute, 1985), p. 271 (noting that from 1953 to 1977 rabbinical courts issued only twelve compulsion orders). For certain Ashkenazic communities, a wife's consent to divorce is now theoretically needed, but a rebellious wife's consent is not necessary. See Raday, *supra* note 36, p. 212. "Rebellious" may be defined so broadly in this context as to eviscerate any requirement of the wife's consent. A husband may remarry despite not having his wife's consent to divorce, and his remarriage is not defined as biga-

mous. Cohn, *supra* note 208, p. 172 (citations omitted). If, however, a wife fails to obtain a *get*, she may not remarry without committing bigamy. See Greenberg, *supra* note 208, p. 12.

217. Greenberg, *supra* note 208, p. 12. In the United States, civil courts have just begun to penalize husbands for withholding the religious divorce writ in order to obtain financial concessions from the wife. See Ronald Sullivan, "Refusing to Agree to a Religious Divorce Proves Costly," *N.Y. Times*, 5 Oct. 1994, p. B3. For example, New York statutes require that if a marriage is solemnized by a religious leader, then an individual must take all steps to remove barriers to remarriage, see N.Y. Dom. Rel. Law §253 (McKinney 1986): 253; *Friedenberg v. Friedenberg*, 523 N.Y.S. 2d 578 (App. Div. 1988), and that effective barriers to remarriage must be taken into account in equitable distribution of property and maintenance, see N.Y. Dom. Rel. Law §236B (5)(h), (6)(d) (McKinney supp. 1993); see also *Avitzur v. Avitzur*, 58 N.Y.2d 108 (1983) (forcing husband to appear before rabbinical courts with respect to dispute concerning a *get*).

218. Raday, *supra* note 36, p. 213. There is a concept of a rebellious husband *(mored)*, but this is narrowly construed in terms of failure to fulfill basic marital obligations, whereas *moredet* is more widely defined. Moreover, the sanctions imposed on a *moredet* are much stricter and more onerous. *Ibid.* This concept of a "rebellious wife" in fundamentalist Judaism is similar to the concept in Christianity and Islam, particularly in that it is founded on an underlying concept of obedience of the wife to the husband. See *supra* notes 88 (Christianity), 181-90 (Islam) and accompanying text.

219. See David M. Feldman, *Birth Control in Jewish Law* (New York: New York University Press, 1968), p. 63; Greenberg, *supra* note 208, p. 22. A wife who is "rebellious" for denying sexual relations suffers greater financial detriment in this context than a man who fails in his duty to have conjugal relations. See Feldman, *supra*, p. 63 n. 23; see generally Hardacre, "Impact," *supra* note 76, p. 132.

220. Yuval-Davis, *supra* note 24, p. 219. It was not a sufficient defense to failure to do domestic chores that the husband was living with another woman at the time. For discussion of this and other such cases, see Yuval-Davis, *supra* note 24, p. 219 (citing S. Aloni, *Nushim Kivneh Adam* [*Women as Humans*] (Jerusalem: Mabat, 1976) (Hebrew)).

221. See Yuval-Davis, *supra* note 24, p. 219; Greenberg, *supra* note 208, p. 12; Raday, *supra* note 36, p. 211.

222. Hazleton, *supra* note 212, pp. 177-78.

223. Denise L. Carmody, "Today's Jewish Women," in *Today's Woman in World Religions, supra* note 6, pp. 245, 252 (quoting Galia Golan, "Movement toward Equality for Women in Israel," *Tikkun* 2, no. 1 [1987]: 19-20).

224. Greenberg, *supra* note 208, pp. 36-37; see also Levinson, *supra* note 23, pp. 45-46. After their extensive study of the *haredim*, Heilman and Friedman concluded that this was the primary reason for the modesty laws. See Heilman and Friedman, *supra* note 203, p. 217.

225. See Heilman and Friedman, *supra* note 203, pp. 214-15, 226, 233, 237, 239; Aran, *supra* note 15, p. 306; Levinson, *supra* note 23, pp. 57, 60; cf. Neusner, *supra* note 203, p. 170.

226. "From their beginnings the *haredim* stressed 'modesty' in women's dress. . . . To this day, the neighborhoods of the *haredim* are plastered with signs warning visitors, particularly the women among them, to be 'modest' in their dress." Heilman and Friedman, *supra* note 203, p. 217; see also Greenberg, *supra* note 208, pp. 36-37. The rules regarding a

woman's dress are strict. Her body must be substantially covered if she goes out in public. See Heilman and Friedman, *supra* note 203, p. 217; Yuval-Davis, *supra* note 24, p. 212; Aran, *supra* note 15, pp. 306, 312-13. Upon marriage, a woman must cover her hair or shave her head and cover it with a wig, see Heilman and Friedman, *supra* note 203, p. 217; Yuval-Davis, *supra* note 24, p. 212; Aran, *supra* note 15, p. 306. "There continue to be calls to do away with wigs in favor of shaved heads and kerchiefs" in an effort for women to show more virtue. Heilman and Friedman, *supra* note 203, p. 218.

227. See Levinson, *supra* note 23, pp. 51, 60.

228. See Heilman and Friedman, *supra* note 203, p. 218; see also Berman, *supra* note 209, p. 122.

229. Yuval-Davis, *supra* note 24, p. 212.

230. See Heilman and Friedman, *supra* note 203, p. 218 (noting how computers and modems may be important to *haredi* women who wish to be employed without needing to leave their homes).

231. For a discussion of the various political parties associated with fundamentalist groups, see Heilman and Friedman, *supra* note 203, pp. 225, 246-50; Aran, *supra* note 15, p. 326; see also Liebman, *supra* note 204, pp. 70-71 (discussing religious party groups).

232. This is particularly true in the recent 1996 elections, which the right-wing Likud party won by such a slim majority that the small parties of the Ultra-Orthodox effectively hold the balance of power. See Julian Ozanne, "Israel Braces for Retreat from Secularization: The Orthodox Right Is Making the Formation of a Government a Religious Issue," *Fin. Times*, 13 June 1996, p. 4; Julian Ozanne, "Netanyahu Would Look to Smaller Parties," *Fin. Times*, 31 May 1996, p. 4; Liebman, *supra* note 204, pp. 70-71, 82-84 (discussing power of religious parties in 1990 elections); Carmody, *supra* note 223, pp. 250-51.

233. See England, *supra* note 204, pp. 178-79. For example, state financial support of religious schools (which for most sects are open only to boys) has increased enormously because of the religious groups' political power. Yuval-Davis, *supra* note 24, pp. 206-7; Heilman and Friedman, *supra* note 203, pp. 236-37, 240, 249, 251. *Haredim* have also fought against universal army service for women (religious girls did not belong in the licentious, unsegregated environment of the army) and complete Sabbath observance in areas near *haredi* neighborhoods (no driving, etc.). Heilman and Friedman, *supra* note 203, p. 240.

234. See Heilman and Friedman, *supra* note 203, pp. 219, 235, 248, 250-51 (discussing *haredim*); Liebman, *supra* note 204, p. 74 (discussing *haredim*); Sprinzak, *supra* note 204, p. 486 (discussing GE); Aran, *supra* note 15, p. 319 (discussing GE). The *halakhah* "sees itself as applying to everybody, gentile as well as Jew, everywhere, at everytime." England, *supra* note 204, p. 171 (footnote omitted).

235. Aran, *supra* note 15, p. 319. The drafter of the Constitution was imprisoned for participating in a plot to blow up the Muslim mosque on the Temple Mount. *Ibid.* GE has established an institute whose stated purpose is "to promote the full application of ancient Hebrew law in the modern national state." *Ibid.* This includes not only the complete details of biblical worship, "but also the institution of the Bible as the standard of conduct of public systems normally regulated by the state." *Ibid.*

236. The Rabbinical Courts Jurisdiction (Marriage and Divorce) Law 210, 7 L.S.I. 139 (1952-53), placed marriage and divorce of Jews under the exclusive jurisdiction of the Rabbinical Courts. See Raday, *supra* note 36, p. 209; Amnon Rubinstein, "Law and Religion in

Israel," in *Jewish Law in Ancient and Modern Israel, supra* note 204, pp. 194-98; Strum, *supra* note 216, p. 491. The King's Order in Council, 1922-1947; s. 52, also placed jurisdiction of marriage and divorce in Shari'ah courts for Muslims and in Christian denominational courts for Christians. See Raday, *supra* note 36, p. 209.

237. There is civil law governing issues of matrimonial property, and this may be superimposed on the personal law systems. It is in practice overridden, however, as a result of the husband's bargaining power deriving from his unilateral ability to grant a divorce. See Raday, *supra* note 36, p. 216; see also Rosen-Zvi, *supra* note 213, pp. 347-96.

238. See Heilman and Friedman, *supra* note 203, p. 235: State funding of religious education and a network of state religious schools, see State Education Law, 5713-1953, 7 L.S.I. 113 (1952-53); State Education Regulations (Religious State Education Council), 5713-1953, K.T. 5723, 1423; Jewish Sabbath and Holidays as prescribed days of rest in the state, on which no Jew may be employed, see Days of Rest Ordinance, 1948; 1 L.S.I. 18 (1948); Hours of Work and Rest Law, 5708-1951, 5 L.S.I. 125 (1950-51) 18A; Jewish dietary laws enforced for a variety of public institutions, see Pig-Raising Prohibition Law, 5722-1962, 16 L.S.I. 93 (1961-62); Kosher Food for Soldiers Ordinance, 5709-1949, 2 L.S.I. 37 (1948-49); military-service exemptions for yeshivah-kollel students, *supra* note 233; see Heilman and Friedman, *supra* note 203, p. 240.

239. Aran, *supra* note 15, p. 319 (GE wants to expand religious courts' jurisdiction to cover everything, not just marriage and divorce). "Despite the fact that many Israeli citizens do not consider themselves religious . . . , the Hasidim have worked with other Orthodox Jews to make the precept of the religious law (halakah *[sic]*) binding in Israeli civil life." Carmody, *supra* note 223, p. 251. Cf. Aran, *supra* note 15, p. 319; IWRAW, *Women's Watch* 7, no. 1 (1993): 3 (noting that new proposed Israeli Constitution states that sex discrimination prohibitions do not apply to marriage and divorce, which remain with religious courts).

240. Carmody, *supra* note 223, p. 251 (quoting Galia Golan, "Movement toward Equality for Women in Israel," *Tikkun* 2, no. 1 [1987]: 19-20). Secular Israelis have avoided the exclusive jurisdiction of the religious courts by marrying or divorcing outside the state. Until now, the state has recognized the foreign civil marriage or divorce, but fundamentalists wish to stop this practice. See Raday, *supra* note 36, p. 214.

241. See Strum, *supra* note 216, p. 483.

242. It has been suggested that the conflict between women's rights and religious freedom sets "tenets of equality against values of liberty." Donna J. Sullivan, "Gender Equality and Religious Freedom: Toward a Framework for Conflict Resolution," 24 *N.Y.U. J. Int'l L. & Pol.* 795 (1992). This, however, implies that women's equality is the only right at stake in this conflict, whereas women's liberty is also at stake. Women's submissive status and inability to move beyond the realms of male authority affect their liberty rights of freedom of association and of political and religious belief. See *infra* notes 343-66 and accompanying text.

243. See supra note 2.

244. UN Charter art. 103 ("In the event of conflict between obligations of Members . . . under the . . . Charter and their obligations under any other international agreement, their obligations under the . . . Charter shall prevail.").

245. Vienna Convention on the Law of Treaties, opened for signature 23 May 1969,

art. 31, 1155 U.N.T.S. 331, 341, UN Doc. A/Conf. 39/27 (1969) (entered into force 27 Jan. 1980). This and many other articles of the Vienna Convention are generally agreed to represent customary law. See Malcolm N. Shaw, *International Law,* third ed. (Cambridge: Grotius Publications, 1991), p. 561.

246. A balancing approach attempts to identify factors of importance related to the text but not necessarily in the text, which are then weighed, in a process that is not itself guided by the text, to determine an outcome. See, e.g., Sullivan, *supra* note 242, pp. 821-23; Donna J. Sullivan, "Advancing the Freedom of Religion or Belief through the UN Declaration on the Elimination of Religious Intolerance and Discrimination," 82 *Am. J. Int'l L.* 487 (1988): 510. Balancing approaches may be helpful in contexts where there is no great diversity among the disputants because there is greater chance of agreement in identifying which factors are important. Although a balancing procedure is often used in the context of U.S. Constitutional law, there is no equivalent in international law and limited authority for introducing a balancing approach into international law.

247. As of December 31, 1995, 184 states were parties to the UN Charter. See *Multilateral Treaties Deposited with the Secretary-General: Status as of 31 December 1995,* UN Doc. ST/LEG/SER.E/14, UN Sales No. E.96.V.5 (1996), pp. 3-10 [hereinafter *Multilateral Treaties*]. Basic Charter norms are also considered applicable to nonmember states because these norms have entered into customary law. See *infra* notes 281, 282, 292 and accompanying text.

248. The preamble "reaffirms faith in fundamental rights, in the dignity and worth of the human person, in the equal rights of men and women and of nations large and small. . . ." UN Charter 1.0.

249. UN Charter art. 1(3). This is the first mention of religion. UN Charter article 76(c) provides parallel objectives to article 1(3) by its encouragement of respect for human rights and fundamental freedoms in the context of the international trusteeship system. The Charter also requires studies to produce recommendations in order to promote the realization of human rights and fundamental freedoms without distinction. UN Charter art. 13(1) (b).

250. UN Charter art. 56.

251. UN Charter art. 55(c).

252. Although a few scholars argued that the human rights provisions of the Charter, particularly article 56, do not impose legal obligations, see, e.g., Manley O. Hudson, "Integrity of International Instruments," 42 *Am. J. Int'l. L.* 105 (1948): 105-8, this view is now generally discredited and article 56 is understood to impose a legal duty which members cannot disregard and violate. See Oscar Schachter, "International Law Implications of U.S. Human Rights Policies," 24 *N.Y.L. Sch. L. Rev.* 63 (1978): 67-69; Egon Schwelb, "The International Court of Justice and the Human Rights Clause of the Charter," 66 *Am. J. Int'l. L.* 337 (1972): 350; Hersch Lauterpacht, *International Law and Human Rights* (New York: Garland Publishing, 1973), pp. 147-49; Georges Scelle, "Summary Records and Documents of the First Session Including the Report of the Commission to the General Assembly (23rd Mtg.) [1949]," 1 *Y.B. Int'l L. Comm'n* 163, ¶76, p. 169, UN Doc. A/CN.4/Ser.A/1949; F. Blaine Sloan, "Human Rights, The United Nations and International Law," 20 *Nordisk Tidsskrift for International Ret, Acta Scandinavica juris gentium* (1950): 30-31. The International Court of Justice (ICJ) has also accepted this interpretation. See *infra* note 256;

Schwelb, *supra*, p. 349 (noting that ICJ adopted this approach in case of *Legal Consequences for States of the Continued Presence of South Africa in Namibia (South West Africa) Notwithstanding Security Council Resolution 276*, 1971 I.C.J. 16, ¶131 at 57 [21 June]). Although article 56 is understood as imposing a legal obligation on members, scholarly opinion is not uniform with respect to the scope of the legal obligation. See *infra* notes 265-93 and accompanying text.

253. See *supra* note 250.

254. Sloan, *supra* note 252, p. 31.

255. Vienna Convention on the Law of Treaties, opened for signature 23 May 1969, art. 31(1), 1155 U.N.T.S. 331, 341, UN Doc. A/Conf. 39/27 (1969) (entered into force 27 Jan. 1980). Even a state that has signed a treaty but not yet ratified it must not undermine its object and purpose. *Ibid.*, at art. 18. *A fortiori*, a member of the United Nations must not do so. See also Louis B. Sohn, "John A. Sibley Lecture: The Shaping of International Law," 8 *Ga. J. Int'l & Comp. L.* 1 (1978): 18-19 [hereinafter Sohn, "John A. Sibley Lecture"] (noting that article 56 language of "pledge" has "the force of positive international law and creates basic duties which all members must fulfill in good faith").

256. The ICJ has indicated that the language of "pledging" in article 56 is a substantive legal obligation with respect to article 55(c) rights. Although the ICJ was dealing with South Africa's Mandate under the trusteeship system (UN Charter arts. 75-85), the language that it used with respect to human rights — "pledged itself to observe and respect" — is found in articles 55(c) and 56 rather than in article 76(c). The ICJ stated: "Under the Charter of the United Nations, the former Mandatory [South Africa] had *pledged itself to observe and respect . . .* human rights and fundamental freedoms for all without distinction as to race. To establish instead, and to enforce, distinctions, exclusions, restrictions and limitations exclusively based on grounds of race . . . which constitute a denial of fundamental human rights is a flagrant violation of the purposes and principles of the Charter." *Legal Consequences for States of the Continued Presence of South Africa in Namibia (South West Africa) Notwithstanding Security Council Resolution 276* (1970), 1971 I.C.J. 16, ¶131, at 57 (21 June) (emphasis supplied). The ICJ's references to a denial of fundamental human rights and a violation of the purposes and principles of the Charter clearly indicate that the Court was referring to direct obligations of a state under the Charter and not merely those deriving from South Africa's Charter obligations as a trustee. See *infra* note 261; Schwelb, *supra* note 252, pp. 348-49.

257. See also David Little, "Religion — Catalyst or Impediment to International Law? The Case of Hugo Grotius," 87 *Am. Soc'y Int'l l. Proc.* 322 (1993): 323 (discussing religious freedom rights in the context of the language of the Universal Declaration).

258. See also Little, *supra* note 257, p. 323 ("In short, the secularity of human rights [in the Universal Declaration], carefully specified in this way, appears to be a corollary of the principle of nondiscrimination, which is fundamental to the whole idea of human rights.").

259. There is nothing to prevent religious laws providing inspiration for international legal standards, and various religions have influenced the formation of international law. See Mark W. Janis, ed., *The Influence of Religion on the Development of International Law* (Boston: Nijhoff, 1991). Moreover, international law does not require that states be secular or that church and state be separated. A religious state, with its own municipal

religious laws, merely needs to conform to international human rights standards. See *infra* notes 424-25 and accompanying text (discussing that municipal law is no defense to a state's violation of international treaty obligations). States and UN studies have acknowledged a danger in a state recognizing a single, particular religion in that the mere recognition discriminates against other religions. See, e.g., *United Nations General Assembly, Draft Declaration on the Elimination of All Forms of Religious Intolerance: Report of the Secretary-General 17*, 31 UN Doc. A/9134 (1973) (statements of Finland and Sweden); Arcot Krishnaswami, *Study of Discrimination in the Matter of Religious Rights and Practices*, UN Doc. E/CN.4/Sub. 2/200/Rev. 1, UN Sales No. E.60.XIV.2 (1960), p. 47. Nonetheless, the existence of a state religion is not per se a violation of international law as long as there is "no discrimination against persons practicing other religions." *Summary Records of the 328th Meeting* (1981-82), [1989] 1 *Y.B. Hum. Rts. Comm* ¶39, at 241, UN Doc. CCPR/C/10/Add. 2, p. 39 at 241 (discussing Morocco's report under the International Covenant on Civil and Political Rights, 16 Dec. 1966, 999 U.N.T.S. 171 [hereinafter ICCPR]). For this reason, it is particularly important at the international level that no one religion be preferred over any other and that no one religion is determinative of human rights. For an example of a religious state specifically stating its intentions to abide by international law in the event of a conflict with municipal religious law, see *infra* note 427 (discussing Tunisia).

260. Later human rights treaties generally use the term "discrimination" rather than "distinction." "Without distinction" appears, however, in article 2(1) of the ICCPR. The ICCPR elsewhere specifically prohibits "discrimination," and drafting debates make clear that there was no attempt to distinguish these two terms. See B. G. Ramcharan, "Equality and Nondiscrimination," in *The International Bill of Rights: The Covenant on Civil and Political Rights*, ed. Louis Henkin (New York: Columbia University Press, 1981), pp. 246, 259. Human Rights Committee interpretations of these provisions also make clear that the terms are used interchangeably. See Human Rights Committee, *General Comments adopted by the Human Rights Committee Under Article 40, ¶4 of the International Covenant on Civil and Political Rights, Addendum: General Comment 18* [37] (non-discrimination) (adopted 21 Nov. 1989), UN GAOR, 45th Sess., Supp. No. 40, at 173, ¶1, at 173, UN Doc. A/45/40, CCPR/C/21/Rev.1/Add.1 (1990) [hereinafter Human Rights Committee, General Comment Non-Discrimination]. "Discrimination" is the principal concept also used in such human rights treaties as the International Covenant on Economic, Social and Cultural Rights, see 16 Dec. 1966, 993 U.N.T.S. 3, and the Convention on the Elimination of All Forms of Discrimination Against Women (CEAFDAW), G.A. Res. 34/180, UN GAOR, 34th Sess., Supp. No. 46, at 193, art. 1, UN Doc. A/34/46 (1979); 19 I.L.M. 33 (1980) [hereinafter CEAFDAW]. (The abbreviation "CEAFDAW" is used instead of "Women's Convention" because the latter term suggests that this treaty serves only to benefit women, whereas all society is richer economically, socially, and ethically if all members are capable of full participation, and free to the "full development of the human personality." See Universal Declaration art. 26(2)). For example, CEAFDAW article 1 defines "discrimination against women" as meaning "any distinction, exclusion or restriction made on the basis of sex which has the effect or purpose of impairing or nullifying the recognition . . . of equality of men and women. . . ."

261. Legal Consequences for States of the Continued Presence of South Africa in Namibia (South West Africa) Notwithstanding Security Council Resolution 276 (1970),

1971 I.C.J. 16, ¶131, at 57 (21 June). The fact that the ICJ was dealing with South Africa's actions in "a territory having an international status" does not imply that South Africa could therefore impose apartheid elsewhere. A state's duty under the Charter applies uniformly and universally. See Schwelb, *supra* note 252, pp. 348-49.

262. Charter art. 55(c).

263. See *infra* notes 265-93 and accompanying text.

264. See *supra* note 248 and accompanying text. The Charter uses the terms "fundamental human rights" in the preamble, and "human rights and fundamental freedoms" in the articles 1(3), 13(b), 55(c), 62(2), and 76(c). There is no indication that a substantive difference between "fundamental human rights" and mere "human rights" was intended. If such a difference were intended, then the Charter, although recognizing "fundamental" human rights in the preamble, proceeds to extend protection to all (not just "fundamental") human rights in the substantive articles. At the same time, it extends protection to "fundamental" freedoms but not other freedoms. This interpretation results in a disjointed, haphazard understanding of the Charter, and makes the preamble seem at odds with the substantive articles. Whereas, if the terms are read to be interchangeable, then the preamble and subsequent articles appear as an intelligible and comprehensive whole. Thus, there is no hierarchy in the Charter between fundamental human rights and human rights. See also Theodor Meron, "On a Hierarchy of International Human Rights," 80 *Am. J. Int'l.L.* 1 (1986): 5.

265. *Jus cogens,* or peremptory norms, are a subset of international customary law, see *infra* notes 267-73 and accompanying text, and are those norms accepted and recognized by the international community from which no derogation is permissible and which may be modified only by subsequent norms of the same fundamental character. States may not contract out of these norms. See Vienna Convention on the Law of Treaties, 23 May 1969, 1155 U.N.T.S. 331, UN Doc. A/CONF 39/27 (1969), 8 I.L.M. 679 (1969) (entered into force 27 Jan. 1980); Ian Brownlie, *Principles of Public International Law,* fourth ed. (Oxford: Clarendon Press, 1990), pp. 512-25. These peremptory norms address, for the most part, actions which shock the conscience of the international community, and suggest the need for universal jurisdiction and international criminal liability. See R. Y. Jennings and A. Watts, eds., *Oppenheim's International Law,* ninth ed. (London: Longmans, 1992), pp. 7-8, §2. Peremptory norms are considered to prohibit genocide; slavery; the murder or causing disappearance of individuals; torture or other cruel, inhuman, or degrading treatment or punishment; prolonged arbitrary detention; and systematic racial discrimination such as apartheid. American Law Institute, *Restatement of the Law Third: The Foreign Relations Law of the United States* (vol. 2), §702, p. 161, §702, Comment n, p. 167 (1987) [hereinafter *Restatement*]; Theodor Meron, *Human Rights and Humanitarian Norms as Customary Law* (New York: Oxford University Press, 1989), pp. 23, 94-98; see Brownlie, *supra,* pp. 512-25.

266. Thus, killing half the members of a racial group violates the *jus cogens* prohibition of genocide whether the victims are chosen without sexual distinction, or are all women, or all men.

267. There is a tendency to find human rights principles as customary law only if they meet the higher burden of proof of being *jus cogens.* This confers the benefit of not allowing states to agree to violate human rights norms among themselves. It is, however, un-

desirable to prevent human rights norms becoming part of customary law because they do not meet the higher standard of *jus cogens.* A human rights norm which is part of international customary law is nonetheless binding on states. For example, the prohibition of hate speech is arguably at least a local customary law of Europe, but is not at the level of being *jus cogens.* This does not prevent European states, and possibly new neighbors, from being bound by the law.

268. Statute of the International Court of Justice, art. 38(1)(b); see Colombian-Peruvian Asylum Case, 1950 I.C.J. 266 (20 Nov.).

269. North Sea Continental Shelf Cases *(Germ. v. Den.; Germ. v. Neth.),* 1969 I.C.J. 3.

270. Military and Paramilitary Activities in and against Nicaragua *(Nicar. v. U.S.),* 1986 I.C.J. 14, 98 (27 June).

271. See Military and Paramilitary Activities in and against Nicaragua *(Nicar. v. U.S.),* 1986 I.C.J. 14, 98 (27 June); Meron, *supra* note 265, p. 113; see also *Filartiga v. Peña-Irala,* 630 F.2d 876 (2d. Cir. 1980) (reviewing UN declarations and actions as evidence of *opinio juris* intertwined with state practice); Anne F. Bayefsky, "General Approaches to the Domestic Application of Women's International Human Rights Law," in *Human Rights of Women, supra* note 128, pp. 351, 361 (discussing necessary evidence for *opinio juris* and state practice regarding norms of customary law affecting women).

272. This minimum list of human rights norms as customary international law includes the following prohibitions: genocide; slavery or the slave trade; murder or causing the disappearance of individuals; torture or other cruel, inhuman, or degrading treatment or punishment; prolonged arbitrary detention; systematic racial discrimination; and consistent patterns of gross violations of internationally recognized human rights. See *Restatement, supra* note 265, at 702, at 161; Bayefsky, *General Approaches, supra* note 271, p. 361 (adding freedom from loss of consortium to list); see also Barcelona Traction, Light and Power Co., Ltd. *(Belg. v. Spain)* (New Application), 1970 I.C. J. 3, ¶¶33, 34, at 32 (Feb. 5) (finding prohibition against racial discrimination is customary norm). The Restatement states that the list of norms "is not closed," *Restatement, supra* note 265, at §702, Comment a, p. 162, and "[m]any other rights will be added in the course of time." Meron, *supra* note 265, at 95, 99.

273. Brownlie, *supra* note 265, p. 598 and n. 3; Ramcharan, *supra* note 260, p. 249; see also Anne F. Bayefsky, "The Principle of Equality or Non-Discrimination in International Law," 11 *Hum. Rts. L. J.* 1 (1990): 19.

274. *Restatement, supra* note 265, §702, Comment i, at 165; see Brownlie, *supra* note 265, pp. 598-99 (noting that prohibition against race discrimination is a principle based in part on articles 55 and 56 of Charter, Universal Declaration, and other international Covenants). It is unclear whether nonsystematic racial discrimination violates customary international law. Compare *Restatement, supra* note 265, §702, Comment i, at 165 (limiting racial nondiscrimination norm to systematic discrimination) with Barcelona Traction, Light and Power Co., Ltd. *(Belg. v. Spain)* (New Application), 1970 I.C. J. 3, ¶¶33, 34, at 32 (Feb. 5) (finding racial nondiscrimination is the norm of customary law).

275. The *Restatement* acknowledges that religion and race are treated alike under the Charter such that there is a "strong case that systematic discrimination on the grounds of religion as a matter of state policy is also a violation of customary law." See *Restatement,*

supra note 265, §702, Comment j, at 165. But it fails to note that sex is treated the same as race and religion. See *Restatement, supra* note 265, §702, Comment l, at 165.

276. *Restatement, supra* note 265, §702, Comment l, at 166; see Brownlie, *supra* note 265, p. 599; see also Myres S. McDougal et al., "Human Rights for Women and World Public Order: The Outlawing of Sex-Based Discrimination," 69 *Am. J. Int'l L.* 497 (1975): 509-31 (finding that prohibition of sex discrimination is becoming the fairly accepted norm).

277. The most recent pronouncement of equality being at the United Nations Fourth World Conference on Women held in Beijing in 1995. See *Beijing Declaration and Platform for Action,* Preamble ¶¶3, 8, 9, 13, 15, 32 (1995).

278. See Bayefsky, *Equality, supra* note 273, pp. 20-23, 21 n. 100 (listing such treaties); Bayefsky, *General Approaches, supra* note 271, p. 369 n. 1 (listing such treaties); see also Brownlie, *supra* note 265, pp. 598-99 (noting that prohibition against sex discrimination is based on the same set of multilateral instruments as the prohibition against race discrimination).

279. See, e.g., *Dow v. Attorney General,* Civ. App. No. 4/91, Law Rep. of the Commonwealth 1992, at 623 (Court of Appeal Botswana, 3 July 1992) (holding that sex discriminatory nationality laws violated international principles of women's equality); Case of Abdulaziz, Cabales and Balkandali, 94 Eur. Ct. H. R. (Ser. A) 8, ¶78, at 38 (28 May 1985) (Judgment) ("it can be said that the advancement of the equality of the sexes is today a major goal in the member States of the Council of Europe"); *Reed v. Reed,* 404 U.S. 71 (1971) (finding that sex discrimination is subject to scrutiny under U.S. Constitution); see also McDougal, *supra* note 276, pp. 509-31.

280. See Military and Paramilitary Activities in and against Nicaragua *(Nicar. v. U.S.),* 1986 I.C.J. 14, 98 (27 June). Shame, however, has not prevented states arguing that their denials of equality to women under conventional law are due to different concepts of equality. For example, Egypt has declared that its interpretation of Islamic law gives an equivalency of rights and duties to ensure the "complementarity which guarantees true equality between the spouses." *Multilateral Treaties, supra* note 247, at 169. It nonetheless had to admit that its religious concept of "equivalency" diverged from the concept of equality during marriage and at divorce under the treaty. See *Report of the Committee on the Elimination of Discrimination Against Women,* UN GAOR, 39th Scss., Vol. II (Third Sess.), Supp. No. 45, at 29, UN Doc. A/39/45 (1984). However, states presenting a religious fundamentalist viewpoint, such as Sudan, see *infra* notes 423, 425, seem to be claiming that they are setting forth a new rule by their activities to replace the human rights concepts under international law. Thus, the Sudan representative to the Human Rights Committee stated that "the Covenant should be adapted to the Islamization movement, which was recent, and the wording of the Covenant's provisions, which dated from a bygone era, should be amended." UN Human Rights Committee, *Summary Record of the Consideration of the Initial Report of the Sudan, Continued, 42d Sess., 1067th mtg.,* ¶74, at 18, UN Doc. CCPR/C/SR.1067 (1991). This argument must be rejected. First, it is not a sufficient defense to treaty violations. See *infra* notes 424-25 and accompanying text. Second, the Islamization movement is based on an interpretation of Islam that is fourteen centuries old, see Hélie-Lucas, *supra* note 6, p. 54, and thus represents a retreat from the Charter, subverting it in violation of the pledge in articles 55 and 56. See *supra* notes 250-56 and accompanying text. Third, it also violates articles 55 and 56 of the Charter, which prevent any particular religion being

privileged over others or being determinative of human rights standards. See *supra* notes 257-59 and accompanying text. Fourth, such a declaration cannot be considered as *opinio juris* with respect to the creation of a customary norm regarding sex discrimination since such a declaration violates the Charter, and obviously *opinio juris* may not attach to anything that would be a Charter violation.

281. Louis B. Sohn, "The New International Law: Protection of the Rights of Individuals Rather than States," 32 *Am. U. L. Rev.* 1 (1982): 13 [hereinafter Sohn, "The New International Law"] ("The Charter was not meant to be a temporary document, to be easily and perpetually amended, but, rather, to be a lasting expression of the needs of humanity as a whole"). Virtually all states in the world are bound by the Charter. See UN Charter art. 103. The Charter itself has been taken as evidence of *opinio juris* and state practice, and even as having become part of customary law. See Military and Paramilitary Activities in and against Nicaragua *(Nicar. v. U.S.),* 1986 I.C.J. 4, 98 (27 June) (holding that certain articles of Charter are norms of customary law); Rosalyn Higgins, *Problems and Process: International Law and How We Use It* (New York: Oxford University Press, 1994), pp. 30-32; Sohn, "The New International Law," *supra,* pp. 13-14 (arguing that the Charter is customary international law and *jus cogens*).

282. See *supra* pp. 179-81. If the nondiscrimination principles are part of customary law, then they bind all states, including nonmembers of the United Nations. John P. Humphrey, "The Implementation of International Human Rights Law," 24 *N.Y.L. Sch. L. Rev.* 31 (1978-79): 32.

283. Legal Consequences for States of the Continued Presence of South Africa in Namibia (South West Africa) Notwithstanding Security Council Resolution 276 (1970), 1971 I.C.J. 16, ¶131, at 57 (21 June). The fact that the ICJ was dealing with South Africa's imposition of apartheid in the territory of Namibia did not limit to only such situations the ICJ's determination that systematic racial discrimination violated the Charter. South Africa's systematic racial discrimination was a violation whether imposed on a territory or elsewhere. See *supra* notes 256, 261.

284. The general rule is that a treaty "shall be interpreted in good faith in accordance with the ordinary meaning to be given to the terms of the treaty in their context and in the light of its object and purpose." Vienna Convention on the Law of Treaties, opened for signature 23 May 1969, art. 31 (1), 1155 U.N.T.S. 331, UN Doc. A/CONF 39/27 (1969) (entered into force 27 Jan. 1980).

285. The Universal Declaration was adopted by the General Assembly, consisting of all the original members save eight abstainers, within three and half years of the Charter. G.A. Res. 217A (III), UN GAOR, 3rd Sess., pt. 1, at 71, UN Doc. A/180, at 71 (1948). It was adopted on December 10, 1948, with forty-eight states voting in favor, none against, and eight abstaining (Byelorussian S.S.R., Czechoslovakia, Poland, Saudi Arabia, Ukrainian S.S.R, U.S.S.R., Union of South Africa, and Yugoslavia). The communist states of Europe that had initially abstained later expressly accepted the Universal Declaration in the Final Act of the Conference on Security and Cooperation in Europe (Helsinki 1975).

286. Some commentators have argued that because General Assembly Declarations are not legally binding, they therefore have no legal effect. See Stephen M. Schwebel, "The Effect of Resolutions of the UN General Assembly on Customary International Law," 301-2 *Am. Soc'y Int'l L. Proc.* (1979); Gerald Fitzmaurice, "The Future of Public International

Law and of the International Legal System in the Circumstances of Today: Special Report," in *Institut de Droit International, Livre du Centenaire* (Basel: Karger, 1973), pp. 270-74. According to this argument, the Universal Declaration would not even impose a legal obligation on members who voted for it, and certainly does not bind members who have not approved it. At the time of its adoption, the U.S. representative declared that the Universal Declaration was not a treaty and imposed no legal obligation. 19 Dep't State Bull. 751 (1948); see Bayefsky, *General Approaches, supra* note 271, p. 362 (stating that General Assembly resolutions, like those of the Universal Declaration, do not alone constitute international legal obligation); see also Lauterpacht, *supra* note 252, pp. 408-17.

287. See Higgins, *supra* note 281, pp. 22-38 (arguing that General Assembly resolutions, although not binding, have legal effect). Falk similarly argues that although General Assembly resolutions are not per se binding, they are nonetheless indications of general customary law and serve as a source of evidence. See Richard Falk, "On the Quasi-Legislative Competence of the General Assembly," 60 *Am. J. Int'l L.* 782 (1966): 785.

288. See Myres McDougal et al., *Human Rights and World Public Order* (New Haven: Yale University Press, 1980), pp. 272-74. With respect to General Assembly declarations, Falk argues that the General Assembly has quasi-legislative capacity and thus makes "norm-positing" resolutions. See Falk, *supra* note 287, p. 791. Others, however, reject viewing the General Assembly as a quasi-legislative body. See, e.g., Gaetano Arangio-Ruiz, "The Normative Role of the General Assembly of the United Nations and the Declaration of Principles of Friendly Relations," *Recueil des Cours* 431, 729-30 (III, 1972).

289. See Sohn, "The New International Law," *supra* note 281, pp. 16-17; Sohn, "John A. Sibley Lecture," *supra* note 255, pp. 18-19; see also Schwelb, *supra* note 252, p. 337. The Universal Declaration has been subsequently affirmed "as an obligation for the members of the international community" in the Proclamation of Teheran, see Final Act of the International Conference on Human Rights 3, ¶2, at 4, UN GAOR, 23rd Sess., Supp. No. 41, at 1, UN Doc. A/CONF. 32/41 (1968); UN Sales No. E.68.XIV.2, which itself was subsequently affirmed by the General Assembly "as a reaffirmation of the principles embodied in the Universal Declaration of Human Rights," G.A. Res. 2442 (XXIII), 19 Dec. 1968; UN GAOR, 23rd Sess., Supp. No. 18 (A/7218), at 49, UN Doc. A/7218 (1968); see also "Montreal Statement of the Assembly for Human Rights," reprinted in 9 *J. Int'l Comm'n Jurists* 94 (1968): 94-95. For a discussion of the legal status and effect of the Universal Declaration, particularly in light of these subsequent affirmations, see Louis B. Sohn and Thomas Buergenthal, *International Protection of Human Rights* (Indianapolis: Bobbs-Merrill, 1973), pp. 518-19, 522. Furthermore, member states recently reaffirmed their commitment to the Universal Declaration by the General Assembly adopting a resolution "Strengthening of the rule of law," declaring "that, by adopting the Universal Declaration of Human Rights, member states have pledged themselves to achieve, in cooperation with the United Nations, the promotion of universal respect for and observance of human rights and fundamental freedoms. . . ." G.A. Res. 50/179, UN Report: A/50/635/Add. 2, 22 Dec. 1995, in Resolutions adopted on the reports of the Third Committee 400 (1996).

290. Sohn, "The New International Law," *supra* note 281, p. 17; see McDougal, *supra* note 288, p. 274; John P. Humphrey, *Human Rights and the United Nations: A Great Adventure* (Dobbs Ferry: Transnational Publishers, 1984), pp. 64, 65, 75-76 [hereinafter Humphrey, *Human Rights*]; Humphrey, *supra* note 282, pp. 32-33 ("Universal Declaration of Human

Rights . . . is now part of customary law of nations not because it was adopted as a resolution of the General Assembly but because of juridical consensus from its invocation as law on countless occasions); Louis B. Sohn, "Protection of Human Rights through International Legislation," in 1 *René Cassin, Amicorum Discipulorumque Liber* (Paris: A. Pedone, 1969), p. 325. For an analysis which accepts "Professor Sohn's method [as] perfectly legitimate," see Meron, *supra* note 265, pp. 82-99. The argument that the Universal Declaration is part of customary law is that declarations adopted by an overwhelming majority of the General Assembly demonstrate consensus and constitute *opinio juris* that the provisions are generally acceptable to the international community, and the subsequent practice of a reasonable number of states and acquiescence by others show states' willingness to abide by the principles. See Louis B. Sohn, "'Generally Accepted' International Rules," 61 *Wash. L. Rev.* 1073 (1986): 1077-79, 1078 n. 3; see also Antonio Cassese, "The Geneva Protocols of 1977 on the Humanitarian Law of Armed Conflict and Customary International Law," 3 *U.C.L.A. Pac. Basin L.J.* 55 (1984): 58-68, 113-17 (arguing that the birth of certain customary international norms may occur from previous state practice combined with consensus at treaty conference). Implicit recognition by nonmember states of the binding nature of the human rights obligations of the Charter with respect to nonmember states constitutes acquiescence, and thus the nonmember is bound by these obligations. See Schachter, *supra* note 252, p. 69. *Opinio juris* and state practice make clear the customary law status of the Universal Declaration. For example, the ICJ has relied upon the obligatory nature of the principles of the Universal Declaration and the Charter. See Case Concerning United States Diplomatic and Consular Staff in Tehran *(U.S. v. Iran),* 1980 I.C.J. 3, 42 (May 24); see also Humphrey, *Human Rights, supra,* pp. 75-76. The obligatory status of these principles has also been recognized in UN reports and declarations, see *supra* note 289; Meron, *supra* note 265, p. 83 n. 9, p. 87 n. 18 (listing such numerous UN reports and statements), and by governments, see, e.g., *J.O. Débats parlementaires, Conseil de la République* 418 (1957) (representative of France), *quote reprinted in* Meron, *supra* note 265, p. 82 ("Although these conventions cannot be invoked [against Saudi Arabia and Yemen, which] abstained or were absent when the United Nations General Assembly adopted the Universal Declaration of Human Rights in 1948, it nevertheless remains that slavery is prohibited under the general principles of the Charter relating to fundamental human rights"). It has also been recognized by national courts. See, e.g., *Filartiga v. Peña-Irala,* 630 F.2d 876, 883 (2d. Cir. 1980) (holding that Universal Declaration was authoritative statement of international community and prohibition on torture is customary norm of international law). For a further discussion of arguments concerning customary international law, see Meron, *supra* note 265, pp. 79-135.

291. Louis B. Sohn, Supplementary Paper, "A Short History of United Nations Documents on Human Rights," in *The United Nations and Human Rights, 18th Report of the Commission,* ed. Commission to Study the Organization of Peace (Metuchen: Scarecrow Press, 1968), pp. 39, 71-72.

292. See *supra* notes 281, 282 and accompanying text; Sohn, "The New International Law," *supra* note 281, p. 17.

293. See *supra* notes 249-56 and accompanying text. Members must not act contrary to the object and purpose of the Charter. *Ibid.*

294. Universal Declaration art. 2.

295. See *supra* notes 257-59 and accompanying text.

296. Article 32 of the Vienna Convention on the Law of Treaties allows recourse to supplementary means of interpretation including preparatory work in cases of ambiguity or obscurity in the meaning of treaty language. Vienna Convention on the Law of Treaties, opened for signature 23 May 1969, art. 32, 1155 U.N.T.S. 331, 341, UN Doc. A/Conf. 39/27 (1969) (entered into force 27 Jan. 1980). Although the Universal Declaration is not a treaty, it is reasonable to apply the same procedures because of its status as a law-creating instrument.

297. *Summary Records of Meetings of the Third Committee Sept. 21-Dec. 8, 1948,* Official Records of the Third Session of the General Assembly, Part I, at 55, UN Doc. (A/C.3/ SR.) 84-180 (1948); see Humphrey, *Human Rights, supra* note 290, p. 67. These suggestions were made by Christians: the Brazilian delegation and Father Beaufort of the Netherlands. Humphrey, *Human Rights, supra* note 290, p. 67; see also UN Doc. A/C.3/215.

298. See Humphrey, *Human Rights, supra* note 290, p. 67; *Summary Records of Meetings of the Third Committee Sept. 21–Dec. 8, 1948,* Official Records of the Third Session of the General Assembly, Part I, at 108-25, UN Doc. (A/C.3/SR.) 84-180 (1948).

299. See Little, *supra* note 257, p. 323.

300. For a full discussion of article 18 see *infra* notes 351-57 and accompanying text.

301. See Humphrey, *Human Rights, supra* note 290, pp. 67-68.

302. *Ibid.,* p. 68.

303. *Ibid.*

304. *Ibid.,* p. 73.

305. *Ibid.* For example, Iraq has subsequently relied on the legal principles of the Charter and the Universal Declaration to denounce South Africa's apartheid policy as "a massive and ruthless denial of human rights" such that South Africa should be expelled from the UN. See UN, Security Council Official Records, 29th Year, 1808th Mtg., Oct. 30, 1974, UN Doc. S/PV.1808, ¶146, at 17; UN, Security Council Official Records, 29th Year, 1807th Mtg., Oct. 30, 1974, UN Doc. S/PV.1807, ¶31, at 5. Saudi Arabia apparently abstained from the vote because of its objection to article 18 including the right to change one's religion although it made no public explanation of this. Thus, at the most, Saudi Arabia could be seen as a persistent objector to the customary law of the right to change religion, but even this stretches the definition of persistent objector because "evidence of objection must be clear and there is probably a presumption of acceptance which is to be rebutted." Brownlie, *supra* note 265, p. 10. Certainly, its abstention cannot insulate it from being bound by other norms of customary international law deriving from the Universal Declaration. See *supra* note 290 (French representative noting that Saudi Arabia was bound by prohibition of slavery in Universal Declaration and Charter).

306. See *supra* notes 245-246 and accompanying text.

307. Universal Declaration art. 18.

308. Universal Declaration art. 26.

309. Universal Declaration art. 16(1).

310. For example, according to the Human Rights Committee, identical treatment is not required under the ICCPR and not every differentiation will amount to discrimination. See Human Rights Committee, *General Comment Non-Discrimination, supra* note 280, ¶8, p. 174.

311. See South West Africa Cases (Second Phase) *(Eth. v. S. Afr.; Liber. v. S. Afr.),* 1966

I.C.J. 6, 306-16 (18 July) (dissenting opinion of Judge Tanaka); see also Human Rights Committee, *General Comment Non-Discrimination, supra* note 260, ¶13, p. 175. For a general discussion of the standards to be employed in sex discrimination, see Bayefsky, *Equality, supra* note 273, p. 12.

312. South West Africa Cases (Second Phase) *(Eth. v. S. Afr.; Liber. v. S. Afr.)*, 1966 I.C.J. 6, 306, 309, 314 (18 July) (dissenting opinion of Judge Tanaka) (finding that "the practice of apartheid is fundamentally unreasonable and unjust. The unreasonableness and injustice do not depend upon the intention or motive."). Moreover, some analyses of equality impose the further requirement that a distinction which otherwise meets the requirements of an allowable distinction must also be invoked for a legitimate purpose. See Human Rights Committee, *General Comment Non-Discrimination, supra* note 260, ¶13, p. 175 (stating that differentiation will be justified only if the "criteria for such differentiation are reasonable and objective and if the aim is to achieve a purpose which is legitimate under the Covenant."). The Human Rights Committee has justified affirmative action on this basis. *Ibid.,* ¶10.

313. The article 29 approach applies to all acts attributable to a state, not just "laws." For a discussion of acts attributable to a state, see Section IV.C.

314. Universal Declaration art. 29(2). Article 29(2) uses the connector "and" rather than "or," which implies that limitations are permissible only if other individuals' rights are not recognized and society's interests are not met. In other human rights treaties, however, the "and" has become an "or." See, e.g., ICCPR art. 18(3). It might be argued that the "and" in article 29(2) should therefore be understood as an "or" as if the clause is providing separate paragraphical alternatives, but this interpretation creates an ellipsis. Since there is some ambiguity with respect to this term, I use, for the purpose of argument, an interpretation which favors religious fundamentalism throughout. That is, I demand an "and" interpretation to justify any constraint on religion, but accept an "or" interpretation as justifying a limitation on women's rights. These interpretations are made in the context of an article 29 analysis as applied to religious fundamentalist laws. See *infra* notes 367-410 and accompanying text.

A further requirement is that limitations must be determined by law. Universal Declaration art. 29. At the very least, this means that they may not be imposed arbitrarily, but under a law that gives clear notice as to the consequences of any proscribed action. See *Olsson v. Sweden,* 130 Eur. Ct. H.R. (ser. A) at 30 (1988) (discussing comparable limitations clause in article 8 of the European Convention for the Protection of Human Rights and Fundamental Freedoms, 4 Nov. 1950, 213 U.N.T.S. 221). Religious fundamentalist laws generally give ample notice of the consequences of violation, and thus this requirement is not normally at issue except for laws that operate extra-legally. See *supra* notes 189-190 and accompanying text and *infra* notes 322-325 and accompanying text (discussing laws absolving husbands who kill their wives for moral disobedience).

315. See generally Alexandre Charles Kiss, "Permissible Limitations on Rights," in *The International Bill of Rights: The Covenant on Civil and Political Rights, supra* note 260, pp. 290, 305-8 (discussing the meaning of democracy in context of ICCPR limitations).

316. Universal Declaration art. 29(3).

317. So, for example, in the case of a religious law that discriminates against a particular race, the importance to the religion of the right to discriminate is not a factor to be

considered because this would subvert the "due recognition" standard being based on international law. It has been argued, in the context of a balancing approach to women's rights and religious freedom, that a factor to consider is "the importance of the religious law or practice to the right of religious freedom . . . [and] assessments of the significance of a religious practice should proceed from the significance accorded that practice by the religion or belief itself." Sullivan, *supra* note 242, p. 822 (footnote omitted). This factor is impermissible under international law and, moreover, is unworkable on a practical basis.

318. For a discussion of how the international standard of due recognition has been worked out in the context of racial discrimination and religious rights, see *infra* notes 326-334, 372-408 and accompanying text.

319. Universal Declaration art. 30. This is very similar to the wording in article 5(1) of the ICCPR, which has been understood to mean that even when individuals engage in the destruction of the rights guaranteed, the individuals "do not lose all rights, but only those that directly promote the destructive activities." Thomas Buergenthal, "To Respect and Ensure: State Obligations and Permissible Derogations," in *The International Bill of Rights: The Covenant on Civil and Political Rights, supra* note 260, pp. 72, 89.

320. A state is permitted to limit the actions of such groups within the guidelines of article 30. See *supra* note 319 and accompanying text. It may also be argued, however, that a state *must* limit such groups. Article 30 was originally "designed to enable the state to protect itself against individuals relying on the human rights guarantees to promote activities seeking to establish totalitarian regimes." Buergenthal, *supra* note 319, pp. 86-87 (footnote omitted). Since article 30 denies to private actors the right to destroy other rights in the Declaration, it is arguable that article 30 grants to everyone the corresponding right to be free from the intimidating actions of any such individuals or groups who are attempting to destroy rights. For example, a group may act toward an individual in a threatening and intimidating way that does not yet invade a right under another article of the Universal Declaration but nonetheless results in the silencing and coercing of the individual into foregoing rights for fear of reprisal. Such groups may create an atmosphere of fear such that others are too frightened to exercise their rights. If the state fails to act against such destructive and terrorist groups under article 30, then the right to be free of the actions of these groups is empty and also threatens to undermine individuals' other rights under the Universal Declaration. Article 30 might therefore be understood to impose an affirmative obligation on a state to ensure that nonstate actors do not engage in activities aimed at destroying the rights of others.

321. "Religious fundamentalist laws" in this section means all religious fundamentalist laws and acts discussed in Part III that are attributable to a state. See *supra* note 313. For a discussion of acts attributable to a state, see Section IV.C.

322. See *supra* note 265.

323. Nigel S. Rodley, *The Treatment of Prisoners under International Law* (New York: Oxford University Press, 1987), p. 148.

324. See *supra* notes 189-90 and accompanying text (discussing Iraq's and Kurdistan's laws).

325. This same analysis applies to the state flogging women for breaking modesty code laws. There is strong evidence that flogging is a violation of the *jus cogens* prohibition against torture and ill-treatment. See Rodley, *supra* note 323, p. 254.

326. See *supra* p. 178.

327. See Legal Consequences for States of the Continued Presence of South Africa in Namibia (South West Africa) Notwithstanding Security Council Resolution 276 (1970), 1971 I.C.J. 16, ¶131, at 57 (21 June). "Apartheid" is based on the separation of each culture requiring geographical segregation based on race such that blacks were permitted in "white areas" only if they were performing an essential economic service for whites. George M. Fredrickson, *White Supremacy: A Comparative Study in American and South African History* (New York: Oxford University Press, 1981), pp. 175, 240-41. Under apartheid, Africans of color were denied most civil and political rights, employment rights, and property rights. See *infra* notes 389-403, 438 and accompanying text; Legal Consequences for States of the Continued Presence of South Africa in Namibia (South West Africa) Notwithstanding Security Council Resolution 276 (1970), 1971 I.C.J. ¶130, at 57.

328. See *infra* notes 391-400 and accompanying text.

329. See *infra* notes 391-400 and accompanying text.

330. See Legal Consequences for States of the Continued Presence of South Africa in Namibia (South West Africa) Notwithstanding Security Council Resolution 276 (1970), 1971 I.C.J. ¶¶ 128-29, at 56-57.

331. See Legal Consequences for States of the Continued Presence of South Africa in Namibia (South West Africa) Notwithstanding Security Council Resolution 276 (1970), 1971 I.C.J, ¶129, at 57. This accords with Judge Tanaka's earlier dissenting opinion where he found that apartheid was fundamentally unreasonable and unjust without regard to motive or purpose, whether the intent was oppressive or benevolent. South West Africa Cases (Second Phase) *(Eth. v. S. Afr.; Liber. v. S. Afr.)*, 1966 I.C.J. 6, 306-16 (18 July) (dissenting opinion of Judge Tanaka); see *supra* note 312 and accompanying text.

332. See Legal Consequences for States of the Continued Presence of South Africa in Namibia (South West Africa) Notwithstanding Security Council Resolution 276 (1970), 1971 I.C.J. ¶¶ 129, 130, at 57.

333. See *infra* notes 390-400 and accompanying text.

334. See Legal Consequences for States of the Continued Presence of South Africa in Namibia (South West Africa) Notwithstanding Security Council Resolution 276 (1970), 1971 I.C.J. ¶131, at 57 ("To establish .. [such] distinctions . . . exclusively based on grounds of race . . . which constitute a denial of fundamental human rights is a flagrant violation of the purposes and principles of the Charter"); see *supra* notes 253-60 and accompanying text and *infra* notes 372-410 and accompanying text.

335. See *supra* p. 178 and *infra* notes 438-40 and accompanying text (discussing similarity of the denial of rights to Africans of color under apartheid to the denial of rights of women under religious fundamentalist laws).

336. See *supra* notes 313-18 and accompanying text.

337. The justification normally offered for such laws is that they constitute the exercise of religious belief and freedom protected under the Universal Declaration. For example, Iran stated in its report to the Human Rights Committee that its strict dress code for women was intended to ensure respect for the country's religious beliefs and was not intended to repress or penalize women. See UN Human Rights Committee, 46th Sess., *Summary Record of the 1195th Mtg.: Second Periodic Report of the Islamic Republic of Iran*, UN Doc. CCPR/C/SR.1195, ¶21, at 7 (1992).

338. See South West Africa Cases (Second Phase) *(Eth. v. S. Afr.; Liber. v. S. Afr.)*, 1966 I.C.J. 6, 306-16 (18 July) (dissenting opinion of Judge Tanaka); see also Human Rights Committee, General Comment Non-Discrimination, *supra* note 260, ¶13, at 175. The Human Rights Committee imposes the further requirement that any distinction must be for a legitimate purpose. The distinctions that religious fundamentalism imposes on women, however, fail to satisfy the requirements of being reasonable or just, and based on objective criteria, see *infra* notes 341-42 and accompanying text, and so there is no need to consider legitimacy of purpose in determining whether discrimination exists.

339. See *supra* notes 48-54, 56-59 (Buddhism), 75-87, 92, 95-99 (Christianity), 112-13, 119-24, 129-32, 149 (Hinduism), 159-69, 173, 179 (Islam), 207-8, 210-12, 224-30 (Judaism) and accompanying text.

340. See *supra* notes 257-59 and accompanying text.

341. For example, in the context of the ICCPR, see *S.W.M. Broeks v. the Netherlands* (adopted 9 April 1987, 29th Sess.), Communication No. 172/1984, Report of the Human Rights Committee, UN GAOR, 42d Sess., Supp. No. 40, 139, ¶8.2, at 145, ¶8.4, at 147, ¶¶14, 15, at 150, UN Doc. A/42/40, at 139 (1987) (rejecting notion that a prevailing view in the society's culture that men are naturally "breadwinners" justifies differential treatment).

342. Even if fundamentalists allege that the obedience and modesty laws are not intended to make women unequal, lack of intent is irrelevant to laws discriminatory on their face. See *supra* notes 312, 331 and accompanying text. For example, in the context of the ICCPR, see *S.W.M. Broeks v. the Netherlands* (adopted 9 April 1987, 29th Sess.), Communication No. 172/1984, Report of the Human Rights Committee, UN GAOR, 42d Sess., Supp. No. 40, 139, ¶¶14, 15, 16, at 150, UN Doc. A/42/40, at 139 (1987) (finding that lack of intent is irrelevant to laws that are discriminatory on their face).

343. Universal Declaration art. 3.

344. For example, in the context of the ICCPR's guarantee of the security of the person, the Human Rights Committee has declared that "it cannot be the case that, as a matter of law, States can ignore known threats to the life of persons under their jurisdiction, just because he or she is not arrested or otherwise detained. States parties are under an obligation to take reasonable and appropriate measures to protect them." See *W. Delgado Páez v. Colombia*, Communication No. 195/1985 (adopted 12 July 1990, 39th Sess.), Report of the Human Rights Committee, Vol. II, Comm. No. 195/1985, UN GAOR, 45th Sess., Supp. No 40, at 43, ¶5.5, at 47, UN Doc. A/45/40 (1990) (holding that anonymous threats and an attack on a state school teacher, following harassment by ecclesiastical and educational authorities, constituted a violation of article 9 of the ICCPR, which guarantees security of the person); see *infra* notes 418-19 and accompanying text (discussing the relevance of *Delgado* to the issue of state accountability for violative actions by nonstate actors). The Committee specifically rejected that the right to security of the person found in the first sentence of ICCPR article 9(1) was in any way limited to the circumstances of the second sentence of article 9(1) referring to arrest and detention. See *Delgado Páez v. Colombia*, ¶5.5, at 147. Article 3 in the Universal Declaration has no such potentially limiting provision in any event.

345. Universal Declaration art. 8.

346. Universal Declaration art. 18.

347. Universal Declaration art. 19.

348. Article 20 gives everyone the right to freedom of peaceful assembly. Universal Declaration art. 20(1).

349. Article 21 gives everyone the right to take part in government, directly or through freely chosen representatives, the right of equal access to public service, and the right to vote in periodic elections. Universal Declaration art. 21.

350. The only exception is that, in some cases, a husband may not demand that his wife do something that would violate other strong norms of the religion. See Maududi, *The Meaning of the Qur'an* (Vol. II), *supra* note 164, p. 325 n. 58. There are no strong fundamentalist norms that require women to vote or to be involved in political matters, so nothing within the religion prevents the husband from limiting his wife's action with respect to all political matters.

351. Universal Declaration art. 19.

352. Canada and the United States define "refugee" consistently with the 1967 Protocol Relating to the Status of Refugees, 31 Jan. 1967, 19 U.S.T. 6223, 606 U.N.T.S. 267, thus conforming their national law to their international obligations. See, e.g., *I.N.S. v. Cardozo-Fonseca,* 480 U.S. 421, 436-37 (1987). The recognition of gender-related asylum, formalized through administrative guidelines in Canada and the United States, has been developing in other national courts and through pronouncements of international organizations. For example, the United Nations High Commission on Refugees concluded that states "are free to adopt the interpretation that women asylum-seekers who face harsh and inhumane treatment due to their having transgressed the social mores of the society in which they live may be considered as a 'particular social group' within the meaning of . . . the United Nations Refugee Convention." UN Doc. HRC/IP/2/Rev. 1986, at Conclusion No. 39, (XXXVI), ¶(k) (8 July 1985); see generally A. Johnson, "The International Protection of Women Refugees: A Summary of Principal Problems and Issues," 1 *Int'l J. Refugee L.* 221 (1989). Thus, in these contexts, there is increasing awareness that gender-based persecution may take the form of reprisals against women for contravening their society's norms. I would like to thank Minty Chung for her help and advice with regard to the law and practice of political asylum and refugee cases.

353. See, e.g., *In the Matter of A and Z: In Deportation Proceedings* (A 72-190-893; A 72-793-219) (Exec. Office for Immigration Review, Arlington, Va., U.S.A.) (20 Dec. 1994) 14 (unpublished opinion), reported in 72 *Interpreter Releases* 521 (17 Apr. 1995) (holding that a Jordanian woman and her son were entitled to asylum in U.S. due to persecution by her husband "for their political belief in the importance of individual freedom . . . for women and children."); *In the Matter of M.K.: In Deportation Proceedings* (A 72-374-558) (Exec. Office for Immigration Review, Arlington, Va., U.S.A.), 19 (9 Aug. 1995) (unpublished opinion) ("'Political opinion' includes not only a woman's attitude about her government, but also includes her opinion relating to the treatment and status of women generally within her country or culture, or within her social, religious, or ethnic group. . . . 'Political opinion' includes . . . her refusal to conform to religious or cultural norms or the roles assigned women within her country or culture."); Decision of the Federal Office for the Recognition of Foreign Refugees 439-26428-86 (Federal Republic of Germany) (24 Nov. 1988) (granting refugee status to an Iranian woman and holding that "the ideologically based power of men over women results in a general political repression of women in defiance of their individual liberties and human rights.").

354. See *Fatin v. INS*, 12 F.3d 1233, 1242 (3rd Cir. 1993) ("feminism qualifies as a political opinion").

355. The judge stated:

> She is not content to be a slave. . . . The emancipation of women is one of the most important world-wide political and social movements of this century. Precisely because of its importance, the freedom and equality of women is dangerous and threatening politics to her husband, his society, and his government. . . . [Her] husband has beaten and abused [her] . . . for three decades, but [she] . . . remains unbowed . . . and seeks protection . . . for . . . political belief in the importance of individual freedom.

In the Matter of A and Z: In Deportation Proceedings (A 72-190-893; A 72-793-219), at 14 (Exec. Office for Immigration Review, Arlington, Va., U.S.A.) (20 Dec. 1994) (unpublished opinion), reported in 72 *Interpreter Releases* 521 (17 Apr. 1995). See also Rhonda Copelon, "Intimate Terror: Understanding Domestic Violence As Torture," in *Human Rights of Women, supra* note 128, pp. 116, 120-21 (discussing that wife-battering is related to, and triggered by, women's expressions of capacity and power, and by their "rebellions" small and large).

356. In the asylum context, actions of nonstate actors may be attributed to the state from the state's unwillingness to control the actors. See U.S. Department of Justice: Immigration and Naturalization Service International Division, *Memorandum: Considerations for Asylum Officers Adjudicating Asylum Claims from Women* 16 (26 May 1995). Thus, courts have found states complicit in the reprisals women suffer at the hands of their husbands, nonstate actors, because of states' failure to provide a remedy, even if the failure is due to state cultural and religious norms. See Convention Refugee Determination Decision, 1993 C.R. D.D. No. 307 (No. T93-08296) (Immig. and Refugee Board of Canada, Convention Refugee Determination Div.) (Toronto, Ontario, Canada) (29 Sept. 1993) (holding that an Argentine woman subjected to years of violence from a "machismo" husband met refugee status and that the state did not have the impetus to provide effective remedy in part due to Roman Catholic norms that limited women to the domestic sphere and mandated men as heads of their family); see also *supra* note 353 and accompanying text. Systematic failure to provide a remedy may also be grounds in international human rights law for attributing nonstate third party acts to the state. I discuss the issue of state accountability for acts of nonstate actors under general international human rights law in Section IV.C. See *infra* notes 412-20 and accompanying text; see generally Celina Romany, "State Responsibility Goes Private: A Feminist Critique of the Public/Private Distinction in International Human Rights Law," in *Human Rights of Women, supra* note 128, pp. 85, 100.

357. See, e.g., *In the Matter of M.K.: In Deportation Proceedings* (A 72-374-558) (Exec. Office for Immigration Review, Arlington, Va., U.S.A.) 13-15 (9 Aug. 1995) (unpublished opinion) (holding that spouse abuse was attributable to the state and that a wife was "persecuted by being punished with spousal abuse for attempting to assert her individual autonomy and resisting mandated female subservience."); *In the Matter of A and Z: In Deportation Proceedings* (A 72-190-893; A 72-793-219) (Exec. Office for Immigration Review, Arlington, Va., U.S.A.) 18 (20 Dec. 1994) (unpublished opinion), reported in 72 *Interpreter Releases* 521 (17 Apr. 1995); see also *supra* note 351.

358. Universal Declaration art. 21.

359. See *supra* note 201 (discussing limits on women's right to vote in Kuwait and Algeria).

360. See, e.g., Iqbal, *supra* note 36, pp. 115-19 (arguing that under Islamic law women are prohibited from running for public office under modesty codes).

361. Women who claim that they support laws of obedience and modesty codes call into question the reliability of their own position. There is no way that an outside observer can evaluate whether or not this political position is her own since she is subject to obedience rules and corresponding coercive violent sanctions. The very existence of the rules undermines the credibility of a woman who supports such rules while subject to them.

362. See *supra* notes 4-6, 23 and accompanying text.

363. See *supra* notes 6, 23 and accompanying text.

364. As a U.S. circuit court declared in a political asylum case concerning an Iranian woman who had been harassed by Iranian authorities for "some strands of hair outside her veil or 'chador,' which the Iranian regime requires all women to wear," it is "clear that being forced to conform to, or being sanctioned for failing to comply with, a conception of Islam that fundamentally is at odds with one's own also can rise to the level of persecution. . . . Indeed, when a member of a religion is forced to comply with an interpretation of her faith with which she disagrees, . . . the individual may suffer not only the general 'torture' of conscience . . . , but also the additional consequence of having imposed upon her a particular conception of the dictates of her own religion." *Fisher v. I.N.S.*, 37 F.3d 1371, 1381 (9th Cir. 1994) (remanding to the Immigration Board for consideration an Iranian woman's claim of well-founded fear of persecution on account of her religious beliefs).

365. Universal Declaration art. 23; see *supra* notes 172, 182 and accompanying text (discussing codes requiring a wife to have her husband's permission to work).

366. Universal Declaration art. 13.

367. See *supra* notes 314-18 and accompanying text.

368. See *supra* notes 295, 317 and accompanying text.

369. See *supra* notes 257-59, 295, 317 and accompanying text.

370. For example, the activities recognized as core to the manifestation of religious belief in article 6 of the UN Declaration on the Elimination of Religious Intolerance and Discrimination include the freedom, *inter alia,* to worship, and to maintain places of worship; to maintain charitable institutions; to make and use necessary articles related to the rites and customs of a religion; to issue and disseminate publications concerning the religion; to teach a religion in a place suitable for this purpose; to solicit financial support; to train leaders; to observe religious holidays; to have communications at the national and international level with other members of the religion. See UN Declaration on the Elimination of Religious Intolerance and Discrimination, G.A. Res. 36/55, 36 UN GAOR, 36th Sess., Supp. 51, at 171, UN Doc. A/36/51 (1981). The Human Rights Committee has recognized a similar list, focusing on acts that are integral and close to the basic affairs of religion. Human Rights Committee, General Comments Adopted under Article 40, Paragraph 4, of the ICCPR: General Comment No. 22 (48) (art. 18), UN GAOR, 48th Sess., Supp. 40, UN Doc. A/48/40 (Pt. I) (1993). The Committee recognizes the right to wear distinctive dress, and does not deal with mandatory modesty dress codes.

371. See *supra* note 370.

372. See also Sullivan, *supra* note 242, p. 811.

373. See supra note 318 and accompanying text.

374. Slavery was justified under traditional Buddhism and was considered legitimate under Hindu law. See Dev Raj Chanana, *Slavery in Ancient India, As Depicted in Pali and Sanskrit Texts* (New Delhi: People's Pub. House, 1960), pp. 2-3, 26-30, 39-63, 87. With respect to Christianity, Islam, and Judaism, see David B. Davis, *Slavery and Human Progress* (New York: Oxford University Press, 1984), pp. 86-90; Fredrickson, *supra* note 327, p. 10. These religions relied on Genesis 9:24-25 where Noah awakens from his drunkenness and curses Ham, his son, that Canaan (Ham's son) shall be a "servant of servants" of his brethren, and on Leviticus 25:44-46 where God tells Moses that the Hebrews should not sell their own brethren but should buy their slaves "of the nations that are around you." See Davis, *Slavery and Human Progress, supra,* pp. 86-90. By the Middle Ages, Jewish, Muslim, and Christian writers all separately identified the curse of Noah on Canaan as referring specifically to the "black children of Ham" understood to be black Africans, *ibid.,* p. 87, although they justified the institution in general and did not limit it to black Africans. Christianity and Islam also justified taking infidels and captives of war as slaves, and consequently each enslaved prisoners of war taken from the other, a practice that continued for six centuries including through the Crusades and Jihads in the eleventh, twelfth, and thirteenth centuries. See David B. Davis, *The Problem of Slavery in Western Culture* (Ithaca: Cornell University Press, 1966), p. 41. I would like to thank Robert J. Cottrol for his help and advice with regard to the subject of the institution and history of slavery.

375. With respect to Christianity, see Davis, *Problem of Slavery, supra* note 374, pp. 101-2. By the middle of the eighteenth century, Christian doctrine and institutions in general played an important part in the procedures of slave control and enforcement of slave codes in the New World. See Lester B. Scherer, *Slavery and the Churches in Early America 1619-1819* (Grand Rapids: Eerdmans, 1975), pp. 15-16, 66-68; Davis, *Problem of Slavery, supra* note 374, pp. 88, 95-96; see also Fredrickson, *supra* note 327, p. 141 (discussing the Christian doctrine of spiritual equality, which still, conveniently, allowed for hierarchical orders on earth). Canon law endorsed slavery to the extent that a bishop was not allowed to manumit a slave belonging to the RCC unless he made up the loss from his own property. Davis, *Problem of Slavery, supra* note 374, p. 95. With respect to Islam, see Nehemia Levtzion, "Slavery and Islamization in Africa: A Comparative Study," in *Slaves and Slavery in Muslim Africa,* vol. I: *Islam and the Ideology of Enslavement,* ed. John R. Willis (London: F. Cass, 1985), pp. 182, 187, 188-95; see generally John R. Willis, "Preface," in *Slaves and Slavery in Muslim Africa,* vol. I: *Islam and the Ideology of Enslavement, supra,* p. viii (noting that Islam justified slavery not only on the basis of the Old Testament, but also on the Sunnah (the model of the prophet Muhammad), "who was at once a slaveholder and a practitioner of polygamy and concubinage."); John R. Willis, "Introduction: The Ideology of Enslavement in Islam," in *Slaves and Slavery in Muslim Africa,* vol. I: *Islam and the Ideology of Enslavement, supra,* pp. 1, 4 [hereinafter Willis, "Introduction"]; Robert W. July, *A History of the African People* (New York: Scribner's, 1970), pp. 97-99, 148-156, 165, 217-23.

376. Scherer, *supra* note 375, pp. 76-78, 98-100; see also Fredrickson, *supra* note 327, pp. 185, 201-2 (discussing doctrine that found that some men were incapable of governing themselves and therefore were better off in slavery, particularly as they benefited from being under the care of Christians).

377. See Fredrickson, *supra* note 327, p. 84; Scherer, *supra* note 375, pp. 95-100; Davis, *Problem of Slavery, supra* note 374, pp. 203-5.

378. See Fredrickson, *supra* note 327, p. 172; Davis, *Slavery and Human Progress, supra* note 374, pp. 111-12, 234, 260-61; see generally Thomas V. Peterson, *Ham and Japheth: The Mythic World of Whites in the Antebellum South* (Metuchen: Scarecrow, 1978).

379. See Davis, *Problem of Slavery, supra* note 374, pp. 473-74; Scherer, *supra* note 375, pp. 142-44; see, e.g., *infra* note 382; see also Fredrickson, *supra* note 327, pp. 150-62.

380. See Davis, *Slavery and Human Progress, supra* note 374, pp. 309-10; see generally United Nations Economic and Social Council, The Work of the League of Nations for the Suppression of Slavery, UN Doc. E/AC.33/2, at 2-3 (23 Jan. 1950), LNP, C.426.M157.1925.VI, 71-74.

381. See Davis, *Slavery and Human Progress, supra* note 374, pp. 314, 319.

382. For example, Christian Reconstructionists who hope to establish a Christian nation with a legal system based upon the Mosaic laws of the Bible, see *supra* notes 71 and 94, support slavery because it is part of those laws. On a Christian Reconstruction website, there is an anthology of writings by Reconstructionists concerning "God's Laws." See Anthology of Quotations (visited 8 Feb. 2005) http://www.serve.com/thibodep/cr/words.htm. With respect to slavery, Reconstructionist thought is that "[t]he bible permits slavery . . . [and] biblical laws concerning slavery are among the most beneficent in all the Bible." See David Chilton, Slavery (visited 8 Feb. 2005) http://www.serve.com/thibodep/cr/slavery.htm, extracted from David Chilton, *Productive Christians in an Age of Guilt-Manipulators* (Tyler, Tex.: Institute for Christian Economics, 1981), pp. 61-62.

Chilton reviews how it is appropriate under Christian law — including Exod. 21:16, 20-27; 22:1-3; Lev. 25:39, 44-46; Num. 31:32-35; Deut. 21:10-14 — to obtain slaves, and how to care for slaves. See *ibid.* Rushdoony, one of the main Reconstructionist leaders, see *supra* note 71, was eulogized in the *Daily Oklahoman* newspaper at his death in 2001, despite his wanting to found the state on biblical law (including slavery as a lawful institution), because, as one Christian commentator wrote, "Oklahoma is one of the few states where influential people have little fear that their credibility will be undermined by being openly identified with Rushdoony. . . ." See Bruce Prescott, *Christian Reconstructionism* (Westminister Presbyterian Church, 11 Apr. 2002) (visited 8 Feb. 2005) http://www.mainstreambaptists.org/dominionism.htm. Christian Reconstructionist thought is central to another sect led by Douglas Wilson of the Christ Church in Idaho. See Mark Potok, *Taliban on the Palouse?: A Religious Empire Based in Idaho Is Part of the Far-Right Theological Movement Fueling Neo-Confederate Groups* (visited 8 Feb. 2005) http://www.splcenter.org/intel/intelreport/article.jsp?aid=376. Wilson, with co-Religionist Steven Wilkins, is tightly linked with the Reconstructionists and the Coalition on Revival, another group endorsing Reconstructionist theology. See *ibid.* The theology of Wilkins and Wilson, which combines an endorsement of the antebellum South with Reconstructionist theories, is now at the center of the neo-Confederate movement. See *ibid.* Reconstructionist theology has gained legitimacy when endorsed by state government representatives. For example, State Representative Bill Graves of Oklahoma City has written articles for the Reconstructionist Foundation Newsletter, see Prescott, *supra,*and an Alabama State senator defended flying the Confederate flag at the capitol of Alabama by quoting biblical passages on slavery (including Leviticus 25:44-46), by arguing the benefits of Southern farmers converting slaves to Christianity, and by arguing that "[t]hose bitter about slavery . . . 'are obviously bitter and hateful against God and his word, because they reject what God says and embrace what mere humans say concerning slavery.'" "Alabama House Candidate Quits After Slavery Defense," *Wash. Post,* 12 May 1996, p. A11 (explaining that the state senator ended his plans to run for U.S. Congress but did not resign as state senator). For the text of Davidson's article, reprinted with approval on CSAnet: The E-voice of the Old South, where they "do not apologize for being Southern, for being Christian, or for being of Anglo-Celtic descent," see CSANET, *About CSAnet* (visited 8 Feb. 2005) http://www .pointsouth.com/csanet/aboutcsa.htm, see Charles Davidson, *The Confederate Battle Flag: A Symbol of Racism?* (visited 8 Feb. 2005) http://www.pointsouth.com/csanet/confeder-ate_flag.htm.

383. See, e.g., Iqbal, *supra* note 36, pp. 158-63 (discussing that Islamic law allows for slavery of prisoners of war and that men are free to have "sexual relations" with their female slaves and to sell them); Maududi, *Purdah, supra* note 158, p. 21 n. 1 (arguing that if one's enemy refuses to give compensation for slaves or to release Muslim prisoners, then it is lawful under Islam to keep a slave); see also Abdulahi Ahmed An-Naim, *Toward an Islamic Reformation: Civil Liberties, Human Rights, and International Law* (Syracuse: Syracuse University Press, 1990), p. 175 ("Muslim tribesmen of southwestern Sudan feel justified in capturing non-Muslims from southern Sudan and keeping them in secret slavery").

384. See *supra* notes 317-18 and accompanying text.

385. See *supra* pp. 178, 180-81, 182.

386. A comparison between the ideology of slavery and the ideology of women's subordination is not only apt, but is so complete that some sects themselves have compared slavery to the servile state of women in simultaneous justification of both systems of domination. For example, Muslim ideology has explicitly compared the condition of the slave to the servile status of a wife to her husband: "a comparison is drawn between the dominion imposed by the husband through which his wife is caused to surrender her sexual self, and the sovereignty established by the master whereby the slave is compelled to alienate his right to dispose. . . . The master buys his slave, whereas in marriage, the husband purchases his wife's productive part. For the security of dower, the woman's sexual self is enslaved — for the protection of his lord, the slave's person is secured." Willis, "Introduction," supra note 375, p. 1. On contemporary religious fundamentalism, see Iqbal, *supra* note 36, pp. 158-63 (making comparison of female slaves to wives).

387. See *supra* note 376 and accompanying text.

388. See *supra* note 376 and accompanying text.

389. See Fredrickson, *supra* note 327, pp. 18, 37, 65, 73.

390. Fredrickson, *supra* note 327, pp. 42, 48, 147-48, 163-72; T. Dunbar Moodie, *The Rise of Afrikanerdom: Power, Apartheid, and the Afrikaner Civil Religion* (Berkeley: University of California Press, 1975), pp. 3-4, 19.

391. Fredrickson, *supra* note 327, pp. 37, 170; see Moodie, *supra* note 390, pp. ix, 22-26.

392. Fredrickson, *supra* note 327, p. 171 (quoting a local official's report on the treatment of servants by settlers; Landdrost Albert to Gov. Janssens, as quoted in J. S. Marais, *Maynier and the First Boer Republic,* p. 73); see Moodie, *supra* note 390, p. 29; see also *supra* note 374 (discussing Ham's curse). One participant in the Great Trek explained the necessity of migration because of "our slaves . . . being placed on an equal footing with Chris-

tians, contrary to the laws of God and the natural distinctions of race and religion."
Fredrickson, *supra* note 327, p. 171 (quoting from W. M. Macmillan, *The Cape Colour Question: A Historical Survey* [London: Faber and Gwyer, 1927], p. 81).

393. Fredrickson, *supra* note 327, pp. 174-75; Moodie, *supra* note 390, pp. 6, 15, 199-200, 245. A visiting missionary described the Boers in the independent Boer republics, see *infra* note 395 and accompanying text, as having "persuaded themselves . . . that they are God's chosen people, and that the blacks are wicked and condemned Canaanites over whose head the divine anger lowers continually." John MacKenzie, *Ten Years North of the Orange River, 1859-1869* (London: F. Cass, 1971 [1871]). They found it obvious that heathens and black Africans could not be members of their divinely chosen select group. Moodie, *supra* note 390, pp. 28-29. The survivors of the battle covenanted to God to celebrate the victory every year thereafter, and accordingly the Day of the Covenant remains an important national holiday of Afrikaners. Moodie, *supra* note 390, pp. 20-21.

394. Fredrickson, *supra* note 327, p. 176; see Moodie, *supra* note 390, p. 7.

395. Fredrickson, *supra* note 327, p. 177 (quoting Constitution of South African Republic); see Moodie, *supra* note 390, p. 7.

396. Fredrickson, *supra* note 327, p. 191; see Moodie, *supra* note 390, pp. 7-11, 26-38.

397. See Moodie, *supra* note 390, pp. 7-11, 26-38; see also Fredrickson, *supra* note 327, p. 193 (quoting President of Transvaal, Paul Kruger, in 1882).

398. Fredrickson, *supra* note 327, p. 193; see July, *supra* note 375, p. 493 (noting Kruger's religious view of the Boers as God's chosen people as the genesis of apartheid and nationalism); see Moodie, *supra* note 390, pp. 7-11, 26-38, 79, 104, 178, 199-200, 215. At the centenary celebration of the Day of the Covenant, a reenactment of the Great Trek galvanized thousands of Afrikaners into forming an association dedicated to promoting the Afrikaner race and culture and preserving the rule of the white race. See Moodie, *supra* note 390, pp. 178-89, 199-200.

399. Moodie, *supra* note 390, pp. 247, 248. When South Africa emerged as a self-governing union, the white supremacy laws of segregation, traceable back to the earlier Boer republics and slaveholding mentalities, were established. See Fredrickson, *supra* note 327, pp. 238, 239-40, 249.

400. See Moodie, *supra* note 390, pp. 260-61, 265-66, 269-70, 280-85. Despite a small group of Dutch Reformed theologians (the "enlightened ones") questioning apartheid in 1961, they were still a minority in Afrikanerdom in the mid 1970s. *Ibid.*, p. 292.

401. See *infra* notes 436-43 and accompanying text (discussing potential expelling of South Africa from the United Nations); see generally John Dugard, *The South West Africa/Namibia Dispute: Documents and Scholarly Writings on the Controversy between South Africa and the United Nations* (Berkeley: University of California Press, 1973).

402. See *supra* notes 327-35 and accompanying text (discussing *Legal Consequences for States of the Continued Presence of South Africa in Namibia [South West Africa] Notwithstanding Security Council Resolution 276* [1970], 1971 I.C.J. Rep. 16, ¶131, at 57 [21 June]); *infra* notes 436-43 and accompanying text.

403. See *supra* notes 327-35.

404. See *supra* notes 257-59, 295-306, 317 and accompanying text.

405. See *supra* notes 317-18, 384 and accompanying text.

406. See *supra* notes 315-17 and accompanying text.

407. Even without considering the negative impact of religious fundamentalist movements on women, fundamentalist movements promote an intolerance of other religions through elevation of their own religion over all others. The religious intolerance manifested by religious fundamentalists to those in their own religion and to outsider religions is contrary to democratic principles and to the object and purpose of the Universal Declaration.

408. See *supra* notes 346-61 and accompanying text.

409. For example, many states have submitted reservations to CEAFDAW that are contrary to the very aim of the treaty itself. A large number of the explicit and all-encompassing reservations resulted from religious fundamentalist influence. See UN-NGO Group on Women and Development, *Women and Human Rights,* pp. 116-20 (prepared by Katarina Tomasevki, 1993).

410. As has been argued, see *supra* notes 319-20, article 30 may be interpreted to impose an affirmative duty on states concerning religious fundamentalist laws. Thus, in order to protect citizens' right to be free of the intimidating and silencing threat of such groups, a state is obliged to stop the destructive activities of such groups.

411. See Kenneth Roth, "Domestic Violence As an International Human Rights Issue," in *Human Rights of Women, supra* note 128, pp. 326, 329-35; Dorothy Q. Thomas and Michele E. Beasley, "Domestic Violence As a Human Rights Issue," 58 *Alb. L. Rev* 1119 (1995): 1121-34; Rebecca J. Cook, "State Responsibility for Violations of Women's Rights," 7 *Harv. Hum. Rts. J.* 125 (1994): 151. The ICJ distinguished the first and third situations of accountability in *Case Concerning United States Diplomatic and Consular Staff in Tehran (U.S. v. Iran),* 1980 I.C.J. 3, 29 (May 24). The "militants" who first attacked the American embassy in Tehran were not official agents of Tehran, and thus the state was not accountable for the attack. Once the state authorities approved the occupation and adopted a state policy to continue it, the attack was attributable to Iran. *Ibid.,* pp. 35-36. This constitutes the first situation of accountability where the state is directly involved. The third type of situation was demonstrated by Iran's failure to protect the embassy from attack by the militants, contrary to its duty to do so under the Vienna Convention on Diplomatic Relations. *Ibid.,* pp. 30-32.

412. A state is also accountable under customary law for state policy. See *Restatement, supra* note 265, §702, Comment b, p. 162. The Restatement takes the position that a state is not responsible for private acts in violation of customary law unless the state "required, encouraged, or condoned such private violations, but mere failure to enact laws prohibiting private violations of human rights would not ordinarily constitute encouragement or condonation." *Ibid.*

413. See *supra* note 176.

414. See *supra* note 236 and accompanying text. The recent elections in Israel increased the power of the religious fundamentalist parties, who seek to broaden the jurisdiction of the religious courts. This is likely to worsen the problem of discriminatory religious law.

415. India enforces discriminatory laws through its delegation to Christian and Muslim religious courts of jurisdiction in these matters, and has bowed under Muslim religious fundamentalist pressure to limit further women's rights under Muslim family laws. See *supra* notes 93, 152; Singh, *supra* note 128, pp. 384-85 (discussing passage of Muslim

Women's Act due to Muslim fundamentalist pressure, which overruled the Supreme Court decision in *Shah Bano* and denied Muslim women maintenance on divorce beyond the period of *iddat*). With respect to Hinduism, the recent elections in India enlarged the representation of the BJP, which advocates implementation of discriminatory Hindu laws relating to marriage, divorce, and *sati* and may put India in further violation of its international responsibilities.

416. See Roth, *supra* note 411, pp. 333-35. The state is discriminating against female victims of assault crimes by failure to prosecute men.

417. See *supra* note 345 and accompanying text.

418. *W. Delgado Páez v. Colombia*, Communication No. 195/1985 (adopted 12 July 1990, 39th Sess.), Report of the Human Rights Committee, Vol. II, Comm. No. 195/1985, UN GAOR, 45th Sess., Supp. No. 40, at 43, ¶5.5, at 47, UN Doc. A/45/40 (1990) (holding that anonymous threats and an attack on a state school teacher, following harassment by ecclesiastical and educational authorities, constituted a violation of article 9 of ICCPR). The Committee specifically rejected that the right to security of the person found in the first sentence of article 9(1) was in any way limited to the circumstances of the second sentence of article 9(1) referring to arrest and detention. See *Delgado Páez v. Colombia*, ¶5.5, at 47. Roth raises this issue of limitation regarding article 9, see Roth, *supra* note 411, p. 335, but *Delgado* explicitly rejects it. Because the threats and attacks were by unknown persons, Delgado did not allege state action. *Delgado Páez v. Colombia*, ¶2.8, at 44, ¶2.9, at 45; see also Michael Singer, "Jurisdictional Immunity of International Organizations: Human Rights and Functional Necessity Concerns," 36 *Va. J. Int'l L.* 53 (1995): 148-49 (discussing state accountability for private action under *Delgado* as encompassing liability for actions of international organizations). *Delgado* also rejects Roth's notion that the security of the person protects only against violence just short of murder. Cf. Roth, *supra* note 411, p. 335.

419. *Delgado Páez v. Colombia*, ¶5.6, at 48, ¶6, at 49.

420. India and Egypt have taken this approach over many years. India has attempted to deal with Hindu fundamentalism by enacting civil laws of marriage and divorce that do not discriminate (or discriminate much less than traditional and fundamentalist Hindu norms) and legislation specifically banning certain discriminatory Hindu religious practices such as *sati*, dowry deaths, and the prohibition of widow remarriage. See *supra* notes 128, 135, 140, 147; *infra* note 421. Egypt's new educational initiative attempts to reclaim classrooms from fundamentalists, particularly the Muslim Brotherhood. See David Gardner, "Investing in the future," *Fin. Times*, 20 May 1996, p. VIII (Supp. Egypt). This new literacy crusade (52 percent of all Egyptians, but 70 percent of Egyptian women are illiterate) emphasizes skills, agility, and innovation in order to encourage independence of mind in place of rote and passive learning. *Ibid.* It also incorporates a ban on *hejab* dress or the veil from girls' primary schools, *ibid.*, raising a question whether this violates the girls' right to religious freedom. A law banning religious dress in general would clearly violate rights to religious freedom concerning a basic manifestation of religious belief. There is no way of knowing, however, whether the desire of a young child in the religious fundamentalist context to wear *hejab* dress is her own belief or merely the manifestation of obedience to her father. See *supra* note 361. Thus, banning the veil for primary school in order to eliminate the discriminatory effect of such modesty laws and to discourage submissive and passive behavior in the child as part of the learning experience is an important educational

imperative of the state. It may be concluded, therefore, that banning particular dress in state schools is permissible because of the strong needs of the state to prepare citizens for full participation in state democratic affairs.

421. For example, India reported to the Human Rights Committee that it passed laws making dowry deaths a recognizable offense and making the harassment of a woman for property an illegal act of cruelty for which her husband may be prosecuted. See Human Rights Committee, *Summary Record of the 1041st Meeting: Second Periodic Report of India,* ¶¶49-52, CCPR/C/SR.1041; see Indian Penal Code 304B (criminalizing dowry deaths), 498B (criminalizing cruelty to a woman by her husband or a relative of her husband). The Committee regarded these laws as part of India's positive duty under the ICCPR, and the only question was whether India had done enough, especially in enforcing the laws and in educating the populace to a perspective which would improve women's status. See Human Rights Committee, *Summary Record of the 1041st Meeting: Second Periodic Report of India,* ¶52. For a discussion of the Indian government's failure to enforce these laws, see Singh, *supra* note 128, pp. 375, 388-93. The Committee did not find that the civil marriage laws (which attempt to provide equality between the sexes by outlawing religious practices), the laws criminalizing dowry deaths, and the aiding and abetting of *sati* were violations of the right to religious freedom. In fact, the issue was not even raised.

422. The approach is similar to that of India in enacting a law that outlawed the Hindu prohibition on widow remarriage. See *supra* note 146.

423. Since the Iranian Revolution, Iran has repeatedly made the claim that Islamic law takes precedence over international law. See, e.g., UN GAOR 3d Comm., 36th Sess., 29th mtg. at 4-5, 6, UN Doc. A/C.3/36/SR.29 (1981); UN GAOR Hum. Rts. Comm., 37th Sess., Supp. No. 40, ¶300, at 66, UN Doc. A/37/40 (1982); UN GAOR Hum. Rts. Comm., 37th Sess., 56th mtg., ¶¶53-55, at 16, UN Doc. A/C.3/37/SR.56 (1982); UN ECOSOC Comm'n on Human Rts., 44th Sess., Provisional Agenda, Annex II, Agenda Item 12, UN Doc. E/CN.4/1988/12 (1988); Subcomm'n on Prevention of Discrimination and Protection of Minorities, 39th Sess., Agenda Item 6, ¶¶1-10, at 6-8, UN Doc. E/CN.4//Sub.2/1987/35 (1988); see Theodor Meron, "Iran's Challenge to the International Law of Human Rights," 13 *Hum. Rts. Internet Rep.* 9 (1989). Sudan has also asserted this position in the context of the ICCPR. See UN Human Rights Committee, *Summary Record of the Consideration of the Initial Report of the Sudan, Continued, 42d Sess., 1067th mtg.* ¶2, at 2, ¶13, at 5, ¶74, at 18, UN Doc. CCPR/C/SR.1067 (1991). Saudi Arabia has generally avoided signing any human rights treaty, but it does make general comments about religious law taking precedence over international law. See UN GAOR 3d Comm., 3d Sess., 124th mtg. at 363-65, UN Doc. A/C.3/SR.124 (1948); UN GAOR 3d Comm., 3d Sess., 125th mtg. at 367-70, UN Doc. A/C.3/SR.125 (1948) (opposing international guarantees of women's rights in marriage and inheritance).

424. See Vienna Convention on the Law of Treaties, opened for signature 23 May 1969, art. 27, 1155 U.N.T.S. 331, 341, UN Doc. A/Conf. 39/27 (1969) (entered into force 27 Jan. 1980).

425. Report of the Committee of Experts on the Application of Conventions and Recommendations, International Labour Conference, 71st Sess., Report III, Pt. 4A, at 290 (1985) (rejecting Iran's assertion of primacy of religious law over international human rights law); UN Human Rights Committee, *Summary Record of the Consideration of the*

Initial Report of the Sudan, Continued, 42d Sess., 1067th mtg. ¶25, at 8, ¶30 at 9, ¶¶36-37, at 10-11, ¶39, at 11, ¶46, at 13, UN Doc. CCPR/C/SR.1067 (1991) (statements by members of Human Rights Committee that Sudan could not assert Islamic law as justification for failure to comply with the ICCPR); see Sullivan, *supra* note 242, pp. 832-34; Meron, *supra* note 423, p. 8. These claims must be resolutely rejected because if this "argument is raised to the level of theoretical discourse, there is a serious danger that many other states following fundamental religions, or groups (e.g., the Israeli fundamentalist/extremist Gush Emunim . . .) will raise similar arguments to defeat the primacy of international law and divert attempts of the international community to bring about compliance with international law." Meron, *supra* note 423, p. 8.

426. For example, Bangladesh has made the following reservation to CEAFDAW: "The Government of . . . Bangladesh does not consider as binding upon itself the provisions of articles 2, 13(a) and 16.1(c) and (f) as they conflict with Sharia law based on Holy Quran and Sunna." UN Doc. CEDAW/SP/1992/2 at 9; *Multilateral Treaties, supra* note 247, p. 169. Articles 2, 13(a) and 16.1(c) require equal rights of men and women to family benefits, equal rights in marriage, dissolution of marriage, guardianship, and custody. For the argument that these reservations are invalid, see Sara Hossain, "Equality in the Home: Women's Rights and Personal Laws in South Asia," in *Human Rights of Women, supra* note 128, pp. 465, 470. Other states have made similar broad reservations. See UN Doc. CEDAW/SP/1992/2, 1 Nov. 1991, ¶¶11, 15, 16 (reservations of Egypt, Iraq, and Libya); *Multilateral Treaties, supra* note 247, p. 169 (Egypt), ¶171 (Iraq), ¶172 (Libya). Israel has also made a reservation to the ICCPR on the basis of religious laws governing personal status. *Multilateral Treaties, supra* note 247, p. 125.

427. *Multilateral Treaties, supra* note 247, p. 169 (emphasis supplied). Contrast Tunisia, which regards Islamic law as a source of law and social progress, but has acknowledged that in the event of a conflict between Tunisia's law and the ICCPR the Shari'ah could not supplant the positive law of the ICCPR. See *Report of the Human Rights Committee,* UN GAOR, 42d Sess., Supp. No. 40, ¶108, at 26, UN Doc. A/42/40 (1987).

428. For example, Sweden objected to the reservations entered by the government of Iraq on the ground that the reservations are incompatible with the object and purpose of the Convention and "would inevitably result in discrimination against women on the basis of sex, which is contrary to everything the Convention stands for," *Multilateral Treaties, supra* note 247, p. 173, and other states, such as Finland, Federal Republic of Germany, Mexico, the Netherlands, Norway, and Sweden have also objected to Libya's reservation to CEAFDAW. See *Multilateral Treaties, supra* note 247, p. 171 (Germany), p. 172 (Mexico, the Netherlands, Norway, Sweden); Sullivan, *supra* note 242, p. 807. For commentators' arguments, see Hossain, *supra* note 426; Belinda Clark, "The Vienna Convention Reservations Regime and the Convention on Discrimination against Women," 85 *Am. J. Int'l L.* 281 (1991); Rebecca Cook, "Reservations to the Convention on the Elimination of All Forms of Discrimination against Women," 30 *Va. J. Int'l L.* 643 (1990).

429. See *supra* notes 249-56 and accompanying text.

430. See Vienna Convention on the Law of Treaties, opened for signature 23 May 1969, art. 26, 1155 U.N.T.S. 331, 341, UN Doc. A/Conf. 39/27 (1969) (entered into force 7 Jan. 1980).

431. See *supra* notes 257-59 and accompanying text.

432. See *supra* notes 257-59 and accompanying text. A number of these states (Afghanistan, Egypt, Iran, Iraq, Israel, Pakistan, Syria) voted for the Universal Declaration with the full knowledge that the Universal Declaration did not endorse any particular religion as its source of rights, see *supra* notes 285, 303-6 and accompanying text, in accordance with the Charter. Other states with strong fundamentalist movements also voted for the Universal Declaration; these include Chile, Colombia, India, Thailand, and the United States.

433. Some of these states have long been UN members and have benefited from their membership. Their relatively recent assertions of the absolute priority of religious law are due to domestic pressure from religious fundamentalists. Human rights and fundamental freedoms are fragile and constantly under assault from a variety of sources. The challenge to protect human rights will always be great, and changes in municipal government are not an excuse to violate international law. As other countries begin to feel the pressure of religious fundamentalism, this problem of states violating the Charter will only increase.

434. Section IV.B established that religious fundamentalist norms (laws and acts which are attributable to the state according to Section IV.C) of marriage, divorce, and modesty requiring that wives submit to their husbands and obey them violate the Charter and the Universal Declaration. Section IV.D established that some states are in violation of the Charter for their declarations and reservations to treaties to the effect that their particular religious law is supreme over international law and determinative of the interpretation of the prohibition of sex discrimination.

435. See *supra* notes 327-35, 372-405 and accompanying text.

436. UN Charter art. 5.

437. UN Charter art. 6.

438. For the debates, see UN SCOR, 29th Sess., 1796th mtg. UN Doc S/PV. 1796 (1974); UN SCOR, 29th Sess., 1800th mtg., UN Doc. S/PV. 1800 (1974); UN SCOR, 29th Sess., 1807th mtg., UN Doc. S/PV. 1807 (1974); UN SCOR, 29th Sess., 1808th mtg., UN Doc. S/PV.1808 (1974).

439. See, e.g., UN SCOR, 29th Sess., 1796th mtg., ¶¶8-18, at 2-4, ¶35, at 5; ¶41, at 6, ¶47, at 7, ¶56, at 8, UN Doc. S/PV. 1796 (1974); UN SCOR, 29th Sess., 1800th mtg., ¶17, at 3, ¶¶31-33, at 5, ¶46, at 6, UN Doc. S/PV. 1800 (1974); UN SCOR, 29th Sess., 1807th mtg., ¶3, at 1, ¶11, at 2, ¶19, at 3, UN Doc. S/PV. 1807 (1974); UN SCOR, 29th Sess., 1808th mtg., ¶3, at 1, ¶5, at 2, ¶26, at 4, ¶¶33-34, at 5, ¶45, at 6, ¶51, at 6, ¶87, at 11, ¶113, at 13, ¶126, at 15, ¶129, at 15, UN Doc. S/PV. 1808 (1974).

440. Section III discusses these limits on rights within each religion, and Section IV.B and IV.C establish their legal consequences.

441. See UN SCOR, 29th Sess., 1808th mtg., ¶¶ 48-111, at 6-13, ¶154, at 17-8, UN Doc. S/PV. 1808 (1974).

442. See "U.N. Secretariat Summary of U.N. Credentials Practice Through 1973," 1973 *U.N. Jurid. Y.B.* 139 (1973): 140-41. For the debate of the General Assembly's final rejection of South Africa's credentials in 1974, see UN GAOR, 29th Sess., 2281st. plen. mtg., at 840-41, 854-55 (12 Nov. 1974). The presenting of credentials by governments to the Secretary General before the opening of a new session of the General Assembly is normally a routine procedure. Rule 27 of the General Assembly's Rules of Procedure deals with the

submission of credentials. See UN Doc. A/520/Rev. 15 (1985); see also 1985 *U.N. Jurid. Y.B.* 128 (1985).

443. The UN Legal Counsel expressed the opinion that the General Assembly could not suspend membership without following articles 5 and 6 of the Charter, which require action by the Security Council. The conclusion was that suspension of membership through the credentials process would be contrary to the Charter, particularly since there were no rival claimants to represent South Africa in the United Nations. See UN Legal Counsel, "Opinion on Rejection of Credentials," 1970 *U.N. Jurid. Y.B.* (1970): 169-70. Nonetheless, the General Assembly did exactly this with the result that South Africa could not participate, and by so doing, set a precedent. A subsequent initiative by some Arab states to take the same approach to Israel's credentials in the early 1980s was not successful because there was no broad-based support for the move.

444. For example, the International Labour Organization, Food and Agriculture Organization, United Nations Educational, Scientific, and Cultural Organization, World Health Organization, International Civil Aviation Organization, Universal Postal Union, International Telecommunication Union, Intergovernmental Maritime Consultative Organization (since 1982 named International Maritime Organization, see 1982 *U.N. Jurid. Y.B.* 126 [1982], UN Doc. ST/LEG/SER.C.20), and World Meteorological Organization all took measures to try to deny membership or certain privileges of membership to South Africa because of its policy of racial discrimination. Some were more successful than others. See, e.g., World Meteorological Organization Resolution Suspending South African Rights and Privileges, WMO Congress, May 1975, Res. 38 (Cg. VII), Seventh World Meteorological Congress, Abridged Rep. with Res. 136; Universal Postal Union, Resolution C 6, 1979, Compendium of Congress Decisions (Paris 1947-Hamburg 1984), at 30 (1985) (expelling South Africa).

445. For example, the World Bank, in linking economic reforms to "good governance," refused to make new loans to Malawi until progress had been made on "basic freedoms and human rights" by its one-party "life president." World Bank Press Release, Paris, 13 May 1992; "Donors withdraw support until Malawi ends human-rights abuses," *Afr. Business* (June 1992): 5.

Notes to Chapter 10

1. J. M. Potgieter, "Gedagtes oor die nie-Christelike Aard van Menseregte," *Tydskrif Vir Hedendaagse Romeins-Hollandse Reg* (August 1989): 52-53. There were, of course, also several important interventions supportive of human rights. Significant among these was Johan van der Vyver, *Seven Lectures on Human Rights* (Cape Town: Juta, 1976); and John Dugard, *Human Rights and the South African Legal Order* (Princeton, N.J.: Princeton University Press, 1978).

2. *The Gospel Defence League Newsletter,* Cape Town: June 1989.

3. Bernard Lategan, Johann Kinghorn, Lourens du Plessis, and Etienne de Villiers, *The Option for Inclusive Democracy: A Theological-Ethical Study of Appropriate Social Values for South Africa* (Stellenbosch: Centre for Hermeneutics, University of Stellenbosch, 1987).

4. David Novak, "Religious Human Rights in Judaic Texts," in *Religious Human Rights in Global Perspectives,* ed. John Witte Jr. and Johan D. van der Vyver (The Hague: Martinus Nijhoff, 1996), p. 178.

5. S. D. Goitein, "Human Rights in Jewish Thought and Life in the Middle Ages," in *Religious Human Rights in Global Perspectives,* ed. Witte and van der Vyver, p. 247.

6. The centuries-long naked anti-Semitism of European society, in turn, resulted in Jewish individuals and groups giving expression to this pursuit of rights through Zionist national self-determination, aimed at producing a Jewish state where the rights of Jews would be clearly protected and dependent on none but Jews. See Leslie C. Green, "Jewish Issues on the Human-Rights Agenda in the First Half of the Twentieth Century," in *Essays on Human Rights: Contemporary Issues and Jewish Perspectives,* ed. David Sidorsky (Philadelphia: Jewish Publication Society of America, 1979), p. 298.

7. Rifaat Hassan, "Rights of Women Within Islamic Communities," in *Religious Human Rights in Global Perspectives,* ed. Witte and van der Vyver, p. 366.

8. Abdullahi A. An-Na'im, "The Synergy and Interdependence of Human Rights, Religion and Secularism." Reprinted at http://www.polylog.org/them/2/fcs7-en.htm.

9. Hassan, "Rights of Women," in *Religious Human Rights in Global Perspectives,* ed. Witte and van der Vyver, p. 371.

10. David Novak takes the argument a step further in claiming that a *reclaimed religious foundation* for human rights might, in fact, provide a way beyond the liberalism/communitarianism debate. See Witte and Van der Vyver, *Religious Human Rights in Global Perspectives,* p. 200.

Johan van der Vyver's survey of prospective antecedents for human rights provides important insights in this regard. He suggests that group rights in the sense that the "self-determination of peoples" is a recognized norm of international law, can be traced back to the simultaneous development in both Reformed and Roman Catholic traditions through the legacies of Abraham Kuyper (1837-1920) and Leo XIII's (1878-1903) encyclical, *Rerum Novarum.* Johan van der Vyver, "The Jurisprudential Legacy of Abraham Kuyper and Leo XIII," *Journal of Markets and Morality* 5, no. 1 (2002): 211-49.

11. Max Horkheimer, *Die Sehnsucht nach dem ganz Anderen.* Quoted in Charles Davis, *Theology and Political Society* (London: Cambridge University Press, 1980), p. 18.

12. In Dugard, *Human Rights and the South African Legal Order,* p. 402.

13. Dugard, *Human Rights and the South African Legal Order,* p. 24. Interestingly, the Orange Free State Constitution turned away from parliamentary supremacy, to entrench certain individual rights under the protection of the Supreme Court. In reality, however, the court never saw fit to overrule the actions of the Volksraad, and the guarantee of rights was extended only to "citizens," a category which, according to the customs and practice of the Republic, excluded blacks.

14. This meant that only African voters who met certain educational and economic requirements were permitted to vote. As the number of the African voters increased, these qualifications were raised.

15. Dugard, *Human Rights and the South African Legal Order,* p. 33.

16. Dugard, *Human Rights and the South African Legal Order,* p. 31.

17. South African House of Assembly Debates, May 16, 1983, cols. 7065-74.

18. Albie Sachs, "A Bill of Rights for South Africa: Areas of Agreement and Disagreement," *Columbia Human Rights Law Review* 21, no. 1 (1989): 13-44.

19. African National Congress, *Constitutional Guidelines for a Democratic South Africa* (1988).

20. South African Law Commission, Working Paper 25, Project 58, *Group and Human Rights* 235 (1989).

21. Chinua Achebe, *Morning Yet on Creation Day: Essays* (London: Heinemann, 1975).

22. See Augustine Shutte, *Ubuntu: An Ethic for a New South Africa* (Pietermaritzburg: Cluster, 2001).

23. St. Augustine, *Expositions on the Book of Psalms*, vol. 11 (Oxford: A Library of the Fathers, 1848), p. 194.

24. Quoted in Richard Niebuhr, *Christ and Culture* (New York: Harper Torchbooks, 1951), p. 84.

25. Charles Villa-Vicencio, *The Spirit of Freedom: Conversations on Politics, Religion and Values* (Berkeley: University of California Press, 2001).

26. Villa-Vicencio, *The Spirit of Freedom*, pp. 261-73.

27. Villa-Vicencio, *The Spirit of Freedom*, pp. 143-57.

28. Villa-Vicencio, *The Spirit of Freedom*, pp. 199-207.

29. Villa-Vicencio, *The Spirit of Freedom*, pp. 47-59.

30. Lourens du Plessis, "A Christian Assessment of Aspects of the Bill of Rights in South Africa's Final Constitution," *Journal of Theology for Southern Africa* 96 (1996): 59. See also Martin Prozesky, "Religious Justice at Last," *Journal of Theology for Southern Africa* 92 (1995): 11-21.

31. Republic of South Africa Constitution of 1983, Act 110.

32. Constitution of the Republic of South Africa of 1996, Act 108.

33. Cornelius van Peursen, *Him Again*, trans. Annebeth Macky-Gunning (Richmond, Va.: John Knox, 1969), p. 13.

34. Albert Nolan, *God in South Africa: The Challenge of the Gospel* (Cape Town: David Philip, 1988).

35. Abdullahi A. An-Na'im, "The Synergy and Interdependence of Human Rights, Religion and Secularism." Reprinted at http://www.polylog.org/them/2/fcs7-en.htm.

36. Julian Huxley, *Religion without Revelation* (New York: Harper, 1957), p. 58.

37. Martin Heidegger, *Existence and Being*, ed. Werner Brock (Chicago: Regnery Gateway, 1968), pp. 280-90.

38. Paul Tillich, *The Courage to Be* (New Haven: Yale University Press, 1965), p. 106.

39. I am particularly indebted to Hans Engdahl for his thoughts and insights on the work of Derrida.

40. John D. Caputo, *The Prayers and Tears of Jacques Derrida: Religion without Religion* (Bloomington: Indiana University Press, 1997).

41. Harold Coward and Toby Foshay, eds., *Derrida and Negative Theology* (Albany: State University of New York Press, 1992), p. 59.

42. Jacques Derrida, *The Gift of Death* (Chicago: University of Chicago Press, 1995), p. 84.

43. Emmanuel Levinas, *Totality and Infinity* (Pittsburgh: Duquesne University Press, 1969), pp. 195f.

44. Karl Barth, *The Epistle to the Romans,* trans. E. C. Hoskyns (London: Oxford University Press, 1960), p. 330.

45. See Graham Ward, *Barth, Derrida and the Language of Theology* (Cambridge: Cambridge University Press, 1995).

46. See An-Na'im, "The Synergy and Interdependence of Human Rights, Religion and Secularism."

47. Don Cupitt, *The Long-Legged Fly* (London: SCM Press, 1987), p. 2.

48. Cupitt, *The Long-Legged Fly,* "Author's Note."

49. Dietrich Bonhoeffer, *Letters and Papers from Prison* (London: Fontana, 1964), p. 91.

50. Dag Hammarskjöld, *Markings* (London: Faber and Faber, 1963), p. 31.

51. Johan Baptist Metz, *Faith in History and Society: Toward a Practical Fundamental Theology,* trans. David Smith (London: Burns and Oates, 1980).

52. A speech delivered at the Witwatersrand University Graduation Ceremony (September 1, 1998). Transcript released by UN Office of the High Commissioner for Human Rights, Johannesburg.

53. Frederik van Zyl Slabbert, "Truth without Reconciliation, Reconciliation without Truth," in *Provocations of Amnesty,* ed. C. Villa-Vicencio and Erik Doxtader (Cape Town: David Philip, 2002).

54. From Tina Rosenberg, "A Reporter at Large: Recovering from Apartheid," *New Yorker,* 18 November 1996. Quoted in Martha Minow, *Between Vengeance and Forgiveness* (Boston: Beacon, 1998).

55. Donald Shriver, *An Ethic for Enemies* (Oxford: Oxford University Press, 1995), p. 13.

56. Johan Degenaar, "How Can the Human World Live Its Difference?" in *Race and Reconciliation in South Africa,* ed. William E. Van Vugt and G. Daan Cloete (Lanham, Md.: Lexington Books, 2000), p. 163.

57. Hammarskjöld, *Markings,* p. 31.

Notes to Chapter 11

1. Arendt's point of departure is the idea that political thought within our Western tradition has been formed primarily from the perspective of thinking ego, such that all its concepts and habits have been constituted as if disconnected from the experiential basis of *vita activa,* where they are originally coming from. "Ich habe Verdachtniss," she wrote to her teacher and lifelong friend Karl Jaspers in 1956, "dass diese abendlandische Philosophie nie einen reinen Begriff des Politischen gehabt hat und auch nicht haben konnte, weil sie notgedrungen von dem Menschen sprach und die Tatsache der Pluralität nebenbei behandelte." *Hannah Arendt Karl Jaspers Briefwechsel* (München: Pieper Verlag, 1985), p. 203. The major task of our own political thought, then, according to Arendt, is to bring "die Tatsache der Pluralität" back to our attention. She suggests reexamining and rethinking our elementary political concepts, brought to us from the past, from the perspective of

the acting ego. Arendt's analysis of the dichotomy between the *vita activa* and the *vita contemplativa* can be found in the Prologue and the first chapter of her fundamental work, *The Human Condition* (Chicago: University of Chicago Press, 1958), pp. 1-21.

2. "With the term *vita activa,* I propose to designate three fundamental human activities: labor, work, and action. They are fundamental because each corresponds to one of the basic conditions under which life on earth has been given to man.

Labor is the activity which corresponds to the biological process of the human body, whose spontaneous growth, metabolism, and eventual decay are bound to the vital necessities produced and fed into the life process by labor. The human condition of labor is life itself.

Work is the activity which corresponds to the unnaturalness of human existence, which is not imbedded in, and whose mortality is not compensated by, the species' ever-recurring cycle. Work provides an "artificial" world of things, distinctly different from all natural surroundings. Within its borders each individual life is housed, while this world itself is meant to outlast and transcend them all. The human condition of work is worldliness.

Action, the only activity that goes on directly between men without the intermediary of things or matter, corresponds to the human condition of plurality, to the fact that men, not Man, live on the earth and inhabit the world. While all aspects of the human condition are somehow related to politics, this plurality is specifically *the* condition — not only the *conditio sine qua non* but the *conditio per quam* — of all political life." Arendt, *The Human Condition,* p. 7.

3. There is, to be sure, the whole tradition of Western philosophy and theology, both in its classical Greek form and in its later Christian modifications, which can be consulted here. What I would like to recommend here instead, as a primary source in the search for the constitution of that inner world we dive into in the moment of contemplation, is the corpus of "fragments" of Pre-Socratic philosophy. (Their classical edition in English is available under the title *Ancilla to the Pre-Socratic Philosophers: A Complete Translation of the Fragments in Diels Fragmente der Vorsokratiker* [Cambridge: Harvard University Press, 1983].) The Pre-Socratic fragments can obviously be read in many different ways. No matter what they say about the "origins" of cosmos or how they explain the processes either taking place in the human world or belonging to "physis," they bear testimony to *prima facie* encounters with that space that opens for a "philosopher" who has embarked on adventures of *vita contemplativa* and descends, leaving all "things" he is busy with in his daily life behind, to the inner world of his thoughts. The two greatest examples of this descent are perhaps the way of truth embarked upon by Parmenides, and Heraclitus's explorations of the divine *Logos* and of the *apeirontic* (infinite) depth of the immortal soul. A concise and reasonably short interpretation of elementary noetic problems of Parmenides and Heraclitus can be found in Eric Voegelin's *Order and History: The World of the Polis,* vol. 15 of *The Collected Works of Eric Voegelin* (Columbia: University of Missouri Press, 2000), pp. 274-313.

4. The Aristotelian "definition" was in fact formulated only by Porphyry, but its real source can indeed be found in Aristotle's *Politics: logon de monon anthrōpos echei tōn zōōn* (*physis* "has endowed man alone among the animals with the power of speech"): *Politics* 1253a9-10, English trans. E. T. Sinclair and Trevor Saunders (New York: Penguin Classics, 1981).

5. This distance can be measured in all sorts of ways and discussed in all sorts of con-

texts, but it is basically the distance of "spectator," mentioned in the following anecdote from the life of Pythagoras reported by Diogenes Laertius ("Life of Pythagoras," *The Lives and Opinions of Eminent Philosophers,* trans. C. D. Yonge, http://classicpersuasion.org): "Having been asked by Leon, the tyrant of the Phliasians, who he was, he replied, 'A philosopher.' And he adds, that he used to compare life to a festival. 'And as some people came to a festival to contend for the prizes, and others for the purposes of traffic, and the best as spectators; so also in life, the men of slavish dispositions,' said he, 'are born hunters after glory and covetousness, but philosophers are seekers after truth'" (8:VI).

6. The scope of the problem referred to here is enormous within our Western civilization, not speaking about the conceptions of "eternity" in the non-European traditions. I limit myself here consciously to the short but inspiring analysis concerning the dichotomy "eternity versus immortality" in Arendt, *The Human Condition,* pp. 17-21.

7. This thesis comes from Czech philosopher Jan Patočka, whose contributions to the contemporary dialogue on human rights will be discussed in Section IV of this essay. Patočka writes, "History arises and can arise only insofar as there is *aretē,* the excellence of humans who no longer simply live to live but who make room for their justification by looking into the nature of things and acting in harmony with what they see — by building a *polis* on the basis of the law of the world which is *polemos,* by speaking that which they see as revealing itself to a free, exposed yet undaunted human (philosophy)." Jan Patočka, "The Beginning of History," in *Heretical Essays in the Philosophy of History,* trans. Erazim Kohák, ed. James Dodd (Chicago: Open Court, 1996), p. 43.

8. I am consciously borrowing this term from Heidegger's *Sein und Zeit* (Tübingen: Max Niemeyer Verlag, 1993). Heidegger's *"Frage nach dem Sinn des Seins"* and the following *"Fundamentale Daseinsanalyse,"* where the concept *In-der-Welt-Sein* is introduced, represent, in my view, the basic point of departure for any serious attempt to think through the relationship between God and human rights.

9. The Declaration of Independence, quoted from *The American Republic: Primary Sources,* ed. Bruce Frohnen (Indianapolis: Liberty Fund, 2002), p. 189.

10. Aristotle, *Politics* 1252b21-22.

11. Aristotle, *Politics* 1252b28.

12. Aristotle, *Politics* 1252b29-30.

13. Aristotle, *Politics* 1253a37-39.

14. Cf., for instance, Herodotus, *Historiai* 3:142, where a well-meant but unfortunately in the end rather unsuccessful attempt to establish the "democratic" form of government on the island of Samos is described by Maendrius, who "had taken hold of rule entrusted him by Polycrates," as follows: "To me, as you too know, the scepter and all the power of Polycrates have been entrusted and it is possible for me to rule you, but I what for my part rebuke my neighbor for, I myself will not do according to my ability; for neither Polycrates pleased me by being lord over men similar to himself nor any other who acts like that. Now, Polycrates fulfilled his portion, but *I put the rule in your midst and proclaim the equality before the law for you.*" Trans. Shlomo Felberbaum, Lost Trails, www.losttrails.com (emphasis added).

15. Patočka, *Heretical Essays,* pp. 28-29.

16. In the following paragraph I am using some formulations from my own article "Totalitarianism and Authoritarianism," *Encyclopedia of Violence, Peace and Conflict,* vol. 3 (San Diego: Academic Press, 1999), pp. 541-58.

17. *Esti d' ho archōn phylax tou dikaiou, ei de tou dikaiou, kai tou isou.* Aristotle, *Nicomachean Ethics* 1134b1-2, trans. Terence Irwin (Indianapolis: Hackett, 1985). The famous Aristotelian classification of correct and deviated constitutions can be found in the third book of *Politics* (1279a22-1279b10): "Sovereignty necessarily resides in one man, or in a few, or in the many. . . . The usual names for right constitutions are as follows: (a) Monarchy aiming at the common interest: kingship *(basileia)*. (b) Rule of more than one man but only a few: aristocracy *(aristokratia)*. . . . (c) Political control exercised by the mass of the populace in the common interest: polity *(politeia)*. . . . The corresponding deviations are: from kingship, tyranny *(tyrannis)*; from aristocracy, oligarchy *(oligarchia)*; from polity, democracy *(dēmokratia)*."

18. "The laws, if rightly established, ought to be sovereign" *(dei tou nomous einai kyrious keimenous orthōs)*. Aristotle, *Politics* 1282b1-2.

19. Patočka, *Heretical Essays,* p. 29.

20. *Metechein kriseōs kai archēs.* Aristotle, *Politics* 1275a23.

21. *Polin de tō toioutōn plēthos hikanos pros autarkeian zōēs, hōs haplōs eipein.* Aristotle, *Politics* 1275b20-21.

22. *Polis koinōnia tōn eleutherōn.* Aristotle, *Politics* 1279a21.

23. The household *(oikia)* is the "association of persons, established according to nature for the satisfaction of daily needs" *(hē men oun eis pasan hēmeran synestēkia koinōnia kata physin estin).* Aristotle, *Politics* 1252b12-14. The village is the "association of a number of houses for the satisfaction of something more than daily needs. It comes into being through the process of nature in the fullest sense, as offshoots of the households are set up by sons and grandsons." Aristotle, *Politics* 1252b15-18.

24. What from our modern perspective is especially disturbing in Aristotle's descriptive account of Greek *koinōnia* is the natural conception of the institution of slavery. It seems to be unthinkable for Aristotle that the household, serving the satisfaction of all needs connected with the physical being of man and the continuation of human life in the succession of generations within a family or tribe, could exist without the relation between master and slave *(despotēs kai doulos).* In the several chapters of Book I of *Politics,* Aristotle, when speaking about "economics" *(peri oikonomias,* the matters of household), seems to accept entirely the conventional beliefs of his time concerning this topic: "These considerations will have shown what the nature and functions of the slave [*hē physis tou doulou kai tis hē dynamis*] are: any human being that by nature belongs to another [*hō gar mē autou physei all' allou anthrōpos ōn*] is by nature a slave [*houtos physei doulos estin*]; and a human being belongs to another whenever, in spite of being a man, he is a piece of property [*hos an ktēma ē anthrōpos ōn*], i.e., a tool having a separate existence and meant for action [*organon praktikon kai chōriston*]." Aristotle, *Politics* 1254a13-17.

25. Cf. Aristotle, *Nicomachean Ethics* 1181b15.

26. *Tou te eu zēn kai tēs eudaimonias ephientai pantes.* Aristotle, *Politics* 1331b39 (emphasis added).

27. *Pantes anthrōpoi tou eidenai oregontai physei.* Aristotle, *Metaphysics* 980a21, trans. W. D. Ross, the Internet Classics Archive (www.classics.mit.edu).

28. *Dittēs dē tēs aretēs ousēs, tēs men dianoētikēs tēs de ēthikēs.* Aristotle, *Nicomachean Ethics* 1103a14-15.

29. Cf. Voegelin, *Order and History: The World of the Polis,* chap. 2 ("The Hellenic Polis"), pp. 181-94; and cf. Jean-Pierre Vernant, *Les origines de la pensée grecque* (Quadrige, 4th edition, 1981).

30. Voegelin, "The Hellenic Polis," *Order and History,* demonstrates this trend on the constitutional reform of Cleisthenes from 508 B.C., which "divided the Attic territory into ten regions and constituted their inhabitants as ten new *phylai.* Each of the ten *phylai* was subdivided into ten districts, the *dēmoi.* Citizenship was now made dependent on membership in one of the *dēmoi* . . . the net effect was a successful democratization of the constitution breaking the power of the old gentilitian structure" (p. 184). "Nevertheless," he notes a couple of lines later, "only the power of the aristocratic *genē* was broken, not the gentilitian spirit of the institutions. The *dēmos,* in spite of its territorial basis, was a corporation of persons just like the older blood relationships. The Athenian still had his citizenship, not through the legal act making his person a member of the *polis,* but by the virtue of his membership in a *demos*" (p. 184).

31. Voegelin, "The Hellenic Polis," *Order and History,* p. 183.

32. Voegelin, "The Hellenic Polis," *Order and History,* pp. 188-89.

33. Patočka, "The Beginning of History," *Heretical Essays,* p. 39.

34. *Dia gar tō thaumazein hoi anthrōpoi kai nyn kai to prōton erxanto philosophein.* Aristotle, *Metaphysics* 982b12-13.

35. *To d'eidenai kai to epistasthai autōn heneka.* Aristotle, *Metaphysics* 982a30-31.

36. *Dia to eidenai to epistasthai ediōkon kai ou chrēseōs tinos heneken.* Aristotle, *Metaphysics* 982B20-21.

37. *Ho d'aporōn kai thaumazōn oietai agnoein.* Aristotle, *Metaphysics* 982B17-18.

38. *To pheugein tēn agnoian.* Aristotle, *Metaphysics* 982b20.

39. *Autēn hōs monēn ousan eleutherian tōn epithēmōn.* Aristotle, *Metaphysics* 982b27.

40. *Kai ho philomythos philosophos pōs estin.* Aristotle, *Metaphysics* 982b18-19.

41. Patočka refers here ("The Beginning of History," *Heretical Essays,* p. 40, citing Aristotle, *Metaphysics*) to Parmenides, the Eleatic philosopher who in his famous poem describes the travel of a thinker to the well-spoken path of the Goddess *(es hodon polyphēmon daimonos),* the road "lying far indeed from the beaten paths of humans" *(tōn d'hodōn — hē gar ap' anthrōpōn ektos patou estin),* where he can "learn all things [*panta*], both the persuasive, unshaken heart of (Objective) Truth [*ēmen alētheiēs eukykleos atremes hētor*] and the (subjective) beliefs of mortals, in which there is no true trust" *(ēde brotōn doxas tais ouk eni pistis alēthēs).* Parmenides, *Peri physeos,* in Hermann Diels, *Die Fragmente der Vorsokratiker* (Berlin: Zweite Auflage, 1906), English trans. and ed. Allan F. Randall, the Classic Internet Library.

42. Patočka, "The Beginning of History," *Heretical Essays,* p. 41.

43. "For I do nothing but go about persuading you all, old and young alike, not to take thought for your persons and your properties, but first and chiefly to care about the greatest improvement of the soul" *(ouden gar allo prattōn perierchomai ē pethōn hymōn kai neoterous kai presbyterous mēte sōmatōn epimeleistai mēte chrēmatōn proteron mēde houto sphodra hōs tēs psychēs hopōs aristē estai).* Plato, *Apology of Socrates* 30a8-30b1, trans. Benjamin Jowett, the Internet Classics Archive (www.classics.mit.edu).

44. Plato, *Apology of Socrates* 30c6.

45. *En akadēmeia to siōpōmenon agaton zētein kai dia geōmetrias eudaimonia*

genesthai ("To look for an undisclosed good in Academy and to became happy with the help of geometry"). These references come from one of the most hilarious but also very illuminating descriptions of the clash between the philosophical way of life and leadership in the political domain, Plutarch's account of the life of Dion, a relative of and an adviser to the Sicilian king Dionysios II. Dion twice brought his teacher Plato to Sicily in order to educate and to convince the ruler to subordinate his activities as a statesman to the guidance of philosophy. Plutarch, *Lives,* vol. 6, trans. Bernadotte Perrin (Cambridge, Mass.: Harvard University Press, reprint 1970), Dion XIV:1-6, p. 29.

46. There is no space here to look more closely at this phenomenon that has influenced substantively the whole tradition of Western philosophy and seems to have always played an important role in the human rights discourse. As a rather anecdotal illustration of how estranged the relationship between the *polis* and the philosopher in the post-Socratic era can be, let us take the example of Diogenes of Sinope (412-323 B.C.). The eccentric life of this Cynic philosopher (cf. Diogenes Laertius, "Life of Diogenes," *The Lives and Opinions of Eminent Philosophers,* trans. C. D. Yonge, http://classicpersuasion.org) — who allegedly lived for years in Athens in a large tub — shows more than clearly what is at stake. He transformed philosophy into a colorful mélange of often provocative opinions of both stateless and homeless persons, showing, first of all, the distance of their holder from all ephemeral political matters, his disdain not only for his fellow-citizens but also for his fellow-philosophers, his disenchantment not only about Athens or any other concrete political body but about the whole of human civilization. From the records of his numerous conversations with various interlocutors, it is apparent that he believed that as a philosopher he was doomed to remain a stranger in the world of the Greek *polis.* This enstrangement, however, could be overcome (the adherents to Hegel's dialectics might be inclined to say *aufgehoben*) according to Diogenes by making resort to the person's place in the cosmos, by making the claim that the ultimate source of human dignity is not in citizenship, a good passport in our modern terminology, but in human nature. One of these conversations recorded by Diogenes Laertius is particularly telling in our context: "The question was put to him what countryman he was, and he replied, 'A Citizen of the world *[kosmopolitēs].*'" Diogenes Laertius, "Life of Diogenes."

47. In the following paragraphs I will be following the analysis of Cicero's political thought by James E. Holton in *History of Political Philosophy,* ed. Leo Strauss and Joseph Cropsey, third ed. (Chicago: University of Chicago Press, 1987), pp. 155-75.

48. Polybius, *The Histories,* 6 vols., trans. W. R. Paton, The Loeb Classical Library (London: W. Heinemann, 1922-1927).

49. Thucydides, *The History of the Peloponnesian War,* trans. Richard Crawley, the Internet Classics Archive, http://classics.mit.edu.

50. Strauss and Cropsey, *History of Political Philosophy,* p. 164.

51. Strauss and Cropsey, *History of Political Philosophy,* p. 155.

52. Cf. note 1, referring to the Arendt's evaluation of the Western tradition of political thought.

53. Strauss and Cropsey, *History of Political Philosophy,* p. 159.

54. Strauss and Cropsey, *History of Political Philosophy,* p. 157.

55. The dialogue described in *The Republic* (Cicero, *The Republic,* trans. C. W. Keyes, Loeb Classical Library [Cambridge: Harvard University Press, 1928]) allegedly took place

during a Roman holiday in 129 B.C. among members of the Scipionic circle; the dialogue recorded in the *Laws* (Cicero, *Laws,* trans. C. W. Keyes, Loeb Classical Library [Cambridge: Harvard University Press, 1928]) was to take place among Cicero himself, his brother, and an Epicurean friend.

56. *Laws* I.37, in Strauss and Cropsey, *History of Political Philosophy,* p. 171.

57. Cicero, *The Republic* III.33, in Strauss and Cropsey, *History of Political Philosophy,* p. 169.

58. Charter 77 was published on January 1, 1977. The movement ceased to exist in 1992.

59. Patočka, *Heretical Essays,* p. 120.

60. T. G. Masaryk, *The Making of a State* (New York: Howard Fertig, 1969), p. 372.

61. The Battle on White Mountain took place in 1620. The armies of revolting Czech Estates were defeated by the Austrian Emperor Ferdinand II.

62. The most profound analysis of the modern Czech nation, reborn "from below" in the enlightened eighteenth century, can be found in Jan Patočka's booklet *Co jsou Češi? Malý přehled fakt a pokus o vysvětlení (Was Sind die Tschechen? Kleine Tatsachesbericht und Erklarungsversuch)* (Praha: Panorama, 1992).

63. Cf. T. G. Masaryk, *Česká otázka/Naše nynější krize* (The Czech Question/Our Present Crisis) (Praha, 1948). The most penetrating study of Masaryk available in English was written by Canadian historian H. Gordon Skilling (*T. G. Masaryk: Against the Current, 1882-1914* [London: Macmillan, 1994]).

64. Václav Havel, *Stories and Totalitarianism, Open Letters: Selected Writings 1965-1990,* trans. Paul Wilson (New York: Alfred Knopf, 1991), pp. 331-32.

65. Cf. Václav Havel, "Dear Dr. Husak," *Stories and Totalitarianism,* pp. 50-83.

66. Cf. Milan Kundera, "Tragedy of Central Europe," *New York Review of Books,* April 26, 1984.

67. International Covenant on Civil and Political Rights and International Covenant on Economic, Social, and Cultural Rights.

68. This and following quotations are from the Declaration of Charter 77 from January 1, 1977.

69. Václav Havel, *Stories and Totalitarianism,* p. 330.

70. Cf. Marcus Tullius Tusculan, *Disputations* IV: 23-32, in Eric Voegelin, "Wisdom and the Magic of the Extreme," in *The Collected Works of Eric Voegelin,* vol. 12: *Published Essays 1966-1985,* p. 322.

71. The concept of "parallel *polis*" comes from Václav Benda, whose seminal essay on this topic published in early 1980 initiated an important and substantive discussion in the dissidents' circles. Benda's essay "The Parallel Polis" and other contributions to this debate (including my text "Jan Patočka versus Václav Benda," which is being used here as my own point of departure) can be found in *Civic Freedom in Central Europe: Voices from Czechoslovakia,* ed. H. G. Skilling and Paul Wilson (London: Macmillan, 1991).

72. The English version of this text can be found in *Good-bye, Samizdat: Twenty Years of Czechoslovak Underground Writing,* ed. Marketa Goetz-Stankiewicz (Evanston, Ill.: Northwestern University Press, 1992), pp. 142-44, or in *Jan Patočka: Philosophy and Selected Writings,* ed. and trans. Erazim Kohak (Chicago: University of Chicago Press, 1989), "Two Charter 77 Texts, The Obligation to Resist Injustice," pp. 340-43.

73. Goetz-Stankiewics, *Good-bye, Samizdat*, p. 143.

74. Erazim Kohak, *Jan Patočka: Philosophy and Selected Writings*, p. 341.

75. Goetz-Stankiewics, *Good-bye, Samizdat*, p. 143.

76. Goetz-Stankiewics, *Good-bye, Samizdat*, p. 143.

77. Goetz-Stankiewics, *Good-bye, Samizdat*, p. 144.

78. Hannah Arendt, *The Origins of Totalitarianism*, "Preface to the First Edition" (New York: Harcourt Brace Jovanovich, 1973), p. ix.

79. Hannah Arendt, "On the Nature of Understanding," *Essays in Understanding 1930-1954* (New York: Harcourt, Brace, and Company, 1994), p. 322.

Notes to Chapter 12

1. William Penn, *The Great Case of Liberty of Conscience (1670)*, quoted in William Wistar Comfort, *William Penn: 1644-1718* (Philadelphia: University of Pennsylvania Press, 1944), p. 120.

2. Mary Maples Dunn, *William Penn: Politics and Conscience* (Princeton, N.J.: Princeton University Press, 1967), p. 54.

3. From an unpublished working paper by IGE Research Associate Dane Shelly.

4. John Milton, *Areopagitica*, Part IV.

5. James Madison, "To the Honorable the General Assembly of the Commonwealth of Virginia: A Memorial and Remonstrance" (20 June 1785); quoted in *The Founders Constitution*, vol. 5, Amendment 1 (Religion), Document 43 (http://press-pubs.uchicago.edu/founders/documents/amendI_religions43.html).

6. Rhode Island State, *Charter of Rhode Island and Providence Plantations* (15 July 1663); quoted by the Avalon Project at Yale Law School (http://www.yale.edu/lawweb/avalon/states/rio4.htm).

7. Paul Johnson, "God and the Americans," *Commentary* (January 1995): 25-45.

8. Jeremy Gunn, in *Facilitating Freedom of Religion or Belief: A Deskbook*, ed. Tore Lindholm et al. (Leiden: Martinus Nijhoff, 2004), p. 722.

9. Gunn, *Facilitating Freedom of Religion or Belief*, p. 722.

10. International Religious Freedom Act of 1998 — H.R. 2431, Section 2 (b) (1). The full text of this act is archived at http://usinfo.state.gov/usa/infousa/laws/majorlaw/intlrel.html.

11. Gunn, *Facilitating Freedom of Religion or Belief*, p. 740.

12. Gunn, *Facilitating Freedom of Religion or Belief*, p. 746.

13. The modern notion of universal human dignity has been codified only in the twentieth century, but it has deep roots in various theological traditions. Universality is perhaps most fully developed in Judeo-Christian thought, but virtually every other world religion has some concept of a universal human dignity, either stemming from a theistic view of creation — like Islam's — or from some version of the Golden Rule, as we see in the Asian religions. Each of these traditions fed into the Universal Declaration and its clear statement that all human beings — of whatever race, creed, income, or locality — possess an inviolable worth that transcends the authority of the state.

14. Jacques Maritain, *Man and the State* (Chicago: University of Chicago Press, 1951), p. 77.

15. The authors of the Universal Declaration understood that religious freedom touches upon the most fundamental of human quests — the search for ultimate meaning and purpose that is at the heart of what it means to be human. It is a search in which virtually every human being engages, most in the context of religious belief and worship. And, for religious and nonreligious alike, it is a quest that provides the context for much else of value in life.

16. Paul A. Brink, "Debating International Human Rights," *The Brandywine Review of Faith and International Affairs* 1, no. 2 (Fall 2003): 20.

17. In becoming members of the UN, states voluntarily assume obligations of the Charter and other international norms of human rights. No state can therefore claim it is immune to international scrutiny of its human rights record. While some states may claim that this is a violation of sovereignty, international spotlighting of human rights problems cannot reasonably be considered a violation, since there is no enforcement provision within the UN system other than moral persuasion.

18. This is understandable at one level but, unfortunately, short-sighted. As noted earlier, religious freedom and security play complementary roles in a values-based civil society. Giving countries a "pass" on religious freedom violations in exchange for security demonstrates a profound misunderstanding of both issues.

19. When I first came to the State Department, the only other staff were two part-time employees. The only budget we had after two years, excluding salaries, was an $82,000 travel budget. The commission, on the other hand, has received $3 million a year for each year of its existence.

20. See Chris Seiple, "Toward a World Safe for Religion and Politics," Institute for Global Engagement (21 February 2003): http://www.globalengagement.org/issues/2003/02/safe.htm.

21. See "Iran's President Pushes Reform in New Challenge to Hard-Liners," *Associated Press Online* (28 August 2002), found at http://www.kommersant.ru/FirstFaces/FF30082002.htm.

22. Chalmers Johnson, *Blowback* (New York: Henry Holt, 2000), p. 94.

23. Ziauddin Sardar and Merryl Wyn Davies, *Why Do People Hate America?* (Cambridge: Icon, 2002), p. 11.

24. Sardar and Davies, *Why Do People Hate America*, p. 13.

25. Sardar and Davies, *Why Do People Hate America*, p. 35.

26. Sardar and Davies, *Why Do People Hate America*, p. 105.

27. Sardar and Davies, *Why Do People Hate America*, p. 201.

28. Stephen L. Carter, *The Culture of Disbelief* (New York: Basic, 1993), p. 3.

29. Taken from a private conversation with Tom Farr.

30. Carter, *The Culture of Disbelief*, p. 109.

31. Carter, *The Culture of Disbelief*, p. 93.

32. These events were all recorded during China's fiftieth anniversary of the Communist party. The irony was intense. It was not one of business's finest hours!